Communications
in Computer and Information Science 1487

More information about this series at http://www.springer.com/series/7899

Nibras Abdullah · Selvakumar Manickam ·
Mohammed Anbar (Eds.)

Advances in Cyber Security

Third International Conference, ACeS 2021
Penang, Malaysia, August 24–25, 2021
Revised Selected Papers

 Springer

Editors
Nibras Abdullah ⓘ
Hodeidah University
Hodeidah, Yemen

Selvakumar Manickam ⓘ
Universiti Sains Malaysia
Penang, Malaysia

Mohammed Anbar ⓘ
Universiti Sains Malaysia
Penang, Malaysia

ISSN 1865-0929   ISSN 1865-0937   (electronic)
Communications in Computer and Information Science
ISBN 978-981-16-8058-8   ISBN 978-981-16-8059-5   (eBook)
https://doi.org/10.1007/978-981-16-8059-5

This Springer imprint is published by the registered company Springer Nature Singapore Pte Ltd.
The registered company address is: 152 Beach Road, #21-01/04 Gateway East, Singapore 189721, Singapore

Preface

This volume contains the papers from the Third International Conference on Advances in CyberSecurity (ACeS 2021). The event was organized by the National Advanced IPv6 Centre at Universiti Sains Malaysia, Penang, Malaysia, which specializes in cybersecurity, the Internet of Things, wireless communication, and other emerging network technologies. The year 2021 continued to see the ravaging effect of the COVID-19 pandemic worldwide, with domestic and international travel being barred. Because of this, ACeS 2021 once again had to be organized fully online. Nevertheless, going virtual also removed financial barriers, allowing the session to be carried without any form of fee for the presenters and participants. The conference was carried out with breakout sessions involving presenters and participants from around the world. ACeS 2021 focused on existing and newly emerging cybersecurity areas associated with advances in systems and infrastructures, lifestyle, policy, and governance. The conference encouraged the interaction of researchers, practitioners, and academics to present and discuss work on cybersecurity, especially in new, emerging domains such as the Internet of Things (IoT), Industry 4.0, blockchains, and cloud and edge computing. The conference attracted a total of 92 submissions from authors in countries including Albania, Bangladesh, Belgium, Canada, China, Germany, India, Indonesia, Iraq, Italy, Jordan, Kuwait, Malaysia, Mexico, New Zealand, Nigeria, Norway, Oman, Pakistan, Rwanda, Saudi Arabia, the USA, Vietnam, and Yemen.

All submissions underwent a strict peer-review and paper selection process, resulting in the acceptance of 36 submissions (39% of the total submissions). The accepted submissions were presented online at the conference held during August 24–25, 2021. All the accepted papers were peer-reviewed by three qualified reviewers chosen from our Technical Program Commitee based on their qualifications and experience.

The proceedings editors wish to thank the dedicated organizing committee members and all reviewers for their contributions and commitment. We also would like to thank Springer for their trust and for publishing the proceedings of ACeS 2021.

August 2021

Nibras Abdullah
Selvakumar Manickam
Mohammed Anbar

Organization

Organizing Committee

Honorary Chairs

Bahari Belaton   Universiti Sains Malaysia, Malaysia
Selvakumar Manickam   Universiti Sains Malaysia, Malaysia
Mohammed Anbar   Universiti Sains Malaysia, Malaysia

General Chair

Nibras Abdullah   Hodeidah University, Yemen

Program Chair

Nibras Abdullah   Hodeidah University, Yemen

Publication Chairs

Ola A. Al-wesabi   Hodeidah University, Yemen
Manmeet Mahinderjit Singh   Universiti Sains Malaysia, Malaysia
Taief Alaa Hamdi Al Amiedy   Universiti Sains Malaysia, Malaysia

Technical Chairs

Iznan Husainy Hasbullah   Universiti Sains Malaysia, Malaysia
Asyraf Mustaqim Bin Abd Manaf   Universiti Sains Malaysia, Malaysia

Publicity and Public Relations

Wan Tat Chee   Universiti Sains Malaysia, Malaysia
Lokman Mohd Fadzil   Universiti Sains Malaysia, Malaysia
Shankar Karuppayah   Universiti Sains Malaysia, Malaysia

Secretariat

Malar Devi Kanagasabai   Universiti Sains Malaysia, Malaysia

Webmaster

Asamoah Kwaku Acheampong   Universiti Sains Malaysia, Malaysia

Technical Program Committee

Abdulghani A. Ahmed	De Montfort University, UK
Abdullah Rashid	University of Basrah, Iraq
Abdulwahab Almazroi	University of Jeddah, Saudi Arabia
Ahmed Hintaw	AlSafwa University College, Iraq
Ahmed K. Al-Ani	Xiamen University Malaysia, Malaysia
Alhamza Alalousi	College of Applied Sciences, Oman
Ali Abdulrazzaq K.	University of Mosul, Iraq
Ali Bin Salem	Neijiang Normal University, China
Andrea Visconti	Università degli Studi di Milano, Italy
Aws Naser Jaber	Universiti Malaysia Kelantan, Malaysia
Badiea Abdulkarem Mohammed Al-Shaibani	University of Hail, Saudi Arabia
Baidaa Khudayer	Buraimi University College, Oman
Basim Ahmad Alabsi	Najran University, Saudi Arabia
Belal Al-Fuhaidi	University of Science and Technology, Yemen
Brahim Raouyane	Hassan II University of Casablanca, Morocco
Esraa Saleh Hasoon AL-omari	Wasit University, Iraq
Fathey Mohammed	Universiti Utara Malaysia, Malaysia
Fatina Shukur	University of Kufa, Iraq
Gamil Qaid	Future University, Yemen
Ghada Almukhaini	Sur College of Applied Sciences, Oman
Hala Al-Baroodi	Ministry of Education, Iraq
Hedi Hamdi	Jouf University, Saudi Arabia
Hicham Toumi	Hassan II University of Casablanca, Morocco
Hussain A.Younis	University of Basrah, Iraq
Je Sen Teh	Universiti Sains Malaysia, Malaysia
Kamal Ibrahim Ahmed Alieyan	Universiti Sains Malaysia, Malaysia
Karim Hashim	Mustansiriyah University, Iraq
Lateef Qudr	AlSafwa University College, Iraq
Lee Wai Kong	Universiti Tunku Abdul Rahman, Malaysia
Leon Bock	TU Darmstadt, Germany
Lim Seng Poh	Universiti Tunku Abdul Rahman, Malaysia
Loai Kayed Hassen Bani-Melhim	Majmaah University, Saudi Arabia
Lokman Bin Mohd Fadzil	Universiti Sains Malaysia, Malaysia
Luca Davoli	University of Parma, Italy
Lutfi Khanbary	University of Aden, Yemen
Mahmoud Khalid Baklizi	The World Islamic Sciences and Education University, Jordan
Mathias Fischer	University of Hamburg, Germany
Md Saiful Islam	King Saud University, Saudi Arabia
Mie Mie Su Thwin	University of Computer Studies, Yangon, Myanmar

Misbah Liaqat	Air University, Pakistan
Moatsum Alawida	Universiti Sains Malaysia, Malaysia
Mohamed Abdulnabi	APU, Malaysia
Mohammed A. Awadallah	Al-Aqsa University, Palestine
Mohammed Abdo Mohammed Mahdi	University of Hail, Saudi Arabia
Mohammed Aleidaroos	Sieyun Community College, Yemen
Mohammed Al-Mashraee	Free University Berlin, Germany
Mohammed Al-Shalabi	The World Islamic Sciences and Education University, Jordan
Mohammed Anbar	Universiti Sains Malaysia, Malaysia
Mohammed Azmi Al-Betar	Al-Balqa Applied University, Jordan
Mohammed Faiz Aboalmaaly	AlSafwa University College, Iraq
Mohammed Zaki Hasan	University of Mosul, Iraq
Mohd Arfian Ismail	Universiti Malaysia Pahang, Malaysia
Mohd Najwadi Yusoff	Universiti Sains Malaysia, Malaysia
Mosleh Abualhaj	Al-Ahliyya Amman University, Jordan
N. K. Sakthivel	Nehru Institute of Engineering and Technology, India
N. P. Gopolan	National Institute of Technology, Thiruchirapalli, India
Narayanan Kulathu Ramaiyer	Universiti Malaysia Sarawak, Malaysia
Nasrin Makbol	Universiti Sains Malaysia, Malaysia
Nathan Balasubramanian	Universiti Sains Malaysia
Navaneethan C. Arjuman	Universiti Sains Malaysia
Nibras Abdullah	Hodeidah University, Yemen
Nurul Hidayah Ab Rahman	Universiti Tun Hussein Onn Malaysia, Malaysia
Ola A. Al-wesabi	Hodeidah University, Yemen
Omar Abdulmunem Ibrahim	University of Mosul, Iraq
Omar Elejla	Islamic University of Gaza, Palestine
Ooi Boon Yaik	Universiti Tunku Abdul Rahman, Malaysia
P. Jayasree	Madras Insititute of Technology, India
Pantea Keikhosrokiani	Universiti Sains Malaysia, Malaysia
Raja Kumar Murugesan	Taylor's University, Malaysia
Rajni S. Goel	Howard University, USA
Randa Jabeur Ben Chikha	Al Jouf University, Saudi Arabia
Rayan Yousif Yacob Alkhayat	University of Mosul, Iraq
Redhwan Saad	Ibb University, Yemen
Reem Baragash	Universiti Sains Malaysia, Malaysia
Roa'a M. Al-airaji	University of Babylon, Iraq
Robert Janz	University of Groningen, The Netherlands
Saad Alfadhli	Imam Al-Kadhum College, Iraq
Saadun Hussein	Mosul University, Iraq
Sabri Mohammed Abdhood	Universiti Sains Malaysia, Malaysia
Sadik Ali Al-Taweel	University of Science and Technology, Yemen

Saif Almashhadi	Universiti Sains Malaysia, Malaysia
Sajid Latif	University Institute of Information Technology, Pakistan
Salah Salem Bin Dahman	Alsaher Community College, Yemen
Salah Shaman Alghyaline	The World Islamic Sciences and Education University, Jordan
Salam Al-Emari	Umm Al-Qura University, Saudi Arabia
Satya N. Gupta	ITU-APT Foundation of India, India
Selvakumar Manickam	Universiti Sains Malaysia, Malaysia
Seng Poh Lim	Universiti Tunku Abdul Rahman, Malaysia
Shahzad Ashraf	Hohai University, China
Sibghat Bazai	Massey University, New Zealand
Steffen Haas	University of Hamburg, Germany
Sudhir Kumar Sharma	Institute of Information Technology and Management, India
Suliman Mohamed Fati	Prince Sultan University, Saudi Arabia
Sunil Kumar Khatri	Amity University, India
Supriyanto Praptodiyono	Universitas Sultan Ageng Tirtayasa, Indonesia
Syaril Nizam Omar	Universiti Sains Islam Malaysia, Malaysia
Taha Rassem	Universiti Malaysia Pahang, Malaysia
Taief Alaa Hamdi Al Amiedy	Universiti Sains Malaysia, Malaysia
Talal Saeed Qaid	Hodiedah University, Yemen
Tim Grube	TU Darmstadt, Germany
Vasaki Ponnusamy	Universiti Tunku Abdul Rahman, Malaysia
Waheed Ali H. M. Ghanem	Universiti Malaysia Terengganu, Malaysia
Waled Almakhawi	University of Siegen, Germany
Yagasena Appannah	Quest International University, Malaysia
Yean Li Ho	Multimedia University, Malaysia
Yousef Sanjalawe	Northern Border University, Saudi Arabia
Yu Beng Leau	Universiti Malaysia Sabah, Malaysia
Zeyad Ghaleb Almekhlafi	University of Hail, Saudi Arabia

Contents

**Digital Forensics and Surveillance, Botnet and Malware, DDoS,
and Intrusion Detection/Prevention**

Ambient Cloud and Edge Computing, SDN, Wireless and Cellular Communication

**Governance, Social Media, Mobile and Web, Data Privacy, Data Policy
and Fake News**

Internet of Things, Industry 4.0 and Blockchain, and Cryptology

A Blockchain Framework to Increase the Security and Verifiability of Educational Certificates

Faraz Masood[(✉)] ⓘ and Arman Rasool Faridi ⓘ

Department of Computer Science, Aligarh Muslim University, Aligarh,
Uttar Pradesh 202002, India
fmasood@myamu.ac.in

Abstract. Education not only means acquiring knowledge or skills, but it also includes acquiring morals, beliefs and values. Nowadays, most people think that gaining an educational certificate means that they are qualified, and because of that, some people make fake certificates to get the job. There is no easy way to validate these certificates, mainly when people belong to different countries. With the spread of coronavirus worldwide, travel restrictions were imposed between nations and within the nation itself. As a result, numerous educational activities, such as conferences, seminars etc., have been postponed. However, the organisers opted to hold these events over the Internet due to the pandemic's numerous limitations. Many of these activities offer certificates of participation, but it is not easy to verify the authenticity of these certificates and the coordinating institutes and attendees. Similarly, there are problems with attending several events at the same time. Many such challenges are explored thoroughly. Then a framework is proposed along with the algorithms that will explain in detail how these challenges can be solved using blockchain technology. As a result, a comparison of the proposed framework is made with the frameworks discussed in the literature and found that the proposed framework is much better in solving the discussed challenges. The article concludes with the future directions for implementing such a framework in the real world.

Keywords: Blockchain · COVID-19 · Education · Hyperledger · Smart contracts

1 Introduction

With the spread of COVID-19, many countries have implemented lockdown and travel bans. Due to this, it was challenging for educational institutions to operate traditionally. Therefore, not only online teaching has increased, but conferences, workshops, seminars, and faculty development programs (FDPs) are also being conducted online. Figure 1 shows the increase in search of online meeting applications, especially during the lockdown period in various parts of the world. To attend these events, participants have to register, and after attending the event, organisers ask the participants to fill up the feedback form or give a quiz and, based on that, provide the certificate to the participants.

© Springer Nature Singapore Pte Ltd. 2021
N. Abdullah et al. (Eds.): ACeS 2021, CCIS 1487, pp. 3–17, 2021.
https://doi.org/10.1007/978-981-16-8059-5_1

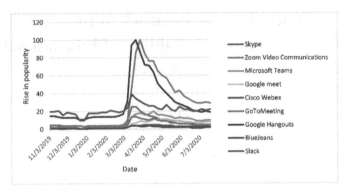

Fig. 1. Trend showing the rise in online meeting applications. (https://trends.google.com/)

There are many problems with this system. Participants can apply with any institution name whether or not they belong to that particular institution, and there is no easy way to verify these details. Similarly, the participants cannot verify the organisers. Also, the validity of the certificates cannot be verified, and many people may participate in multiple events simultaneously. To overcome these problems, this paper proposes the use of blockchain technology.

Blockchain technology is a distributed ledger maintained in a decentralised way that can store transactions, records, logs, metadata of big files etc. Blockchain stores data that is timestamped and immutable, which is not maintained by an individual but a group of people or nodes, and no one can modify the data without coming to a consensus with the majority of the nodes [1, 2]. Data is stored in the form of blocks that are chained together and secured using cryptographic principles. After its launch, blockchain has been expected to be the next disruptive technology that can disrupt sectors like banking, energy trading, logistics and many more [3, 4].

Blockchain is considered to be of three types based on usage: public, private, and consortium blockchains [5–7]. Any user with the appropriate software can access the network, read, write, or send and receive data within public blockchains. Public blockchains are made of a decentralised network that has no single authority to regulate the flow, as the public blockchains have no authorisation. Any transaction stored in a public blockchain is entirely accessible, meaning that anyone can access the transaction details. However, privacy is maintained [8, 9].

For private blockchains, only approved users are given access to the chain [10]. This is also called permissioned blockchain, as it prevents the engagement of unauthorised users in the network. The system can be operated by more than one person or organisation. Read and write permissions are held centralised to a specific person, but we use consensus, immutability, and security features of the blockchain.

In Consortium blockchains, the network is restricted, but it is not controlled by a single entity [11]. In this, some individuals or organisations have read and write access with certain restrictions. Since it is semi-decentralised, a group of sanctioned individuals control a blockchain consortium rather than a single entity. We will be using this type of blockchain in our proposed framework.

This paper proposes a framework in which it has been assumed that the highest educational authority C_a of the country will issue the public and private keys to the institutions, students and faculties. Only institutions can add data to the blockchain. Institutions can also read data of the participants if they have permission to do so. Participants can access the information whenever required with the help of their keys. Privacy of the participants will also be maintained, and the process of verification will be fast and reliable.

In this paper, we first discussed all the challenges of the current system for maintaining the certificates. After that, related work is explored. Then the foundation of the proposed framework has been built. The final framework has been presented along with the algorithms. Later, we explained how the proposed framework would address the discussed challenges, along with the future directions for the implementation of the framework.

2 Motivation: Challenges in the Existing System

Due to the spread of Novel Coronavirus, the world is facing many challenges that impact the economy and all walks of life, including the education system, especially that of the developing countries. Some are intelligently turning this disaster into an opportunity by organising educational events online like online webinars, FDPs etc., and people are participating in these events from home saving their travel time and money. However, this sudden change from offline mode to online mode raised many challenges that can harm event organisers and the participants.

The following discussion focuses on the challenges that can be addressed using blockchain technology:

- C1:- *As everything is online, so the main challenge for the organisers is to validate the information of the participants. It is possible that participants may pretend to be belonging to an institution but actually not and gets a participation certificate mentioning that institution name. This may be the cause of concern to the organisers as they may issue the certificate to the fake participant.*
- C2:- *Participants can not verify the details of the organisers. Some fake institutions may be conducting an event to take personal data by pretending to be a prestigious institutions. Participants get the certificates from these institutions and may write them in their profiles. This may be a cause of concern to the participants as they received the certificate from fake organisers, which may hamper their reputation.*
- C3:- *There is no easy way to verify the validity of the certificates. Suppose participant claims to attend an event then there is no easy way for the other institutions to verify the details.*
- C4:- *When applying for a job, an individual has to present a hard copy of all the certificates he has acquired. There is no single platform where all these certificates are present, along with the details of the events. Suppose a person participated in an online certification program, then what are the contents covered by that program and his performance should be easily verifiable.*

– C5:- *The main problem with online events is that an individual can participate in multiple events that are going on simultaneously. If there are multiple events at different times on a single day, then it may be valid, but if the events are at the same time, then it should not be considered valid, and one of the participation should be rejected.*

So, it is necessary to tackle these challenges as online events are expected to be the new normal even after the pandemic is over.

3 Related Work

Before studying the existing systems, it is necessary to check whether blockchain solves these challenges. For this, we will use the model proposed by [12]. Yes, following the model, we need to share consistent data in which more than one entity will contribute. That data should not be altered later, and blockchain will not store sensitive data. It will be mentioned in our framework, which will have read and write permissions and audit the data. So that means it is appropriate to use blockchain to solve the challenges discussed.

A literature survey is done to identify whether such type of system is proposed earlier or not. For this, it was necessary to explore the uses of blockchain in the online education system and find the proposed solution for storing certificates and digital records in the blockchain. A good amount of work is proposed and implemented concerning the usage of blockchain for storing land records [13–15]. Similarly, a lot of work is going on to connect medical records with blockchain to increase security and availability [16, 17]. Blockchain can also be used to secure data related to applications of the Internet of things [18–21], as well as it can deal with the security aspects of cloud computing [22–24]. Some work is also done for issuing digital certificates using blockchain [25–27].

In [28] authors explained how blockchain could be beneficial in the education system. An analysis of the use of artificial intelligence, big data and blockchain in the education system is discussed in [29]. Authors in [30] discuss the use of blockchain for learning logs that can be used in data analytics. The benefits and challenges of using blockchain are discussed in [31].

In [32], authors have provided a solution for the assessment of e-learning and certification of the blockchain but is mainly focussed on the course of study completion based on the performance in online courses. In [33], authors proposed integrating blockchain in the education system, trying to make the educational assessments and personalised curricula more manageable but not include the certification process.

Authors in [34] focus on the digital storage and authentication of educational records, but other institutions can not participate in the system. Similarly, in [35] authors suggest a system to store and retrieve the educational records. In [36], the authors discussed the quiz on blockchain but missed the storage and issuance of the certificate. In [37, 38] tries to give the whole solution of adopting blockchain in the education system and employers' involvement.

4 Proposed Framework

The proposed framework includes mainly five types of stakeholders. The first one is the country's highest education authority, C_a, which permits the institutions to read and write on the blockchain. C_a also permit the institutions to issue keys to the participants or provides keys themselves. The second one is the participant P. P can be a student, faculty or any other staff belonging to an institution. The third one is I_p, the institution of P, i.e. from where he belongs. The next one is the institution where P has participated I_o, and the last one is other institutes I_n where P may want to show his certificates.

4.1 Building the Solution

To begin with, C_a issue the keys to the authorised organisations. So every authorised organisation has a key pair and can digitally sign using their private keys. Similarly, every P will be provided with their key pair. Now, let us suppose P wants to participate in any event.

Partial Solution. P will apply for the event. After attending the event, I_o will digitally sign the certificate, and that certificate will be stored in the blockchain. A separate portal will be provided for I_n and I_p to search with the public key of P. Now, this solution has many problems. With this system, we can achieve a solution for challenges C2, C3 and C4 but cannot achieve a solution for C1 and C5.

Partial Solution. P will apply for the event, but for that, he has to take permission from I_p. A smart contract will be written such that I_p will digitally sign the details of P along with the details of the event. I_o will only allow participants who have initiated the smart contract from their organisation. When the event is over, I_o will digitally sign the certificate, and that certificate, along with other details, will be stored in the blockchain. So here, when both I_o and I_p are signing the participant's details, challenge C1 is also appropriately handled.

Partial Solution. To solve C5, only those contracts should be finalised in which there is no clash in timing. Both I_o and I_p can verify timing details. So whenever P attends two events that are clashing with each other and which are against the rules, then the smart contract will first verify the details about the clashing events from the blockchain using the public key of P, and if there is a match, a new certificate will not be added. If there is no clash, then the certificate will be added to the blockchain. For P and I_n, a separate portal will be provided to search all the certificates acquired by P. So by this, all the challenges are covered, but some problems which do not exist in the current system may arise. This system has a problem that P may later deny that he has not attended that event.

Partial Solution. In this solution, the smart contract will be initiated by P by signing and uploading the event's details. Then it is verified and signed by the I_p, and now I_o will allow only those participants whose details are digitally signed by P and I_p, then they may be allowed to join the event. After the event is over, certificates will be digitally signed by I_o along with other details like quiz score etc., and if there is no conflict, then all the details will be stored in the blockchain. The unfinished smart contracts will be removed without adding anything to the blockchain once the predefined deadline is over. Now similar to the solution above, a separate portal will be provided to search for the details of the P using his public key, and also, this solution solves the challenges C1, C2, C3 and C4. Now only one issue is left, which is the privacy of P. As to search the certificates of an individual, we proposed a portal that will be public, and anyone can search using the public key, so there is a need to handle this issue.

Partial Solution. Everything will be done according to last partial solution, and personal details of the P will include the public key and the address generated using the private key. This address will be added to the blockchain, and P will be searchable using this address only instead of the public key. While applying for a job or any other purpose, if P wants to share his details, he will write the address of all the certificates he has obtained. Then these certificates can be obtained from blockchain, and the privacy of P will be maintained.

Complete Solution. First, when P is interested in joining an event, he will create an address and initiate the smart contract after adding his personal details, address, the public key, and event details along with time and date. All these details will be signed using the private key of P. Now, these details will be verified and signed by I_p. After that, P will inform I_o about the contract details. If I_o finds everything according to the requirements, it can allow P to join the event. Once the event is over and P has fulfilled all the criteria, I_o digitally signs the details like attendance, exam score, and even screenshots of participation. If there is no conflict in timing and other rules, the contract will be completed, and the certificate and other details will be added to the blockchain.

A separate portal will be provided, which will call the blockchain API and helps to download or view certificates based on the address given in the search bar. This solution will deal with all the challenges, maintaining the privacy of P.

4.2 System Design

Figure 2 depicts the basic architecture of the system. Here, C_a create users in the system and provides with public-private key pair. First, it checks whether the user is already present in the system. If yes, then it will provide the public key to the user. Only C_a can search by user name and other details. However, it cannot access the private key of the user. So the users must store private keys properly. If the user is not added to the system, it will be added, and the system automatically return keys to the newly added user. This process is shown in Algorithm 1.

Algorithm 1 Adding a new user to the system

Require:

C_a *has proper permissions to add a new user.*

Ensure:

Proper permissions are given to the user based on the type of user.

if the user has already been added to the system, **then**

  return Public key.

else

  if the user has proper documentation, **then**

    return Public and Private key pair.

  else

    Ask for proper documentation.

  end if

end if

Once the keys are issued, and I_o wants to organise an event, it publishes the advertisement with all the information. If P wants to attend that event, he will start a smart contract with all the necessary details, including a public key, generated address, event details, personal details, I_p, I_o, etc. It will then be sent to I_p. After validating the details, I_p will sign the details, and P sends the smart contract details to I_o.

If I_o finds everything valid, it will allow P to participate in the event. The whole process is shown in Algorithm 2.

Algorithm 2 Register to attend the event

Require:

P, I_o and I_p are added to the system.

Ensure:

Valid P should be allowed to attend the event.

P will generate the address from the private key.

P will start the smart contract by digitally signing the required details. I_p will verify the details.

if I_p found all the details valid, **then**

  I_p Sign the details.

  P informs I_o about the contract.

  if I_o found all the details valid, **then**

    Allow P to attend the event.

  else

    I_o will reject the request, and the smart contract will be terminated without adding anything to the blockchain.

  end if

else

  I_p will reject the request, and the smart contract will be terminated without adding anything to the blockchain.

end if

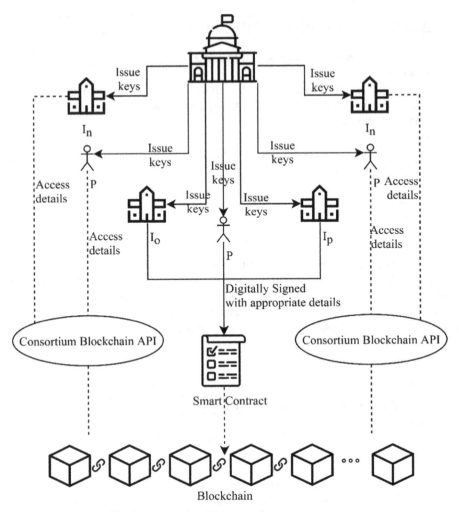

Fig. 2. Proposed architecture using smart contracts.

Once the event is over, the I_o will check whether P has met all the requirements to achieve the certificate including payment details. If all the requirements are fulfilled then, I_o will add all the details, including the score, event details, event timing, certificate details etc. I_o will sign the details, and if the P does not already have an entry for that time on the blockchain, these details will be added to the blockchain. Now smart contract will automatically verify that there is an entry for that time or not. However, this can be only done if there is a unique field that is searchable. So for this only, we will add a public key in the details, but no one can read it.

It will be used internally by the system, and the system will automatically check whether there is an entry in the blockchain or not. If the details exist in that time, then the smart contract will be terminated without adding anything in the blockchain, as shown in Algorithm 3.

Algorithm 3 Generation of the certificate.

Require:

        P, I_o and I_p are added to the system.

Ensure:

        Only a valid certificate will be added to the system.

I_o will check whether *P* has met all the requirements of the event.

if I_o found all the requirements are met, **then**

  I_o will sign the details.

  if a Simultaneous event is present in blockchain, **then**

      The smart contract will be terminated; nothing will be added to the blockchain.

  else

      The system will add the certificate along with all details in the blockchain.

  end if

else

      The smart contract will be terminated without adding anything to the blockchain.

end if

Suppose *P* wants to retrieve the certificate, so he has to provide the address generated while applying for the event. A portal will be provided to search the certificate by address. *P* will go to the portal and search using the address.

Algorithm 4 *P* wants to retrieve the certificate from the blockchain.

Require:

        P has the address of the certificate.

Ensure:

        Valid event details should be retrieved.

P will call blockchain API with the address.

 if the address is found, **then**

   Display retrieved details to the user.

 if *P* wants to download the certificate, **then**

  Give the private key

  if the private key is valid, **then**

   Return certificate

  else

   Show error message

  end if

 else

   Return

 end if

 else

 Display error message.

end if

If the address is valid, he will be provided with the event's details and his performance. If he wants to download the certificate, P can download it using his private key, which is signed by all I_o, I_p and P. This process is shown in Algorithm 4.

Now suppose P wants to share his certification details with I_n, then he has to share all the certificate addresses. I_n will go to the same portal and can verify the details using these addresses. By this, P does not need to share xerox copies while applying for the job. I_n cannot download the certificate but can verify the details. This process can be seen in Algorithm 5.

Algorithm 5 I_n wants to verify certificate details of P.

Require:
> I_n has the addresses of the certificates.

Ensure:
> *Valid event details should be retrieved.*

I_n will call blockchain API with the address.

if the address is found **then**

Return certificate along with other details.

else

Display error message.

end if

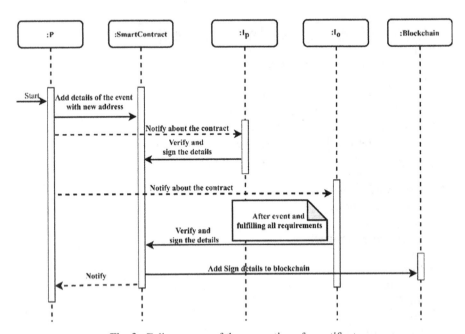

Fig. 3. Full sequence of the generation of a certificate

So by this, the whole process will be complete. The whole sequence considering the positive cases can be seen in Fig. 3. To summarise, P will initiate the process, the smart contract will be terminated after the completion of the event, and only when everything is valid then details will be added in the blockchain.

4.3 Security and Privacy Issues

Main issues of making things public are security and privacy issues. In our system, we are using blockchain, and its main feature is to provide security of data using cryptographic algorithms. So the only concern is privacy unless the blockchain system is compromised.

As discussed above, a separate public portal will be provided to retrieve the certificates and other details, but if we use the public key for searching, this may lead to privacy issues for P because anyone may access all the participant's details from the public key. So the first option is to provide them with login credentials, but this may cause problems to verify the details by I_n. Hence we propose to generate a new address for every new application. We use a similar approach as used by Bitcoin. We will follow the steps shown in Fig. 4 to generate the new address. It depends upon P whether he wants to generate a new address for every event or not:

- P will generate a random number.
- Add random number and public key.
- Perform SHA-256 hashing on that.
- Carry out RIPEMD-160 hashing on SHA-256 outcome.
- Execute SHA-256 hash on the RIPEMD160 extended result.
- Execute SHA-256 hash on previous SHA-256 hash.
- Take the preceding 4 bytes of SHA-256 hash. This is Address Checksum.
- To get the RIPEMD-160 hash extended, add the checksum bytes at the end of the RIPEMD-160 hash.

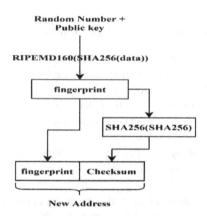

Fig. 4. Address generation process.

5   Discussion

Now we discuss whether our framework will be able to solve the discussed challenges in Sect. 2.

5.1   Verification of the Participant's Information

As the smart contract is initiated by P and signed by him and not only that, it is signed by the I_p as well. Therefore the information of P is verified before applying for the event.

5.2   Verification of the Organisers

I_o gets key only after verification by C_a. I_o can sign the details only if it is authorised. This way I_o is verified.

5.3   Validation of the Certificates

All the details, including event details, quiz score, attendance etc., are signed by I_o and added to the blockchain, which can not be modified. All these details cannot be changed once added to the blockchain. P and I_n can search the details by using the address generated by P. So if the details are present on the blockchain, that means the certificate is valid.

5.4   Reducing Paper Usage and Retrieval of Certificate Details

As for the job application, we need to share the certification details, so instead of hard copies, P will share all the addresses of all the certificates he has obtained. By this, all the details can be retrieved using these addresses, which will contain the certificate and other details like topics covered, quiz scores, etc.

5.5   Restriction on Attending Simultaneous Events

As events are online, it is possible that P can attend two events that are going on simultaneously. Now he will get the participation certificate for both events. Suppose the first event generates the certificate and added the details to the blockchain. When the second event tries to enter the details, it will not be added, and P will not get the second certificate. Hence once P knows that only one certificate can be generated, he will not attend both the events.

In this way, all the challenges can be addressed and resolved by our framework. In Table 1, we have compared our work with the previous works and found that most of the previous works focus on the storage of records and mainly dealt with the use of blockchain within an institution. Most of the discussed challenges have not been dealt in many of the previous works. Only [37] is partially able to solve the three challenges out of the five discussed challenges. However, the proposed system handles all these challenges, the solution is secure, and privacy is also maintained.

Table 1. Comparison of the research work with the proposed solution

Papers	Challenges				
	C1	C2	C3	C4	C5
[28, 29, 31]	✗	✗	✗	✗	✗
[30]	✗	✗	✗	✓	✗
[32–35]	✗	✗	✓	✓	✗
[36, 38]	✗	✗	✓	✗	✗
[37]	✗	✓	✓	✓	✗
Proposed	✓	✓	✓	✓	✓

6 Conclusion and Future Directions

With the travel restrictions due to the spread of COVID-19 in various parts of the world, it is not possible to attend various events. So there is an increase in the number of online meetings, conferences, workshops etc. Some events provide a participation certificate, and these are needed for promotions and jobs. So first, we have listed out the challenges that the current system faces for the validity of organisations, participants and certificates. Even if the event is offline, there is no easy way to verify the details of the events, and the person has to share duplicate hard copies of the certificates for any job or promotion. Our framework will use smart contracts and store information in the blockchain. So that all the details can be easily verified and retrieved from a single portal. We have maintained the privacy aspects of the participants, as well.

This paper suggested and covered mainly all the aspects to adopt the new system. In Future, attempts will be made to implement the proposed framework in Hyperledger Fabric [39]. Once it is unit tested, the plans are to deploy and test the system at department levels, then to university level and once successful, it will be presented to the research and development department of the country for approval. Once it is approved, then attempts will be made to implement it all over the country.

References

1. Nakamoto, S.: Bitcoin: A Peer-to-Peer Electronic Cash System—Satoshi Nakamoto Institute (2008)
2. Raval, S.: Decentralized Applications: Harnessing Bitcoin's Blockchain Technology. O'Reilly Media Inc., Sebastopol (2016)
3. Swan, M.: Blockchain: Blueprint for a New Economy. O'Reilly Media Inc., Sebastopol (2015)
4. Casino, F., Dasaklis, T.K., Patsakis, C.: A systematic literature review of blockchain-based applications: current status, classification and open issues. Telematics Inform. **36**, 55–81 (2019). https://doi.org/10.1016/j.tele.2018.11.006
5. Gramoli, V.: From blockchain consensus back to Byzantine consensus. Future Gener. Comput. Syst. **107**, 760–769 (2020). https://doi.org/10.1016/j.future.2017.09.023
6. Zhang, S., Lee, J.-H.: Analysis of the main consensus protocols of blockchain. ICT Express **6**, 93–97 (2020). https://doi.org/10.1016/j.icte.2019.08.001

7. Sankar, L.S., Sindhu, M., Sethumadhavan, M.: Survey of consensus protocols on blockchain applications. In: 2017 4th International Conference on Advanced Computing and Communication Systems (ICACCS), pp. 1–5 (2017)

8. Kus Khalilov, M.C., Levi, A.: A survey on anonymity and privacy in bitcoin-like digital cash systems. IEEE Commun. Surv. Tutor. **20**, 2543–2585 (2018). https://doi.org/10.1109/COMST.2018.2818623

9. Conti, M., Sandeep Kumar, E., Lal, C., Ruj, S.: A survey on security and privacy issues of bitcoin. IEEE Commun. Surv. Tutor. **20**, 3416–3452 (2018)

10. Hao, Y., Li, Y., Dong, X., Fang, L., Chen, P.: Performance analysis of consensus algorithm in private blockchain. In: 2018 IEEE Intelligent Vehicles Symposium (IV), pp. 280–285 (2018)

11. Dib, O., Brousmiche, K.-L., Durand, A., Thea, E., Hamida, E.: Consortium Blockchains: overview, applications and challenges. Int. J. Adv. Telecommun. **11**, 51–64 (2018)

12. Yaga, D., Mell, P., Roby, N., Scarfone, K.: Blockchain technology overview. Natl. Inst. Stand. Technol. 1–68 (2018)

13. Pongnumkul, S., Khonnasee, C., Lertpattanasak, S., Polprasert, C.: Proof-of-Concept (PoC) of land mortgaging process in blockchain-based land registration system of Thailand. In: Proceedings of the 2020 The 2nd International Conference on Blockchain Technology, pp. 100–104. ACM, New York (2020)

14. Yapa, I., Heanthenna, S., Bandara, N., Prasad, I., Mallawarachchi, Y.: Decentralized ledger for land and property transactions in Sri Lanka Acresense. In: 2018 IEEE Region 10 Humanitarian Technology Conference (R10-HTC), pp. 1–6 (2018)

15. Nandi, M., Bhattacharjee, R.K., Jha, A., Barbhuiya, F.A.: A secured land registration framework on Blockchain. In: 2020 Third ISEA Conference on Security and Privacy (ISEA-ISAP), pp. 130–138 (2020)

16. Azaria, A., Ekblaw, A., Vieira, T., Lippman, A.: MedRec: using blockchain for medical data access and permission management. In: 2016 2nd International Conference on Open and Big Data (OBD), pp. 25–30 (2016)

17. Xia, Q., Sifah, E.B., Asamoah, K.O., Gao, J., Du, X., Guizani, M.: MeDShare: trust-less medical data sharing among cloud service providers via blockchain. IEEE Access **5**, 14757–14767 (2017)

18. Liu, C.H., Lin, Q., Wen, S.: Blockchain-enabled data collection and sharing for industrial IoT with deep reinforcement learning. IEEE Trans. Ind. Inform. **15**, 3516–3526 (2019). https://doi.org/10.1109/TII.2018.2890203

19. Singh, M., Singh, A., Kim, S.: Blockchain: a game changer for securing IoT data. In: 2018 IEEE 4th World Forum on Internet of Things (WF-IoT), pp. 51–55 (2018)

20. Liang, X., Zhao, J., Shetty, S., Li, D.: Towards data assurance and resilience in IoT using blockchain. In: MILCOM 2017 - 2017 IEEE Military Communications Conference (MILCOM), pp. 261–266 (2017)

21. Li, R., Song, T., Mei, B., Li, H., Cheng, X., Sun, L.: Blockchain for large-scale internet of things data storage and protection. IEEE Trans. Serv. Comput. **12**, 762–771 (2019)

22. Kirkman, S.: A data movement policy framework for improving trust in the cloud using smart contracts and blockchains. In: 2018 IEEE International Conference on Cloud Engineering (IC2E), pp. 270–273 (2018)

23. Liang, X., Shetty, S., Tosh, D., Kamhoua, C., Kwiat, K., Njilla, L.: ProvChain: a blockchain-based data provenance architecture in cloud environment with enhanced privacy and availability. In: 2017 17th IEEE/ACM International Symposium on Cluster, Cloud and Grid Computing (CCGRID), pp. 468–477 (2017)

24. Kanimozhi, E.A., Suguna, M., Mercy Shalini, S.: Immediate detection of data corruption by integrating blockchain in cloud computing. In: 2019 International Conference on Vision Towards Emerging Trends in Communication and Networking (ViTECoN), pp. 1–4 (2019)

25. Huynh, T.T., Tru Huynh, T., Pham, D.K., Khoa Ngo, A.: Issuing and Verifying Digital Certificates with Blockchain. In: International Conference on Advanced Technologies for Communications, 2018-October, pp. 332–336 (2018). https://doi.org/10.1109/ATC.2018.858 7428
26. Cheng, J., Lee, N., Chi, C., Chen, Y.: Blockchain and smart contract for digital certificate. In: 2018 IEEE International Conference on Applied System Invention (ICASI), pp. 1046–1051 (2018)
27. Chowdhury, M.J.M., Colman, A., Kabir, M.A., Han, J., Sarda, P.: Blockchain as a notarization service for data sharing with personal data store. In: 2018 17th IEEE International Conference on Trust, Security and Privacy in Computing and Communications/12th IEEE International Conference on Big Data Science and Engineering (TrustCom/BigDataSE), pp. 1330–1335 (2018)
28. Chen, G., Xu, B., Lu, M., Chen, N.-S.: Exploring blockchain technology and its potential applications for education. Smart Learn. Environ. 5(1), 1–10 (2018). https://doi.org/10.1186/ s40561-017-0050-x
29. Williams, P.: Does competency-based education with blockchain signal a new mission for universities? J. High. Educ. Policy Manag. 41, 104–117 (2019). https://doi.org/10.1080/136 0080X.2018.1520491
30. Ocheja, P., Flanagan, B., Ueda, H., Ogata, H.: Managing lifelong learning records through blockchain. Res. Pract. Technol. Enhanc. Learn. 14(1), 1–19 (2019). https://doi.org/10.1186/ s41039-019-0097-0
31. Malibari, N.A.: A survey on blockchain-based applications in education. In: 2020 7th International Conference on Computing for Sustainable Global Development (INDIACom), pp. 266–270. IEEE (2020)
32. Li, C., Guo, J., Zhang, G., Wang, Y., Sun, Y., Bie, R.: A blockchain system for E-learning assessment and certification. In: Proceedings of the 2019 IEEE International Conference on Smart Internet Things, SmartIoT 2019, pp. 212–219 (2019). https://doi.org/10.1109/Sma rtIoT.2019.00040
33. Lam, T.Y., Dongol, B.: A blockchain-enabled e-learning platform. Interact. Learn. Environ. 0, 1–23 (2020).https://doi.org/10.1080/10494820.2020.1716022
34. Zhao, G., Di, B., He, H.: Design and implementation of the digital education transaction subject two-factor identity authentication system based on blockchain. International Conference on Advanced Communication Technology ICACT 2020, pp. 176–180 (2020). https://doi.org/ 10.23919/ICACT48636.2020.9061393
35. Han, M., Li, Z., He, J.S., Wu, D., Xie, Y., Baba, A.: A novel blockchain-based education records verification solution. In: Proceedings of the 19th Annual SIG Conference on Information Technology Education, pp. 178–183. ACM, New York (2018)
36. Shen, H., Xiao, Y.: Research on online quiz scheme based on double-layer consortium blockchain. In: Proceedings of the 9th International Conference on Information Technology in Medicine and Education ITME 2018, pp. 956–960 (2018). https://doi.org/10.1109/ ITME.2018.00213
37. Lizcano, D., Lara, J.A., White, B., Aljawarneh, S.: Blockchain-based approach to create a model of trust in open and ubiquitous higher education. J. Comput. High. Educ. 32(1), 109–134 (2019). https://doi.org/10.1007/s12528-019-09209-y
38. Sharples, M., Domingue, J.: The blockchain and kudos: a distributed system for educational record, reputation and reward. In: Verbert, K., Sharples, M., Klobučar, T. (eds.) EC-TEL 2016. LNCS, vol. 9891, pp. 490–496. Springer, Cham (2016). https://doi.org/10.1007/978-3-319-45153-4_48
39. Androulaki, E., et al.: Hyperledger fabric: a distributed operating system for permissioned blockchains. In: Proceedings of the Thirteenth EuroSys Conference, p. 15. Association for Computing Machinery, New York (2018)

A Conceptual Model to Identify Illegal Activities on the Bitcoin System

Khaled Gubran Al-Hashedi[1], Pritheega Magalingam[1(✉)], Nurazean Maarop[1], Ganthan Narayana Samy[1], and Azizah Abdul Manaf[2]

[1] Advanced Informatics Department, Razak Faculty of Technology and Informatics, Universiti Teknologi Malaysia, Kuala Lumpur, Malaysia
gyakhaled2@live.utm.my, {mpritheega.kl,nurazean.kl, ganthan.kl}@utm.my
[2] Department of Cybersecurity, College of Computer Science and Engineering, University of Jeddah, Jeddah, Saudi Arabia
aaabdmanaf@uj.edu.sa

Abstract. Soon after its inception in 2009, Bitcoin was used as a tool by malicious attackers who exploit its pseudo-anonymity to establish untraceable frauds. Recently, several Bitcoin users and institutions have confirmed that thousands of Bitcoins were lost due to the failure to implement a fraud detection system, causing significant damage to individuals or institutions and resulting in bankruptcy. The anonymous nature of the Bitcoin system makes it a desirable option for malicious people to carry out illegal activities, making it difficult for law enforcement to detect suspicious behavior and making the current fraud detection techniques impractical. Thus, identifying illegal activities becomes an important factor to protect the reputation of the Bitcoin system. In this paper, we propose a model to identify illegal transactions in the Bitcoin system. Firstly, we collect illegal addresses for data labeling purposes from different sources such as online public bitcoin forums and related datasets from previous papers and then verify them with a raw Bitcoin dataset. Secondly, we introduce new types of features by using a time-based approach to segment transactions into time slices over a period in addition to the most meaningful features of the prior studies. Thirdly, we evaluate the proposed model on five popular supervised classifiers (KNN, SVM, RF, XGB, and KNN). Finally, this paper considers the problem of class imbalance and attained better optimization when using an adaptive oversampling technique (ADASYN). Results obtained from this study demonstrate that RF and XGB outperform KNN, SVM, and NN in terms of detection rate.

Keywords: Bitcoin · Fraud detection · Machine learning · Cybercrime · Illicit addresses

1 Introduction

Throughout the entire history of electronic financial systems, individuals have utilized different payment methods in electronic commerce. Numerous companies involved in

© Springer Nature Singapore Pte Ltd. 2021
N. Abdullah et al. (Eds.): ACeS 2021, CCIS 1487, pp. 18–34, 2021.
https://doi.org/10.1007/978-981-16-8059-5_2

e-commerce use digital currencies as a technique for executing sales and purchases [1]. The reason for creating an innovative currency is to transfer money via peer-to-peer protocol with no need for intermediate servers such as a financial institution or a bank. Bitcoin is a new type of virtual currency introduced first by an anonymous name of a person or group known as Satoshi Nakamoto 2008 and formally launched in 2009 [2]. Bitcoin is deemed the most prevailing and acknowledged among numerous competitors. As of December 2017, Bitcoin occupied more than 44% of the cryptocurrency market. In this context, the number of bitcoins currently available in the world is estimated to be 16.7 million bitcoins, and the total market value of bitcoins is as high as 268 billion US dollars [3].

Bitcoin introduced the concept of a decentralized network that is entirely functional based on peer-to-peer (p2p) protocol, where miners solve complex computational puzzles to generate digital Bitcoin. Since its inception in 2009, Bitcoin has become increasingly popular in terms of use and value. Even though it works well as an effective and reliable system, Bitcoin still faces some challenges as a payment system. The first challenge is related to fraudulent activities and the theft of Bitcoin [4]. Bitcoin is non-refundable after it has been traded without beneficiary approval due to its irrevocable nature [5]. In case of losing or stealing Bitcoin, Bitcoin owners may not be aware of what happened to the coin, as users whose funds have been lost or stolen can be only identified by anonymous Bitcoin addresses [6].

The second challenge for Bitcoin is illegal exchange. Bitcoin is not only used by criminals to perform fraudulent activities. On the contrary, it has been used as a platform to participate in illegal drug purchases, money laundering, terrorist financing, and many more [7]. However, the Federal Bureau of Investigation (FBI) stated that most cyber-crimes are being carried out employing digital currencies on the Silk Road [8]. The Silk Road is known as the dark web's secret marketplace, with questionable trades, such as the sale of weapons and other illegal commodities, without being traced [9]. Thus, the Silk Road scheme could collect approximately $1.2 billion illegally through tax evasion and money laundering [10]. The term Bitcoin has frequently appeared in numerous head-lines in multiple media sources highlighting fraud, malware (ransomware) or dark web markets. Consequently, several Bitcoin users and institutions have recently confirmed that thousands of Bitcoins were lost due to the failure to implement a fraud detection system, causing significant damage to individuals or institutions and resulting in bankruptcy [11–14].

Due to the anonymous nature of the Bitcoin system, Bitcoin becomes a desirable option for malicious people to carry out illegal activities that make it difficult for law enforcement to detect suspicious behavior, because the identity of the owner is anony-mous and does not require any personal information [6, 15], unlike current banking systems that require real world identities associated with users [16]. This poses a real challenge for the financial authorities, as the current fraud detection techniques might not be feasible to identify illegal activities on an anonymous network, where thousands of transactions are made every minute [4, 17, 18]. Regardless of these challenges, the entire transactions are publicly accessible for anyone, and several studies found methods to deanonymize Bitcoin users. Recently, some studies have been proposed to identify illegal activities in the Bitcoin network using different methods. This includes unsupervised methods [8, 10, 19–21] and semi-supervised methods [15]. However, these methods adopted by recent studies do not fulfill the function of identifying illegal activities as they were not efficient during the evaluation and validation process, resulting in low precision and accuracy. This is because the small amount of labeled data creates obscurities in the interpretation of abnormal financial behavior.

Thus, this paper proposes a model for identifying illegal activities in the Bitcoin system by first collecting illegal addresses for labeling purposes from public online Bitcoin forums and websites in addition to the datasets of related work. We carried out addresses filtration by checking each illegal address through the website "www.bitcoinabuse.com" [22] which provides an open online database of bitcoin addresses employed by malicious people. Then, all the collected illegal addresses with the original dataset were verified. Once the address is matched with the original dataset, it is automatically labeled as illegal. Besides, new informative features based on time-slice have been extracted along with the basic features of related papers. All experiments are implemented using five popular supervised classifiers (SVM, RF, NN, XGB, and KNN) and performance metrics (precision, recall, and f1) were applied to evaluate the performance of the proposed model. Finally, the problem of class imbalance was discussed by applying an adaptive oversampling technique (ADASYN).

In summary, the following contributions are proposed:

– This paper reviews some Bitcoin illicit activities studies of bitcoin and summarizes vulnerabilities of the Bitcoin system.
– It constructs a large dataset of illicit addresses from different sources.
– It proposes new types of features based on time-slice.
– It evaluates the performance of the proposed model based on five popular supervised classifiers in addition to addressing the problem of class imbalance.

The remainder of the paper is organized as follows: Sect. 2 discusses related work and the criminal activities in the Bitcoin system. Section 3 discusses the methodology used in this paper, demonstrating data collection and pre-processing, and describes the extracted features. Section 4 illustrates the experiment setup and interprets the result of the experiment. Finally, the conclusion is stated in Sect. 5.

2 Related Work

The task of detecting illicit activities play a vital role in the security and integrity of financial systems. Over the last few years, the issue of illicit activity detection in the financial domain has been studied by many [4, 18, 23–25]. Due to the novelty of Bitcoin, several publications mainly concentrated on detecting illicit behaviors on the Bitcoin network employing different approaches. In this paper, the focus is given to the methods that involve the Bitcoin dataset. Studies of detecting illegal activities in the Bitcoin network are classified into two groups. The first group is to identify suspicious users and transactions. The second group is to identify certain types of illicit activities such as fraud, money laundering, hack, darknet markets, ransomware, human traffickers, suspicious users, Ponzi scams, and mixing services.

Zambre and Shah [14] conducted a study by analyzing blockchain transactions to detect abnormal behavior of users carrying out fraudulent activities on Bitcoin networks employing K-means algorithm. Pham and Lee [19] examined three different types of unsupervised methods to discover malicious activities in the Bitcoin system include K-Means clustering, unsupervised Support Vector Machines, and Mahalanobis distance-based method. Besides, Pham and Lee [20] in their subsequent study applied Laws of Power Degree & Densification by adopting K-Means clustering to discover the existence of irregularities when its curved shape does not follow a particular law and Local Outlier Factor method used to measure the local deviation of a given data point regarding its neighbours.

Monamo et al. [10] studied the application of Trimmed K-Means clustering to reveal suspicious behaviours in the Bitcoin transactions based on patterns recognition with the adoption of K-Means for grouping the data into clusters with aiming to improve the ability of detection. In their subsequent study, Monamo et al. [21] suggested a multifaceted method by applying the unsupervised learning algorithm applying kd-trees and Trimmed K-Means.

For Botnets identification, Zarpelão, Miani et al. [26] examined a method to detect botnets in the Bitcoin system by launching DDoS attacks. The method was evaluated on legitimate samples to build the classification model using One-class Support Vector Machine. For ransomware identification, Liao, Zhao et al. [27] proposed a novel approach to analyze ransomware in the Bitcoin network and transactions by applying a topological network.

For illegal users' identification, Yang, Dong et al. [25] conducted a study to reveal the identity of illegal activities using the heuristic user address clustering method. Zhang, Zhou et al. [28] suggested a multi-resolution clustering system called BITSCOPE to identify illegal user activities that use Bitcoin. Irwin and Turner performed an optimal solution to identify illicit Bitcoin users and the transactions. Turner and Irwin [23] investigated several experiments on the Bitcoin network to discover illicit activities of users using heuristics and graph analysis techniques. Li, Cai et al. [18] presented a study to discover the illegal addresses in the Bitcoin system by collecting a large number of illegal addresses and applied various machine learning algorithms.

For fraud identification, Bartoletti, Pes et al. [29] utilized data mining techniques to discover addresses associated with Ponzi schemes. Lin, Wu et al. [30] suggested a classification model using a supervised technique for identifying the abnormal addresses in the Bitcoin system. Nerurkar, Bhirud et al. [24] examined several supervised learning techniques for identifying illicit activities in the Bitcoin network by collecting a dataset of 1216 Bitcoin users and classified them into 16 classes. For the Darknet market identification, Janze [31] examined the evolution of Bitcoin and Darknet markets by designing a dynamic research model. Table 1 outlines all the related studies of identifying illegal activities in the Bitcoin system.

Table 1. List of published studies on Bitcoin.

Ref.	Dataset	Description	Feature extracted
[14]	Public	Identifying the peculiar behavior of users on Bitcoin	Network based features
[19, 20]	Public	Detecting malicious activities on Bitcoin	Network and transaction-based features
[10, 21]	Public	Identifying fraudulent activities on Bitcoin	Transaction features
[26]	Private	Detecting botnets in the Bitcoin network	Transaction features
[27]	Private	Detection ransomware in Bitcoin	Transaction features
[25]	Private	Identifying illegal Bitcoin user	Transaction features
[28]	Private	Identifying illegal Bitcoin user	Transaction features
[18]	Private	Detection illicit addresses in Bitcoin	Transaction features, topological features, and
[29]	Private	Identifying Bitcoin fraud associated with Ponzi schemes	temporal features
[30]	Private	Detection of abnormal addresses in Bitcoin	Transaction and network features
[24]	Public	Detection of illicit activities in Bitcoin	Transaction features
[31]	Private	Analyzing of Bitcoin and Darknet markets	Transaction features

2.1 Bitcoin Criminal Activities and Vulnerabilities

Due to the significant increase in the value and use of Bitcoin, users and researchers have expressed interest in the reliability, integrity, and security of the Bitcoin system by asking various questions. Böhme et al. [32] considered several problems related to the use of Bitcoin in a decentralized network. These problems have caused concern for many Bitcoin users because Bitcoin is designed to allow money transfers without any authentication. One of these problems is the adoption of Bitcoin without using any third-party services such as the traditional financial system, which increases the potential for cybercrimes risks. According to the European Central Bank, the unregulated use of Bitcoin may open up new avenues for scammers, money laundering, crimes, terrorist financing, and ransomware [6, 33]. With the remarkable adoption and fast expansion of cryptocurrencies, particularly Bitcoin, which has set record levels of value in recent years, the amount of abuse reports has also increased [13]. The term Bitcoin has frequently appeared in numerous headlines in multiple media sources highlighting fraud, malware (ransomware), or dark web markets. However, law enforcement and the government have expressed serious concern about adopting cryptocurrencies as a tool in criminal activity and suspected purchasing [34]. Table 2 shows the main security threats in the Bitcoin system.

Table 2. A list of the main security threats in the Bitcoin system.

Ref.	Attack	Description	Targets	Attack effect
[35]	51% ATTACK or Goldfinger	Attackers get control of more than 50% of the Bitcoin network	Bitcoin network, mining pools	Prevent current and future transactions from being confirmed by other miners
[36–38]	Selfish Mining or Block Discarding Attack	Violates Bitcoin forking feature to collect more revenues	Honest miners	Honest miners are forced to make wasted calculations, with >50% leading to a Goldfinger attack
[39, 40]	Block Withholding	A rogue miner may submit only partial work information and act fraudulently, instead of submitting a full part proof of the dishonest miner's work	Honest miners	Dishonest miners attempt to rise their profit by lowering the returns of other miners
[41]	Double spending	Spending the same Bitcoin twice by sending two inconsistent transactions	Sellers or merchants	This attack causes merchants to waste their funds and drive out honest users
[42, 43]	Transaction malleability	The attacker changes the transaction content before confirming it to the blockchain	Bitcoin Exchange	The bad user gets more exchanges which cause loss of Bitcoin faced by the good users due to the changes of the unique identifier of the transaction by the hacker
[11, 44]	DDoS	An extensive attack to make a network resource unavailable	Bitcoin components	Disrupting Bitcoin system by sending endless demands from various network sources

3   Proposed Model

One of the most significant problems facing researchers during their proposing a fraud detection model is what kind of machine learning method or statistical data to use. However, if the wrong method is selected, the system may fail, or the false detection rate may be affected. For this paper, it is important to do some preliminary research on the previous work, which may assist to lay the foundation for the investigation by obtaining and analyzing the previous research literature related to the detection of fraud in the Bitcoin system. Thus, searching in various academic journals through online databases was conducted. This includes the IEEE Xplorer Library, Science Direct, Web of Science, and Google Scholar. This focuses on previous work related to detecting Bitcoin fraud. Therefore, it is necessary to conduct a comparative study of previous work, and through a critical analysis of each study to understand what dilemmas exist in the current fraud detection system. This covers the advantages and disadvantages of each method. Next, each study was reviewed and investigated individually to understand the problems that exist in the current studies. This section briefly summarizes the proposed conceptual model for detecting illegal activities in Bitcoin as shown in Fig. 1.

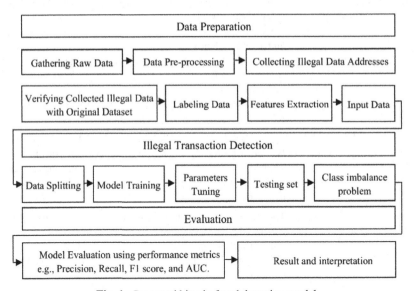

Fig. 1. Proposed bitcoin fraud detection model.

3.1   Data Collection and Pre-processing

This section consists of two steps. The first step is to collect the right data. A publicly raw available Bitcoin dataset proposed by ELTE Bitcoin Project was collected [45]. The collected Bitcoin dataset comprises the whole blockchain transactions from genesis transactions till 2014. Even though the obtained dataset comprises a large amount of data and attributes, only the most significant files were kept for analysis. These files include the information of users, transactions, addresses, inputs and outputs, values, etc. The dataset contains all blockchain transactions and is made up of eight ".csv" files totaling 8.10 GB. After collecting the data, we performed data cleansing where the incomplete and noise transactions were checked and then each file was analyzed individually to gain insights about the users, their transactions, and related addresses possessed by a single user. Data processing is time-consuming and requires perseverance. It should be noted that before solving this task, the data collected from the Bitcoin network was found to be very large and the most difficult to be used for analysis as it is heterogeneous. Therefore, it is evident that it is necessary to transform the data into homogeneous data. Since the gathered data is deemed as big data, a sophisticated tool like Neo4j [46] was used to handle a large amount of data.

Neo4j is an open-source graph database used to store data in rows and columns with the ability to connect the data into relationships. The graph database will assist to understand and find the flow of a certain relationship and provides a way to extract the required information between addresses and transactions belonging to the same user [47]. For example, to create a table containing all the coin-based transactions with a timestamp, output transaction, input transaction value, address, and users, we need to combine all the different files into one. To better understand the Bitcoin dataset, we have compiled the Bitcoin dataset files in Table 3.

Table 3. A description of a raw Bitcoin dataset.

File name	Description
Blockhash	277.443 lines
Transaction hash	24.618.959 lines
Address	24.618.959 lines
Enumeration of all transactions	30.048.983 lines
List of all transaction inputs	65.714.232 lines
List of all transaction outputs	73.738.345 lines
Timestamp	30.048.983 lines
Contraction	24.618.959 lines

The second step is to collect illegal addresses for data labeling purposes by searching through online bitcoin forums such as bitcointalk.org, reddit.com, and blockchain.info or tags that refer to addresses related to thieves, scammers, wallets, drug, ransomware, Ponzi, a darknet market, blackmail scam, and arms. These websites allow users to discuss and report Bitcoin addresses. This is accomplished by collecting addresses belonging to the same user indicating such malicious activities through online forum tags. To assure the integrity of the collected labeled data, address filtering was carried out by checking each illegal address through the website "www.bitcoinabuse.com" that provides an open online database of bitcoin addresses used by malicious people, which traces bitcoin suspicious addresses used by money laundering, scammers, ransomware, etc. Then, we also verified all collected illegal addresses with the original dataset.

Once the address is matched with the original dataset, it is automatically labeled as illegal. After the carrying out of the filtration, we found some addresses that can be difficult to label as legal or illegal. Therefore, we remove these unconfirmed addresses. However, with recent collected illegal data, we can simply determine a potentially suspicious transaction. In addition, we took into consideration and examined some datasets found in the literature that is relevant to identify illegal activities in Bitcoin. These datasets are used in our paper. For example, in [29], a publicly available dataset containing most of Ponzi schemes illegal addresses. In [48], a dataset of 7122 addresses of ransomware payment was released. In [49], an Elliptic dataset with a total of 11,698 was published. However, these datasets are used in our paper along with the illegal data collected from online bitcoin forums. Overall, we could find a total of 21,325 illegal addresses.

3.2 Feature Extraction

When a bitcoin wallet or account is compromised. A fraudster would like to let others believe that fraud is just an ordinary action. Thus, the fraudster would abuse Bitcoin as much as possible and will organize multiple fake addresses in a short period. Hence, if the transactions are aggregated over some time, abrupt changes can be detected. Aggregation of the transactions, whether it is minimum or maximum, average or total, can reveal a lot of insights resulting in creating hundreds of features generated from transaction data [50–52]. This paper intended to improve the existing detection method by finding suitable features using both transactions and network-based features. As stated by Pham and Lee [20], extracting meaningful features can be improved by identifying a significant portion of the data through the adoption of a time-based approach to examine and discover smaller communities within the Bitcoin network. Therefore, this paper focuses on extracting features by splitting the transactions into time slices in addition to using the most important features found in previous studies [10, 14, 15, 19–21].

Furthermore, the time-slices would contain six features of each feature on a total, one month, one week, one day, one hour, and five minutes basis. For example, the monthly feature will only show the activity of the transactions and addresses within one month. The reason behind choosing these features is to analyze each transaction in a short period of time. Note that all features have incoming and outgoing perspectives, except for 'User' and 'Life duration in minutes'. Overall, we have extracted 100 features. Table 4 illustrates the extracted features from the Bitcoin dataset.

Table 4. List of extracted features.

Feature Name	Description
User	Id of identified user
Life Duration in minutes	Time difference between the first and last transaction
In-totalamount, Out-totalmount	The sum of bitcoins sent and received by the user
In-degree, Out-degree (six periods)	Represents the number of incoming and outgoing transactions
Average Amount incoming, Average Amount outgoing (six periods)	Represents the mean value of bitcoins sent and received by a user
In-maxamount, Out-maxamount (six periods)	Represents the largest value of bitcoins sent and received by the user
In-minamount, Out-minamount (six periods)	represents the smallest value of bitcoins sent and received by the user
In- standard deviation, Out- standard deviation (six periods)	Represents the standard deviation of bitcoins sent and received by the user
In-transaction rate, Out-transaction rate (six periods)	Represents incoming and outgoing transaction frequency for the user
Avg_INC_speed, Avg_ OG speed (six periods)	Represents the speed with which bitcoins flow to or from a user (incoming & outgoing)
In-acceleration, Out-acceleration (six periods)	Represents the acceleration of bitcoin flow to or from a user

4   Experimental Setup

The experiments presented in this paper were conducted on a single computer with a 2.4 GHz CPU and 16 GB of RAM. Experiments and results are carried out with Jupyter notebook compilation environment with Python version 3.6 and related Python library. The final dataset contains 21,325 illegal addresses and 10,000,000 legal addresses that were selected randomly from the original raw dataset. To accurately evaluate the performance of the proposed model, the dataset is divided into a ratio of 0.8 (80%) for the training set and a ratio of 0.2 (20%) for the testing set. This will also help to prevent the model from overfitting because the dataset is highly imbalanced.

4.1   Classifier Models

To demonstrate the effectiveness of our proposed model, we carried out two different experiments. Firstly, all classifiers are implemented on the dataset without fixing the class imbalance problem. In the second experiment, we applied the adaptive over-sampling technique (ADASYN) to balance data. All experiments were implemented using five popular supervised classifiers as follows: Extreme Gradient Boosting (XGB)

[53], Random Forest (RF) [54], Support Vector Machine (SVM) [55], Neural Network [56], and K-nearest neighbor (KNN) [57]. All five classifiers are executed using Python machine learning library - Scikit-learn [58] to RF, SVM, NN, and KNN while XGB was implemented using an external python library which is open source at GitHub.

To evaluate the performance of our proposed model, all classification methods were evaluated and computed via Precision (P), Recall (R), F1 score, and Receiver Operating Characteristic curve (AUC) metrics due to their capability to measure the class imbalanced data.

4.2   Experiment Results

To prove our extracted features and classifiers methods are effective, the following results are demonstrated. There is a total of five methods that are used to identify illicit and licit transactions in the Bitcoin dataset utilized for this paper. Table 5 illustrates the evaluation statistics computed for each method. This paper aims to improve the identification rate between illicit and licit transactions while decreasing false-positive cases.

Table 5.   Results of all classifiers methods.

Method	Precision	Recall	F1
KNN	0.8072	0.6925	0.7647
SVM	0.8389	0.7443	0.7871
RF	**0.8921**	**0.8072**	0.7993
NN	0.7549	0.7018	0.7229
XGB	0.8607	0.7336	**0.8576**

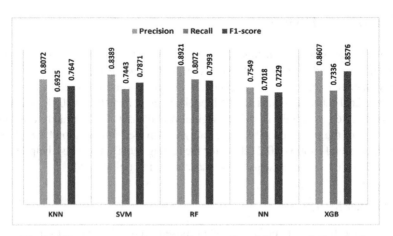

Fig. 2.   Histogram comparing precision, recall, and f1-score of all methods.

Based on the tabular data from Table 5 and a comparative histogram in Fig. 2 of the precision, recall, and F1 scores along with the area under the curve of ROC in Fig. 3, it can be seen that RF and XGB outperform KNN, SVM, and NN in terms of precision, recall, and F1 scores, confirming the effectiveness of the tree-based techniques compared to other techniques. In addition, XGB attained the best result of F1 score which means XGB could correctly identity illicit transactions and achieved low false positives and low false negatives. Although the F1 score of RF is a little worse, the precision and recall metrics are much better. The overall performance of RF is more suitable for application on identifying illegal activities on the Bitcoin dataset. Besides, RF, XGB, and SVM obtained the best result of AUC compared to other methods as shown in Fig. 3.

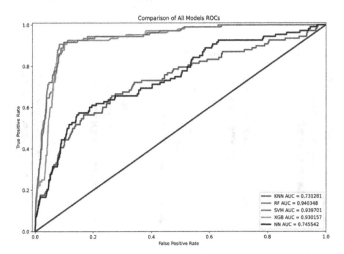

Fig. 3. Comparison of receiver operating characteristic (ROC) curve for all methods.

4.3 Class Imbalance Problem

Imbalance data happens when the data classification is not evenly distributed, as the number of negatives (majority) cases exceeds the number of examples of the positive (minority) class. In the case of an anonymous environment such as the Bitcoin dataset, the Bitcoin dataset is known to be highly skewed because the number of legitimate transactions is much greater than the illegal ones [59]. A basic method to overcome the problem of imbalanced datasets is just to balance them. This is accomplished by utilizing a sophisticated technique called an adaptive oversampling technique (ADASYN). ADASYN [60] is an oversampling approach that can learn from the imbalance dataset by creating synthetic data for minority classes relying upon their distributions. The primary thought is not to duplicate a similar minority class but, it disperses the data by recreating the minority classes that are hard-to-learn minority classes instead of easy-to-learn points [61]. To solve this problem, we apply ADASYN to all methods by calculating the different ratios of the minority to majority samples.

Table 6. Results of all classifiers methods with ADASYN.

Method	Precision	Recall	F1
KNN	0.8572	0.829	0.787
SVM	0.8719	0.8353	0.829
RF	**0.9474**	0.8402	0.8515
NN	0.8389	0.8183	0.7976
XGB	0.9021	**0.8719**	**0.8876**

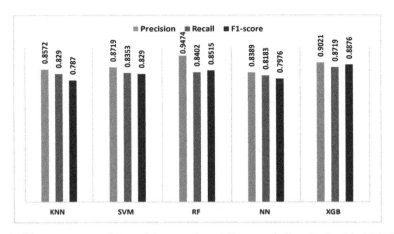

Fig. 4. Histogram comparing precision, recall, and f1-score of all methods with ADASYN.

Table 6 and Fig. 4 illustrate the result after applying the ADASYN method to overcome the problem of class imbalance. Based on the result, it is obvious that the ADASYN enhanced the performance of all methods. Among all methods, RF and XGB attained the best performance compared to the other methods with a noticeable increase in precision, recall, and f1 scores of RF. The best recall and F1 score were achieved by XGB. This is due to the ability to build multiple decision trees from random variants of the same data.

5 Conclusion

The Bitcoin currency is an innovative technology that has lately gained widespread popularity and appeal over similar digital currency such as. It is in return poses a significant challenge in building trust between financial institutions and governments. Bitcoin is a decent innovation yet carries difficulties to the general public where it tends to be utilized as a tool for taking part in illegal activities, unlawful drugs buying, tax evasion, terrorist financing, murder services, and many other things. This paper proposed a model for identifying illegal activities in the Bitcoin system with the aim to expand the prevailing literature in innovative and exploratory ways. First, state-of-art works on identifying illegal activities in the Bitcoin system were reviewed. Then, a discussion of some Bitcoin criminal activities and vulnerabilities was presented. A large dataset that contains illegal addresses for data labeling purposes was constructed by collecting them from different sources such as online public bitcoin forums and related datasets from previous papers. Then a verification method was carried out by checking each address with a raw Bitcoin dataset to ensure that all collected data are valid.

This paper mainly contributes to extracting meaningful features using a time-based approach by splitting transactions in a short period of time "total, monthly, weekly, daily, hourly, and 5 min". In addition, an investigation has been performed on the problem of class imbalance since there is an unequal distribution between the number of illegitimate addresses and legitimate addresses thus an adaptive oversampling technique (ADASYN) was applied to enhance the performance of all classifiers. The proposed model was evaluated using five popular supervised classifiers (KNN, SVM, RF, XGB, and KNN). Lastly, the future work will focus on investigating more illegal activities on the Bitcoin system by applying various types of data mining approaches and expand the analysis by extracting more meaningful features.

Acknowledgment. The authors would like to thank the Ministry of Higher Education (MOHE), Government of Malaysia and Research Management Centre, Universiti Teknologi Malaysia for supporting this work through the Tier-2 Grant, vote number Q.K130000.2656.16J48 and Registration Proposal No: PY/2019/00551.

References

1. Al-Hashedi, K.G., Magalingam, P.: Financial fraud detection applying data mining techniques: a comprehensive review from 2009 to 2019. Comput. Sci. Rev. **40**, 100402 (2021). https://doi.org/10.1016/j.cosrev.2021.100402
2. Nakamoto, S.: Bitcoin: a peer-to-peer electronic cash system (2008)
3. Khalilov, M.C.K., Levi, A.: A survey on anonymity and privacy in Bitcoin-like digital cash systems. IEEE Commun. Surv. Tutorials (2018)
4. Irwin, A.S., Turner, A.B.: Illicit Bitcoin transactions: challenges in getting to the who, what, when and where. J. Money Laundering Control (2018)
5. Hill, A.: Bitcoin: Is Cryptocurrency Viable? (2014)
6. Meiklejohn, S., et al.: A fistful of Bitcoins: characterizing payments among men with no names. In: Proceedings of the 2013 Conference on Internet Measurement Conference, pp. 127–140. ACM (2013)
7. Horst, L.V.D., Choo, K.K.R., Le-Khac, N.A.: Process memory investigation of the Bitcoin clients electrum and Bitcoin core. IEEE Access **5**, 22385–22398 (2017). https://doi.org/10.1109/ACCESS.2017.2759766
8. Christin, N.: Traveling the silk road: a measurement analysis of a large anonymous online marketplace. In: Proceedings of the 22nd International Conference on World Wide Web, pp. 213–224. ACM (2013)
9. Baravalle, A., Lopez, M.S., Lee, S.W.: Mining the dark web: drugs and fake ids. In: 2016 IEEE 16th International Conference on Data Mining Workshops (ICDMW), pp. 350–356 (2016)
10. Monamo, P., Marivate, V., Twala, B.: Unsupervised learning for robust Bitcoin fraud detection. In: Information Security for South Africa (ISSA), pp. 129–134. IEEE (2016)

11. Vasek, M., Thornton, M., Moore, T.: Empirical analysis of denial-of-service attacks in the Bitcoin ecosystem. In: Böhme, R., Brenner, M., Moore, T., Smith, M. (eds.) FC 2014. LNCS, vol. 8438, pp. 57–71. Springer, Heidelberg (2014). https://doi.org/10.1007/978-3-662-447 74-1_5

12. Walch, A.: The Bitcoin blockchain as financial market infrastructure: a consideration of operational risk. NYUJ Legis. Pub. Pol'y **18**, 837 (2015)

13. Tu, K.V., Meredith, M.W.: Rethinking virtual currency regulation in the Bitcoin age. Wash. L. Rev. **90**, 271 (2015)

14. Zambre, D., Shah, A.: Analysis of Bitcoin network dataset for fraud. Unpublished Report (2013)

15. Jobse, F.: Detecting suspicious behavior in the Bitcoin network. Tilburg University (2017)

16. Möser, M., Böhme, R., Breuker, D.: Towards risk scoring of Bitcoin transactions. In: Böhme, R., Brenner, M., Moore, T., Smith, M. (eds.) FC 2014. LNCS, vol. 8438, pp. 16–32. Springer, Heidelberg (2014). https://doi.org/10.1007/978-3-662-44774-1_2

17. Marcin, S.I.: Bitcoin live: scalable system for detecting Bitcoin network behaviors in real time (2015)

18. Li, Y., Cai, Y., Tian, H., Xue, G., Zheng, Z.: Identifying illicit addresses in Bitcoin network. In: Zheng, Z., Dai, H.-N., Fu, X., Chen, B. (eds.) BlockSys 2020. CCIS, vol. 1267, pp. 99–111. Springer, Singapore (2020). https://doi.org/10.1007/978-981-15-9213-3_8

19. Pham, T., Lee, S.: Anomaly detection in Bitcoin network using unsupervised learning methods. arXiv preprint arXiv:1611.03941 (2016)

20. Pham, T., Lee, S.: Anomaly Detection in the Bitcoin System-A Network Perspective. arXiv preprint arXiv:1611.03942 (2016)

21. Monamo, P.M., Marivate, V., Twala, B.: A multifaceted approach to Bitcoin fraud detection: global and local outliers. In: 2016 15th IEEE International Conference on Machine Learning and Applications (ICMLA), pp. 188–194 IEEE (2016)

22. Bitcoin Abuse: Bitcoin Abuse Database (2021). Accessed 1 July 2021

23. Turner, A., Irwin, A.S.M.: Bitcoin transactions: a digital discovery of illicit activity on the blockchain. J. Finan. Crime (2018)

24. Nerurkar, P., Bhirud, S., Patel, D., Ludinard, R., Busnel, Y., Kumari, S.: Supervised learning model for Identifying illegal activities in Bitcoin. Appl. Intell. **51**(6), 3824–3843 (2021)

25. Yang, L., Dong, X., Xing, S., Zheng, J., Gu, X., Song, X.: An abnormal transaction detection mechanim on Bitcoin. In: 2019 International Conference on Networking and Network Applications (NaNA), pp. 452–457 IEEE (2019)

26. Zarpelão, B.B., Miani, R.S., Rajarajan, M.: Detection of Bitcoin-based botnets using a one-class classifier. In: Blazy, O., Yeun, C.Y. (eds.) WISTP 2018. LNCS, vol. 11469, pp. 174–189. Springer, Cham (2019). https://doi.org/10.1007/978-3-030-20074-9_13

27. Liao, K., Zhao, Z., Doupé, A., Ahn, G.-J.: Behind closed doors: measurement and analysis of CryptoLocker ransoms in Bitcoin. In: 2016 APWG Symposium on Electronic Crime Research (eCrime), pp. 1–13. IEEE (2016)

28. Zhang, Z., Zhou, T., Xie, Z.: BITSCOPE: scaling Bitcoin address deanonymization using multi-resolution clustering. In: Proceedings of the 51st Hawaii International Conference on System Sciences (2018)

29. Bartoletti, M., Pes, B., Serusi, S.: Data mining for detecting Bitcoin Ponzi schemes. In: 2018 Crypto Valley Conference on Blockchain Technology (CVCBT), pp. 75–84. IEEE (2018)

30. Lin, Y.-J., Wu, P.-W., Hsu, C.-H., Tu, I.-P., Liao, S.-W.: An evaluation of Bitcoin address classification based on transaction history summarization. In: 2019 IEEE International Conference on Blockchain and Cryptocurrency (ICBC), pp. 302–310. IEEE (2019)

31. Janze, C.: Are cryptocurrencies criminals best friends? Examining the co-evolution of Bitcoin and darknet markets (2017)

32. Böhme, R., Christin, N., Edelman, B., Moore, T.: Bitcoin: economics, technology, and governance. J. Econ. Perspect. **29**(2), 213–238 (2015)
33. Conti, M., Kumar, S., Lal, C., Ruj, S.: A survey on security and privacy issues of Bitcoin. IEEE Commun. Surv. Tutorials (2018)
34. Yin, H.S., Vatrapu, R.: A first estimation of the proportion of cybercriminal entities in the Bitcoin ecosystem using supervised machine learning. In: 2017 IEEE International Conference on Big Data (Big Data), pp. 3690–3699. IEEE (2017)
35. Kroll, J.A., Davey, I.C., Felten, E.W.: The economics of Bitcoin mining, or Bitcoin in the presence of adversaries. In: Proceedings of WEIS, p. 11 (2013)
36. Courtois, N.T., Bahack, L.: On subversive miner strategies and block withholding attack in Bitcoin digital currency. arXiv preprint arXiv:1402.1718 (2014)
37. Eyal, I., Sirer, E.G.: Majority is not enough: Bitcoin mining is vulnerable. Commun. ACM **61**(7), 95–102 (2018)
38. Bahack, L.: Theoretical Bitcoin Attacks with less than Half of the Computational Power (draft). arXiv preprint arXiv:1312.7013 (2013)
39. Rosenfeld, M.: Analysis of Bitcoin pooled mining reward systems. arXiv preprint arXiv:1112.4980 (2011)
40. Bag, S., Ruj, S., Sakurai, K.: Bitcoin block withholding attack: analysis and mitigation. IEEE Trans. Inf. Forensics Secur. **12**(8), 1967–1978 (2017)
41. Karame, G.O., Androulaki, E., Capkun, S.: Double-spending fast payments in Bitcoin. In: Proceedings of the 2012 ACM Conference on Computer and Communications Security, pp. 906–917. ACM (2012)
42. Decker, C., Wattenhofer, R.: Bitcoin transaction malleability and MtGox. In: Kutyłowski, M., Vaidya, J. (eds.) ESORICS 2014. LNCS, vol. 8713, pp. 313–326. Springer, Cham (2014). https://doi.org/10.1007/978-3-319-11212-1_18
43. Andrychowicz, M., Dziembowski, S., Malinowski, D., Mazurek, Ł.: On the malleability of Bitcoin transactions. In: Brenner, M., Christin, N., Johnson, B., Rohloff, K. (eds.) FC 2015. LNCS, vol. 8976, pp. 1–18. Springer, Heidelberg (2015). https://doi.org/10.1007/978-3-662-48051-9_1
44. Johnson, B., Laszka, A., Grossklags, J., Vasek, M., Moore, T.: Game-theoretic analysis of DDoS attacks against Bitcoin mining pools. In: Böhme, R., Brenner, M., Moore, T., Smith, M. (eds.) Financial Cryptography and Data Security, pp. 72–86. Springer, Heidelberg (2014). https://doi.org/10.1007/978-3-662-44774-1_6
45. Kondor, D., Csabai, I., Szüle, J., Pósfai, M., Vattay, G.: Inferring the interplay between network structure and market effects in Bitcoin. New J. Phys. **16**(12), 125003 (2014)
46. Neo4j Graph Platform: Neo4j Graph Platform – The Leader in Graph Databases (2021). Accessed 1 June 2021
47. Magalingam, P., Rao, A., Davis, S.: Identifying a criminal's network of trust. In: 2014 Tenth International Conference on Signal-Image Technology and Internet-Based Systems, pp. 309–316 (2014)
48. Paquet-Clouston, M., Haslhofer, B., Dupont, B.: Ransomware payments in the Bitcoin ecosystem. J. Cybersecur. **5**(1), tyz003 (2019)
49. Weber, M., et al.: Anti-money laundering in Bitcoin: experimenting with graph convolutional networks for financial forensics. arXiv preprint arXiv:1908.02591 (2019)
50. Bahnsen, A.C., Aouada, D., Stojanovic, A., Ottersten, B.: Detecting credit card fraud using periodic features. In: 2015 IEEE 14th International Conference on Machine Learning and Applications (ICMLA), pp. 208–213. IEEE (2015)
51. Bahnsen, A.C., Aouada, D., Stojanovic, A., Ottersten, B.: Feature engineering strategies for credit card fraud detection. Expert Syst. Appl. **51**, 134–142 (2016)

52. Lim, W.-Y., Sachan, A., Thing, V.: Conditional weighted transaction aggregation for credit card fraud detection. In: Peterson, G., Shenoi, S. (eds.) DigitalForensics 2014. IAICT, vol. 433, pp. 3–16. Springer, Heidelberg (2014). https://doi.org/10.1007/978-3-662-44952-3_1

53. Ke, G., et al.: LightGBM: a highly efficient gradient boosting decision tree. In: Advances in Neural Information Processing Systems, vol. 30, pp. 3146–3154 (2017)

54. Breiman, L.: Random forests. Mach. Learn. **45**(1), 5–32 (2001)

55. Hearst, M.A., Dumais, S.T., Osuna, E., Platt, J., Scholkopf, B.: Support vector machines. IEEE Intell. Syst. Appl. **13**(4), 18–28 (1998)

56. Haykin, S., Network, N.: A comprehensive foundation. Neural Netw. **2**(2004), 41 (2004)

57. Lall, U., Sharma, A.: A nearest neighbor bootstrap for resampling hydrologic time series. Water Resour. Res. **32**(3), 679–693 (1996)

58. Pedregosa, F., et al.: Scikit-learn: machine learning in Python. J. Mach. Learn. Res. **12**, 2825–2830 (2011)

59. Devi, D., Biswas, S.K., Purkayastha, B.: A boosting based adaptive oversampling technique for treatment of class imbalance. In: 2019 International Conference on Computer Communication and Informatics (ICCCI), pp. 1–7 (2019)

60. Subudhi, S., Panigrahi, S.: Effect of class imbalanceness in detecting automobile insurance fraud. In: 2018 2nd International Conference on Data Science and Business Analytics (ICDSBA), pp. 528–531. IEEE (2018)

61. Haibo, H., Yang, B., Garcia, E.A., Shutao, L.: ADASYN: adaptive synthetic sampling approach for imbalanced learning. In: 2008 IEEE International Joint Conference on Neural Networks (IEEE World Congress on Computational Intelligence), pp. 1322–1328 (2008)

A Light-Weight Stream Ciphering Model Based on Chebyshev Chaotic Maps and One Dimensional Logistic

Jamal N. Hasoon[1] , Bashar Ahmed Khalaf[2] , Rasha Subhi Hameed[3] ,
Salama A. Mostafa[4(✉)] , and Ali Hussein Fadil[3]

[1] Department of Computer Science, Mustansiriyah University, 10001 Baghdad, Iraq
jamal.hasoon@uomustansiriyah.edu.iq
[2] Department of Medical Instruments Engineering Techniques, Bilad Alrafidain University
College, Ba'aqubah 32001, Diyala, Iraq
bashar@bauc14.edu.iq
[3] Department of Computer Science, University of Diyala, Baqubah 32001, Diyala, Iraq
[4] Faculty of Computer Science and Information Technology, Universiti Tun Hussein Onn
Malaysia, 86400 Parit Raja, Johor, Malaysia
salama@uthm.edu.my

Abstract. This paper investigates the efficiency of consolidating the stream cipher Salsa20 with chaos theory. Subsequently, an enhanced Salsa20 is presented in this paper using two kinds of chaotic maps (1D logistic map and Chebyshev map). The proposed enhanced Salsa20 (ESalsa20) algorithm is developed to be utilized as a lightweight stream cipher that can be implemented in such a way that the speed of encryption is as important as the security. This enhancement is based on the 1D logistic and Chebyshev functions. The XOR-Boolean operation is used in the chaotic layer of the propped encryption algorithm to increase the scrambling of the secret keys. Generally, histogram analysis of the ESalsa20 algorithm shows robust performance against static attacks. According to the obtained results, the ESalsa20 algorithm achieves the best values of NCC 0.3890752653, NAD 0.3689770561, and UQI 0.3777468183 as compared with the original Salsa20 algorithm. Moreover, it achieves the best values of MSE 6957.49, PSN R 9.7224, and AD 78.3394. and UQI. The proposed ESalsa20 also achieves a fast execution time than the Salsa20. As a result, adding the 1D logistic and Chebyshev functions facilitates achieving an accurate diffusion level and making the cipher faster.

Keywords: Salsa20 · Cryptography · Stream cipher · Chaos theory · Chebyshev function · 1D logistic function

1 Introduction

Cryptography plays an important role in data protection, whereas the data is initially exchanged through the Internet. As data grows, the need for more effective encryption algorithms increases [1, 2]. Ciphering algorithms are commonly categorized into two

© Springer Nature Singapore Pte Ltd. 2021
N. Abdullah et al. (Eds.): ACeS 2021, CCIS 1487, pp. 35–46, 2021.
https://doi.org/10.1007/978-981-16-8059-5_3

classes: (1) a block cipher refers to the encryption methods splitting plain data into sequences of blocks. Each block is ciphered by utilizing the same key. (2) a stream cipher refers to encryption by utilizing XOR operation between the plain data and random stream key to obtaining the cipher data [3]. Stream cipher algorithms are one of the fundamental symmetric cryptography, besides block ciphers. The stream cipher has main benefits in the speed and implementation scale of the hardware. Also, it is useful for utilizing in large data transfer [4].

In February 2004, the European Network of Excellence for Cryptology (ECRYPT) was founded to encourage cooperation among researchers included in information security. eSTREAM is a project of the stream cipher of ECRYPT and was founded in 2005 [5]. The major aim of this project is to ease the recommendations of efficient and secure stream ciphers of common and widespread adoption. In the same year, thirty-four candidates of stream ciphers were submitted, and Salsa20 was one of the finalists as a response to the request of eSTREAM for submitting modern stream ciphers. The (20-Round) Salsa20/20 is most faster than the Advanced Encryption Standard (AES) and supplies the best security [6]. The whole Salsa 20/20 versions are recommended by designers of recommended for perfect coding applications. Since the Salsa20/20 is reducing, round variables of the Salsa20/12 and Salsa20/8 are presented. The eSTREAM selected the algorithms of Salsa20/20, Salsa20/12, and Salsa20/8 to be one of the few standards for extensive adoption. Differential attacks have broken the security of Salsa20, so the suitable solution is to utilize a significant chaotic key that is fed each block to be ciphered. This paper presents an enhancement to Salsa20 using 1D logistic and Chebyshev chaotic functions to increase the diffusion of stream key 64-byte [7, 8].

In 2015, a study was carried out by Almazrooie et al. [5] that conducted in which chaos theory is utilized, and faster diffusion can be achieved compared with original Salsa20. Most of the experiences shown that the new algorithm with two iterations is swifter comparing with the basic four-iterations, but it exhibits the same grade of diffusion [9, 10]. In 2016, the Sobti et al. [11] algorithms analyzed the diffusion characteristic of quarter round (QR) operation of both Salsa & Chacha methods, also proposed an alternative design called Modified ChaCha Core (MCC) to create more than a million matrices of diffusion based on the all possible permutations of rotations constants employed in QR. In 2017, applied research by Gaeini et al. [8] to generation pseudorandom numbers and used these random numbers with several encryption algorithms, including Salsa20. This work employed the results of NIST measures and applied different types of attacks to compare different encryption algorithms using the pseudorandom number. The results appeared using random numbers with salsa20 stream cipher algorithm obtain faster implementation more diffusion than the original salsa20.

In 2018, the super salsa stream cipher algorithm was suggested by Mahdi et al. [2] to increase the diffusion of creation stream key of salsa algorithm and guaranty the parlance between fast implementation and complexity algorithm, in this proposed method using an array with size (4, b) instead of using an array with size (4, 4). In 2019, Mohaisen et al. [12] presented a review of variant the recent researches that deal with Stream cipher depending on Chaotic functions and also test the randomness of these chaotic, the results of testing appeared the stream cipher with chaotic function are more improvement of their security and robustness. In 2020, Basha et al. [13] proposed a new algorithm by adjusting the stream cipher Salsa20/4 to improve the polar degrees' security. This algorithm consists of (1) a secret key and (2) diagonal keys stage of $N-1$.

In the prior work of Kubba and Hoomod [3], a hybrid of PRESENT and Salsa20 algorithms has been proposed. Furthermore, for producing more complexity for the proposed system 2D logistics is employed to generate pseudorandom keys. According to the obtained results, it is observed that the proposed system is working efficiently with fast execution time. However, there is a need to test the proposed system with much data and compare the obtained results with the most related work.

In this work, a lightweight ESalsa20 has been proposed and developed as a stream cipher that takes into consideration the speed of encryption. The proposed algorithm is improved based on two types of chaotic functions (1D logistic and Chebyshev), and it achieved an accurate diffusion level, which made the cipher faster. The XOR-Boolean operation is used in the chaotic layer of the propped encryption algorithm to increase the scrambling of the secret keys. According to histogram analysis, the proposed system is robust against static attacks.

The remaining parts of paper are organized as follows: Sect. 2 presents the related methods and materials of this work, including the Salsa20 and chaotic maps. Subsequently, it describes the main contribution of this work that is represented by using two types of chaotic functions to enhance the diffusion of stream secret keys used in the salsa20 cryptography algorithm. Section 3 explains the proposed simulation method, experimental results, evaluation metrics, and discussion, respectively. Lastly, Sect. 4 concludes the proposed work.

2 Methods and Materials

This paper proposes a lightweight ESalsa20 ciphering based on Chebyshev chaotic and 1D logistic functions. The main topics of the research are Salsa20, 1D logistic function, and Chebyshev function.

2.1 Salsa 20

Salsa20 is a stream cipher that has lightweight encryption and data exchanging mechanisms [8]. Keystream on salsa20 algorithms formed of mathematical operation with salsa20 works on 32 bits' word, uses as input 256 bits, key $K = (k0, k1, k2, k3, k4, k5, k6, k7)$ or 128 bits' key $K = (k0, k1, k2, k3)$ and a 64 bits nonce $N = (n0, n1)$, and resulted in a 512 bits' keystream blocks sequence. The CT block is the output of the Salsa20 function in which the nonce, the key, and a sixty-four bits block counter $C = (c0, c1)$ regarding the integer i are taken as input [9].

Based on the length of the key, where τ and σ indicate constants ($\sigma0 = 0x61707865$, $\sigma1 = 0x3320646E$, $\sigma2 = 0x79622D32$, $\sigma3 = 0x6B206574$, $T_0 = 0x61707865$, $T_1 = 0x3120646E$, $T_2 = 0x79622D36$, and $T_3 = 0x6B206574$) [10, 11]. The block of keystream "Z" can be represented as; $Z = X + X$ (20), and $X(r) = \text{Roundr}(X)$ is the round function of Salsa20 and $+$ represents word-wise addition modulo 232. When $Z = X + X(r)$, it is named "r-round Salsa20" or "Salsa20/r". The round function includes the quarter-round (nonlinear) functions as follows; A vector (a, b, c, d) of four words is transformed as [14]:

$$b \leftarrow b \oplus ((a+d)'' < 7) \tag{1}$$

where;

$$c \leftarrow c \oplus ((b+a'' < 9)) \tag{2}$$

where;

$$d \leftarrow d \oplus ((c+b'' < 9)) \tag{3}$$

where;

$$a \leftarrow a \oplus ((d+c'' < 9)) \tag{4}$$

The quarter-round functions are applied to columns (x0, x4, x8, x12), (x5, x9, x13, x1), (x10, x14, x2, x6) and (x15, x3, x7, x11) in odd rounds, and rows (x0, x1, x2, x3), (x5, x6, x7, x4), (x10, x11, x8, x9) and (x15, x12, x13, x14) in even rounds. The procedure of the Salsa20 is fully described in several references [13].

2.2 Chaotic Maps

The disordered state refers to the meaning of Chaos. Mathematically, the map is regarded as a function of evolution with the behavior of some chaotic sort. Additionally, the map refers to a dynamical system of discrete time. Several features are inherent in the chaotic map. The first feature indicates the effect of the butterfly (the sensitivity for the initial conditions). Any small change in the initial conditions will produce a high variation in the output. The second feature indicates the ergodicity in which the obtained output has a similar distribution to any input. The third feature indicates the deterministic, where the deterministic process is capable of causing the behavior of pseudorandom. The final feature indicates the structure complexity. In other words, the ease mathematical functions have extremely high complexity [15]. There are various kinds of information hiding systems proposed and implemented using the sequence of chaotic.

1D Logistic Function: 1D Logistic maps are one of the well-known one-dimensional chaotic maps. It represents an easy dynamical nonlinear equation of complex, chaotic behavior. This equation can be expressed as follows [15, 16]:

$$xn + 1 = FL(u, xn) = u \times xn \times (1 - xn) \tag{5}$$

where u indicates the parameter of control in range $u \in (0,4]$ and x0 indicates the initial value of the chaotic map, xn indicates the chaotic sequence [15].

The bifurcation diagram of the logistic map is illustrated in Fig. 1. In the plot, the horizontal axis shows the "r" bifurcation parameter, while the vertical axis draws the potential population with long-term values of the logistic function. Every bifurcation point indicates a period-double bifurcation [5].

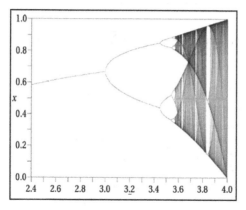

Fig. 1. Bifurcation diagram of the logistic map.

Chebyshev Function: Chebyshev is a chaotic function that has a semigroup property [16].

Definition 1: Chebyshev polynomials; Let, n represented an integer, and x represented a variable with values through the interval [1, 1]. Chebyshev polynomial maps Tn: R → R with n degree is determined by utilizing the next relation of recurrence:

$$T_n(x) = 2xT_{n-1}(x) - T_{n-2}(x) \tag{6}$$

where; $n \geq 2$, $T_0(x) = 1$ and $T_1(x) = x$

Definition 2: Let n represented an integer, and x represented a variable with values through the interval [1, 1]. The polynomial Tn(x): [1, 1] → [1, 1] is determined as follows:

$$T_n(x) = cos(narccos(x)) \tag{7}$$

Definition 3: (Semi-group property): Semigroup is regarded as the most significant property of Chebyshev polynomials which finds that:

$$T_r(T_s(x)) = T_{rs}(x) \tag{8}$$

An immediate consequence of this property is that Chebyshev polynomials commute under composition

$$T_r(T_s(x)) = T_s(T_r(x)) \tag{9}$$

2.3   The Proposed Enhanced-Salsa20 (ESalsa20)

The proposed Enhanced-Salsa20 (ESalsa20) algorithm includes three main layers: generating sequence random numbers based on chaotic maps, key expansion layer, and finally,

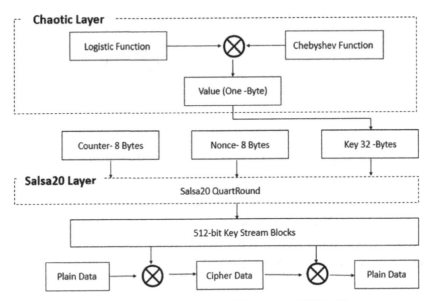

Fig. 2. General block diagram of the proposed ESalsa20.

encryption/decryption layer based on XOR-Boolean operation. Figure 2 illustrates the general block diagram of proposal ESalsa20.

The proposed enhanced Salsa20 (ESalsa 20) based on a chaotic map is demonstrated in Fig. 3. The chaotic key (32 byte) has been generated by utilizing the 1D logistic and Chebyshev functions. In this layer, the first step is the Chebyshev function generates value, converts this value to a binary pulsing padding sequence of zeroes referred to as variable "fixed length" and uses this value to fill one-dimension array called Block1 with size 32 byte. The aims of using fixed length to ensuring all location of Block1 is filling padding, this procedure repeated for the logistic function to fill Block 2 (32 byte) array. The second step is applying XOR-operation between Block1and Block2. The results of XOR –operation convert to decimal which indicates one byte and fills the first location of the secret key array with the size of 32-byte. Repeat steps (1 and 2) for all locations of the secret key array.

In Salsa20 layer takes as input a 32-byte secret stream key K = (k0, k1, k2, k3, k4, k5, k6, k7), an 8-byte nonce N = (n0, n1), and an 8-byte block counter C = (c0, c1). Salsa20's round function itself consists of 4 quarter-round functions. The quarter-round functions can be stated (as shown in Eq. 1, 2, 3, 4, and algorithm 1). The output of this layer is 512 –bits stream key.

The inputs of the Cryptography layer are 512 –bits stream key and plain image. Based on XOR –Boolean operation, it decomposing the input color image into three color channels R, G, and B separately. Each color band represents one domination array that has values in the range [0–255]. Then divided it into N of blocks with a size of 64-byte that is equal to 512-bits of stream key. Then ciphering each color band separately and respectively. The resulting cipher image is the compensation of three cipher color bands. The decryption image inputs are the same stream key 512-bits and cipher image and follow the opposed procedure of the encryption method to obtain the plain image.

2.4 Evaluation Parameters

In cryptography systems, Mean Square Error (MSE), Peak Signal to Noise Ratio (PSNR), Average Difference (AD), Normalized Cross-Correlation (NCC), Universal Image Quality (UQI), Normalized Absolute Error (NAE) represent the most significant parameters utilized to measure the quality of two images. The PSNR evaluates in decibels in which the similarity between two images is measured and is inversely proportional to MSE [18]. PSNR and MSE are given in the following equations [10, 11]:

$$PSNR = 10log_{10}\left[\frac{1^2}{MSE}\right] \tag{10}$$

where;

$$MSE = \frac{1}{[N \times M]^2} \sum_{i=1}^{N} \sum_{j=1}^{M} (x_{ij} - y_{ij})^2 \tag{11}$$

where the image has the maximum intensity of a grayscale image, i.e., 256, Xij and Yij are the intensity of original and cipher image's ijth pixel, respectively. The value of MSE must be enormous, and the value of PSNR must be small.

AD is the metric of the difference between an input image and a ciphering image. If the value of the maximum difference is large, that means the image quality is poor. AD can be determined by Eq. (12) [19]:

$$AD = \frac{1}{M \times N} \sum_{i=1}^{M} \sum_{j=1}^{N} (x(i,j) - y(i,j)) \tag{12}$$

NAE computes the absolute error between the input image and the ciphering image. If the value of normalized absolute error is large, that means a poor quality image. To define the value of NAE by Eq. 13 [20, 21]:

$$NAE = \frac{\sum_{m=1}^{M} \sum_{n=1}^{N} |x(m, n) - y(m, n)|}{\sum_{m=1}^{M} \sum_{n=1}^{N} |x(m, n)|} \tag{13}$$

NCC is a metric of similarity of two-wavelength as a function of the lost time applied to one wavelength. The large value of NCC means the high quality of the image. To calculate the value of NCC by Eq. 14 [12, 22]:

$$NCC = \frac{\sum_{m=1}^{M} \sum_{n=1}^{N} x(m, n).y(m, n)}{\sum_{m=1}^{M} \sum_{n=1}^{N} (x(m, n))^2} \tag{14}$$

UQI is a quality index model that depends on estimating the deformation of two images. It describes distortions according to the luminance distortion, loss of correlation, and contrast distortion [21, 23]. Assume that x indicates the input image, and y indicates the distorted output image. Therefore, the correlation loss is computed via the coefficient of correlation that works on measuring the degree of linear correlation between x and y. Respectively, the contrast and luminance are measured via standard deviation and mean [14, 24]. In mathematics, the UQI is defined by the following equation:

$$UQI = \frac{4\sigma_{xy}\overline{x}\overline{y}}{(\sigma^2 x + \sigma^{2y})[\overline{x}^2 + \overline{y}^2]} \tag{15}$$

3 Simulation and Results

This section presents the experimental work for evaluating the proposed ESalsa20 algorithm. The algorithm is programmed using "C#". The experimental tests are implemented on a PC with Intel (R) Core (TM) i7-5500U, CPU @ 2.40 GHz 2.40 GHz, with RAM of 16.0 GB and system type of 64-bit. The images are used for experimental results are Lena, House, Fruits car, and Baboon images which have RGB color space and size of 256 × 256. The terms of resistance against statistical attacks and analysis of differential attack resistance are used, such as histogram analysis. The outputs of 1D logistic and 1D Chebyshev function are shown in Fig. 3 (a and b).

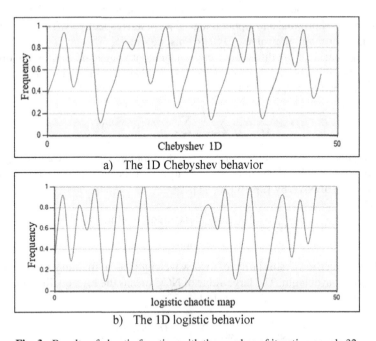

a) The 1D Chebyshev behavior

b) The 1D logistic behavior

Fig. 3. Results of chaotic function with the number of iteration equals 32.

The image histogram refers to the intensity distribution of pixels. It is utilized for identifying the number of pixels with the same value of intensity. The enciphered image

Histogram must have an almost uniform distribution of pixel values and should be distinct from the original image histogram [17]. It shows the distribution of pixels in the encrypted image histogram if it is uniform, and it extremely differs from the distribution of pixels in the original image histogram.

Security of the key used in encryption/decryption color image is produced by using two types of chaotic maps and XOR operation. Therefore, guessing the key is more difficult. The result of the Chaotic map layer is producing a 32-bytes secret key with higher diffusion. The setting parameters of logistic chaotic map for all experiments are $L = 4, x_0 = 0.10$, *number of iteration* = 32, and the setting parameters of the Chebyshev chaotic map for all experiments are $k = 5, x_0 = 0.2$, *and number of iteration* = 32.

MSE, PSNR, AD, NAD, NCC, and UQI are used to evaluate the performance of the encryption algorithm. Further, the performance of the ESalsa20 has been compared with the original Salsa20. Table 1 shows the quantitative analysis between the original test image and its corresponding cipher image using the original Salsa 20 and proposal ESalsa20 encryption techniques in terms of MSE, PSNR, and AD. The proposal algorithm obtains the best value for all experiments, the best values of MSE = 8071.3712272644, PSNR = 9.0613303856, AD = 84.1179318939.

Table 1. Results of original Salsa20 and proposal ESalsa20 based on MSE, PSNR, and AD

Image name	Original Salsa20			Proposal ESalsa20		
	MSE	PSNR	AD	MSE	PSNR	AD
Lena	6880.43730	9.75464	77.94194	6900.22808	9.74216	78.01592
House	6434.39755	10.04572	75.59416	6457.31330	10.03028	75.76188
Fruit	7978.37636	9.11165	83.57535	8071.37122	9.06133	84.11793
Car	6993.34193	9.68395	78.42897	7022.15591	9.66609	78.66592
Baboon	6316.87175	10.12578	74.99343	6336.38470	10.11238	75.13581

Table 2 shows the quantitative analysis between the original test image and its corresponding cipher image using original Salsa 20 and proposal ESalsa20 encryption techniques in terms of NAE, NCC, and UQI. The proposal algorithm obtains the best value for all experiments, the best values of NCC = 0.3890752653, NAD = 0.3689770561, and UQI = 0.3777468183.

The cost of computation for the proposed algorithm is evaluated in the execution time criteria and measured in seconds. Figure 4 illustrates a comparison in the time of execution between the proposed Enhanced-Salsa20 (ESalsa20) and the original Salsa20. As illustrated in Fig. 4, the proposal cipher algorithm is faster than the original algorithm.

Table 2. Results of original Salsa20 and proposal ESalsa20 based on NAD, NCC, and UQI

Image name	Original Salsa20			Proposal ESalsa20		
	NAD	NCC	UQI	NAD	NCC	UQI
Lena	0.36863	0.47054	0.46648	0.36897	0.46836	0.46438
House	0.33815	0.47843	0.46367	0.33890	0.47548	0.46093
Fruit	0.34848	0.39384	0.38264	0.35073	0.38907	0.37774
Car	0.32903	0.44330	0.42120	0.33001	0.44185	0.41970
Baboon	0.35769	0.50109	0.49395	0.35837	0.49920	0.49212

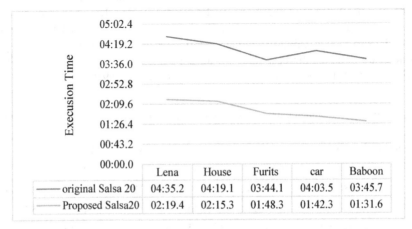

	Lena	House	Furits	car	Baboon
original Salsa 20	04:35.2	04:19.1	03:44.1	04:03.5	03:45.7
Proposed Salsa20	02:19.4	02:15.3	01:48.3	01:42.3	01:31.6

Fig. 4. Comparison between original Salsa20 and ESalsa20 execution time.

4   Conclusion

Progressively, Information and Communication Technology (ICT) progression depends on the advancement of information security. Information security has introduced various ciphering methods to ensure supplying confidential data through computer networks. The main constraints related to the development of ciphering methods are related to the computing resources, including memory usage, CPU time, and force. Salsa20 is one of the efficient, fastest, and modern stream encryption algorithms. It has the desirable characteristics of implementing all ciphering rounds in order to achieve higher diffusions and escape from known attacks. This paper introduces an enhanced version of the Salsa20 algorithm (ESalsa20). The ESalsa20 includes a chaotic layer (1D logistic and Chebyshev chaotic functions) to improve the algorithm's performance and the diffusion speed. Subsequently, it presents the simulation results of the original Salsa20 and the ESalsa20. It then compares the results using Peak Signal to Noise Ratio (PSNR), Average Difference (AD), Mean Square Error (MSE), Normalized Absolute Error (NAE), Universal Image Quality (UQI), execution time, and Normalized Cross-Correlation (NCC). The results show that the ESalsa20 surpasses the original Salsa20 for all the tested evaluation criteria. The ESalsa20 algorithm achieves the best values of NCC 0.3890752653, NAD 0.3689770561, UQI 0.3777468183, MSE 6957.49, PSN R 9.7224, and AD 78.3394 and the fastest execution time. The future work considers further improving the ESalsa20 by including optimization algorithms such as Bat or ant colony algorithm.

Acknowledgment. This paper is supported by the Center of Intelligent and Autonomous Systems (CIAS), Faculty of Computer Science and Information Technology, Universiti Tun Hussein Onn Malaysia (UTHM).

References

1. Gjorgjievska Perusheska, M., Dimitrova, V., Popovska-Mitrovikj, A., Andonov, S.: Application of machine learning in cryptanalysis concerning algorithms from symmetric cryptography. In: Arai, K. (ed.) Intelligent Computing. LNNS, vol. 285, pp. 885–903. Springer, Cham (2021). https://doi.org/10.1007/978-3-030-80129-8_59
2. Mahdi, M.S., Hassan, N.F.A.: Suggested super salsa stream cipher. E. Iraqi J. Comput. Inform. **44**(2), 1–6 (2018)
3. Kubba, Z.M.J., Hoomod, H.K.: A hybrid modified lightweight algorithm combined of two cryptography algorithms PRESENT and Salsa20 using chaotic system. In: The 1st International Conference of Computer and Applied Sciences (CAS), pp. 199–203. IEEE, Baghdad (2019)
4. Kashinath, S.A., Mostafa, S.A., Lim, D., Mustapha, A., Hafit, H., Darman, R.: A general framework of multiple coordinative data fusion modules for real-time and heterogeneous data sources. J. Intell. Syst. **30**(1), 947–965 (2021)
5. Almazrooie, M., Samsudin, A., Singh, M.M.: Improving the diffusion of the stream cipher salsa20 by employing a chaotic logistic map. J. Inf. Process. Syst. **11**(2), 310–324 (2015)
6. Bernstein, D.J.: The Salsa20 family of stream ciphers. In: Robshaw, M., Billet, O. (eds.) New Stream Cipher Designs. LNCS, vol. 4986, pp. 84–97. Springer, Heidelberg (2008). https://doi.org/10.1007/978-3-540-68351-3_8
7. Nugrahtama, A.L., Pramadi, Y.R.: Pramadi, implementation of Salsa20 stream cipher algorithm as an alternative cipher suite SSL-VPN for VOIP security. In: IOP Conference Series: Materials Science and Engineering, vol. 508, no. 1, p. 012132. IOP Publishing (2019)
8. Gaeini, A., Mirghadri, A., Jandaghi, G., Keshavarzi, B.: Comparing some pseudorandom number generators and cryptography algorithms using a general evaluation pattern. Int. J. Inf. Technol. Comput. Sci. **9**(2), 5–31 (2016)
9. Zhao, Y., Zhai, F., Liang, X., Miao, S., Zhu, Y.: A lightweight secure access protocol for collecting terminals in power internet of things based on symmetric cryptographic algorithm. In: Journal of Physics: Conference Series, vol. 1920, no. 1, p. 012051. IOP Publishing (2021)
10. Henriques, M.S., Vernekar, N.K.: Using symmetric and asymmetric cryptography to secure communication between devices in IoT0. In: 2017 International Conference on IoT and Application (ICIOT), pp. 1–4. IEEE (2017)
11. Sobti, R., Ganesan, G.: Analysis of quarter rounds of Salsa and ChaCha core and proposal of an alternative design to maximize diffusion. Indian J. Sci. Technol. **9**(3), 1–10 (2016)
12. Mohaisen, E.L., Mohammed, R.S.: Stream cipher based on chaotic maps. In: 1st International Conference of Computer and Applied Sciences (CAS), pp. 256–261. IEEE, Baghdad (2019)
13. Basha, C.B., Rajaprakash, S.: Enhancing the security using SRB18 method of embedding computing. Microprocess. Microsyst. **77**, 103125 (2020)

14. Kubba, Z.M.J., Hoomod, H.K.: Modified PRESENT Encryption algorithm based on new 5D chaotic system. In: IOP Conference Series: Materials Science and Engineering, vol. 928, no. 3, p. 032023. IOP Publishing (2020)
15. Rajendran, S., Doraipandian, M.: Chaotic map based random image steganography using LSB technique. Int. J. Netw. Secur. 19(4), 593–598 (2017)
16. Yoon, E.J., Jeon, I.S.: An efficient and secure Diffie-Hellman key agreement protocol based on Chebyshev chaotic map. Commun. Nonlinear Sci. Numer. Simul. 16(6), 2383–2389 (2011)
17. Aswad, F.M., Salman, I., Mostafa, S.A.: An optimization of color halftone visual cryptography scheme based on Bat algorithm. J. Intell. Syst. 30(1), 816–835 (2021)
18. Dey, S., Sarkar, S.: Improved analysis for reduced round Salsa and Chacha. Discret. Appl. Math. 227, 58–69 (2017)
19. Fadel, A.H., Hameed, R.S., Hasoon, J.N., Mostafa, S.A., Khalaf, B.A.: A Lightweight ESalsa20 Ciphering based on 1D Logistic and Chebyshev chaotic maps. Solid State Technol. 63(1), 704–717 (2020)
20. Ibtisam, A.T., Hameed, S.M.: A new Color image Encryption based on multi Chaotic Maps. Iraqi J. Sci. 59(4), 2117–2127 (2018)
21. Khalaf, B.A., et al.: An adaptive protection of flooding attacks model for complex network environments. Secur. Commun. Netw. 2021, 1–17 (2021)
22. Babatunde, O.S., Ahmad, A.R., Mostafa, S.A.: A smart network intrusion detection system based on network data analyzer and support vector machine. Int. J. Emerg. Trends Eng. Res. 8(1), 213–220 (2020)
23. Mostafa, S.A., Mustapha, A., Shamala, P., Obaid, O.I., Khalaf, B.A.: Social networking mobile apps framework for organizing and facilitating charitable and voluntary activities in Malaysia. Bull. Electr. Eng. Inform, 9(2), 827–833 (2020)
24. Ismael, H.A., Abbas, J.M., Mostafa, S.A., Fadel, A.H.: An enhanced fireworks algorithm to generate prime key for multiple users in fingerprinting domain. Bulletin of Electrical Engineering and Informatics 10(1), 337–343 (2021)

An Implementation of Robust User Authentication Technique for Big Data Platform

Galal A. AL-Rummana[1]([✉]), Abdulrazzaq H. A. Al-Ahdal[1,2], and G. N. Shinde[3]

[1] School of Computational Sciences, S.R.T.M. University, Nanded, India
Galal300z@gmail.com
[2] Computer Science and Engineering, Hodeidah University, Al Hudaydah, Yemen
[3] Yeshwant College, S.R.T.M. University, Nanded, India

Abstract. Hadoop framework has been developed to manage Big Data on the Cloud. The main components of this framework are MapReduce and Hadoop Distributed File System (HDFS), but Hadoop does not provide any mechanism for robust authentication. The existing authentication protocols are vulnerable to many security threats. Therefore, we suggest an authentication model based on "Inverse Hyperbolic Functions" in this paper. This model is followed by a mechanism that verifies the identity of the user and determines whether the user is permitted for access or not. The security study takes into account both functionality and security needs. Furthermore, (AVISPA) is used to verify the proposed system. Finally, the suggested scheme defends against a variety of attacks, including replay, MITM, DOS, password guessing, insider attack, and phishing.

Keywords: Authentication · Big data security · Hadoop · AVISPA · Inverse Hyperbolic Fun

1 Introduction

Between 2005 and 2020, the digital universe will have grown by a factor of 300, from 130 exabytes to 40,000 exabytes, or 40 trillion gigabytes (more than 5,200 gigabytes for every guy, woman, and child). Every two years, the digital world will nearly double [1]. Obviously, this has attracted the interest of numerous Big Data scholars. To cope with this, numerous distributed file systems were developed, including HDFS [1], which was built to offer a storage service where data could be safely saved across several servers owing to its simple availability (open source). The client can send Big Data via an insecure channel to geographically dispersed servers of a distant third-party using this connection. Because access to the storage service is granted across an insecure communication route, there are certain security concerns. The best solution to the problem is a strong authentication method [2–4].

We can say that the registration phase must first take place in the authentication system, and after the registration, only the authorized person can access the data. There

---

G. N. Shinde—Former Pro-Vice-Chancellor.

N. Abdullah et al. (Eds.): ACeS 2021, CCIS 1487, pp. 47–61, 2021.
https://doi.org/10.1007/978-981-16-8059-5_4

are many schemes discussed on this topic [5, 6, 7, 8, 9, 10, 11]. These options, on the other hand, are either costly in terms of extra hardware or computationally complex.

In fact, it is not enough to specify the username and password to be considered a special and strong identifier, because the hacker can easily perform various attacks to predict the user name and password.

In this scheme, the user is trusted after several steps. After the user enters the username and password, a comparison is made between the entered variables and the variables stored into user's credential cache that were saved during the registration phase.

We generate a session key distribution between the user and the server to ensure mutual authentication the variable η by using this equation $\eta = \log_e(\gamma + \sqrt{\gamma^2 + 1}$ to server, as well as calculate the η^* by using the equation $\eta^* = \sinh^{-1}\gamma$ to user. In the case of equality of the variable η with variable η^* i.e. $\eta = \eta^*$ that means indicates reliability then the session key are distribution. Nonetheless, for joint authentication between the user and the server, the suggested scheme uses time synchronization by calculating T^*, T using this equation $T^* - T \leq \Delta T$. After the two parties are trusted each other, the user can access the data.

- **MOTIVATION**

In the suggested scheme, we established the following aims to address the difficulties and issues that currently exist in authentication schemes that aid Hadoop security.

1. During the registration phase, the proposed protocol must be able to register the server with the user both in Hadoop.
2. The suggested protocol should protect against a variety of well-known attacks, including replay, MITM, DOS, password guessing, and phishing.
3. The authentication work for both the user and the Big Data technology provider should be made more robust and user-friendly in the suggested scheme.
4. The session key between the user and the server should be distributed securely using the suggested protocol.
5. The suggested protocol has to protect the anonymity of user and service server by concealing their true identities from privileged insiders and eavesdroppers.

To achieve the aforementioned goals, a strong authentication framework was introduced. This framework was designed in a way that makes it distinct and achieves the goals so that all the users are registered and saved within the server at the registration stage.

At the authentication stage, not allow unauthorized person to access data. Moreover, the proposed framework resists many of the known security threats mentioned in Objective No. 2, according to the proposed framework policy. The authentication task is more robust and easy to handle, so that each user is registered once on the server.

To improve the robustness and validity of the entity's authentication, we employ the proposed scheme to make the users' original identities fully anonymous. We are proposing a new entity verification scheme that uses key encryption to remedy plain text attack and chosen plain text attacks, to create a secure session between two communicating parties, the proposed model generates and distributes session keys that are valid keys for some fixed time.

- **Hadoop and MapReduce**

Hadoop presents a new approach to store and process big data and it is an open source, as mentioned earlier, it comprises of two main components, the first is the file store FS, called HDFS, and the second is the distributed processing system and it is called MapReduce. HDFS is designed to store very large files that divide files into default 64-bit blocks.

MapReduce is a software framework that performs filtering, sorting and reducing and is considered very convenient for big data. It is used to reduce the cost of security by dividing the input data into several parts. MapReduce can deal with most problems such as consistency and fault tolerance.

The remaining parts of the current study are grouped as follows: The second part of the presentation is a survey of the literature on entity authentication in Hadoop. Section 3 discusses the essential relevant preliminaries, which are useful for characterizing and analyzing the suggested protocol. The suggested scheme is demonstrated in Sect. 4. The suggested protocol's Functionality and Security Requirements are presented in Sect. 5. In Sect. 6, we use the AVISPA tool to simulate the proposed protocol under the CLAtSe backends, describe the attack traces, and explain the suggested scheme's performance analysis. Finally, Sect. 7 brings the paper to a close.

2 Literature Review

Newman et al. [12] they proposed the Kerberos authentication protocol, which registers the user first in the system to take advantage of the services. In this proposal, all messages are encrypted between the user and the server. An authentication request is sent to an authentication server (AS) by a user by sending a plain text containing the "username" [13]. Here, the attack can eavesdrop on the "username" and use it to identify himself to the authentication server as a legitimate user, and the attacker can identify the currently online users from the transmitted messages [14–16]. In addition, the authentication server issues an Authentication Ticket (AT) to the end user after only the "username" has been verified, regardless of the password or any other credentials [14] and this gives attack an opportunity to get an authentication card. To avoid this, a Kerberos-based public key infrastructure called PKINIT [17], has been reported and published in Hadoop. But it does not properly address user, server, and other security threats [16, 18]. To address these issues, PKINIT [17], a public key infrastructure based on Kerberos, has been reported and implemented in Hadoop. However, it does not sufficiently fix the user's and service server's privacy issues, as well as other security challenges [14, 18].

Nivethitha et al. [9] suggested an authentication scheme for Hadoop which is based on a one-time pad key encryption protocol. For safe transmission between the two servers, a random key is used to encrypt the password. The authors say that their scheme makes the Hadoop environment safer because each login generates a new random key for encryption. They also argued that since their scheme requires knowledge of a legitimate random key, an adversary's ability to decode the cypher stored on the server is reduced.

Rahul and GireeshKumar [7] they used their own framework this framework based on cryptographic functions, by giving each client a new key and authenticate all clients and services using this key. They stated that their authentication system protects user privacy, provides a modern way of separating privileges, and meets the minimum security requirements for data stored in HDFS.

Sadasivam et al. [6] suggested a new authentication protocol for Hadoop in a cloud environment, in which simple triangle properties are used and updated two server-based models to boost Hadoop cluster security. They used the authentication server to interpret and alienate the user's password, which was then placed in various back-end servers including the corresponding user.

Different security mechanisms within the Apache Hadoop Stack were described by Sharma and Navdeti [2]. According to Sharma and Navdeti, the Kerberos approach is preferred for providing authentication services in most of the cases.

Srinivas et al. [11] suggested 2PBDC, an elliptic curve cryptography-based privacy-preserving Big Data collection scheme in the cloud. They demonstrate that 2PBDC provides a better balance of stability, functionality, connectivity, and computation overheads.

(SecSVA) Secure Storage, Verification, and Auditing of Big Data in the Cloud Environment was proposed by Aujla et al. [10]. Merkle hashtree-based trusted third-party auditing. They proposed a cloud data storage framework focused on attribute-based secure data deduplication, and Kerberos-based identity authentication and verification.

3   Preliminary and Notation

- **HASH FUNCTION h (.)**

It is mathematical function that can be used to convert arbitrary-sized data (x) into fixed-size values (y), it is a one-way function. Hash values are the values obtained by a hash function.

- **NOTATION**

Table 1 lists and describes the essential notations that are used in the proposed system.

Table 1. Description of the proposed scheme's notations.

ID	Username
PW	password
α, β, γ	random number
S	Big data server
h	One way hash function
$\|$	concatenation operation
$\oplus$	xor operation
T	current time of the user
T^*	current time of the big date server
Mi	Messages
If	Condition operation

4 Proposed Scheme

We have explained this point in the our published study [19] which includes of four phases, registration phase, login phase, authentication phase and one activity called password change phase. The Fig. 1, 2 illustrates these four phases.

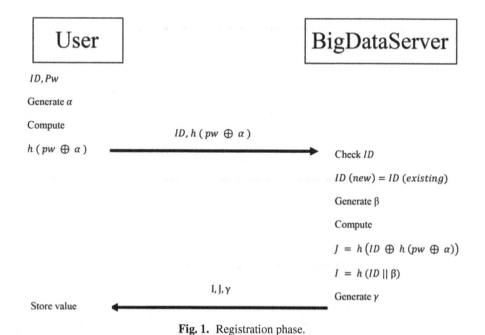

Fig. 1. Registration phase.

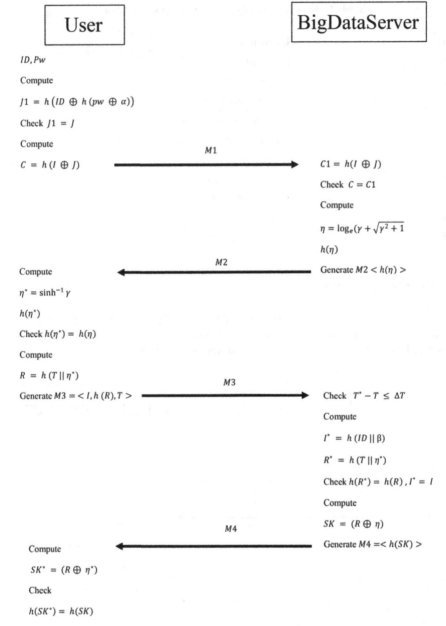

Fig. 2. Login and authentication Phase.

5 Security Discussions

We summarize and analyze our proposed scheme's security review in our published study [19], as well as compare it to other similar schemes. In Table 2, a summary of that comparison can be observed which exposes that our proposed scheme is more secured than other schemes.

Table 2. Security features comparison.

Security features	Choudhury [20]	Algaradi [21]	Jiang [22]	proposed
Identity management	✓	X	X	✓
User privacy	✓	✓	X	✓
Mutual authentication	✓	X	✓	✓
Password change	✓	X	✓	✓
Session key agreement	✓	X	✓	✓
brute-force	X	✓	X	✓
Replay attack	✓	✓	✓	✓
Man in the middle attack	✓	✓	X	✓
Denial of service attack	✓	✓	✓	✓

6 Performance Study

6.1 Protocol Simulation

To check safety measures, a simulation tool should be employed. Several models have used AVISPA to validate the safety of the proposed model. AVISPA is a simple tool that determines whether the security protocol in use is SAFE or UNSAFE.

Farash et al. [23] have described the architecture of this tool. It uses a modular called "HLPSL" to create protocols. A protocol's HLPSL specification is converted into an intermediate format (IF). Each participant takes on the role of a character who interacts with other characters through channels [24].

6.1.1 HLPSL Specification of Our Protocol

In the HLPSL standard, we have two fundamental roles: user and bigdataserver, which represent the user and big data server. Session and environment are the other two responsibilities. Figures 3 illustrate the HLPSL implementation of the user role, while Figs. 4 illustrate the implementation of the bigdataserver role. Figures 5 and 6 depict the functions of session, environment, and aim. We have defined 9 secrecy and 9 authentication objectives to be verified in this implementation, which are the following:

secrecy_of sec_A, secrecy_of sec_I, secrecy_of sec_J, secrecy_of sec_Gamma, secrecy_of sec_C, secrecy_of sec_D, secrecy_of sec_Rh, secrecy_of sec_T, secrecy_of sec_SK.

authentication_on auth_A, authentication_on auth_I, authentication_on auth_J, authentication_on auth_Gamma, authentication_on auth_C, authentication_on auth_D, authentication_on auth_Rh, authentication_on auth_T, authentication_on auth_SK.

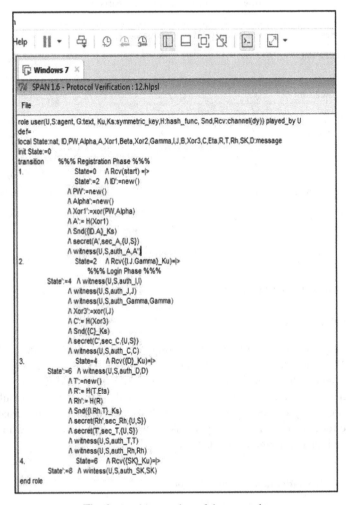

Fig. 3. Implementation of the user role.

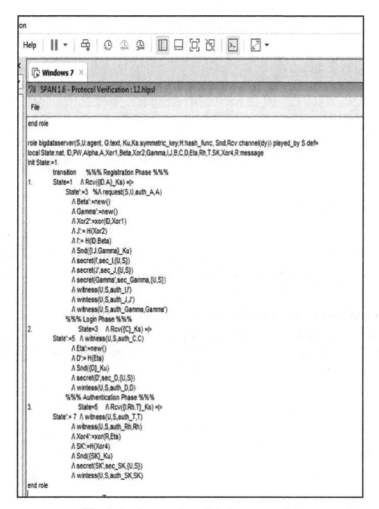

Fig. 4. Implementation of bigdataserver role.

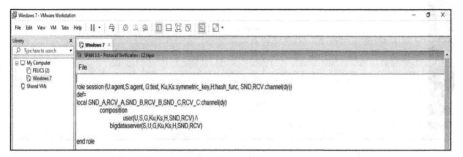

Fig. 5. Implementation of the session role.

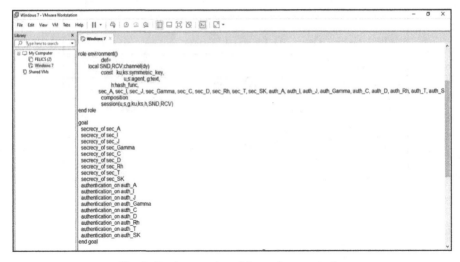

Fig. 6. Implementation of the environment role.

6.1.2 Simulation Results and Discussion

The CLAtSe backend is used to simulate our protocol, as it is in most schemes. Because our protocol employs the XOR operation that is not supported by other backends, the simulation results for these backends have been excluded.

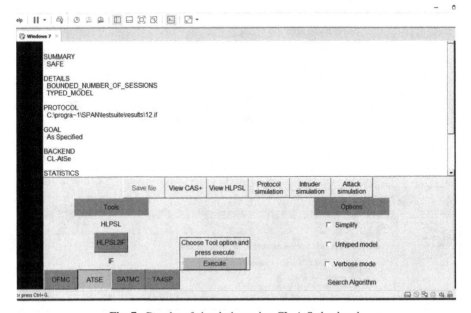

Fig. 7. Results of simulation using CL-AtSe backend.

To check for the replay attack, the CLAtSe backend performs rigorous security verification checks. The simulation results for the CLAtSe backend are shown in Fig. 7, indicating that our protocol is secure from passive and active attacks such as replay and MITM attacks.

6.2 Computation Cost

The computation cost is measured and compared with other similar schemes in order to evaluate the proposed scheme's performance. The computation cost is evaluated for all phases, registration, login and authentication, which are summarized as follows:

The following are the definitions of the notations used in the comparison: hash operation (Th), modular exponentiation (Te), bitwise operation (Tbit), and encryption operation (Tenc). Table 3 shows the data related to the computation cost of the proposed scheme and related scheme. Through the Table 3, we notice that the proposed scheme has only one TEnc and two Te that refers the proposed work is more efficient than other existing schemes [20, 21], and [22]. Graphically computation cost is shown in the Fig. 8.

Computation Cost

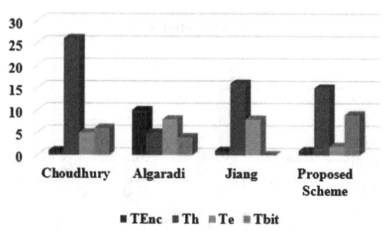

$\blacksquare$ TEnc $\blacksquare$ Th $\blacksquare$ Te $\blacksquare$ Tbit

Fig. 8. Computation cost.

Table 3. Comparison of the computation cost

Scheme	T_{Enc}	T_h	T_e	T_{bit}
Choudhury	1	26	5	6
Algaradi	10	5	8	4
Jiang	1	16	8	0
Proposed Scheme	1	15	2	9

6.3 Communication Cost

Another important aspect to consider when evaluating the scheme's performance is the cost of communication. The communication cost comparison is based on the number of messages exchanged for successful registration and login. The capability of the transmitted message used in the authentication mechanism is included in the proposed scheme's communication overhead as shown in the Table 4. It is noticed that the proposed scheme exchange is less in cost in comparison with other related schemes. Graphically Communication cost is shown in the Fig. 9.

Table 4. Comparison of the communication cost

Scheme	Communication cost
Choudhury	1440
Algaradi	5216
Jiang	1664
Proposed Scheme	1312

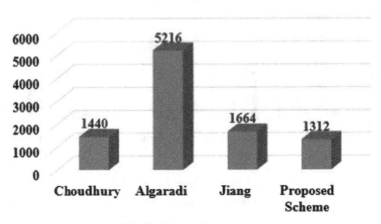

Communication Cost

Fig. 9. Communication cost.

6.4 Storage Overhead Cost

In the proposed schemes, the parameters (ID, pw, c, h(function), time stamp, sk) are stored to be used in the process. Thus the storage cost is $1184 = (9 \times 128 + 1 \times 32)$ bit.

Table 5 shows the results of comparing the suggested technique to the comparable schemes. It demonstrates that the proposed solution has the lowest and best storage cost. The cost of storage is shown graphically in the Fig. 10.

Table 5. Comparison of the storage overhead cost.

Scheme	Storage overhead cost
Choudhury	1568
Algaradi	1504
Jiang	1664
Proposed Scheme	1184

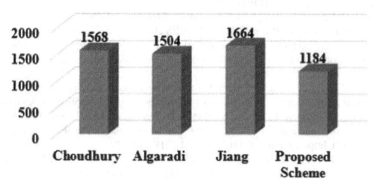

Fig. 10. Storage overhead cost.

7 Conclusion

In this study, we suggest a new authentication model using "Inverse Hyperbolic Functions". To the Hadoop framework to verify the identity of the user. Only the authorized user is allowed to enter after performing several operations according to the mechanism explained in this protocol. After entering the user name and password, the entered data is compared with the data that was stored and saved at the registration stage. Then, to assure mutual authentication and distribution of session keys, as well as a time stamp, arithmetic operations are performed.

The suggested system is provably secure, according to the protocol's security analysis. Furthermore, the proposed protocol's security is tested using the widely known AVISPA protocol simulator tool. All of these security study results suggest that the proposal is resistant to attack. Furthermore, the suggested protocol has been compared to existing state-of art techniques and shown to be effective in terms of communication, computation, and storage costs and proved to be effective.

References

1. Shvachko, K., Kuang, H., Radia, S., Chansler, R.: The hadoop distributed file system. In: 2010 IEEE 26th Symposium on Mass Storage Systems and Technologies (MSST), pp. 1–10. IEEE May 2010

2. Priya, S., Navdeti, C.: Securing big data hadoop : a review of security issues, threats and solution. Int. J. Comput. Sci. Inf. Technol. **5**, 1 (2015)
3. Jin, S., Yang, S., Zhu, X., Yin, H.: Design of a trusted file system based on hadoop. In: Yuan, Y., Wu, X., Lu, Y. (eds.) ISCTCS 2012. CCIS, vol. 320, pp. 673–680. Springer, Heidelberg (2013). https://doi.org/10.1007/978-3-642-35795-4_85
4. Zhou, H., Wen, Q.: A new solution of data security accessing for Hadoop based on CP-ABE. In: 2014 IEEE 5th International Conference on Software Engineering and Service Science, pp. 525–528. IEEE (2014)
5. O'Malley, O.: Integrating kerberos into apache hadoop. In: Kerberos Conference, pp. 26–27 (2010)
6. Sadasivam, G.S., Kumari, K.A., Rubika, S.: A novel authentication service for hadoop in cloud environment. In: 2012 IEEE International Conference on Cloud Computing in Emerging Markets (CCEM), pp. 1–6. IEEE (2012)
7. Suresh, L.P., Dash, S.S., Panigrahi, B.K.: Artificial Intelligence and Evolutionary Algorithms in Engineering Systems: Proceedings of ICAEES 2014, vol. 2 (2015)
8. Sarvabhatla, M., Chandra, M.R.M., Vorugunti, C.S.: A secure and light weight authentication service in hadoop using one time pad. Procedia Comput. Sci. **50**, 81–86 (2015). https://doi.org/10.1016/j.procs.2015.04.064
9. Somu, N., Gangaa, A., Shankar Sriram, V.S.: Authentication service in hadoop using one time pad. Indian J. Sci. Technol. **7**, 56–62 (2014). https://doi.org/10.17485/ijst/2014/v7sp4.16
10. Aujla, G.S., Chaudhary, R., Kumar, N., Das, A.K., Rodrigues, J.J.P.C.: SecSVA: secure storage, verification, and auditing of big data in the cloud environment. IEEE Commun. Mag. **56**, 78–85 (2018). https://doi.org/10.1109/MCOM.2018.1700379
11. Srinivas, J., Das, A.K., Rodrigues, J.J.P.C.: 2PBDC: privacy-preserving bigdata collection in cloud environment. J. Supercomput. **76**(7), 4772–4801 (2018). https://doi.org/10.1007/s11227-018-2605-1
12. Neuman, C., Kohl, J.: The Kerberos Network Authentication Service (V5), pp. 1–139 (1993)
13. Bellovin, S.M., Merritt, M.: Limitations of the Kerberos authentication system. ACM SIGCOMM Comput. Commun. Rev. **20**, 119–132 (1990). https://doi.org/10.1145/381906.381946
14. Chattaraj, D., Sarma, M., Das, A.K.: A new two-server authentication and key agreement protocol for accessing secure cloud services. Comput. Netw. **131**, 144–164 (2018). https://doi.org/10.1016/j.comnet.2017.12.007
15. Sobh, T., Elleithy, K., Mahmood, A., Karim, M.A.: Novel Algorithms and Techniques in Telecommunications, Automation and Industrial Electronics. Springer, Heidelberg (2008). https://doi.org/10.1007/978-1-4020-8737-0
16. Abdelmajid, N.T., Hossain, M.A., Shepherd, S., Mahmoud, K.: Location-based kerberos authentication protocol. In: 2010 IEEE Second International Conference on Social Computing, pp. 1099–1104. IEEE (2010)
17. Zhu, L., Tung, B.: Public Key Cryptography for Initial Authentication in Kerberos (PKINIT). https://www.hjp.atdocrfcrfc4556.html
18. Chattaraj, D., Sarma, M., Das, A.K., Kumar, N., Rodrigues, J.J.P.C., Park, Y.: HEAP: an efficient and fault-tolerant authentication and key exchange protocol for hadoop-assisted big data platform. IEEE Access **6**, 75342–75382 (2018). https://doi.org/10.1109/ACCESS.2018.2883105
19. Al-Rummana, G.A., Al Ahdal, A.H.A., Shinde, G.N.: A robust user authentication framework for bigdata. In: 2021 Third International Conference on Intelligent Communication Technologies and Virtual Mobile Networks (ICICV), pp. 1256–1261. IEEE (2021)
20. Choudhury, A.J., Kumar, P., Sain, M., Lim, H., Jae-Lee, H.: A strong user authentication framework for cloud computing. In: 2011 IEEE Asia-Pacific Services Computing Conference, pp. 110–115. IEEE (2011)

21. Algaradi, T.S., Rama, B.: Static knowledge-based authentication mechanism for hadoop distributed platform using kerberos. Int. J. Adv. Sci. Eng. Inf. Technol. **9**, 772–780 (2019). https://doi.org/10.18517/ijaseit.9.3.5721
22. Jiang, L., Li, X., Cheng, L.L., Guo, D.: Identity authentication scheme of cloud storage for user anonymity via USB token. In: 2013 International Conference on Anti-Counterfeiting, Security and Identification (ASID), pp. 1–6. IEEE (2013)
23. Farash, M.S., Turkanović, M., Kumari, S., Hölbl, M.: An efficient user authentication and key agreement scheme for heterogeneous wireless sensor network tailored for the Internet of Things environment. Ad Hoc Netw. **36**, 152–176 (2016). https://doi.org/10.1016/j.adhoc.2015.05.014
24. Mehra, P.S., Doja, M.N., Alam, B.: Codeword Authenticated Key Exchange (CAKE) light weight secure routing protocol for WSN. Int. J. Commun. Syst. **32** (2019). https://doi.org/10.1002/dac.3879

Blockchain-Based Incentive Mechanism to Combat Fake News

Munaza Farooq, Aqsa Ashraf Makhdomi[✉] ⓘ, and Iqra Altaf Gillani ⓘ

Department of Information Technology, National Institute of Technology Srinagar, Srinagar, India

Abstract. With advancing technology, social media sites have become narratives for news surfacing the digital world. Social media users generally have no qualm for forwarding whatever comes their way. The flexibility of social media platforms offers no way to prove the credibility of a shared piece of information. The authenticity of the news and maintaining netiquette over social media sites have become precedence areas. This has challenged the technology in maintaining the ethics and objectivity of journalism. This paper proposes a shared, decentralized framework that implements an alternate vision to the customary way people share information. In particular, we provide an innovative blockchain and crowd sourcing-based framework for demonstrating the provenance of news surfacing through digital media. Under this platform, the truth is sourced from the crowd, stored, and consequently transformed into a real-time interface. Moreover, using the immutable feature of blockchain, all users are made accountable and valued based on their reputation. Further, nodes are provided with incentives for their rightful behavior and are penalized for their malicious actions. Thus, in this paper, we aim to offer a much-needed layer for secure, reliable information exchange in our present-day social media infrastructure that does not rely on a single source of truth.

Keywords: Fake news · Blockchain · Consensus algorithm · dApp

1 Introduction

Reading and watching the news have been important for individuals to keep themselves informed about the world and current affairs. Traditionally newspapers, radio, and television were the medium through which people consumed information. With the traditional news process, very few people controlled the editing, publication, and amplification stages, so news's credibility was preserved. Nowadays, the mainstream media is mostly being ruled by massive corporations leading towards the centralization of news and its presentation of facts to benefit their financial or political agenda. With the considerable level of corporate media concentration, people have lost their trust in the mainstream media as these networks demonstrate their political preferences leading towards group thinking.

M. Farooq and A.A. Makhdomi—Both authors have equal contribution.

ⓒ Springer Nature Singapore Pte Ltd. 2021
N. Abdullah et al. (Eds.): ACeS 2021, CCIS 1487, pp. 62–77, 2021.
https://doi.org/10.1007/978-981-16-8059-5_5

With trust in traditional news networks at a low point, people have started moving from mainstream media towards social media for accessing news. Social media provides users with an open and distributed platform where they can freely share their content and express themselves. However, with diverse sources and online intermediaries present, infiltration in news-related information management and communication has a considerable impact in shaping an individual's opinions. This has unfolded yet another issue of *reliable information* and *accountability* over the social media networks.

With an increase in online social media usage to network and communicate with people, it has become a conspicuous source for the propagation of disinformation. The low cost, easy access and rapid diffusion of information on social media have enabled the wide propagation of fake news on social media [18]. Because of that, malicious actors of society are using it as a tool to create a narrative that benefits them and suits their agenda. Modern social media platforms are broken and fail to focus on the quality of the user-generated content due to centralized architecture, the situation being akin to a country with no law enforcement agencies. Social media platforms miss adequate regulation, and their roles and responsibilities are still not clearly defined [8]. Although certain social media platforms have added the feature of content moderation, such as flagging the content as instigative or otherwise, but the individual propagating such news can still get away easily.

We aim to offer a much-needed layer for secure, reliable information exchange in our present-day social media infrastructure, which does not rely on a single source of truth by harnessing the three distinctive attributes of blockchain, i.e., *immutability, data provenance,* and *distributed consensus.* The core idea is to provide a platform with reliable and accountable information exchange, where every activity carried out over the network is stored immutably, and data provenance of the activity can always be proved. We have proposed a platform where users can freely express themselves and be accountable for their actions, unlike present-day social networks where no regulations are stated for preserving netiquette over the Internet. Our model rewards users for being truthful and penalizes them for being misleading.

In particular, our major contributions can be summarized as follows:

- We propose a decentralized crowd sourcing and blockchain-based framework for sharing news on social media platforms.
- We use an immutable database for recording events associated with the decentralized application, making sure that the provenance of data can always be tracked down in our proposed model.
- We incorporate the characteristic feature of human behavior associated with fake news and propose an innovative reward generation mechanism to combat the issue.
- We introduce a new consensus rule based on Byzantine Generals Problem [10] to improve the existing blockchain-based fake news solutions by using active users and validators to agree upon the validity of news.

– Finally, we also implement a prototype model in form of a dApp. The experimental results indicate feasible performance by our proposed model especially under the popular Sybil and Byzantine Generals attack.

The rest of the paper is organized as follows. Section 2 discusses the related work on fake news using blockchain and other applied methods. Section 3 presents the design of our proposed model and it details out the appropriate consensus mechanism and reward generation architecture. Section 4 introduces the prototype implementation and experiments conducted on the test network. In the end, Sect. 5 concludes the paper highlighting its key contributions.

2 Related Work

Fake news detection has attracted the interest of researchers in recent years and a number of different approaches have been proposed. In addition, conventional content moderation techniques have been incorporated by several social online platforms (e.g., Mozilla, Facebook, Twitter) and trade associations (e.g., EACA, IAB Europe and WFA). All these have made progress in their commitment to tackle fake news [8]. For instance, Google has announced the Google News Initiative to support the news industry in quality journalism. However, these techniques used by the social media platforms for flagging content as instigative or otherwise assumes a centralized regulator which removes the content immediately. Machine learning based algorithms [1,4,9,13,19] were the foremost approaches developed to check the fake news menace. In this approach, fake news detection is formulated as a classification or regression problem, with the former being used more frequently. However, the classification is usually restricted to binary classification where the news is checked for being either real or fake. The challenge here is related to the partly fake or partly real news. Similarly, regression problems face the challenge of converting the discrete labels of news datasets to numeric scores of truthfulness.

Although, all these machine learning based approaches have been effective in fake news detection to a greater extent, however, most of these are centralized with a single source controlling identification, prevention and detection of fake news. This is troublesome as the decision made by a single central authority mostly tends to be skewed. To overcome this challenge, the decentralized architecture of blockchain is effective as there is no central authority to skew the results and the control is completely distributed.

In this distributed direction, Qayyum et al. [15] proposed an open protocol for tracking the credibility of news by introducing the concept of Proof of Truthfulness (PoT), where any node in the network can verify whether a content is or not part of a blockchain. In particular, they store the content in a Merkle tree i.e., a binary tree built using hash pointers. Moving the work ahead in this direction several works have been proposed to trace the origin of news source [6,17] by using the decentralized blockchain framework to combatting the spread of fake news [2,11,12,14,16]. Our proposed approach for the fake news detection is also based on blockchain distributed architecture. We will discuss the approach in detail in Sect. 3.

3 Our Model

In this section, we present our proposed model in detail. In particular, we first discuss our proposed framework. After that, we define our proposed consensus rule, and finally we present the reward mechanism that is used by our model.

3.1 Proposed Framework

We have used blockchain to create a decentralized news network, where a distributed ledger records information about transactions in a block, and the blocks are interlinked through secure cryptographic functions. The distributed ledger based on blockchain acts as an immutable record of timestamped transactions, enabling our model to track the provenance of data so that users know that their data has not been altered. For example, transactions include account creation, uploading posts, access to posts, upvoting, downvoting, and network affordances to facilitate communication.

The blockchain [20] acts as an immutable database with an implicit trust mechanism, determining the integrity and transparency of news without third party involvement. Each action of user has a signature associated with it which ensures that the content published by the author or voting done by users will be stored permanently on the distributed ledger and will be made available to other users in the same form as it was published. It becomes impossible for a user to change its "*incorrect votes*" into "*correct votes*" or to alter the "*fake news*" and make it appear "*true*" after publishing it. Other users can always analyse the news source from the blockchain and be sure about its validity. This indelible recording of events in the system is essential for users being accountable for the content they share, i.e., a user can't simply delete an inappropriate post once he has posted it. Authorized users will always trace a post to a certain user adding the feature of accountability to the system.

Apart from providing the features of "accountability" and "provenance" which help our proposed model to determine the origin of data and at the same time make users answerable for their actions, blockchain can also execute *Smart Contract* [3], which automates agreement between various nodes of the network. Smart Contracts play a significant role in combating fake news as they enforce agreement among all the network participants without intermediary's involvement. The agreements include set of rules that enforce the consensus mechanism and reward generation required to authenticate the news article, and thereupon propose rewards and punishments to the desired participants.

Even though blockchain guarantees provenance and immutability of data, the nodes can still act in a malicious manner and detect the status of news incorrectly. These nodes can either act individually or they could collude with the peer nodes in order to advance in their direction of getting successful. To determine the status of news in the presence of these nodes, each node is associated with a reputation score, which helps our model to determine their integrity and thereupon resolve the authenticity of news. Further the nodes are administered with the amount of voting proportional to their reputation score. Thus by using reputation score along with blockchain, our model provides the means for storing and retrieving news articles along with their status (*Verified/Fake*) with absolute credibility. Blockchain makes sure that the provenance of news article could be followed by going through the blocks in a sequential manner, and the nodes in turn distinguish between fake and verified news.

Since social media platforms are crowded with news articles it would not be possible to verify the authenticity of each news article. Our model verifies $(u + v) * n_{u+v}$ number of news in parallel, where u is the number of users in our model, v is the number of validators and n_{u+v} is the number of news articles that have been assigned to each user/validator node. By allocating each user multiple news our model increases the number of news that can be verified simultaneously. Further in order to resolve conflict regarding the news that need to be verified first, our model gives priority to those news which have become viral.

3.2   System Architecture

Figure 1 illustrates the framework of our proposed model. As can be seen by the figure, the user upload the data on blockchain through dApp which acts as an interface for retrieving data through Smart Contracts of blockchain. After the news is uploaded by a user, its authenticity is checked by the user and validator nodes with the help of consensus mechanism described in Sect. 3.3. Thereupon the nodes are provided with appropriate rewards by the reward generation mechanism detailed out in Sect. 3.4.

3.3   Consensus Rule

We have defined our consensus rule based on *Byzantine Generals Problem* [10] which is defined in distributed systems as a "description of a situation where involved parties must agree on a single strategy in order to avoid complete failure, but where some of the involved parties are corrupt and disseminating false information or are otherwise unreliable". This means for any m, Algorithm $A(m)$ reaches consensus if there are more than $3m$ generals and at most m traitors. This implies that the algorithm can reach consensus as long as $\frac{2}{3}$rd of the actors are honest [10]. Since Blockchain is also a distributed system, to reach a consensus on a news article and to avoid the 51% attack [7], wherein a user or a group of users maliciously control the network for a complete failure of the network our model proposes consensus rules which are modified with the number of users connected to the network (u) and number of validators (v), based on the $\frac{2}{3}$rd rule of Byzantine Generals Problem. The consensus algorithm states that for associating verified tag to a news article $\frac{2}{3}$rd of active users in the network and $\frac{1}{3}$rd of the active validators should have upvoted the article and for associating fake tag to a news article $\frac{2}{3}$rd of active users in the network or $\frac{1}{3}$rd of the active

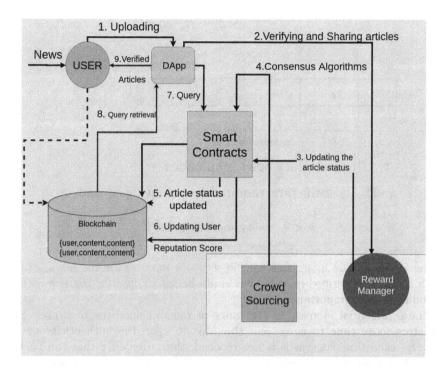

Fig. 1. Proposed framework

validators should have downvoted the article within a random time slot T and if they do not agree during this time slot then a backoff procedure is implemented wherein another time slot is selected with wider duration and this process will continue until the active users and/or validators agree upon the authenticity of the news. For determining the time window T during which active users and validators will find out the authenticity or fakeness of the news we have used a *sliding window approach*, (see Fig. 2), wherein we define a contention window that will move forward until consensus is reached.

Figure 3 illustrates the flow of actions in our proposed consensus mechanism. In this figure, we can see that after a news post is uploaded on the dApp, we note the current time unit t_i as the time for the start of consensus. We start a counter for users and validators to reach consensus, by generating a random number r_i. The random number will denote the time for which active users and validator nodes could decide the status of news. By selecting the time interval after which news status is determined at random the number of nodes that decide the authenticity of news will be dynamic, as each node who is active during the time period can join the network and vote for news article. This dynamic time interval will prevent collusion among nodes as they do not know the ratio of user and validator nodes they need to collude with in order to change the status of news. The random number $r_i \in (1, 2^i) * z$ where z is the lease time defined

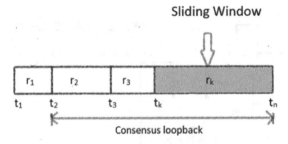

Sliding Window

t_1 : Time at which news is uploaded

and t_n - t_1 is the time required for achieving consensus

Fig. 2. Sliding window approach

by the network. The lease time can be setup in minutes for the news articles which need to be verified quickly or it could be set to days for the news where reliability is more important.

The exponential increase in the range of random numbers gives users and validators more time to agree and thus decide upon the authenticity of the news. So each time consensus is not reached, the probability that the backoff time will become longer increases, and the time for collaboration among nodes in the network will increase. Since the time at which network will check the consensus among nodes and mine no one knows the results due to the random time slot based contention window method, our model does not allow nodes to collude with each other.

3.4   Reward Generation Mechanism

Our proposed model uses *reputation score* as a trust measure to determine the credibility of a node. We propose a dynamic reputation system where an initial score of zero is assigned to each node, and the score evolves as the node verifies trustworthy news. The change in reputation score varies dynamically for each news post depending upon the number of user and validator nodes which took part in the consensus process. Our model gives a reputation score of $\{-2I, 0, I/0\}$ to correct, unknown and incorrect decisions made by the user/validator nodes respectively. The incentives (I) for a particular news post are a logarithmic function of X, where X = number of upvotes for the news if news is authentic and number of downvotes if the news is fake i.e. $I = \log(X)$. We have used Incentive as log function of X to reduce its exponential growth in the network. Every user node who has participated in the news post's consensus will see an increase in the reputation score by I units, i.e., if a user has a reputation score of R_{t-1} units, after verifying a news correctly, his reputation score will be $(R_t = R_{t-1} + I)$ units.

The reputation score of validator node is not increased on their correct detection as it could advance their reputation score to such a degree that it becomes

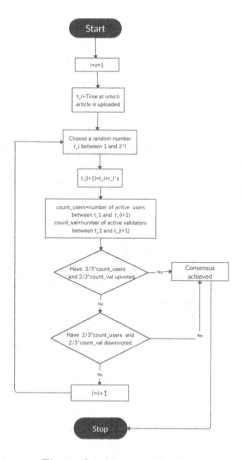

Fig. 3. Consensus mechanism

impossible for other nodes to surpass it. This could concentrate the power of voting among a handful of nodes within a few iterations. However, for incorrect detection, both user and validator nodes are penalized for their actions and their reputation score is deducted by $2I$ units, i.e. if their reputation score before the transaction was R_{t-1}, the reputation score after the transaction will be $(R_t = R_{t-1} - 2I)$ units. Thus our incentive mechanism makes sure that the malicious behavior of node costs them twice as compared to what they had gained from honest behavior. If the nodes did not vote for the news post their reputation score remains unchanged.

Further our model categorizes nodes dynamically into user or validator nodes after each news post. It does so by comparing the reputation score of the nodes with the dynamic threshold of the network. The threshold (t_h) for our model is the running average of all the incentives I of the news post.

$$t_h = \frac{(n_t - 1) * I_{t-1} + \log(X_i)}{n_t}$$

where n_t is the number of news articles our model has verified till time instant t, I_{t-1} denotes the running average of all the incentives till time instant $t-1$ and t_h denotes the new running average. As can be seen by the equation, threshold increases with an increase in the number of news posts, as the running average will increase, which will eventually make our network more reliable.

After the status of news is determined the nodes are categorized into user or validator by comparing their reputation score with the threshold.

– If the reputation score of a user node surpasses the threshold ($R_t > I_t$) it is labelled as *validator* node.
– If reputation score of validator node does not exceed the threshold ($R_t \leq I_t$) it is downgraded to *user* node.

This dynamic categorization of nodes ensures the nodes cannot continue with their wrong over a period of time as they would be checked for their behavior after each status of news is decided. By defining the threshold as running average we are making sure that users which have actively taken part in the consensus process are adept to act as validator nodes, henceforth more value is assigned to their votes in the consensus process.

Initially the network will not have adequate number of validator nodes, so our model will rely on web scrapping from leading reputed dailies to verify the news. User votes will only increase or decrease their reputation score and will not be used for authentication purposes. If the user votes in accordance with the leading dailies, its reputation score will increase, otherwise its reputation score will be decreased. Those users who are consistent in voting and vote according to the leading dailies, their reputation score will surpass the threshold defined by the network, and be given a validator tag. By the time the network will have 33% of validator nodes, web scraping will be replaced by achieving consensus among validator nodes and user nodes. Thereupon credibility of news will be decided based upon the consensus among these nodes.

4   Prototype Implementation

We have developed our system as a decentralized application (dApp) which is an end to end to application on the blockchain that offers access to individuals, applications, and frameworks, not necessarily known to one another to execute peer to peer transactions. It has a user interface as its front-end and a back-end that incorporates blockchain and Smart Contract, with blockchain giving it decentralized architecture.

4.1   Implementataion and Basic Components of dApp

The decentralized web based application has been developed using *MetaMask, Truffle,* and *Web3.js*. While MetaMask facilitates access of blockchain to dApp with normal browser, Truffle provides set of tools for developing Ethereum Smart

Contracts, and Web3.js is the official Ethereum JavaScript API which is used to interact with Ethereum Smart Contracts.

The proposed dApp has an interactive interface that allows for viewing on desktops or tablets. It consists of three main components:

- The front-end component, which interacts with the user.
- An Ethereum blockchain, that stores the user data and metadata about media resources.
- Ethereum Smart Contracts, written in Solidity, which read and write metadata about media objects on the blockchain.

4.2 Overall Working of dApp

Figure 4 captures the overall working of our decentralized App. When a user posts an article via dApp, a block is created, which contains information about user's account ID, hash of the article, previous hash and the timestamp. Once the article is posted, active validators and users can take part in voting process. When users or validators vote for an article, another block is created that stores the hash of the events, i.e., votes that could be upvote or downvote and the account ID of users who voted, timestamp, and the hash of previous block. After a random time slot it is checked whether the consensus has been reached or not. If consensus is reached, another block is added to blockchain which updates the status of news i.e., news gets verified or fake tag. However, if the consensus is not reached during the time interval than another random time slot is selected wherein more users and validators are appended to vote for the news post and this process will continue until consensus is reached. Once the consensus is reached, the reputation score of the participants is updated.

4.3 Performance Evaluation

We analyze the performance of our consensus protocol based on the following metrics:

Time Complexity: To evaluate the performance of our model we need to determine the time it takes to execute various functions. The process of upvoting, downvoting or reading a news article takes constant amount of time as these functions involve operations of reading or writing to the blockchain once. However, the time taken to decide upon the authenticity of news builds upon the consensus function which in turn depends upon the agreement among user and validator nodes. If our model includes m validator nodes and n user nodes the consensus function takes $\mathcal{O}(m + n)$ time to execute as it needs to check the decision of $m + n$ nodes from blockchain before coming to a decision.

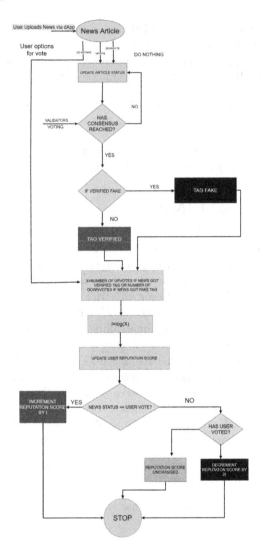

Fig. 4. Flow diagram of overall working of our proposed model

Scalability: Scalability is the property of a system to adapt to the growing load by utilizing the network resources properly. Our model is scalable as it adjusts to growing load of news by letting the nodes to vote for multiple news simultaneously. Thus news classification is done in a parallel manner by the available nodes, which enhances the performance of our network. Figure 5 demonstrates the scalability of our proposed model. As can be seen by the figure with increase in number of user and validator nodes our model is able to classify more number of news articles in parallel thereby displaying the scalable nature of our model.

Fairness: Fairness in our proposed model is a measure of the following aspects:

- The consensus outcome should not be concentrated within the hands of a few people.
- There should be impartial selection of nodes.
- The model should not discriminate against correct and honest members.

Our model satisfies these aspects by dividing the power of decision making to the two sets of nodes (user and validator) which drive their decision simultaneously. The consensus outcome is decided only when both set of nodes stipulate decision, otherwise the decision is delayed until the next consensus window is reached. The nodes are selected on the basis of reputation score earned by the users. Only the nodes with reputation score greater than the threshold are suitable to become validator nodes. The method of node selection and updation is done dynamically after each news post and it cannot be tweaked by any authority. Also, our model provides incentives for honest behaviour of nodes while the malicious ones are penalized.

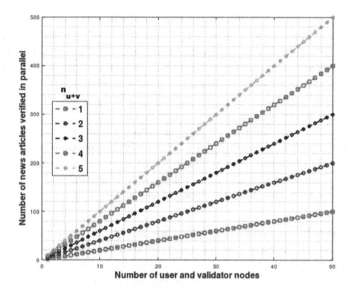

Fig. 5. Scalability of our model

4.4 Defense Against Attacks

1. Byzantine Generals Attack: In Byzantine Generals attack, the nodes vote maliciously in order to disrupt the proper flow of network. Since every distributed system is susceptible to this attack, we devised a consensus mechanism wherein for associating verified tag to a news article $\frac{2}{3}rd$ active users in the network and

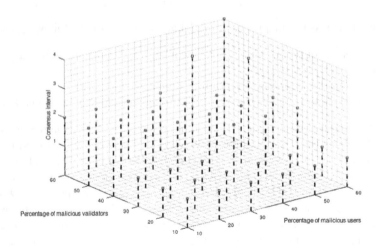

Fig. 6. Contention window over which consensus takes place in presence of malicious nodes

$\frac{1}{3}rd$ of the active validators should have upvoted the article and for associating fake tag to a news article $\frac{2}{3}rd$ of active users in the network or $\frac{1}{3}rd$ of the active validators should have downvoted the article within a random time slot. As Fig. 6 shows when the number of malicious users or validators are less than 30% the news got verified in the first slot of sliding window. When the number of malicious nodes increased beyond 30% it took more time for news to get verified as the duration of next time slot increased giving nodes more time to agree upon a decision. However, if the percentage of malicious user nodes and validator nodes will increase beyond 70% and 30% simultaneously, our model could misclassify the news. This is a theoretical attack considering the fact that the nodes are selected randomly and probability of selecting colluding malicious nodes decreases with increase in number of users.

2. Sybil Attack: In sybil attack [5], the attacker forges a large number of identities in the blockchain network and tries to affect the consensus outcome. In our proposed model, since the nodes are selected based on their reputation score, the likelihood for such an attack to succeed is very rare. Even when there are attacker nodes selected among the user nodes, the news voted by the user nodes will simultaneously be voted by validator nodes. Therefore, our consensus algorithm can resist the Sybil attack with an impressive probability.

Efficiency of Our Model Under These Attacks: Figure 7 shows the efficiency of our proposed model under Sybil and Byzantine Generals attack. Initially, when there are few number of user and validator nodes, these attacks lead to decrease in efficiency of our proposed model. This happens primarily due to the fact that probability of malicious nodes and nodes with multiple fake identities occupying a single slot of sliding window and outdoing the desired percentage of 30% for validators and 70% for users to change the decision in their favor is more when their are few number of nodes. However as the number of nodes increase, the efficiency of our proposed model is found to increase progressively. After the number of user and validator nodes are found to surpass 35 and 15 respectively, our model is found to classify 99% of news accurately.

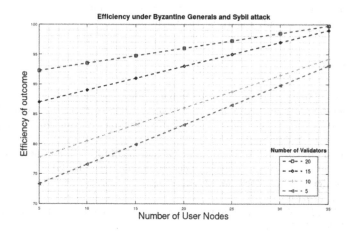

Fig. 7. Efficiency in presence of Byzantine Generals and Sybil attack

5   Conclusion and Future Work

We have proposed a framework for incentivizing user behavior on social networks to achieve two objectives: *combating fake news* and *accountability for sharing data*. While the current architecture of social networking does not offer much in terms of privacy, security, and trust, the intrinsic architecture of blockchain ensures that the user can tweak the criterion of sharing in the proposed framework for a secure, trusted, and rewarding networking experience. Our proposed prototype is uniquely capable of recording metadata about digital media on blockchain so that it becomes trivial to prove their authenticity in a manner that can be trusted. Our model's ultimate aim is to make content creators accountable for what they create and reward/penalize them for their behavior through our blockchain based incentive mechanism wherein we provide incentives to nodes after following their actions through blockchain. The experimental results of our proposed model indicate its scalability and flexibility. Moreover, under Sybil and Byzantine Generals attack as the number of user and validation nodes increase beyond the desired threshold value, our proposed model is able to classify 99% of news articles accurately in a prompt manner.

Moving this work ahead, our proposed model can be expanded to crawl over different web sources and categorize their news articles based upon the metadata structure associated with the current news article which has been classified either as verified or fake. Further our model can be used as a framework/API by web based news portals to authenticate their news articles and provide appropriate rewards and punishments to their content writers for their fitting behavior. They could likewise stop traffic flow to those portals which result in propagation of fake news.

Acknowledgement. Authors would like to thank the anonymous reviewers for their useful suggestions especially regarding the future work.

References

1. Ahmed, H., Traore, I., Saad, S.: Detection of online fake news using N-gram analysis and machine learning techniques. In: Traore, I., Woungang, I., Awad, A. (eds.) ISDDC 2017. LNCS, vol. 10618, pp. 127–138. Springer, Cham (2017). https://doi.org/10.1007/978-3-319-69155-8_9

2. Christodoulou, P., Christodoulou, K.: Developing more reliable news sources by utilizing the blockchain technology to combat fake news. In: 2020 Second International Conference on Blockchain Computing and Applications (BCCA), pp. 135–139. IEEE (2020)

3. Cong, L.W., He, Z.: Blockchain disruption and smart contracts. Rev. Financ. Stud. **32**(5), 1754–1797 (2019)

4. Conroy, N.K., Rubin, V.L., Chen, Y.: Automatic deception detection: methods for finding fake news. Proc. Assoc. Inf. Sci. Technol. **52**(1), 1–4 (2015)

5. Douceur, J.R.: The sybil attack. In: Druschel, P., Kaashoek, F., Rowstron, A. (eds.) IPTPS 2002. LNCS, vol. 2429, pp. 251–260. Springer, Heidelberg (2002). https://doi.org/10.1007/3-540-45748-8_24

6. Dwivedi, A.D., Singh, R., Dhall, S., Srivastava, G., Pal, S.K.: Tracing the source of fake news using a scalable blockchain distributed network. In: 2020 IEEE 17th International Conference on Mobile Ad Hoc and Sensor Systems (MASS), pp. 38–43. IEEE (2020)

7. Eyal, I., Sirer, E.G.: Majority is not enough: bitcoin mining is vulnerable. In: Christin, N., Safavi-Naini, R. (eds.) FC 2014. LNCS, vol. 8437, pp. 436–454. Springer, Heidelberg (2014). https://doi.org/10.1007/978-3-662-45472-5_28

8. Fraga-Lamas, P., Fernández-Caramés, T.M.: Leveraging distributed ledger technologies and blockchain to combat fake news. arXiv preprint arXiv:1904.05386 (2019)

9. Gilda, S.: Evaluating machine learning algorithms for fake news detection. In: 2017 IEEE 15th Student Conference on Research and Development (SCOReD), pp. 110–115. IEEE (2017)

10. Lamport, L., Shostak, R., Pease, M.: The byzantine generals problem. In: Concurrency: The Works of Leslie Lamport, pp. 203–226 (2019)

11. Mikeln, M., Perović, L.: Eventum: platform for decentralized real-world data feeds (2018)

12. Murimi, R.M.: A blockchain enhanced framework for social networking. Ledger **4**, 67–81 (2019)

13. Ozbay, F.A., Alatas, B.: Fake news detection within online social media using supervised artificial intelligence algorithms. Phys. A Stat. Mech. Appl. **540**, 123174 (2020)

14. Paul, S., Joy, J.I., Sarker, S., Ahmed, S., Das, A.K., et al.: Fake news detection in social media using blockchain. In: 2019 7th International Conference on Smart Computing and Communications (ICSCC), pp. 1–5. IEEE (2019)
15. Qayyum, A., Qadir, J., Janjua, M.U., Sher, F.: Using blockchain to rein in the new post-truth world and check the spread of fake news. arXiv preprint arXiv:1903.11899 (2019)
16. Shae, Z., Tsai, J.: AI blockchain platform for trusting news. In: 2019 IEEE 39th International Conference on Distributed Computing Systems (ICDCS), pp. 1610–1619. IEEE (2019)
17. Shang, W., Liu, M., Lin, W., Jia, M.: Tracing the source of news based on blockchain. In: 2018 IEEE/ACIS 17th International Conference on Computer and Information Science (ICIS), pp. 377–381. IEEE (2018)
18. Shu, K., Sliva, A., Wang, S., Tang, J., Liu, H.: Fake news detection on social media: a data mining perspective. ACM SIGKDD Explor. Newsl. **19**(1), 22–36 (2017)
19. Tacchini, E., Ballarin, G., Della Vedova, M.L., Moret, S., de Alfaro, L.: Some like it hoax: automated fake news detection in social networks. arXiv preprint arXiv:1704.07506 (2017)
20. Wang, S., Ouyang, L., Yuan, Y., Ni, X., Han, X., Wang, F.Y.: Blockchain-enabled smart contracts: architecture, applications, and future trends. IEEE Trans. Syst. Man Cybern. Syst. **49**(11), 2266–2277 (2019)

g-EoN: A Non-salient Approach Towards Encryption Using Gamma Function

$$\Gamma\left(-\frac{\alpha}{\beta}\right) = -\frac{\beta}{\alpha}\,\Gamma\left(\frac{\beta-\alpha}{\beta}\right)$$

Abhilash Kumar Das[✉] and Nirmalya Kar[✉]

National Institute of Technology Agartala, Agartala, India
nirmalya@ieee.org

Abstract. Cryptography is the art of presenting secret information under code obfuscation. This can be achieved by various algorithms which convert human readable text into non-legible text. This paper presents a cryptosystem that adopts the Gamma function and tabular modeling to carry out both the encryption and decryption using two common keys namely Primary Common Key (PCK) and Secondary Common Key (SCK). The encryption outputs two ciphers when a message P and PCK is given as input. The value Key VK is generated by Value Key Generator (VKG). Cipher C_1 uses modular arithmetic followed by Gamma function and Cipher C_2 uses Gamma function in Gamma Cryptor Module (GCM). The result of VKG is given to GCM. During decryption, it requires both the ciphers $C_1 C_2$ and a Value key VK for generating the plaintext back.

Keywords: Gamma function · Value key generator · Gamma cryptor module · Encryption · Decryption

1 Introduction

A cryptosystem is designed in such a way that it returns the plaintext back by its decryption process. Till this age, most of the algorithms for cryptosystems have used a direct relationship between ciphertext and plaintext. The secrecy of the plaintext is due to the hardness of dicrete logarithm problem (DLP). For ex. RSA [1] uses the following equations.

$$C = P^e \,(\text{mod } N) \tag{1}$$

$$P = C^d \,(\text{mod } N) \tag{2}$$

put the value of C in Eq. 2

$$P = (P^e \,(\text{mod } N))^d \,(\text{mod } N) \tag{3}$$

$$P = P^{ed} \,(\text{mod } N) \tag{4}$$

$$\therefore P = P \,(\text{mod } N) \tag{5}$$

where e and d are co-prime to each other.

© Springer Nature Singapore Pte Ltd. 2021
N. Abdullah et al. (Eds.): ACeS 2021, CCIS 1487, pp. 78–94, 2021.
https://doi.org/10.1007/978-981-16-8059-5_6

Another cryptosystem namely Elgamal [2] was introduced in 1984 by Tather Elgamal. It is also based on DLP [3]. It provides randomised encryption of plaintext. It is used for establishing key exchange. It also uses direct relationship between plaintext and ciphertext. The Elgamal encryption is given by the following equations.

$$e_2 = e_1 (\text{mod } p) \tag{6}$$
$$C_1 = e_1^r (\text{mod } p) \tag{7}$$
$$C_2 = (e_2^r \times M) \text{ mod } p \tag{8}$$
$$M = [C_2 \times (C_1^d)^{-1}] \text{ mod } p \tag{9}$$

Substitute in the Eq. 9 from the Eq. 7, Eq. 8 and Eq. 6.

$$M = [C_2 \times ((e_1^r (\text{mod } p))^d)^{-1}] \text{mod } p$$
$$= [(e_2^r \times M) \text{ mod } p \times ((e_1^r (\text{mod } p))^d)^{-1}] \text{mod } p$$
$$= [((e_1 (\text{mod } p))^r \times M) \text{ mod } p \times ((e_1^r (\text{mod } p))^d)^{-1}] \text{mod } p$$
$$= [(e_1^{rd} \text{mod } p \times M) \text{mod } p \times (e_1^{rd} \text{mod } p)^{-1} \text{mod } p]$$
$$\therefore M = M \text{mod } p$$

where e_1, e_2 are the public key, d is the private key, p is a very large prime number and M is the message. So, in this paper it has been focused to remove the direct relationship between plaintext and ciphertext. The proposed algorithm uses an intermediate specific value to connect the ciphertext and plaintext. A table has been constructed to translate simple plaintext into intermediate values.

Block ciphers like AES [4] and DES [5] uses many rounds of encryption where first round is of initial permutation and after 16 rounds of rigorous permutations of 64-bits. The output cipher is transmitted to the receiver. But in our proposed model, Gamma Crypt Module (GCM) is introduced to bring randomness over short differences in plaintext e.g. 1234, 5678 etc. Also it resists linear and differential cryptanalysis because the proposed algorithm is a stream cipher [6].

The proposed algorithm uses Diffie Hellman Key Exchange [7,8] for key exchanging. It uses the following equations.

$$Key_1 = (\alpha^x \text{mod } p)^y \text{mod } p$$
$$Key_2 = (\alpha^y \text{mod } p)^x \text{mod } p$$
$$\therefore Key_1 = Key_2 = PCK$$

where α is primitive root modulo p and PCK can take value from 1 to $(p-1)$.

In [9], the author has used a dynamic table to generate the ciphertext. There is a limitation of overflow of ciphertext values if larger key values are used to generate the table e.g. 2371. Here, the 2371 is splitted and used as seed value to generate the dynamic table. The ciphertext for plaintext '99' will be so large that it may get overflown. So, in our proposed model, modular arithmetic has been used to keep the values maximum upto 2^{20} which is a very big number.

Thus, the probability of redundancy is reduced to much extent. This avoids such risk of overflow.

The proposed model is designed in such a way that it provides *the avalanche effect* as seen in AES and DES encryption. The avalanche effect turns out to bring randomness among slight changes in plaintext. If there is a slight change of unit distance of plaintext, it should reflect a drastic change in ciphertext. In [10] and [11], the author have designed an algorithm to bring Zero Knowledge Proof (ZKP) on Diffie Hellman Key Exchange. The author have taken various situations for ZKP, demonstrating the reliability of Diffie Hellman Key Exchange. In paper [12], the authors have used the Diffie Hellman key exchange for node to node connectivity authentication in a Wireless Sensor Network (WSN). Also, they have used concepts of cryptosystem and clustering head mechanisms for eliminating the weaknesses in Diffie Hellman Key exchange. In [13], the author has proposed three different approaches that help securely integrating Diffie Hellman Key Exchange into Digital Signatures.

In later sections, few graph plots of plaintext with the ciphertext has been shown. They depicts randomness and non redundancy of ciphertext for different plaintext.

2   Proposed Methodology

This section describes the proof and design architecture of the proposed model.

2.1   Gamma Function

The mathematical Gamma Function is defined as

$$\Gamma(a) = \int_0^\infty x^{a-1} e^{-x} dx \tag{10}$$

It is also known as Euler's integral of the second kind [14,15]. The reduction formula for Gamma function is given as

$$\begin{aligned}
\Gamma(n+1) &= \int_0^\infty x^n e^{-x} dx \\
&= \left[-x^n e^{-x}\right]_0^\infty + \int_0^\infty n\, x^{n-1} e^{-x} dx \\
&= n \int_0^\infty x^{n-1} e^x dx \\
&= n\, \Gamma(n)
\end{aligned}$$

$$\Gamma(n+1) = n\, \Gamma(n) \tag{11}$$

The Gamma Function works as if $\Gamma(n)$ is known for an interval say $1 < n \le 2$, then $2 < n \le 3$ can be found out [16]. It is also valid for negative values of n. If $\Gamma(n)$ is known for an interval say $-1 < n < 0$ then for interval $-2 < n < -1$, $\Gamma(n)$ can be found. In general, $\Gamma(n+1) = n!$ for $n > 0$.

2.2 Equation of Cryptosystem

The following equations are used for encryption and decryption respectively.

$$C_1 = \Gamma\left(\frac{-VK(\mathrm{mod}SCK)}{SCK}\right) \tag{12}$$

$$C_2 = \Gamma\left(\frac{-VK}{SCK}\right) \tag{13}$$

$$VK = -SCK \times \left(\frac{C_1}{C_2}\right) \tag{14}$$

The Eq. 12 and Eq. 13 gives the ciphertext for corresponding VK where as Eq. 14 gives the decryption of $(C_1 \cdot C_2)$ into VK. Here, SCK is the Secondary Common Key, VK is the Value key and $C_1 C_2$ are the two ciphertext.

2.3 Proof of Cryptosystem

The idea of cryptography is derived from reduction formula in Eq. 11. Suppose $\Gamma(72/101)$ is calculated where Value Key VK = 72 and Secondary Common Key SCK = 101. [17] Since, no direct formula is there to solve this except the integral. But the equation can be modified as $\Gamma(-29(\mathrm{mod}101)/101)$ for the critical condition $0 < VK \leq SCK$. Now, if noted carefully then $\Gamma(-29(\mathrm{mod}101)/101)$ is equal to $\Gamma(72/101)$ for $0 < VK \leq SCK$. For generalization,

$$n\,\Gamma(n) = \Gamma(n+1) \tag{15}$$

put n $= \left(\frac{-VK}{SCK}\right)$ in Eq. 15 where VK < SCK

$$\frac{-VK}{SCK}\,\Gamma\left(\frac{-VK}{SCK}\right) = \Gamma\left(\frac{-VK+SCK}{SCK}\right)$$

$$\Gamma\left(\frac{-VK}{SCK}\right) = -\left(\frac{SCK}{VK}\right) \times \Gamma\left(\frac{-VK+SCK}{SCK}\right)$$

$$VK = -SCK \times \frac{\Gamma\left(\frac{-VK+SCK}{SCK}\right)}{\Gamma\left(\frac{-VK}{SCK}\right)}$$

$$\therefore VK = -SCK \times \left(\frac{C_1}{C_2}\right)$$

Thus, the proof is valid.

2.4   Architectural Model

This section describes the flowchart diagram in the context of encryption and decryption. The sender sends the plain message P which is provided as input to the Value Key Generator (VKG). The output of the VKG is generated by the usage of the Primary Common Key (PCK). The output is then transferred to the Gamma Cryptor Module (GCM). The GCM encrypts the VK into cipher C_1 and C_2 using another common key namely Secondary Common Key (SCK). Here, the encryption ends whereas for decryption the reverse procedure is followed (Fig. 1).

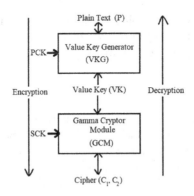

Fig. 1. The diagram shows the architecture of the proposed encryption model

Value Key Generator (VKG). This section describes the conversion of plaintext P into VK. This requires VKG which uses a Sheet Table (ST) which is dynamically created during encryption. In [9] the author has used a similar kind of table to convert plaintext into cipher. The following lines describe the formation of the sheet table of dimension 10×10. PCK is required for creating the sheet table. The CK is splitted into two parts. For e.g. 42 is the PCK then '4' is placed in ST[0][0] and '2' is placed in ST[0][1]. The first row is occupied by fibonacci sequence [18] till the last column ST[0][9]. For the next corresponding row, the first column ST[1][0] is occupied by the last fibonacci sequence. The rest of ST's memory location is occupied by the Eq. 16. The ST is created by ST-Generate function. The resultant table gives the sheet values of PCK.

$$ST[i][j] = (ST[i][j-1] + ST[i-1][j] + ST[i-1][j-1]) \mathrm{mod}(2^{20}) \qquad (16)$$

$\forall i, j \in [1, 9]$

Gamma Cryptor Module (GCM). This section describes the encryption and decryption using the Gamma function. The encryption takes VK from the VKG and SCK. C_1 is generated by the Eq. 12 where as C_2 is generated by the

*	0	1	2	3	4	5	6	7	8	9
0	4	2	6	8	14	22	36	58	94	152
1	153	159	167	181	203	239	297	391	543	789
2	790	1102	1428	1776	2160	2602	3138	3826	4760	6092
3	6093	7985	10515	13719	17655	22417	28157	35121	43707	54559
4	54560	68638	87138	111372	142746	182818	233392	296670	375498	473764
5	473765	596963	752739	951249	156791	482355	898565	380051	3643	852905
6	852906	875058	127608	783020	842484	433054	765398	995438	330556	138528
7	138529	817917	772007	634059	162411	389373	539249	202933	480351	949435
8	949436	857306	350078	707568	455462	1007246	887292	580898	215606	596816
9	596817	306407	465215	474285	588739	1002871	800257	171295	967799	731645

Fig. 2. The table shows the Sheet Values with the PCK as '42'

Eq. 13. C_1 and C_2 is concatenated to get the cipher. For the decryption part, VK is given by Eq. 14. The VK is sent back to the VKG for further decryption process in reverse (Fig. 3).

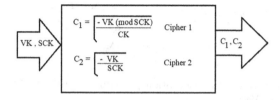

Fig. 3. The diagram shows the inner organization of GCM

2.5 Encryption Procedure

Plaintext is considered as numbered characters e.g. 90, 827, 123. If the number of digits is even then the digits are paired up. For example, 9081, here '90' and '81' are considered separately. But if the number of digits is odd then add an initial zero '0' to the number. For example, number 90123 is considered then adding zero to the front made it 090123. Lastly, all the digits are paired up as 09, 01 and 23.

RULE 1 $\implies$ If the number of digits in the plaintext $(d_0, d_1, ..., d_n)$ is odd then append '0' at the front of the d_0. Now, the number of digits is even.

RULE 2 $\implies$ If the number of digits is odd then use Rule(1) else pair all the digits.

Suppose that a common key has been exchanged whose value is 45 and the plaintext is 18. ST is generated by using PCK as described earlier in VKG subsection. The plaintext is broken down into 2 parts e.g. '1' to be mapped to row and '8' to be mapped to the column of the ST. The plaintext is transferred to the VKG and it maps the plaintext for corresponding row and column of the

ST according to Fig. 4. The intersection of the row and the column will give the VK. The following will describe the transformation of VK into cipher $(C_1.C_2)$. The C_1 is generated by the Eq. 12 and C_2 is generated by Eq. 13 taking VK and plaintext as an input. The C_1 is concatenated with C_2 to get the cipher $(C_1 \cdot C_2)$.

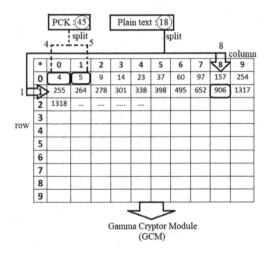

*	0	1	2	3	4	5	6	7	8	9
0	4	5	9	14	23	37	60	97	157	254
1	255	264	278	301	338	398	495	652	906	1317
2	1318	...	....	......	....					
3										
4										
5										
6										
7										
8										
9										

Gamma Cryptor Module (GCM)

Fig. 4. The diagram shows the encryption procedure with PCK '45' and translation of plaintext '18' into Value Key 'VK'

2.6   Decryption Procedure

This section describes the decryption of $(C_1.C_2)$ to get back to the original plaintext. The first stage of decryption occurs in GCM. The cipher C_1 and C_2 is used along with the SCK to decrypt the cipher into VK is given by Eq. 14. The result of Eq. 14 gives the VK which is given to the VKG for decryption. It should be noted that ST is generated at the receiver's side as well. This requires the PCK which is exchanged by Diffie Hellman Key Exchange approach [7,8]. The ST is generated at the receiver by the help of PCK as well. In VKG, the VK for a particular plaintext 'P' is searched in the ST linear row major order. At some point of time the VK will be found. Lastly, return the corresponding row and column index of the VK giving the plaintext P as concatenation of row index $P[0]$ and column index $P[1]$ to form $(P[0], P[1])$ tuple.

3   Various Algorithms Used in Cryptosystem

The following algorithm gives the Gamma values for $0 < n < 1$. This algorithm will create a 2-D matrix of order (length(table) × 2) which provides Gamma Values of n in the 2nd column. This length of table is created dynamically for

$c = 0.0001$ to ∞. Here, ∞ is the maximum value for an integer data type. The incremental factor is taken as $h = 0.001$ and $e = 2.718$.

Algorithm 1. The following algorithm gives the Gamma values for $0 > n > -1$. This algorithm provides only Gamma values of negative numbers in the above range.

---

assign table = empty list, $c = 0.0001$, $e = 2.718$, $h = 0.001$;
for i from 0 to ∞ **do**
   row = empty list
   row.append(c)
   row.append($e^{-c} \times c^{n-1}$)
   assign $c = c + h$
   table.append(row)
end for
assign sum = 0
for i from 1 to length(table)-1 **do**
   sum = sum + table[i][1]
end for
result = $\frac{h}{2}$(table[0][1]+table[length(table)-1][1]+2×sum)
return result

The algorithm ST-Generate(PCK, P) uses Primary Common Key and plaintext to generate value key VK. Suppose that PCK is a tuple (PCK[0], PCK[1]) where PCK is the concatenation of PCK[0] and PCK[1]. Note that PCK[0] and PCK[1] are not equal. The line no. (11) in ST-Generate function does the mod with 2^{20} where 20 is the total number of digits of row [0:9] and column [0:9]. P is also a tuple (P[0], P[1]) where P is the concatenation of P[0] and P[1].

Algorithm 2. GammaNeg(n)

---

assign factor = 1
while $n < 0$ **do**
   assign factor = factor $\times n$
   assign $n = n + 1$
end while
assign result = $\frac{\text{Gamma}(n)}{\text{factor}}$
return result

Generate-SCK(ST). Return a random number between number i.e. maximum of all values in ST and ∞.

4 Proposed Algorithm and Complexity Analysis

This section provides steps of the algorithm for both the encryption and decryption (see Fig. 5 and Fig. 6 for reference). At the last details about the computational complexity has been discussed. During the decryption, the VKG searches

Algorithm 3. ST-Generate(PCK,P)

Declare arr[10][10], i, j
arr[0][0] = PCK[0], arr[0][1] = PCK[1]
for i, j ∈ [0:9] **do**
  if (not((i = 0 and j = 0) or (i = 0 and j=1)) **then**
    if i=0 **then**
      arr[i][j]=arr[i][j-2]+arr[i][j-1]
    else
      if j=0 **then**
        arr[i][j]=arr[i-1][9]+1
      else
        arr[i][j]=(arr[i][j-1]+arr[i-1][j]+arr[i-1][j-1])$\mathtt{mod}\ 2^{20}$
      end if
    end if
  end if
end for
Print (arr [i][j] $\forall i, j \in [0,9]$)
Return the VK which is the intersection of $P[0]^{th}$ row and $P[1]^{th}$ column.

for the VK in the ST. This is shown as shaded cells in the VKG module in Fig. 6. The searching is done in row major order.

The algorithm for encryption is stated in Algorithm 4. The complexity of enciphering is of polynomial time $O(n \cdot k)$. Let the plaintext be $P = (d_0, d_1, d_2...., d_n)$. At the first step, the digits are paired up. Thus, decrease the length of plaintext by half. ST is generated dynamically which takes order of $O(\frac{n}{2} \times 100k)$. Now, for each pair of VK, ciphertext is generated by the Eq. 12. and Eq. 13 which takes $O(k)$. So, overall time complexity for enciphering is $O(n \times 100 \cdot k \times k) = O(n \cdot k)$.

Algorithm 4. The enciphering algorithm uses VKG and GCM to translate plaintext into ciphertext. Here, parameters are PCK is taken from key exchange and SCK is based on the ST table formed i.e. a random number between maximum of all VK(s) and ∞.

Initialize the key exchange and get the PCK.
Generate the ST based on the PCK exchanged.
Take the plaintext as digits $P = (d_0, d_1, d_2...., d_n)$.
Convert the plaintext as paired digits by rule no.(1) and (2).
while plaintext paired digits are left in the buffer **do**
  Send each paired digits to VKG to convert plain into $VK = (VK_0, VK_1, ..., VK_{\frac{n}{2}})$.
  Send the VK of above step to the GCM to translate it into ciphertext $(C_1 \cdot C_2) = (C_{01}, C_{02}, C_{11}, C_{12}, ...C_{n1}, C_{n2})$.
end while

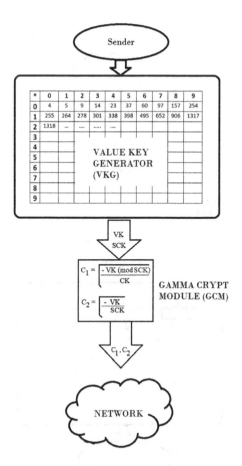

Fig. 5. Flowchart for encryption procedure

The algorithm for decryption is stated in Algorithm 5. The complexity for decryption is also $O(n \cdot k)$. At first in GCM, each ciphertext pair $(C_1 \cdot C_2)$ in translated into VK(s) by Eq. 14 which takes $O(\frac{n}{2} \times k)$ time. Then, for each VK search the whole ST table generated in receiver side. So that VK(s) are converted into plaintext. This requires $O(100 \times k)$ for comparing with 100 VK(s) in the ST in worst case. Overall, the time complexity for decryption is $O(k \times \frac{n}{2} \times 100 \cdot k) = O(n \cdot k)$.

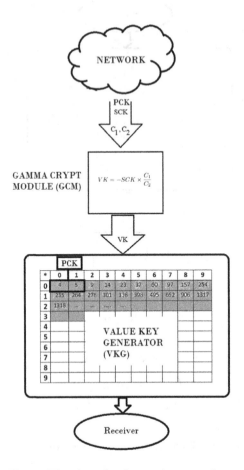

Fig. 6. Flowchart for decryption procedure

Algorithm 5. The deciphering algorithm uses VKG and GCM in reverse to translate ciphertext into plaintext. Here, PCK and SCK are same as before taken during encryption.

$(C_{01}, C_{02}, C_{11}, C_{12}, ...C_{n1}, C_{n2})$ is in cipher buffer.
while ciphertext is left in the buffer **do**
    Send each (C_{i1}, C_{i2}) to the GCM to translate back to VK.
    Send each of the VK $(VK_0, VK_1, ..., VK_{\frac{n}{2}})$ of above step to the VKG to convert
    back to initial plaintext $P = (d_0, d_1, d_2...., d_n)$.
end while

---

5   Implementation Details

Suppose the PCK exchanged is '42'. The sender generated a ST shown in Fig. 2. Consider a plaintext '543' such that it is split into pair number. Therefore, '0' is added at the front of the number i.e. the number becomes '0543'. So, 2 tuple pairs $[(0,5),(4,3)]$ of number is ready as input to VKG.

By referring to Fig. 2 '05' refers to '22' and '43' refers to '111372'. Now, these VK are sent to the GCM where they are converted to cipher C_1 and C_2. The GCM requires a SCK to encipher the plaintext. The function Generate-SCK generates a SCK for enciphering the VK. The maximum VK out of all Sheet Values in ST is '1007246' with corresponding plaintext '85'. A random is generated between '1007246' and ∞ = 99999999 i.e. '1202678'. According to the Eq. 12 and Eq. 13, C_1 = 0.999968 and C_2 = −54665.475990. The ciphertext is (0.999968, −54665.475990). Similarly, for '43' the ciphertext is (1.062645, −11.475235).

The decryption starts with (C_1, C_2) and GCM where the VK is generated by Eq. 14. For the first cipher pair (0.999968, -54665.475990), the VK = 22.0 and for the second pair (1.062645, −11.475235) VK = 111372.0. The VKs are searched in the ST created at the receiver's side. Here it returns the concatenation of corresponding row and column $[(0,5),(4,3)]$ as plaintext for each VK.

6   Statistical Analysis

The Value Keys from ST of PCK = 42 for plaintext from 1 to 100 has been analyzed. To check the randomness and unpredictibleness of the VK(s) for corresponding plaintext, Root Mean Square Error, Kurtosis and Skewness has been taken into consideration (Figs. 7, 8, 9).

Root Mean Square Error(RMSE). The RMSE is given by the following Eq. 17.

$$RMSE = \sqrt{\frac{1}{N} \Sigma_{i=1}^{N}(x_i - \mu)^2} \tag{17}$$

The RMSE tells about the standard deviation of set of points from the mean value. In other words, it gives a measure of farness from the regression line. Here, the x_i is the Value keys (VK) and N = 100 $\forall$ Sheet Values of PCK = 42. The RMSE value came to be 345374.361535. The RMSE is larger enough. Therfore, it is very difficult to guess the VK for corresponding plaintext.

Kurtosis. The Kurtosis [19] is given by the following Eq. 18.

$$Kurtosis = \frac{1}{N} \Sigma_{i=1}^{N}\left(\frac{x_i - \mu}{\sigma}\right)^4 \tag{18}$$

There are 3 types of measures of kurtosis.

1. Platykurtic ($K < 0$)
2. Mesokurtic ($K = 0$)
3. Leptokurtic ($K > 0$)

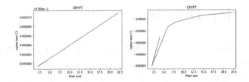

Fig. 7. Plot of C_1 and C_2 w.r.t plaintext from 1 to 5

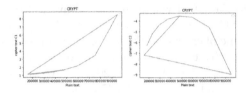

Fig. 8. Plot of C_1 and C_2 w.r.t plaintext from 45 to 55

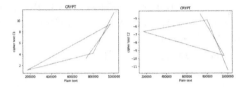

Fig. 9. Plot of C_1 and C_2 w.r.t plaintext from 95 to 100

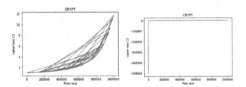

Fig. 10. Plot of C_1 and C_2 w.r.t plaintext from 1 to 100

```
PLAIN: 480351
Key: 1007346
C1=1.695968995446474
C2=-3.5566233518552557
Plain decrypted:480351
```

Fig. 11. The snapshot of C_1 and C_2 for plaintext $= 78$

Taking the same data set as consideration, Kurtosis value came to be 1.926 which is greater than 0. This means it comes under leptokurtic curve. The leptokurtic curve Fig. 12 specifies broader fluctuations resulting in less potential to predict the VK for some plaintext.

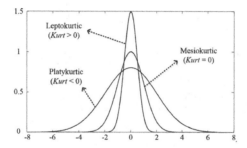

Fig. 12. The diagram shows the various types of kurtosis

Skewness. The skewness [20] is given by the following Eq. 19.

$$Skewness = \frac{1}{N} \Sigma_{i=1}^{N} \left(\frac{x_i - \mu}{\sigma} \right)^3 \tag{19}$$

There are 3 types of skewness.

1. Negative skewness
2. Normal
3. Positive skewness

The data set has given skewness to be 0.6611 which is positive. It means that most of the VK values are greater than the mean value of all VK(s). The skewness values lies in Weibull random numbers ($Gamma = 1.5$) as shown in Fig. 13.

7 Analysis of Attacks

7.1 Known Plaintext Attack

The intruder has the plaintext and the ciphertext pair. According to the Eq. 12 and Eq. 13, there is no direct relationship between the plaintext and ciphertext. The VK is related to C_1 and C_2 with the SCK. To crack the ciphertext, the intruder needs the VK and cipher pair. But to find out VK, the intruder needs the PCK to generate the ST. The VK is found out by corresponding plaintext. So, it's difficult to get the VK cipher pair (VK, C_1, C_2).

7.2 Regression Analysis Attack

For instance, plaintext from 1 to 100 with its corresponding cipher has been taken for regression analysis [21].

$$a\Sigma x_i^4 + b\Sigma x_i^3 + c\Sigma x_i^2 = \Sigma x_i^2 y_i \tag{20}$$

$$a\Sigma x_i^3 + b\Sigma x_i^2 + c\Sigma x_i = \Sigma x_i y_i \tag{21}$$

$$a\Sigma x_i^2 + b\Sigma x_i + c \cdot n = \Sigma y_i \tag{22}$$

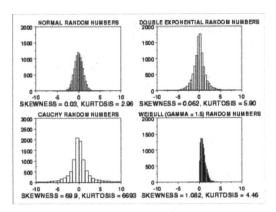

Fig. 13. The diagram shows various scenarios of skewness

Algorithm 6. Algorithm for Regression

Calculate Σx_i, Σy_i, Σx_i^2, Σx_i^4, $\Sigma x_i y_i$, $\Sigma x_i^2 y_i$, and Σx_i^3.

Substitute values in Eq. 20, Eq. 21 and Eq. 22.

Form an augmented matrix $[A : B]$ where A is 3×3 and B is 3×1.

$$[A : B] = \begin{bmatrix} a\Sigma x_i^4 & b\Sigma x_i^3 & c\Sigma x_i^2 & : & \Sigma x_i^2 y_i \\ a\Sigma x_i^3 & b\Sigma x_i^2 & c\Sigma x_i & : & \Sigma x_i y_i \\ a\Sigma x_i^2 & b\Sigma x_i & c \cdot n & : & \Sigma y_i \end{bmatrix}$$

Convert the [A:B] into echelon form.

Solve for a, b and c.

Substitute in $f(x) = a + bx + cx^2$ for quadratic fitting.

Now, the ciphertext value for corresponding plaintext '78' has been predicted. The Fig. 11 gives the actual results for key = 1007346. The predicted result for plaintext '78' is $C_1 = 3.4947230055810192$ and $C_2 = 8547.159814527055$ which is different from what is depicted in Fig. 11. This concludes that after regression analysis it's difficult to get even close to the accurate values of C_1 and C_2. This unpredictable regression analysis is due to the modular arithmetic in ST generation algorithm in line number (11).

8   Results and Discussions

This section discusses about the plotting of ciphertext for plaintext from 1 to 100. From Fig. 10 it is seen that some chaotic nature is created when plaintext from 1 upto 100 is plotted with ciphertext C_1. On the other hand, the difference between two consecutive ciphertext is very less but uniqueness lies in decimal points. Primarily, when it comes to encrypt numbers "123", it returns the ciphertext as $(0.999959 \cdot -503652.545991 \cdot 1.000978 \cdot -567.754159)$ for $PCK = 42$ and $SCK = 1007346$.

9   Conclusion

To strengthen our cryptosystem, the direct relationship between plaintext and ciphertext has been removed and replaced by VKG. In addition, a novel cryptosystem GCM has been introduced which turns out to bring randomness in ciphertext for consecutive VK(s). However, it resists cryptanalysis to much extent by providing chaotic nature to the ciphertext. Also, the computational complexity is of order polynomial time $O(n \cdot k)$. This cryptosystem will assist as a perfect application for securing essential social security numbers and PINs of debit cards and credit cards in the cloud databases.

References

1. Mathur, S., Gupta, D., Goar, V., Kuri, M.: Analysis and design of enhanced RSA algorithm to improve the security. In: 3rd International Conference on Computational Intelligence & Communication Technology (CICT), pp. 1–5. IEEE (2017)
2. Mallouli, F., Hellal, A., Saeed, N.S., Alzahrani, F.A.: A survey on cryptography: comparative study between RSA vs ECC algorithms, and RSA vs El-Gamal algorithms. In: 6th IEEE International Conference on Cyber Security and Cloud Computing (CSCloud)/5th IEEE International Conference on Edge Computing and Scalable Cloud (EdgeCom), pp. 173–176. IEEE (2019)
3. Amadori, A., Pintore, F., Sala, M.: On the discrete logarithm problem for prime-field elliptic curves. Finite Fields Appl. **51**, 168–182 (2018)
4. Indrayani, R., Ferdiansyah, P., Satria, D.A.: Effectiveness comparison of the AES and 3DES cryptography methods on email text messages. In: International Conference on Information and Communications Technology (ICOIACT), pp. 66–69. IEEE (2019)
5. Buchanan, W.J., Li, S., Asif, R.: Lightweight cryptography methods. J. Cyber Secur. Technol. **1**(3–4), 187–201 (2017)
6. Dooley, J.F.: History of Cryptography and Cryptanalysis: Codes, Ciphers, and Their Algorithms. Springer, Heidelberg (2018)
7. Abusukhon, A., Anwar, M.N., Mohammad, Z., Alghannam, B.: A hybrid network security algorithm based on Diffie Hellman and Text-to-Image Encryption algorithm. J. Discret. Math. Sci. Cryptogr. **22**(1), 65–81 (2019)
8. Ali, S., et al.: An efficient cryptographic technique using modified Diffie-Hellman in wireless sensor networks. Int. J. Distrib. Sens. Netw. **16**(6) (2020)
9. Das, A.K., Das, A., Kar, N.: An approach towards encrypting paired digits using dynamic programming and Diffie-Hellman key exchange. In: Saha, A., Kar, N., Deb, S. (eds.) ICCISIoT 2019. CCIS, vol. 1192, pp. 170–181. Springer, Singapore (2020). https://doi.org/10.1007/978-981-15-3666-3_15
10. Wu, H., Zheng, W., Chiesa, A., Popa, R.A., Stoica, I.: DIZK: a distributed zero knowledge proof system. In: 27th USENIX Security Symposium, pp. 675–692 (2018)
11. Major, W., Buchanan, W.J., Ahmad, J.: An authentication protocol based on chaos and zero knowledge proof. Nonlinear Dyn. **99**(4), 3065–3087 (2020). https://doi.org/10.1007/s11071-020-05463-3
12. Joshi, P., Verma, M., Verma, P.R.: Secure authentication approach using Diffie-Hellman key exchange algorithm for WSN. In: International Conference on Control, Instrumentation, Communication and Computational Technologies (ICCICCT), pp. 527–532. IEEE (2015)

13. Harn, L., Mehta, M., Hsin, W.J.: Integrating Diffie-Hellman key exchange into the digital signature algorithm (DSA). IEEE Commun. Lett. **8**(3), 198–200 (2004)
14. Artin, E.: The Gamma Function. Courier Dover Publications, New York (2015)
15. Karatsuba, E.A.: On the asymptotic representation of the Euler gamma function by Ramanujan. J. Comput. Appl. Math. **135**(2), 225–240 (2001)
16. Lanczos, C.: A precision approximation of the gamma function. J. Soc. Ind. Appl. Math. Ser. B Numer. Anal. **1**(1), 86–96 (1964)
17. Mortici, C.: A continued fraction approximation of the gamma function. J. Math. Anal. Appl. **402**(2), 405–410 (2013)
18. Horadam, A.F.: A generalized Fibonacci sequence. Am. Math. Mon. **68**(5), 455–459 (1961)
19. DeCarlo, L.T.: On the meaning and use of kurtosis. Psychol. Methods **2**(3), 292 (1997)
20. Groeneveld, R.A., Meeden, G.: Measuring skewness and kurtosis. J. R. Stat. Soc. Ser. D (Stat.) **33**(4), 391–399 (1984)
21. Chatterjee, S., Hadi, A.S.: Regression Analysis by Example. John Wiley & Sons, Hoboken (2015)

Image Encryption-Compression Method Based on Playfair, OTP and DWT for Secure Image Transmission

Haidar Raad Shakir[1](✉) ⬤ and Suhad Abbas Yassir[2] ⬤

[1] University of Thi-Qar, Nasiriyah, Thi-Qar, Iraq
haidar.raad@utq.edu.iq
[2] Shatra Technical Institute, Southern Technical University, Nasiriyah, Thi-Qar, Iraq
suhad.yasir@stu.edu.iq

Abstract. Digital image cryptography has the greatest priority with the rise and authenticity of the multimodal data. Encryption is known to be a very critical step in the security of multimedia applications. This paper proposes the Playfair, and OTP based image encryption-compression method using integer Haar transform. Initially, the proposed method encrypts the image using integer Haar transform with the One Time Pad (OTP) algorithm and the Playfair encoding. Finally, Inverse Discrete Wavelet Transform (IDWT) is applied to get the ciphered encoded image. The decoding part is driven automatically by inverting the operations of the encoding part. The quality of encrypted-decrypted images is assessed using Histogram Analysis, NPCR, UACI, PSNR, SSIM, GLCM correlation coefficient and Entropy. It is evident from visual inspection of the images and quality assessment parameters that the proposed method works effectively.

Keywords: Image encryption · One Time Pad · DWT · Playfair · Compression

1 Introduction

The protection and privacy of digital images, taken from digital devices, are of greatest priority with the rise in the velocity, quantity, and authenticity of gathered multimodal data [1]. Encryption is known to be a very critical step in the security of multimedia applications [2–8]. The protection of multimedia systems relies on the potency of the encryption algorithm. Therefore, there is a need for a robust encryption method to maintain the data secrecy and integrity from attackers or other third-party users [9–17]. Cryptography is a way to encrypt messages, such that a single key can only be used by the transmitter and the receiver to decrypt the correct message [18]. Cryptography deals entirely in correspondence with any kind of third-party application. It deals with problems such as encryption, authentication, and key distribution [19]. Image Encryption is a way of increasing the anonymity of the images by converting them from their previous state to an encrypted form that cannot be identified by any other entity, this image is known as an encrypted image [20]. Image encoding has a wide range of applications in various fields like, healthcare [21], digital images [22] and military communications [24], etc.

© Springer Nature Singapore Pte Ltd. 2021
N. Abdullah et al. (Eds.): ACeS 2021, CCIS 1487, pp. 95–113, 2021.
https://doi.org/10.1007/978-981-16-8059-5_7

2 Related Studies

In this scope, a variety of encryption solutions have been proposed [1, 9–11, 24–28]. Belazi et al. [9] suggested an Advanced Encryption Standard (AES) S-box scheme based on Discrete Wavelet Transform (DWT) and chaotic permutation. The proposed scheme consisted of four steps (i) image decomposition, block permutation, DWT decomposition, (ii) substitution phase, (iii) chaotic permutation, and (iv) reconstruction phase. The work utilized Discrete Wavelet Transform (DWT) to decompose space into cAP, cVP, cHP, and cDP sub-bands. Among all the sub-bands, the cAP is the only technique that is encrypted, as it includes a substantial part of the data. While the other substrings (cVP, cHP, and cDP) remain unchanged. This work demonstrates the robustness of the proposed cryptosystem, which is ideal for real-time use. Chakravarthy et al. [10] proposed to use Integer Wavelet Transform (IWT) with the Playfair Cipher for Image Encryption. In this article, pre-processed data (e.g. text or image) is initially sent to the generic cryptographic engine, where IWT transformed it to the sub-bands i.e. LL, HL, LH, and HH combinations. After initial pre-processing, Playfair cipher produces the key-matrix and the ciphertext/image. This study suggested an improved Playfair cipher in the spatial and frequency domain using IWT that provides better-desired error metrics. Alawida et al. [29] also suggested the novel image cipher based on the disruption of a hybrid, chaotic system to encrypt images. In this technique, the hybrid system cascades and combines to create 1D chaotic maps which preserve the phase space of their underlying images. Then, these new maps are used to directly replace existing encryption methods based on chaos. According to the chaotic performance evaluation, the novel hybridization approach has more complexity and sensitivity. Alawida et al. also presented a new SVD-based image watermarking technique [32]. In [30], the authors employed a chaotic map to address the false positive issue (FPP), which is the major disadvantage of SVD-based watermarking schemes. A secret key is first derived from both the host and watermark images, and this key is then utilized to build a new chaotic matrix. Finally, throughout the extraction procedure, this secret key is utilized for authentication. As the security level of chaos-based encryption is determined by its underlying digital chaotic map, Alawida et al. [31] present a hybridization of a tent map with a deterministic finite state machine, i.e. digital one-dimensional chaotic system called TM-DFSM to improve its chaotic characteristics. They claimed that a TM-DFSM-based picture encryption system can conduct both confusion and diffusion operations in a single pass and has a large key space. A cipher picture created by changing a single bit of the plain image or secret key will be completely different.

Kumar et al. [11] have proposed work for Color Image Encryption using Multiresolution Singular Value Decomposition (MSVD), Discrete Wavelet Transform (DWT) and Arnold transform into a fractional Fourier domain. In this work, the original color image is initially divided into its primary color elements, i.e. Red (R), Green (G), and Blue (B). Furthermore, each part is encrypted separately using DWT, MSVD, and Arnold transform into a fractional domain. In this research, different encryption and decryption keys are used which include (i) the FrFT keys, (ii) the MSVD and DWT sub-bands, (iii) the values and arrangement of 4×4 matrix, created by MSVD in the DWT sub-bands, (iv) the use of Arnold Transform and (v) the arrangement of many sub-images. At the time of decryption, proper knowledge of all keys, along with the method of arrangement, is required for the correct decryption of encrypted images. Wang et al. [25] also suggested a color image encryption algorithm based on a structural chaotic calculation matrix and random step mask. In this work, the Chebyshev chaotic sequence is used to produce the flip permutation matrix, the sampling subset, and the chaotic cyclic matrix. In his proposed method, Compressive Sensing (CS) compresses and encrypts the original image simultaneously and re-encrypts it using a two-dimensional fractional Fourier transform. Another image encryption algorithm, based on CS and iterative chaotic map with infinite collapse modulation map (2D-SLIM), was proposed by Xu et al. [27]. Firstly, the plain image is transformed into the coefficient matrix using discrete wavelet transform (DWT). The permutation of row and column is then applied to achieve a good scrambling effect. Then, a measurement matrix is calculated using chaotic 2D-SLIM map sequences which permutes the coefficient matrix. Finally, the Galois field multiplication based on diffusion algorithm is designed to encrypt the compressed matrix and obtain small-size and high-security cipher images. Zhang et al. [32] proposed two-dimensional Compressive Sensing (2D-CS) and Fourier transform fraction (FrFT) to encrypt the color images. In this scheme, the Kronecker Products (KP) are used to expand the low dimensional seed matrices to generate random phase masks by randomly controlling the chaotic map. The original image is encrypted and compressed concurrently with 2D CS and re-encrypted with FrFT. The proposed encryption scheme provides fast speed, low complexity, and high protection.

Recently, Albahrani et al. [33] has suggested a new approach of image encryption based on modified Playfair and chaotic scheme. In his study, image encryption was achieved using chaos theory in diffusion and confusion processes. The diffusion method was conducted using a chaotic cross-map to permute the matrix of each color image channel. The confusion method was used to update the Playfair method to generalize the classical algorithm. The novelty of this method is that it combines cascade of processes and multiple encryption schemes to produce fast and robust encoding and a perfect reconstruction in the decoding. The integer Haar transform, the one-time pad (OTP), and the Playfair algorithm had the ability to reconstruct the encoded image perfectly on the decoder site. Finally, the arithmetic coding algorithm makes the final image represented in a binary code, not understandable to most of the ciphering detection algorithm. It also increases the robustness of the overall method by providing additional compression features which makes the encoded image to be valid for transmission and storage with less amount of data.

In the proposed method, initially on the encryption side, integer Haar transform is applied to decompose the original image into LL, LH, HL, and HH sub-band. Then the encryption of the LL sub-band is done with the one-time pad (OTP) algorithm and the Playfair encoding on other sub-bands (LH, HL, and HH). Finally, IDWT is applied to get the ciphered encoded image. The decoding part is driven automatically by inverting the operations of the encoding part. The decoding starts by reversing the arithmetic coding and the corresponding decryption algorithm. These are named as OTP for LL section, Playfair decipher LH, HL, and HH sections to get the recovered image. The time taken by the algorithm is 71 s per image for encoding and decoding. The most time-consuming process is the arithmetic coding and decoding process which takes 55 min for the encoding and decoding processes. The Playfair algorithm takes only one second for the encoding and decoding processes. This analysis was conducted on HP core i5 laptop with 2.67 GHz processor and 4 GB of RAM.

The remaining structure of this paper is as followed: Sect. 3 discusses the methodology of the proposed work in detail and information about the data set used to test the proposed method. Section 4 gives a brief review of the quantifying parameters used in this work. Section 5 presents the results with detailed analysis and discussion and Sect. 6 summarizes the proposed work.

3 Material and Methods

The encryption and decryption part of the proposed algorithm is done based on the two methods i.e. one-time-pad and Playfair for encryption and decryption along with the arithmetic coding.

3.1 Encryption Algorithms

The integer Haar transform outputs the LL in scalar values which contains the global component of the entire image. OTP (One-time pad) algorithm is used for the encoding of the LL. The code must be agreed on both encoder and decoder present on both sides. For the rest of the planes, the integer Haar transform outputs 8 different decompositions of each plane, i.e. 8 decompositions for the HL, and 8 different decompositions for the HH. The encryption is done on each of the sub-planes from 8 to 2 corresponding planes, which are HH, LH, and HL. The last decomposition is not encoded which corresponds to the least significant bit and sent without encryption because it always comes with an odd number of values not compressed directly with the Playfair algorithm. Figure 1 shows the encryption side block diagram of the proposed method.

The Haar wavelet transform is one of the orthogonal transforms that decomposes a signal to time-frequency sub-bands based on the following equation [43]:

$$H_r(t) = \begin{cases} \frac{1}{\sqrt{N}} * 2^{\frac{m}{2}}, & \frac{k-1}{2^m} < t < \frac{k-\frac{1}{2}}{2^m} \\ -\frac{1}{\sqrt{N}} * 2^{\frac{m}{2}}, & \frac{k-\frac{1}{2}}{2^m} < t < \frac{k}{2^m} \\ 0, & otherwise \end{cases} \tag{1}$$

$$H_0(t) = \frac{1}{\sqrt{N}} \tag{2}$$

Where, $r = 0, 1, ..., N-1$, and $N = 2p$ where p is the range of the maximum observation of the given signal, in natural RGB images this range is from 0 to 255, that's why a value of 8 is used for p for such cases of images. k and m represent integer decomposition of the index level r [43].

After passing the image into the integer Haar it gets decomposed into 4 decomposition sub-bands, the sub-bands were termed, LL, LH, HL and HH. Where L stands for low-frequency decomposition sub-band and H for high-frequency decomposition sub-band. Each of the 4 decompositions contains 8 levels ranging from the most significant bit (MSB) part of the decomposition plane to the least significant bit (LSB). Except for

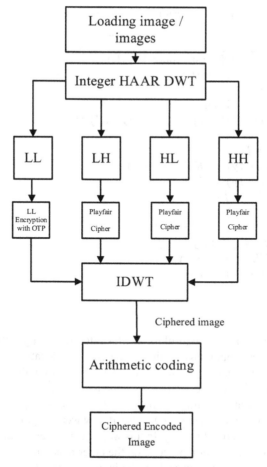

Fig. 1. Encryption block diagram of the proposed method for Encoding Part.

the LL band which is the H0 in the equation above, it's a single scalar that represents the DC content of the entire Haar plane. When addressing the encryption two different algorithms are used for two different scenarios, the LL band is encrypted with OTP algorithm described by the following equation:

$$C = S \oplus K \tag{3}$$

$$C = mod(S)_K \tag{4}$$

Where C is the encrypted output, S and K are the input and the key respectively. The one-time pad algorithm performs bitwise XOR operation denoted in the above equation, it can also be represented by the modulo operation of the input string based on the key (K), in images cases, this K is also 255.

The other planes, namely, HL, LH, and HH are encrypted with the Playfair ciphering algorithm described with the following algorithmic flow (Table 1):

Table 1. Playfair ciphering algorithm for image encryption.

	Input: Plain image (S), Encryption key (K)
	Output: Ciphered image (C)
1	Initialize S, K
2	for each input pixel pairs in S:
3	let I, J be neighboring pixels, Ix, Iy, Jx, Jy are pixel coordinates in the image
4	if $(Ix = Jx)$:
5	$C(Ix, Iy) = K(Ix, Iy + 1)$
6	$C(Jx, Jy) = K(Jx, Jy + 1)$
7	else if $(Jx = Jy)$
8	$C(Ix, Iy) = K(Ix + 1, Iy)$
9	$C(Jx, Jy) = K(Jx, + 1, Jy)$
10	else $(Ix != Jx)	(Iy != Jy)$
11	$C(Ix, Iy) = K(Iy, Ix)$
12	$C(Jx, Jy) = K(Jy, Jx)$
13	End

In few words, the Playfair algorithm, as illustrated in the algorithmic flow above, works by changing the input image by the key based on the location of the input entries in the key. If the entries are at the same raw of the key they will be ciphered by the next pair of key entries with one increment. Same happens for the column, if the input entries happened to be at the same column of the key, they are replaced with the key at the same column but increasing raw value, else, if they were diagonal, they get replaced by the opposite corner value of the key. In this way, it can generate different encryption results each time. The decryption process, on the other hand, just reverses this process by decreasing the index of key entry where the input was found.

One of the major strengths of the algorithm is that the Playfair encrypts inside the sub-band planes, the, LH, LH, and HH. The algorithm encrypts each plane from the second plane to the N−1 plane, the LSB plane of each sub-band is left without encryption because it's always an odd number.

3.2 Encryption Keys

The keys for the OTP method are generated randomly with a random number generator taken between 0 to 255 to be used to XOR with the LL plane.

The Playfair keys are generated with selectable plane dimensions. A single scalar dimension corresponds to the $M \times M$ (M^2) number of elements distributed randomly across the plane. The range for key values would be between $-\frac{M}{2}^2$ and $\frac{M}{2}^2 - 1$. As an example, when the scalar dimension value is 32, the corresponding key values will range from −512 to 511.

Changing the plane dimension will directly change the total number of keys in the dictionary. This change will make the encryption more robust but it will also increase the time complexity as the matrix size will be bigger. Another affected parameter is the encoding using the Arithmetic coding algorithm as the operation is directly related to the maximum value that appears in the input sequence, the bigger the maximum value more time it takes to encode the input sequence. Figure 2 shows the decryption side block diagram of the proposed method.

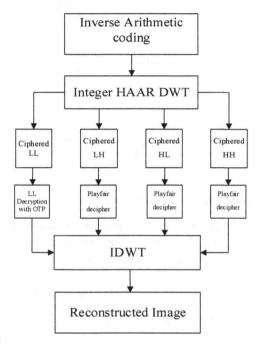

Fig. 2. Proposed method decryption block diagram for decoding part

The decoding part is driven automatically by inverting the operations of the encoding part. The decoding part starts by reversing the arithmetic coding algorithm. The recovered image is fed to an integer Haar transform which will result in the output of Haar planes, but for the encrypted image. The Haar encrypted planes are then deciphered using the corresponding decryption algorithm as in the encodings part; namely, OTP for LL part, Playfair decipher LH, HL, and HH parts. Final notes between the data to be sent to the decoder for proper reconstruction are:

1. The OTP keys.
2. The Playfair cipher keys.
3. The arithmetic coding doesn't need keys, but it needs the dimensions of the input image to be sent to the decoder for proper reconstruction of the image size.
4. The value of the Playfair cipher dimension is also needed by the arithmetic coding algorithm as it uses it to avoid negative values, so it's added in the encoder and then subtracted in the decider.

4 Quantifying Parameters

4.1 Peak Signal to Noise Ratio (PSNR)

PSNR [34] calculates the peak signal-to-noise ratio, in decibels, between reference images (I_{ref}) and reconstructed image (I_{recon}). Higher value of the PSNR shows better Signal-to-Noise ratio of the reconstructed image. PSNR has been calculated from the following formula:

$$PSNR_{db} = 10\log_{10}\left(\frac{max(I_{rec})^2}{MSE}\right) \qquad (5)$$

where,

$$MSE = \frac{\sum \|I_{ref}(x, y)| - |I_{recon}(x, y)\|^2}{\sum |I_{ref}(x, y)|} \qquad (6)$$

4.2 Structural Similarity Index Measure (SSIM)

Structural similarity (SSIM) [35] is an error measure for image similarity. In terms of structural differences between the reference and the reconstructed image, it gives an error approximation [35]. SSIM can be calculated as:

$$SSIM = \frac{\left(2\mu_{I_{ref}}\mu_{I_{rec}} + K_1\right)\left(2\sigma_{I_{ref}}\sigma_{I_{rec}} + K_2\right)}{\left(\mu_{I_{ref}}^2 + \mu_{I_{rec}}^2 + K_1\right)\left(\sigma_{I_{ref}}^2 + \sigma_{I_{rec}}^2 + K_2\right)} \qquad (7)$$

where μ is the mean value, $K1$ and $K2$ are the normalization constants for images, $\sigma_{I_{ref}}^2$ and $\sigma_{I_{rec}}^2$ are the variance values and $\sigma_{I_{ref}}$ & $\sigma_{I_{rec}}$ is the covariance.

4.3 Gray-Level Co-occurrence Matrix (GLCM) Correlation

Gray-level co-occurrence matrices (GLCMs) [35] correlation is defined over an image to be the distribution of co-occurring pixel values (grayscale values, or colors) at a given offset. It is used as an approach to texture analysis [36].

$$GLCM\ correlation = \sum_{i,j=0}^{N-1} P_{i,j}\left[\frac{(i - u_i)(i - u_j)}{(\sigma_i^2)(\sigma_j^2)}\right] \qquad (8)$$

The GLCM correlation indicates the linear dependency of the linear dependency between the grey levels and the neighboring pixels where u_i represents the horizontal mean in the matrix, u_j represents the vertical mean in the matrix, σ_i^2 and σ_j^2 represents dispersion around the mean of combinations of target and neighbor pixel.

4.4 Histogram Analysis

The histogram shows the pixel values distributed in an image. Consistent distribution of histogram values is required to provide an encrypted image impossible for the attacker to know about the image. Via uniform distribution of pixel value in an encoded file, the suitability of the proposed encryption approach is observed.

4.5 Information Entropy Analysis

The entropy of information assesses random variable insecurity as follows:

$$E = \sum_{i=1}^{256} P(i) log\left(\frac{1}{P(i)}\right) \tag{9}$$

here $P(i)$ is the probability of the presence of pixel i. To test images, a larger entropy value means a higher degree of safety. Usually, an entropy value very similar to 8 is considered secure from a brute force attack.

4.6 NPCR Analysis

The pixel discrepancy between the original images and the encrypted images is evaluated by the Pixel number change rate (NPCR) as follows:

$$NPCR = \frac{\sum_{i,j} D(i,j)}{MN} \times 100 \tag{10}$$

Where, $D(i, j)$ is:

$$D(i,j) = \begin{cases} 0 \ P(i,j) = C(i,j) \\ 1 \ P(i,j) \neq C(i,j) \end{cases} \tag{11}$$

The pixel values of the original and encrypted images are p(i, j) and C(i, j), respectively. The higher pixel randomization results in a higher NPCR score.

4.7 UACI Analysis

The Unified Average Changing Index (UACI) evaluates the average intensity of the variations between the original and the encrypted image as follows:

$$D(i,j) = \begin{cases} 0 \ P(i,j) = C(i,j) \\ 1 \ P(i,j) \neq C(i,j) \end{cases} \tag{12}$$

Here $P(i, j)$ and $C(i, j)$ are pixel values of the original and encrypted images, and L is the largest pixel value of both images. The values of both NPCR and UACI indicate the resistance of the encryption method against the differential attack.

5 Results and Discussion

The proposed encryption-decryption method is tested on the seven different natural images that are Lena, Baboon, Pepper, Plan, House, Building, and Water. Seven different metrics were utilized; namely, peak signal to noise ratio PSNR, structural similarity index SSIM, the gray level co-occurrence matrix correlation (GLCM), Histogram analysis, Information Entropy Analysis, NPCR Analysis, and UACI Analysis to assess the quality of the proposed scheme. Each of the metrics was assessed twice, once between the original image and the encrypted image (denoted as - 1), and once between the original image and recovered image (denoted as - 2). Except for the GLCM correlation which is calculated for each image individually.

In Fig. 3, Experimental results in terms of GLCM array of Original images and Encrypted images are given. The first column shows the Original images, the column with GLCM array of original images shows the correlation matrix of original images, the Encrypted images column shows the corresponding image encryption, and the GLCM array of Encrypted images show the image encryption correlation matrix. The scatter plot of GLCM array of the original images gives a strong correlation between the adjacent pixels; but, the GLCM array scatter plot of the encrypted images shows a weaker correlation between the adjacent pixels. However, the scatter plot of GLCM array of the original images and the corresponding successfully decrypted image demonstrates the strong correlation between the adjacent pixels of the GLCM array as shown in Fig. 4.

Figure 5 shows Experimental results in terms of the GLCM array of original images and Encrypted images. The first column shows the original images, the column with GLCM array of original images shows the correlation matrix of original images, the Encrypted images column shows the corresponding image encryption and the GLCM array of Encrypted images shows the image encryption correlation matrix. The scatter plot of GLCM array of the original images gives a strong correlation between the adjacent pixels; but, the GLCM array scatter plot of the encrypted images shows a weaker correlation between the adjacent pixels. However, the scatter plot of GLCM array of the original images and the corresponding successfully decrypted image demonstrates the strong correlation between the adjacent pixels of the GLCM array as shown in Fig. 4.

Figure 5 shows the experimental results in terms of Histogram analysis of Original images, Encrypted images, and Decrypted images without key attack. The first column shows the Original images, the second column shows the histogram of the original images, the third column shows the Encrypted images, column four shows the corresponding encrypted image histogram and columns five and six show the successfully decrypted image and decrypted image histogram. The original images histogram shows the pixel distribution according to the number of pixels intensities and number of specific pixels. However, the encrypted images histogram analysis shows a uniform pixel values distribution over the number of specific pixels. This uniform distribution confirms that it would be difficult for the attacker to encode the data.

To further evaluate and validate the encoding process of the proposed method, Fig. 6 gives the experimental results in terms of Histogram analysis of Original images, Encrypted images, and Decrypted images with a key attack. The original images histogram shows the pixel distribution according to the number of pixels intensities values and the number of pixels and the encrypted images histogram analysis shows a uniform

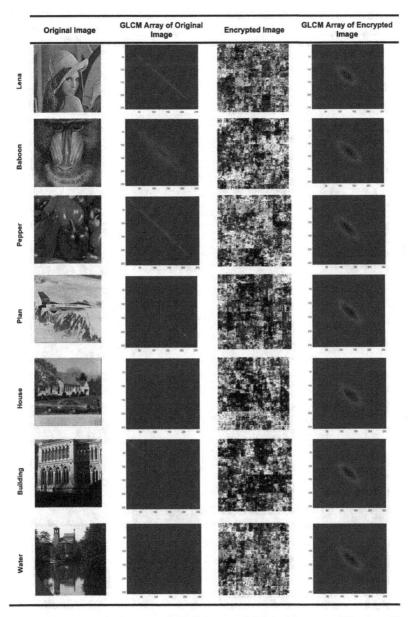

Fig. 3. Experimental results in terms of GLCM array of Original image and Encrypted images. Original image column shows the Original images, GLCM array of original images shows the correlation matrix of original images, Encrypted images column shows the corresponding image encryption and the GLCM array of Encrypted images show the image encryption correlation matrix

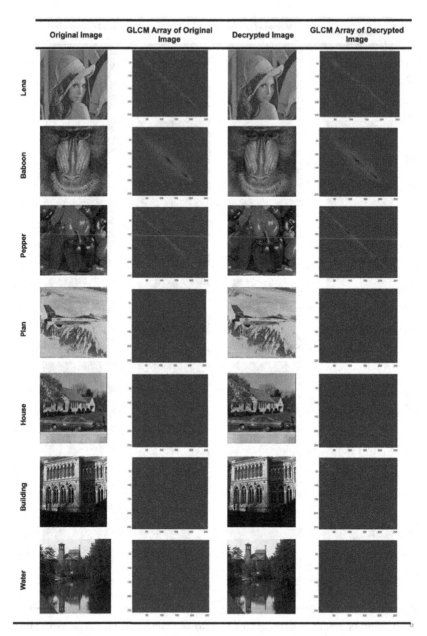

Fig. 4. Experimental results in terms of GLCM array of Original image and Decrypted images. Original image column shows the Original images, GLCM array of original images shows the correlation matrix of original images, Decrypted images column shows the corresponding successfully decrypted image and the GLCM array of decrypted images show the image successfully decrypted image correlation matrix

pixel values distribution over the number of specific pixels in the fourth column of Fig. 6. This time a key security attack is applied and when decrypted the encrypted image and a loss of some information is obverse in the decrypted images. However, the proposed algorithm successfully defends the encrypted image information as shown in Fig. 6 (Column 5). Also, the key attacked decrypted image histogram analysis shows some changes in the histogram with respect to the original image, still maxim information is restored as shown in Fig. 6 (Column 6).

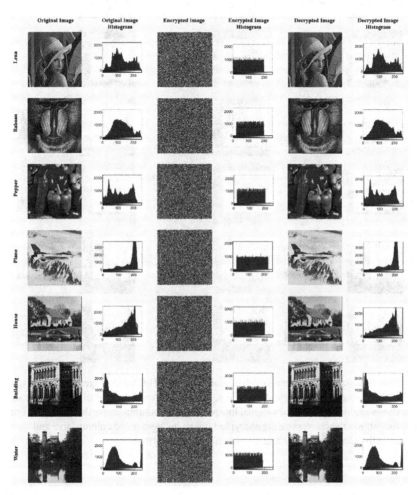

Fig. 5. Experimental results in terms of Histogram analysis of Original images, Encrypted images, and Decrypted images without key attack. The original image column shows the Original images, the second column shows the histogram of the original images, the third column shows the Encrypted images, column four shows the corresponding encrypted image histogram and column five and six show the successfully decrypted image and decrypted image histogram.

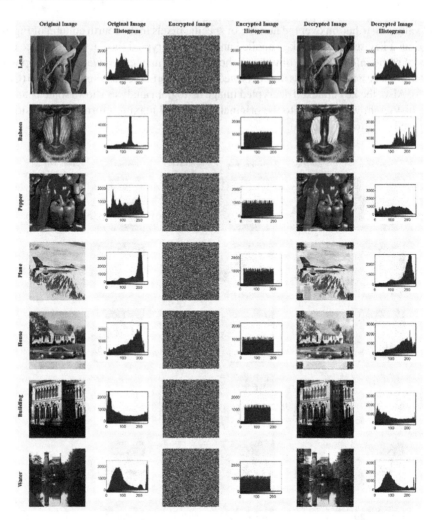

Fig. 6. Experimental results in terms of Histogram analysis of Original images, Encrypted images, and Decrypted images with a key attack. First, column shows the Original images, the second column shows the histogram of the original images, the third column shows the Encrypted images, column four shows the corresponding encrypted image histogram and columns five and six show the successfully decrypted image and decrypted image histogram.

Results in terms of quality parameters were assessed twice, once between the original image and the encrypted image, and once between the original image and recovered image. Except for the GLCM correlation which is calculated for each image individually. Table 2 and Table 3 give the NPCR, UACI, PSNR, SSIM, GLCM correlation, and entropy results for Encrypted-Decrypted images without and with a key attack, respectively.

The NPCR and UACI values confirm that the proposed method successfully recovers the encrypted image. Also, results in terms of PSNR show higher PSNR between the original image and decrypted image (PSNR-2). The higher the PSNR, the closer is the image to the original image, which means that the two images are identical. Similarly, the SSIM value follows the same trend as PSNR, SSIM - 2 value of 1 shows that the original and encrypted images are identical. The GLCM value calculates the correlation of pixels of the image to itself, it ranges between 0 to 1, the higher the correlation value (Corr-2) means that the pixels of the image are more correlated and homogeneous which is natural for the images. The lower the correlation value means that the pixels of the image are distributed randomly with little correlation to each other which is seen int the encrypted images results (Corr-1). Furthermore, results in terms of entropy are also quite close to the value of 8 (Entr-2) that illustrate that the proposed method successfully encrypted the resultant images.

With key attack results Table 3, The NPCR and UACI values are still reasonable which confirms that the proposed method successfully recovers the encrypted image. Also, results in terms of PSNR show a very low PSNR, however, PSNR is still better for the decrypted image as given under PSNR - 2 as compared to the PSNR -1. Results in terms of SSIM show that SSIM - 2 value is higher which confirms that the original and encrypted images are similar. Also, the GLCM value is higher (Corr-2) than the Corr-1 value that confirms that the pixels of the encrypted images are more correlated and homogeneous with the original images. In addition, entropy results are also very close to 8 (Entr-2) which shows that the proposed method encrypted the resulting images successfully.

Table 2. NPCR, UACI, PSNR, SSIM, GLCM correlation and Entropy Results for the proposed Encryption-Decryption Scheme without key attack

	NPCR		UACI		PSNR		SSIM		Correlation		Entropy	
	NPCR-1	NPCR -2	UACI-1	UACI-2	PSNR-1	PSNR-2	SSIM-1	SSIM-2	Corr-1	Corr-2	Entr-1	Entr-2
Lena	0.996	0.996	0.334	0.334	9.348	99.099	0.002	1.00	0.0064	0.945	6.961	7.937
Baboon	0.996	0.996	0.334	0.334	10.592	99.099	0.004	1.00	0.0008	0.873	6.927	7.937
Pepper	0.996	0.995	0.334	0.334	9.569	99.099	0.001	1.00	0.0024	0.963	6.950	7.937
Plan	0.996	0.995	0.334	0.334	8.729	99.099	0.001	1.00	0.0018	0.936	6.105	7.937
House	0.996	0.995	0.334	0.334	8.474	99.099	0.001	1.00	0.0015	0.918	6.772	7.937
Building	0.996	0.996	0.334	0.334	8.003	48.960	0.001	1.00	0.0015	0.861	6.888	7.937
Water	0.996	0.996	0.334	0.334	9.197	99.099	0.001	1.00	0.0059	0.945	6.763	7.937

Table 3. NPCR, UACI, PSNR, SSIM, GLCM correlation and Entropy Results for the proposed Encryption-Decryption Scheme with key attack

	NPCR		UACI		PSNR		SSIM		Correlation		Entropy	
	NPCR-1	NPCR-2	UACI-1	UACI-2	PSNR-1	PSNR-2	SSIM-1	SSIM-2	Corr-1	Corr-2	Entr-1	Entr-2
Lena	0.993	0.945	0.269	0.032	9.596	12.402	0.002	0.867	0.005	0.945	6.961	7.937
Baboon	0.996	0.999	0.260	0.077	9.933	9.132	0.003	0.386	0.004	0.874	6.927	7.937
Pepper	0.996	0.9839	0.2770	0.045	9.4184	11.527	0.0020	0.7691	0.001	0.964	6.951	7.937
Plan	0.996	0.9934	0.3193	0.031	8.3891	12.724	0.0022	0.5625	0.001	0.936	6.106	7.937
House	0.996	0.9567	0.2956	0.047	8.8952	11.612	0.003	0.5371	0.002	0.918	6.772	7.937
Building	0.997	0.9861	0.3158	0.039	8.5025	11.295	0.002	0.6792	0.004	0.861	6.888	7.937
Water	0.996	0.9921	0.2759	0.051	9.2005	11.168	0.001	0.519	0.003	0.945	6.763	7.937

The proposed method results are compared with other methods which are presented in [38–42] in terms of NPCR (Table 4) and Correlation of Encrypted Image (Table 5) for the Lena, Baboon, and Pepper images, respectively. Both Table 4 and Table 5 show that the proposed method gives better results than [39, 41], and [42] for Lena and baboon images.

Table 4. Performance evaluation in terms of NPCR of the proposed method with other methods

	Proposed	[38]	[39]	[40]	[43]	[41]	[42]
Lena	0.9961	0.9964	0.9954	0.9972	0.9969	0.9960	0.9954
Baboon	0.9961	--	--	0.9964	--	--	--
Pepper	0.9959	--	--	--	0.9970	--	--

Table 5. Performance evaluation in terms of Correlation of Encrypted Image of the proposed method with other methods

	Proposed	[38]	[39]	[40]	[43]	[41]	[42]
Lena	0.0064	0.0009	0.0025	0.0098	0.0013	--	--
Baboon	0.0008	--	--	0.0096	--	--	--
Pepper	0.0024	--	--	--	0.0030	--	--

When comparing the method to the state of the art methods, we can find that it performs within an average of most of the work, we have superior performance to some of the state of the art algorithms like [38, 39, 41, 43] and [42] but we have results that show lower metrics than [40] which motivates the algorithm for further development.

6 Conclusions

In this paper, a color Image encryption-decryption method based on Playfair and one-time pad algorithms using the integer Haar transform has been proposed to efficiently encrypt images. The visual assessment in terms of Histogram analysis confirms that the proposed method is able to recover the encrypted images successfully. Also, the results obtained metric values, namely, NPCR, UACI, PSNR, SSIM, GLCM correlation coefficient, and Entropy makes it evident that the proposed method works effectively.

References

1. Sneha, P.S., Sankar, S., Kumar, A.S.: A chaotic colour image encryption scheme combining Walsh–Hadamard transform and Arnold–Tent maps. J. Ambient Intell. Human. Comput. **11**(3), 1289–1308 (2019). https://doi.org/10.1007/s12652-019-01385-0
2. Yasser, I., Mohamed, M.A., Samra, A.S., Khalifa, F.: A chaotic-based encryption/decryption framework for secure multimedia communications. Entropy **22**, 1–23 (2020). https://doi.org/10.3390/e22111253
3. Dongare, A.S., Alvi, A.S., Tarbani, P.N.M.: An efficient technique for image encryption and decryption for secured multimedia application. Int. Res. J. Eng. Technol. **4**, 3186–3190 (2017)
4. Ullah, A., Jamal, S.S., Shah, T.: A novel scheme for image encryption using substitution box and chaotic system. Nonlinear Dyn. **91**(1), 359–370 (2017). https://doi.org/10.1007/s11071-017-3874-6
5. Aljawarneh, S., Yassein, M.B., Talafha, W.A.: A resource-efficient encryption algorithm for multimedia big data. Multimedia Tools Appl. **76**, 22703–22724 (2017). https://doi.org/10.1007/s11042-016-4333-y
6. Haider, M.I., Ali, A., Shah, D., Shah, T.: Block cipher's nonlinear component design by elliptic curves: an image encryption application. Multimedia Tools Appl. **80**(3), 4693–4718 (2020). https://doi.org/10.1007/s11042-020-09892-5
7. Sultana, S.F., Shubhangi, D.C.: Video encryption algorithm and key management using perfect shuffle. Int. J. Eng. Res. Appl. **7**, 01–05 (2017). https://doi.org/10.9790/9622-0707030105
8. Abdelfatah, R.I., Nasr, M.E., Alsharqawy, M.A.: Encryption for multimedia based on chaotic map: several scenarios. Multimedia Tools Appl. **79**(27–28), 19717–19738 (2020). https://doi.org/10.1007/s11042-020-08788-8
9. Belazi, A., Abd El-Latif, A.A., Rhouma, R., Belghith, S.: Selective image encryption scheme based on DWT, AES S-box and chaotic permutation. In: IWCMC 2015 - 11th International Wireless Communications and Mobile Computing Conference, pp. 606–610 (2015). https://doi.org/10.1109/IWCMC.2015.7289152
10. Chakravarthy, S., Venkatesan, S.P., Anand, J.M., Ranjani, J.J.: Enhanced playfair cipher for image encryption using integer wavelet transform. Indian J. Sci. Technol. **9** (2016). https://doi.org/10.17485/ijst/2016/v9i39/86519
11. Vaish, A., Kumar, M.: Color image encryption using MSVD, DWT and Arnold transform in fractional Fourier domain. Optik (Stuttg) **145**, 273–283 (2017). https://doi.org/10.1016/j.ijleo.2017.07.041
12. Sangavi, V., Thangavel, P.: An image encryption algorithm based on fractal geometry. In: Procedia Computer Science, pp. 462–469 (2019)

13. Wang, C., Zhang, X., Zheng, Z.: An efficient image encryption algorithm based on a novel chaotic map. Multimedia Tools Appl. **76**(22), 24251–24280 (2016). https://doi.org/10.1007/s11042-016-4102-y
14. Chai, X., Yang, K., Gan, Z.: A new chaos-based image encryption algorithm with dynamic key selection mechanisms. Multimedia Tools Appl. **76**(7), 9907–9927 (2016). https://doi.org/10.1007/s11042-016-3585-x
15. Huang, X., Ye, G.: An image encryption algorithm based on irregular wave representation. Multimedia Tools Appl. **77**(2), 2611–2628 (2017). https://doi.org/10.1007/s11042-017-4455-x
16. Sheela, S.J., Suresh, K.V., Tandur, D.: Image encryption based on modified Henon map using hybrid chaotic shift transform. Multimedia Tools Appl. **77**(19), 25223–25251 (2018). https://doi.org/10.1007/s11042-018-5782-2
17. Patro, K.A.K., Acharya, B., Nath, V.: Secure multilevel permutation-diffusion based image encryption using chaotic and hyper-chaotic maps. Microsyst. Technol. **25**(12), 4593–4607 (2019). https://doi.org/10.1007/s00542-019-04395-2
18. Sindhu, S.: Cryptographic algorithms : applications in network security. Int. J. New Innov. Eng. Technol. **7**, 18–28 (2017)
19. Fadhel Hamood, S., Mohd Rahim, M.S., Farook Mohammado, O.: Chaos image encryption methods: a survey study. Bull. Electr. Eng. Inform. **6**, 99–104 (2017). https://doi.org/10.11591/eei.v6i1.599
20. Kumar, M., Saxena, A., Vuppala, S.S.: A survey on chaos based image encryption techniques. In: Hosny, K.M. (ed.) Multimedia Security Using Chaotic Maps: Principles and Methodologies. SCI, vol. 884, pp. 1–26. Springer, Cham (2020). https://doi.org/10.1007/978-3-030-38700-6_1
21. Roy, M., Mali, K., Chatterjee, S., Chakraborty, S., Debnath, R., Sen, S.: A study on the applications of the biomedical image encryption methods for secured computer aided diagnostics. In: Proceedings - 2019 Amity International Conference on Artificial Intelligence, AICAI 2019, pp. 881–886. Institute of Electrical and Electronics Engineers Inc. (2019)
22. Malik, M.G.A., Bashir, Z., Iqbal, N., Imtiaz, M.A.: Color image encryption algorithm based on hyper-chaos and DNA computing. IEEE Access **8**, 88093–88107 (2020). https://doi.org/10.1109/ACCESS.2020.2990170
23. Bagul, A., Sonawane, P., Sawant, L., Doshi, R.: Advance security in cloud computing for military weapons. Int. Res. J. Eng. Technol. **4**, 1511–1513 (2017)
24. Fuqua, P.B.: Dear Author. Int. J. Psychoanal. Self Psychol. **4**, 398–400 (2009). https://doi.org/10.1080/15551020902995363
25. Wang, X., Su, Y.: Color image encryption based on chaotic compressed sensing and two-dimensional fractional Fourier transform. Sci. Rep. **10**, 1–19 (2020). https://doi.org/10.1038/s41598-020-75562-z
26. Mathur, S.K., Srivastava, S.: Extended 16x16 playfair cipher algorithm for secure key exchange using RSA algorithm. Int. J. Sci. Innov. Res. **5**, 75–81 (2017)
27. Xu, Q., Sun, K., He, S., Zhu, C.: An effective image encryption algorithm based on compressive sensing and 2D-SLIM. Opt. Lasers Eng. **134**, 106178 (2020). https://doi.org/10.1016/j.optlaseng.2020.106178
28. Yao, S., Chen, L., Zhong, Y.: An encryption system for color image based on compressive sensing. Opt. Laser Technol. **120**, 105703 (2019). https://doi.org/10.1016/j.optlastec.2019.105703
29. Alawida, M., Samsudin, A., Teh, J.S., Alkhawaldeh, R.S.: A new hybrid digital chaotic system with applications in image encryption. Signal Process. **160**, 45–58 (2019). https://doi.org/10.1016/j.sigpro.2019.02.016

30. Alshoura, W.H., Zainol, Z., Teh, J.S., Alawida, M.: A new chaotic image watermarking scheme based on SVD and IWT. IEEE Access **8**, 43391–43406 (2020). https://doi.org/10.1109/ACCESS.2020.2978186

31. Alawida, M., Teh, J.S., Samsudin, A., Alshoura, W.H.: An image encryption scheme based on hybridizing digital chaos and finite state machine. Signal Process. **164**, 249–266 (2019). https://doi.org/10.1016/j.sigpro.2019.06.013

32. Zhang, D., Liao, X., Yang, B., Zhang, Y.: A fast and efficient approach to color-image encryption based on compressive sensing and fractional Fourier transform. Multimedia Tools Appl. **77**(2), 2191–2208 (2017). https://doi.org/10.1007/s11042-017-4370-1

33. Albahrani, E.A., Maryoosh, A.A., Lafta, S.H.: Block image encryption based on modified playfair and chaotic system. J. Inf. Secur. Appl. **51** (2020). https://doi.org/10.1016/j.jisa.2019.102445

34. Ghrare, S.E., Ali, M.A.M., Ismail, M., Jumari, K.: Diagnostic quality of compressed medical images: objective and subjective evaluation. In: 2008 Second Asia International Conference on Modelling & Simulation (AMS), pp. 923–927. IEEE (2008)

35. Elahi, S., kaleem, M., Omer, H.: Compressively sampled MR image reconstruction using generalized thresholding iterative algorithm. J. Magn. Reson. **286**, 91–98 (2018). https://doi.org/10.1016/j.jmr.2017.11.008

36. Nanni, L., Brahnam, S., Ghidoni, S., Menegatti, E., Barrier, T.: Different approaches for extracting information from the co-occurrence matrix. PLoS One **8**, 83554 (2013). https://doi.org/10.1371/journal.pone.0083554

37. Chai, H.Y., Wee, L.K., Swee, T.T., Hussain, S.: Gray-level co-occurrence matrix bone fracture detection. WSEAS Trans. Syst. **10**, 7–16 (2011)

38. Samhita, P., Prasad, P., Abhimanyu Kumar Patro, K., Acharya, B.: A secure chaos-based image encryption and decryption using crossover and mutation operator. Int. J. Control Theory Appl. **9**, 17–28 (2016)

39. Huang, C.K., Liao, C.W., Hsu, S.L., Jeng, Y.C.: Implementation of gray image encryption with pixel shuffling and gray-level encryption by single chaotic system. Telecommun. Syst. **52**, 563–571 (2013). https://doi.org/10.1007/s11235-011-9461-0

40. Es-Sabry, M., El Akkad, N., Merras, M., Saaidi, A., Satori, K.: A new image encryption algorithm using random numbers generation of two matrices and bit-shift operators. Soft Comput. **24**(5), 3829–3848 (2019). https://doi.org/10.1007/s00500-019-04151-8

41. Zhang, X., Wang, L., Cui, G., Niu, Y.: Entropy-based block scrambling image encryption using DES structure and chaotic systems. Int. J. Opt. **2019** (2019). https://doi.org/10.1155/2019/3594534

42. Verma, O.P., Nizam, M., Ahmad, M.: Modified multi-chaotic systems that are based on pixel shuffle for image encryption. J. Inf. Process. Syst. **9**, 271–286 (2013). https://doi.org/10.3745/JIPS.2013.9.2.271

43. Mondal, B., Kumar, P., Singh, S.: A chaotic permutation and diffusion based image encryption algorithm for secure communications. Multimedia Tools Appl. **77**(23), 31177–31198 (2018). https://doi.org/10.1007/s11042-018-6214-z

Improving Security and Performance of Distributed IPFS-Based Web Applications with Blockchain

Vu Le, Ramin Moazeni, and Melody Moh[✉]

San Jose State University, San Jose, CA 95192-0249, USA
melody.moh@sjsu.edu

Abstract. While cloud computing is gaining widespread adoption these days, some challenges are emerging around security, performance, and reliability of centralized cloud resources. Decentralized services are introduced as an effective way to overcome the limitations of cloud services. Blockchain technology with its associated decentralization is used to develop decentralized application platforms. The InterPlanetary File System (IPFS) is built on top of a distributed system consisting of a group of nodes that shares the data and takes advantage of blockchain to permanently store the data. The IPFS is very useful in transferring remote data. This work focuses on applying blockchain technology onto the IPFS for improving its security and performance. It illustrates different types of blockchain and their advantages and challenges; it also describes the proposed design and its detailed implementation. For performance evaluation, we show the performance gains, analyze security enhancements, and discuss the tradeoffs between security and performance. We believe that the presented work is significant towards more secured, efficient web applications utilizing the emerging blockchain technologies.

Keywords: Blockchain technology · Distributed system · Decentralized service · Interplanetary File System (IPFS)

1 Introduction

Traditional centralized cloud resources have been used widely by the government and businesses these days. Popular services such as Amazon AWS and Google Cloud can provide high reliability and security to the user. However, there are certain limitations with using centralized cloud resources because the centralized cloud can be a single point of failure, as shown by many such examples in the past. Take, for example, a careless mistake committed by a cloud operator can cause the cloud, and all the companies and organizations relying on the cloud resource, essentially half of a country, to shut down for up to an entire day. Similarly, a power outage, a data loss, or a network attack on these services can potentially disrupt the operations, causing huge damages to user data and business activities. A survey was conducted by RightScale in 2018; it asked 997 technical professionals about the challenges of adopting cloud technology. The survey

N. Abdullah et al. (Eds.): ACeS 2021, CCIS 1487, pp. 114–127, 2021.
https://doi.org/10.1007/978-981-16-8059-5_8

showed some interesting findings. Security was the top concern mentioned by 77% of them, and 55% of them faced performance challenges while using cloud technology [3].

In this paper, we address the security and performance challenges of distributed systems. There are several blockchain-based solutions to mitigate the drawbacks of centralized cloud resources. The computing resources need to be decentralized and performed by multiple parties, so blockchain processes the right characteristics and functionalities as a blockchain is stored on a ledger that is shared between all participating nodes on a network. In addition, any transaction that takes place on the blockchain requires consensus of all the nodes, so it is also very secure. It is important that there is no single entity which controls the blockchain, so it does not have the single point of failure issue as in other regular cloud storages.

A new file system called interplanetary file system (IPFS) has been invented and can process large files in a decentralized and effective manner. IPFS runs on a peer-to-peer network where each peer provides its own storage. It helps prevent data losses since the same data is available on multiple peer nodes [11]. Based on the above reasons, IPFS combined with blockchain technology can serve as a great solution to address the security and performance concerns of cloud technology.

This work describes the design of applying blockchain to IPFS to support secured distributed web applications, including applying smart contracts for access control [16]. The detailed implementation is depicted, including encryption/decryption schemes, smart contracts, remote application migration, and memory cache for key values. Performance and security analyses are presented, with a discussion of tradeoffs between the two.

The rest of the paper is organized as follows. Section 2 goes over preliminary background information and related work about blockchain technology, smart contracts, IPFS, distributed hash table, and memory cache. Section 3 demonstrates the high-level architectural design of the web application as well as how each component is designed. Section 4 talks about the implementation of each improvement method in our application. In Sect. 5, we detail our experiments and analyze the performance and security aspects of our application. Finally, Sect. 6 presents the conclusion and future work.

2 Background and Related Work

2.1 Background

Blockchain Technology
Blockchain technology is an open source and distributed system that enables transactions between two parties in a secure, verifiable, and trusted way, as illustrated in Dragonchain [2]. The underlying system behind blockchain is a distributed peer- to-peer network. There is no centralized authority that controls the network. Each node in the network performs its work independently. A new node needs to be verified by existing nodes before it joins the blockchain network. All the nodes are required to reach a consensus on a transaction before the transaction is recorded on a ledger that is shared among all the participating nodes. A consensus is made by each participant solving a complex puzzle and providing a proof of work or proof of stake to a server. The server checks the proof from each participant and rewards the ones with the correct proofs [1]. Once

the proof has been approved by the server, the transaction is confirmed, and a new block which contains the hash code and the transaction is added to the ledger, as illustrated by Tar [17]. The new block creation process is called mining. A node gets rewarded with money for successfully mining a block first, so all the completing nodes race to process a transaction and create a new block; refer to Salman et al. (2019) [13]. Data on the blockchain is immutable, so it will never change after it is written to the ledger. One limitation of blockchain is that it relies on continuous communications between nodes in the network, so its performance will be largely impacted in areas with a low bandwidth or slow connection, explained by Hu et al. [5].

Note that although blockchain is a great solution for decentralized computing resources, storing data on a blockchain alone is expensive because the same data needs to be propagated to and processed on other nodes in a blockchain network. As there is a large amount of data on the Internet now and getting larger in the future, a node will need a more powerful CPU, higher bus speed, higher bandwidth, and a bigger storage to process all the data, which will increase the cost to operate blockchain.

Smart Contracts

Smart contracts are computer programs that are used to execute blockchain based transactions. Smart contracts contain executable code written in Solidify. Solidity is a statically typed language that makes use of variables, functions, and structures. The code follows a mutual agreement between two par- ties involved in a transaction. Contracts are compiled and deployed to an environment which is capable of running the contracts whenever a transaction takes place. As an example, for Ethereum blockchain, smart contracts are deployed and executed in the Ethereum virtual machine (EVM) [9]. The code in a smart contract is publicly available on the ledger in a blockchain, so a new node which joins the blockchain later will receive a copy of the smart con- tract. There is no centralized authority controlling smart contracts, but instead they are distributed across multiple nodes on the network. It ensures trust and anonymity of any smart contract triggered operations. Before a smart contract executes a transaction, a transaction fee is required and, in the Ethereum case, the fee is paid in ether, also known as gas. The transaction fee is higher for smart contracts with more complex logic.

Interplanetary File System

Interplanetary file system is a distributed file system where we can store any computer file or data for later access. Unlike a file system on a computer, IPFS divides a file into multiple chunks of data and distributes the chunks across different nodes on IPFS. While other file systems use a location-based address to look up a file, IPFS uses a content-based address where a file's address is based on the hash of the file's content. A single unit of data on IPFS is a block. IPFS constructs a directed acyclic graph to link all the blocks in a file, which facilitates data retrieval. IPFS maintains a distributed hash table to know where to find the data or the path which leads closer to the data [7].

When a node downloads data from IPFS, the node can store the data locally and will serve as a new provider of the data. Therefore, when the node's nearby computer requests the data, the node can send the data to the requesting computer, just as any other nodes on IPFS can do.

Distributed Hash Table

.A distributed hash table stores key-value mappings to help IPFS find a peer node having the requested data or find a path leading to a node. Each node on the IPFS network maintains its distributed hash table and uses it to find and return the value when requested for a key. A key can be a data unique identifier, an Interplanetary Name System (IPNS) key, or a peer ID.

2.2 Related Work

In order to protect the privacy of users' data on the network, Rahulamathavan et al. (2017) proposed an attribute-based encryption method. The data owner creates user groups and assigns an access policy that consists of certain user attributes to each group. A user must possess all the specified attributes that satisfy the policy to access the data [12]. This encryption technology does not look at users' identity and does not work in a decentralized network as it requires the centralized access policy server. Smart contracts can solve this problem by their ability to work on a decentralized network and customized implementation logic for user verification in every transaction.

The usage of smart contracts has been previously proposed for access control between smart devices in the Internet of Things (IoT). Song et al. (2019) comes up with an attribute-based access control scheme that checks device attribute information and decides whether to allow a device to join an IoT network. This scheme uses blockchain and smart contracts to store and manage access control policies [15]. In addition, Nakamura et al. (2020) proposes a capability-based access control using smart contracts in the IoT. In this scheme, the author suggests having smart contracts manage capability tokens. There is a token created for each capability or action, and smart contracts will verify the ownership and validity of the token from the access requestor to grant them access or not [10].

The paper Shen et al. (2019) analyzes the I/O performance of IPFS and notices a bottleneck in IPFS data retrieval because of the resolving and downloading operations. When a node in IPFS receives a data retrieval request, if the data is not local on the node, it needs to perform a lookup to find the storage node of the data. If the data size to download is larger than 256KB, IPFS will break it into multiple blocks of 256KB each. When all the blocks arrive at the requesting node, they will be re-aggregated to a file of the original size, so the block size also affects the I/O performance of IPFS [14].

In the paper, Hassanzadeh-Nazarabadi et al. (2019), the author used the distributed hash table concept to design a blockchain architecture called LightChain. LightChain is a permissionless blockchain where any node can join the network. Any new transaction or block addition to this blockchain will be recorded in the distributed hash table of a peer in an on-demand manner, so each peer does not have to store the entire blockchain locally [4]. The distributed hash table provides efficient data lookup, but it may take a noticeable latency when it requires many table lookups to retrieve the data.

3   Application Design

The application consists of the following components, as shown in Fig. 1:

- Web client: the user interface that runs on a browser where the user can interact with and perform operations in the application.
- Web server: the web server has all the implementations to support file upload and download
- IPFS data storage: a distributed data storage that stores and manages the data.
- Blockchain: a local Ethereum blockchain to host smart contracts and record user activities from the application

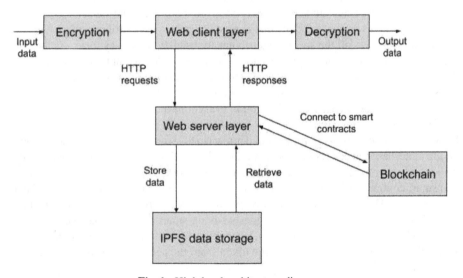

Fig. 1. High level architecture diagram

Smart contracts are used to verify the user's identity and write transactions' hash codes to the blockchain. The contracts are deployed to and running on the blockchain network, as illustrated in Fig. 2.

Figure 3 shows the sequence diagram of data retrieval in IPFS: The web application server uses an IPFS client to talk to a remote IPFS network of nodes or the local IPFS daemon. In our experiments, we run the IPFS daemon locally, so we can test the code changes we make to improve the performance of IPFS data retrieval. We add key-value memory cache to two APIs in IPFS. One API is to get the root file node from a file hash, and the other API is to find provider nodes that can provide the corresponding data from a key. A key is the content addressed identifier of a file. Besides querying data, the web application also utilizes the IPFS client's Add API to add new data to IPFS.

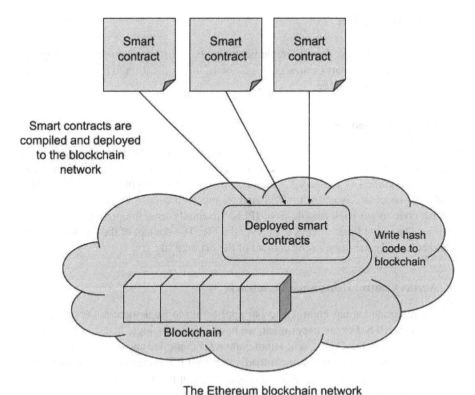

Fig. 2. Smart contracts in the Ethereum blockchain

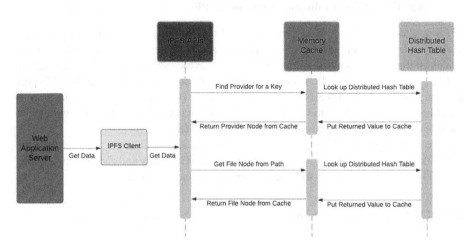

Fig. 3. Sequence diagram of data retrieval in IPFS

4   Implementation

This section describes the detailed implementation, including encryption and decryption, access control using Smart Contracts, migration of the application to Remote IPFS, and the key-value memory cache.

4.1   Encryption and Decryption

We used encryption and decryption to protect the privacy of the data we upload to IPFS. We first generated a pair of a public key and a private key using OpenSSL commands. We used the public key to encrypt a file and uploaded the encrypted file to IPFS. After the file was successfully added to IPFS, and we received a hash code in return, we used the hash code to get back the file from IPFS. We finally used the private key from the previously generated pair of keys to decrypt the file. The content of the downloaded file should be exactly the same as the content of the original file.

4.2   Access Control Using Smart Contracts

We have integrated smart contracts to our application to implement the access control of the data on IPFS. For our experiment, we have written the logic in a smart contract to check the user's email address. The smart contract is compiled and deployed to our local blockchain. When a user tries to download a file from IPFS, they are prompted to enter their email address. This email address is sent to the application server, and the server calls a method on the smart contract for email verification. If the verification succeeds, the server proceeds with fetching the requested data from IPFS. Otherwise, we show an error message to the user that they do not have access to the requested data.

4.3   Migration of the Application to Remote IPFS

IPFS provides a great way to decentralize the hosting of an application where multiple nodes can host the application, so the application can be accessed in case one or a few nodes go down. Whereas the centralized server provides access to a website through an HTTP protocol, an application running on IPFS will be accessed through the IPFS peer to peer protocol or the IPFS Gateway API. It is even better that once the application is on IPFS, we can pin it to the local node using the hash output from IPFS in order to make sure the application stays on the IPFS network [8].

We have used a tool on fleek.co to deploy our application to a distributed IPFS network. Once deployed, we create a domain name on GoDaddy and change the CNAME record in our domain's DNS to have a better URL to access the application.

4.4   Key-Value Memory Cache

Method getFileNodeFromPath

This method takes an IPFS hash path to a file and resolves to a file root node that points to the start of the file. The method queries the directed acyclic graph (DAG) which is the underlying data structure of IPFS and returns a node pointer to the file. Since the hash path is based on the file content and is the same for the same content, we can put the hash path and the resolved file node in the cache. Future requests with the same hash path will hit the cache and immediately return the file node.

This method first resolves the given path to the last valid resolvable path. It uses the content identifier in the last resolvable path to query the DAG. The DAG will return a root node that contains links to other nodes in the graph representing the requested data. When receiving the root node, the method creates a new Unix file system-based file node. This node can represent different hierarchies of the file system, such as a file, a directory, or a symbolic link to a file.

Method findProvidersAsync

While getFileNodeFromPath returns the file root node to a specific given hash path, this findProvidersAsync method searches for peers that are close to the current node and can provide a given key. The method takes a content addressed identifier and a count, then returns a set of peers that have or know where to get the requested content. A content addressed identifier is formed by a version, a content type, and the hash of the content. The count specifies how many peers we want to get. If the count is zero, the method returns an unbounded number of peers. Because the content identifier is unique for the same content, we cache the content identifier and the set of peer providers. Therefore, future calls to this method with the same identifier will be able to directly get the providers from the cache.

This method internally tries to find providers from the local network as well as the wide area network. In each network, it creates a channel which is responsible for sending back a peer's address when it is found. Since a peer can be found again and again, the method keeps a local map that stores a newly found peer. We just ignore the peer that has already been found and is in the map. If at the end of the method, we cannot find any new peers, we publish a query event to the query event channel. The query event has the context of the initial data request.

5   Performance and Security Analysis

5.1   Security Analysis

In the first experiment, thanks to the encryption mechanism, only people whose email addresses are not in the blacklist will be able to download from IPFS. It protects the data from being accessed by certain users who we have already blacklisted.

In the second experiment, we used smart contract-based access control to verify the user's identity before giving them permission to download a file on IPFS. When we downloaded a file from IPFS, we were required to enter an email address for the smart contract to validate. For experimental purposes, we created a blacklist of email addresses which should be blocked from accessing our data on IPFS. When the entered email address passed the verification, we showed a success message to the user and started downloading the file from IPFS. When we deliberately put an email address which is in the email blacklist, it would fail the verification by the smart contract. We showed a failure message to the user and did not allow them to download the file.

We have migrated the web application from the localhost to a remote IPFS network, so the web application can be accessed even though the local server is not running. We also set up an SSL connection and a custom URL https://sjsu-cs298.on.fleek.co for secured and easy access to the application.

5.2 Performance Analysis

We experimented uploading and downloading files of different sizes and measured the time it took to get the data from IPFS with and without the cache. For each file, we ran the same experiment 10 times and took the average latency. The results are shown in Fig. 4.

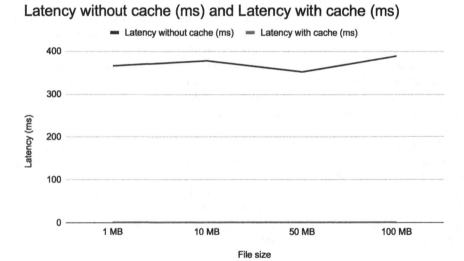

Fig. 4. Comparison between IPFS file retrieval latency with cache and without cache

We can see that without the cache, the average latency fluctuates from 300 ms to 400 ms. In our experiment, sometimes it can take up to a few seconds to get the root file node because it depends on when the lookup algorithm finds the node.

We also measure the download latency for different file sizes, shown in Fig. 5. With the cache, it only takes about 10 ms to get the root file node, and the latency is pretty consistent. The latency that the user observes when downloading a file from the application will be higher due to the Internet latency to transfer the data. With the Internet download speed of about 90 Mbps in our experiments, the Internet latency is insignificant and not noticeable for a 1 Mb file, and it is increasing as the size of a file gets bigger.

We also tried varying the expiration time of the memory cache; the results are shown in Fig. 6. We pre-uploaded 100 different text files of about 1 Mb each to IPFS. We tried

Internet download latency (ms) vs. File size (Mb)

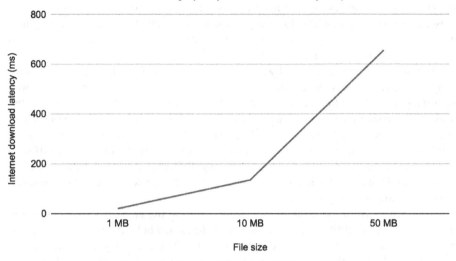

Fig. 5. Internet download latency for different file sizes

setting the expiration time to 10 s, 30 s, 1 min, and 5 min, and for each expiration time, we ran a script to continuously download random files from the pre-uploaded files on IPFS and measured the latency. The resulting latency is drawn in the chart below. As the chart illustrates, when the expiration time increases, the latency decreases because more entries are kept in the cache, and we get more cache hits in the download operation.

Latency (ms) vs. Expiration time (seconds)

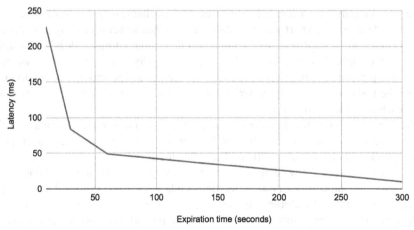

Fig. 6. Latency vs. expiration time of the memory cache

However, we do not want to have a very large expiration time as the cache will maintain a lot of entries that are not frequently accessed. From our experiments, the reasonable expiration time should be at the minimum of 1 min to about 2–3 min because at 1 min, we can already get a significant latency reduction from more than 200 ms to about 50 ms. From 1 min and above, the latency is only gradually decreasing.

The memory cache is backed by a key-value map in the Go language. Since a map can have a dynamic size, when more data is added to the map, the map will get more slots internally. Therefore, the maximum amount of data in the cache will depend on the available heap size and the operating system where IPFS is running. For example, a map in a 32-bit operating system can have 2^{31} - 1 slots, and a map in a 64-bit operating system can have 2^{63} - 1 slots. Because of the above reason, initializing a map with a different size for our memory cache will not result in any difference in terms of the latency to get the data. However, the size of the cache is limited by the heap size and the memory available in the operating system.

Note that there is a possible disadvantage of using the memory cache. When the data requested from IPFS is too large that the cache cannot hold, it will result in a cache miss. When many cache misses are happening, it will slow down the performance of IPFS. Depending on the application's use cases, if IPFS with the integrated memory cache is not a good fit, we can consider other alternative distributed file systems, such as Ceph, GlusterFS, and HDFS. HDFS stands for Hadoop distributed file system which can store, process large unstructured data, and provide high throughput access. Ceph is a POSIX-compliant network file system that offers high performance, large data storage, and is highly compatible with legacy applications. GlusterFS is also a fast and scalable distributed file system which has caching of data and metadata. GlusterFS can be integrated with HDFS to process large data for data analysis purposes [6].

5.3   Tradeoff Between Performance and Security

There is a computing cost for each added security mechanism in the application, so it incurs a tradeoff between performance and security. When an additional layer of security is integrated, the application's server has to do more computing work in the security check, so the application can run a little slower. If security is more important, we need to sacrifice performance of the application, and vice versa. Therefore, it is important to choose the right balance between performance and security to meet the requirements and use cases of the application.

We have measured the performance impact in our application for each security method. We upload and download files of 1 Mb in size. The encryption and decryption using OpenSSL each takes about 50 ms. The call to the smart contract to verify the user's identity takes between 20 to 70 ms. Because the identity check by the smart contract is simple, assuming no network failures, the time it takes is small enough to be acceptable and very consistent in the aforementioned range of 20 and 70 ms. In short, the security implementation adds an additional 50 ms to the file upload flow and an extra 70 ms to 120 ms when downloading a file.

As we know from the experiments, IPFS with the memory cache only takes about 10 ms to resolve the root file node, so the additional latency from the security protection is about 7 to 12 times longer on average for a file download. From the user experience, the added latency of about 100 ms in a download should not be noticeable. However, if we want to upload a very large file, we may need to split it into chunks and encrypt each chunk at a time because there is a size limit in OpenSSL encryption. This splitting and encrypting of a large file may add a significantly longer latency for uploading a file, which is something we need to consider.

6 Conclusion and Future Work

Our research and experiments show that it is imperative to protect the security and privacy of data on a distributed network, and we have used several methods in our application to improve it. Data encryption ensures the data can only be seen by the authorized user who has the right key to decrypt the data. Access control by smart contracts provides another layer of security check to verify the user's identity before giving the user permission to access the data. Combining the two methods can significantly improve the security and lower the risk of data being stolen by malicious users. Some future work to be done in this area will be to add more access control policies to smart contracts to verify the user's identity, such as verify the user's public key and signature. We can also have a blockchain based service that encrypts and manages the user's secret key, and an application which wants to access the data can call the service to get the key and decrypt it. This key management service can use smart contracts' access control to authenticate the user before sending them the key [18, 19].

Besides the security concern, our experiments demonstrate performance improvement in IPFS by using key-value memory caching. The cache helps significantly reduce the time it takes to find a data provider or the root node of an underlying directed acyclic graph in IPFS, which in turn makes it faster to retrieve data from IPFS. In the future, another way we can try to add on top of caching is to use recursive lookup instead of the current iterative lookup. When the iterative lookup asks a node for the associated value of a key, if the node does not have the value, it will return a list of other nodes closer to the requested value. The same process continues until it finds a node that actually has the value and can return it. With the recursive lookup, when we ask a node for a value, and the node does not have the value, it will ask another closer node which will ask another closer node. Once the value is found, it will be returned to the original requestor following the same chain of requests in the reversed order. The recursive lookup can reduce a lot of network traffic between nodes and the latency in processing requests and responses in each node, so it will certainly improve the performance of data retrieval in IPFS.

The performance can degrade when extremely large data files are transferred because the entire data will not fit in the memory cache. We will more likely experience cache misses. Another future work is to find a solution to handle this situation and try to achieve the optimized performance of the cache as well as IPFS when requesting large data from IPFS.

References

1. Shermin, V.: Blockchains & Distributed Ledger Technologies. BlockchainHub (2019). https:// blockchainhub.net/blockchains-and-distributed-ledger-technologies-in-general/.   Accessed 12 Apr 2020
2. Dragonchain: What different types of blockchains are there? (2019). https://dragonchain.com/ blog/differences-between-public-private-blockchains/. Accessed 11 Apr 2020
3. Durcevic, S.: Cloud computing risks, challenges & problems businesses are facing. Datapine.com (2019). https://www.datapine.com/blog/cloud-computing-risks-and-challenges/. Accessed 17 Apr 2021
4. Hassanzadeh-Nazarabadi, Y., Kupcu, A., Ozkasap, O.: LightChain: a DHT-based Blockchain for Resource Constrained Environments. ArXiv abs/1904.00375 (2019)
5. Hu, Y., et al.: A delay-tolerant payment scheme based on the ethereum blockchain. IEEE Access 7(6), 33159–33172 (2019). https://doi.org/10.1109/access.2019.2903271
6. John, B.K.: Ceph vs. GlusterFS vs. MooseFS vs. HDFS vs. DRBD. ComputingForGeeks (2020). https://www.datapine.com/blog/cloud-computing-risks-and-challenges/. Accessed 4 June 2021
7. Khudhur, N., Fujita, S.: Siva - The IPFS search engine. In: 2019 Seventh International Symposium on Computing and Networking (CANDAR), Nagasaki, Japan, pp. 150–156 (2019). https://doi.org/10.1109/CANDAR.2019.00026. https://doi.ieeecomputersociety.org/ 10.1109/CANDAR.2019.00026
8. Kohorst, L.: Decentralizing your Website. Medium (2020). https://towardsdatascience.com/ decentralizing-your-website-f5bca765f9ed. Accessed 27 Mar 2021
9. Lipton, A., Levi, S.: An Introduction to Smart Contracts and Their Potential and Inherent Limitations. The Harvard Law School Forum on Corporate Governance (2018). https://corpgov.law.harvard.edu/2018/05/26/an-introduction-to-smart-contracts-and-their-potential-and-inherent-limitations/. Accessed 27 Mar 2021
10. Nakamura, Y., Zhang, Y., Sasabe, M., Kasahara, S.: Exploiting smart contracts for capability-based access control in the internet of things. Sensors 20(6), 1793–1793 (2020). https://doi. org/10.3390/s20061793
11. Naz, M., Al-Zahrani, F.A., Khalid, R., Javaid, N., Qamar, A.M., Afzai, M.K.: A Secure data sharing platform using blockchain and interplanetary file system. Sustainability 11, 7054 (2019). https://doi.org/10.3390/su11247054
12. Rahulamathavan, Y., Phan, R.C., Rajarajan, M., Misra, S., Kondoz, A.: Privacy-preserving blockchain based IoT ecosystem using attribute-based encryption. In: Proceedings of IEEE International Conference on Advanced Networks and Telecommunications Systems, pp. 1–6 (2017)
13. Salman, T., Zolanvari, M., Erbad, A., Jain, R., Samaka, M.: Security services using blockchains: a state of the art survey. IEEE Commun. Surv. Tutor. 21(1), 858–880 (2019). https://doi.org/10.1109/comst.2018.2863956
14. Shen, J., Li, Y., Zhou, Y., Wang, X.: Understanding I/O performance of IPFS storage: a client's perspective. In: IEEE Access, p. 24 (2019)
15. Song, L., Li, M., Zhu, Z., Yuan, P., He, Y.: Attribute-based access control using smart contracts for the internet of things. ScienceDirect, p. 2019 (2019)
16. Steichen, M., Fiz, B., Norvill, R., Shbair, W., State, R.: Blockchain-based, decentralized access control for IPFS. In: IEEE Access, p. 15 (2019)
17. Tar, A.: Proof of Work, Explained. Cointelegraph (2018). https://cointelegraph.com/explai ned/proof-of-work-explained. Accessed 3 Apr 2021

18. Wang, S., Zhang, Y., Zhang, Y.: A blockchain-based framework for data sharing with fine-grained access control in decentralized storage systems. IEEE Access **6**, 38437–38450 (2018)
19. Zheng, W., Zheng, Z., Chen, X., Dai, K., Li, P., Chen, R.: NutBaaS: a blockchain-as-a-service Platform. IEEE Access **7**(10), 134422–134433 (2019). https://doi.org/10.1109/access.2019.2941905

Internet of Things (IoT) Security Challenges and Solutions: A Systematic Literature Review

Rao Faizan Ali[iD], Amgad Muneer[(⊠)][iD], P. D. D. Dominic[iD], Shakirah Mohd Taib[iD],
and Ebrahim A. A. Ghaleb

Department of Computer and Information Sciences, Universiti Teknologi PETRONAS,
32160 Seri Iskandar, Malaysia
amgad_20001929@utp.edu.my

Abstract. The Internet of Things (IoT), often known as the Internet of Everything, is a new technological paradigm visualized as a worldwide network of interconnected machines. IoT brings another dimension into Information Technology (IT), where machines can communicate with various machines and humans. Researchers and IT industry produced various IoT devices, architectures. Different ways are introduced to implement and use IoT concepts. IoT is getting more intention in ideas like smart homes and smart cities, raising security concerns. This article aims to gather the reported security issues, the classification of those issues, and the solutions that were provided against those IoT security issues.

Keywords: Internet of Things (IoT) · IoT security · IoT security challenges ·
IoT security solutions

1 Introduction

Internet of Things (IoT) refers to the network of interrelated physical devices connected to the Internet or other devices that have the ability to collect, share and act on data without human-to-human or human-to-computer interaction. The term IoT was proposed to uniquely identify the connected devices using radio-frequency identification (RFID) [1]. Devices, which are connected via IoT vary in their shapes or sizes. A smart home is the best example where electricity, ovens, fridge, television, security alarm, and other devices are connected to one IoT platform. Due to technological advancements, it has now become possible to connect home appliances, cars, even heart monitors, and others.

Devices with embedded sensors are connected to an IoT platform. The IoT platform then applies analytic to the collected data from various devices [2] and shares valuable information to the application for decision making or research purposes [3]. IoT is so sophisticated that it can decide what information is useful and what is not. The smart home concept is based on this advancement of IoT where various smart devices in the home are connected to one IoT device [4]. that gathers data from the connected devices and lets users make decisions. Users can make decisions like controlling home temperature, playing music, control lighting, checking who is at the door etc. In recent years, there has been rapid growth in IoT application development due to the RFID and

© Springer Nature Singapore Pte Ltd. 2021
N. Abdullah et al. (Eds.): ACeS 2021, CCIS 1487, pp. 128–154, 2021.
https://doi.org/10.1007/978-981-16-8059-5_9

Wireless Sensor Network (WSN). RFID enables the labelling of devices so that they can be uniquely identified, and with WSN, every device, object becomes wireless identifiable object. WSN enables communication among the devices in or out of the network [1]. With the increasing involvement of IoT in different fields of life, information security breaches and attacks also increased [5–7].

This research aims to present a comprehensive survey in the domain of IoT from the information security perspective. Due to the rapid growth of IoT applications, there are serious concerns in the areas of security and privacy while using IoT [6, 8–10]. Several studies conducted on IoT security in recent years. It is essential to collect the state-of-the-art IoT security challenges, the solutions proposed against those challenges and highlight the challenges that are still open and needs attention. To conduct an adequate review, a basic search string is formalized to collect relevant research available in IoT security. We focused on different publications from renowned journals and conferences.

We divided this research into four main sections. In Sect. 2, we shed some light on the architecture of IoT. Section 3 describes the security concerns for IoT. Section 4 presents the research methodology followed for this survey, security challenges reported in IoT architecture, classification of IoT Security issues according to the IoT layered architecture. It also provides the solutions available to these security issues. Finally, Sect. 5 delivers the conclusion of this study.

2 IoT Architecture

IoT works in three layers. There are different opinions about the number of layers in IoT architecture, but it fundamentally consists of three-layer architecture, as shown in Fig. 1; Perception Layer, Network Layer, and Application Layer [7]. All these three layers define the basic idea behind IoT.

2.1 Perception Layer

It is a physical layer, often called the sensor layer. It works like a human sensor e.g., eyes for watching, ears for listening, nose for sniffing etc. Actuators, Edge devices, and Sensors are used in this layer responsible for interacting with the environment, identifying objects in the environment, collecting data, processing that data into useful information, and passing it to the network layer.

2.2 Network Layer

This layer is also called the data transmission layer. The responsibility of these layers is to collect the data from the perception layer and transmit it to other smart devices, cloud, internet gateways or IoT hubs for data processing or storage purposes. The medium for transmission can be either be wired or wireless. It works like a bridge between the physical layer and the application layer. Figure 1 shows the three fundamental layers of IoT.

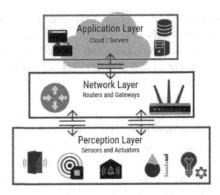

Fig. 1. Three fundamental layers of IoT

2.3 Application Layer

This layer provides the processed data to the end-user via an interface. This layer gets the data from servers and cloud platforms and presents it to the end-user to view the gathered data. Smart home, smart TV, smartwatch are examples of applications that use the application layer. Due to the need and usage of IoT at scale, researchers started proposing multi-layer IoT architecture. It includes 3-layer, 4-layer, 5-layer, and others. The four-layer architecture consists of one layer, whereas five-layer architecture added two more layers; the business and the processing layers. The order of layers in 5-layer architecture can be seen in Fig. 2. The responsibility of the remaining two layers in three-layer architecture is the same.

2.4 Business Layer

This layer works as a manager of IoT. It manages the applications, business flows, business models, data creation, storage, user privacy, access controls, etc.

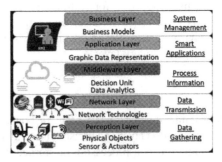

Fig. 2. Five-layer architecture

2.5 Processing Layer

It is also called the middle-ware layer, where data is processed, analytic are performed. It receives the data from the transport layer and processes the data into useful information. The primary responsibility of this layer is to remove the unwanted data and store only useful information. Figure 3 shows different architectures proposed over time.

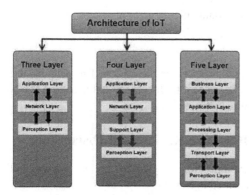

Fig. 3. Different IoT architectures

There is not a single architecture that is considered as a standard or agreed by the researchers. That is why several architectures are available to date. The reason behind proposing five-layer architecture is security and privacy, which previous architectures were not seemed to fulfil [11].

3 IoT Security Concerns

The security of IoT is related to the principles that should be enforced to achieve a secure communication network. These principles are as follows:

3.1 Authentication, Authorization and Confidentiality

Every object in the IoT platform needs to be identified by the system and other objects. Every object needs to be authenticated before interacting with the system or other objects in the IoT platform [12, 13]. Ensuring the data is available to authorized persons or objects is a critical task. Management of data is also vital to protect and manage that data so that the authorized objects will get their data [14]. A key management system needs to be enabled for ensuring confidentiality.

3.2 Data/Service Availability

The idea of smart devices emphasizes the availability of data and services to provide data or processing services whenever required.

3.3 Privacy

Due to the diverse nature of objects, including networks, devices connecting to one platform make the stored data vulnerable to attackers.

3.4 Integrity

There is a lot of data exchange among the objects. Ensuring the data is coming from the proper object and it is being sent to the object that is asking is also essential. IoT must ensure the integrity of data during transmission.

4 Systematic Literature Review and Discussion

A methodology is developed for carrying out this research in IoT security issues and their solutions, as presented in Fig. 4.

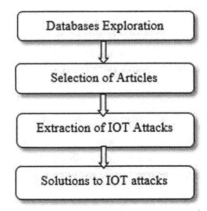

Fig. 4. Research methodology

The details of each component defined within the methodology are as follows:

4.1 Database Exploration

As stated in Table 1, some of the famous databases were explored to get the desired articles. Table 3 explains the search strings used to extract the required research articles from the databases by using AND, OR operators along with the search strings called advance search.

Research parameters for the research are finalized. Table 2 presents the research strings followed for extracting the number of articles from the selected databases.

Table 1. Databases explored

No.	Database name	Address
1	IEEE explore	https://ieeexplore.ieee.org/
4	ACM library	https://dl.acm.org/
3	Research gate	https://www.researchgate.net/
4	Science direct	https://www.sciencedirect.com/

Table 2. Research parameters

No.	Parameter
1	IoT security
2	IoT security issues
3	Abusing IoT security
4	Vulnerabilities in IoT
5	IoT security attacks
6	Security issues in IoT
7	Security issues in IoT layers
8	Security issues in IoT architecture

4.2 Articles Selection

A criterion is defined for the selection of articles for this research. The criteria are as follows:

Table 3. Research parameters

No.	Criteria
1	Assessment of relevancy
2	Number of citations
3	Time frame of publication

Total 68 papers were selected in the first place based on the defined criteria in Table 3. Table 3 presents the criteria for selecting the articles, which contains three points. The first is related to the relevancy level, which is used to determine whether the articles are related to the expected or now. The second point checks for a number of citations. The third point checks for the date of its publication to check whether the article is within a timeframe from 2013–2020 or not. Based on these two points, collected articles were filtered.

4.3 IoT Security Issues

A number of recent IoT survey papers were selected to find out IoT security issues. Majority of survey papers discussing the same security issues found in earlier survey papers. Duplication of IoT security issues were removed, only unique IoT security issues were kept so that an idea about IoT security issues become apparent. An essential point of this research is that; it combines the issues not previously covered by any survey. All the layers in IoT architecture are susceptible to a number of security attacks or threats. These attacks/threats could be active; they directly stop the services or passive; they can continuously monitor IoT services without stopping them. Various IoT researchers reported several security challenges in IoT. Table 4 depicts those issues along with the short description.

Table 4. IoT security issues

Reference	Security issue	Layer	Description
[15]	Replay attack	Perception layer	This attack has been made by altering, spoofing the identity information of connected devices to IoT
[6]	Malware in IoT	Processing layer	This attack has been made when the user executes an unwanted, non-scanned executable
[44]	DNS cache poisoning attack	Network layer	This attack is DNS spoofing where altering cashed DNS details of neighbour objects
[45]	Man-in-the-middle attack	Network layer	The attacker gain access to communication and silently alters the communication between objects
[6]	Lightweight cryptosystems and security protocols	Network layer	Due to the usage of the lightweight cryptosystem, the IoT systems become vulnerable to the attacks
[46]	Heterogeneous devices connect	Network layer	Heterogeneous devices connecting to the IoT system make it easier for an attacker to exploit the system
[6]	Android malware	Application layer	Due to the heterogeneity of android users on the network, this attack becomes possible

(continued)

Table 4. (*continued*)

Reference	Security issue	Layer	Description
[47]	Eavesdropping	Application layer	It is a real-time attack where the attacker gains access to live phone calls, messages etc.
[45]	Node capture attack	Perception layer	The attacker gains access to the key node and can extract sensitive information
[18]	Fake node or malicious node	Perception layer	The attacker adds a node into the IoT system and tries to stop the network
[48]	Timing attack	Perception layer	This attack is possible when the device has low computational resources. The attacker observes the response time of the device and extracts weaknesses
[4, 49]	Denial of Service (DoS) attack	Network layer	This attack is made by flooding the network with fake requests. As a result, the network first gets slower to respond to genuine users and finally stops responding
[1]	Storage attack	Network layer	The storage where data is stored can be attacked, and the data could be tempered
[50]	Exploit attack	Network layer	Any attack which includes illegal code, set of commands to steal the confidential information
[51]	Cross site scripting	Application layer	This attack is made by injecting script or code from the client-side, which will execute on the server-side
[45]	Malicious code attack	Application layer	It is the code written intentionally in application to harm the system
[7]	The ability to deal with mass data	Application layer	Due to the many objects transmitting data, it becomes possible for the attacker to analyze and intercept the data
[51]	Malicious insider attack	Network layer	This attack is made from inside the network by an unauthorized user to steal information of authorized users

(*continued*)

Table 4. (*continued*)

Reference	Security issue	Layer	Description
[45]	Exhaustion	Processing layer	The attacker uses exhaustion to exhaust the system resources to disrupt the network
[45]	Business logic attack	Business layer	The attacker alters the business logic after observing it
[52]	Zero-day attack	Business layer	This attack refers to finding the loophole in the implementation of the business model
[47]	Data privacy and identity authentication	Application layer	This attack happens during device communication
[53]	Malicious data	Application layer	This attack is made by putting data that has malicious code. When it is stored in the system, it gets evoked and try to exploit the system
[18]	Traffic analysis	Network layer	This attack is made after analyzing the traffic on the system
[47]	Compatibility	Network layer	The diverse nature of different network components used in the system makes it challenging to impose network protocols correctly
[54]	Network topology	Network layer	This attack is made after analyzing the network topology
[55]	Brute force	Network layer	This attack becomes possible when weak or hard-coded passwords are used for the system
[56]	Firmware hijacking	Application layer	This attack turns the system into various exceptions like buffer overflow/underflow
[49]	Micro probing	Perception layer	This attack is applied by attaching tiny needles to the internal wiring of a chip

(*continued*)

Table 4. (*continued*)

Reference	Security issue	Layer	Description
[57]	Jamming adversaries	Network layer	This attack fails the networks to work appropriately by emitting radio frequency without following any protocols
[45]	Sybil and spoofing attacks	Perception layer	A Sybil node with a fake identity pretending to be an authorized object of the system consumes network resources, resulting in access denied to other objects
[57]	Insecure interface	Perception layer	Insecure implementation of the communication interface could lead to attackers access the system
[53]	Sleep deprivation attack	Perception layer	This attack is made by making the devices always awake, resulting in too much energy consumption and ultimately no battery left when necessary to perform some operation
[57]	Session hijacking	Network layer	The attacker can hijab the session and enforce denial of service
[57]	Cloud security	Network layer	Privacy in the cloud can be attacked and compromised
[57]	RPL routing attack	Network layer	IPV6 RPL is vulnerable to noisy nodes within the network
[57]	Transport security	Network layer	Without end-to-end security on the network layer, it is vulnerable to attackers
[57]	Buffer reservation attack	Perception layer	The receiver contains the store for incoming packet processing, and an attacker sends the incomplete packet, which results in a denial-of-service attack

4.4 Proposed Solutions to IoT Security Issues

This section provides an overview of the security solutions available to the highlighted IoT problems. The precise details and analysis of the available solutions are presented in Table 5.

Replay attack [15] occurs when some intruder pretends to be the original user of the system and starts communicating with other users of the system. It is performed during the authentication process. The authors in [15] proposed a framework that detects and mitigates the issue if it exists. Detection involves Universally Unique Identifier (UUI) for identifying objects uniquely, Timestamp; current time of the event and Battery Depletion

Table 5. Solutions to IoT security issues

Year	Author	Threat	Solution	Critical analysis
2017	Rughoobur et al.	Replay attack	A lightweight replay attack detection framework for battery dependent IoT devices designed for healthcare	Although the provided solutions are good for detecting replay attack based on battery consumption, it could be better if the author provides the mitigation as well
2018	HaddadPajouh et al.	Malware in IOT	A deep recurrent neural network based approach for internet of things malware threat hunting	Using a deep learning approach to detect security issues is fine, but a feasible solution that can be implemented in a smart home or smart city could be more impressive
2016	Sforzin et al.	DNS cache poisoning attack	RPiDS: Raspberry Pi IDS a fruitful intrusion detection system for IoT	This idea is quite impressive; the author designed a device for intrusion detection. It is a novel idea; no such other solution is reviewed so far
2016	Sforzin et al.	Man-in-the-middle attack	RPiDS: Raspberry Pi IDS a fruitful intrusion detection system for IoT	Same as above

(continued)

Table 5. (*continued*)

Year	Author	Threat	Solution	Critical analysis
2017	Thirumalai et al.	Lightweight cryptosystems and security protocols	Memory Efficient Multi Key (MEMK) generation scheme for secure transportation of sensitive data over cloud and IoT devices	The authors provided a solution to cryptosystem security concerns. The proposed solution is good in that it reduces the computational resources required for RSA. Thus, the solution can be used in low storage or processing power device
2016	Pham et al.	Heterogeneous devices connect	Management architecture for heterogeneous IoT devices in home network	Security is a management problem that the authors did in their solution, but it still requires improvement
2014	Ham et al.	Android malware linear	SVM-based android malware detection for reliable IoT services	The proposed model detects android malware that was the intention, but no solution achieves 99 percent accuracy so far, and this one too
2017	Siby et al.	Node capture attack	IoT Scanner: detecting privacy threats in IoT neighborhoods	The proposed solution monitors different events performed by the devices and presents the data in visualizations. It could be better if the author provided the mitigation process as well

(*continued*)

Table 5. (*continued*)

Year	Author	Threat	Solution	Critical analysis
2018	Rizal et al.	Fake node or malicious node network	Forensics for detecting flooding attack on Internet of Things (IoT) device	The authors proposed a good framework that detects the security issues and stops them from causing a threat
2019	Takarabt et al.	Timing attack	Cache-timing attacks still threaten IoT devices	The authors proposed a low-level memory leakage solution that is a novel idea to avoid vulnerability from the very start
2018	Brun et al.	Denial of Service (DoS) attack	Deep learning with dense random neural network for detecting attacks against IoT-connected home environments	The authors proposed a machine learning module with improved accuracy, which seems an excellent solution to detect security issues
2019	Dwivedi et al.	Storage attack	A decentralized privacy-preserving healthcare blockchain for IoT	The authors proposed a solution to break the data into blocks and perform crypt algorithms. This seems a costly solution that requires evaluation on real-world devices

(*continued*)

Table 5. (*continued*)

Year	Author	Threat	Solution	Critical analysis
2018	Rathore et al.	Exploit attack	Semi-supervised learning based distributed attack detection framework for IoT	The authors proposed a fog-based distributed solution that detects vulnerabilities, but it requires experiments on small and large-scale devices
2017	Kornfeld et al.	Cross-site scripting	Securing vulnerable home IoT devices with an in-hub security manager	The proposed solution works like a controller for all the IoT connected devices. Reporting about the specific vulnerability only is the good thing in the provided solution
2015	Li et al.	Malicious code attack	A hybrid malicious code detection method based on deep learning	The solution provides detection of the malicious code attack, which is simply malware or some other executable. It is an elegant solution
2013	Liu et al.	The ability to deal with mass data	A novel approach to IoT security based on immunology	The researchers proposed a dynamic solution that detects intruders by using the features and then takes action. It is a well-thought solution

(*continued*)

142   R. F. Ali et al.

Table 5. (*continued*)

Year	Author	Threat	Solution	Critical analysis
2017	Sohal et al.	Malicious insider attack	A cybersecurity framework to identify malicious edge device in fog computing and cloud-of things environments	The proposed solution detects malicious edge devices by analyzing their activity. Event-based detection is a good thing in an IoT environment
2018	Burn et al.	Exhaustion	Deep learning with dense random neural network for detecting attacks against IoT-connected home environments	The solution is based on deep learning that analyzes the packets, their route and the execution time. Although more features need to be added in this solution, it could be more efficient and accurate
2019	Takarabt et al.	Business logic attack	Cache-timing attacks still threaten IoT devices	Vulnerabilities in Low-level implementations of the devices or smartphones can lead to a potential attack. The authors proposed a solution to prevent them. It is a good idea to secure them at the very start

(*continued*)

Table 5. (*continued*)

Year	Author	Threat	Solution	Critical analysis
2018	Sharma et al.	Zero-day attack	A framework for mitigating zero-day attacks in IoT	The authors proposed a model that automatically updates the system when it needs it. That is a good solution, but if the user does not want the updates, there are no configurations available that need to be added
2017	Siby et al.	Malicious data	IoTScanner: detecting privacy threats in IoT neighborhoods	The proposed solution monitors different events performed by the devices and presents the data in visualizations. It could be better if the author provided the mitigation process as well
2019	Stiawan et al.	Brute force	Investigating brute force patterns in IoT network	The authors proposed a system for the identification of brute force attacks. These patterns are beneficial in diagnosing brute force attacks as well as avoiding them

(*continued*)

Table 5. (*continued*)

Year	Author	Threat	Solution	Critical analysis
2017	Siby et al.	Passive monitoring	IoTScanner: detecting privacy threats in IoT neighborhoods	The proposed solution monitors different events performed by the devices and presents the data in visualizations. It could be better if the author provided the mitigation process as well
2018	Brun et al.	Sleep deprivation attack	Deep learning with dense random neural network for detecting attacks against IoT-connected home environments	The proposed solution is a notification system that notifies the users about when a device consumes too much battery. It is a good idea, but vulnerabilities are not there
2019	Dwivedi et al.	Cloud security	A decentralized privacy-preserving healthcare blockchain for IoT	The provided solution helps secure the data on the cloud, but it seems costly and needs to be evaluated with medium-scale data for its effectiveness
2017	Siby et al.	Traffic analysis	IoTScanner: detecting privacy threats in IoT neighborhoods	The proposed solution monitors different events performed by the devices and presents the data in visualizations. It could be better if the author provided the mitigation process as well

(*continued*)

Table 5. (*continued*)

Year	Author	Threat	Solution	Critical analysis
2017	Rughoobur et al.	Replay attack	A lightweight replay attack detection framework for battery dependent IoT devices designed for healthcare	A framework is proposed that performs detection and mitigation of replay attacks. The provided solution is a complete package, but its evaluation at different scales is required
2018	HaddadPajouh et al.	Malware in IoT	A deep recurrent neural network based approach for internet of things malware threat hunting	Although the provided solutions are suitable for detecting replay attack based on battery consumption, it could be better if the author also provides the mitigation
2016	Sforzin et al.	DNS cache poisoning attack	RPiDS: Raspberry Pi IDS a fruitful intrusion detection system for IoT	The authors proposed a solution that includes designing a separate device that will handle the vulnerability detection process separately. It will be working in passive mode. It is a better solution
2016	Sforzin et al.	Man-in-the-middle attack	RPiDS: Raspberry Pi IDS a fruitful intrusion detection system for IoT	Same as above

(*continued*)

Table 5. (*continued*)

Year	Author	Threat	Solution	Critical analysis
2017	Thirumalai et al.	Lightweight cryptosystems and security protocols	Memory Efficient Multi Key (MEMK) generation scheme for secure transportation of sensitive data over cloud and IoT devices	The authors proposed a system that uses a traditional cryptosystem, but instead of using them in their full strength, the authors reduce their computational powers. Although the solution seems quite promising, its effectiveness needs to be judge thoroughly
2016	Pham et al.	Heterogeneous devices connect	Management architecture for heterogeneous	Security is a management problem. That is what the author did in his solution, but still, it requires improvement
2014	Ham et al.	Android malware	Linear SVM-based android malware detection for reliable IoT services	The provided solution is not very attractive because it is just ranking and detecting the malware
2016	Xu et al.	Eavesdropping	Security enhancement for IoT communications exposed to eavesdroppers with uncertain locations	The authors proposed a solution to validate the original users of the system. The proposed solution seems reasonably good, but its evaluation needs to be made at different scales

(*continued*)

Table 5. (*continued*)

Year	Author	Threat	Solution	Critical analysis
2017	Siby et al.	Node capture attack	IoTScanner: detecting privacy threats in IoT neighborhoods	The proposed solution monitors different events performed by the devices and presents the data in visualizations. It could be better if the author provided the mitigation process as well
2018	Rizal et al.	Fake node or malicious node	Network forensics for detecting flooding attack on Internet of Things (IoT) device	The authors proposed an excellent framework that detects the security issues and stops them from causing a threat
2019	Takarabt et al.	Timing attack	Cache-timing attacks still threaten IoT devices	Vulnerabilities in Low-level implementations of the devices or smartphones can lead to a potential attack. The authors proposed a solution to prevent them. It is a good idea to secure them at the very start
2018	Brun et al.	Denial of service (DoS) attack	Deep learning with dense random neural network for detecting attacks against IoT-connected home environments	The proposed solution is a notification system that notifies the users about when a device consumes too much battery. It is a good idea, but vulnerabilities are not there

(*continued*)

Table 5. (*continued*)

Year	Author	Threat	Solution	Critical analysis
2019	Dwivedi et al.	Storage attack	A decentralized privacy-preserving healthcare blockchain for IoT	The provided solution helps secure the data on the cloud, but it seems costly and needs to be evaluated with medium-scale data for its effectiveness

Rate Monitor; to analyze the battery usage by the IoT components involved. Replay Attack mitigation is done by only responding to the requests with a valid device Id and MAC address [16].

Malware in IoT [6] increased from 2015 and went beyond it. A well-known firm Kaspersky reported 120000 malware attacks in 2018. They also gave the reason for these attacks; the devices either had unpatched vulnerabilities or used default passwords. The solution to these malware's is mainly related to energy consumption patterns and OpCode. Authors in [17] proposed a framework that uses a deep learning model for IoT malware detection. Authors prepared a dataset, extracting Opcode, extracting features, classifying the threats, and then selecting the top 10 Opcodes targeted by the attackers. The accuracy of detection is relatively better than others [17].

Domain Name System or DNS works as the translator for the devices capable of connecting to the IoT framework for various services. IoT, as we know, has small storage and processing power, so DNS security models cannot be implemented. It poses threats like DNS Cache Poisoning and Man-In-The-Middle attacks [18, 19]. Authors in [20] proposed a device that can monitor traffic, logging regular and malicious traffic traces. The proposed solutions notify malicious traffic based on the system administrators' defined rules and packet sizes that are configurable.

IoT has small memory and processing power. That is why only lightweight crypto systems are used in this platform that attract the attackers' attention and invite threats because these solutions are not suited well [6]. Authors in [21] proposed a Memory Efficient Multi Multi-key generation scheme that helps secure information transmission between IoT devices and the cloud. The proposed scheme is based on RSA, which is asymmetric cryptography. The proposed scheme does not have a private key, so there is no need to calculate the inverse. The reason behind excluding the private key is the limitation of IoT devices.

IoT promotes connectivity among devices with heterogeneous nature, which is a good thing, but on the other hand, it poses threats. When many different types of devices connected to a network, it becomes difficult to manage such a network. Authors in [22] proposed a management framework for classifying the devices and managing the local operations on sensitive and sleepy devices. The authors validate the framework developing the Constrained Application Protocol device.

IoT devices are managed via smartphones that use various Operating Systems like Samsung/Huawei, or other brands made with Android-based cell phones. Similarly, the apple phone has its operating system. The number of android users is more than the apple users. A well-known android threat is detected on IoT devices called Android Malware that exploits the system and attempts to breach user privacy or gain personal information. Hackers have now started targeting mobile devices as well. The authors proposed a machine learning-based solution that uses a support vector machine to detect android malware as it is ranked higher among all other cell phone OS threats [23].

IoT is widely used in many areas like transportation, healthcare, markets, and others. It has the ability to connect various types of devices to multiple locations. Exposing the identity of the user, its privacy, or other information is unacceptable. Due to the ability of device-to-device, human-to-device, radio propagation makes the communication vulnerable to eavesdropping attacks. Authors in [24] have proposed a solution that detects eavesdropping by determining the distribution of eigenvalues of an original user of the system. The authors validate the solutions and claim that the proposed solution has a performance edge over all other existing solutions.

Ubiquitous communication in IoT devices is managed due to the heterogeneous devices connected to a platform. This way of communication leads to many threats, and node capturing is one of those attacks. The Authors proposed a solution for passive monitoring. According to the authors, this sort of attack will be passive, not active. The proposed solution is an IoTScanner that listens to the signals available in the network without performing anything. IoTScanner works as a traffic interceptor that continuously sends data to the server for processing, storage, and decision-making. It just captures the traffic and then visualizing the data in a meaningful way for decision making. Detection or protection is not part of the IoTScanner [25].

Connecting various devices, various integration standards in connected devices bring challenges to forensic investigation. Fake Node, Malicious Node or Node Tempering attack happens when a person (possibly a hacker) change/configure the device based on their intentions. As a result, the device will not work as expected and can threaten the whole system. The authors [26] propose a forensic model that not only detects Malicious node attacks but many others as well. The proposed solution logs the files of all the actions (legal and illegal) performed by the devices for investigation purposes that can also be imported in Wireshark [26].

IoT devices rely heavily on cryptographic systems for their confidentiality, availability, and integrity. When deploying such cryptosystems in real-time machines, the vulnerabilities begin to show, especially in IoT. These vulnerabilities are behavior-based, such as calculations, time consumption, and battery consummations that can trigger hints in the attacker's mind about the underlying implementations of the system. According to the authors in [27], some solutions were proposed in this regard: high-level countermeasures to prevent these attacks, but low-level residual leakage of such information still exists. The authors propose a methodology to identify the weaknesses in cryptographic system implementations that leak sensitive information.

Denial of Service (DOS), Denial of Sleep (also called sleep deprivation) attacks is flooding-type attacks where the device is flooded with requests until it stops responding and consumes all its energy (battery) to respond to these flooding requests. It is sometimes called an exhaustion attack as well. This can bring a lot of other attacks like Broadcast attacks, Replay attacks, and others. Authors in [28] have proposed a machine learning-based model that detects such attacks. It uses a dense random neural network with deep learning that inspects the packet and gives the probability of an attack.

The advancement in technology is very impressive on the one hand, and on the other hand, it also poses new security challenges to IoT. Attacking storage is one of a kind. Although data could be stored in databases deployed on the cloud, it can also be tempered or removed due to third-party involvement. The authors provide a mechanism to overcome this issue by storing the transactions in blocks, calculating their hash, and storing them. Hence, if any change is made to those blocks of data, then it can easily be tracked due to the hashing mechanism [19].

IoT systems are vulnerable to many vulnerabilities, including encryption, decryption mechanisms, intruding into the network, and flooding requests. Whenever an attack happens, it exploits the vulnerabilities found in the system because every attack targets some specific vulnerabilities and then exploits them. The Authors proposed a fog-based distributed attack detection mechanism for IoT. The proposed solution also solved the problem of labelled data in IoT. The author also suggests that the proposed framework can be enhanced via a deep learning algorithm for eliminating the manual assignment of features [29].

Malicious code is an application or executable developed by intruders/attackers to alter the system's functionality. Trojans, Viruses are types of such applications. These applications are getting smarter day by day, and it becomes difficult to detect and eliminate such applications from a layman system [30, 31]. Therefore, the authors in [32] have proposed a deep learning model that uses DBN to detect malicious code and AutoEncoder for data dimensionality reduction. Authors in [32] claim that the proposed model increases the correct detection rate when compared to other existing models.

IoT faces more problems than the typical networks do. Due to the nature of the IoT network, it becomes difficult to secure the network. There are many security issues in IoT, but none provides a dynamic solution. Authors in [33] have proposed such a system that will detect the danger in the system and react and mitigate that danger instantly. It first identifies the threats, applies rules of immunology. Thus, the proposed model secures the IoT in a novel way [33].

Decreasing latency in data generation and processing is called fog computing, enabling smart applications to continue their processing over network devices, including routers, switches, or gateways to cloud-enabled data centers. Outside attacks of the network are more accessible to detect than the attacks performed by insiders. The authors say that insider attack needs to be identified before they exploit any vulnerability in the system. So, the system will be secure. The authors in [34] proposed a framework based on Markov models for detecting such attacks.

If a vulnerability is detected in one of the IoT devices, it can expose the entire architecture to the attacker. A zero-day attack refers to the time between detecting and fixing the vulnerability, *i.e.,* antivirus updates or patching a solution to fix some problems. Meanwhile during finding the solution and fixing in the device can lead to exploits of many types. Zero-day attack varies from situation to situation. If identified by the ethical hackers, aka white hackers, they will not expose it until it got fixed. On the other hand, if bad people aka black hat hackers find this vulnerability, they will surely destroy the system. A context graph-based distributed diagnosis solution for classification of context was provided to identify the threat and notify the end-users about it [24].

Before providing a solution, it is better to understand a security concern from both perspectives *i.e.* from the client and the attacker perspectives. Authors in [30, 31, 35–39] emphasize attacker perspectives to understand how they choose their methods for scanning the vulnerability and tools to exploit those vulnerabilities. The authors investigated the patterns behind the brute force Dos/DDoS attacks and presented an idea about when these sorts of attacks will happen. Lastly, machine learning [40] and deep learning [41–43] have used in many field, and they have showed promising results in overcoming IoT security issues.

5   Conclusion and Future Directions

The main objective of this paper was to gather all the security issues reported in IoT. The classification of those security issues is also performed. After collecting all those reported issues, another research was conducted to understand how many solutions were available to tackle those security challenges. All the solutions were gathered and presented in Table 5.

Mainly provided solutions were addressing a single security issue. Although there were solutions that offer a complete framework for more than one security issue, those were mostly related to diagnosing or detecting these security issues. Only one solution is available that performs detection and mitigation of security issues at the complete time. The future direction of this work is to classify all the problems highlighted based on their severity levels and then provide an accumulated solution that will address those security issues based on severity.

Another critical point is related to the validation sections in all the solutions. None of the solutions were implemented in a real-time environment like in a safe home or in a safe city to be judged effectively. Another future direction is to implement the solution in a real-world IoT network.

References

1. Ashton, K.: That 'internet of things' thing. RFID J. **22**, 97–114 (2009)
2. Alqourabah, H., Muneer, A., Fati, S.M.: A smart fire detection system using IoT technology with automatic water sprinkler. Int. J. Electr. Comput. Eng. **11**, 2994–3002 (2021)
3. Shahzad, K., Shareef, K., Ali, R.F., Nawab, R.M.A., Abid, A.: Generating process model collection with diverse label and structural features. In: 2016 Sixth International Conference on Innovative Computing Technology (INTECH), pp. 644–649. IEEE (2016)
4. Chong, G., Zhihao, L., Yifeng, Y.: The research and implement of smart home system based on internet of things. In: 2011 International Conference on Electronics, Communications and Control (ICECC), pp. 2944–2947. IEEE (2011)
5. Zhang, C., Green, R.: Communication security in internet of thing: preventive measure and avoid DDoS attack over IoT network. In: Proceedings of the 18th Symposium on Communications & Networking, pp. 8–15 (2015)

6. Zhang, Z.-K., Cho, M.C.Y., Wang, C.-W., Hsu, C.-W., Chen, C.-K., Shieh, S.: IoT security: ongoing challenges and research opportunities. In: 2014 IEEE 7th International Conference on Service-Oriented Computing and Applications, pp. 230–234. IEEE (2014)

7. Zhao, K., Ge, L.: A survey on the internet of things security. In: 2013 Ninth International Conference on Computational Intelligence and Security, pp. 663–667. IEEE (2013)

8. Muneer, A., Fati, S.M., Fuddah, S.: Smart health monitoring system using IoT based smart fitness mirror. Telkomnika 18, 317–331 (2020)

9. Naseer, S., Ali, R.F., Muneer, A., Fati, S.M.: IAmideV-deep: valine amidation site prediction in proteins using deep learning and pseudo amino acid compositions. Symmetry (Basel) 13, 560 (2021)

10. Naseer, S., Ali, R.F., Fati, S.M., Muneer, A.: iNitroY-deep: computational identification of nitrotyrosine sites to supplement carcinogenesis studies using deep learning. IEEE Access 9, 73624–73640 (2021)

11. Alshohoumi, F., Sarrab, M., AlHamadani, A., Al-Abri, D.: Systematic review of existing IoT architectures security and privacy issues and concerns. Int. J. Adv. Comput. Sci. Appl. 10, 232–251 (2019)

12. Fati, S.M., Muneer, A., Mungur, D., Badawi, A.: Integrated health monitoring system using GSM and IoT. In: 2018 International Conference on Smart Computing and Electronic Enterprise (ICSCEE), pp. 1–7. IEEE (2018)

13. Muneer, A., Fati, S.M.: Automated health monitoring system using advanced technology. J. Inf. Technol. Res. 12, 104–132 (2019)

14. Qadri, I., Muneer, A., Fati, S.M.: Automatic robotic scanning and inspection mechanism for mines using IoT. In: IOP Conference Series: Materials Science and Engineering, p. 12001. IOP Publishing (2021)

15. Puthal, D., Nepal, S., Ranjan, R., Chen, J.: Threats to networking cloud and edge datacenters in the Internet of Things. IEEE Cloud Comput. 3, 64–71 (2016)

16. Rughoobur, P., Nagowah, L.: A lightweight replay attack detection framework for battery depended IoT devices designed for healthcare. In: 2017 International Conference on Infocom Technologies and Unmanned Systems (Trends and Future Directions) (ICTUS), pp. 811–817. IEEE (2017)

17. HaddadPajouh, H., Dehghantanha, A., Khayami, R., Choo, K.-K.R.: A deep recurrent neural network based approach for internet of things malware threat hunting. Futur. Gener. Comput. Syst. 85, 88–96 (2018)

18. Deogirikar, J., Vidhate, A.: Security attacks in IoT: a survey. In: 2017 International Conference on I-SMAC (IoT in Social, Mobile, Analytics and Cloud) (I-SMAC), pp. 32–37. IEEE (2017)

19. Dwivedi, A.D., Srivastava, G., Dhar, S., Singh, R.: A decentralized privacy-preserving healthcare blockchain for IoT. Sensors. 19, 326 (2019)

20. Alessandro, S., Felix, G., Mauro, C., Jens-Matthias, B.: Raspberry Pi IDS: a fruitful intrusion detection system for IoT. In: 2017 13th IEEE International Conference on Advanced and Trusted Computing (ATC 2016), pp. 1–9 (2016)

21. Thirumalai, C., Kar, H.: Memory efficient multi key (MEMK) generation scheme for secure transportation of sensitive data over cloud and IoT devices. In: 2017 Innovations in Power and Advanced Computing Technologies (i-PACT), pp. 1–6. IEEE (2017)

22. Pham, C., Lim, Y., Tan, Y.: Management architecture for heterogeneous IoT devices in home network. In: 2016 IEEE 5th Global Conference on Consumer Electronics, pp. 1–5. IEEE (2016)

23. Ham, H.-S., Kim, H.-H., Kim, M.-S., Choi, M.-J.: Linear SVM-based android malware detection for reliable IoT services. J. Appl. Math. 2014, 10p. (2014)

24. Sharma, V., Kim, J., Kwon, S., You, I., Lee, K., Yim, K.: A framework for mitigating zero-day attacks in IoT. arXiv Prepr. arXiv:1804.05549 (2018)

25. Siby, S., Maiti, R.R., Tippenhauer, N.O.: IoTScanner: detecting privacy threats in IoT neighborhoods. In: Proceedings of the 3rd ACM International Workshop on IoT Privacy, Trust, and Security, pp. 23–30 (2017)

26. Rizal, R., Riadi, I., Prayudi, Y.: Network forensics for detecting flooding attack on internet of things (IoT) device. Int. J. Cyber-Secur. Digit. Forensics 7, 382–390 (2018)

27. Takarabt, S., et al.: Cache-timing attacks still threaten IoT devices. In: Carlet, C., Guilley, S., Nitaj, A., Souidi, E. (eds.) C2SI 2019. LNCS, vol. 11445, pp. 13–30. Springer, Cham (2019). https://doi.org/10.1007/978-3-030-16458-4_2

28. Brun, O., Yin, Y., Gelenbe, E., Kadioglu, Y.M., Augusto-Gonzalez, J., Ramos, M.: Deep learning with dense random neural networks for detecting attacks against IoT-connected home environments. In: Gelenbe, E., et al. (eds.) Euro-CYBERSEC 2018. Communications in Computer and Information Science, vol. 821, pp. 79–89. Springer, Cham (2018). https://doi.org/10.1007/978-3-319-95189-8_8

29. Rathore, S., Park, J.H.: Semi-supervised learning based distributed attack detection framework for IoT. Appl. Soft Comput. 72, 79–89 (2018)

30. Ali, R.F., Dominic, P.D.D., Ali, S.E.A., Rehman, M., Sohail, A.: Information security behavior and information security policy compliance: a systematic literature review for identifying the transformation process from noncompliance to compliance. Appl. Sci. 11, 3383 (2021)

31. Dong, K., Ali, R.F., Dominic, P.D.D., Ali, S.E.A.: The effect of organizational information security climate on information security policy compliance: the mediating effect of social bonding towards healthcare nurses. Sustainability 13, 2800 (2021)

32. Li, Y., Ma, R., Jiao, R.: A hybrid malicious code detection method based on deep learning. Int. J. Secur. Its Appl. 9, 205–216 (2015)

33. Liu, C., Zhang, Y., Zhang, H.: A novel approach to IoT security based on immunology. In: 2013 Ninth International Conference on Computational Intelligence and Security, pp. 771–775. IEEE (2013)

34. Sohal, A.S., Sandhu, R., Sood, S.K., Chang, V.: A cybersecurity framework to identify malicious edge device in fog computing and cloud-of-things environments. Comput. Secur. 74, 340–354 (2018)

35. Ali, R.F., Dominic, P.D.D., Ali, K.: Organizational governance, social bonds and information security policy compliance: a perspective towards oil and gas employees. Sustainability 12, 8576 (2020)

36. Shahzad, K., et al.: A process model collection and gold standard correspondences for process model matching. IEEE Access 7, 30708–30723 (2019)

37. Ali, R.F., Dominic, P., Karunakaran, P.K.: Information security policy and compliance in oil and gas organizations—a pilot study. Solid State Technol. 63, 1275–1282 (2020)

38. Ali, R.F., Dominic, P.D.D., Ali, S.E.A., Naseer, S.: Information security behavior of IT professionals (role of polices and compliance). Solid State Technol. 63, 21601–21608 (2020)

39. Naseer, S., Faizan Ali, R., Dominic, P.D.D., Saleem, Y.: Learning representations of network traffic using deep neural networks for network anomaly detection: a perspective towards oil and gas IT infrastructures. Symmetry (Basel) 12, 1882 (2020)

40. Muneer, A., Fati, S.M.: A comparative analysis of machine learning techniques for cyberbullying detection on Twitter. Futur. Internet. 12, 187 (2020)

41. Naseer, S., Ali, R.F., Khan, Y.D., Dominic, P.D.D.: iGluK-deep: computational identification of lysine glutarylation sites using deep neural networks with general pseudo amino acid compositions. J. Biomol. Struct. Dyn. 1–14 (2021)

42. Muneer, A., Ali, R.F., Fati, S.M., Naseer, S.: COVID-19 recognition using self-supervised learning approach in three new computed tomography databases. J. Hunan Univ. Nat. Sci. 48, 227–234 (2021)

43. Muneer, A., Fati, S.M.: Efficient and automated herbs classification approach based on shape and texture features using deep learning. IEEE Access 8, 196747–196764 (2020)

44. Sivaraman, V., Gharakheili, H.H., Vishwanath, A., Boreli, R., Mehani, O.: Network-level security and privacy control for smart-home IoT devices. In: 2015 IEEE 11th International conference on wireless and mobile computing, networking and communications (WiMob), pp. 163–167. IEEE (2015)
45. Nawir, M., Amir, A., Yaakob, N., Lynn, O.B.: Internet of Things (IoT): taxonomy of security attacks. In: 2016 3rd International Conference on Electronic Design (ICED), pp. 321–326. IEEE (2016)
46. Conti, M., Dehghantanha, A., Franke, K., Watson, S.: Internet of things security and forensics: challenges and opportunities (2018)
47. Mahmoud, R., Yousuf, T., Aloul, F., Zualkernan, I.: Internet of Things (IoT) security: current status, challenges and prospective measures. In: 2015 10th International Conference for Internet Technology and Secured Transactions (ICITST), pp. 336–341. IEEE (2015)
48. Ahemd, M.M., Shah, M.A., Wahid, A.: IoT security: a layered approach for attacks & defenses. In: 2017 international conference on Communication Technologies (ComTech), pp. 104–110. IEEE (2017)
49. Ibrahim, A., Sadeghi, A.-R., Tsudik, G., Zeitouni, S.: DARPA: device attestation resilient to physical attacks. In: Proceedings of the 9th ACM Conference on Security & Privacy in Wireless and Mobile Networks, pp. 171–182 (2016)
50. ul Sami, I., Ahmad, M.B., Asif, M., Ullah, R.: DoS/DDoS detection for E-healthcare in Internet of Things. Int. J. Adv. Comput. Sci. Appl. 9, 297–300 (2018)
51. Arasteh, H., et al.: IoT-based smart cities: a survey. In: 2016 IEEE 16th International Conference on Environment and Electrical Engineering (EEEIC), pp. 1–6. IEEE (2016)
52. Palani, K., Holt, E., Smith, S.: Invisible and forgotten: zero-day blooms in the IoT. In: 2016 IEEE International Conference on Pervasive Computing and Communication Workshops (PerCom Workshops), pp. 1–6. IEEE (2016)
53. Vashi, S., Ram, J., Modi, J., Verma, S., Prakash, C.: Internet of Things (IoT): a vision, architectural elements, and security issues. In: 2017 International Conference on I-SMAC (IoT in Social, Mobile, Analytics and Cloud)(I-SMAC), pp. 492–496. IEEE (2017)
54. Al-Sarawi, S., Anbar, M., Alieyan, K., Alzubaidi, M.: Internet of Things (IoT) communication protocols. In: 2017 8th International Conference on Information Technology (ICIT), pp. 685–690. IEEE (2017)
55. Kolias, C., Kambourakis, G., Stavrou, A., Voas, J.: DDoS in the IoT: mirai and other botnets. Comput. (Long. Beach. Calif.) 50, 80–84 (2017)
56. Wurm, J., Hoang, K., Arias, O., Sadeghi, A.-R., Jin, Y.: Security analysis on consumer and industrial IoT devices. In: 2016 21st Asia and South Pacific Design Automation Conference (ASP-DAC), pp. 519–524. IEEE (2016)
57. Khan, M.A., Salah, K.: IoT security: review, blockchain solutions, and open challenges. Future Gener. Comput. Syst. 82, 395–411 (2018)

Pluggable Authentication Module Meets Identity-Based Identification

Jason Chia[1($\boxtimes$)], Ji-Jian Chin[2], and Sook-Chin Yip[1]

[1] Faculty of Engineering, Multimedia University Cyberjaya, 63100 Selangor, Malaysia
scyip@mmu.edu.my
[2] Faculty of Computing and Informatics, Multimedia University Cyberjaya,
63100 Selangor, Malaysia
jjchin@mmu.edu.my

Abstract. Pluggable authentication modules (PAMs) primarily provide authentication services to system software on a machine. PAM simplifies the job for both software developers and system administrators by providing a unified method to manage user access to the system. Therefore, software developers do not need to write user authentication subroutines because they can safely rely on well-studied and tested modules to provide the required services. The default authentication mechanism provided by PAM is password-based; while this is sufficient, the security is highly dependent on the strength of the password, which can vary based on the individual or the organization setting the associated password policies. To address this problem, we present an identity-based identification (IBI) module that works as a PAM, specifically for Linux-PAM. The security of the authentication mechanism provided by our work is only dependent on the fixed cryptographic strength of the user keys, which is generally much more secure than passwords. In addition, IBI also has comparatively simpler operations and provides easier ways to manage users compared to existing cryptographic alternatives.

Keywords: Access control · Linux security · Identity-based identification · Pluggable authentication modules · System administration

1 Pluggable Authentication Modules

Pluggable authentication modules (PAM) constitutes a unified authentication framework proposed under OSF-RFC 86.0 [1, 2]. It is an open framework supported by many operating systems such as GNU/Linux[1], FreeBSD, NetBSD, macOS, AIX

---

[1] GNU/Linux is often referred to as Linux, which is just the kernel of the operating system.

Supported by the Ministry of Higher Education of Malaysia through the Fundamental Research Grant Scheme under Grant FRGS/1/2019/ICT04/MMU/02/5.

© Springer Nature Singapore Pte Ltd. 2021
N. Abdullah et al. (Eds.): ACeS 2021, CCIS 1487, pp. 155–175, 2021.
https://doi.org/10.1007/978-981-16-8059-5_10

operating system, HP-UX, and Solaris. Modules in the PAM framework are implemented as dynamically loaded shared libraries which are used by the PAM library when a PAM-aware[2] application requests for authentication services [3].

The first PAM implementation is the Linux-PAM project in 1996 by Marc Ewing for the Red Hat Linux operating system and has been since maintained by Andrew Morgan [4]. Figure 1 shows the architecture of PAM and its relationship with system utilities and authentication mechanisms. Referring to the Fig. 1, Linux-PAM interfaces with system applications such as `login`, `sudo`, `ftp`, etc., through the PAM application programming interface (PAM API). The PAM API provides service functions (i.e., `pam_authenticate`) for the applications to use the authentication mechanism provided by the service modules. On the other end, PAM provides a service provider interface (PAM SPI) which enables authentication service providers (e.g., Kerberos, OAuth 2.0) to provide authentication mechanisms to PAM. Service providers implement service handlers (i.e., `pam_sm_authenticate`) which handles service calls by the PAM library whenever a user application invokes the corresponding service function [5].

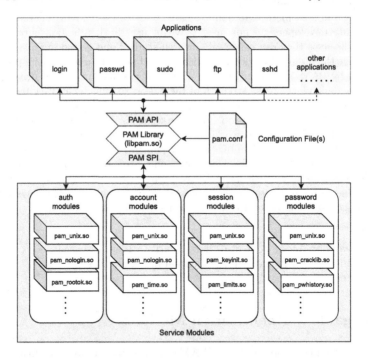

Fig. 1. An overview of the Linux-PAM framework.

As shown in Fig. 1, Linux-PAM breaks PAM into 4 service types: `auth`, `account`, `session`, and `password`. Each of the services are concerned with a different aspect of user authentication [6]. A detailed description of the 4 service types are provided as follows:

---

[2] An application using PAM for authentication.

- **auth** is responsible for authenticating the user. It also grants group membership or other privileges to the authenticating users.
- **account** is responsible for determining if the authenticated user should be granted access by checking for password aging, account expiration, and access time.
- **session** is responsible for setting up/tearing down the user authenticated sessions (e.g., activity logging, mounting directories).
- **password** updates the authentication token associated with the user.

Figure 1 also shows that a service type can be serviced by multiple service modules, with 3 example modules given for each of the service types. Additionally, a service module may also serve multiple service types. For example, the module **pam_unix.so** provides all 4 services, while **pam_nologin.so** provides **auth** and **account** services. The behavior of the PAM library is controlled by a configuration file **pam.conf**, which dictates which of the service module is responsible for the different types of services required by the applications.

Note that without the PAM approach, system application programmers would have to write their authentication subroutines. In addition, the system administrator is stuck with the limited list of authentication mechanisms provided by the application programmer. It is not an overstatement to say that Linux-PAM is the cornerstone to the security of the GNU/Linux distributions. Given the widespread use of the GNU/Linux operating system to run the massive amounts of servers powering the Internet [7,8], Linux-PAM thus also plays a crucial role in securing a significant portion of the infrastructure of the Internet.

2   Related Works

Table 1 shows an overview of common **auth** modules for PAM. We first notice that half of them rely on password-based authentication. The use of

Table 1. Overview of commonly available **auth** modules for PAM.

Module name	Mechanism	Setup requisite (optional)
pam_unix.so [4]	Password	-
pam_unix2.so [4]	Password	(NIS server)
pam_ldap.so [9]	Password, SASL	LDAP server
pam_krb5.so [10]	Password, Pre-shared keys	Kerberos KDC server
pam_sasl.so [11]	Based on SASL plugins	based on SASL plugins
OAuth2 [12–14]	Authentication token	OAuth2 identity provider
pam_yubico.so [15]	Yubikey specific mechanism	Yubico hardware security keys
pam_u2f.so [16]	FIDO U2F	FIDO U2F compliant hardware security keys
pam_pkcs11.so [17]	X.509 certificates	Public key infrastructure
pam_ussh.so [18]	SSH certificates	SSH certificate authority

password-based authentication is inherently not a bad thing. It is simple to configure and the majority of users are familiar with the concept of passwords. In addition, passwords are also cheaper to setup than other modules such as hardware security keys and digital certificates. However, password-based authentication mechanisms are not ideal as it has always been the easiest attack vector for attackers [19,20]. Password-based authentication is as secure as the password chosen by the users, which is always a tradeoff between usability and security; users are prone to make mistakes in handling their passwords [21–23].

The use of hardware security keys improves the security of password-based authentication, but it comes at a cost. These hardware tokens are well-made and typically cost US$30 to US$50 per piece. While the initial setup cost is relatively high for this method, the hardware security keys are built and tested to secure strong cryptographic keys on behalf of the user. It lowers the risk of attack through an account because it is significantly harder to crack such a device. Additionally, the cryptographic keys do not ever leave the hardware. In other words, one must physically possess the security key for authentication to succeed [24]. It is not easy for small and medium enterprises to finance equipping their employees with these security devices. It is even more difficult for an individual who may treat their online identity with nonchalance.

It leads us to the use of cryptographic keys that are stored on a disk. This approach has the benefit of a fixed security strength as compared to passwords. It is because the users do not have to bear high costs as compared to hardware security keys. It is the middle ground between the two approaches mentioned previously. However, we only found two readily available modules that are developed for Linux-PAM, which are the PKCS11 module [17] and Uber's SSH certificate modules [18]. These two cryptography-based modules use the notion of a digital certificate for user authentication. A digital certificate is a public key with identification information signed by another public-private key-pair [25,26]. This requires a fairly complicated setup known as a public key infrastructure (PKI), which consists of a certificate authority (CA) that effectively certifies the user's public keys in the system. The whole setup is configured to prevent attackers from misrepresenting as owners of random-looking keys, which is the basis for man-in-the-middle attacks [27]. Figure 2 illustrates the visual representation of how authentication is achieved through the use of digital certificates. Particularly steps 1–4 set up a certificate for Peggy (i.e., who wants to prove herself to Victor) while steps 6–7 allow Victor to ensure that Peggy indeed owns the public key which will be used by her during authentication, and is **NOT** the authentication process itself. Finally, step 8 authenticates that Peggy indeed possesses the secret key(s) corresponding to her verified public key. These processes that made up the interactions are complex and require high expertise to get it right; failing to perform one or more steps could lead to a vulnerability in the authentication procedure. This required expertise would also translate to a higher cost as PKI services are known to charge a considerable sum only to issue certificates, more so for a dedicated setup for large corporate networks.

The problems discussed in this section lead us to a question: *Is there a method of realizing an authentication module for PAM that is as secure as state-of-the-art cryptographic methods, yet remains low cost, simplistic and practical?* We answer this question positively with our work which utilizes identity-based identification (IBI) schemes and their hierarchical variants (HIBI) in PAM.

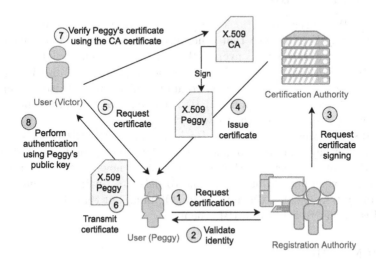

Fig. 2. Authentication using X.509 digital certificates.

3 Paper Organization and Our Contributions

The rest of this paper is organized as follows. Section 4 gives an introduction of the concept and the review on identity-based identification (IBI) literature along with the rationale of using it in PAM. Section 5 goes in-depth on the design and implementation of the module, followed with discussions in Sect. 6. Finally, we provide some concluding remarks in Sect. 7. In short, the main contributions of this paper are two-fold:

1. Investigation on the effectiveness of using IBI and HIBI as a pluggable `auth` module for PAM.
2. Software design and implementation of the IBI and HIBI module for PAM.

4 Identity-Based Identification (IBI)

Identity-based identification (IBI) is an identity-based cryptographic primitive that is first formalized by Kurosawa and Heng [28] and Bellare et al. in 2004 [29]. Identity-based cryptography was first conceived by Shamir in 1984 [30], where he presented a cryptographic scheme that uses the identity strings of users as their public keys. As a result, the verifier no longer needs to verify the public key first as it is already indicative of who the owner is. Identity-based cryptographic schemes require a trusted authority that resembles a certificate authority to issue user keys that corresponds to their identity strings. We refer users to read Bellare et al. [29] for in-depth information about IBI.

4.1   Literature on IBI

Research in IBI consists of various frameworks for design and security, such as a seminal work by Yang in 2008 that generalized construction of IBI schemes [31], and a generic transform to convert IBI with passive security into concurrent security by Fujioka et al. in 2012 [32]. Cryptographers have also investigated ad-hoc schemes arising from various computationally intractable assumptions [33–36]. More recently, we published two IBI schemes that are tightly secure against active attacks in our earlier works [37,38].

In 2018, Vangujar et al. proposed a hierarchical IBI (HIBI) scheme which allows the user key generator to delegate user key generation to trusted entities [39,40]. It creates a scenario that closely mimics how digital certificates are issued today, whereby a root CA is able to delegate certificate issuance to an intermediary CA. Besides, the authors in [40] found out that the security model of HIBI is similar to that of an IBI scheme.

4.2   PAM + IBI?

Here, we answer our research question: *Is there a method of realizing an authentication module for PAM that is as secure as the state-of-the-art cryptographic methods, yet remains low cost, simplistic and practical?*. We discover that IBI and HIBI schemes satisfy the requirements. Let's first tackle the question of *is it as secure as what state-of-the-art cryptographic methods have to offer*? IBI is built from the same building blocks (i.e., elliptic curve cryptography, big integers) as digital certificates. It also goes through the same rigorous processes as defined by the standards of modern cryptography, which includes precise definitions and security reduction proofs [41].

How about its simplicity and practicality in comparison with the use of digital certificates? As noted by Youngblood, the main argument in support of identity-based cryptography is that it removes the necessity for additional preparation (i.e., explicit verification of public key before authentication) before using the scheme [42]. It is visualized in Fig. 3: Peggy would like to authenticate herself to Victor. Steps 1–4 constitute the setup of the system similar to the case of digital certificates with reference to Fig. 2. However, steps 6–7 shown in Fig. 2 is not required with the case of IBI because the public key of Peggy is Peggy's identity. This eliminates the transmission of the X.509 certificate and verification of Peggy's public key by Victor. IBI has effectively moved the important task of verifying the public key upstream to be handled by the cryptographic protocol instead of handling it in an ad-hoc manner as it was done with digital certificates. Thus, IBI schemes are relatively simpler compared to the use of digital certificates [43].

In terms of practicality, our previous work showed how to implement IBI schemes using a well-known and high-speed elliptic curve known as Curve25519 [44]. The results indicated that the implemented IBI protocols can be deployed on lightweight credit-card-sized computers with practical run-time and memory efficiency. When we consider the setup and operating costs, setting up an IBI will be cheaper compared to PKI as it does not require certificate issuance, management and revocation. In terms of operating costs, the use of IBI will lower the network bandwidth, storage, and computational requirements because certificates need not be transmitted, stored, or verified.

Based on our discussions, it is obvious that IBI is an attractive candidate to be implemented for PAM. However, there are some notable disadvantages for IBI compared with digital certificates [43]. We briefly discuss a few of these drawbacks before we proceed to the design of our PAM for IBI:

1. Key escrow problem: Unlike conventional public key cryptography, users do not generate their keys. The key generation center (KGC) is responsible to generate all user keys. Thus, IBI suffers from what is known as the key-escrow problem.
2. Single point of failure: If the KGC is compromised, every user in the system must renew user keys. This argument also applies to the case of digital certificates when a CA is compromised, but the damage is less severe in the sense that only the certificates have to be revoked without renewing the private keys.
3. Identity corruption: When a user key is compromised, the user can never reuse the same identity because the attacker has the corresponding key to that identity. The user can only reuse the same identity if the KGC decides to renew the master keys. In other words, all users will also need to renew keys. Another solution proposed by Boneh and Franklin is to append an expiry date to the user identity [45]. Particularly, all users will need to renew their user keys periodically.

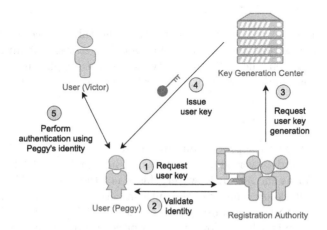

Fig. 3. Authentication using IBI.

5   Design and Implementation

In this section, we discuss the software design consideration and implementation of a PAM-IBI, pam_ibi.so. PAM-IBI is implemented using the C programming language as it is the direct approach used on Linux to compile shared object libraries. Figure 4 shows the software stack of the implementation. To incorporate the support of multiple IBI algorithms, which includes HIBI, an IBI library is developed to be used in the PAM implementation. The library provides a generic call interface based on the definition of the Kurosawa and Heng IBI model [28]. For example, MKGEN is implemented as a function that calls the lower layer cryptographic implementation for key generation of the desired IBI scheme. As for the interactive algorithms PROVE and VERIFY, the functions take in byte buffers unsigned char * and return the required responses based on a state structure. It decouples the library implementation from any transport mechanism, leaving that up to the application developer. It also enables further enhancement of PAM-IBI to support various kinds of remote authentication mechanisms.

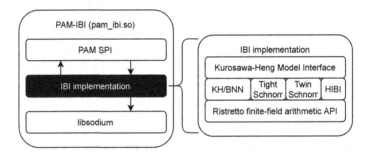

Fig. 4. Implementation stack for PAM-IBI.

As the goal of our module is authentication, the only service provider interface (SPI) callback that is relevant to this work is pam_sm_authenticate [46]. Libsodium[3] is chosen due to its maturity as a cryptographic library and the availability of basic arithmetic functions for Curve25519 over Ristretto [47].

5.1   Authentication Flow

Typically, Peggy (i.e., the prover) initiates a protocol with Victor (i.e., the verifier). In a standard server-client architecture, one would model Peggy as the client and Victor as the server. However, this is not the case for PAM. The user does not generally know when will the authentication process happens because this is always up to the software developer. Let's consider a useful Linux program known as sudo which allows users to perform operations as other users

---

[3] Libsodium is a fork of the popular NaCL written by Daniel Bernstein.

temporarily. sudo can be configured to keep the user authenticated for a certain period after a successful authentication attempt. It is a convenient feature because the user will not have to input their password multiple times when executing a sequence of sudo commands. Notice, in this case, it is up to sudo to decide *when* should it authenticate the user. Thus, we conclude that it is more suitable to model the authenticator as the client, which initiates the authentication process when it wants to authenticate the user.

Figure 5 shows how a user of the PAM-aware process can use PAM-IBI to authenticate a user on a local machine. The IBI agent acts on behalf of the user (i.e., who owns the process) to authenticate an IBI prover. The IBI agent is not part of the PAM-IBI stack but is part of the IBI suite that can be shipped together with the module for user convenience.

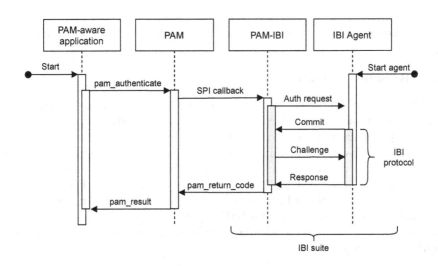

Fig. 5. Authentication mechanism with PAM-IBI.

Our design approach is similar to that of how SSH authenticates a user through password-less logins using agents. To log in to an SSH server using SSH keys, the user will first need to start a background process known as an SSH agent. The SSH agent is loaded with the user's SSH private key capable of performing digital signatures. The SSH agent listens on a local Unix socket, which is accessed by the SSH client to authenticate itself to the SSH server. The SSH agent is implemented as a socket server and attempts to authenticate itself whenever probed by the SSH client [48]. Figure 6 shows the SSH client-server interaction and the role of the SSH agent. It is a similar authentication architecture used by pam_ussh.so, which relies on an SSH agent to perform authentication on behalf of the user [18].

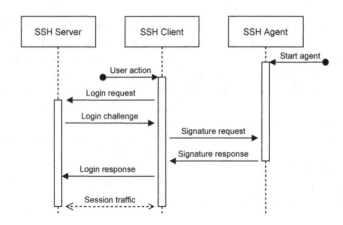

Fig. 6. An overview of SSH password-less authentication with SSH agent. The SSH agent method was used by Uber Technologies' pam_ussh.so for user authentication.

5.2 IBI Software Suite

PAM-IBI only covers the verification aspect of what we are trying to achieve. It is in line with the goal of PAM, which is to provide authentication services. For example, pam_unix.so does not handle Unix account creation, deletion, and password change. It merely provides its services to utilities that do the actual work (i.e., useradd, userdel, passwd). However, no utilities can set up IBI and issue user keys. Therefore, we cannot have a verification mechanism without providing methods to create user credentials! Unlike pam_ussh.so and pam_pkcs11.so, which can rely on SSH key generation utilities and openssl, respectively, to create user credentials; we must provide our own set of basic utilities in our implementation.

KGC Tool. The KGC tool provided as part of a command-line utility tool ghibc, boasts several functionalities for the system administrator: to generate master key-pairs, issue and validate user keys. Figure 8 shows how to setup master keys using the utility. The cat command is used to show the contents of the keys, which is base64 encoded. The keys are encrypted using a one-time pad (OTP) encryption scheme, shown in Fig. 7. Before encoding the bytes as base64, the utility tool first prompts a master passphrase and generates 16-byte salt. The passphrase and salt are fed into the scrypt208 with sha256 key derivation hashing function [49]. scrypt allows variable hash output length, which is suitable for our simple OTP encryption scheme. We fix the output size of scrypt such that an encryption key that is as long as the IBI key material is obtained. The process is then followed by a bitwise XOR encryption. We chose this method because the OTP encryption scheme is a simple and secure encryption scheme for short plain texts; in this work, the key materials are only roughly 64–160 bytes long depending on the IBI scheme that is used.

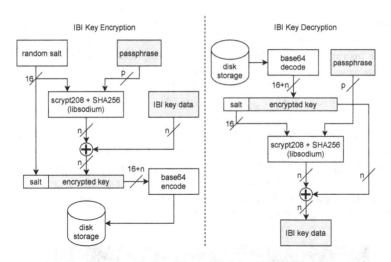

Fig. 7. OTP encryption scheme for IBI key storage (encrypt, decrypt).

```
user@machine: ghibc keygen -s master
Enter master passphrase:
Master key generated to files master and master.pub
user@machine: ls -la
total 16K
drwxr-xr-x 2                 4.0K Jun  2 00:49 .
drwxr-xr-x 3                 4.0K Jun  2 00:49 ..
-rw-r--r-- 1                  114 Jun  2 00:49 master
-rw-r--r-- 1                   49 Jun  2 00:49 master.pub
user@machine: cat master
AVhoANMsO2N/gQGZcCrhCnCFecaFu5/nlwUAI86IVqxqDZr/x0dLxns6ZZiaDzwUQDhWOkH844ps
QbSsU57ySPDQ41HPXXT9phO/EaVz/c/OTB0=
user@machine: cat master.pub
AAFwiooEuVc8pzSZHN7Li0ST85gUn7IfcIZBAqTNCnOFXA==
user@machine: |
```

Fig. 8. A series of commands demonstrating the KGC tool's key-generation function.

Figure 9 shows how user key issuance is performed using the utility tool. A system administrator would first need to enter the master passphrase, then enter the passphrase to encrypt the user key. The encryption uses the same OTP scheme as the encryption of the master secret keys.

```
user@machine: ghibc issue -s sk -u test.key -i test_user
Enter master passphrase:
Enter user passphrase:
User key for test_user: file test.key generated.
user@machine: |
```

Fig. 9. Issuing a user key using the KGC tool.

IBI Agent. The IBI agent we provide is a part of a command-line utility tool, ghibc. It takes in one argument that is the file path to the user key. When started, it prompts the user for a decryption passphrase used to derive the OTP decryption key. The decrypted key material is placed into a pointer location protected by sodium_malloc to be used in the IBI protocol.

The agent subsequently opens a Unix TCP socket on the user's home directory that is only readable by the user (i.e., with octal permission 0600) and performs authentication on behalf of the user. Figure 10 shows usage of the utility from the command line. Note that the behavior is similar to that of the SSH agent, which exports the authentication socket path and agent process ID when it is run from the terminal. Therefore, the IBI agent is the best run when a user physically logs in to the machine as one of the command shell initialization scripts (i.e., the .bashrc or .profile file).

```
user@machine: ghibc agent -u test.key
Enter user passphrase:
GHIBC_AUTH_SOCK=/home/        /.ghibc/agent.sock; export GHIBC_AUTH_SOCK;
GHIBC_AGENT_PID=200599; export GHIBC_AGENT_PID;
echo Agent pid 200599
```

Fig. 10. Running the IBI agent from the command-line.

5.3   IBI Key Structure

The master secret key (MSK) is used to issue user keys. For the HIBI scheme, it is used to issue the root user key, which can further issue lower-level keys. The MSK can be thought of as the private key of a digital signature scheme. However, the master public key (MPK) is more than a public key of a digital signature scheme; it is also the key used for all authentication procedures of the scheme. Thus, the MPK is more of a CA certificate and is a crucial component in setting up an IBI scheme. To support various IBI schemes in our implementation, the keys should also contain identification information about the protocol used. The following structure is used for both MSK and MPK:

```
typedef struct __ds_k {
        uint8_t an; //algorithm number
        uint8_t t; //key type (private/public)
        void *k; //key pointer
} ds_k_t;
```

The key pointer is assigned a *secure memory area* from calling sodium_malloc. It places an additional guard page and a canary[4] right before the pointer, which makes it less likely for sensitive data to be accessible [50]. In addition, calling sodium_free on the pointer would automatically zero out the contents of the pointed addresses. Due to the different key size requirements of different IBI

---

[4] A watched variable to indicate memory access violation or buffer overflow attacks.

schemes, the type void is used to allow the pointer to point to the different low-level cryptographic key structures. For instance, the following are two key structures for the Schnorr-IBI protocol [29] and Twin-Schnorr protocol [35]. It allows the key pointer to refer to the different structures easily.

```
struct __schnorr91_pk {
        unsigned char *A;
};
struct __schnorr91_sk {
        struct __schnorr91_pk *pub;
        unsigned char *a;
};
struct __twin15_pk {
        unsigned char *A;
        unsigned char *B2; //second base
};
struct __twin15_sk {
        unsigned char hf;
        struct __twin15_pk *pub;
        unsigned char *a1;
        unsigned char *a2;
};
```

The following is the structure for user keys. The user identity is stored on the key for the user's convenience to retrieve the corresponding identity of that key. Note that in the HIBI schemes, a user key can further hierarchically issue user keys. It complicates the structural design because one needs to store the current user's identity and all its ancestor keys to authenticate. In this work, we solve this problem by storing the ancestral identity on the low-level cryptographic implementation structure because it only exists in the HIBI schemes. It provides the benefit of dealing with the same key structure from a high-level perspective and simplifies design.

```
typedef struct __ibi_uk {
        uint8_t an; //algo type
        void *k; //key pointer
        size_t mlen;
        uint8_t *m; //user id
} ibi_u_t;
```

The structure of the low-level cryptographic key implementation for the HIBI scheme is shown below. The first byte is used to distinguish a hierarchical key, followed by the hierarchy level and the ancestral name (hn). The HIBI presented by Vangujar et al. is built using a Twin Schnorr which already has a key structure implemented in our scheme; for that reason, the HIBI contains an IBI key pointed by the void pointer. One may also notice that a public variable is also stored on the HIBI key. The reason for doing so is to ensure that the user only needs their user key for authentication without needing to keep the MPK.

```
struct __hibi19_uk {
        uint8_t hf;
        uint8_t hl; //hier level: 0-root
        uint8_t *A; //public variable
        size_t hnlen; //hier name length
        uint8_t *hn; //hier name
        void *d; //key (twin15 design)
};
```

5.4   Hierarchical IBI

The main reason for including a hierarchical IBI scheme in our work is to provide a feature that presents in the digital certificate authentication mechanism. Typically, a root CA, which is one with a self-signed certificate will delegate different portions of a domain to a different sub-CA, known as intermediate CAs. These allow a domain to be partitioned into multiple authorities, which resembles that of an organizational hierarchy. Fujioka et al. [39] and subsequently, Vangujar et al. presented a hierarchical version of IBI schemes. Our module pam_ibi.so supports HIBI using the scheme by Vangujar et al. [40].

Figure 11 shows an example of how the identities of the implemented HIBI relate with each other. Each identity is characterized by 3 components: its identity string ID, the ancestor name, and a fully qualified name (FQN). An FQN is formed by appending the ancestral name to the identity separated by a dot and performing key issuance using the ancestor's user key. Therefore, the master keys need not be involved. Instead of the identity string, the FQN is used during authentication. At the root level, the keys are identical to the conventional IBI scheme because they have no ancestors, and thus their FQN is their identity.

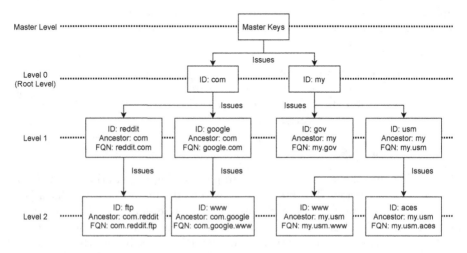

Fig. 11. An example of identities and their relations in an hierarchical IBI scheme. FQN: Fully qualified name.

6 Discussion

The implemented PAM `pam_ibi.so` is installed under the security directory (i.e., `/usr/lib/security` or `/lib/security`). Configuration is straight forward, with an example shown below for configuring `sudo` to use `pam_ibi.so` for authentication under the PAM configuration file for `sudo`, `/etc./pam.d/sudo`.

```
auth required pam_ibi.so /etc/ibi_mpk/master.pub
account include system-auth
session include system-auth
```

From an initial test run, the change causes authentication for `sudo` to fail if the user's IBI agent is not up started or the IBI agent does not possess the corresponding user key to their identity. This behavior is also similarly exhibited by `pam_ussh.so` and `pam_pkcs11.so`. Thus, `pam_ibi.so` is a good substitute for password authentication in Linux-PAM.

6.1 Setup Comparison

`pam_ibi.so` has an obvious advantage over digital certificate-based authentication mechanisms designed for PAMs because the system administrator can opt to use the user's Unix account name as their user key identities. In other words, when the PAM prompts for a username, the user can literally type their public key (i.e., identity) into the prompt, which is then authenticated by their IBI agent. It is not possible for digital certificates because the certificate is very long as shown in Fig. 12.

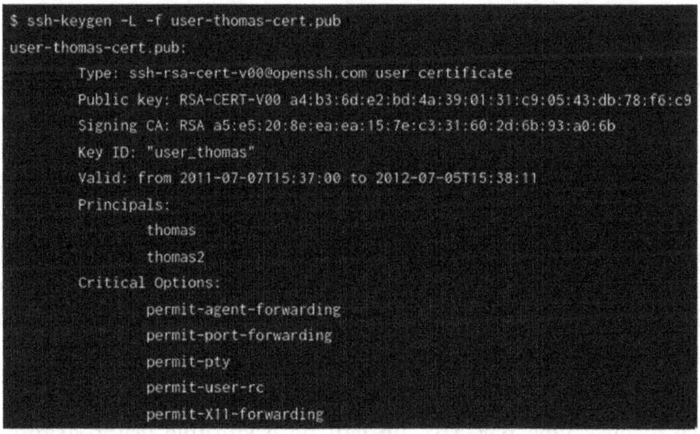

Fig. 12. Image source: https://blog.habets.se/2011/07/OpenSSH-certificates.html

In addition, generating such a certificate is also no simple feat. The user will first perform key-generation on their machine, then send the certificate signing request (in case of PKCS#11) or the public key (in case of SSH certificates) to a CA, and finally configuring their login agent to use the certificate. For PKCS#11 login mechanisms, the administrator has to set up a mapping between Unix accounts and their certificates[5].

6.2 Security Comparison

The security of pam_ibi.so is similar to pam_ussh.so and pam_pkcs11.so as they all provide cryptography-based authentication mechanisms. However, when compared to hardware security key modules such as pam_u2f.so, the users of these modules are relatively more secure than the on-disk storage method of the cryptographic modules. Mistakes made by the user (e.g., accidentally sending their unencrypted user keys over anonymous FTP transfers) can jeopardize their login security. It is not the case for hardware security keys because the user cannot physically make such a mistake as the cryptographic keys never leave the hardware module.

pam_ibi.so is not susceptible to dictionary attacks as compared to the password-based security module because its authentication mechanism is non-password-based. In terms of key security, the XOR encryption key generation method using random salt prevents specialized cracking attacks such as the rainbow table attacks.

Unlike the OAuth2 modules, pam_ibi.so does not rely on third parties to facilitate authentication. However, The OAuth2 approach is much more scalable when it handles a large group of machines. The same argument applies to pam_ussh.so, pam_pkcs11.so and pam_u2f.so. Nevertheless, we address this problem in the next section.

6.3 Recommended Use Cases

In Sect. 5.2, we point out that while pam_ibi.so can be used independently as an authentication module, it is best combined with existing access control mechanisms to augment the benefits it brings to the table. The main problem for cryptographic modules is that they do not offer access control policies as the higher-level protocols that change based on organizational sizes and requirements. Specifically, the cryptographic modules that we discussed cannot provide account and session type services out of the box. A possible method to address this issue is by the use of mature access control mechanisms such as LDAP or through the local account management provided by pam_unix.so.

LDAP. We discuss how pam_ibi.so can be a suitable cryptographic module candidate when it comes to integration with LDAP or pam_unix.so. As mentioned in Sect. 6.2, for pam_pkcs11.so to work with pam_unix.so for login, the administrator must configure a mapper file. It adds additional complexity to the

---

[5] See Sect. 3.2 "User Matching" on OpenSC's PAM PKCS#11 operation manual.

setup and could leave room for human error. Since `pam_ibi.so` has user identities as public keys, the KGC management policies are simplified as the issued keys can follow the LDAP directory names assigned to users without needing to configure a mapper file. It is important because PAM will cache the authenticated username after the `auth` service is achieved successfully. The cached username is used by the latter service types such as `account` and `session`, which is treated as the real identity of the user. Henceforth, a configuration oversight could lead to potential vulnerability.

Scalability. For a large number of nodes in a network, it becomes a challenge to manage the distribution of the MPK across the machines. It is the same problem for digital certificates as the CA certificate will also need to be distributed across the machines. A solution is to use `pam_ibi.so` with a network file system (NFS) to host the MPK on a network file server marked read-only, then configure the machines to mount the network file location and point the configuration file in the mounted path. This solution introduces a single point of failure, whereby if an attacker manages to replace the MPK on the NFS, they will be able to gain authentication over the entire network easily. We recommend using a containerized approach to this problem by deploying `pam_ibi.so` with frameworks such as Kubernetes. Thus, a successful MPK replacement on one of the nodes is still insufficient for the attacker to gain authentication on healthy nodes.

Multi-factor Authentication. Recently, Hamilton and Olmstead showed that PAM can be used to create multi-factor authentication schemes [51]. Their scenario involves using `pam_unix.so` and `pam_google_authenticator.so`[6] as a test case to provide authentication to access a running MySQL server instance. For increased security on mission-critical servers, `pam_ibi.so` is a simple yet effective candidate for second-factor authentication to complement password-based logins.

6.4   Storage Efficiency Comparison

The most practical aspect to compare the performance of the cryptographic modules would be the *key sizes*. Since our implementation uses Curve25519 that has equivalent 128-bit security, we shall compare the lower limits of the alternative PKCS11 and SSH certificate sizes using NIST key size recommendations [52]. Particularly, we will select the lowest possible key size for the respective implementations for performance comparisons. For PKCS11 certificates, ECDSA offers the lowest security key size using a 256-bit NIST curve. The keys and certificates are generated using `openssl` and measured using `wc` for the size of bytes. For SSH certificates, `ssh-keygen` is used to generate the keys and the algorithm `Ed25519` is used as the same primitive as our implementation (i.e., Curve25519). The key sizes were sampled using the `wc` command-line utility.

---

[6] The module is not mentioned in our survey as the developers maintain it as a demo project rather than an actual authentication use case.

The results are shown in Fig. 13 for storage size comparison, where user public indicates a X.509 certificate for pam_pkcs11.so, a SSH certificate for pam_ussh.so and the user identity for pam_ibi.so. Note that there is no lower limit for a user's public for IBI because the public key is the user's identity, which needs not be stored. Master public would indicate the CA certificate for pam_ussh.so and pam_pkcs11.so, or the MPK for pam_ibi.so. The result shows that foregoing certificates in favor of identity-based cryptography can lead to significant savings in storage requirements. The most significant saving is that user certificates are no longer required and thus eliminating the need to manage a certificate database.

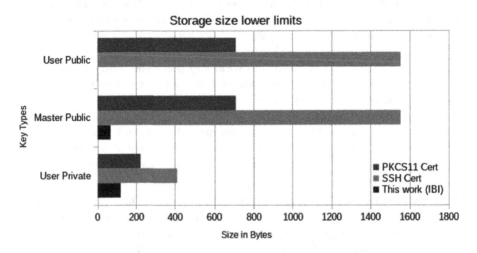

Fig. 13. Storage size comparison amongst the known cryptographic modules for PAM and our IBI implementation.

7 Conclusion

In this work, we have presented a pluggable module for PAM which works using IBI. We found the module to be highly efficient and convenient to be used by both system administrators and users. Therefore, we propose PAM-IBI as an alternative to existing cryptographic pluggable modules for PAM. While PAM-IBI can function as a standalone authentication module, it can enhance existing access control protocols such as LDAP. Using IBI, our result shows that it makes PAM relatively easier to configure compared to existing cryptographic alternatives, in addition to significant savings in key and certificate storage spaces.

Acknowledgments. The authors would like to acknowledge the support of the Ministry of Higher Education of Malaysia through the Fundamental Research Grant Scheme under Grant FRGS/1/2019/ICT04/MMU/02/5.

References

1. Samar, V., Schemers, R.: Unified login with pluggable authentication modules (PAM). RFC 86.0, Open Software Foundation, October 1995. https://opensource. apple.com/source/pam/pam-31/pam/doc/specs/rfc86.0.txt.auto.html
2. Samar, V.: Unified login with pluggable authentication modules (PAM). In: Proceedings of the 3rd ACM Conference on Computer and Communications Security, CCS 1996, New York, NY, USA, pp. 1–10. Association for Computing Machinery (1996). https://doi.org/10.1145/238168.238177
3. Garfinkel, S., Spafford, G., Schwartz, A.: Pluggable Authentication Modules, pp. 114–116. O'Reilly (2003)
4. Kukuk, T., Mráz, T., Levin, D.V., Morgan, A.G.: Pluggable authentication modules for Linux, December 1997. https://www.linuxjournal.com/article/2120. Accessed 1 Dec 1997
5. Geisshirt, K.: Pluggable Authentication Modules: The Definitive Guide to PAM for Linux SysAdmins and C Developers. Packt Publishing, Birmingham (2007)
6. Morgan, A.G., Kukuk, T.: The Linux-PAM system administrators' guide, August 2010. http://www.linux-pam.org/Linux-PAM-html/Linux-PAM_SAG.html
7. Comparison of the usage statistics of Linux vs. windows for websites. https://w3techs.com/technologies/comparison/os-linux,os-windows. Accessed 27 May 2021
8. OS/Linux distributions using Apache. https://secure1.securityspace.com/s_survey/data/man.202104/apacheos.html. Accessed 1 May 2021
9. PADL Software Pty Ltd: pam_ldap(1) Linux User's Manual (2000)
10. Cusack, F., Salomon, A., Allbery, R.: pam-krb5, March 2021. https://www.eyrie. org/~eagle/software/pam-krb5/
11. Mantova, V. (2013). http://www1.maths.leeds.ac.uk/~pmtvlm/pam-sasl.html. Accessed 23 July 2013
12. Kukushkin, A.: pam-oauth2 (2017). https://github.com/CyberDem0n/pam-oauth2
13. Velissek, O.: pam-oauth2-device (2018). https://github.com/ondrejvelisek/pam_oauth2_device
14. Motoki, S.: pam-exec-oauth2 (2017). https://github.com/shimt/pam-exec-oauth2
15. Lindfors, K., Josefsson, S., Thulin, F., S., H., Babioch, K.: pam-yubico (2008). https://github.com/Yubico/yubico-pam
16. Mauro, A.D., Martelletto, P., Michaelsson, L., Bierbaumer, B.: pam-u2f (2014). https://github.com/Yubico/pam-u2f
17. Strasser, M., Martinez, J.A.: pam_pkcs11(8) Linux User's Manual (2005)
18. Moody, P., Harrington, B., Shuffler, S.: pam-ussh (2018). https://github.com/uber/pam-ussh
19. Witts, J.: The top 5 biggest cyber security threats that small businesses face and how to stop them, May 2021. https://expertinsights.com/insights/the-top-5-biggest-cyber-security-threats-that-small-businesses-face-and-how-to-stop-them/
20. Tunggal, A.T.: What is an attack vector? 16 common attack vectors in 2021, May 2021. https://www.upguard.com/blog/attack-vector
21. Password security best practices in 2021, November 2020. https://www. swisscyberforum.com/blog/is-your-password-secure/
22. Most hacked passwords revealed as UK cyber survey exposes gaps in online security. National Cyber Security Centre, April 2019. https://www.ncsc.gov.uk/news/most-hacked-passwords-revealed-as-uk-cyber-survey-exposes-gaps-in-online-security

23. Swinhoe, D.: The 15 biggest data breaches of the 21st century. CSO, January 2021. https://www.csoonline.com/article/2130877/the-biggest-data-breaches-of-the-21st-century.html

24. Srinivas, S., Balfanz, D., Tiffany, E., Czeskis, A.: Universal 2nd factor (U2F) overview, April 2017. https://fidoalliance.org/specs/fido-u2f-v1.2-ps-20170411/fido-u2f-overview-v1.2-ps-20170411.html

25. Pkcs #11 v2.20: Cryptographic token interface standard. RSA Laboratories Public Key Cryptography Standards, June 2004

26. Igoe, K., Stebila, D.: X.509v3 Certificates for Secure Shell Authentication. RFC 6187, March 2011. https://rfc-editor.org/rfc/rfc6187.txt

27. Conti, M., Dragoni, N., Lesyk, V.: A survey of man in the middle attacks. IEEE Commun. Surv. Tutor. **18**, 1 (2016)

28. Kurosawa, K., Heng, S.-H.: From digital signature to ID-based identification/signature. In: Bao, F., Deng, R., Zhou, J. (eds.) PKC 2004. LNCS, vol. 2947, pp. 248–261. Springer, Heidelberg (2004). https://doi.org/10.1007/978-3-540-24632-9_18

29. Bellare, M., Namprempre, C., Neven, G.: Security proofs for identity-based identification and signature schemes. In: Cachin, C., Camenisch, J.L. (eds.) EUROCRYPT 2004. LNCS, vol. 3027, pp. 268–286. Springer, Heidelberg (2004). https://doi.org/10.1007/978-3-540-24676-3_17

30. Shamir, A.: Identity-based cryptosystems and signature schemes. In: Blakley, G.R., Chaum, D. (eds.) CRYPTO 1984. LNCS, vol. 196, pp. 47–53. Springer, Heidelberg (1985). https://doi.org/10.1007/3-540-39568-7_5

31. Yang, G., Chen, J., Wong, D.S., Deng, X., Wang, D.: A new framework for the design and analysis of identity-based identification schemes. Theoret. Comput. Sci. **407**(1), 370–388 (2008)

32. Fujioka, A., Saito, T., Xagawa, K.: Security enhancements by OR-proof in identity-based identification. In: Bao, F., Samarati, P., Zhou, J. (eds.) ACNS 2012. LNCS, vol. 7341, pp. 135–152. Springer, Heidelberg (2012). https://doi.org/10.1007/978-3-642-31284-7_9

33. Chin, J.-J., Heng, S.-H., Goi, B.-M.: An efficient and provable secure identity-based identification scheme in the standard model. In: Mjølsnes, S.F., Mauw, S., Katsikas, S.K. (eds.) EuroPKI 2008. LNCS, vol. 5057, pp. 60–73. Springer, Heidelberg (2008). https://doi.org/10.1007/978-3-540-69485-4_5

34. Tan, S.-Y., Heng, S.-H., Phan, R.C.-W., Goi, B.-M.: A variant of Schnorr identity-based identification scheme with tight reduction. In: Kim, T., et al. (eds.) FGIT 2011. LNCS, vol. 7105, pp. 361–370. Springer, Heidelberg (2011). https://doi.org/10.1007/978-3-642-27142-7_42

35. Chin, J.J., Tan, S.Y., Heng, S.H., Phan, R.: Twin-Schnorr: a security upgrade for the Schnorr identity-based identification scheme. Sci. World J. **2015**, 237514 (2015)

36. Chin, J.J., Tan, S.Y., Heng, S.H., Phan, R.C.W.: Twin-beth: security under active and concurrent attacks for the beth identity-based identification scheme. Cryptogr. Commun. **8**(4), 579–591 (2015)

37. Chia, J., Chin, J.: An identity based-identification scheme with tight security against active and concurrent adversaries. IEEE Access **8**, 61711–61725 (2020)

38. Chia, J., Chin, J.J., Yip, S.C.: A pairing-free identity-based identification scheme with tight security using modified-Schnorr signatures. Symmetry **13**(8) (2021). https://www.mdpi.com/2073-8994/13/8/1330

39. Fujioka, A., Saito, T., Xagawa, K.: Applicability of OR-proof techniques to hierarchical identity-based identification. In: Pieprzyk, J., Sadeghi, A.-R., Manulis, M. (eds.) CANS 2012. LNCS, vol. 7712, pp. 169–184. Springer, Heidelberg (2012). https://doi.org/10.1007/978-3-642-35404-5_14

40. Vangujar, A., Chin, J., Tan, S., Ng, T.: A hierarchical identity-based identification scheme without pairing. Malays. J. Math. Sci. **13**, 93–109 (2018)

41. Katz, J., Lindell, Y.: Introduction to Modern Cryptography, 2nd edn. Chapman & Hall/CRC, Boca Raton (2014)

42. Youngblood, C.: An introduction to identity-based cryptography, March 2005. https://courses.cs.washington.edu/courses/csep590/06wi/finalprojects/youngblood_csep590tu_final_paper.pdf

43. Bai, Q.-H.: Comparative research on two kinds of certification systems of the public key infrastructure (PKI) and the identity based encryption (IBE). In: Cross Strait Quad-Regional Radio Science and Wireless Technology Conference (CSQRWC), pp. 147–150, July 2012

44. Chia, J., Chin, J.-J., Yip, S.-C.: Evaluating pairing-free identity-based identification using curve25519. In: Anbar, M., Abdullah, N., Manickam, S. (eds.) ACeS 2020. CCIS, vol. 1347, pp. 179–193. Springer, Singapore (2021). https://doi.org/10.1007/978-981-33-6835-4_12

45. Boneh, D., Franklin, M.: Identity-based encryption from the Weil pairing. In: Kilian, J. (ed.) CRYPTO 2001. LNCS, vol. 2139, pp. 213–229. Springer, Heidelberg (2001). https://doi.org/10.1007/3-540-44647-8_13

46. Morgan, A.G., Kukuk, T.: The Linux-PAM module writers' guide, August 2010. http://www.linux-pam.org/Linux-PAM-html/Linux-PAM_MWG.html

47. Bernstein, D., Lange, T., Schwabe, P.: The security impact of a new cryptographic library. IACR Cryptology ePrint Archive 2011, 646, January 2011

48. Ylonen, T.: The secure shell (SSH) protocol architecture. RFC 4521, January 2006. https://www.rfc-editor.org/rfc/rfc4251.txt

49. Percival, C., Josefsson, S.: The scrypt Password-Based Key Derivation Function. RFC 7914, August 2016. https://rfc-editor.org/rfc/rfc7914.txt

50. Denis, F.: Secure memory, May 2018. https://libsodium.gitbook.io/doc/memory_management

51. Hamilton, C., Olmstead, A.: Database multi-factor authentication via pluggable authentication modules. In: 2017 12th International Conference for Internet Technology and Secured Transactions (ICITST), pp. 367–368 (2017)

52. Elaine, B.: Recommendation for Key Management, Part 1: General, 5th edn. U.S. Department of Commerce, National Institute of Standards and Technology (2020)

Using Knowledge Synthesis to Identify Multi-dimensional Risk Factors in IoT Assets

Gerard Ward[✉] ⓘ and Lech Janczewski ⓘ

University of Auckland, Auckland 1010, New Zealand
{gerard.ward,l.janczewski}@auckland.ac.nz

Abstract. The mass implementation of the Internet of Things (IoT) creates a new computing paradigm where ubiquitous networks of devices with embedded sensors and actuators support innovative business models. This research uses a combination of natural language processing and corpus linguistics techniques to support identification of the risk factors present in multi-dimensional industrial IoT assets (IIoT). The methods reviewed are found to streamline the manual stages traditionally associated with robust knowledge synthesis processes such as PRISMA. The methods explored can help decision makers and researchers to systematically identify trends and directions in the literature across the broad domain of IoT. The resulting findings can then contribute to risk management planning in what is an emerging and complex field, particularly the industrial use of IoT, and for which historic risk data is immature.

Keywords: Internet of Things (IoT) · Cybersecurity · Industrial Internet of Things (IIoT) · Industry 4.0 · Risk analysis · PRISMA · Natural language processing · Corpus linguistics · Knowledge synthesis · CIA Triad

1 Introduction

The Internet of Things (IoT) and its industrial variant, the Industrial IoT (IIoT) are information system and device paradigms that support new business models. These paradigms enable organisations to deterministically optimise the performance of process assets, and initiate new customer relationships. The literature abounds with use-cases of IIoT-enabled assets improving performance, reducing mundane tasks, limiting exposure to workplace hazards, and addressing declining work forces [1–6].

The technical characteristics of IoT systems are described as being things-orientated with a focus on identity and integration [7]. IoT systems rely extensively on the Internet, using Internet Protocol (IP)-based communications to enable wide network connectivity. Wide connectivity supports the scale and utilisation of data necessary to deliver real-time value [7]. The resulting benefits are considered to deliver business model agility through the provision of "real-time, high data volume, multilateral communication and interconnectedness between cyber-physical systems and people" [8]. In the era of IoT, this unrestrained vertical and horizontal flow of data across the enterprise represents a step change compared to the hierarchal data structures that have historically characterised

© Springer Nature Singapore Pte Ltd. 2021
N. Abdullah et al. (Eds.): ACeS 2021, CCIS 1487, pp. 176–197, 2021.
https://doi.org/10.1007/978-981-16-8059-5_11

information technology (IT) and operational technology (OT) systems. To support the optimisation of deterministic processes the IIoT ensemble extends its IT and OT cores by incorporating artificial intelligence (AI).

The layering of these technologies creates complex systems and gives rise to risk from differing technical cores being bound by the need for tight data integration. In the context of IIoT, risks are those factors that could disrupt IoT-dependent business processes, thus affecting the achievement of organisational objectives [9]. Therefore, risk management requires information that can inform the appropriate risk controls needed to maintain the normal operation of safety critical and data security critical systems, or reduce that risk profile to within acceptable limits.

One of the first stages in a risk assessment is identification [10, 11], not only of the enterprise assets and the associated business processes, but also the issues and risks particular to the classes of technology implemented. Therefore, there is a need to be able to analyse and categorise new classes of risk [12], for which historic information may be limited given that IoT and IIoT are new computing paradigms.

With regard to information system data, risk has traditionally been mapped against the critical data security objectives of confidentiality, integrity and availability, which information security practitioners refer to as the CIA Triad (CIA) [13]. Following the identification of data risks relevant to CIA, management will choose from risk controls categorised as escalate, avoid, mitigate, transfer, or accept [14]. Selection of an appropriate control strategy will be based on a considered evaluation of risk factors, organisational objectives, and the cost-benefit ratio of the available control options.

The question then arises as to how issues and risks particular to the data created and consumed in IIoT systems can be enumerated. This exploratory research undertakes knowledge synthesis [15] bound by the process discipline required in clinical medical trials to:

- Consider a novel adaptation of tools and techniques from natural language processing (NLP) and corpus linguistics.
- Complete a preliminary review of the directions in literature that address multi-dimensional data risk, which can assist future research.

To encapsulate the sequential use of NLP for semantic reduction (SR) and corpus linguistics analysis (CL) in this research, the label SRCL is used to describe the end-to-end reduction and evaluation processes.

Given the transformative impact on society that is predicted to result from IoT technologies, IoT and IIoT are referred to as Industry 4.0, the fourth industrial revolution [16]. This research uses the term IIoT to encapsulate the characteristics and benefits of Industry 4.0, which is also referred to as Industrie 4.0, I4.0, or IoT industrial assets. In terms of network data, Industry 4.0 is distinct from the Industry 3.0 data hierarchies that emerged during the 1970s to support IT and OT [16].

This exploratory research is structured as follows:

- Section 2 discusses risk management in the context of IIoT.
- Section 3 sets out the methods from NLP and corpus linguistics that are adapted to analyse two classes of IoT- and IIoT-related documentation.

- Section 4 discusses an IIoT reference model to elaborate the attributes of this new computing paradigm, and Sect. 5 analyses data risk in the context of the CIA Triad to illuminate specifics particular to the IIoT ensemble.
- Sections 6 and 7 present the findings and conclusions of this exploratory research to test whether semantic reduction and visualisation tools are an effective method for examining risk in the context of IIoT systems.

2   Review of the Issues Confronting IIoT Risk Management

For those enterprises where management has invested in IIoT, risk management is a vital part of ensuring that the firm can realise and maintain its benefits. The US government's Office of Management and Budget defines risk as "the effect of uncertainty on objectives" [17]. Risk management involves structured efforts directed at identifying and implementing appropriate controls to limit the exploitation of vulnerabilities that could otherwise prevent objectives from being achieved.

With regard to data, the ISO/IEC 27000 series, a set of IT-centric risk standards states that "the information security risk assessment process" needs "to identify risks associated with the loss of confidentiality, integrity and availability for information within the scope of the information security management system" [18]. These are the data risks encapsulated in the CIA Triad [13].

In setting out organisational risk management challenges regarding cyber resilience, the World Economic Forum (WEF) [19] urges firms to examine whether their risk management adequately accounts for the risks posed by IIoT, including enlarged attack surface; connectivity; supply chain risk; the internal risk management processes of monitoring; and best practice. In the context of CIA, system and data integrity must also be considered, as well as confidentiality and availability [19].

While risks can be positive [14], in this research risk is considered as a negative issue. Underlying negative risk are vulnerabilities that can be exploited by threat-actors, and the risk of latent defects that may be inadvertently triggered. Relative to a firm's risk appetite, risk exposure is checked using the risk controls set out in the introduction [14].

Illustrating the uptake of industrial IoT technologies, and therefore the need for IIoT data risk controls, Microsoft [20] conducted a survey in 2020 of 3,000 firms operating in energy, retail, manufacturing, and healthcare across the US, UK, Germany, France, China, and Japan. The survey indicated that 91% of respondents had implemented IoT projects incorporating AI directed at optimising productivity [20]. Also, IIoT projects implemented included predictive maintenance and edge computing strategies [20]. Edge computing refers to decentralised application data processing [21]. By processing data at the edge of a network close to physical processes, the volume of data requiring transmission across a wider area network is reduced [21].

The WEF [19] notes that with AI becoming more ubiquitous and sophisticated, the potential exists "to amplify existing risks or create new ones" as "IIoT connects billions of devices" [19]. Despite the increasing rate of adoption, IoT and IIoT are relatively new fields. The term IoT was only coined in 1999 by MIT to describe networks of ubiquitous sensors incorporated into real-time platforms [7]. The introduction to this research noted that such systems are multi-dimensional because of the tight integration of the different technical cores of IT, OT, and AI. The multidisciplinary nature of the ensemble means that considering risk across the system requires extensive consideration of business processes and technical factors. This research therefore examines state-of-the-art knowledge synthesis methods to determine whether SRCL can assist in the analysis of data security risk. The following research question (RQ) is proposed:

- RQ: How can the risk factors resulting from the integration of IIoT digital and physical processes be effectively and efficiently synthesised?

3   Research Method: Knowledge Synthesis

To understand how knowledge synthesis can support efficient, accurate, and reproducible analysis of the state of the art, this exploratory research adapts processes from NLP and corpus linguistics to approximate the robust standards required in health sciences. This methodology follows Design Science principles, whereby the building and evaluation of artefacts is designed to address specific needs in the pursuit of utility [22]. Specifically, it aims to develop a system that can support repeatable knowledge synthesis, and that can be used iteratively to extend the enumeration of risk as the pool of knowledge across the emergent and complex technical domain known as IIoT enlarges.

3.1   Extending Current Review Processes

Authoritative publications from the Centre for Reviews and Dissemination (CRD) [23] and the Cochrane Collaboration [24] prescribe research structures appropriate to medical clinical trials. Extending Cochrane, the preferred reporting items for systematic reviews (PRISMA) supports the systemisation and reproducibility of the research methods used [15]. The objective of the PRISMA statement covering reporting guidelines is to provide a "systematic approach to map evidence on a topic and identify main concepts, theories, sources, and knowledge gaps" [15]. In summary, PRISMA's objective is to direct systematic reviews to reduce risk resulting from the analysis of clinical trials.

Research in information technology is increasingly applying these frameworks to bring structure and rigour to systematic literature reviews. Recent examples of IoT-related literature reviews that used PRISMA canvassed use-cases including smart cities [25], agriculture [26], home medical devices [27], use in medical rehabilitation [28], privacy attacks on IoT systems [29], and reviewing vulnerabilities in IoT protocols [30]. Figure 1 illustrates the traditional funnel flow for processing literature as prescribed by PRISMA [24, 31].

However, in each of these examples the knowledge synthesis stage (Fig. 1 – 4. *Included*) still relies on manual processing. While the upfront use of broad Boolean search criteria (Fig. 1 – 1. *Identification*) to create a sub-set of literature from academic databases can assist the control of selection bias, the determination of relevance based on titles, abstracts, main contents, and conclusions ultimately requires manual evaluation.

In the context of risk management, bias is identified as the potential for inaccuracy because human judgment has a tendency to "misperceive and systematically underestimate risks" [32]. Given the scale of investment in IIoT, and the losses that could result if

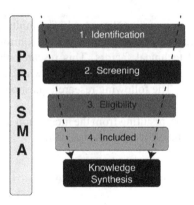

Fig. 1. PRISMA knowledge synthesis process stages

vulnerabilities are not adequately controlled, the next section sets out the methods that SRCL supports to bring greater fidelity to the process of knowledge synthesis, and thus reduce the risk of human-introduced misperception and under-estimation.

3.2 Datasets Used for Measurement

The authoritative data sources selected to create two corpora were:

1. ***Corpus A: IoT and IIoT Reference Models*** – to frame technical consideration the following resource documents are examined:

   - RAMI4.0 [33].
   - ITU-T Y.2060 - Overview of the Internet of things [34].
   - Industrial Internet Reference Architecture V 1.9 [35].
   - OpenFog Reference Architecture for Fog [36].

   These four documents are not an exhaustive list of IoT and IIoT reference models, but rather a set against which to measure directions in literature in this exploratory research.

2. ***Corpus B: Academic Literature*** – peer-reviewed articles in English were drawn from IEEE and Elsevier ScienceDirect. Being exploratory research, the literature set compromises 110 papers[1] published from 2020, with high-level generalised terminology used to ensure the identification of a broad selection of literature. The 110 papers selected were drawn randomly from the IEEE (10 papers) and ScienceDirect (100 papers) section results. Prior to analysis, the reference management software EndNote[2] was used to confirm that no duplicate research articles had been downloaded.

---

[1] A list of these 110 papers is available on request from the authors of this research. When directly cited, that paper is referenced within this research.

[2] endnote.com.

In selecting the 110 papers from literature, the Boolean criteria applied were "Industrial Internet of Things" or "IIoT" or "I4.0" or "Industry 4.0" or "Industrie 4.0" AND "risk management".

3.3 Semantic Reduction and Meta Data Methods (SRCL)

Final paper selection was not based solely on manual evaluation, thus differentiating the research method using SRCL from the six PRISMA-based research articles described in Sect. 3.1 [26–31]. In SRCL, identification of relevant knowledge uses frequency count and metadata visualisation to map the colocation of relevant keywords to other words in a topic-relevant corpus.

Semantics is defined as the study of meaning of language [37]. Semantic reduction in the context of this research is the process of being able to reduce the technical language to a more contextually rich form [38, 39] (the SR in SRCL). Corpus linguistics (the CL in SRCL) is the science of compiling and analysing collections of language to identify their nature, structure, and use [40].

For the first stage of SRCL processing, a tool was developed in Python with NLP capability to complete the semantic reduction [38]. In the semantic reduction stage, all content other than body text and commonly used words (such as if, but, and, of) were removed [38]. In this research all pronouns were also removed, and semantic reduction criteria were refined over numerous iterations until a further 23 terms were removed; e.g., vol, university, Wang, shown, Figure, Table, page.

Following semantic reduction, LancsBox, the corpus linguistics tool created by the University of Lancaster [41] to assist meta-analysis visualization was used to analyse the resulting corpora. Corpus linguistics undertakes lexico-grammatical analysis of all language elements in the corpus including commonly used words [42], which in this research were removed during the reduction (SR) stage. This approach differentiates the traditional application of corpus linguistics from the SRCL method.

3.4 Iterative Analysis

The iterative nature of SRCL approximates that of the Spiral Method [13], a project methodology. The Spiral Method (Spiral) is characterised by progressive and repeated analysis of projects to support systemisation and reproducibility, which are key objectives of Cochrane and PRISMA [24, 31]. These objectives resonate in the design of SRCL, given Spiral's use in "complex, high risk, and expensive" projects [13]. However, SRCL is intended to reduce the resource overhead associated with literature syntheses.

To contrast the processes prescribed under PRISMA [24, 31], where literature is processed through the four stages effectively in a funnel as illustrated in Fig. 1, Fig. 2 sets out the SRCL processes that approximate Spiral. Figure 2 shows that while the identification of literature is identical between the two processes, SRCL uses iterations to identify the themes and directions from the literature, until the researcher is satisfied that all themes have been explored and elaborated.

Table 1 shows that three of the literature reviews in *Other PRISMA Research* [27, 28, 30], which relied on manual evaluation, saw the average paper count reduce from 296 in

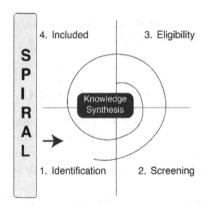

Fig. 2. SRCL knowledge synthesis process stages

the Identification stage to 96 in the Included stage, a reduction of 67.5%. In contrast, in Table 1, the column titled *SRCL* illustrates that the 110 papers used in this explanatory research remained in the corpus throughout; no matter what themes specific to IIoT the paper contained, relevance was identified during the SRCL evaluation stages. Relevance was measured based on the findings using meta data visualisation, which is presented in Sect. 6.

Table 1. Comparison of manual literature synthesis versus SRCL

Count of papers from literature	Other PRISMA research				SRCL
	[27]*	[28]*	[30]*	Average	
Identification	209	463	213	295	110
Screening	159	463	213	278	110
Eligibility	62	206	186	151	110
Included	41	159	88	96	110

*Citation with the papers and author(s) details set out in References.

A search of Google Scholar using the terms IoT, IIoT, risk assessment, NLP, and corpus linguistics listed approximately 18,000 results. However, a check of the top nine papers returned contained no reference to NLP, semantic reduction, or corpus linguistics. To the best of our knowledge, this research presents the first survey of the current state of IIoT risk management that uses the tools and techniques set out above. The only research using corpus linguistics (not including semantic reduction or bound by PRISMA), outside of traditional linguistics, that we identified was a literature review covering aquaculture [43].

The next section presents an IIoT reference model to provide context for the IIoT concepts when discussing the findings in Sect. 6.

4   The New Computing Paradigm (A Reference Model)

To explain the IIoT paradigm, and inform best practice, reference models have been created [33]. As an example, Fig. 3 shows the Reference Architecture Model Industrie 4.0 (RAMI4.0) published by the German national organisation for standardisation [33].

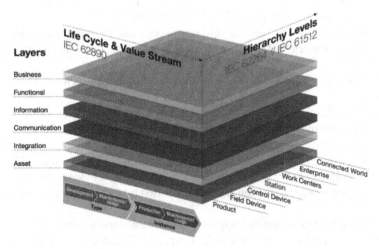

Fig. 3. Reference architecture model Industrie 4.0 (RAMI4.0)

RAMI4.0 incorporates the asset life cycle that approximates a factory-type IIoT use-case, and is set out to illustrate the multi-dimensional nature of physical and digital convergence present in the IIoT ensemble [44].

The levels and layers shown in Fig. 3 are summarised as:

1. *Life Cycle & Value Stream* are specific to the assets and the business processes that support manufacturing from product development to the product completion stage [33, 45].
2. *Hierarchy Levels* extends the traditional definitions of factory automation (IEC 62264 and IEC 61512) from just IT and OT systems to integrate IoT-type field devices, or larger ecosystems such as multiple factories [33, 45]. Many of the digital systems that integrate these OT components to provide feedback about the state of the processes are categorised as cyber physical systems (CPSs) [46]. CPSs incorporate an embedded system but with Internet connectivity [47] such that the CPS can integrate with other systems both vertically within the hierarchy, and horizontally with peer layer systems.
3. *Layers* refers to the intersection of the physical controls that integrate OT (physical control) with AI, and IT systems supporting the organisation's management. The functions that each layer encapsulates [33, 48] are summarised as:

   - *Business layer* – a wrapper that includes business models, strategic decisions, planning and procurement, legal and regulatory conditions, and the processes that orchestrate these commercial inputs.

- *Functional layer* – the runtime of technical processes.
- *Information layer* – event-driven tasks including pre-processing, rules, data analysis, and the quality assurance processes necessary to maintain data integrity [33].
- *Communication layer* – approximates the seven layers of the conceptual OSI data model to account for the communication stacks and data protocols adapted to, or that are specialist to, IoT and IIoT [33, 49].
- *Integration layer* – supports the transition from the "physical world to the information world" [33] e.g., a physical event triggers a virtual event in higher layers.
- *Asset layer* – the devices that control physical processes such as CPS.

For Industry 3.0-type OT systems, data security considerations are addressed under ISA-99, a reference model that includes definitions and metrics, policies and procedures, security requirements of systems, and components [50]. ISA-99 aligns with ISA-95 (IEC 62264) covering the interface between enterprise and control systems [51]. While RAMI4.0 is built upon ISA-95, in the Industry 4.0 era it is extended to provide for real-time and autonomous decision-making supported by CPS and Internet-routed data [48].

Highlighting ongoing threats against OT technologies, a report by Kaspersky Labs [52] ics-cert.kaspersky.com/media/Kaspersky-Threat-landscape-for-industrial-automation-systems-statistics-for-H2-2020-En.pdf states that the percentage of attacked industrial control systems (ICS) in the second half of 2020 was 33.4%, an increase of 0.85% compared to the first half of 2020. The enlarged IIoT network surface places greater reliance on the insecure routable Internet Protocol (IP) and IoT IP adapted protocols [49], increasing the number of possible attack vectors that a threat actor could exploit.

RAMI4.0 states that the need for security is an elementary aspect of IIoT, and needs to be defined across the three axes shown in Fig. 3 [33]. Furthermore, it emphasises that the "confidentiality, integrity of the data, functions and availability of the technical functionality must be ensured" [33]. While RAMI4.0 [33] sets out its aspirational data security state as a reference model for the risk factors inherent in the ensemble it describes, possible threat controls are not elaborated. Therefore, to better appraise the key differences in the technical cores of a generalised IIoT ensemble, the next section introduces the critical and competing information characteristics that are necessary to maintain safety-critical and data security-critical systems.

5   IIoT Data Risk

Alongside the references in RAMI4.0 [33] to security, stating that data must incorporate the critical data security characteristics of CIA, the influential National Institute of Standards and Technology (NIST) advocates that risk management analysis should weight the characteristics of CIA to identify and enumerate data vulnerabilities [53].

5.1 Critical IIoT Characteristics

While originally an IT construct, [54], the CIA Triad has been situationally modified to ensure its relevance to OT. As OT systems prioritise data availability and data integrity over confidentiality in support of process correctness [55], ISA-99 rotates the CIA to emphasise AIC (prioritise Availability, then Integrity, then Continentality) in support of safety and the quality of system performance [56]. Process correctness is vital for OT as failings in ICS that support assets such as critical infrastructure may not only risk injury or the loss of life, but also significant economic damage [57].

In autonomous IIoT ensembles, AI supports process determinism informed by real-time sensor data, which following analysis within the AI core, returns instruction sets to the actuators necessary to control physical movement. It is this presence of feedback loops that characterises CPSs in what are tightly integrated and highly coupled systems [58]. Therefore, to ensure process safety, AI should prioritise AIC in lockstep with OT to emphasise safety.

With data being the catalyst that integrates IIoT, the IEEE [21] notes that open data exchange across all elements of the business process is necessary for the success and accuracy of the value-creating process that IoT and IIoT business models support [21]. Open data exchange marks a big change in how data is being consumed under IIoT. Whereas in Industry 3.0 time-series data produced by OT systems was typically temporal, for IIoT business processes that data is now an enduring asset given IIoT is data-centric [59]. As a result, no ensemble-produced data should be discarded; rather it should be retained for future use, even if the future purpose is unclear at the date of creation. Given the volume of information that time-series data can account for, data lakes can be used as repositories for this structured and unstructured data at scale, and can be cloud hosted [60].

Therefore, data security will need to account for the confidentiality and integrity of this archived time-series data [61], particularly if it needs to inform greater accuracy in CPS algorithms, and machine learning (ML) in AI systems.

5.2 Primary and Secondary Risk

Elaborating the theme of data security critical considerations, the risks posed by failings in IoT and IIoT business processes can be a source of both primary and secondary loss. AI is a data-driven model reliant on accuracy and timelines, so primary loss can result from disruption to, or inaccuracy in, the data the AI algorithms consume.

The risk of secondary loss is present in data that may contain personally identifying information (PII). Failings in PII data management can result in significant financial sanction – an emerging class of data risk – given an increasing array of regulation. For example, in 2018 the European Parliament [62] data.europa.eu/eli/reg/2016/679/2016-05-04 introduced the General Data Protection Regulation (GDPR), which imposes significant fines for failing to secure PII [63]. Europe's cybersecurity legislation, the NIS Directive, compels essential services to ensure high system availability to reduce the risk of outage across the commercial sectors of utilities, healthcare, transportation, financial services, online marketplaces, search engines, and cloud providers [64]. Effective from

2020, California's IoT law requires manufacturers of IoT endpoints to ensure a minimum set of "security features" [65]. Failure to do so will result in punitive sanctions [65]. During 2021, the New York Privacy Act [66] was introduced, which requires data controllers to uphold a fiduciary duty to the individuals whose data they hold, which is effectively the same duty of care as that between doctors and patients [67].

Consideration of these secondary losses are highly relevant to IIoT when PII is present to facilitate interactions; e.g., in RAMI4.0-type use-cases, customers may be billed for products upon dispatch, or PII is present in HR systems that are integrated into the business layer [33].

6 Findings

The discussion of key findings is set out in two sub-sections. Section 6.1 discusses the consistency of process resulting from the use of SRCL; and Sect. 6.2 presents the synthesised themes and collocated concepts flowing from the anchor words in CIA.

6.1 Systemisation and Reproducibility

The process of semantic reduction satisfies an essential requirement of Cochrane and PRISMA [24, 31]; that robust research methodologies should incorporate pre-specified scientific designs that are reproducible.

Table 2 compares the pre-processed and post-SRCL word counts, to show that once the corpus is semantically conditioned, the total word count reduces by 47%. To meet the reproducibility requirements, it was essential that on the multiple occasions the SRCL processes were rerun against the corpora A and B source documents, the resulting words counts and results were identical across each iteration.

Table 2. Comparison of word counts pre and post SRCL processing.

Corpora references	Pre-semantic processing (words)	Following SRCL conditioning (words)	Reduction (%)	
A. Reference models	79,886	41,431	38,455	48%
B. Literature	1,035,669	544,999	490,670	47%
Total	**1,115,555**	**586,430**	**529,125**	**47%**

To illustrate how the SRCL process assists knowledge synthesis, Fig. 4 shows the keyword-in-context function from LancsBox [41], the software package used for dissection and analysis of corpora. The example in Fig. 4 shows a sample of 22 research articles that reference the anchor term *integrity* as per the CIA Triad. Bordered in blue is the name of the source document, which means the researcher can rapidly drill down to appraise that paper's themes.

For researchers, this SRCL approach means the anchor word's context and frequency of use informs a preliminary set of eligibility criteria (aligning with the Spiral shown in Fig. 2) to consider relevance for inclusion prior to completing knowledge synthesis.

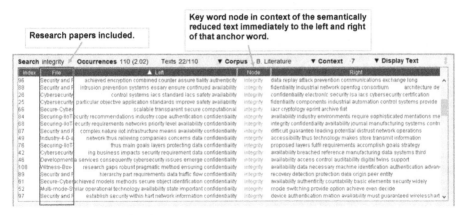

Fig. 4. Example of keyword-in-context search

As this research forms part of a program of research centered on IIoT risk management, SRCL will be used to update directions in the literature at key junctures in the program. Also, the use of SRCL means that the themes identified in the literature can be incrementally updated as new literature becomes available.

6.2 Knowledge Synthesis Examples

Figure 5 presents the visual analysis of Corpus A against the critical information characteristics of *confidentiality, integrity,* and *availability*; where the terms are applied as anchor words. Based on the colocation of the anchor words with concepts within the corpus, and within a defined word span subject to a minimum word frequency count, Fig. 5 shows the common collocate is *data*. For integrity, a key security consideration is *authentication*, and for availability it is the concept of *reliability*. Interestingly there are no comparable colocation themes emerging for confidentiality, particularly authentication, which is an implicit part of the IT-centric 27001 [18] series that controls the risk of unauthorised data access.

In Fig. 5, the presence of the term *fog* is unsurprising as the Corpus A document set includes a fog reference architecture [36]. Fog refers to decentralised computation located between the data source and cloud hosted environments [36], and is distinct from edge computing as discussed in Sect. 2.

Contrasting with Fig. 5, Fig. 6 shows CIA as anchor words in corpus B, which incorporates the exploratory 110 papers drawn from the current academic literature.

Elaborating themes, Fig. 6 shows additional concepts specific to CIA with the shared collocates including *loss; security; information* and *data*; as bordered in blue. Illustrating the application of SRCL in knowledge synthesis, to understand the relevance of the of the term *loss*, there are 203 references to the term across 36 of the 110 papers analysed.

References to *loss* include primary and secondary losses [68] as introduced in Sect. 5 of this research. Extending the risks introduced in Sects. 5.1 and 5.2, risk considerations

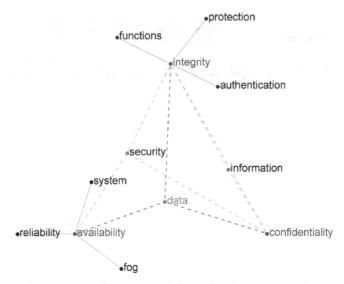

Fig. 5. Corpus A bound by the information characteristics of CIA

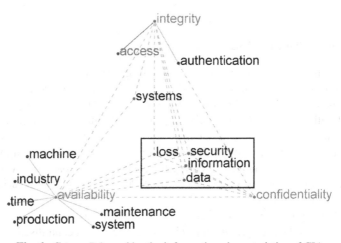

Fig. 6. Corpus B bound by the information characteristics of CIA

present in the literature consider the potential for diminution in an enterprise's competitive advantage following the negative financial and reputational impacts of IIoT asset failure [68]. This is relevant to controlling risk in the RAMI4.0 [33] business layer.

Other analysis considers *loss* avoidance by using AI in trainable generative adversarial networks (GAN) to identify threats against critical processes. The resulting taxonomy of GAN architectures [69] can help in the selection of appropriate risk controls relevant to the protection of critical processes in the functional, integration, and asset layers of RAMI4.0 [33]. AI is regarded as an essential part of IoT and IIoT initiatives [20].

Additionally, [70] proposes a data structure that enables the analysis of OT runtime data in ICS to support process sequence and coordinated sampling rates, thereby reducing errors. This will be important for process integrity across the functional, information, integration and assets layers in RAMI4.0 [33]. Also, time-series data was a key concept discussed in respect of safety critical process introduced in Sect. 5.1 covering primary risk.

From Fig. 6, another theme of interest is the extension of authentication from both corpora A and B, to include in B *access* (Fig. 7).

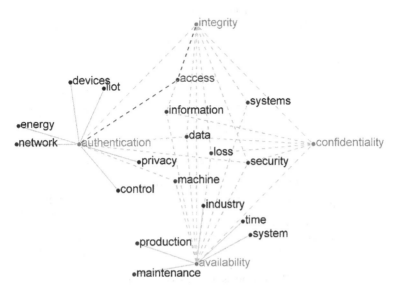

Fig. 7. Corpus B bound by CIA and authentication

In corpus B, access is referenced 539 times over 63 papers. Considerations specific to access applicable to RAMI4.0 included the asset layer's support for CPS fog nodes [71]. Establishing adequate trust relationships to facilitate access to third-party hosted fog and cloud data is vital to both safety-critical and data-critical sub-systems within the RAMI4.0 [33] hierarchy. This aligns with the characteristics of IIoT as noted in the introduction, in that IoT systems are focused on identity and integration [7]. Also, [71] notes the importance of ensuring data integrity for raw data stored in data lakes. Additionally, [71] discusses energy consumption given that robust authentication processes may impose additional computational load in resource-constrained edge devices, creating a risk in remotely deployed devices where physical replacement is challenging.

To help in maintaining data integrity, [72] discusses the use of secure objects that feature encrypted payloads, so that if CPS nodes or intermediary hosts are compromised, confidentiality and integrity are not threatened. Noting the requirements of availability and time critical as shown in Fig. 8, [72] advocates the use of defense-in-depth threat protections via network segmentation to improve performance. However, [72] does not analyse where such technical protections sit alongside the IEEE [21] concept of the open data exchange necessary for value creation. Nonetheless, encrypted payloads do control the confidentiality and integrity risk resulting from the enlarged network's surface reliance on insecure Internet-routed IP traffic [49] as referenced in Sect. 4.

These considerations illustrate the multi-dimensional risk that results from the integration of the IIoT technical cores to achieve real-time, high data volume, multi-layer interconnectedness between CPS, people, and processes [8].

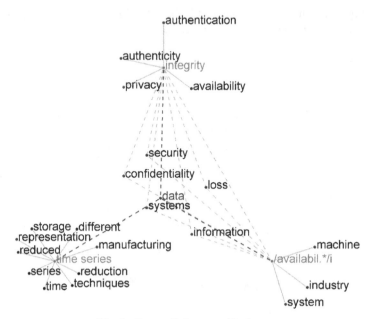

Fig. 8. Corpus B time-specific themes

The significance of *time* was discussed in Sect. 5.1, to synthesise relevant themes covering process accuracy. To synthesise this theme the anchor term *time-series* was introduced alongside integrity and availability in Fig. 8 (using a * wild card to capture the terms availability and availabilities). Relevant to the retrofitting of legacy industrial assets with IoT capability to support predictive maintenance, [73] identifies the data risks as data accuracy sufficient to train ML; the extent of data volumes required; and managing data latency and scalability where network bandwidth constraints exist, providing another example of multi-dimensional risk considerations.

Demonstrating the specificity of IIoT fault detection, [74] discusses the use of neural networks (a key algorithmic technique in AI) in the diagnosis of machine bearing faults. Illustrating knowledge synthesis, in Fig. 8, *manufacturing* and *machine* share a collocated node. Additionally, [74] notes that while predictive accuracy needs to be high, there is a desire to reduce data storage requirements. Elaborating that theme, [75] proposes a novel architecture that reduces time-series dimensionality to accommodate the high concurrency throughput and writing of data to disk, but only requires low read rates for data archived in data lakes. This may represent a risk control for issues related to the storage of data en mass as introduced in Sect. 5.1, provided it satisfies the future data integrity considerations implicit in the RAMI4.0 [33]. Also, reducing storage requirements [74] helps with cost management, since data lakes are offered as hosted services based on volumetric charging by third-party providers including Microsoft Azure, AWS, IBM and Cortex.

Finally, Fig. 9 examines references to the anchor term *risk management*, which framed part of the Boolean literature criteria in the PRISMA identification stage (Fig. 1). Collocates include *legal*, with 117 references across 125 of the 110 papers sampled. Considering the legal risk [76] brings more specificity to the legal considerations in the sub-components of the technical cores of IT, OT, and AI. For example, [76] elaborates legal risk in the cloud, big data, and CPS [76]. This helps in the identification of possible regulatory risk. Other legal considerations include German enterprises reshoring production facilities [77] and poor government policy frameworks [78]. The need to ensure themes are current is illustrated by corpus A only setting out two generalised references to legal issues: general regulatory [33]; licenses and patents [35].

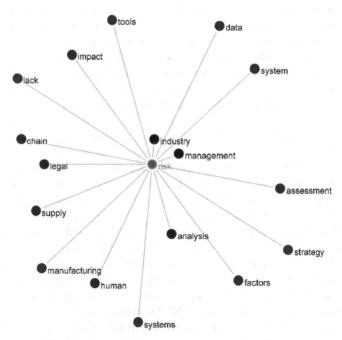

Fig. 9. Corpus B risk management-specific collocates

This section has discussed the findings of the SRCL knowledge synthesis to show examples of interrelated risk themes that reflect the nature of IIoT multi-dimensional integration. The next section presents the conclusions of this research.

7 Conclusion and Implications

Industrial IoT and IIoT represent comparatively new information system paradigms that address asset optimisation, among other business drivers. Although research covering IIoT is extensive, since it is by design a multi-dimensional layering of different technologies with differing priorities, considering risk across these ensembles is challenging. The WEF [19] notes the challenge of risk management given the enlarged network surface and multi-dimensional integration that characterises IIoT. Additionally, the historic data that often informs risk controls is immature given the relative newness of IoT and IIoT, and continuing system innovation.

To address the research question of what methods could support knowledge synthesis, a novel adaption of NLP and corpus linguistics processes was incorporated into the SRCL's processes and tested. While exploratory, the research findings suggest that SRCL's spiral process flow satisfies PRISMA's requirement for systemised and reproducible knowledge synthesis processes. SRCL was found to do so efficiently and effectively, thereby also satisfying the utility of artefact criteria associated with Design Science. In addition, SRCL was aided by the capability to visually map themes across iterative analysis. This will also enable the concepts in comparatively more static reference models (corpus A) to be refreshed as new considerations in the literature (corpus B) emerge. The practical importance of this research is thus the exploration of a high-utility method that can reduce the need for manual, and potentially subjective, screening of relevant literature when undertaking systematic literature reviews.

This research found that identifying a whole ensemble set of IIoT risk factors requires substantial effort. Therefore, any method that can assist the integration of themes in literature is desirable. For example, the collection and future use of time-series data involves considerations beyond those specific to the related disciplines of OT, IT, and big data analysis. Furthermore, as much of an IIoT system's data may be hosted in the cloud by third parties, the considerations related to trust relationships and secondary losses become increasingly significant. While the issues flowing from the retrofitting of industrial IoT to legacy process assets were only touched on in this research, it may be that the risk considerations flowing from retrofits differ from the risk issues arising in a greenfield IIoT implementation. The risk factors identified will inform future work in a program focused on IIoT risk management. Having a consistent risk factor baseline may help reduce the bias risk [32] with regard to underestimating threats.

While exploratory, the combination of NLP, semantic reduction, and corpus linguistics is expected to provide a valuable contribution to risk practitioners and researchers alike. A knowledge synthesis method that can support more rapid yet detailed analysis of risk themes in the emergent domain of IIoT will help the consideration and currency of appropriate risk controls.

References

1. NASA. https://spinoff.nasa.gov/Spinoff2019/pdf/Spinoff508_2019.pdf. Accessed 1 Mar 2020
2. PortEconomics. https://www.porteconomics.eu/the-impact-of-emerging-digital-technolog ies-on-logistics-centres-business-models/. Accessed 22 Mar 2020

3. Shah, S.: https://www.ft.com/content/12bea95d-2171-4619-a483-1cf7ec306be9. Accessed 12 Apr 2020
4. Hastie, H.: https://www.smh.com.au/business/companies/no-more-training-wheels-rio-tinto-launches-world-s-biggest-robot-20190614-p51xxj.html. Accessed 15 Mar 2020
5. Paris, C.: https://www.wsj.com/articles/rules-for-robot-cargo-ships-could-be-years-away-regulator-says-11559843777. Accessed 20 Nov 2019
6. Gapper, J.: https://www.ft.com/content/c895c9ef-ebec-4fa1-a048-082382194c70. Accessed 27 June 2021
7. Borgia, E.: Review: the Internet of Things vision: key features, applications and open issues. Comput. Commun. **54**, 1–31 (2014). https://doi.org/10.1016/j.comcom.2014.09.008
8. Schuh, G., Anderl, R., Dumitrescu, R., Krüger, A., ten Hompel, M.: Industrie 4.0 maturity index. Managing the digital transformation of companies – UPDATE 2020. acatech National Academy of Science and Engineering (2020). https://www.acatech.de/publikation/industrie-4-0-maturity-index-update-2020/download-pdf/?lang=en
9. Hopkin, P.: Fundamentals of Risk Management: Understanding, Evaluating and Implementing Effective Risk Management. Kogan Page, London (2018)
10. British Standards: BS ISO/IEC 27003:2017 Information technology. Security techniques. Information security management systems. Guidance. BSI Standards Limited, Gunnersbury, London (2017)
11. British Standards: BS EN ISO/IEC 27000:2017 Information technology. Security techniques. Information security management systems. Overview and vocabulary. BSI Standards Limited, Gunnersbury, London (2017)
12. Radanliev, P., De Roure, D., Nurse, J., Montalvo, R.M., Burnap, P.: Standardisation of cyber risk impact assessment for the Internet of Things (IoT) (2019). https://doi.org/10.13140/RG.2.2.27903.05280
13. Warsinke, J.: CISSP: Certified Information Systems Security Professional. Wiley, Hoboken (2019)
14. Project Management Institute: A Guide to the Project Management Body of Knowledge (PMBOK Guide) - Sixth Edition. Project Management Institute, Newtown Square, Pennsylvania (2017)
15. Tricco, A.C., et al.: PRISMA extension for scoping reviews (PRISMA-ScR): checklist and explanation. Ann. Intern. Med. **169**, 467–473 (2018). https://doi.org/10.7326/m18-0850
16. Henning, K., Wahlster, W., Helbig, J.: Recommendations for implementing the strategic initiative INDUSTRIE 4.0. German Academy of Science and Engineering (2013). https://www.din.de/blob/76902/e8cac883f42bf28536e7e8165993f1fd/recommendations-for-implementing-industry-4-0-data.pdf
17. Office of Management and Budget: Circular No. A-11 l Preparation, Submission, And Execution of the Budget. Executive Office of the President. U.S. Department of Commerce, Washington, DC (2016). https://obamawhitehouse.archives.gov/sites/default/files/omb/assets/a11_current_year/a11_2016.pdf
18. British Standards: BS ISO/IEC 27001:2005 Information technology—Security techniques—Information security management systems—Requirements. BSI Standards Limited, London (2005)
19. World Economic Forum: Advancing Cyber Resilience in Aviation: An Industry Analysis. World Economic Forum (2020). https://www.weforum.org/whitepapers/advancing-cyber-resilience-in-aviation-an-industry-analysis
20. Microsoft: IoT Signals (2020). https://azure.microsoft.com/mediahandler/files/resourcefiles/iot-signals/IoT%20Signals_Edition%202_English.pdf. Accessed 5 June 2021
21. IEEE: Standard for Adoption of OpenFog Reference Architecture for Fog Computing. IEEE Std 1934-2018, pp. 1–176 (2018). https://doi.org/10.1109/IEEESTD.2018.8423800

22. Hevner, A.R., March, S.T., Park, J., Ram, S.: Design science in information systems research. MIS Q. **25**, 75–105 (2004). https://doi.org/10.2307/25148625
23. Centre for Reviews and Dissemination: Systematic reviews: CRD's guidance for undertaking reviews in health care. University of York, York (2009)
24. Higgins, J.P.T., Cochrane Collaboration, i.b.: Cochrane Handbook for Systematic Reviews of Interventions. Wiley, Hoboken (2019)
25. Adiyarta, K., Napitupulu, D., Syafrullah, M., Mahdiana, D., Rusdah, R.: Analysis of smart city indicators based on prisma: systematic review. IOP Conf. Ser. Mater. Sci. Eng. **725**, 012113 (2020). https://doi.org/10.1088/1757-899x/725/1/012113
26. Navarro, E., Costa, N., Pereira, A.: A systematic review of IoT solutions for smart farming. Sensors **20**, 4231 (2020). https://doi.org/10.3390/s20154231
27. Thongprasert, A., Jiamsanguanwong, A.: New product development processes for IOT-enabled home use medical devices: a systematic review. Eng. J. **25**(2), 15–48 (2021). https://doi.org/10.4186/ej.2021.25.2.15
28. Gradim, L.C.C., José, M.A., Cruz, D.M.C.d., Lopes, R.d.D.: IoT services and applications in rehabilitation: an interdisciplinary and meta-analysis review. IEEE Trans. Neural Syst. Rehab. Eng. **28**, 2043–2052 (2020). https://doi.org/ https://doi.org/10.1109/TNSRE.2020.3005616
29. Zagi, L.M., Aziz, B.: Privacy attack on IoT: a systematic literature review. In: 2020 International Conference on ICT for Smart Society (ICISS), Manhattan, pp. 1–8. IEEE (2020)
30. Torres, N., Pinto, P., Lopes, S.I.: Security vulnerabilities in LPWANs—an attack vector analysis for the IoT ecosystem. Appl. Sci. **11**, 3176 (2021). https://www.mdpi.com/2076-3417/11/7/3176
31. Nawijn, F., Ham, W.H.W., Houwert, R.M., Groenwold, R.H.H., Hietbrink, F., Smeeing, D.P.J.: Quality of reporting of systematic reviews and meta-analyses in emergency medicine based on the PRISMA statement. BMC Emerg. Med. **19**, 19 (2019). https://doi.org/10.1186/s12873-019-0233-6
32. Hubbard, D.: The Failure of Risk Management: Why It's Broken and How to Fix It. Wiley, Hoboken (2020)
33. Deutsches Institut für Normung: Architecture Model Industrie 4.0 (RAMI4.0). DIN SPEC 91345:2016-04. Deutsches Institut für Normung, Berlin (2016)
34. International Telecommunication Union: Overview of the Internet of Things. Telecommunication Standardization Sector. ITU-T Y.2060. International Telecommunication Union, Geneva (2012)
35. Industrial Internet Consortium: The Industrial Internet of Things - Volume G1: Reference Architecture. IIC:PUB:G1:V1.80:20170131. Industrial Internet Consortium, Milford, MA (2019)
36. Industrial Internet Consortium: OpenFog Reference Architecture for Fog Computing. OPFRA001.020817. OpenFog Consortium Architecture Working Group (2017). https://site.ieee.org/denver-com/files/2017/06/OpenFog_Reference_Architecture_2_09_17-FINAL-1.pdf
37. University of Sheffield, All about linguistics: what does semantics study? https://all-about-linguistics.group.shef.ac.uk/branches-of-linguistics/semantics/what-does-semantics-study
38. Antony, B.: Developing cybersecurity capability forensic risk modelling for the internet of things. School of Engineering, Computer and Mathematical Sciences, Ph.D. thesis, Auckland University of Technology, Auckland (2021). https://openrepository.aut.ac.nz/handle/10292/14085
39. Giora, R., Shen, Y.: Degrees of narrativity and strategies of semantic reduction. Poetics **22**, 447–458 (1994). https://doi.org/10.1016/0304-422X(94)90020-5
40. Kennedy, G.: Corpus linguistics. In: Smelser, N.J., Baltes, P.B. (eds.) International Encyclopedia of the Social & Behavioral Sciences, pp. 2816–2820. Pergamon, Oxford (2001)

41. Brezina, V., Timperley, M., McEnery, A.: LancsBox v.5.1 Manual. A new-generation corpus analysis tools for researchers, students and teachers. Lancaster University, Bailrigg (2020). https://docplayer.net/194829601-Lancsbox-5-1-manual.html

42. Anthony, L.: Introducing corpora and corpus tools into the technical writing classroom through Data-Driven Learning (DDL). In: Flowerdew, J., Costley, T. (eds.) Discipline Specific Writing, pp. 162–180. Routledge, Oxford (2016)

43. Cordeiro, C.M.: A corpus-based approach to understanding market access in fisheries and aquaculture: a systematic literature review. Int. J. Econ. Manag. Eng. **13**, 1324–1333 (2019)

44. Castillón, D.C., Martín, J.C., Suarez, D.-M., Martínez, Á.R., Álvarez, V.L.: Automation trends in industrial networks and IIoT. In: Butun, I. (ed.) Industrial IoT, pp. 161–187. Springer, Cham (2020). https://doi.org/10.1007/978-3-030-42500-5_4

45. Hankel, M., Rexroth, B.: The reference architectural model Industrie 4.0 (RAMI 4.0). ZVEI, April 2015. https://przemysl-40.pl/wp-content/uploads/2010-The-Reference-Architectural-Model-Industrie-40.pdf

46. Veeramany, A., Hutton, W.J., Sridhar, S., Gourisetti, S.N.G., Coles, G.A., Skare, P.M.: A framework for development of risk-informed autonomous adaptive cyber controllers. J. Comput. Inf. Sci. Eng. **19** (2019). https://doi.org/10.1115/1.4043040

47. Jazdi, N.: Cyber physical systems in the context of Industry 4.0. In: 2014 IEEE International Conference on Automation, Quality and Testing, Robotics, pp. 1–4 (2014). https://doi.org/10.1109/AQTR.2014.6857843

48. Moghaddam, M., Cadavid, M.N., Kenley, C.R., Deshmukh, A.V.: Reference architectures for smart manufacturing: a critical review. J. Manuf. Syst. **49**, 215–225 (2018). https://doi.org/10.1016/j.jmsy.2018.10.006

49. Figueroa-Lorenzo, S., Añorga, J., Arrizabalaga, S.: A survey of IIoT protocols: a measure of vulnerability risk analysis based on CVSS. ACM 53, Article 44 (2020). https://doi.org/10.1145/3381038

50. Flammini, F.: Resilience of Cyber-Physical Systems: From Risk Modelling to Threat Counteraction. Springer, Cham (2019). https://doi.org/10.1007/978-3-319-95597-1

51. Quadrini, W., Negri, E., Fumagalli, L.: Open interfaces for connecting automated guided vehicles to a fleet management system. Procedia Manuf. **42**, 406–413 (2020). https://doi.org/10.1016/j.promfg.2020.02.055

52. Kaspersky Labs: Threat landscape for industrial automation systems. Statistics for H2 2020 (2021). https://ics-cert.kaspersky.com/reports/2021/03/25/threat-landscape-for-industrial-automation-systems-statistics-for-h2-2020/

53. Paulsen, C., Byers, R.: Glossary of key information security terms. NISTIR 7298 Revision 3. NIST, Gaithersburg (2019)

54. McCumber, J.: Information systems security: a comprehensive model. In: Proceedings 14th National Computer Security Conference, pp. 328–337. National Institute of Standards and Technology, Gaithersburg (1991). http://csrc.nist.gov/publications/history/nissc/1991-14th-NCSC-proceedings-vol-1.pdf

55. Lee, E.A., Seshia, S.A.: Introduction to Embedded Systems: A Cyber-Physical Systems Approach. MIT Press, Cambridge (2017)

56. Flaus, J.-M.: Cybersecurity of Industrial Systems. ISTE, London (2019)

57. Eden, P., et al.: A cyber forensic taxonomy for SCADA systems in critical infrastructure. In: Rome, E., Theocharidou, M., Wolthusen, S. (eds.) Critical Information Infrastructures Security. LNCS, vol. 9578, pp. 27–39. Springer, Cham (2016). https://doi.org/10.1007/978-3-319-33331-1_3

58. Törngren, M., Sellgren, U.: Complexity challenges in development of cyber-physical systems. In: Lohstroh, M., Derler, P., Sirjani, M. (eds.) Principles of Modeling. LNCS, vol. 10760, pp. 478–503. Springer, Cham (2018). https://doi.org/10.1007/978-3-319-95246-8_27

59. Ilyas, A., Santurkar, S., Tsipras, D., Engstrom, L., Tran, B., Madry, A.: Adversarial examples are not bugs, they are features. In: Wallach, H., Larochelle, H., Beygelzimer, A., d'Alche-Buc, F., Fox, E., Garnett, R. (eds.) Advances in Neural Information Processing Systems 32, pp. 125–136 (2019)
60. Prabhu, C.S.R.: Fog Computing, Deep Learning and Big Data Analytics-Research Directions. Springer, Singapore (2019). https://doi.org/10.1007/978-981-13-3209-8
61. Radanliev, P., De Roure, D., Cannady, S., Mantilla Montalvo, R., Nicolescu, R., Huth, M.: Analysing IoT cyber risk for estimating IoT cyber insurance. In: Living in the Internet of Things: Cybersecurity of the IoT-2018. IET Conference Proceedings. The Institution of Engineering and Technology, London (2018). https://www.econstor.eu/handle/10419/193692
62. European Parliament: General Data Protection Regulation (GDPR). In: Council, E.P.a.o.t. (ed.) Regulation (EU) 2016/679 of the European Parliament and of the Council, Regulation (EU) 2016/679 of the European Parliament and of the Council. European Parliament, Brussels (2018)
63. Lubin, A.: The Insurability of Cyber Risk. SSRN 3452833 (2019). https://doi.org/10.2139/ssrn.3452833
64. Urquhart, L., McAuley, D.: Avoiding the internet of insecure industrial things. Comput. Law Secur. Rev. **34**, 450–466 (2018). https://doi.org/10.1016/j.clsr.2017.12.004
65. California State Senate: Senate Bill No. 327. Chapter 886, Version 1.0. DoD Standards, Sacramento, CA (2018)
66. State of New York: New York Privacy Act (2021). https://legislation.nysenate.gov/pdf/bills/2021/a680
67. Federman, H.: Moving beyond notice and choice to welcome a fiduciary standard. iapp (2021). https://iapp.org/news/a/moving-beyond-notice-and-choice-to-welcome-a-fiduciary-standard/
68. Corallo, A., Lazoi, M., Lezzi, M.: Cybersecurity in the context of industry 4.0: a structured classification of critical assets and business impacts. Comput. Ind. **114**, 103165 (2020). https://doi.org/10.1016/j.compind.2019.103165
69. Terziyan, V., Gryshko, S., Golovianko, M.: Taxonomy of generative adversarial networks for digital immunity of Industry 4.0 systems. Procedia Comput. Sci. **180**, 676–685 (2021). https://doi.org/10.1016/j.procs.2021.01.290
70. Sølvsberg, E., Øien, C.D., Dransfeld, S., Eleftheriadis, R.J., Myklebust, O.: Analysis-oriented structure for runtime data in Industry 4.0 asset administration shells. Procedia Manuf. **51**, 1106–1110 (2020). https://doi.org/10.1016/j.promfg.2020.10.155
71. Sengupta, J., Ruj, S., Bit, S.D.: A secure fog-based architecture for industrial internet of things and Industry 4.0. IEEE Trans. Ind. Inform. **17**, 2316–2324 (2021). https://doi.org/10.1109/TII.2020.2998105
72. Mosteiro-Sanchez, A., Barcelo, M., Astorga, J., Urbieta, A.: Securing IIoT using defence-in-depth: towards an end-to-end secure Industry 4.0. J. Manuf. Syst. **57**, 367–378 (2020). https://doi.org/10.1016/j.jmsy.2020.10.011
73. Dalzochio, J., et al.: Machine learning and reasoning for predictive maintenance in Industry 4.0: current status and challenges. Comput. Ind. **123**, 103298 (2020). https://doi.org/10.1016/j.compind.2020.103298
74. Wang, Y., Yan, J., Sun, Q., Jiang, Q., Zhou, Y.: Bearing intelligent fault diagnosis in the industrial internet of things context: a lightweight convolutional neural network. IEEE Access **8**, 87329–87340 (2020). https://doi.org/10.1109/ACCESS.2020.2993010
75. Villalobos, K., Ramírez-Durán, V.J., Diez, B., Blanco, J.M., Goñi, A., Illarramendi, A.: A three level hierarchical architecture for an efficient storage of Industry 4.0 data. Comput. Ind. **121**, 103257 (2020). https://doi.org/10.1016/j.compind.2020.103257
76. Habrat, D.: Legal challenges of digitalization and automation in the context of Industry 4.0. Procedia Manuf. **51**, 938–942 (2020). https://doi.org/10.1016/j.promfg.2020.10.132

77. Unterberger, P., Müller, J.M.: Clustering and classification of manufacturing enterprises regarding their Industry 4.0 reshoring incentives. Procedia Comput. Sci. **180**, 696–705 (2021). https://doi.org/10.1016/j.procs.2021.01.292
78. Majumdar, A., Garg, H., Jain, R.: Managing the barriers of Industry 4.0 adoption and implementation in textile and clothing industry: interpretive structural model and triple helix framework. Comput. Ind. **125**, 103372 (2021). https://doi.org/10.1016/j.compind.2020.103372

Novel Maturity Model for Cybersecurity Evaluation in Industry 4.0

Alexander Kreppein[1](✉), Alexander Kies[1], and Robert H. Schmitt[1,2]

[1] Fraunhofer Institute for Production Technology IPT, Steinbachstr. 17, 52074 Aachen, Germany
alexander.kreppein@ipt.fraunhofer.de

[2] Laboratory for Machine Tools and Production Engineering (WZL) of RWTH Aachen University, Campus-Boulevard 30, 52074 Aachen, Germany

Abstract. The opportunities offered by Industry 4.0 for manufacturing companies are enormous but are in danger of remaining unexploited due to inadequate IT security measures. Increasing networking in the production environment leads to a growing number of attack surfaces that need to be protected by appropriate security measures. The overarching goal of this paper is therefore to provide companies with an easy-to-use tool with which they can self-assess their own cybersecurity maturity level, identify vulnerabilities and, based on this, implement secure, digitally networked production themselves. The Fraunhofer IPT has therefore developed the "Production Security Readiness Check", which is presented in this article and the result of a study of 28 companies that have carried out the check is highlighted.

Keywords: Industry 4.0 · IT security · Cybersecurity · ICS security · Networked production · Security level · Maturity assessment

1 Introduction

The industrial production is currently undergoing a change towards a digital and networked production within the fourth industrial revolution, the Industry 4.0. The shift from the so-called automation pyramid to a networked production is illustrating this change (see Fig. 1) [1]. In this process, networking technologies that originate from the IT (information technology) environment, such as Ethernet or Wi-Fi are being adopted and used in an OT (operation technology) environment, resulting in the IT-OT convergence. Alongside with the benefits also comes a threat in terms of cybersecurity. The physical separation between process and control levels ("air gap") is continuously decreasing, thus leading to the opening of previously closed systems. On the one hand this enables cross-company networking, but also leads to an increased number of security gaps and corresponding attack surfaces [2]. From an IT perspective, this means that field devices are now directly accessible from the Internet via Ethernet and Wi-Fi and therefore vulnerable to attacks. Additionally, mobile devices that are used in an OT environment increase the multitude of interfaces and thus must be taken into account with regard to cybersecurity.

© Springer Nature Singapore Pte Ltd. 2021
N. Abdullah et al. (Eds.): ACeS 2021, CCIS 1487, pp. 198–210, 2021.
https://doi.org/10.1007/978-981-16-8059-5_12

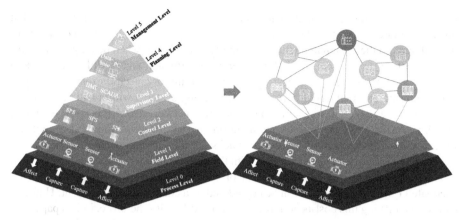

Fig. 1. The resolution of the automation pyramid into a production network [3]

The potential of a networking production is estimated to be 30 million euros for cross-company networking and 126 billion euros by 2025 for the internal digitalization of the production [4, 5]. Thus, exploiting the potential that Industry 4.0 holds is a key criterion for competitiveness in international comparison [1]. In order to do so, companies must

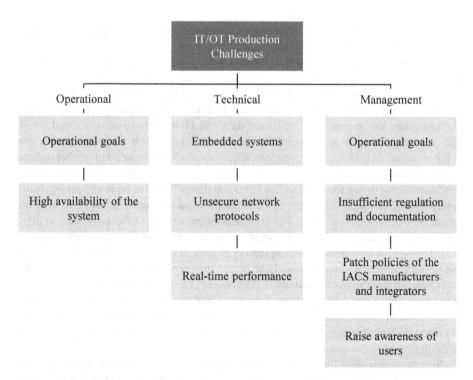

Fig. 2. Challenges with IT/ OT Systems for manufacturing companies [9]

overcome the current challenges, which are not only limited to technical measures, but must also address operational and managerial challenges. Figure 2 gives an overview of the different challenges manufacturing companies are facing when dealing with cyber-security within their organization. Moreover, for an efficient and flexible collaboration between companies, a major aspect will be overcoming organization-related breaks in manufacturing and delivery processes by networking systems within and across companies [6]. The vulnerabilities of isolated corporate networks, which become the target of cyber attacks every day, represent an enormous risk for all partners [7]. The direct financial damages resulting from cyber attacks for the German economy can be estimated at 103 billion euros per year [8]. With the value creation potential of a networked production on the one hand, and the risk of cyber attacks on the other hand, finding adequate IT security measures can be considered as a cost-benefit investment. Unfortunately, quantifying this cost-benefit relationship is difficult. Therefore, in this paper, we give an insight into a developed cybersecurity framework for manufacturing companies. The framework identifies IT and OT risks to which companies are exposed to as well as evaluates the security level on which they currently are. In this way, in addition to the current status of IT and OT security in production, the reasons for the low level of implementation of security measures can also be determined.

2   State of the Art

The German government is also focusing on the importance of IT security. In its "High-Tech Strategy 2025", it attaches great importance to security in the digital world. According to this strategy, secure information technology is an innovation driver and a necessary prerequisite for the competitiveness of Germany as a business location. Only new, holistic IT security solutions can exploit the full potential of digitalization in the field of Industry 4.0 [10]. The "Data Strategy of the Federal Government" published in 2021 also considers the guarantee of structural data and IT security to be existential for all stakeholders. Technical implementation via norms and standards play a significant role in this context [11]. The security-relevant requirements for IT systems are either defined by the company – for example, if critical manufacturing data is to be stored and processed confidentially – or are specified in laws and standards. There is currently no generally applicable IT security law in Germany. Instead, the legal requirements for IT security are spread across various laws [12]. The commencement of the "IT Security Act" in 2015 was therefore intended to drive improvements in the security of IT systems in companies [13]. The core of the law addresses operators of critical infrastructures and providers of tele-communications – the industrial sector and the corresponding value chains, on the other hand, are not explicitly named as addressees [12, 14]. A legal basis for industrial production outside of the regulations for critical infrastructures that concern IT security is not defined [15]. Figure 3 shows the most important bodies which promote IT security through the publication of standards and norms – world-wide, at Europe level or in Germany.

Recent studies show that the industrial sector has the lowest level of security precautions compared to banks, insurance companies and telecommunications, even though it is the most frequently attacked sector [17, 18]. Figure 3 shows that several norms,

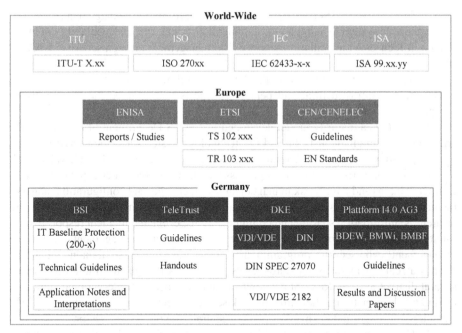

Fig. 3. International and national IT security laws, standards and bodies sorted by their regions of validity [16]

standards and security measures exist to prevent or avoid precisely such threats and attacks. However, only a fraction of companies implements these norms, standards and measures. Depending on the study and the standard, implementation rates vary between 4.5% and 45% [18–21].

It can be concluded that there are proposed security measures for the industrial sector, each with a different level of detail and abstraction. However, the current low level of implementation in companies and an industrial landscape that is still vulnerable to IT attacks leads to the assumption that a practicable solution for implementing cybersecurity measures has not yet been established. Therefore, a framework is presented that enables companies from the manufacturing industry to determine their own cybersecurity level in a first step, based on which concrete measures can be derived afterwards.

3 Related Work

The most influential standards and methodologies that address cybersecurity are the Cybersecurity Capability Maturity Model (C2M2), ISO/IEC 27001, NIST CSF (all with a worldwide focus) and the BSI IT Baseline Protection (originated in Germany) which is why they are presented in this section (see Fig. 3).

The International Standard ISO/IEC 27001 develops a set of requirements for the "establishment, implementation, maintenance and continuous improvement of an information security management system" [22] as well as access and identify IT security risks. Additionally, the ISO/IEC 27001 defines an information management system as the responsible system to maintain the confidentiality, integrity, and availability of information. It focuses on information security risk management through security standards [22].

In alignment with ISO 27001, the BSI IT Baseline Protection covers technical, organizational, infrastructural and personnel aspects to guarantee the IT security of companies from different sectors [23, 24].

The C2M2 is a maturity model developed by the US Department of Energy (DOE) and considers simultaneously IT and OT technology systems and their environments, focusing predominantly on the implementation and management. The C2M2 is built on on a continuous risk management process and measures the cyber capabilities of 10 distinct domains and covers risk management; asset, change, and configuration management; identity and access management; threat and vulnerability management; situational awareness; information sharing and communications; event and incident response; continuity of operations; supply chain and external dependencies management; work-force management; cybersecurity program management. Based on these domains the model defines a scale of maturity indicator levels [25, 26]. Although the framework covers several distinct areas it does not acknowledge entire aspects of international standards as IEC 62443 or national standards as IT Baseline Protection. And even though C2M2 considers OT assets and environments it concentrates on the energy sector.

The Cybersecurity Framework (CSF) for improving critical infrastructure is a maturity model developed by the National Institute of Standards and Technology (NIST). NIST presents five cybersecurity functions, namely identify, protect, detect, respond, and recover and introduces the idea of Cybersecurity Tiers. The concept of the 4 Tiers is that an organization can be classified in 4 stages or sophistication degrees on which cybersecurity management practices are implemented and in which extent [27]. NIST CSF considers IT, operational environments as well as the risks of ICS Systems. The NIST CSF framework also has some drawbacks, for example it is missing relevant sub-categories [28]. Additionally, Kosutic [29] remarks that NIST CSF does not establish which documents and records should be used when applying the model, as well as does not focus on how to further improve the management system.

4   Research Design

To identify existing vulnerabilities for manufacturing companies, the Fraunhofer Institute for Production Technology IPT developed the "Production Security Readiness Check" (PSRC) [30, 31]. The PSRC is based on the C2M2 [32] and common cybersecurity standards such as ISO 27001, IEC 62443, NIST CSF and the BSI IT-Baseline Protection [14, 22, 27, 33]. To map these norms, standards, and security measures into an easy-to-use tool for measuring the cybersecurity status of manufacturing companies, the key aspects were determined and clustered into nine domains into which the PSRC can be divided (see Fig. 4).

Each domain consists of cybersecurity practices which are referred to as building blocks in the PSRC and are assigned a maturity level. The higher the maturity level, the more demanding the implementation of the individual building blocks. The scale

Fig. 4. The nine domains of the Production Security Readiness Check

ranges from 0 ("not implemented") to 3 ("fully implemented"). For each module, a gap analysis is performed in which companies compare the actual security status of production with the target security status in a self-assessment. The target security status is derived from a consideration of the risk of attack – critical infrastructures, for example, are subject to a different risk of attack than standard manufacturing small and medium-sized enterprises (SME) [30, 31]. There are four categories of attack threats - script kiddies, motivated hackers, professional organizations, and cyber powers - that differ in criticality to enterprise cybersecurity and each has a different impact on the actions to be taken [34]. In the PSRC, these categories are determined individually by enterprises depending on the threat of attack. For the PSRC, an attack threat from the third category was assumed, so that the target security status is based on this category. The gaps resulting from the comparison with the actual security status can be critical, moderate or low.

As part of a study, the PSRC was subsequently applied to survey potential companies for the collection of research data. Using a company contact database, companies were pre-filtered based on three criteria (number of employees >20, existence of an email contact address, manufacturing industry). After being contacted, 28 companies completed the PSRC. A (telephone) interview was subsequently arranged with selected companies, in order to be able to derive the reasons for a respective result in more detail.

5 Results

We first provide an overview of the results from the survey of all surveyed SME (n = 16, cf. Fig. 5), followed by an overview showing the PSRC results with the participating large enterprises (LE) (n = 12, cf. Fig. 5). The median and mean of each implementation status achieved in the different domains is summarized in Table 1.

Table 1. Implementation status of all cybersecurity practices across all domains

PSRC domain	SME		LE	
	Mean	Median	Mean	Median
Risk management	0.85	0.63	1.12	0.93
Asset, change and configuration management	1.13	0.98	1.47	1.55
Identity and access management	1.56	1.54	1.63	1.66
Threat and vulnerability management	1.05	0.83	1.27	1.21
Situation awareness	0.93	0.63	0.95	0.77
Information exchange and communication	0.83	0.34	0.84	0.64
Response to events/incidents and continuity of production	0.95	0.61	1.17	0.90
Supply chain management	0.80	0.40	0.95	0.87
Human risk factor	0.79	0.23	0.77	0.54

Within *risk management* of SME (median: 0.63), cybersecurity is predominantly actively addressed in the office network. In production, the risk of cyberattacks was recognized, but only actively addressed in a few cases. SME have difficulties holistically grasping the threat landscape posed by cyber attacks. Managing the risk of cyber attacks has a reactive rather than proactive character.

The *asset, change and configuration management* domain has a higher median implementation level (0,98) for the participating SME. This can be explained by the fact that managing enterprise assets – regardless of IT security – is a common process in many companies.

Compared to all other domains, the *identity and access management* domain achieved the highest median implementation level among the surveyed SME (median: 1.54). In this domain, mature directory services such as Windows Active Directory already exist to help companies manage the entire life cycle - from creation to deactivation - of logical and physical access. In terms of access management, processes for managing access and identities are well established in many companies. A few companies additionally apply the need-to-know principle when granting access.

Regarding the *threat and vulnerability management*, SME (median: 0.83) apply activities in an ad hoc manner. However, the majority is overwhelmed by the acceleration of asset update cycles. There are huge differences in how vulnerabilities are handled on different components: While Windows components are subjected to active patch management, companies omit to actively patch industrial software, e.g. PLC controllers.

In the domain *situational awareness* (median of SME: 0.63), companies had to evaluate their activities around logging and monitoring. Logging and monitoring are carried out, but not in a comprehensive or goal-oriented framework: Production is not considered separately, but logging is performed company-wide in the IT and OT network.

SME take a specific approach due to their limited resources: They outsource some of the logging and monitoring activities to service providers who periodically evaluate the logged data.

Information exchange and communication regarding cybersecurity issues can be described as inadequate overall: This domain has the second lowest median implementation level (median of SME: 0.34) of all domains and holds particular potential for improvement. Most participating SME rely solely on their own resources and obtain information independently without being active in an exchange network.

Responses to cyber events and incidents, as well as activities around continuity of production, are also not sufficiently implemented (median SME: 0.61). Due to sophisticated attack methods, participating companies fear that they will fail to detect a large number of attacks. Forward thinking to prevent incidents in general is only slowly becoming established.

When it comes to cybersecurity practices in relation to *supply chain management*, the SME surveyed are not familiar with measures in this domain (median SME: 0.40). When new equipment is procured, security requirements are only rarely listed in the specifications. The IT department is also rarely involved in procurement processes. Responsibilities as to who is responsible for the security of the system after delivery are insufficiently defined between the manufacturer and the operator of a system.

The *human risk factor* domain has the lowest level of implementation at SME (median: 0.23), although cybersecurity training is a topic at all companies surveyed. On average, however, there is a lack of consistent implementation. The existence of malware is merely pointed out on the intranet, but active, repetitive training does not take place. Many employees lull themselves into a deceptive sense of security that the IT department will protect them against risks.

From a global perspective, it can be observed that LE have to deal with similar challenges in terms of cybersecurity. However, the overall implementation level (see Fig. 5) and also within the individual domains is considerably higher than among the SME surveyed. This is primarily due to the fact that LE often have their own IT departments that are responsible for realizing appropriate measures.

In the *risk management* domain, the situation is comparable to that of SME: Cybersecurity is considered in the office network, but is treated only partially in production. A holistic approach is rarely followed here either.

Especially in LE, the management of enterprise assets in defined processes has already become established. This can also be seen in the median score of the LE surveyed in the *asset, change and configuration management* domain, which at 1.55 is higher than that of SME.

The implementation level is even higher at the median in the *identity and access management* domain (1.66). This can be attributed to the same factors that contribute to the high median for SME: mature directory services, established asset management processes, and the application of the need-to-know principle.

LE often have a structured approach to eliminating vulnerabilities and threats as part of *threat and vulnerability management* (median: 1.21). However, even LE are being impacted by the acceleration of asset update cycles. If testing is nevertheless carried out, large companies in particular make use of support from the respective manufacturers

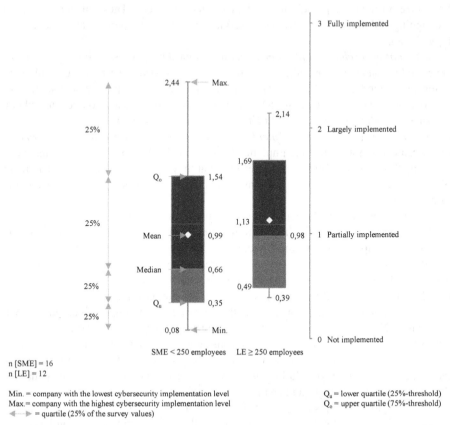

n [SME] = 16
n [LE] = 12

Min. = company with the lowest cybersecurity implementation level Q_u = lower quartile (25%-threshold)
Max. = company with the highest cybersecurity implementation level Q_o = upper quartile (75%-threshold)
◀— ▶ = quartile (25% of the survey values)

Fig. 5. Implementation status of all cybersecurity practices across all domains in the SME and LE surveyed

at the time of patching. Nevertheless, the exact effects of a patch on a plant cannot be predicted. This is due to the difficulty that companies do not have test systems and devices on site in multiple versions.

In the *situational awareness* domain, the median implementation status of the LE surveyed (0.77) is only slightly higher than that of the SME. It can be stated here that LE in particular use so-called security information and event management systems to support the company in monitoring. LE with a high volume of data use common log file analysis tools, but have difficulty configuring thresholds for alerts and warnings to protect the enterprise from cyber attacks. Defining the normal behavior of a network and distinguishing false alarms from true alarms must be done largely by hand. Many manufacturers of production equipment do not clearly communicate to the operating companies what they need to, should or can monitor.

Even LE have major problems actively communicating cybersecurity issues and exchanging information with partners. This also led to the second lowest level of implementation in the *information exchange and communication* domain (median: 0.64).

Preventive measures to ensure continuous production are increasingly being developed at large companies with the help of business continuity management. Nevertheless, even in the domain *response to events and incidents and continuity of production*, there is still need for action regarding cybersecurity. The median score of the 12 large companies surveyed was 0.90.

The implementation status of cybersecurity measures to protect the organization in the area of *supply chain management* was not satisfactory, even among LE. Accordingly, there is an enormous need for action, especially in cross-company cooperation, as otherwise all cooperating partners are exposed to risks in the event of possible attacks.

However, even in LE, the *human risk factor* represents the greatest area of attack (median 0.54). Again, employee training courses are not implemented with the utmost consistency, and employees rely on the supposed protection offered by an in-house IT department in LE.

6 Discussion for Future Analysis

The study has shown that with the help of the PSRC, the security level of the individual companies in the manufacturing sector can be recorded in detail and it can also contribute to improving the security level by highlighting their own weak points.

In order to point out to companies how they can securely participate in digitally networked production and at the same time protect themselves against cybersecurity risks in line with their needs, new approaches with concrete measures will be necessary. Ultimately, the overarching goal is to enable companies to implement secure, digitally networked production themselves. For this reason, the Fraunhofer IPT developed the PSRC and will extend its research in this area.

It is possible to adapt the PSRC for different industry sectors and their specific requirements. The selected data acquisition methodology based on a self-assessment proved to be suitable in principle. However, the details of the PSRC could be better addressed in an on-site workshop at the companies.

In the future, companies want to - and can - use the uniquely documented actual implementation status as a benchmark reference for the further implementation of cybersecurity practices. The PSRC can be consulted as a "working tool" at defined intervals, as it can be updated to document progress in the establishment of further cybersecurity practices and the improvement of existing ones. It enables companies to query their (new) current security level at any time and to identify the vulnerabilities that continue to exist.

It has also been observed that the high level of detail in the PSRC sometimes led to issues when answering the questions for SME without an in-house IT department. In the future, the scope and complexity of the tool should therefore be adapted according to the respective target group in order to ensure appropriate feasibility while at the same time guaranteeing high quality results.

7 Conclusion

Increasing digitalization and networking are creating new opportunities and growth potential. Industrial companies in particular can benefit from this in the form of additional value creation. Regardless of the great growth potential, the digitalization rate in the production of large German companies is only just under 30% (SME at 20%) [35]. In addition to opportunities, however, there are various risks that inhibit companies from digitally connecting their production. One of the three main obstacles to networking is IT security [36]. Whereas the primary focus to date has been on the functional safety of production machinery, cybersecurity is now increasingly coming to the fore due to the shift from closed to open cyber-physical systems (CPS) [37].

For this reason, a holistic cybersecurity framework for manufacturing - the PSRC - was developed based on current norms and standards, which clarifies for manufacturing companies the current security level they are at and the IT and OT risks they are exposed to. Based on the current implementation status of the companies' cybersecurity practices, the PSRC offers options for action that companies can use to improve their security level in order to meet the previously defined target implementation status.

To develop the PSRC, the most important IT protection goals (confidentiality, integrity, availability), legal requirements and (inter)national norms and standards were analyzed and summarized. Based on this, the specific requirements and challenges of IT security in production were addressed. This knowledge was then used to develop the framework. The PSRC contains nine domains (cf. Fig. 4), each with different cybersecurity practices to be fulfilled by the company. Depending on the implementation status of the individual domains, companies can achieve different levels of maturity in their cybersecurity implementation.

To determine and improve the current level of security, the PSRC was sent to companies in the manufacturing sector. The sample of respondents consisted of 28 manufacturing companies from different sectors, 16 of which were SME and 12 of which were LE. The study has shown that the PSRC can be used to record the security level of individual companies in the manufacturing sector in detail. By revealing the vulnerabilities in organizations, the PSRC can thus contribute to improving the security level. With regard to the evaluation, it can be stated that the implementation status of cybersecurity activities does not meet the required level, neither in SME nor in LE. For example, the risk posed by the human factor to cybersecurity is hugely underestimated across companies - the implementation level in this domain is clearly the lowest. A particular challenge lies in the fact that organizational measures in the form of training must not be neglected when technical security measures are introduced. Otherwise, there is a very high probability that employees will not understand the meaning of a newly introduced technical measure and will therefore not accept it or even avoid it. Nor does the interaction of companies with their peers take place in this subject area to the extent that a positive impact on cybersecurity would require. The exchange of information via corporate networks is a lever that companies could use relatively easily to benefit from the experience of others. In this respect, there is an enormous need for action across all industries in the different domains presented in this paper – although some companies are already working intensively on cybersecurity in certain domains.

References

1. Flatt, H., Schriegel, S., Jasperneite, J., Trsek, H., Adamczyk, H.: Analysis of the cybersecurity of industry 4.0 technologies based on RAMI 4.0 and identification of requirements. In: 2016 IEEE 21st International Conference on Emerging Technologies and Factory Automation (ETFA). 2016 IEEE 21st International Conference on Emerging Technologies and Factory Automation (ETFA), Berlin, Germany, 06–09 September 2016, pp. 1–4. IEEE (2016). https://doi.org/10.1109/ETFA.2016.7733634

2. Gatzke, M., Stark, J., Weigelin, L.: Künstliche Intelligenz, Blockchain, 5G und Cyber Physical Security, Wuppertal (2018)

3. Heinrich, B., Linke, P., Glöckler, M.: Grundlagen Automatisierung. Sensorik, Regelung, Steuerung, 2nd edn. Lehrbuch. Springer Vieweg, Wiesbaden (2017)

4. Lichtblau, K., et al.: Industrie 4.0-readiness. Aachen, Köln (2015)

5. Mohr, N., Morawiak, D., Köster, N., Saß, B.: Die Digitalisierung des deutschen Mittelstands (2017)

6. Bischoff, J., et al.: Erschließen der Potenziale der Anwendung von 'Industrie 4.0' im Mittelstand, Mühlheim an der Ruhr (2015)

7. Meyer, L., Seiz, M.: Industrie 4.0 im Mittelstand, München (2019)

8. Barth, M., et al.: Spionage, Sabotage, Datendiebstahl – Wirtschaftsschutz in der vernetzten Welt, Berlin (2020)

9. Hahn, A.: Operational technology and information technology in industrial control systems. In: Colbert, E.J.M., Kott, A. (eds.) Cyber-security of SCADA and Other Industrial Control Systems. AIS, vol. 66, pp. 51–68. Springer, Cham (2016). https://doi.org/10.1007/978-3-319-32125-7_4

10. Forschung und Innovation für die Menschen – Die Hightech-Strategie 2025 (2018). https://www.bmbf.de/upload_filestore/pub/Forschung_und_Innovation_fuer_die_Menschen.pdf. Accessed 17 Mar 2021

11. Datenstrategie der Bundesregierung. Eine Innovationsstrategie für gesellschaftlichen Fortschritt und nachhaltiges Wachstum, Berlin (2021). https://www.bundesregierung.de/resource/blob/992814/1845634/5bae389896531854c579069f9a699a8f/datenstrategie-der-bundesregie-rung-download-bpa-data.pdf. Accessed 17 Mar 2021

12. Schneider, F.: IT-Sicherheit 2018: Pflichten für Unternehmen (2018). https://www.cmshs-bloggt.de/tmc/it-recht/it-sicherheit-2018-sicherheit-fuer-unternehmen/. Accessed 17 Mar 2021

13. IT-Sicherheitsgesetz und Datenschutz-Grundverordnung: Handreichung zum "Stand der Technik" technischer und organisatorischer Maßnahmen. Revidierte und erweiterte Ausgabe 2018 (2018). https://www.teletrust.de/fileadmin/docs/fachgruppen/ag-stand-der-technik/TeleTrusT-Handreichung_Stand_der_Technik_-_Ausgabe_2018.pdf. Accessed 17 Mar 2021

14. Schutz Kritischer Infrastrukturen durch IT-Sicherheitsgesetz und UP KRITIS (2017). https://www.bsi.bund.de/SharedDocs/Downloads/DE/BSI/Publikationen/Broschueren/Schutz-Kritischer-Infrastrukturen-ITSig-u-UP-KRITIS.pdf?__blob=publicationFile&v=7. Accessed 17 Mar 2021

15. IT-Sicherheit für die Industrie 4.0. Produktion, Produkte, Dienste von morgen im Zeichen globalisierter Wertschöpfungsketten. Studie im Auftrag des Bundesministeriums für Wirtschaft und Energie. Abschlussbericht (2016). https://www.bmwi.de/Redaktion/DE/Publikationen/Studien/it-sicherheit-fuer-industrie-4-0.pdf?__blob=publicationFile&v=4. Accessed 17 Mar 2021

16. Niemann, K.-H., Hoh, M.: Anforderungen an die IT-Sicherheit von Feldgeräten. Schutzlösungen für hoch vernetzte Produktionsanlagen. atp edition **59. Jg.**, 42–53 (2017)

17. Live Security Studie 2017/2018. Eine repräsentative Untersuchung von Bitkom Research im Auftrag von F-Secure, Berlin (2018)

18. Digitalisierung und IT-Sicherheit in deutschen Unternehmen. Eine repräsentative Untersuchung, erstellt von der Bundesdruckerei GmbH in Zusammenarbeit mit KANTAR EMNID, Berlin (2017)
19. The State of Industrial Cybersecurity 2018 (2018)
20. VDMA Studie Status Quo der Security in Produktion und Automation, Frankfurt am Main (2013). https://industrialsecurity.vdma.org/viewer/-/v2article/render/26700821. Accessed 17 Mar 2021
21. Protecting Industrial Control Systems, Heraklion (2011)
22. DIN EN ISO/IEC 27001:2017-06, Informationstechnik_- Sicherheitsverfahren_- Informationssicherheitsmanagementsysteme_- Anforderungen. Beuth Verlag GmbH, Berlin
23. BSI-Standard 200-1. Information Security Management Systems (ISMS), Bonn (2017). https://www.bsi.bund.de/EN/Topics/ITGrundschutz/itgrundschutz_node.html. Accessed 6 Aug 2021
24. BSI-Standard 200-2. IT-Grundschutz-Methodik, Bonn (2017). https://www.bsi.bund.de/SharedDocs/Downloads/DE/BSI/Grundschutz/BSI_Standards/standard_200_2.pdf?__blob=publicationFile&v=2
25. Cybersecurity Capability Maturity Model (C2M2) (2014). https://www.energy.gov/sites/prod/files/2014/03/f13/C2M2-v1-1_cor.pdf. Accessed 6 Aug 2021
26. Le, N.T., Hoang, D.B.: Can maturity models support cyber security? In: 2016 IEEE 35th International Performance Computing and Communications Conference (IPCCC), pp. 1–7 (2016)
27. National Institute of Standards and Technology: Cybersecurity Framework (CSF) (2018). https://www.nist.gov/cyberframework. Accessed 6 Aug 2021
28. Almuhammadi, S., Alsaleh, M.: Information security maturity model for nist cyber security framework. In: CS & IT-CSCP 2017, pp. 51–62 (2017)
29. Kosutic, D.: Which one to go with – Cybersecurity Framework or ISO 27001? (2014). https://advisera.com/27001academy/blog/2014/02/24/which-one-to-go-with-cybersecurity-framework-or-iso-27001/. Accessed 6 Aug 2021
30. Kiesel, R., Heutmann, T., Dering, J., Kies, A., Vollmer, T., Schmitt, R.H.: Cybersecurity in der vernetzten Produktion. Fraunhofer-Institut für Produktionstechnologie IPT, Aachen (2020)
31. Kiesel, R., Kies, A., Kreppein, A., Schmitt, R.H.: IT-Sicherheit in der vernetzten Produktion. Unzureichende Sicherheitsmaßnahmen gefährden den digitalen Wandel. ZWF Zeitschrift für wirtschaftlichen Fabrikbetrieb (2021)
32. Schwab, W., Poujol, M.: The State of Industrial Cybersecurity 2018 (2018)
33. DIN Deutsches Institut für Normung e. V.: DIN EN IEC 62443. IT-Sicherheit für industrielle Automatisierungssysteme. Beuth Verlag GmbH, Berlin. Accessed 2020
34. Leszczyna, R., Egozcue, E., Tarrafeta, L., Fidalgo Villar, V., Estremera, R., Alonso, J.: Protecting Industrial Control Systems, Heraklion (2011)
35. Lichtblau, K., Schleiermacher, T., Goecke, H., Schützdeller, P.: Digitalisierung der KMU in Deutschland, Köln (2018)
36. Icks, A., Schröder, C., Brink, S., Dienes, C., Schneck, S.: Digitalisierungsprozesse von KMU im Verarbeitenden Gewerbe, Bonn (2017)
37. Security on the Industrial Internet of Things. How companiescan defend themselves against cyber attacks, Bonn (2016)

Digital Forensics and Surveillance, Botnet and Malware, DDoS, and Intrusion Detection/Prevention

A Review on TLS Encryption Malware Detection: TLS Features, Machine Learning Usage, and Future Directions

Kinan Keshkeh[1]([✉]) [ID], Aman Jantan[1], Kamal Alieyan[2],
and Usman Mohammed Gana[1]

[1] School of Computer Sciences, Universiti Sains Malaysia, Gelugor, Pulau Pinang, Malaysia
kinan.keshkeh@student.usm.my, Aman@usm.my
[2] Faculty of Computer Sciences and Informatics, Amman Arab University, Amman, Jordan
k.alieyan@aau.edu.jo

Abstract. With the growth of internet encryption to protect users' privacy, malware has evolved to employ encryption protocols such as TLS/SSL to obfuscate the contents of malicious communications. Unfortunately, decrypting network data before it reaches the signature-based Intrusion Detection System (IDS) to identify TLS-based malware is impractical since it adds infrastructure complexity and compromises user privacy. As a result, various studies have moved to investigate anomaly-based detection without decryption using different TLS features and techniques such as Machine Learning (ML). This paper aims to review TLS-based malware anomaly detection studies and analyze the employment of TLS features and machine learning in these works to understand the field's current state better. Furthermore, this study highlights the strengths of the related research and offers several recommendations on its shortcomings and TLS features for future effective detection systems.

Keywords: Malware · TLS · Encryption · TLS features · Intrusion detection system · Machine learning

1 Introduction

Malware is any program that is intended to harm a particular device, server, or computer network, whether it is a virus, spyware, or anything else.[1] Based on AV-TEST Institute[2], the total number of discovered malware has been tremendously growing over the last few years, from 2012 to 2021.

With the massive expansion of malware, malware developers chose to embrace the continued development of encryption protocols by adopting TLS protocol to disguise

---

[1] "Defining Malware: FAQ | Microsoft Docs". https://docs.microsoft.com/en-us/previous-versions/tn-archive/dd632948(v=technet.10)?redirectedfrom=MSDN (accessed Apr. 29, 2021).
[2] "Malware Statistics & Trends Report | AV-TEST". https://www.av-test.org/en/statistics/malware/ (accessed Apr. 29, 2021).

© Springer Nature Singapore Pte Ltd. 2021
N. Abdullah et al. (Eds.): ACeS 2021, CCIS 1487, pp. 213–229, 2021.
https://doi.org/10.1007/978-981-16-8059-5_13

their malicious communication. According to Sophos Labs[3], approximately 23% of all malware types and 44% (nearly a half) of info stealing malware use TLS when they transmit or receive commands from C&C (Command and Control) server, during the installation of malicious payloads, or when they are retrieving the data returned by that payload.

An Intrusion Detection System (IDS) is a common network protection system that searches for anomalous activity and alerts if any malware is found. IDSs are either Network-based IDS (NIDS) or Host-based IDS (HIDS). Also, IDSs detect attacks using two methods: (1) signature-based detection, which uses databases with predefined known attack patterns, and (2) anomaly-based detection, which detects unknown suspicious behavior by comparing it to the network's normal activity.

Although Network-based intrusion detection (NIDS) is a valuable technology, they have significant drawbacks when detecting TLS-based malware due to the unavailability of clear-text metadata. Decrypting network traffic before it reaches the signature-based NIDS could be considered an option for detecting TLS -based malware, but unfortunately, it has numerous flaws that make it impractical. TLS traffic decryption increases network infrastructure complexity, impacts the security of connections negatively [1], and causes all devices to trust the certificate used by the decryptor.

However, anomaly-based NIDS is a feasible TLS-based malware detection that does not require any decryption. The integration of Machine Learning (ML) algorithms into the anomaly-based NIDS yields a robust system. ML applies a mathematical modeling approach to the available traffic features to learn past data patterns before predicting the possible anomaly malicious behavior using new data [2]. As a result, feature extraction and machine learning that employs these features are two critical components in developing anomaly-based NIDS.

This paper investigates and compares numerous TLS features used to identify TLS-based malware in order to gain a deeper understanding of their applications. In addition, the paper discusses several ML algorithms that have been applied in the study area. The review also examines the related studies' limitations and strengths in all aspects and makes recommendations based on them. An overview is also provided on malware taxonomy, malware analysis, and TLS protocol.

The following are the remaining sections of this paper: Sect. 2 provides a summary of the existing related reviews. Section 3 describes the paper methodology. Section 4 contains background about malware taxonomy and analysis and TLS protocol. Section 5 discusses the usage of TLS features and ML algorithms in TLS-based malware detection. Section 6 compares the strengths and shortcomings. Section 7 presents the discussion and future directions. Finally, Sect. 8 is the conclusion of this review.

---

[3] L. Nagy, "Nearly a quarter of malware now communicates using TLS – Sophos News", Feb. 18, 2020. https://news.sophos.com/en-us/2020/02/18/nearly-a-quarter-of-malware-now-communicates-using-tls/ (accessed May 02, 2021).

2   Existing Reviews on TLS-Based Malware Detection

In the research field of TLS-based malware detection, one study conducted by Singh et al. [3] provides a comparative investigation on the ideas and techniques for malware detection in HTTP over TLS traffic. They discussed features-based, flow-based approaches, and machine learning-based studies. They found that most research employed statistical features, and deep learning should be employed. However, the comparison they performed is fairly basic and does not contain feature specifics, particularly TLS features. Furthermore, they did not compare the strengths and drawbacks of each study in all aspects, nor did they analyze machine learning algorithms, but rather classified the techniques and disadvantages for each work individually. Table 1 summarizes what Singh et al. [3] review lacks and what this paper provides.

Table 1. A comparison of Singh et al. [3] review with this paper

	TLS features analysis	Comparison of weaknesses & limitations	Comparison of machine learning algorithms
This review	✓	✓	✓
Singh et al. [3]	✗	✗	✗

3   Methodology

The Scopus and Google Scholar sources were searched using a query string based on the abstract and title, with a date range of 2015 to 2020. The decision to proceed with five-year papers was made in order to examine current malware trends and detection techniques. "((https OR ssl OR tls OR encrypted OR encryption) AND (bot OR botnet OR malware))" is the query string used. The words "bot" and "botnet" were added to broaden the search scope and produce additional publications. Following that, the irrelevant papers were eliminated using a selection procedure that included reading and evaluating the abstract, conclusion, and introduction. Finally, for this study review, 23 papers were gathered and used.

4   Background

4.1   Malware Taxonomy

Malware is a harmful code or program that corrupts files, exhausting system resources or steals credentials. Malware has lately expanded in quantity, and it is critical to understand its taxonomy to identify it. Therefore, malware is classified into a set of generic malware groups; some of them are as follows:

- **Coin miners** that allow criminals to penetrate a corporation and illegally mine coins.

- **Exploits** and exploit kits that make use of software flaws to circumvent the machine's security defences and exploit the computer.
- **Phishing** that attempts to get sensitive information using seemingly legitimate channels such as emails, directories, texting, or other forms of electronic interaction.
- **Ransomware** which encrypts data and seeks to extort money from victims by demanding money, generally in the form of cryptocurrency, to give them the decryption key.
- **Rootkits** that may conceal themselves as well as their destructive actions on a computer.
- **Trojans** that appear like legitimate apps.
- **Worms** propagate over the network by taking advantage of vulnerabilities [4].
- **Virus** is harmful software that replicates from one device to another.
- **Bots** are automated programs that communicate with other network services to offer information that a human being would otherwise carry out [5].

In fact, any of the above malware types can be categorized as TLS-based malware if the communication traffic is encrypted using the TLS protocol. Trojans, such as "Trick-Bot", "Dridex", and "IcedID", Ransomeware, and Botnets are the most frequent forms of TLS-based malware.

4.2 Malware Analysis Techniques

Static Analysis. The static analysis of malware is a process focused on inspecting without running a malware program. Using software such as IDA Pro, the disassembly of the binary file is done, and the program logic is then examined. This strategy does not require a lot of resources, so it saves time. However, most malware variants now aim to circumvent this sort of analysis by relying on parameters that are difficult to determine statically, such as the present system date and indirect jump instructions [6], among other things.

Dynamic Analysis. It is the method of running a given malware sample in a managed environment and tracking its behavior to evaluate the malicious activity [6]. In this type of analysis, system behavior and network traffic are monitored for any unusual changes. In addition to solving the static analysis issues, an advantage of this analysis is that it can analyze large datasets as it can be automated. The first step in implementing this sort of analysis is to install network sensors that gather traffic by making a copy of it, evaluate it, and then take relevant actions. Some of the traffic collection techniques are: port mirroring, network TAP, and host capturing.

4.3 TLS Protocol

The TLS protocol is a cryptographic protocol that provides privacy, integrity, and confidentiality of communication, and it is widely used to secure HTTP web traffic. Currently, the last version of TLS is v1.3. Although TLS v1.3 has been launched recently for further security improvements, the most widespread version of TLS is TLSv1.2. The TLS protocol lies below the application layer and above the transport layer, mainly TCP. TLS Handshake Protocol handles TLS session establishment by sending two round trips of clear-text messages between a client and a server to agree on many parameters, as illustrated in Fig. 1.

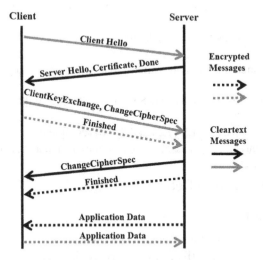

Fig. 1. TLSv1.2 handshake messages

The client begins with a Client Hello message which contains:

- **Ciphersuites** are the client cryptographic algorithms that are supported [7].
- **Compression methods**.
- **Server Name Indication (SNI)** is an extension to specify the server to be connected to.
- **Client version** is the TLS version selected by the client.
- **Extensions** have many types that determine the information the client needs from the server. Some of the extensions are Elliptic Curve (EC) Point Formats, EC Supported Groups, and Signature Algorithms.

The Server returns several messages:

- **ServerHello** has the Server selected Ciphersuites and compression methods.
- **Certificate** determines the chain of TLS certificates the Server sends to the client. It also checks the authenticity, non-repudiation, and integrity using a digital signature. Each certificate has fields for verifying the legality of the issuer and receiver, determining the validity duration, and categorizing the validity levels.
- **ServerKeyExchange** is needed when certain key exchange methods (e.g., Diffie-Hellman) are used and when the Server does not have a certificate [8].

Then the client replies with several messages:

- **ClientKeyExchange** enables the server to create the final symmetric session key. For example, at RSA, the client must create a random string of bytes called a pre-master password, then encrypt and transmit it with the server's public key [8].
- **ChangeCipherSpec** informs the Server that all subsequent communications must be encrypted with the session key.
- **Finished** lets the server know that the client has completed the handshake.

Finally, the server ends the handshake with:

- **ChangeCipherSpec** informs the client that the session key must encrypt all subsequent messages.
- **Finished** lets the client know that the Server has completed the handshake.

Following these steps, the TLS v1.2 handshake is complete, and both parties will have a session key and start communicating with an authenticated and encrypted connection.

5   TLS-Based Malware Detection

5.1   TLS Features Usage

Researchers have made use of the fact that TLS transmits certain metadata in plain text during the handshake process (Fig. 1) by analyzing it and extracting features for use in detection. The metadata is present in various TLS handshake messages exchanged between the client and server, as explained in the following subsections.

Client TLS Handshake Messages. One of the essential messages the client sends during the handshake process is the Client Hello message. It is used to fingerprint what application is being used for the TLS user as it is sent in a clear text [7]. Different TLS clients use specific values of Client Hello message fields; therefore, the TLS client application can be fingerprinted, and the same goes for malware [7]. TLS Client Hello has also been used, as the first message in the TLS handshake phase, to achieve fast early detection since its features can be accessed at the initial TLS communication time. One of the earlier studies is [9], in which researchers presented a MalDetect-enhanced fast detector. It only analyses the first eight packets of the TLS handshake process, including Client Hello, to detect malware before it has a practical impact. Many Client Hello fields have been used as features in the literature, such as client version, compression methods, extensions, ciphersuites, and others which are shown in Fig. 2 with the usage percentages.

Client Ciphersuites. Most of the literature studies have used Ciphersuites advertised by the client or chosen by the server in their detection systems (e.g., [7, 9–14]). The significance of ciphersuites derives from the concept that the client ciphersuites used by benign software and malware are remarkably distinct, as malware tends to encrypt network traffic using simpler algorithms. Additionally, using feature selection, Zheng et al. [15] and Jenseg [7] found that Ciphersuites are among the most insightful TLS features. However, some studies such as [12, 16–19] have neglected the significance of ciphersuite use.

Client Extensions. Counting and recording extensions the client advertises has been an essential operation to some scholars like in studies by [9, 10, 16, 17, 20, 21]. One of the important extensions is SNI (Server Name Indication), an extension used to define the Server to access if several HTTPS websites are located behind a single IP address. In [17] study, Bazuhair et al. used the feature of just checking whether SNI is an IP or not, whereas Dai et al. [16] examined if the SNI IP same as the destination IP and also whether SNI exists in the server certificate SANs (Subject Alternative Name). Interestingly, in the identification system based on multi-view features proposed by Dai et al. [16], researchers concentrated primarily on statistical features such as measuring ratio, mean, and the number of TLS handshakes and server certificates. Moreover, the SNI has also been used to generate additional domain name features, such as the study by Prasse et al. [22], where they extracted the same feature set as the one used by Franc et al. [23], from SNIs. These features also include the total length of vowel-free substrings, the ratio of vowel changes, the presence of non-base-64 characters, the prevalence ratio of particular domain and subdomain letters, the proportion of non-letter characters, and others [22]. In comparison to Prasse et al. [22], who used previously known SNI features, Bortolameotti et al. [24] applied an n-gram technique on the Server Name making new features that help in the detection of randomly created domains. N-gram is a method that works by splitting the domain name into overlapped sets of substrings of length n; for example, the domain "example.org" consists of the 3-g "xam", "exa", "amp", ..., and "org" [22]. Nevertheless, the sparsity problem that occurs when the value of n increases and storage problems associated with the large vocabulary size will cause researchers to be more careful and reconsider using n-gram. The SNI features used in the studies reviewed are illustrated in Table 2.

Table 2. TLS client Hello SNI features utilized in research examined

Ref.	SNI analysis features
[17]	Is IP?
[16]	1. Ratio of existing SNI 2. Is IP or destination IP? 3. Is in SANs (Subject Alternative Name)?
[15]	1. Is Empty? 2. By DGA (Domain Generation Algorithm)? 3. In Alexa 1M? IP?
[25]	1. Is IP? destination IP? 2. Is in SANs?
[14, 18, 24]	SNI n-gram
[7, 9, 10, 12, 13, 19–22, 26–32]	✕

Server Hello and Certificate Analysis. Server Hello and certificate's messages include important clear-text information like the chosen ciphersuite, approved extensions, and the server certificate chain fields. A variety of features are extracted from

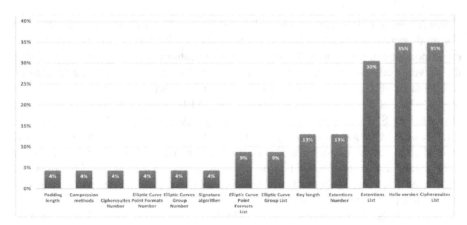

Fig. 2. TLS handshake client features usage in studies reviewed

this essential information and used in the related literature. A comparison of server certificate features is illustrated in Table 3; Server Hello features usage is clarified in Fig. 3. Researchers have found several differences in the Server Hello message and certificates between benign and malicious traffic. In one recent study by Anderson et al. [10], millions of TLS encrypted flows of 18 malware families were analyzed using the sandbox. They have reported some differences in ciphersuites, SubjectAltName (SAN), and validity periods between the malware and benign traffic. More variations have been discovered in server certificate fields that encouraged researchers to use them as features in the malware detection systems, such as the number of certificates (e.g., studies by [9, 17]), the number of SANs (e.g., studies by [9, 10, 20]) and Signature algorithm [9].

Certificate Validity Level. Server certificates have certain validity levels like Domain, Organization, and Extended Validations (DV, OV, EV) as well as Self-signed. The OV and EV certifications are quite trustworthy because they go through an internationally standardized identity authentication process included in the certification as opposed to DV and Self-signed ones [33]. In [30] study, which focused only on TLS certificate analysis, the malware TLS traffic has 0% and less than 0.7% of the EV and OV certificates, respectively. Similarly, in [26] study, researchers used this classification of certificates in their TLS-based malware detection system. They analyzed 1,685 benign and malicious TLS-based Android apps from Androzoo [34] and VirusShare[4] datasets, discovering that most of the malware tends to communicate with untrusted server certificates whose validity levels are either DV or Unknown (when the Server refuses the connection). Examining self-signed certificates in suspicious TLS traffic has piqued the researchers' curiosity in that field. For instance, in [16, 20, 24, 30] studies, researchers considered determining whether the certificate is self-signed as a feature that indicates the existence of malware communication. Another analysis has done by the Cisco research team study (Blake Anderson et al., 2018) on the enterprise data. They resulted in around 0.09 percent of TLS sessions using a self-signed certificate in enterprise data, whereas around 0.7 percent of TLS sessions using a self-signed certificate in malicious data, which is more

---

[4] https://virusshare.com/.

prevalent than enterprise data [10]. In comparison to these findings of the Cisco team [10], Kato et al. [26] showed a higher proportion (more than 80%) of malicious Android applications that interact using unknown server certificates, including self-signed ones. This discrepancy in results may be attributable to differences in the two databases or malware categories used.

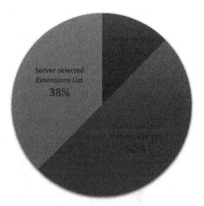

Fig. 3. TLS handshake Server Hello features usage in the research field

Certificate Validity Period. The server certificate validity period has been used as a feature in several studies. For example, Bortolameotti et al. [24] extracted the feature from the university gateway traffic dataset and verified the validity period of the x509 server certificate chain at the time of capture. Another example is [30] study, where they used a detection approach based only on analyzing certificate features, including the certificate validity period. They calculated the period as the days between "not before" and "not after" certificate fields and utilized it as a detection feature. Their training dataset was made of one million legitimate, five thousand phishing and 3,000 malware certificates obtained from many sources: Vaderetro[5] for confirmed phishing certificates, abuse.ch[6], censys.io[7] for blacklisted certificates, and Alexa[8] top one million for the full one million website certificates.

Table 3. A comparison of TLS server certificate features that were used in detection

Ref.	Subject & issuer analysis	Certificate version	CN domain analysis	Check certificate validity level if it is:	Certificate validity	Public key algorithm	Public key length
[26]	✗	✗	✗	EV, OV, SS	✗	✗	✗
[17]	✗	✗	✗	SS	In days & Ratio	✗	✗
[16]	✗	Ratio of the high version	Is CN in SANS?	SS	In days	✗	The length as a number
[9]	✗	Version number	✗	SS	Mean	Ratio	Mean
[19]	✗	✗	✗	✗	✗	✗	✗
[12]	✗	✗	✗	✗	✗	✗	✗
[27]	✗	✗	✗	✗	✗	✗	✗
[28]	✗	✗	✗	✗	✗	✗	✗
[13]	✗	✗	✗	SS	In days	✗	✗
[7]	✗	✗	✗	✗	✗	✗	✗
[29]	✗	✗	✗	✗	✗	✗	✗
[30]	calc. euclidean distance/ Kolmogorov-Smirnov	✗	Is.com ? IP? what is the Entropy?	DV, OV, EV, SS	In days	✗	✗
[14]	✗	✗	✗	✗	✗	✗	✗
[31]	✗	✗	✗	✗	✗	✗	✗
[10]	✗	✗	✗	SS	In days	✗	✗
[25]	✗	✗	Is CN in SANS?	SS	Mean & Std	✗	Mean
[18]	✗	✗	✗	✗	✗	✗	✗
[21]	✗	✗	✗	✗	✗	✗	✗
[22]	✗	✗	✗	✗	✗	✗	✗
[32]	✗	✗	✗	✗	✗	✗	✗
[20]	✗	✗	✗	SS	In days	✗	✗
[24]	✗	✗	In Top 100? Uses DGA?	SS	Valid or not?	✗	✗
[15]	✗	✗	✗	✗	✗	✗	✗

(✗) indicates that the study does not use the feature.
EV: Extended Validation; OV: Organization Validation; SS: Self-signed; DV: Domain Validation;
DGA: Domain Generation Algorithm.

5.2 Machine Learning Usage

Machine learning is a component of artificial intelligence used to solve problems using mathematical models. There are two major categories of machine learning: supervised and unsupervised. Supervised learning works by learning labeled examples to predict new future events. It has the ability to alter the model and correct it by comparing its output with the desired output. In contrast, unsupervised learning aims to find regularities without labeling data elements in the input. In fact, supervised problems can be either regression or classification problems, whereas unsupervised learning problems are either association or clustering problems [35].

Regression. It is one of the simplest algorithms that predict real values based on a continuous variable(s) [36]. One regression algorithm that has been employed in the relevant literature is Linear Regression. Unfortunately, as revealed in the [21] study, it performed badly because of its dependency on extracted feature scaling and the inability to simulate nonlinear functions.

Classification. The classification process consists of several phases: Splitting the data into training and testing parts, pre-processing, feature extraction, learning, and classification. In classification, the selection of features is necessary to determine the features' quality and illustrate the utility of individual features in predicting the objective of a problem [37]. Several classification algorithms, including Logistic Regression, SVM, K-NN, Decision Tree, Random Forest, and Boosting, have been employed in the literature. Logistic Regression did exceptionally well, as shown in [7, 20] investigations, and especially when its two regularizations, l2-regularization and l1-regularization, were applied, as shown in [10, 13, 15] studies. Also, SVM performance has been low compared to other algorithms as in studies [16, 21, 25, 29] and K-NN performance has been acceptable but not excellent such as in [13, 31, 32, 38] research works. However, Decision Tree has been better than SVM and K-NN [7, 16, 21], besides having several subtypes like J48 (C4.5), CART (Classification And Regression Trees), and Alternative Decision Tree (ADTree), which are used in the study of [24]. Furthermore, both Boosting algorithms and Random Forest have the highest overall performance in the related literature, as shown in [7, 31]. Random Forest was also used to filter and choose the most useful features.

Neural Networks. Neural Networks can be supervised or unsupervised. They simulate how human brains function in operations like learning, memorizing, ..etc. Neural Networks have been used in many studies as the only main algorithm in [19, 30] studies. Convolutional Neural Network (CNN) is a form of Neural Network that is frequently used to analyze images. In conjunction with Perlin noise in [20], CNN has created a powerful detector that outperforms the previous method. The Long Short-Term Memory (LSTM) subtype of CNN considers long-term associations in information sequences. It also produced promising results when combined with domain-name characteristics in studies by [22, 30].

6 Strengths and Weaknesses of the TLS-Based Malware Detection Studies

Aside from TLS features and ML uses, TLS-based Malware Detection studies were critically evaluated to determine the weaknesses and strengths based on several metrics such as detection accuracy, speed, dataset specifications, and real-world performance. Table 4 presents a summary of the evaluation.

Table 4. The strengths and weaknesses of the reviewed literature

Ref	Strengths	Weaknesses
[17]	Reducing False Negative while improving the accuracy	Slowness due to the use of CNN
[16]	Enhancing ML model by reducing unimportant features using feature selection	No testing on real and recent traffic
[29]	The feature engineering process is simple and fast (the number of features is small)	No TLS handshake features usage
[25]	Including real traffic in the dataset	Weak connection periodicity calculation
[21]	Creating an enhanced feature set to boost the performance of Linear Regression	• No TLS certificate features usage • Running malware was limited to 5 min only for each type
[15]	• Boosting accuracy and speed of detection by adding two layers: one to filter benign flows and another to identify malware families • Detect unknown malware • Using content, size, periodicity based features • Using private and public dataset	Depending on Random Forest only for evaluation
[26]	Including certificate validation level features	Limited if malware uses OV, EV certificates
[30]	• Focusing on TLS server certificate features • Improving the accuracy of SVM model of Splunk (Ryan Kovar & Dave Herrald) company	Relying only on TLS certificate features
[9]	• Fast detection because of using the first 8 packet of a flow • Ability to detect new threats by updating the classifier parameters online	Relying only on Random Forest
[19]	Enhancing detection using Haar wavelet transforms in combination with an adversarial autoencoder	No TLS handshake features
[12]	Increasing detection performance by using additional ML classifiers that enhance traffic by categorizing HTTP transaction labels	No TLS certificate and handshake features

(continued)

Table 4. (*continued*)

Ref	Strengths	Weaknesses
[27]	Determine malware beaconing in TLS traffic by applying Discrete Fourier transform based on frequency	• No TLS certificate and handshake features • No use of ML
[18]	Detemine malware beaconing in TLS traffic by applying Discrete Fourier transform based on frequency	Lacks using time or size based TLS features
[13]	• Training & testing the detector on real bening dataset • The approach is robust and resilient against attackers' changing	Using an unbalanced dataset (the number of malware flows is not equal to benign flows)
[7]	Depending on only resilient network features which are hard or impossible to change by hackers	• Unbalanced and small dataset • Using only the count feature of TLS handshake
[14]	• Using AdaBoost ML algorithm • Extending the prior work with HTTP features by including TLS features • Analysis of malware and benign feature values using histogram	• Not combine TLS & HTTP features • Limited TLS handshake features usage (only two)
[31]	Ability to detect mlaware using large weblogs and Hadoop cluster	Limited number of TLS features and no TLS certificate features usage
[10]	• Using large dataset of millions of TLS flows and 18 mlaware families • Analysis of malware and benign feature values using histogram	• Using unrobust features which can be changed to be benign by attackers
[18]	• Ability to detect unknown and new, unknown malware • Capturing traffic from the network rather than from the client device	• Limited TLS handshake features usage (domain name only) • Relying on Neural Networks only
[22]	• Ability to detect unseen malware using LSTM algorithm • Testing and training on real traffic	Limited TLS handshake features usage (domain name only)
[32]	Supporting large volumes of high-dimensional data by implementing. Three MapReduce-based and one centralized approximate k-NN join methods	• K-NN was not performing well in high-dimensional dataset • Lacks using enough TLS features
[20]	• Improving detection performance by using DNS & HTTP contextual data with 0.00% false discovery rate • Build a not overfitted detector proven to be so by validation on real-world dataset	No periodic behaviour detection

(*continued*)

Table 4. (*continued*)

Ref	Strengths	Weaknesses
[24]	Detecting zero day attacks and unknown malware	• Lacks using other certificate and TLS handshake features • Only use FNR & TPR for performance evaluation

7   Discussion and Future Directions

This study examines numerous papers related to TLS-based malware anomaly detection, and in addition to reviewing TLS features and ML algorithms, it analyzes the relevant research's strengths and limitations. TLS-based malware is considered one of the most destructive Internet attacks, and it is trying to enhance its human simulation by changing the values of different features. Therefore, analyzing TLS features is a must as it is the input of detection techniques. The review shows in Fig. 2, Fig. 3, Table 2, and Table 3 several uncommon TLS features in both client and server communications. It can be concluded that more research, using several datasets, is thus required to determine the real information gain of infrequently used features in TLS-based malware detection. The need for further studying on the seldom-used features is also emphasized by examining the two Client Hello features, "Elliptic Curves Group Number" and "Ciphersuites Number". Although these features have been utilized rarely (Fig. 3), listing them in the top 20 essential features in [7, 15] research raises intriguing questions. Furthermore, the outcomes of this review research suggest that the most extensively utilized features, which have exceptionally high utilization rates, should not be neglected because they are employed in the majority of associated works due to their significance.

Additionally, by comparing the strengths of reviewed studies in Table 4, it can be inferred that the majority of research concentrated on enhancing classification performance metrics as misclassifying malware in real life can pose a big threat and cost a lot of money. Furthermore, numerous studies examined developing detectors capable of detecting unknown or new malware, which would increase the efficiency of their techniques. However, few studies only, such as [9, 15, 29] have considered improving detection speed (using initial packets, filtering layer, reducing features) and supporting detection in large datasets such as [10, 31, 32] studies. Hence, there is abundant room for advancement in terms of detection speed and detection in large datasets.

Finally, evaluating all studies' weaknesses in Table 4 highlights the necessity for more research to address them. The limited use of TLS features by quantity or category is a recurrent issue in the related literature. This might be due to resource constraints or the researchers' desire to focus on other variables rather than TLS features. Nonetheless, the problem of not utilizing enough features remains. Another clear constraint is the reliance on a single ML algorithm in the testing phase, such as Random Forest [9, 15], Neural Networks [18], or one type of TLS feature like TLS certificate [26]. Researchers will not be able to identify the best algorithm for the study if they depend on only one or two ML algorithms. The findings indicate that more research is needed to get a complete picture of TLS-based malware detection.

8 Conclusion

Malware that communicates using TLS has grown dramatically due to the increasing use of encryption protocols such as TLS/SSL. Many studies have been conducted recently on TLS-based malware anomaly detection since signature-based NIDS cannot access encrypted data, and decryption data is inapplicable. Researchers proposed several approaches to develop an effective detection model in related studies by leveraging several TLS feature sets in different techniques, including ML. However, as malware evolves and the threat posed by it grows, research in this area requires further development and enhancement. This paper attempted to review the proposed approaches in the field to develop a better comprehension of TLS features and ML algorithms and analyze the strengths and weaknesses.

It can be concluded that TLS features should be carefully chosen in terms of type and quantity and that researchers should not depend just on one or two ML algorithms but should test and compare many of them. The paper has raised important questions about the seldom-used TLS features and suggested further enhancements of the detection speed and ability to support detection in a huge database. All of the observations of this review may aid the research community in building new tools and methods for alleviating TLS-based malware threats.

References

1. Durumeric, Z., et al.: The security impact of HTTPS interception. In: NDSS (2017). https://doi.org/10.14722/ndss.2017.23456
2. Kok, S.H., Abdullah, A., Jhanjhi, N.Z., Supramaniam, M.: A review of intrusion detection system using machine learning approach. Int. J. Eng. Res. Technol. **12**(1), 8–15 (2019)
3. Singh, A.P., Singh, M.: A comparative review of malware analysis and detection in HTTPs traffic. Int. J. Comput. Digit. Syst. **10**(1), 2210–3142 (2021). https://doi.org/10.12785/ijcds/100111
4. Understanding malware & other threats - Windows security | Microsoft Docs. https://docs.microsoft.com/en-us/windows/security/threat-protection/intelligence/understanding-malware. Accessed 20 Sept 2020
5. What Is the Difference: Viruses, Worms, Trojans, and Bots? https://tools.cisco.com/security/center/resources/virus_differences. Accessed 08 Oct 2020
6. Gadhiya, S., Bhavsar, K.H.: Techniques for malware analysis. Int. J. Adv. Res. Comput. Sci. Softw. Eng. **3**, 2277–3128 (2013)
7. Jenseg, O.: A machine learning approach to detecting malware in TLS traffic using resilient network features. Master's thesis, NTNU (2019)
8. Patrick, N.: The TLS Handshake: taking a closer look - Hashed Out by The SSL Store[TM] (2019). https://www.thesslstore.com/blog/explaining-ssl-handshake/. Accessed 08 July 2020
9. Liu, J., Zeng, Y., Shi, J., Yang, Y., Wang, R., He, L.: Maldetect: a structure of encrypted malware traffic detection. Comput. Mater. Contin. **60**(2), 721–739 (2019). https://doi.org/10.32604/cmc.2019.05610
10. Anderson, B., Paul, S., McGrew, D.: Deciphering malware's use of TLS (without decryption). J. Comput. Virol. Hack. Tech. **14**(3), 195–211 (2017). https://doi.org/10.1007/s11416-017-0306-6
11. Senecal, D., Kahn, A., Segal, O., et al.: Bot detection in an edge network using Transport Layer Security (TLS) fingerprint. Google Patents (2019)

12. Anderson, B., McGrew, D.: Leveraging point inferences on HTTP transactions for HTTPS malware detection. Google Patents (2019)
13. Roques, O., Maffeis, S., Cova, M.: Detecting malware in TLS traffic. Ph.D. diss., Imperial College London (2019)
14. Calderon, P., Hasegawa, H., Yamaguchi, Y., Shimada, H.: Malware detection based on HTTPS characteristic via machine learning. In: ICISSP 2018 – Proceedings of 4th International Conference on Information Systems Security Privacy, vol. 2018-Janua, no. Icissp, pp. 410–417 (2018). https://doi.org/10.5220/0006654604100417
15. Zheng, R., et al.: Two-layer detection framework with a high accuracy and efficiency for a malware family over the TLS protocol. PLoS ONE 15(5), e0232696 (2020). https://doi.org/10.1371/journal.pone.0232696
16. Dai, R., Gao, C., Lang, B., Yang, L., Liu, H., Chen, S.: SSL malicious traffic detection based on multi-view features. In: ACM International Conference on Proceeding Series, pp. 40–46 (2019). https://doi.org/10.1145/3371676.3371697
17. Bazuhair, W., Lee, W.: Detecting malign encrypted network traffic using perlin noise and convolutional neural network. In: 2020 10th Annual Computing and Communication Workshop and Conference, CCWC 2020, January 2020, pp. 200–206 (2020). https://doi.org/10.1109/CCWC47524.2020.9031116
18. Prasse, P., Gruben, G., Pevny, T., Sofka, M., Scheffer, T.: Malware detection by HTTPS traffic analysis. Math. Fak. Potsdam Univ. (2017). https://doi.org/10.1109/OCEANS.2001.968684
19. Puuska, S., Kokkonen, T., Alatalo, J., Heilimo, E.: Anomaly-based network intrusion detection using wavelets and adversarial autoencoders. In: Lanet, J.-L., Toma, C. (eds.) SECITC 2018. LNCS, vol. 11359, pp. 234–246. Springer, Cham (2019). https://doi.org/10.1007/978-3-030-12942-2_18
20. Anderson, B., McGrew, D.: Identifying encrypted malware traffic with contextual flow data. In: AISec 2016 - Proceedings of the 2016 ACM Workshop on Artificial Intelligence and Security Co-located with CCS 2016, pp. 35–46 (2016). https://doi.org/10.1145/2996758.2996768
21. Anderson, B., McGrew, D.: Machine learning for encrypted malware traffic classification: Accounting for noisy labels and non-stationarity. In: Proceedings of the ACM SIGKDD International Conference on Knowledge Discovery and Data Mining, vol. Part F1296, pp. 1723–1732 (2017). https://doi.org/10.1145/3097983.3098163
22. Prasse, P., Machlica, L., Pevny, T., Havelka, J., Scheffer, T.: Malware detection by analysing network traffic with neural networks. In: Proceedings of the 2017 IEEE Symposium on Security and Privacy Workshops, SPW 2017, vol. 2017-Decem, pp. 205–210 (2017). https://doi.org/10.1109/SPW.2017.8
23. Franc, V., Sofka, M., Bartos, K.: Learning detector of malicious network traffic from weak labels. In: Bifet, A., et al. (eds.) ECML PKDD 2015. LNCS (LNAI and LNB), vol. 9286, pp. 85–99. Springer, Cham (2015). https://doi.org/10.1007/978-3-319-23461-8_6
24. Bortolameotti, R.: C&C botnet detection over SSL. Master's thesis, University of Twente (2014)
25. Strasák, F.: Detection of HTTPS malware traffic. Bachelor's thesis, Czech Technical University in Prague, pp. 1–49 (2017)
26. Kato, H., Haruta, S., Sasase, I.: Android malware detection scheme based on level of SSL server certificate. In: 2019 IEEE Global Communications Conference, GLOBECOM 2019 - Proceedings, no. 2, pp. 379–389 (2019). https://doi.org/10.1109/GLOBECOM38437.2019.9013483
27. Fehrman, B., Woody, E., et al.: Connection information. Google Patents (2020)
28. Senecal, D., Kahn, A., Segal, O., et al.: Bot detection in an edge network using Transport Layer Security (TLS) fingerprint. Google Patents, vol. 1 (2019)

29. De Lucia, M. J., Cotton, C.: Detection of Encrypted Malicious Network Traffic using Machine Learning. In: Proceedings of the IEEE Military Communications Conference, MILCOM, vol. 2019-Novem, pp. 1–6 (2019). https://doi.org/10.1109/MILCOM47813.2019.9020856

30. Torroledo, I., Camacho, L. D., Bahnsen, A. C.: Hunting malicious TLS certificates with deep neural networks. In: Proceedings of the ACM Conference on Computer and Communications Security, pp. 64–73 (2018). https://doi.org/10.1145/3270101.3270105

31. Kohout, J., Komárek, T., Čech, P., Bodnár, J., Lokoč, J.: Learning communication patterns for malware discovery in HTTPs data. Expert Syst. Appl. **101**, 129–142 (2018). https://doi.org/10.1016/j.eswa.2018.02.010

32. Maroušek, J.: Efficient kNN classification of malware from HTTPS data. Master's thesis, Charles University, Faculty of Mathematics and Physics (2017)

33. What is an Extended Validation Certificate? :: What is an Extended Validation Certificate? :: GlobalSign GMO Internet, Inc. https://www.globalsign.com/en/ssl-information-center/what-is-an-extended-validation-certificate. Accessed 08 Oct 2020

34. Allix, K., Bissyandé, T. F., Klein, J., Le Traon, Y.: AndroZoo: collecting millions of android apps for the research community. In: Proceedings - 13th Working Conference on Mining Software Repositories, MSR 2016, pp. 468–471 (2016). https://doi.org/10.1145/2901739.2903508.

35. Brownlee, J.: Supervised and unsupervised machine learning algorithms (2016). https://machinelearningmastery.com/supervised-and-unsupervised-machine-learning-algorithms/. Accessed 03 June 2021

36. Commonly Used Machine Learning Algorithms | Data Science. https://www.analyticsvidhya.com/blog/2017/09/common-machine-learning-algorithms/. Accessed 28 Sept 2020

37. Kononenko, I., Kukar, M.: Machine Learning and Data Mining. Horwood Publishing (2007)

38. Yao, B., Li, F., Kumar, P.: K nearest neighbor queries and KNN-joins in large relational databases (almost) for free. In: Proceedings - International Conference on Data Engineering, pp. 4–15 (2010). https://doi.org/10.1109/ICDE.2010.5447837

A Short Review: Issues and Threats Pertaining the Security of SCADA Systems

Qais Saif Qassim[1]([⊠]), Norziana Jamil[2], Mohammed Najah Mahdi[2], Zaihisma Che Cob[2], Fiza Abd Rahim[3], and Lariyah Mohd Sidek[4]

[1] University of Technology and Applied Sciences – Ibri, Ibri, Sultanate of Oman
qais.aljanabi@ibrict.edu.om
[2] College of Computing and Informatics, Universiti Tenaga Nasional, Kajang, Malaysia
[3] School of Computing, Universiti Teknologi Malaysia, Skudai, Malaysia
[4] Institute of Energy Infrastructure, Universiti Tenaga Nasional, Kajang, Malaysia

Abstract. SCADA systems are commonly used to track and manage utilities in vital national infrastructures including electricity generation and delivery, transportation networks, water supply and manufacturing, and manufacturing facilities. Cyber-attacks that threaten data privacy in SCADA networks, such as unauthorised misuse of sensor or control signals, may have a significant effect on the functioning of sensitive national infrastructure by causing device operators to make incorrect decisions, which could result in disastrous outcomes. Therefore, the cyber-security of SCADA systems has been an active topic of research for the past decades due to the potentially disastrous impact on the environment, public safety, and economy when these systems are breached or compromised. This paper examines the current security posture of SCADA systems from the perspective of data and cybersecurity and to propose recommendations for enhancing protection measures.

Keywords: SCADA · Security · Vulnerabilities · Cyber-attacks · Encryption · Authentication

1 Introduction

SCADA systems are used to automate and track industrial processes in a variety of national infrastructures, including electric power, oil and gas processing, water transmission and distribution [1]. As shown in Fig. 1 [2], a typical SCADA system consists of a control centre and many geographically scattered industrial devices located at remote field sites. Remote Terminal Unit (RTU), Programmable Logic Controllers (PLC), and Intelligent Electronic Device (IED) are among other widely used industrial devices in remote sites [3]. Commonly, sensor readings are received by the RTU from field devices in analogue format, then later converted into digital format to be sent to the corresponding control centre.

© Springer Nature Singapore Pte Ltd. 2021
N. Abdullah et al. (Eds.): ACeS 2021, CCIS 1487, pp. 230–247, 2021.
https://doi.org/10.1007/978-981-16-8059-5_14

Additionally, the RTU has the ability to produce alarms and commit changes based on pre-programmed instructions in some situations. The PLC, like the RTU, is a digital computer system that tracks and regulates field devices and commits adjustments by following hard-coded commands to regulate solenoids, actuators, and valves.

The control centre, on the other hand, which includes the SCADA server, collects data from RTUs and/or PLCs and sends instructions to them, as well as processing and storing data to be presented to human operators to support their decisions. Human operators monitor and manage the controlled device through a Human-Machine Interface (HMI) at the control centre. Furthermore, various computer software systems, such as billing and inventory control applications, are incorporated with the SCADA server to handle corporate and business functions [4]. Since the control centre performs essential functions, any downtime, service disruption, or compromise of its functions can have catastrophic implications for public security and safety, national security, and the economy [2]. As a result, all connection to the SCADA network from the outside must be secured and covered.

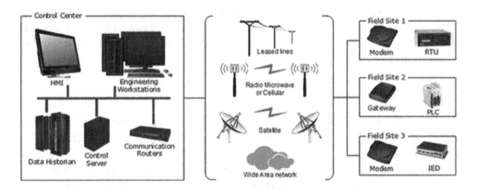

Fig. 1. General architecture of a SCADA system

SCADA systems were disconnected from other networks and external access prior to the Internet networking revolution in the SCADA domain and cloud-based ICS/SCADA applications, as well as the trend of linking these systems to real-time business and management information systems [3]. Additionally, proprietary communication protocols and industrial devices were used, promoting the idea of protection by obscurity. As a result, cyber-security was never a major concern for these systems; instead, the focus was on creating a dependable, real-time, and safe industrial control system. Nonetheless, today's technological developments, as well as the emergence of real-time data sharing and analysis, have paved the way for enterprise and business network inter-networking capabilities with SCADA systems [3,5]. This inter-connectivity made remote control, management, and monitoring of industrial processes within the supervised system far more effective. The disadvantage of this convergence is that it has exposed the industrial domain to numerous security threats. As a result, new security vulnerabilities have been discovered [2]. Furthermore, because of the interconnection with corporate and business networks, malicious parties were able to access and manipulate the vulnerabilities of the systems [6]. In the past, these issues were not considered in SCADA systems [2,3].

SCADA security has become a critical concern as a result of current SCADA system technological developments, as well as a growing number of active breaches and cyber-attacks that have had catastrophic and devastating effects on various critical infrastructures, industries, and dependent economies in recent years, as evidenced by the well-known Stuxnet attack. To withstand cyber sabotage, ICS/SCADA must be well-secured and protected against potential cyber-attacks using adequate security defence measures and smart attack detection/prevention mechanisms. This paper provides a quick yet comprehensive overview of the SCADA security landscape, vulnerabilities, and security threats, as well as the potential and potential efforts to achieve cyber-security assurance in the industrial environment, especially in the electric power grid system. The following is how the rest of the paper is organised: The second section gives an overview of a typical SCADA scheme. Section 3 examines some of the reported security incidents to demonstrate the importance of protecting these systems. Section 4 looks at some of the most common security flaws in SCADA systems and their communication protocols. Finally, Sect. 5 brings the analysis to a close by highlighting several potential future projects.

2   Related Works

Numerous existing works discuss and review the current state of SCADA security. In this section, we review some of the remarkable studies in this field of study. Table 1 presents a summary of the selected related works.

Ghosh et al. [7] have presented a comprehensive SCADA attack classification considering the impact on confidentiality, integrity and availability on these systems. Moreover, they have discussed the various security standards and schemes that have been proposed to protect the SCADA networks. Additionally, the study has explored the potential threats to these systems. The main conclusion drawn from the study was that the main security threats towards the SCADA systems are a lack of defence against Denial of Service attack and weak key exchange protocol. A similar study has been conducted by Pliatsios et al. [8]; the research has presented a broad review on SCADA implementations, protocol vulnerabilities, security threats, and the current posture of SCADA attack prevention initiatives. The main highlights drawn from the study are the lack of mature security tools tailored to the requirements of SCADA systems.

Another similar study on SCADA security was published by Volkova et al. [9]. The paper presented a comprehensive review of the security of the most important control system communication protocols. The survey investigated the security of several protocols, including DNP3, IEC 60870-5-104 and IEC 61850, which are protocols used in power systems. The study also proposed a security assessment methodology based on the IEC 62351 standard.

Another comprehensive security analysis on SCADA-specific protocol has been published by Rosa et al. [4]. The authors have analysed a widely used PLC protocol, namely, PCOM. The study has investigated the security gap of PCOM protocol and has demonstrated several mitigation strategies to encounter specific attack scenarios defined in the study. Another remarkable study on the security of SCADA systems has been reported by Bhamare et al. [10]. The study covered the efforts made by academia and industry to provide the necessary support for the transition from stand-alone systems to cloud-based environments. A review paper presenting case studies of major attacks on SCADA systems in the last 20 years was recently published by Alladi [11]. The study reviewed the Stuxnet attack on the Iranian nuclear facility, the German mill attack, the BlackEnergy attack on the Ukrainian power facility, and the attack on the petrochemical plant in Saudi Arabia in 2017.

Table 1. Summary of the related works

Study	Summary/Contribution	Findings/Conclusion
Ghosh et al. [7]	Presented SCADA attack classification based on CIA triad and discussed the various SCADA security standards and schemes	The main security threats toward the SCADA systems are a lack of defence against Denial of Service attack and weak key exchange protocol
Pliatsios et al. [8]	Presented a broad review on SCADA protocol vulnerabilities, and security threats	The lack of mature security tools tailored to the requirements of SCADA systems
Volkova et al. [9]	Presented a comprehensive review of SCADA protocols, including DNP3, IEC 60870-5-104 and IEC 61850	New rigorous methodologies and tools need to be devised for the sake of validating whether the IEC62351 has been implemented correctly
Rosa et al. [4]	Investigated the security gap of PCOM protocol and demonstrated several mitigation strategies to encounter specific attack scenarios	It was found that PCOM lacks security features such as confidentiality or integrity and is vulnerable to several types of network attacks
Bhamare et al. [10]	Reviewed the development of the secure cloud-based ICS leveraging the advancements in the field of machine learning techniques	Lack of proper security in novel multicloud platforms may cause high costs associated with the security breaches in the real-time industry platforms
Alladi [11]	Presented a review of major attacks on SCADA systems in the last 20 years	Most of the SCADA attacks involve injecting malware into the system

3   SCADA Security Posture

The use of common IT frameworks, communications, and protocols that have known security flaws and deficiencies has broadened the landscape of SCADA attacks over the last two decades, making these systems targets for attackers seeking remote access and in-depth awareness of the systems' weaknesses, defence mechanisms, and sensitive properties. With technological advancements, SCADA vendors have changed how they implement new technologies, especially in data communications, to improve access and efficiency while lowering costs. This has a major impact on the security of these systems, making them more vulnerable to wide range of both cyber and industrial attacks.

The limitations and weaknesses in the communications protocols of SCADA systems have been the focus and target of cyber-attacks [12]. Failure to enforce appropriate security protocols and defend these networks from emerging cyber and physical threats has disastrous consequences. As a result, providing sufficient protections against SCADA threats by upgrading these systems' defences and defence mechanisms is an emergent and necessity to deter cyber-attacks against SCADA systems [13].

Traditional security measures such as restricted physical access, encryption, continuous security patching, perimeter networks, and firewalls are all applicable in industrial control domain, but must be checked in accordance with standard SCADA system security and performance criteria. Such that, the priority order of SCADA security objectives has different order than conventional IT systems, where system's availability is paramount for SCADA, followed by integrity and confidentiality. Thus, due to the remote terminals' limited computing capacity, low data transfer speeds, and the need for real-time and high-speed communication, it's difficult to use traditional cryptographic techniques for data communication [14].

Cyber-attacks usually target SCADA system components that are critical to the SCADA security requirements. In other words, the availability of the control system will be targeted first, followed by its credibility, and then the confidentiality of the system's data, such as measurement readings and control commands. All cyber-attacks on SCADA systems aim to gain unauthorised access to the production network in order to gain privilege and access to confidential industrial data, interrupt SCADA system services, or cause physical damage to SCADA systems and critical infrastructure [15]. Attacks on these systems may use a wide range of techniques to achieve their objectives. Phishing, social engineering, session hijacking, bypassing network protection, and leveraging security device vulnerabilities are all tactics that attackers may use. Attackers can also compromise domain controllers or attack exposed servers, clients, or remote terminals. External intelligence agencies, malicious insiders, hackers, for-profit attackers, hacktivists, or industrial spies are usually the ones who plan and carry out these attacks.

4   Review of Most Known SCADA Attacks

Table 2 lists a compilation of the most known and recorded SCADA security incidents, techniques used, the target countries and the impacts on the security objectives. The security breaches were gathered through surveying security reports, research articles, and online publications, as well as reported news articles [1,3,16–18]. As depicted in Table 1, the recorded security incidents against SCADA and critical infrastructures cut across several critical infrastructure and industrial sectors. It also shows that most of the recorded incidents were intended to violate the system's availability and disrupt the normal operation of the industrial control system. From the list of cyber-attacks, one also can conclude that most of the reported attacks were conducted to sabotage and destruct the target system; the table also shows that various attack techniques have been considered; however, virus was the commonly used attack technique.

Table 2. Cyber-security incidents in history on SCADA and ICS systems

Year	Attack	Objective	Target
2010	Stuxnet	Destruction	Iran's Natanz uranium enrichment facility
2011	Night Dragon	Data leakage	Five global energy and oil firms
2011	DUQU	Data leakage	Several potential ICS targets
2012	Flame	Data leakage	Several ICS targets in the middle east
2012	Shamoon	Destruction	Saudi Aramco SCADA
2013	Havex	Data leakage	Energy and petrochemical industries
2014	German Steel Mill	Destruction	Steel mill in Germany
2015	BlackEnergy	Destruction	Ge intelligent platforms
2016	CrashOverride	Destruction	Ukraine's power grid
2017	Triton	Destruction	Schneider Electric's Safety controllers

4.1   Stuxnet of 2010

To many countries, Stuxnet was the trigger to reconsider the protection defence mechanisms of the national critical infrastructures. Stuxnet was the first cyber-attack in which malware could cause significant physical damage outside of a controlled testing environment. In 2010, Stuxnet deliberately targeted Iran's Natanz uranium enrichment facility. The malware, which was believed to be smuggled into the facility using a USB flash drive, was designed to replicate its code to infect other computers looking for a specific PLC model without human intervention. The impact of Stuxnet was enormous, and it was able to destroy several centrifuges by causing them to burn themselves out.

4.2   Night Dragon of 2011

NightDragon is a code-name of a multi-exploit attack targeted five global energy and oil firms. The attack was reported by McAfee security researchers in 2011. It was reported that the attack was utilising social engineering, spear-phishing attacks, trojans and various OS vulnerabilities, as well as remote administration tools. Night Dragon is designed to extract specific pieces of information and intellectual property. The main goal of the attack was to harvest and collect sensitive information concerning oil and gas field bids and operations. Although the attack didn't use any zero-day vulnerabilities, it was however very successful, and the exfiltrated data has enormous potential value to competitors.

4.3   DUQU of 2011

After about one year of the infamous Stuxnet attack, the Laboratory of Cryptography and System Security (CrySyS) in Hungary has reported malicious malware that re-uses a substantial portion of the Stuxnet code. Duqu's purpose was to gather intelligence data and assets from industrial control system manufacturers to conduct a future attack more easily. According to McAfee, one of Duqu's actions is to steal digital certificates from the compromised computers to help future malware appear as secure software.

4.4   Flame of 2012

Flame malware was discovered in many Middle East countries after two years of operation being undetectable. Researchers have agreed that Flame was designed primarily to collect sensitive from passively compromised systems. In addition to installing a backdoor to allow the attackers to tweak the toolkit and add new functionality. It was reported that Flame malware could spread to other network-connected systems and can record audio and take display screenshots as well as log keyboard activities and sniff network traffic.

4.5   Shamoon of 2012

During the third quarter of 2012, Saudi Aramco has reported a destructive malware attack on their facilities, leaving over 30,000 computer systems unusable. The malware (then called Shamoon) was an information-stealing malware with a destruction module. It was targeting the operational networks rather than the ICS or SCADA systems. Once triggered, it starts to perminantly overwrite the Master Boot Record (MBR) and partition tables and other important system files. Within two weeks, Shamoon was able to hit another ICS facility in Qatar, RasGas, which one of the largest liquefied natural gas (LNG).

4.6   Havex of 2013

Havex was designed to snoop on systems controlling industrial equipment, presumably so that hackers could work out how to mount attacks on the gear. The code was a remote access Trojan, or RAT, which is an acronym for software that lets hackers take control of computers remotely. Havex targeted thousands of US, European, and Canadian businesses, and especially ones in the energy and petrochemical industries.

4.7   German Steel Mill

In 2014 an attack using spear-phishing and social engineering targeted a steel mill in Germany. The attack was initiated on the business network and gain access to the production network. The attack targeted the blast furnace to prevent it from being able to shut down safely. Thus, it caused massive damage to the plant and render failures of several control systems.

4.8   BlackEnergy of 2015

Back energy is one of the most sophisticated and modular malware. It has evolved over time since 2004 from a simple DDoS toolkit to quite sophisticated malware for targeting critical infrastructures. It has been found that Black Energy performs passive Internet scanning looking for a specific type of SCADA HMI, namely GE Intelligent Platforms HMI/SCADA-CIMPLICITY. The analysis has shown that the Back Energy malware targets a known vulnerability in these systems, allowing remote attackers to execute arbitrary code via a crafted message to a specific TCP port. It was used to launch an attack in December 2015 on several Ukranian power companies that helped trigger blackouts. Additionally, the malware was used to gather intelligence about the power companies' systems, and to steal log-in credentials from employees.

4.9   CrashOverride of 2016

CRASHOVERRIDE (also known as Industroyer) is another sophisticated malware framework targeting the SCADA systems and the power grid. IS was used to leverage an attack on Ukraine's power grid in 2016. CRASHOVERRIDE is considered the first-ever known malware targeting the power grids. It is equipped with modules specific to the electrical power grid protocol stacks, including IEC 101, IEC 104, and IEC 61850. The malware can open circuit breakers on RTUs and force them into an infinite loop keeping the circuit breakers open even if grid operators attempt to shut them. This is what causes the impact of de-energising the substations.

4.10   Triton of 2017

Triton malware has been designed to target Schneider Electric's Safety controllers called Triconex Safety Instrumented Systems (SIS). Which are autonomous control systems that independently proctor the performance of physical systems; once a dangerous state is detected, these systems can issue immediate actions automatically. It is worth mentioning that Triton malware was first discovered at a Saudi Arabian petrochemical plant in December 2017. Moreover, its main goal is to prevent the safety mechanisms of the industrial control systems from executing their intended function, resulting in a physical consequence and human life loss.

5   SCADA Vulnerabilities

ICS/SCADA, as a cyber-physical system, can be described as complex networked control systems that combine physical control devices of critical national infrastructures with cyberspace computing and networking systems. SCADA systems are now used in an increasing number of essential infrastructures to manage, supervise, and track the physical and electronic processes of these systems. However, SCADA central and terminal devices, as well as their communication protocols, have significant security flaws that malicious adversaries may exploit to carry out a variety of cyber-attacks without leaving any evidence of the attack, suspicious activity, or part failure. This section serves two folds; first, it presents the most common SCADA vulnerabilities related to its design and implementation. It shed light on the security weaknesses found in three commonly used communication protocols. The review of previously published studies and reviewing the adversaries related to SCADA systems and the various vulnerabilities and attacks targeting these systems, it can be possible to classy the vulnerabilities into several categories as listed below and illustrated in Fig. 2:

1. Vulnerabilities associated with legacy software; many SCADA systems are still utilising outdated operating systems and vulnerable communication protocols and devices.
2. Vulnerabilities associated with default configurations; several SCADA systems were found using default configurations and passwords, making it easy for attackers to enumerate and compromise.
3. Lack of encryption, device identification, and safe data handling; legacy SCADA communication protocols and controllers lack the ability to encrypt the data in transmit and fail to determine the remote devices' true identity vulnerable to bogus data and command injection attacks.
4. Web interface attacks; being connected to the Internet and the needs to manage these systems from remote locations through a simple web interface resulted in making these systems vulnerable to a wide range of web applica-

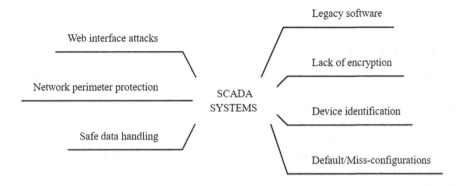

Fig. 2. SCADA systems' vulnerabilities

tions attacks such as cross-site scripting and SQL injection attacks as well as DDoS attacks.

5. Lack of boundary protection; many SCADA attacks reported during the last few years showed weak boundaries between ICS and enterprise networks.

Although the industry has responded with cybersecurity device standards such as IEC 62351, DNP3.0/Secure Authentication or ISA/IEC 62443, the majority of SCADA system implementations are legacy implementations with inadequate capability to properly secure and protect information. Despite widespread understanding of the challenges and effects, industry players must continue to be concerned by continuously assessing risks against costs and benefits. This problem is compounded in industries where long equipment design life cycles are needed, as well as overlapping operational, repair, safety, and security requirements. Nevertheless, for inadequately protected equipment, some of the commonly seen technical vulnerability are following [3,18]:

- Multiple entry points: There will be several access points to all of these networks, including the SCADA network, when a SCADA system implements network interconnectivity, which means the system is linked to corporate networks, business partner's networks, and/or any other networks [19]. A skilled attacker can exploit any of these connections and gain access to the SCADA physical network. A SCADA network is connected to the outside networks through a gateway, yet it does not mean the only way out to the outside world is through that gateway. There might likewise be other unforeseen connections. Hence, many of the gateways also do not include security protection mechanisms. Once the attackers reside in the network it could harm the security properties of the entire system. Usually attackers will gain access to the network through vulnerabilities on other networks such as corporate, vendors and/or customer's network. As an example of attack scenario, an attacker uses a remote access port utilised by vendor for maintenance to get inside the network.

- Transmission Control Protocol/Internet Protocol (TCP/IP) over a wired or wireless communication medium is used by the majority of currently deployed SCADA systems. Due to economic and technological advantages, SCADA have begun to move from proprietary to open international standard communication protocols over the years, but this transition has also increased network vulnerabilities. Moreover, since many SCADA protocols lack encryption, if attackers gain access to the network, they can be able to eavesdrop on the network and obtain sensitive data and control commands. By altering the control commands, they may later use this data to send false messages and compromise data integrity.

- Using commercial hardware and software components: Using Commercial-On-The-Shelf (COTS)-based hardware and software saves money and time when designing a network. This, however, has the potential to damage the SCADA network. COTS are insecure in general because they aren't equipped for sensitive control systems.

– Lack of user awareness: by using social engineering attack tactics, attackers use insiders to gain access to the network. Persuading an internal user to click on a URL in an e-mail from a workstation connected to the Internet and with access to the SCADA network is a common technique. Using this method, the attackers may spread malware or even gain unauthorised access. If an attacker has gained access to the SCADA network, any malicious attack may be used to crash or disrupt the SCADA and cyber-physical networks.

Unprotected communication protocols and channels are considered the weakest and the most fragile part among other ICS/SCADA components from the security perspective. This is because the majority of legacy SCADA systems were implemented and deployed before the advent of open computers and communication networks so that the technologies and protection mechanisms used in SCADA systems have not evolved as fast as those in the conventional computer and communication networks leaving these systems vulnerable to a wide range of attacks [20]. Cybersecurity risk will be severely heightened if existing SCADA implementations utilise the traditional ICT technologies for communication and part of its components are being interfaced with public networks such as the Internet without adequately hardened cybersecurity design architecture, cyber-attacks of traditional ICT systems may cause catastrophic consequences to physical services or even create a national disaster by permitting remote attackers to monitor and control sensitive critical national infrastructures. For instance, the system could be vulnerable to denial-of-service (DoS) attack, which leads to severe time delays and serious degradation of control performances [20]. Therefore, it is critical to ensure the security, robustness, and safety of the industrial control systems. The remaining of this section highlights major SCADA security weaknesses in commonly used communication protocols.

One of the popular ICS and SCADA systems' protocols is the Distributed Network Protocol 3.0 (DNP3). It is first and foremost used in the communication between the master control station and the remote substations [21]. The DNP3 protocol was considered the most comprehensive effort to achieve open, standards-based interoperability among various SCADA components and vendors [22]. Although new DNP 3.0/SA employs secure authentication, many older devices that use DNP3 in SCADA implementations typically do not employ encryption, authentication and authorisation mechanisms [15,23]. In fact, most of the DNP3 devices assume that all messages are valid. Additional examples of possible threats and vulnerabilities are highlighted here as follows [14,21]:

– Being an open-standard protocol allows terminal devices to communicate using a wide range of secured and unsecured protocols like TCP, UDP and HTTP. This may result in having more threats and vulnerabilities in the ICS and SCADA environments.
– Old generation DNP3-based SCADA systems were designed without security considerations such as message authentication. This weakness makes the SCADA system vulnerable to operational data manipulation, resulting in catastrophic disruption of normal system operations.

One of the most commonly used protocol in electrical SCADA system is the IEC 60870-5-101. It is an international industrial standard which has been released about twenty years ago by the IEC. The protocol is primarily used in the energy sector and is being used until today. The IEC 60870-5-101 supports point-to-point and multi-drop communication links carrying bit-serial low-bandwidth data communications. On the other hand, IEC 60870-5-104 is an extension to the IEC 60870-5-101 with changes to the network layer, link layer and physical layer, which enables communication to be done via a standard TCP/IP network. Given that both protocols are very similar, they, therefore, share the same security vulnerabilities. The industry attempts to mitigate the risk of attack by coming up with the IEC 62351 standard that provides authentication for control and critical messages for both IEC 60870 and DNP 3.0. However, the situation is no better off as devices that support IEC60870 are in a similar predicament as those describe for DNP 3.0. Listed below are the security vulnerabilities that exist in both protocols [24, 25].

- Weak or non-existent checksum: The checksum is used to ensure that the data being transmitted is accurate. It can say if the data has been tempered during transmission to the receiver. Just a one-byte checksum is used in IEC 60870-5-101. However, in IEC 60870-5-104, there is no checksum field as it relies only on the protocol checksum provided by the conventional TCP and IP protocols.
- Lack of built-in security mechanisms in both protocols for providing security at the application layer and data link layer. Both protocols are only designed to provide communication, and no security mechanisms such as encryption or authentication are included in their design.
- Communication vulnerabilities at data transit level: Both protocols are widely used in situations where the communication medium has limited bandwidth, restricting the maximum frame duration that can be sent at a given time. The use of communication medium such as twisted-pair copper cable or radio waves (both are common in SCADA implementation) makes it easy for data transmitted to be eavesdropped or fake data to be injected into the medium.

6   SCADA Vulnerability Use Case

In this section, we are demonstrating a simple command injection attack targeting SCADA substation running over IEC104 communication protocol to prove the mentioned vulnerabilities. The main goal of this proof-of-concept attack is to demonstrate the consequences of lack of device identification and encryption of the mentioned protocol. Figure 3 illustrate the deployed testbed and the steps involved in launching the attack.

The experimental testbed includes several SCADA key components: a real-time digital simulator to emulate the power system, generate data and receive commands, master and local HMI, an RTU and several engineering workstations for testing and analysis purposes. In this testbed, an Opal-RT model OP5600, a specialised hardware/software simulator, simulates the IEEE New England

39-Bus power system in real-time. At the bay level, the functions of both the controller and RTU are modelled using the Real-Time Application Platform (RTAP), which is a proprietary platform used for modelling and simulating industrial control system devices. The state of the emulated power system and RTU can be monitored and controlled through the master (station level) and local HMI (bay level), which are modelled using Station Level Operator Interface (SLOI). SLOI is a proprietary platform used to visualise the power system simulated by the Opal-RT simulator and receive and send commands from RTU and Controller (RTAP). In this work, the SCADA network is designed to bridge the substation (bay level) and the control centre (station level) through a network switch. Therefore, all the SCADA testbed components are considered in the same network, and the components are connected to a local area network through an Ethernet switch.

Command injection attacks can result in catastrophic consequences. For example, an adversary can alter the control set-point to make devices operate at critical levels. Moreover, he/she can adjust alarm values stored in PLC registers to disable alarms by changing alarm set-points levels to values in line with the altered high and low set points. An attacker can also forge reading values on the control centre to trick system operators and let the attack go unnoticed.

Once the attacker gained access to the SCADA network, a crafted IEC104 payload can be injected into the operational network to control the actuators located at the physical system. In this case study, we are managing a circuit breaker on the simulated electrical power network. Figure 4 demonstrates the utilisation of an open-source software application (Packet Sender) to inject the crafted command.

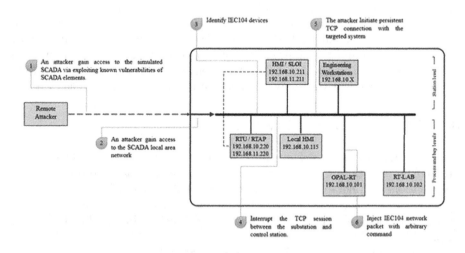

Fig. 3. Command injection attack scenario

Fig. 4. Packet Sender settings of injecting control command

Upon a successful injection, a distribution of the voltage level can be noticed as an effect of unintentionally disconnecting the circuit breaker, as illustrated in Fig. 5. For more details, readers can refer to our previously published paper in [15] and [13].

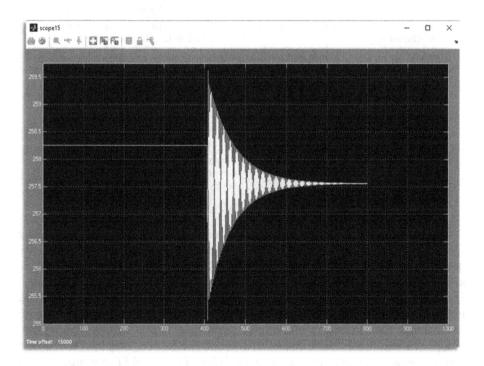

Fig. 5. Voltage distribution as a result of disconnecting a circuit breaker

7 SCADA Security Recommendations

In modern SCADA systems, new technologies play a vital and invaluable role in providing the necessary support for SCADA systems to control and operate various critical industrial infrastructures. Therefore, it is essential to engage necessary technology security capabilities to protect the system from cyber-attacks and eventual sabotage [3]. Potential security countermeasures may include implementing a secured network architecture with segregation in mind; or security enforcement via firewalls, intrusion detection systems and cryptography, as well as other cyber-security protection mechanisms, among other various SCADA security enhancement techniques (Table 3).

Table 3. Summary of SCADA security recommendations

SCADA vulnerabilities	Recommended countermeasure	Recommended actions
Legacy software	Risk analysis and mitigation	Understand the potential risk and put suitable plan to upgrade or maintain the software that possess higher risk
Lack of encryption	Link encryption	Implement security gateway or utilise IPSec and SSL technologies
Device identification	Digital signature	Implement security gateway or utilise IPSec and SSL technologies
Default or Miss-configurations	Audit and monitor data access	Perform continuous security auditing to preserve the secrecy of the system
Web interface attacks	Audit and monitor data access	Perform penetration testing on regular bases
Network perimeter protection	Segregation of assets	Utilise data and user access control mechanisms and apply network-security by design principles
Safe data handling	Anonymisation	Apply data leakage prevention mechanisms and store data as anonymised or synthesised data

The architecture of a SCADA network might offer a strategy for enhancing the security capabilities of the whole system only if a careful and deliberate design were considered [26]. A secured SCADA network architecture could be accomplished by implementing some form of segregation of assets. The zones-and-conduits concept segregates SCADA assets into interrelated groups based on unique services or applications; it also controls the communication flow between separate groups, thereby minimising the potential attack surface of any given group. On the other hand, firewalls, intrusion detection systems, and access controls, among different protection approaches of standard IT systems, are still valuable in protecting SCADA and industrial networks. Firewalls, for example, different trust levels in a network using a defined configuration policy. At the same time, IDS monitors network traffic and system activities for suspicious activities and raises alerts when such action is discovered. It might be better to consider deploying an intrusion detection system along with a firewall to achieve the defence-in-depth security approach for a higher protection level. However, extra precautions must be taken to identify potential setup issues and threats like exploitable backdoors and misconfiguration, and possible network/traffic latency in SCADA operations due to complexities of firewall rule sets along with IDSs' deep packet inspections. Data communication delays are quite intolerable in SCADA because of the potential impacts on security objectives.

Cryptography and authentication, such as offered by IEC 62351, have proved unquestionable data protection and confidentiality method in standard IT systems, and have been adopted in the industrial control systems to aid the security of these systems by guarding against unauthorised information disclosure, manipulation of sensitive data, and also help achieve end-to-end secure communication in SCADA network. Previous researches have shown valuable results while transmitting industrial communication protocols over a secure encrypted channel, such as transmitting DNP3 over SSH. However, several issues related to computational capability and communication latency are still common problems of these systems.

8 Conclusion

Modern SCADA infrastructure has become increasingly exposed to various security risks, either directly connected to the Internet or via data exchange interfaces with management and business IT systems. As a result, inflicting substantial damage or widespread disruption may be quite possible. Therefore, SCADA systems require the design and deployment of numerous security protection measures. Efforts to potentially secure SCADA networks and control and monitoring terminals should focus on traditional IT security mechanisms for detecting malicious activities and responding to potential threats. Moreover, efforts should be drawn to intelligent systems that can proactively identify security vulnerabilities, potential risks, and faults that attackers can exploit.

This paper surveyed state of the art in SCADA security, identified research challenges in this emerging area, and motivated the deployment of cyber-security methods and tools to SCADA systems. Considering the current SCADA communication protocol vulnerabilities, previous reported security incidents and potential threats, it seems clear that cyber-attacks against SCADA and critical infrastructure systems will be more nuanced and smarter. Therefore, much work has to be done to protect these systems from possible sabotage and information disclosure. This can be accomplished through strong and yet lightweight data encryption and device-to-device authentication to prevent injection and data modification attacks and ensure the integrity of both; the data and the source.

Acknowledgement. This research is supported by Transdisciplinary Research Grant Scheme (TRGS) 2020, Ministry of Higher Education Malaysia, under the project 'Cyber Threat Modeling and Advanced Persistent Threat Detection for a Resilient Dam Control System Using Context-based Approach and Ensemble Method of Machine Learning Models With Discrete Probability Distribution'.

References

1. Alcaraz, C., Zeadally, S.: Critical infrastructure protection: requirements and challenges for the 21st century. Int. J. Crit. Infrastr. Protect. **8**, 53–66 (2015). http://linkinghub.elsevier.com/retrieve/pii/S1874548214000791
2. Nazir, S., Patel, S., Patel, D.: Assessing and augmenting SCADA cyber security: a survey of techniques. Comput. Secur. **70**, 436–454 (2017). http://linkinghub.elsevier.com/retrieve/pii/S0167404817301293
3. Ani, U.P.D., He, H.M., Tiwari, A.: Review of cybersecurity issues in industrial critical infrastructure: manufacturing in perspective. J. Cyber Secur. Technol. **1**(1), 32–74 (2017). https://doi.org/10.1080/23742917.2016.1252211
4. Rosa, L., Freitas, M., Mazo, S., Monteiro, E., Cruz, T., Simoes, P.: A comprehensive security analysis of a SCADA protocol: from OSINT to mitigation. IEEE Access **7**, 42156–42168 (2019). https://ieeexplore.ieee.org/document/8672892/
5. Krotofil, M., Gollmann, D.: Industrial control systems security: what is happening? In: 2013 11th IEEE International Conference on Industrial Informatics (INDIN), pp. 664–669. IEEE (2013). http://ieeexplore.ieee.org/document/6622963/
6. Tawde, R., Nivangune, A., Sankhe, M.: Cyber security in smart grid SCADA automation systems. In: 2015 International Conference on Innovations in Information, Embedded and Communication Systems (ICIIECS), pp. 1–5. IEEE, March 2015. http://ieeexplore.ieee.org/document/7192918/
7. Ghosh, S., Sampalli, S.: A survey of security in SCADA networks: current issues and future challenges. IEEE Access 7, 135812–135831 (2019). https://ieeexplore.ieee.org/document/8753583/
8. Pliatsios, D., Sarigiannidis, P., Lagkas, T., Sarigiannidis, A.G.: A survey on SCADA systems: secure protocols, incidents, threats and tactics. IEEE Commun. Surv. Tutor. **22**(3), 1942–1976 (2020). https://ieeexplore.ieee.org/document/9066892/
9. Volkova, A., Niedermeier, M., Basmadjian, R., de Meer, H.: Security challenges in control network protocols: a survey. IEEE Commun. Surv. Tutor. **21**(1), 619–639 (2019). https://ieeexplore.ieee.org/document/8472799/
10. Bhamare, D., Zolanvari, M., Erbad, A., Jain, R., Khan, K., Meskin, N.: Cybersecurity for industrial control systems: a survey. Comput. Secur. **89**, 101677 (2020). https://linkinghub.elsevier.com/retrieve/pii/S0167404819302172
11. Alladi, T., Chamola, V., Zeadally, S.: Industrial control systems: cyberattack trends and countermeasures. Comput. Commun. **155**, 1–8 (2020). https://linkinghub.elsevier.com/retrieve/pii/S0140366419319991
12. Coffey, K., Smith, R., Maglaras, L., Janicke, H.: Vulnerability analysis of network scanning on SCADA systems. Secur. Commun. Netw. **2018**, 1–21 (2018). https://www.hindawi.com/journals/scn/2018/3794603/
13. Qassim, Q.S., Jamil, N., Z'aba, M.R., Aba, N., Kamarulzaman, W.A.W.: Assessing the cyber-security of the IEC 60870-5-104 protocol in SCADA system. Int. J. Crit. Infrastr. **16**(2), 91 (2020). http://www.inderscience.com/link.php?id=107242
14. Qassim, Q.S., Jamil, N., Mahdi, M.N., Abdul Rahim, A.A.: Towards SCADA threat intelligence based on intrusion detection systems - a short review. In: 2020 8th International Conference on Information Technology and Multimedia, ICIMU 2020 (2020)
15. Qassim, Q.S., Jamil, N., Daud, M., Ja'affar, N., Kamarulzaman, W.A.W., Mahdi, M.N.: Compromising the data integrity of an electrical power grid SCADA system. In: Anbar, M., Abdullah, N., Manickam, S. (eds.) ACeS 2020. CCIS, vol.

1347, pp. 604–626. Springer, Singapore (2021). https://doi.org/10.1007/978-981-33-6835-4_40

16. Maglaras, L.A., et al.: Cyber security of critical infrastructures. ICT Express **4**(1), 42–45 (2018). http://linkinghub.elsevier.com/retrieve/pii/S2405959517303880

17. Cárdenas, A.A., Amin, S., Lin, Z.S., Huang, Y.L., Huang, C.Y., Sastry, S.: Attacks against process control systems. In: Proceedings of the 6th ACM Symposium on Information, Computer and Communications Security - ASIACCS 2011, p. 355. ACM Press, New York (2011). http://portal.acm.org/citation.cfm?doid=1966913.1966959

18. Cherdantseva, Y., et al.: A review of cyber security risk assessment methods for SCADA systems. Comput. Secur. **56**, 1–27 (2016). http://linkinghub.elsevier.com/retrieve/pii/S0167404815001388

19. Igure, V.M., Laughter, S.A., Williams, R.D.: Security issues in SCADA networks. Comput. Secur. 25(7), 498–506 (2006). http://linkinghub.elsevier.com/retrieve/pii/S0167404806000514

20. Wu, G., Sun, J., Chen, J.: A survey on the security of cyber-physical systems. Control Theory Technol. **14**(1), 2–10 (2016). http://link.springer.com/10.1007/s11768-016-5123-9

21. Drias, Z., Serhrouchni, A., Vogel, O.: Analysis of cyber security for industrial control systems. In: International Conference on Cyber Security of Smart Cities, Industrial Control System and Communications (SSIC), pp. 1–8 (2015)

22. Amoah, R.: Formal security analysis of the DNP3-secure authentication protocol. Ph.D. thesis, Queensland University of Technology (2016). http://eprints.qut.edu.au/93798/

23. Darwish, I., Igbe, O., Celebi, O., Saadawi, T., Soryal, J.: Smart grid DNP3 vulnerability analysis and experimentation. 2015 IEEE 2nd International Conference on Cyber Security and Cloud Computing, pp. 141–147, November 2015. http://ieeexplore.ieee.org/document/7371473/ieeexplore.ieee.org/lpdocs/epic03/wrapper.htm?arnumber=7371473

24. Tan, S.: Electric power automation control system based on SCADA protocols. In: Zhong, Z. (ed.) Proceedings of the International Conference on Information Engineering and Applications (IEA) 2012. LNEE, vol. 218, pp. 137–143. Springer, London (2013). https://doi.org/10.1007/978-1-4471-4847-0_17

25. Pidikiti, D.S., Kalluri, R., Kumar, R.K.S., Bindhumadhava, B.S.: SCADA communication protocols: vulnerabilities, attacks and possible mitigations. CSI Trans. ICT **1**(2), 135–141 (2013). http://link.springer.com/10.1007/s40012-013-0013-5

26. Qassim, Q.S., Jamil, N., Daud, M., Hasan, H.C.: Towards implementing scalable and reconfigurable SCADA security testbed in power system environment. Int. J. Crit. Infrastr. **15**(2), 91 (2019). http://www.inderscience.com/link.php?id=98834

An Improved Secure Router Discovery Mechanism to Prevent Fake RA Attack in Link Local IPv6 Network

Navaneethan C. Arjuman$^{(\boxtimes)}$ (ID), Selvakumar Manickam$^{(\boxtimes)}$ (ID), and Shankar Karuppayah$^{(\boxtimes)}$ (ID)

National Advanced IPv6 Centre (NAv6), Universiti Sains Malaysia, Gelugor, Penang, Malaysia
{nava,selva,shankar}@nav6.usm.my

Abstract. In Stateless Address Auto Configuration (SLAAC) in the IPv6 network, the host obtain the network prefix using Router Discovery (RD) protocol. The standard RD by design do not have trust mechanism to authenticate the legitimate host and router. This design flaw within RD protocol has led to Fake Router Advertisement (Fake RA) attack where the host is denied of the legitimate gateway. In order to address this issue, several prevention techniques such as Trust Neighbour Discovery (Trust-ND), CGA + Internet Protocol Security (IPSec) Authentication Header (AH) NDP mechanism and others have been proposed in the past. However, these techniques also face other vulnerabilities such as high computation cost, hash collision attacks and bootstrapping problem. Hence, this paper review shortcoming of these mechanisms and proposes an improved secure RD mechanism i.e. the SecMac-Secure Router Discovery (SecMac-SRD) mechanism to overcome the Fake RA attacks. SecMac-SRD mechanism provides 60.8% reduction of processing time compare to Trust-ND while preventing Fake RA attacks during the RD process in the link local communication of the IPv6 network.

Keywords: Router discovery vulnerabilities · Router discovery attacks · Secure router discovery prevention mechanism for Fake RA attacks

1 Introduction

In the IPv6 network, every host required to implement Router Discovery (RD) process in order acquire the gateway prefix for the standard address auto-configuration mechanism e.g. the Stateless Address Auto Configuration (SLAAC) mechanism [1]. Since there is no trust mechanism exist in the standard RD process to verify the legitimacy of the gateway router, studies show that the standard RD operation is vulnerable to Fake Router Advertisement (Fake RA) attacks [2].

The host will send out Router Solicitation (RS) messages to all the active routers on the link in the standard RD process [3] and all the gateway received this RS messages will reply Router Advertisement (RA) messages with appropriate gateway configuration [1]. The host will select suitable gateway router based on the nearest next hop value or

© Springer Nature Singapore Pte Ltd. 2021
N. Abdullah et al. (Eds.): ACeS 2021, CCIS 1487, pp. 248–276, 2021.
https://doi.org/10.1007/978-981-16-8059-5_15

based on highest priority value upon receiving all the appropriate RA messages from the gateway routers. Upon selection of the appropriate gateway router to the Internet, all the communication to Internet will flow through this selected gateway router.

The host is not able to verify whether the selected gateway router is valid router since there is no presence of trust mechanism in the standard RD protocol. This shortcoming in the RD process allows the host to be configured to attacker's routers as the new legitimate gateway router [4]. In this scenario, the host will be configured with Fake RA message [1]. This attack scenario will be categorised as Fake RA attack where the host will be denied with the legitimate service [1].

In overcome the above RD vulnerabilities, several researchers in the past introduces several prevention techniques such as SeND's Authorisation Delegation Discovery (ADD), Trust Router Discovery Protocol (TRDP), Router Advertisement Guard (RA-Guard), Trust Neighbour Discovery (Trust-ND) and CGA + IPSEC AH NDP Mechanism.

The ADD mechanism within the SeND [5] introduced router certificate to determine the legitimacy of the gateway router. However, the lengthy certificate process causes high computational cost and eventually leads to DoS attacks [7]. The proposed TRDP [6] claimed to address the shortcoming of SeND by reducing the complexity and computational cost but with the creation of the new ICMPv6 messages and longer router authentication process of TRDP also contribute to higher computational cost [7].

The introduction of RA-Guard which is the layer 2 prevention mechanism [8] able to overcome the higher computational cost compare to SeND and TRDP but RA-Guard also have other issues.

The researcher of Trust-ND mechanism claims Trust-ND is a lightweight mechanism because having lower computational cost compared to SeND and TRDP [7]. Trust-ND uses the trust concept defined in RFC 3756 [2]. But this mechanism also more complex in terms design especially because required additional trust value and trust tag calculations which leads to high computational cost as well. Furthermore, this mechanism also built using SHA-1 hashing algorithm [9] that is very vulnerable to hash collision attack [10, 11].

The recently introduced CGA + Internet Protocol Security (IPSec) Authentication Header (AH) NDP Mechanism [12] which claims to be a lightweight mechanism compared to SeND. But this mechanism also more complex in terms of design because the additional AH process for RS and RA process will leads to high computational cost as well. Furthermore, this mechanism also uses the AH is part of IPSec suite [13] to authenticate the router. AH operates using Security Association (SA)s that was built based on Internet key exchange version 2 which required functional IP address. So when a new host joining the network, the host will not have functional IP address so this scenario leads to bootstrapping problem [14].

This paper review shortcoming of these mechanisms and proposes an improved secure RD mechanism i.e. the SecMac-Secure Router Discovery (SecMac-SRD) mechanism to overcome the Fake RA attacks. Section 2 discuss IPv6 Router Discovery (RD) process and its security vulnerabilities. Section 3 covers design and implementation of the SecMac-SRD mechanism. Section 4 discuss the Test-bed setup for the SecMac-SRD mechanism. Section 5 describe experimental setup, evaluation of SecMac-SRD mechanism as a security solution and discussion regarding the experimental results. Section 5 analyse the experimental results of the proposed SecMac-SRD mechanism. Section 6 discuss regarding the findings of the research work and future work.

2 IPv6 Router Discovery (RD) Process and Its Security Vulnerabilities

The weakness in the RD protocol in the IPv6 address assignment using the SLAAC scheme leads to various attacks in the IPv6 network [15, 16]. The host will receive Fake RA messages because there is presence of bogus routers in the IPv6 network.

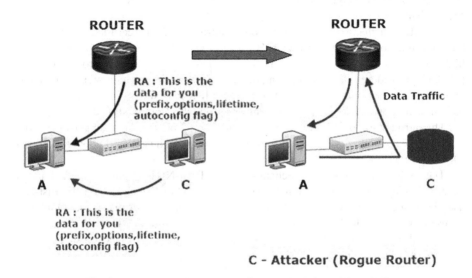

Fig. 1. Router advertisement spoofing attack (Adapted from [17])

In reference to Fig. 1, the Host A will generated RS messages that will be forwarded to all the routers that are active on the link. The same message will be received by Attacker C. The Attacker C whom behave like a legitimate router also reply to the RS message with RA messages with all the required parameters. Upon receiving this RA message from Attacker C, the Host A will select the Attacker C as the default gateway router. In the standard RD process, the selection of gateway router is based on either highest priority or the next nearest hop. The Attacker C will craft RA packet with the highest priority so that the host will select as Attacker C router as the default router gateway. The Host A will be configured with the all the parameters from the Attacker C router. All the data communication of the Host A will goes through Attacker C router before it reaches the actual destination. The attacker able to listen all the communication of the victim Host A to other destination hosts via Attacker C router. This type of attack is also known as Router Advertisement Spoofing [18] attack. Various other attacks such as MITM Attack, DoS attack, DDoS attack, etc. can be initiated using these spoofed information [19, 20].

Since there is no verification mechanism exist in the standard RD protocol to verify the legitimacy of the gateway router, the above-mentioned attacks can be initiated in the IPv6 network. The researchers in the past have proposed several RD security mechanisms to detect, mitigate and prevent the above security issues. The primary focus of this research would be to overcome the RD process vulnerabilities using the prevention mechanism. The following sections analyses in detail the secure RD mechanism that were proposed by the researchers in the past.

2.1 Authorised Delegation Discovery (ADD) Mechanism of SEND

The ADD form as key component of the SeND mechanism. The ADD mechanism was designed based on verification of the legitimate router using the electronic certificate issued by the Certificate Authority (CA). New ICMPv6 messages namely Certificate Path Solicitations (CPS) and Certificate Path Advertisement (CPA) have been introduce by this mechanism to verify the legitimacy of the presented certificate by the router [5–21]. The newly introduced ICMPv6 messages in the mechanism will leads to lengthy certificate path verification process and eventually leads to high computation cost. The requesting host will be busy receiving unnecessary CPAs in the presence of rogue routers. This unnecessary CPA request would require the host to verify again and again the path [21]. The host will busy performing many unnecessary CA validations which eventually leads to higher computation cost and eventually leads to DoS attacks. Furthermore, the only workable SeND solution available now is Easy-SeND. Easy-SeND in the actual implementation unable to perform RD discovery.

2.2 Trusted Router Discovery Protocol (TRDP)

The TRDP mechanism try overcome the limitation of ADD for the computational cost. The CA verification in ADD's is a very lengthy process compare to TRDP which leads to high computation cost. In the TRDP mechanism, Router Access Passport (RAP) were used to verify the legitimacy of Access Router (AR) by the newly joining hosts. ADD uses CPS and CPA messages to verify the certificate path of Certified Authority (CA). Whereas in TRDP, RAPs are issued by upper intermediate router that is linked to CA. Two pair of new ICMPv6 messages known as TRPS/TRPA (Trusted Router Passport Solicitation/Trusted Router Passport Advertisement) and TR2PS/TR2PA (Trusted Router-Router Passport Solicitation/Trusted Router-Router Passport Advertisement) were introduced in the TRDP process [6]. Performance of RD process for TRDP mechanism is better compared to ADD but the router verification process still lengthy compare to RA-Guard. Due to lengthy router verification, this could lead to DoS attacks in the IPv6 network.

2.3 Router Advertisement (RA) Guard

RA-Guard which is the layer 2 secure RD mechanism provides faster router verification compare to ADD and TRDP in the IPv6 network [8]. This mechanism can be implemented together with SeND mechanism as well. This mechanism does not allow RA messages from the unauthorised source [8]. But the RA-Guard mechanism also comes with the following **vulnerabilities**

1. The RA messages that is generated from non RA-Guard enabled devices would not able to block by RA-Guard mechanism.
2. The RA traffic that are channeled through tunnel would not able to block by RA-Guard.
3. The rogue RA messages that are generated for ingress is only can be blocked by RA-Guard and not the rogue egress RA messages.
4. For those devices that already configured with ACL ICMPv6 optimization, unable to configure the RA-Guard feature.
5. For the traffic that are on trunk port with merge mode not supported by the RA-Guard mechanism.

For the traffics that employing IPv6 extension headers, there is an evasion technique that circumvent the RA-Guard implementation [22]. For the forged RA packets that is already fragmented, the RA-Guard is unable to drop the RA messages.

2.4   Trust Neighbour Discovery (Trust-ND)

The Trust-ND mechanism is considered to be lightweight compare to ADD and TRDP in terms of less processing time because it uses shorter SHA-1 hash functions to provide secure RD communication [23]. The Trust-ND mechanism with Trust Value and Trust Option is key security parameters in this mechanism [7]. Trust value is calculated and compared for every host that receives the NDP messages before accepting their NDP messages. This Trust Option is appended to each NDP messages to verify whether NDP messages is valid to ensure the NDP message exchange is secure in the IPv6 networks. The Trust-ND mechanism work based on trust model where each host need to verify the received NDP messages ie. RS, RA, Neighbour Solicitation (NS), Neighbour Advertisement (NA) and Router Redirect (RR) messages is valid before accepting the NDP messages. Based the appended Trust value together with the NDP message, the host will accept or drops the NDP messages. The Trust-ND mechanism was implemented by Praptodiyono et al. [7] using SHA-1 hash function. For the Neighbour Discovery (ND) process, SHA-1 hash function provides faster verifications compare to encryption technique using RSA in the SeND mechanism [24]. Furthermore, the researcher unable to provide comparison results for the RA and RR during the testing of Trust-ND mechanism together using only workable SeND solution that is Easy-SeND mechanism which is limited to the ND process only. Using Easy-SeND solution hosts are unable to participate in the RD process. So the obtained testing results for RA and RR in the Trust-ND mechanism unable to compare with ADD. The Trust-ND mechanism provided performance improvement for ND using small SHA-1 key size to generate the Trust Option [7]. The studies show that SHA-1 hash functions are susceptible to hash collisions attacks although the researcher claimed that Trust-ND is a lightweight mechanism compared to TRDP [9]. Furthermore, the studies show that SHA-1 and MD5 hash functions that are susceptible to hash collisions attacks can be attack by any malicious host using the hash collision vulnerabilities [25]. The Trust-ND mechanism is also vulnerable to hash collision attacks in the IPv6 network communication because it was built on the SHA-1 hash function. Trust-ND also not desired as secure RD solution due to this design issue.

2.5 CGA + IPSEC AH NDP Mechanism

In this secure RD mechanism design, the Yoganguina et al. [12] proposed to use AH to authenticate the RA message. AH is a member of the IPSEC suite [13]. Protection of NDP messages can be implemented using AH to ensure congeniality and integrity of NDP messages. The validity of the NDP messages received from the host can be verified based on AH Security Association (SA)s which is the key feature in protecting the stateless nature of the NDP messages. But the SAs that was built based on Internet key exchange version 2 which required functional IP address. So when a new host joining the network, the host will not have functional IP address so this scenario leads to bootstrapping problem [14]. Without a valid IP address this mechanism would not be able to function. Configuring the IPSEC manually also would be tedious and not scalable [1]. The research conducted by Xinyu, Ting and Yi [26] clearly proof that IPSEC is very vulnerable to DoS attack using legitimate non-spoofed IP address [26]. So this RD mechanism may not be very suitable mainly for those implementation for newly joining hosts in the link local communication of the IPv6 network.

2.6 Drawback of Existing Secure Router Mechanism

The following section categorised drawbacks of the existing mechanism into three main causes as follows:

High Computational Cost
The high computational cost will slow down the operations of any process [32]. The complexity of the mechanism leads to high computational cost. Study shows [7] that the existing mechanisms such as ADD and TRDP have higher computational cost for the secure router verifications process with 3rd party. This 3rd party router verifications are a lengthy process. This will also lead to DoS attacks in the link local communication of the IPv6 network. Even though Trust-ND and CGA + IPSEC AH NDP mechanism claimed to have less computation cost compare to ADD and TRDP but the industry needs even more efficient security mechanisms to meet the demand of new technology such as IoT and 5G networks. Some of the IoT devices uses lower power storage. The high computational cost of the security mechanism will drain the power of the IoT devices. So the proposed security mechanism should use less processing time to reduce the power usage and meets the industry requirements.

Other Inherent Vulnerabilities
Even though the Trust-ND and CGA + IPSEC NDP mechanisms able to secure the RD attacks but these mechanisms suffers from other inherent vulnerabilities such as hash collision attack and bootstrapping problem as explained below.

Hashing Collision Attack

In cryptography, a collision attack on a cryptographic hash tries to find two inputs producing the same hash value, i.e. a hash collision. Although the existing mechanism such as Trust-ND mechanism is able to address the high computational cost issue by introducing a lightweight mechanism using hashing technique but this hashing technique vulnerable to hash collision attack [10]. The validation process of the RS and RA message can be exploited by an attacker taking advantage of this weakness during the RD process. So this will lead to Fake RA attack and other DoS attack in the RD process.

Bootstrapping Problem

Although the existing mechanism such as CGA + IPSEC AH NDP able to prevent Fake RA attack during the RD process but this mechanism itself face issues related to bootstrapping problem where a valid unicast IP address is required before IPSEC AH is initiated. So when new host joining the network, the host would not have valid IP address. So this mechanism would not work well in this scenario. So this mechanism may not suitable to implement in the IPv6 network.

3rd Party Dependency

The existing security mechanisms in the secure RD process such as ADD and TRDP are depend on a 3rd party to verify the certificate. 3rd party verification will incur additional computational cost because required additional processing time.

Due to the constraints possessed by the above mentioned mechanism, the above mechanisms was not widely implemented and the RD process is still vulnerable for exploitation. Therefore, this research proposed an improved secure RD mechanism i.e. SecMac-SRD mechanism to secure the RD process. The proposed mechanism designs would be based on less processing time heuristic based secure RD mechanism that is more efficient in terms computational cost to prevent Fake RA attack in the link local communication of the IPv6 network. The following Section will explain the design and implementation processes of SecMac-SRD Mechanism.

3   Design and Implementation of SecMac-SRD Mechanism

The primary objective of this research to design a less processing time heuristic based secure RD mechanism that is more efficient in terms computational cost to prevent Fake RA attack in the link local communication of the IPv6 network. To fulfill the above design objective, the SecMac-SRD mechanism works as the trusted mechanism to ensure secure RD process in the link local communications of the IPv6 network.

In the RD process, verification required to check the legitimacy of RS and RA message to ensure secure RD process and protect the RD message exchange from Fake RA attack. In order to authenticate the RS and RA messages, the research proposed appropriate hashing technique to secure the RD messages. The selection a hash algorithm to produce quick hash values and immutable is very important to ensure the integrity of the message transaction. In this research, Universal Message Authentication Code (UMAC) has been selected to generate the secure tag to authenticate the RD messages.

UMAC is a higher performance message authentication code (MAC) algorithm that is designed based on Wegman and Carter style [27]. It has a fast "universal" hash function that uses message M as input into a short string. Using a pseudorandom pad, this short string will be masked by XOR that will result in a UMAC tag. The sharing of a randomly-chosen secret hash function of this UMAC tag between the sender and receiver would ensure the communication between sender and receiver is secured. This secure tag generated using keyed hash function H and pseudorandom function F by performing the following computation

$$Tag = H\_K1(M) \ XOR \ F\_K2(Nonce) \tag{1}$$

where K1 and K2 are secret random keys shared by sender and receiver. When the secure tag is generated each time, the Nonce value changes. The sender and receiver needs to synchronize the nonce so that receiver will know which nonce was used by the sender. In order to synchronize the nonce values, the message and tag need to be sent explicitly or use some other non-repeating value such as a sequence number. In order to ensure the lifetime of a UMAC key, a different nonce is used with each message and not necessary to keep the nonce secret.

Researches have proven that UMAC is more efficient compare to the SHA-1 algorithm that used by Trust-ND because SHA-1 hashing algorithm suffers from hash collision attacks. Furthermore, AES-CMAC-96 hashing algorithm bit size is 96 and UMAC bit size is 64 only. So it makes UMAC is an appropriate hashing algorithm with smaller bit size and without hash collision attack vulnerabilities compare to Trust-ND and CGA + IPSEC AH NDP mechanism. So the secure tag that generated used UMAC based hashing algorithms able to secure RD process more efficiently in the RD process in the IPv6 network.

SecMac-SRD mechanism would be appending SecMac-tag to every RS and RA messages that will be generated by host and router to secure the RD message exchange. This Secure-tag that was generated using message authentication code (MAC) that allows the host and router to differentiate between legitimate RS and RA message or fake ones. The standard RS and RA messages in the RD process will be redesign by adding the ICMPv6 Options with the SecMac-tag. Upon appending the SecMac-tag to relevant RS and RA messages with a new added SecMac-tag field would be known as SecMac-RS and SecMac-RA that depicted in the Fig. 2 and 3 accordingly.

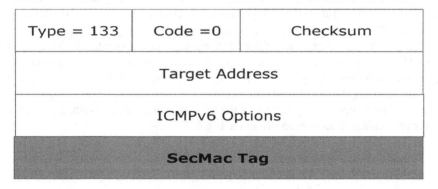

Fig. 2. SecMac-RS message format

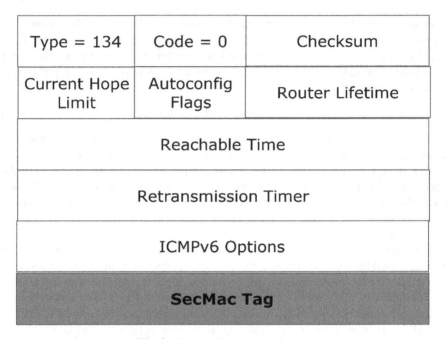

Fig. 3. SecMac-RA message format

In the above mentioned redesigned RD process, the host and router will generate the above mentioned RD messages with appended SecMac-tag that allows the host and router communicate securely. The above mentioned SecMac-tag allows RD messages verification by differentiating the valid or fake RD message. The above redesigned secure RD process allows the host to send valid RS messages with the SecMac-tag to the multicast address group router address FF02::2. Once all the routers received this redesigned RS messages, only the valid routers that was installed with redesigned SecMac-SRD mechanism module able to process this RS message as shown in Fig. 4. The verification process of the RS message with SecMac-tag will be done as shown in Fig. 4. Upon successful verification process of the RS message the router will proceed to the next level of the process of generating secure RA message.

The router will generate redesigned RA message with appended SecMac-tag that is SecMac-RA message based on successful RS verification in the earlier process. The router then will forward SecMac-RA message to the requesting host.

The requesting host will verify the SecMac-RA messages upon receiving this message from the router. The legitimacy of the sending router will be verified through the router verification process as shown in the Fig. 5.

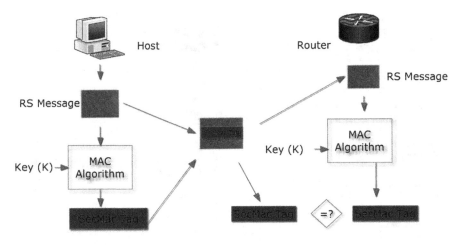

MAC - Message Authentication Code

If same SecMac Tag found then
authenticate the RS otherwise drop

Fig. 4. RS SecMac Tag validation process

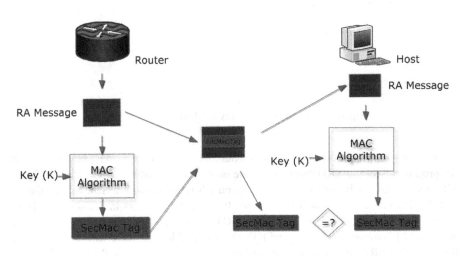

MAC - Message Authentication Code

If same SecMac Tag found then
authenticate the RA otherwise drop

Fig. 5. RA SecMac Tag validation process

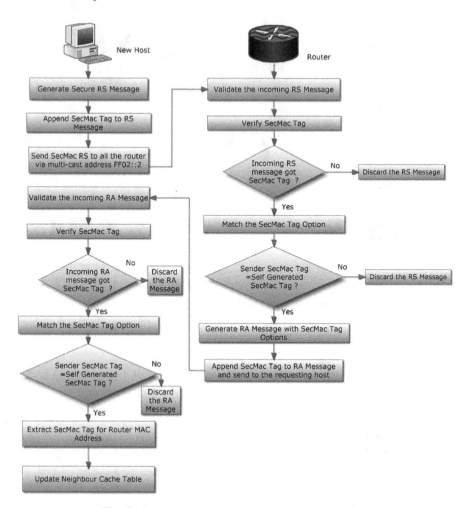

Fig. 6. Secure router discovery mechanism process flow

The entire process flow of the proposed SecMac-SRD mechanism is shown Fig. 6. In the proposed SecMac-SRD mechanism, the new host that have installed with SecMac-SRD mechanism will generate the redesigned RS message with a SecMac-tag that is SecMac-RS message then will forward to all the on link routers in the network. Only routers that have installed with SecMac-SRD mechanism will be able to accept the redesigned RS message and reply with this redesigned RA message with a SecMac-tag that is SecMac-RA message. The requesting host will verify the SecMac-RA then will extract the Router MAC Address then update the Neighbour Cache Table with this valid router. This router will be the default gateway for the requesting host.

The above mention process flow able to overcome Fake RA attacks in the IPv6 network. In the Fake RA attack the victim host will be configured with fake router as the default gateway. Once victim host is configured with fake router then the attacker has a right to deny legitimate service to the host. With redesigned RS and RA messages by appending the SecMac-tag option, only valid router will be configured as legitimate router gateway. The legitimacy of the router is ascertain using the SecMac-tag option which provides integrity checking for the router. If RA message is from the fake router, then this mechanism would drop the request of the router to be default gateway router.

The following section explains the detailed process flow how is the operation of SecMac-SRD mechanism. Please refer to Fig. 6 for a detailed process flow.

1. The newly join host in the network will produce SecMac-RS message with a SecMac-tag that includes Timestamp, Nonce and MAC.
2. The SecMac-RS message will be forwarded to all the on link routers by multicasting to FF02::2 address.
3. The receiving routers will verify whether the received SecMac-RS message has a valid SecMac-tag. If the SecMac-tag is valid then it will proceed to validate the other parameters such as Timestamp, Nonce and MAC. If all the parameters are valid then the router will proceed to produce SecMac-RA message. If each parameter is not valid in the verification process, then it will drop the RS request.
4. Upon successful verification of the RS message then the router will proceed to produce SecMac-RA message by appending RA message with SecMac-tag.
5. The router will forward SecMac-RA message to the requesting host.
6. The host will validate the received SecMac-RA message to authenticate the validity of received RA message.
7. Upon receiving the SecMac-RA message the host will check whether the RA has a SecMac-tag option. Then the host will proceed to verify the other parameters such as Timestamp and Nonce and MAC.
8. Once all the parameters such as Timestamp, Nonce and MAC are verified by the host then the host will proceed to extract router MAC address from the SecMac-RA messages to be updated in the Neighbour Cache Table. This router will be configured as the default gateway for the host.
9. If the validation process is not successful, then the host will not update Neighbour Cache Table with the router information as the default gateway for the host.

4   SecMac-SRD Test-Bed Implementation

The SecMac-SRD mechanism was built using the isolated closed IPv6 network architecture to make sure that the SecMac-tag enabled hosts communicate among themself without the external influence in the Test-bed environment. A closed isolated IPv6 network Test-bed was set up at National Advanced IPv6 Centre (NAv6) in Universiti Sains Malaysia (USM) to test the performance of this mechanism. Figure 7 below shows the Test-bed setup environment.

Figure 7 shows the test-bed environment to test performance of the proposed SecMac-SRD mechanism. In the above test-bed environment, the attack can be originating from any type of host i.e. Windows, Linux, etc. Kali Linux which is a Linux based Operating Systems (OS) used to perform the attack in the above test-bed environment. The Wireshark packet capturing tool has been used to capture and analyse the generated traffic.

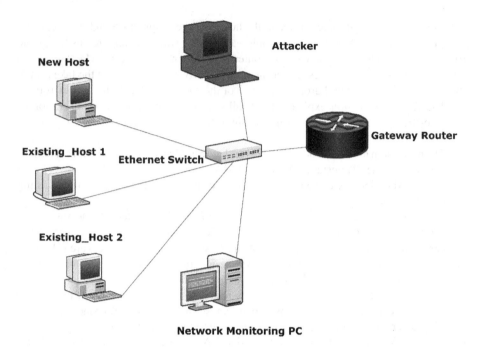

Fig. 7. Test-bed environment setup

In order to implement the above Test-bed, the following hardware and software have deployed based on availability at the NAv6 Centre. The following Table 1 and Table 2 shows the required hardware and software to implement the above mentioned Test-bed environment.

Table 1. Details of hardware requirement for the experimentations

Hardware		Details
Computer Hardware @ per (Host)	CPU	Intel® Core TM i7-4790 CPU@3,6 Ghz
	Memory	8 GB RAM
	Network Interface Card	Intel® Gigabit Ethernet Lan 10/100/1000
	Network Patch cables	Cat5e
Other network devices	Switch	Cisco Catalyst 2960 Fast Ethernet
	Access	Cisco Router C7200

Table 2. Details of software requirement for the experimentations

Operating systems		Role	Tools
Microsoft Windows	Windows 10 Pro (64 bit) Version 1903	Network Monitoring Host	Wireshark
		Test-bed Platform	GNS3
		Virtual Platform	VM Ware Virtual Box
		Programming Tool	Python 2.7.15
Linux Distributions	Kali Linux (Version 2018.4)	Attacker Host	THC IPv6 Attack Toolkit 3.4/ Scapy 2.4.0

The above mentioned SecMac-SRD mechanism was implemented based on RFC 4861 (NDP standard) [28] as shown in the following Fig. 8.

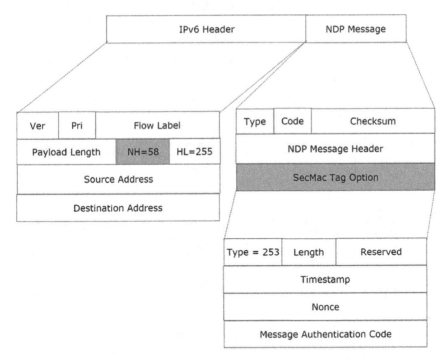

Fig. 8. IPv6 packet with secured RD message generation

The implementation of SecMac-SRD mechanism was carried out in two stages. In the first stage secure RD messages are produced by the sender (host/router). The 2nd stage involved producing secure RD messages by the receiver (host/router). The process of generating secure RD messages consists of appending a SecMac-tag to the RD messages as well as creating an IPv6 header packet and Ethernet frame. SecMac-tag used as new secure tag option to secure the RD process in the SecMac-SRD mechanism. The SecMac-tag that includes parameter such as Timestamp, Nonce and Message Authentication Code (MAC) that was appended to secure RD messages provides security check for all communication between the sender and receiver. Every secure RD message that generated in the above process having three default fields, namely, Type, Length and Reserved as shown in Fig. 8. In terms of RD option types, numeric values of 253 have been assigned as specified in the RFC 4727 [33]. This option type is commonly utilised for experimentation purposes and hence it is the chosen TYPE field value.

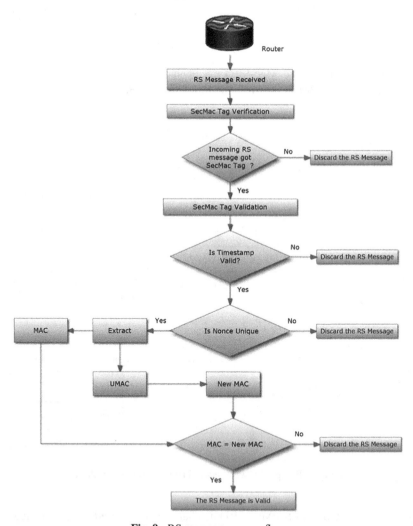

Fig. 9. RS message process flow

The SecMac-SRD mechanism includes three key process that are message verification of the secure RD message, message validation of all the parameters in the SecMac-tag and updating the neighbour cache table as shown Fig. 9 and 10 respectively.

5 Experimental Setup

In order to evaluate the proposed SecMac-SRD mechanism to be qualified as a suitable information security mechanism for securing the RD process, the following experiments was conducted to evaluate the proposed secure RD mechanism. This section discusses the evaluation criteria to be secure RD mechanism and anlayse the recorded results from the experiments.

5.1 Evaluation of SecMac-SRD Mechanism

In order for the proposed SecMac-SRD mechanism to qualify as a suitable information security mechanism for securing the RD process, a standard information security evaluation criterion needed to be established to assess the security capability of the SecMac-SRD mechanism. Information security is defined as protecting information and information systems from unauthorised access, use, disclosure, distribution and modification or destruction [29]. So security experts have outlined that in order to protect the information and information system, the system need to fulfill three key criterion i.e. Confidentiality, Integrity and Availability (CIA) and also known as CIA triad [30, 31]. CIA triad is key requirement in the evaluation for any information protection solutions or systems. According to the security experts, any security mechanism to be considered as viable security solutions or systems need to meets the above three criteria. These same metrics has been used to evaluate the SecMac-SRD implementation to be considered as viable secure RD mechanism to protect all the devices in the link local communication of the IPv6 network where the standard RD do not have trust mechanism to secure the RD messages. SecMac-SRD mechanism provide the required security using the SecMac-tag to secure the RD messages and preventing from the Fake RA attacks. Besides fulfilling the above measurement metrics, the SecMac-SRD mechanism also was measured in terms of processing time to assure that it is the mechanism use less processing time to secure RD messages compare to the existing prevention mechanisms.

5.2 Experimental Results and Discussion

SecMac-SRD mechanism is implemented based on the Test-bed environment as shown in Fig. 7. To ensure the SecMac-SRD mechanism function as security solution and meets all the security requirements, the implementation was carried out in two scenarios. The first scenario was SecMac-SRD mechanism tested under the standard normal condition. The second scenario was SecMac-SRD mechanism was tested during the Fake RA attack. The SecMac-SRD mechanism was tested under normal scenario was to check the efficiency of the proposed mechanism based on the processing time. Under the Fake

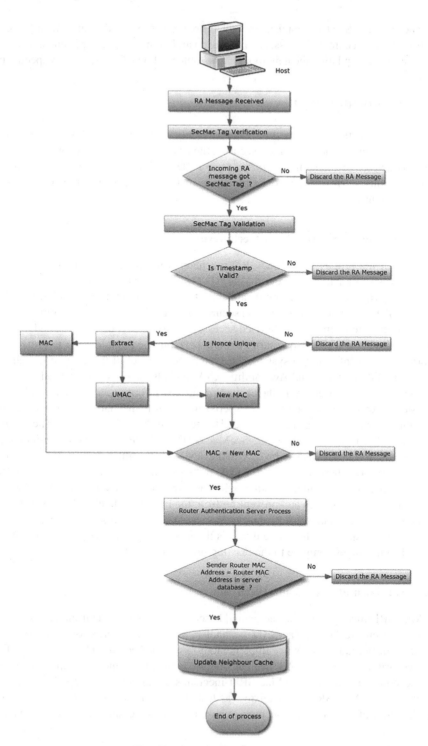

Fig. 10. RA message process flow

RA attack scenario, the proposed mechanism was tested to check the functionality of the proposed mechanism to overcome Fake RA attack.

Experiment Under Normal Scenario

In order to evaluate whether the SecMac-SRD mechanism is an efficient in terms resources i.e. less processing time, this section discuss in details of the computational efficiency of the SecMac-SRD mechanism. The processing time obtained from the experiment for the Standard RD mechanism, SecMac-SRD mechanism and Trust-ND mechanism are compared in this section to evaluated in terms of the performance efficiency of the proposed SecMac-SRD mechanism.

The Standard RD mechanism, SecMac-SRD mechanism and Trust-ND mechanism testing conducted using the same Test-bed environment. All the above mechanism was tested using the same Test-bed environments to ensure that no other external factors affect the results obtained in terms of processing time. Also the same Test-bed environments provide accurate comparison in terms recorded processing time between host and router during the RD process. The recorded results have been analysed to compare the performance of SecMac-SRD mechanism compare against Standard RD and Trust-ND mechanisms.

The router will carry out verification of the received Standard RS to ensure that the RS message from legitimate host. At same time, the message verification for both SecMac-RS and Trust-RS is also be carried out in the same Test-bed environment. The calculation of the total message processing time for the RS message in the router i.e. Ts is done based on subtracting the start processing time from the end processing time of the RS message validation process. So the calculated Ts would be the total message processing time for the RS validation process for the Standard RS, SecMac-RS and Trust-RS messages. The Standard RS, SecMac-RS and Trust-RS processes are repeated several time and recorded. In order to ensure the consistency of the processing time of the RS message, the measurement of Ts was repeated 20 times.

Table 3. RS message processing time in the router

Processing time of RS messages, Ts (milliseconds)			
Router	Standard RS	SecMac-RS	Trust-RS
Mean	0.003	0.634	1.530
Standard Deviation	0.002	0.056	0.171
Overhead	Baseline	0.631	1.527

Table 3 shows the processing time of RS i.e. mean, standard deviation and overhead for message type of Standard RS, SecMac-RS and Trust-RS. In reference to the Table 3, the mean processing time of the SecMac-RS and Trust-RS shows higher value when compare to mean processing time of the Standard RS message. Based on the theoretical analyses this is the expected results. The processing time for SecMac-RS and Trust-RS should be higher because these mechanism process additional parameters such as

SecMac-tag and Trust-tag in the router whereas the Standard RS message does not require to process the additional parameters. So it is expected that mean processing time for the Standard RS would be lower compared to SecMac-RS and Trust-RS. The Table 3 also shows that the mean processing time for SecMac-RS messages is lower than Trust-RS messages. The Trust-RS mean message processing time expected to be higher because Trust-ND has additional parameters to be process compare to SecMac-RS i.e. Trust Value and Trust Option calculation. SecMac-RS provides saving of 0.896 ms compare to Trust-RS messages. This is clearly shows that SecMac-RS generation using UMAC-64 hashing algorithm generates faster results compare to Trust-ND mechanism using SHA-1 hashing algorithm. Standard deviation measures the dispersion of the processing time from the average value (mean). It shows consistency of the processing time measurement for the 20 times experiments. The SecMac-RS shows very smaller deviation i.e. 0.056 in average indicating that SecMac-SRD mechanism has high consistency or stability in generating SecMac-RS message. On the other hand, Trust-RS has deviation of 0.171 in average that shows that Trust-ND mechanism is less consistent compare to SecMac-SRD mechanism. Even though the generation Trust-RS messages was done using the same Test-bed environment, the processing time shows higher variation.

The host also required to perform message verification similar to RS message verification in the router for all the incoming RA messages in the host. The router will generate RA messages in response to the host RS message and similarly the host will verify all the incoming RA message. The host will perform validation of all incoming RA message in the host to valid whether the received RA message is a legitimate RA message from the legitimate router. Similarly, all the RA messages for Standard RA, SecMac-RA and Trust-RA will be validated in this experiment. The calculated Td message processing time will be based on subtraction of the start processing time from the end processing time in the RA message validation process. This is the total message processing time for the RA validation process. For Standard RA, SecMac-RA and Trust-RA, the process is repeated separately for 20 times and recorded in the experiment.

Table 4. RA message processing time in the host

Processing time of RA messages, Td (milliseconds)

Router	Standard RA	SecMac-RA	Trust-RA
Mean	0.003	0.672	1.810
Standard Deviation	0.002	0.067	0.536
Overhead	Baseline	0.669	1.807

Table 4 shows the processing time of RA i.e. mean processing time according to message type i.e. Standard RA, SecMac-RA and Trust-RA. Based on the above theoretical analyses and the recorded results from the experiment, it is logical that the mean processing time of the SecMac-RA should be higher than the processing time of the Standard RA message. This is because SecMac-RA and Trust-RA need to process additional parameters such as SecMac-tag and Trust Option in the host compare to Standard RA message that does not have such additional parameter. So based on theoretical and experiment result comparison, the mean processing time for to SecMac-RA and Trust-RA should be higher compare to mean processing time for the Standard RA. The Table 4 shows that the mean processing time for SecMac-RA messages is lower than Trust-RA messages. SecMac-RA provides saving of 1.138 ms compare to Trust-RA messages. The mean processing time for Trust-RA expected to be higher compare to SecMac-RS because there are two additional process in Trust-ND message verification i.e. Trust Value and Trust Option calculation besides the verification of RA and updating the neighbour cache table. Whereas in SecMac-SRD mechanism there are no additional process involves. The SecMac-SRD mechanism only does host verifications that involves verification of RA messages and updating the neighbour cache table. The SecMac-RA mechanism shows very smaller deviation i.e. 0.067 indicating that SecMac-SRD mechanism has high consistency or stability in generating SecMac-RA message. On the other hand, Trust-RA has deviation of 0.536 in average that shows that Trust-ND mechanism is less consistent compare to SecMac-SRD mechanism. Even though the generation Trust-RA messages was done using the same Test-bed environment, the processing time shows higher variation.

Table 5. Total computational time of router and host

RD process	Processing time, Ts + Td (milliseconds)		
	Standard RD	SecMac-SRD	Trust-ND
Router (RS processing)	0.003	0.634	1.527
Host (RA processing)	0.003	0.672	1.807
Total	0.006	1.306	3.334
Standard Deviation	0.003	1.396	4.397
Overhead	Baseline	1.300	3.328

Table 5 shows the tabulation calculation of total processing time for both RS and RA message verification in the router and the host. It shows the tabulation both RS and RA message processing time for Standard RD, SecMac-SRD and Trust-ND mechanisms. Comparing of the total processing time RS and RA messages validation in the router and the host represents the computational efficiency of the security mechanism. Comparing the processing time of the SecMac-SRD and Trust-ND mechanism against the Standard RD would be the baseline to measure the efficiency of these mechanisms during the RD process. The is the total processing overhead for SecMac-SRD mechanism i.e. 1.300 ms in average. This is the additional processing time required by SecMac-SRD mechanism to verify SecMac-RS and generate SecMac-RA in the router then verify SecMac-RA and then update the neighbor cache table. Whereas for the Trust-ND mechanism, the average total overhead is 3.328 ms. So the overhead incur by Trust-ND higher compare to SecMac-SRD mechanism. Table 5 also shows that standard deviation for the total computation of SecMac-SRD is only 1.396 ms in average compare to Trust-ND which is 4.397 ms. This is deviation is smaller compare to deviation of Trust-ND. This means that the computation of SecMac-SRD messages is more stable compare to Trust-ND messages.

Table 6. Saving of overall processing time by SecMac-SRD mechanism

RD process	Processing time (milliseconds)		Saving time (milliseconds)
	Trust-ND	SecMac-SRD	
Router (RS processing)	1.527	0.634	0.893
Host (RA processing)	1.807	0.672	1.135
Total	3.334	1.306	2.028

Table 6 shows the tabulation saving of total processing time of SecMac-SRD mechanism implementation in comparison with Trust-ND mechanism. In comparison to Trust-ND, SecMac-SRD providing saving of 2.028 times the amount of time that which is translate to 60.8% saving during the secure RD processing in the IPv6 network. With the decreasing of the processing time, it justifies that SecMac-SRD increases the speed of RD message exchange.

The above results discussion clear indicates that the computational cost i.e. the processing time of the secure RD process drastically reduced in the proposed SecMac-SRD mechanism. It can be concluded that the SecMac-SRD mechanism has a lower computational cost compared to Trust-ND mechanism in secure RD process.

Experiment Under Fake RA Attack Scenario

To verify whether the redesigned secure RD message with SecMac-tag able to prevent the Fake RA attack, the SecMac–SRD mechanism was implemented under a closed IPv6 Test-bed and tested under the Fake RA attack scenario. The following section explains how the SecMac-SRD mechanism perform to protect the IPv6 network from Fake RA attack under the Test-bed testing environments.

Under the normal scenario without SecMac-SRD mechanism, the Fake RA attack carried out using the THC attacking tool Fake_router6 within the Kali Linux machine. The attacker sends fake RA packet which is originated from fake router gateway. The victim host will configure to this fake router as the default gateway upon receiving the fake RA message. When victim host received the RA packet with highest priority from fake default gateway, the victim host is forced to accept this fake RA message. Since the Default Router Preference in RA message is set high and all the host in Test-bed will configure this attacker router as a new valid gateway in the link local communication of the IPv6 network as shown in Fig. 11.

Attack Generation During the Fake RA Attack

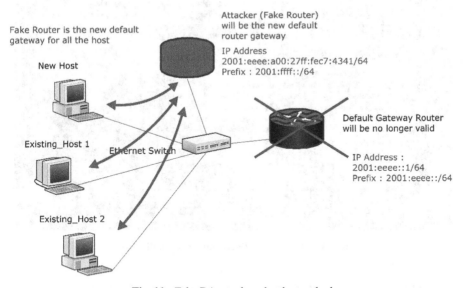

Fig. 11. Fake RA attack under the test bed

The Fig. 11 depicts the scenario how the Fake RA attack is carried out under the Test-bed environment. The above Fake RA attack was carried out using THC attacking tool command Fake_router6 within the Kali Linux machine (acting as the Attacker) by sending Fake RA packets with high priority.

```
Interface 3: Ethernet

Internet Address                          Physical Address    Type
----------------------------------        -----------------   -----------
2001:eeee::1                              ca-01-11-b4-00-08   Reachable (Router)
fe80::c801:11ff:feb4:8                    ca-01-11-b4-00-08   Reachable (Router)
ff02::1                                   33-33-00-00-00-01   Permanent
ff02::2                                   33-33-00-00-00-02   Permanent
ff02::16                                  33-33-00-00-00-16   Permanent
ff02::fb                                  33-33-00-00-00-fb   Permanent
ff02::1:2                                 33-33-00-01-00-02   Permanent
ff02::1:3                                 33-33-00-01-00-03   Permanent
ff02::1:ff7a:66d                          33-33-ff-7a-06-6d   Permanent
ff02::1:ffb1:63e9                         33-33-ff-b1-63-e9   Permanent
ff02::1:ffb4:8                            33-33-ff-b4-00-08   Permanent

netsh interface ipv6>
```

Fig. 12. Neighbour cache table before the Fake RA attack

The Fig. 12 shows the Neighbour Cache Table of the Host before the Fake RA attack.

```
root@kali:~# ifconfig
eth0: flags=4163<UP,BROADCAST,RUNNING,MULTICAST>  mtu 1500
        inet 192.168.39.4  netmask 255.255.255.0  broadcast 192.168.39.255
        inet6 fe80::a00:27ff:fec7:4341  prefixlen 64  scopeid 0x20<link>
        inet6 2001:eeee::a00:27ff:fec7:4341  prefixlen 64  scopeid 0x0<glob
al>
        inet6 2001:eeee::79bd:d282:9480:acaf  prefixlen 64  scopeid 0x0<glo
bal>
        ether 08:00:27:c7:43:41  txqueuelen 1000  (Ethernet)
        RX packets 14606  bytes 15145847 (14.4 MiB)
        RX errors 0  dropped 0  overruns 0  frame 0
        TX packets 7177  bytes 646674 (631.5 KiB)
        TX errors 0  dropped 0 overruns 0  carrier 0  collisions 0

lo: flags=73<UP,LOOPBACK,RUNNING>  mtu 65536
        inet 127.0.0.1  netmask 255.0.0.0
        inet6 ::1  prefixlen 128  scopeid 0x10<host>
        loop  txqueuelen 1000  (Local Loopback)
        RX packets 86  bytes 7144 (6.9 KiB)
        RX errors 0  dropped 0  overruns 0  frame 0
        TX packets 86  bytes 7144 (6.9 KiB)
        TX errors 0  dropped 0 overruns 0  carrier 0  collisions 0
```

Fig. 13. Attacker tool IP configuration (Kali Linux)

The Fig. 13 shows the IP address of the attacking tool i.e. Kali Linux.

```
>>> exit
root@kali:~# fake_router6 eth0 2001:eeee::1/64
Starting to advertise router 2001:eeee::1 (Press Control-C to end) ...
```

Fig. 14. Fake_router6 command

Please refer to Fig. 14 shows how the Fake RA attack was carried out using Fake_router6 command using THC attacking tool in the Kali Linux machine.

```
Internet Address                                 Physical Address    Type
----------------------------------------------   ------------------  ---------
2001:eeee::1                                     ca-01-11-b4-00-08   Stale (Router)
fe80::a00:27ff:fec7:4341                         08-00-27-c7-43-41   Reachable (Router)
fe80::c801:11ff:feb4:8                           ca-01-11-b4-00-08   Reachable (Router)
ff02::1                                          33-33-00-00-00-01   Permanent
ff02::2                                          33-33-00-00-00-02   Permanent
ff02::16                                         33-33-00-00-00-16   Permanent
ff02::fb                                         33-33-00-00-00-fb   Permanent
ff02::1:2                                        33-33-00-01-00-02   Permanent
ff02::1:3                                        33-33-00-01-00-03   Permanent
ff02::1:ff7a:66d                                 33-33-ff-7a-06-6d   Permanent
ff02::1:ffb1:63e9                                33-33-ff-b1-63-e9   Permanent
ff02::1:ffb4:8                                   33-33-ff-b4-00-08   Permanent
ff02::1:ffc7:4341                                33-33-ff-c7-43-41   Permanent
```

Fig. 15. Neighbour cache table after Fake RA attack

In reference the Fig. 15, please take note that the router with the IP address 2001:eeee::1/64 is no longer reachable. The attacker rouge router the IP address 2001:eeee:a00:27ff:fec7:4341/64 is now reachable.

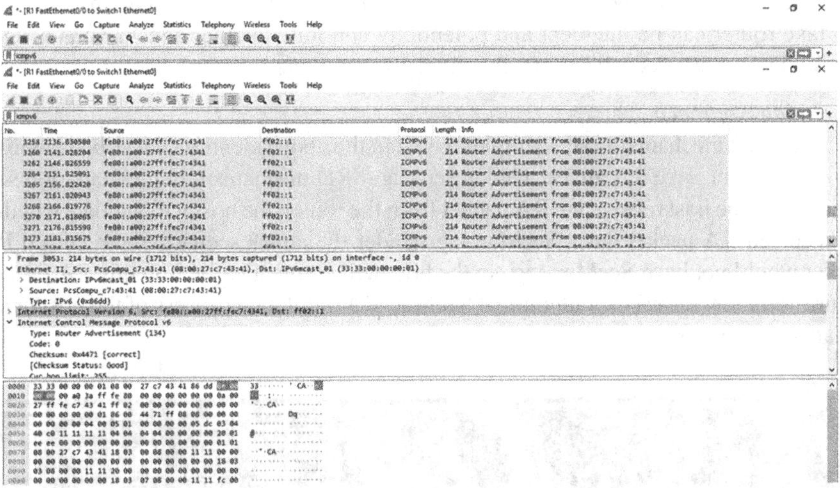

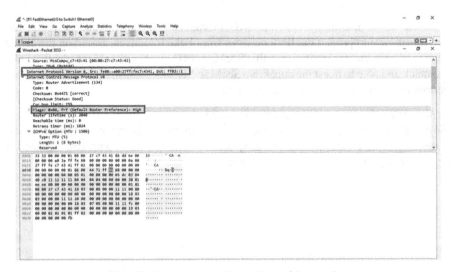

Fig. 16. Screen capture of all RA packets under Fake RA attack

Figure 16 depicts Wireshark screen shot of all the RA packets that were produced during the Fake RA attack using Fake_router6 command. Figure 17 shows the parameter details of one selected RA packet.

Fig. 17. Screen capture RA packets of the attacker

Figure 17 shows that the high setting value for Default Router Preference. Based on the high setting of Default Router Preference, all hosts are required to accept this router as the default gateway. In this scenario, all the host in the network required to communicate with this fake router for all the future communication to other site or Internet. Since this fake router would become the default gateway, all the communications that goes this fake router can be intercept and potentially can initiate other attacks such as DoS attacks, D-Dos attacks, MITM attacks, Reply Attacks, etc.

Prevention Approach
SecMac-SRD mechanism can be implemented in the above mentioned test-bed environment to prevent Fake RA attack. Under SecMac-SRD mechanism implementation scenario, when the host receive the RA packet from the router, the host will validate whether the received RA packet has a SecMac-tag. Under the attack scenario the received RA packet would not have SecMac-tag, so the host will automatically drop this RA packet. Figure 18 below shows the outcome of SecMac-RA validation process of the host under the attack scenario.

```
MsgNum :   1

RA Message detected.
SecMac-tag not found. Ignoring packet.

SecMac-tag RA validation time :    4.05311584473e-06
```

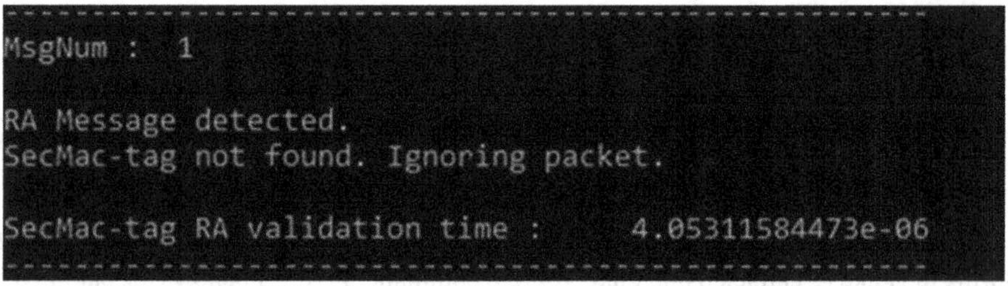

Fig. 18. SecMac-RA validation process in the host

In the above mentioned SecMac-SRD mechanism implementation scenario, the mechanism able to protect the IPv6 network from Fake RA attack. Based on the above mentioned scenario, it clearly shows that SecMac-SRD mechanism able to identify Fake RA attack and able to resist the attack. So SecMac-SRD mechanism qualifies as a viable security mechanism to prevent Fake RA attack.

SecMac-SRD Mechanism Comparative Evaluation
The comparative analysis of the SecMac-SRD mechanism was carried out in terms less processing time, confidentiality, integrity and availability. The comparison based on these three aspects discussed in the following section.

In order to ensure the SecMac-SRD mechanism is efficient mechanism compare other prevention mechanisms, the obtained results from the experiment is compared with the Trust-ND mechanism in terms of the processing time during RD process. The comparative results show that SecMac-SRD mechanism operated with less processing time compare to Trust-ND mechanism. Figure 19 shows comparative results gathered from the experimentation performed with Trust-ND.

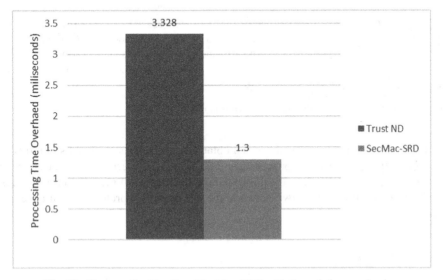

Fig. 19. Comparative Results of SecMac-SRD with the existing mechanism

Based on the above the experiments result analysis, the overall processing time performance of SecMac-SRD mechanism better then Trust-ND mechanism. Apart being less processing time mechanism, SecMAC-SRD mechanism was also proven to be effective in protecting the confidentiality of the RS or RA message content information and maintain integrity of the messages in the RD process. With this security feature, SecMac-SRD mechanism able to protect the IPv6 network from Fake RA attack. This is in contrast with the existing mechanism such as Trust-ND and CGA + IPSEC AH NDP mechanisms. Although Trust-ND and CGA + IPSEC AH NDP mechanisms can fulfill the CIA triad by providing the confidentiality, integrity and availability but these mechanisms suffer from other vulnerabilities such as hash collision and bootstrapping problem. Table 7 below shows the comparative analysis of SecMac-SRD mechanism against the existing mechanism i.e. Trust-ND and CGA + IPSEC in terms of less processing time, confidentiality, integrity and availability.

Table 7. Comparative analysis of SecMac-SRD mechanism with existing mechanism

Mechanism	Less processing time	Confidentiality	Integrity	Availability
Trust-ND	Yes	Yes (Fails under hash collision attack)	Yes (Fails under hash collision attack)	Yes (Fails under hash collision attack)
CGA + IPSEC AH NDP	Yes	Yes (Fails under bootstrapping situation)	Yes (Fails under bootstrapping situation)	Yes (Fails under bootstrapping situation)
SecMac-SRD	Yes*	Yes	Yes	Yes

(Here * sign indicate marginally better in performance).

From the above security analysis and obtained experimentation results in terms of processing time, it is clearly proof that the SecMac-SRD mechanism is an effective viable secure RD mechanism. By implementing SecMac-SRD mechanism in the link local communication of the IPv6 network, the RD process is protected from Fake RA attack.

6 Discussion

This paper presented an improved secure RD mechanism to prevent Fake RA attack in link local IPv6 network. The Test-bed was designed to allow authors to evaluate the effectiveness of the mechanism by carrying Fake RA attack and comparing the performance of SecMac-SRD mechanism against Trust-ND and CGA + IPSEC AH NDP mechanisms. In order to measure the efficiency in terms processing time of SecMac-SRD mechanism, the experiments were conducted using the same Test-bed to comparing performance of Standard RD mechanism, SecMac-SRD mechanism and Trust-ND. Based on the result analysis SecMac-SRD mechanism consumed more processing time compare to Standard RD mechanism and less RD processing time compared to Trust-ND mechanism. The SecMac-SRD mechanism provides 60.8% reduction of average processing time for the RD process compare to RD processing in the Trust-ND mechanism. In order to fulfill the CIA triad security requirement of any secure mechanism, the SecMac-SRD mechanism was tested under Fake RA attack using the same Test-bed environment. The experiments results show that SecMac-SRD mechanism able to resist Fake RA attack in the IPv6 link local network and fulfill the CIA triad by providing the confidentiality, integrity and availability as secure RD mechanism. The comparative results analysis clearly shows that SecMac-SRD mechanism better and viable secure RD mechanism in terms processing time and security features.

With growth of IoT deployment and 5G network implementation, more devices are now connected over the Internet. Currently there is high demand for more secure communication networks with less RD processing time capability. Furthermore, the networks with lower RD processing time and with the low power consumption are great in demand especially in the public networks. Since the SecMac-SRD mechanism use less processing time, it is very suitable for low power sensor network. Hence, this mechanism can be further modified then deployed for the IPv6 addressing of the IoT devices where energy consumption is very low. In order to overcome key management issues, a public key infrastructure is required to distribute the keys within the network. This could be considered as part of future work scope of this research.

Acknowledgement. This research was supported by National Advanced IPv6 Centre (Nav6), Universiti Sains Malaysia (USM) and Ministry of Higher Education Malaysia.

References

1. Arkko, J., Aura, T., Kempf, J., Mäntylä, V.-M., Nikander, P., Roe, M.: Securing IPv6 neighbor and router discovery. In: 1st ACM Workshop on Wireless Security (2002)
2. Nikander, P., Kempf, J., Nordmark, E.: IPv6 neighbor discovery (ND) trust models and threats. RFC 3756 (2004)
3. Chakraborty, M., Chaki, N., Cortesi, A.: A new intrusion prevention system for protecting Smart Grids from ICMPv6 vulnerabilities. In: 2014 Federated Conference on Computer Science and Information Systems, pp. 1539–1547. IEEE (2014)
4. Tian, D.J., Butler, K.R., Choi, J.I., McDaniel, P., Krishnaswamy, P.: Securing ARP/NDP from the ground up. IEEE Trans. Inf. Forensics Secur. **12**(9), 2131–2143 (2017)
5. Arkko, J., Kempf, J., Zill, B., Nikander, P.: Secure neighbor discovery (SEND), pp. 2005-03. RFC 3971, March 2005
6. Zhang, J., Liu, J., Xu, Z., Li, J., Ye, X.M.: TRDP: a trusted router discovery protocol. In: 2007 International Symposium on Communications and Information Technologies, pp. 660–665. IEEE (2007)
7. Praptodiyono, S., Murugesan, R.K., Hasbullah, I.H., Wey, C.Y., Kadhum, M.M., Osman, A.: Security mechanism for IPv6 stateless address autoconfiguration. In: 2015 International Conference on Automation, Cognitive Science, Optics, Micro Electro-Mechanical System, and Information Technology (ICACOMIT), pp. 31–36. IEEE, October 2015
8. Levy-Abegnoli, E., Van de Velde, G., Popoviciu, C., Mohacsi, J.: IPv6 router advertisement guard. RFC 6105 (2011)
9. Polk, T.: Security considerations for the SHA-0 and SHA-1 message-digest algorithms. RFC6194 (2011)
10. Bhargavan, K., Leurent, G.: Transcript collision attacks: breaking authentication in TLS, IKE, and SSH. In: Network and Distributed System Security Symposium—NDSS (2016)
11. Andreeva, E., Mennink, B., Preneel, B.: Open problems in hash function security. Des. Codes Crypt. **77**(2–3), 611–631 (2015). https://doi.org/10.1007/s10623-015-0096-0
12. Yoganguina, B.D., ep Keîta, K.W., Diop, I., Tall, K., Farssi, S.M.: Proposition of a model for securing the neighbor discovery protocol (NDP) in IPv6 environment. In: Gueye, C.T., Persichetti, E., Cayrel, P.-L., Buchmann, J. (eds.) A2C 2019. CCIS, vol. 1133, pp. 204–215. Springer, Cham (2019). https://doi.org/10.1007/978-3-030-36237-9_12
13. Kent, S., Atkinson, R.: IP authentication header, RFC2402 (1998)
14. Shah, S.B.I., Anbar, M., Al-Ani, A., Al-Ani, A.K.: Hybridizing entropy based mechanism with adaptive threshold algorithm to detect ra flooding attack in IPv6 networks. In: Alfred, R., Lim, Y., Ibrahim, A., Anthony, P. (eds.) Computational Science and Technology, vol. 481, pp. 315–323. Springer, Singapore (2019). https://doi.org/10.1007/978-981-13-2622-6_31

15. Nizzi, F., Pecorella, T., Esposito, F., Pierucci, L., Fantacci, R.: IoT security via address shuffling: the easy way. IEEE Internet Things J. **6**(2), 3764–3774 (2019)
16. Shah, J.L.: Secure neighbor discovery protocol: review and recommendations. Int. J. Bus. Data Commun. Netw. (IJBDCN) **15**(1), 71–87 (2019)
17. Pilihanto, A., Wanner, R.: A complete guide on IPv6 attack and defense. SANS Institute (2011)
18. Ullrich, J., Krombholz, K., Hobel, H., Dabrowski, A., Weippl, E.: IPv6 security: attacks and countermeasures in a nutshell. In: 8th USENIX Workshop on Offensive Technologies (WOOT 2014) (2014)
19. Harshita, H.: Detection and prevention of ICMP flood DDOS attack. Int. J. New Technol. Res. **3**(3), 263333 (2017)
20. Chown, T., Venaas, S.: RFC 6104: rogue IPv6 Router Advertisement problem statement. Internet Engineering Task Force (IETF) RFC (2011)
21. AlSa'deh, A., Meinel, C.: Secure neighbor discovery: review, challenges, perspectives, and recommendations. IEEE Secur. Privacy **10**(4), 26–34 (2012)
22. Gont, F.: Implementation advice for IPv6 router advertisement guard (ra-guard). Internet Engineering Task Force (IETF), Technical report (2014)
23. Guo, J., Peyrin, T., Poschmann, A.: The PHOTON family of lightweight hash functions. In: Rogaway, P. (ed.) CRYPTO 2011. LNCS, vol. 6841, pp. 222–239. Springer, Heidelberg (2011). https://doi.org/10.1007/978-3-642-22792-9_13
24. Wang, X., Yin, Y.L., Yu, H.: Finding collisions in the full SHA-1. In: Shoup, V. (ed.) CRYPTO 2005. LNCS, vol. 3621, pp. 17–36. Springer, Heidelberg (2005). https://doi.org/10.1007/11535218_2
25. Turner, S., Chen, L.: Updated security considerations for the MD5 message-digest and the HMAC-MD5 algorithms. RFC 6151 (2011)
26. Yang, X., Ma, T., Shi, Y.: Typical DoS/DDoS threats under IPv6. In: 2007 International Multi-Conference on Computing in the Global Information Technology (ICCGI 2007), p. 55. IEEE (2007)
27. Carter, J.L., Wegman, M.N.: Universal classes of hash functions. J. Comput. Syst. Sci. **18**(2), 143–154 (1979)
28. Narten, T., Nordmark, E., Simpson, W.: H. Soliman," neighbor discovery for ip version 6 (IPv6). RFC 4861, September 2007
29. Andress, J.: The basics of information security: understanding the fundamentals of InfoSec in theory and practice. Syngress (2014)
30. Taherdoost, H., Chaeikar, S., Jafari, M., Shojae Chaei Kar, N.: Definitions and criteria of CIA security triangle in electronic voting system. Int. J. Adv. Comput. Sci. Inf. Technol. (IJACSIT) **1**, 14–24 (2013)
31. Samonas, S., Coss, D.: The CIA strikes back: redefining confidentiality, integrity and availability in security. J. Inf. Syst. Security **10**(3) (2014)
32. Flood, R.L., Carson, E.R.: Dealing with Complexity: An Introduction to the Theory and Application of Systems Science. Springer, Heidelberg (2013)
33. Fenner, B.: Experimental values in IPv4, IPv6, ICMPv4, ICMPv6, UDP, and TCP headers. RFC 4727, November 2006

Analysis of File Carving Approaches: A Literature Review

Nor Ika Shahirah Ramli[1], Syifak Izhar Hisham[1(✉)], and Gran Badshah[2]

[1] Faculty of Computing, College of Computing and Applied Science, Universiti Malaysia Pahang, 26600 Pekan, Pahang, Malaysia
syifakizhar@ump.edu.my
[2] College of Computer Science, King Khalid University, Abha, Saudi Arabia

Abstract. Digital forensics is a crucial process of identifying, conserving, retrieving, evaluating, and documenting digital evidence obtained on computers and other electronic devices. Data restoration and analysis on file systems is one of digital forensic science's most fundamental practices. There is a lot of research being done in developing file carving approaches and different researches focused on different aspects. With the increasing numbers of literature that are covering this research area, there is a need to review this literature for further reference. A review is carried out reviewing different works of literature covering various aspects of carving approaches from multiple digital data sources including IEEE Xplore, Google Scholar, Web of Science, etc. This analysis is done to consider several perspectives which are the current research direction of the file carving approach, the classification for the file carving approaches, and also the challenges are to be highlighted. Based on the analysis, we are able to state the current state of the art of file carving. We classify the carving approach into five classifications which are general carving, carving by specific file type, carving by structure, carving by the file system, and carving by fragmentation. We are also able to highlight several of the challenges for file carving mentioned in the past research. This study will serve as a reference for scientists to evaluate different strategies and obstacles for carving so that they may choose the suitable carving approaches for their study and also future developments.

Keywords: Digital forensic · File carving · File carving approaches' analysis · Challenges in carving

1 Introduction

The development of the current technology nowadays unlocks a new window to the advancement of digital forensic investigation. Digital forensics comprises several phases and procedures, one of the most significant being data acquisition and recovery. In their contents and metadata, files might include key evidence and info making their extraction critical to forensics operations [19]. One of the digital investigation modules is data restoration, which focuses on retrieving data from memory devices such as laptops, PCs, and even thumb drives. Data restoration is one of the aspects that is focused on

N. Abdullah et al. (Eds.): ACeS 2021, CCIS 1487, pp. 277–287, 2021.
https://doi.org/10.1007/978-981-16-8059-5_16

in a digital forensic investigation. File recovery techniques and file carving are two techniques that can be used to restore a file.

The data cannot be normally accessible when it is lost, damaged, deleted, or corrupted. It is possible to lose data due to several factors like viruses, human acts, power overruns, damage to the device, and mechanical system failure [15]. Logic failures and physical failures are the two types of data loss that might occur. The common file recovery method is only suitable if only the presence of the metadata of a file and the metadata has not been corrupted or missing [28]. Else the deleted or corrupted file is possible to be restored by using the file carving technique as this technique utilizes the content of the file rather than the metadata. This is conceivable because when a file is destroyed from an operating system, the system will only be unable to access the file metadata, not the file itself. Moreover, a lot of files that underwent fragmentations cannot be restored by using the standard recovery process without considering the fragmentation as not all files are stored in a continuous and sequential pattern, which completely depend on the free space existing in the system [22]. File carving extracted structured data from the drive's structureless and unallocated raw data portion.

Due to an increase in interdisciplinary research interests in the areas of data recovery and evidence acquisition and processing, we conducted a literature review of carving algorithm performance results in the literature. The review was performed on several papers reporting various file type carving applications in their study and evaluating the experiment's performance. The goal of this article is to review different aspects from the previous research related to the advanced file carving technique. This paper is structured as follows. Section 2 explains the search mechanism of the literature review of different file carving tools in the prior research. Section 3 addresses materials and data extraction based on the literature made from Sect. 2. Section 4 discussed the finding and Sect. 5 concludes this paper.

2 Literature Review

A review has been conducted to assess the present state of the file carving in digital forensic investigation. This study employs a literature review, which is a type of secondary research that involves locating, investigating, and analyzing several published pieces of literature in a given subject. Several databases, notably Google Scholar, IEEE database, and Web of Science, were chosen to limit down the range of prior research on distinct file carving algorithms. These databases were chosen because they have a higher likelihood of locating relevant articles.

Three research questions have been outlined to be answered in this paper. Table 1 shows the research questions of this article.

The criteria to assess the selection of articles include (i) file carving algorithm in general; (ii) classification of the algorithm for file carving; (iii) the latest interval of 10 years. In the end, seven items that meet the defined criteria were identified. Table 2 shows a list of file carving algorithm-related research articles that have been thoroughly analyzed to address predetermined research questions. The search is limited to studies published in the English language. All other unnecessary topic articles were removed. The article is searched using keywords such as file carving, carving framework, carving fragmentation, file restoration, carving analysis, and unallocated space.

Table 1. Research questions

	Research questions
Q1	What is the current state-of-the-arc of file carving algorithm?
Q2	What are the specifications or classifications used for the file carving algorithm?
Q3	What are the challenges of file carving algorithms experienced by past researchers from the prior articles?

3 Materials and Data Extraction

The selection of potential literature is scanned thoroughly and classified based on the search criteria and the journals are identified by using the search string. Both criteria and search string are mentioned in the literature review section. Further filtering is done to keep the articles relevant and appropriate for more in-depth analysis.

Large numbers of literature are identified at the beginning of the review process however further only relevant literature remains for further analysis after screening through the title, abstract, and the body of the literature. The literature is managed by using reference management software, Mendeley to ease the documentation process. Based on Table 2, the literature is simplified into several sections which are author and publication, methodology or approach used by the authors, findings made by the authors, the ID of the answered research question, and carving classification.

4 Discussion

4.1 RQ1: What is the Current State-of-the-Arc of File Carving Algorithm?

In this study, the result of the data extraction from the literature is shown in Table 2. There are different focus areas and challenges highlighted in the previous studies of different emphases (see Fig. 1).

4.2 RQ2: What Are the Specifications or Classifications Used for the File Carving Algorithm?

Based on the literature, advanced generation carving algorithm or second-generation carving algorithm can be classified into five different focuses which are specific file type carving, file system carving, general carving, carving based on structure, and carving based on fragmentation which answers the second research question.

General carving: the algorithm usually focuses on file extension and signature of a file (header-footer) and usually for continuous file fragmentation [1]. Moreover, most algorithms for general carving usually produce high false positives and are usually ineffective.

Specific file type carving: the algorithm focuses on retrieving a particular file type such as JPEG, PDF, GPS [23, 30], network-related file type [7], binary file [14], etc. Different file types have a different structure, for instance, jpeg has a different signature

Table 2. Data extraction of prior research related to file carving algorithm

Authors and publications	Methodology	Finding	Q ID	Classification
FiFTy: large-scale file fragment type identification using convolutional neural networks [24]	Developed a trainable algorithm by utilizing compact neural network architecture	Increased the carving accuracy by 77.5% and reduce the processing time significantly compared to common file carving tool-Sceadan	Q2	Carving based on structure
Forensic tool to study and carve virtual machine hard disk files [12]	Carving algorithm concentrating on the visualization of the virtual machine. This research focuses on understanding the virtual machine file structure and mechanism for the carving process	Although not all VM files can be restored from unallocated space, legitimate data can be extracted and allocated VMDK files can be analyzed. The program may be used to map known locations inside the virtual disc and an image file with the sparse VMDK files	Q2, Q3	Carving based on structure and specific file Type
Statistical byte frequency analysis for identifying jpeg file segments [17]	Developed an algorithm based on statistical byte frequency technique for fragmentation identification rather than file marker (header-footer) with the focus to increase the efficiency and effectiveness of fragments identification	The gap of the fragments is identified by using the k-mean clustering tool. The algorithm increases the accuracy and shortens the total processing time as fragments can be identified faster, less computation is needed compare to searching	Q1, Q2	Carving based on fragmentation

(continued)

Table 2. (*continued*)

Authors and publications	Methodology	Finding	Q ID	Classification
A method for carving fragmented document and image files [26]	Devised a method for carving fragmented document and image data from a FAT32 formatted USB device using pixel matching to locate the adjacent fragment and a total of multiple approaches to calculate the pixel value between two fragments for PNG and dictionary-based approach for TXT file	The approaches used for search and determine best matches takes longer processing time because it needs to go through one cluster at a time	Q2, Q3	Carving based on specific file type
RX_myKarve carving framework for reassembling complex fragmentations of JPEG images [3]	Developed carving file with focused on retrieving intertwined and complex fragmented jpeg files by combining structure-based and content-based carving methods and implementing Extreme Machine Learning as the baseline of the algorithm	By highlighting unique identification and reassembling approaches in the framework, RX_mykarve can carve and fully recover all of the given cases in the DFRWS-2006 dataset	Q2	Carving by structure and fragmentation

(*continued*)

Table 2. (*continued*)

Authors and publications	Methodology	Finding	Q ID	Classification
A comparative study of support vector machine and neural networks for file type identification using n-gram analysis [29]	This paper compares two different classifiers, Support Vector Machine (SVM) and Neural Network (NN) in n-gram approach for file carving identification	SVM works better than NN in terms of scalability and better handling in memory usage cost	Q2, Q3	Carving based on the structure
Hash-based carving: searching media for complete files and file fragments with sector hashing and hashdb [13]	Developed an algorithm focused on hash-based carving. The algorithm uses two approaches where one act as an identifier (Hash-Sets) and one as an assembler (Hash-Run)	Able to function to reduce the processing time by the only search for target file and with a high success rate for target file with large database of block hashes	Q2	Carving by structure
On efficiency of artifact lookup strategies in digital forensics [20]	The algorithm built for rapid file retrieval using multiple tactics such as hash-based carving's database, hierarchical Bloom filter trees, and flash hash maps	The approach improves the runtime performance and applicability, as well as the efficiency of lookups. Extensibility and maintenance, on the other hand, have proven to be a struggle	Q2, Q3	Carving by structure

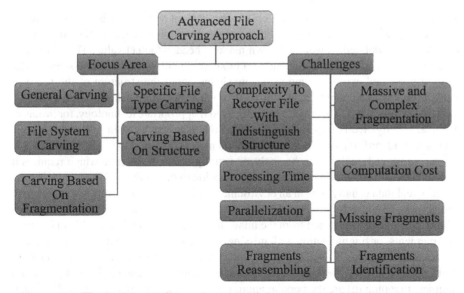

Fig. 1. Advance file carving approach focus area and challenges

and different file structure than pdf. Therefore, most of the research usually focuses on jpeg recovery as it is much easier to carve as compared to txt with no specific header [26]. Therefore, it is not suitable to use a carving algorithm specific to jpeg for text as the algorithm might not even be able to read the structure of the file.

File system carving: the algorithm focuses on carving files based on the file system such as NTFS [10, 18, 33], FAT [26], HDPS [4], ReFS [25], Btrfs [8], and others. The different file system has a different structure and different mechanism.

Carving based on structure: this algorithm focuses on the structure of the file and the architecture of the file to be carved. The idea behind this carving is that one algorithm fits all-can be used for different or multiples different types of files and different file systems [2, 3, 35]. This algorithm usually includes a certain level of automation or learning in the algorithm.

Carving based on fragmentation: this algorithm considers the level of fragmentation that the file underwent. This algorithm considers the condition of the file structure for instance typical carving algorithms are not efficient to be used in the highly fragmented file. This classification also includes the carving of a file with a missing header or footer. This type of file is known as an orphaned file [11, 31]. Moreover, common carving algorithms are not able to carve missing fragments under the usual circumstances. Therefore, a specified carving algorithm is needed to cater to the peculiar scenario.

4.3 RQ3: What Are the Challenges of File Carving Algorithms Experienced by Past Researchers from the Prior Articles?

As according to the literature review, most of the research conducted focused on the recovery for multimedia files compared to documents, binary files, and virtual systems.

There is only one research focused on the recovery of virtual machines. Multimedia files such as JPEG are a popular choice among researchers because the structure of the file is well defined as well as known marker (header-footer) value. Therefore, it is easier to demonstrate the functionality and to experiment with different concepts. The method presented exploits some prior knowledge about the structure of the file type itself; however, document files such as.txt do not have a distinguished header, making it harder to be recovered. This issue can be resolved if appropriate technology, for instance, artificial intelligence is implemented, such as the usage of SVM in [29] increases the accuracy in identifying.doc files by 98.22% on n = 2 compared to 68.58% for NN.

As mentioned, real data to be analyzed usually exists in the state which requires it to be processed to a certain process, in this situation to be carved and recovered. This is because real data usually runs in an environment where it can be corrupted, fragmented, and deleted. Even for fragmented data, the data may be in a state or scenario that makes it hard to be directly extracted from the image file for instance embedded file in between the fragments, or fragmentation with missing fragments, or fragmentation with missing header and et cetera. This scenario increases the complexity of the carving process itself. Different researchers resort to different solutions. Fragments identification and fragment mapping [6] are the popular approaches that are currently being used by many researchers.

The challenges with the fragments identification and mapping cause the growing relevance of including fragmentation and learning capability for file carving [21]. File fragments of different file formats need to be categorized, as is the ability to determine the kind of file of a fragment of the file. Byte frequency distribution [32] and Shannon entropy [9] are among content-based file fragment categorization techniques which are popular and used by the majority of the research. To improve the efficiency of fragment detection and hence raise the carving success rate, decision machine models such as decision tree, machine learning [3, 24, 32], and even neural networks [16, 24, 32] are also being used.

Reducing processing time [34], algorithm optimization, and scalability are among the challenges that have been highlighted by several studies. Different approaches are done to reduce processing time and increase algorithm optimization. Using the hash-based approach [5, 20], semantic carving and smart carving are among several approaches that focus on recovering targeted files making it more practical and more efficient in identifying and recovering the file. Using accelerator and parallelization concepts [27] is also efficient in reducing the overall processing time. Bayne, Ferguson, and Sampson increase the efficiency and overcome the parallelization problem by combining their pattern matching framework with accelerator thus reducing both processing time and allowing parallelization feature [5]. Fragments reassembling also proved to be a challenge in the past study.

5   Conclusion

Based on the analysis being done, research questions are answered. The first research question is being answered when a few challenges are being highlighted by the prior research that affects file carving approaches. This includes parallelization capability to reduce computing time, pattern matching for the target file, scalability of the database for pattern machine if dealing with massive data, fragments identification and fragments assembling to increase carving yield, and complex scenarios of file fragmentation and file structure that affect the overall operation of a carving framework or algorithm. Moreover, the second research question is answered when we are able to recognize and categorize carving approaches based on their classification for different datasets and for the different environments that might need a particular approach to solve them. To be firm, there is no such thing as one method that fits all for the time being as there are various aspects and conditions that still need to be considered. Perhaps the usage of machine learning and neural networks might be able to solve several of the challenges highlighted but it is too early to say that is the exact answer. Based on the past research, we can see clear evidence that by combining several different carving methods, the carving success rate can be increased as well as the overall carving efficiency. Machine learning, automation, content-based carving, and smart carving are among few aspects that hold huge potential to be focused on for future research, and this answers the third research question.

Acknowledgment. This research work is supported by an RDU grant of Universiti Malaysia Pahang, 'Authentication Watermarking in Digital Text Document Images Using Unique Pattern Numbering and Mapping' (RDU190366).

References

1. Afrizal, A., et al.: Analysis and implementation of signature based method and structure file based method for file carving. Indones. J. Comput. **6**, 13–22 (2021). https://doi.org/10.34818/indojc.2021.6.1.457
2. Alherbawi, N., et al.: A survey on data carving in digital forensic. Asian J. Inf. Technol. **15**(24), 5137–5144 (2016)
3. Ali, R.R., Mohamad, K.M.: RX_myKarve carving framework for reassembling complex fragmentations of JPEG images. J. King Saud Univ. Comput. Inf. Sci. **33**(1), 21–32 (2021). https://doi.org/10.1016/j.jksuci.2018.12.007
4. Alshammari, E., et al.: A new technique for file carving on hadoop ecosystem. In: Proceedings of 2017 International Conference on New Trends Computing Sciences, ICTCS 2017, January 2018, pp. 72–77 (2017). https://doi.org/10.1109/ICTCS.2017.16
5. Bayne, E.: Accelerating digital forensic searching through GPU parallel processing techniques. Abertay University (2017)
6. Bayne, E., et al.: OpenForensics: a digital forensics GPU pattern matching approach for the 21st century. In: DFRWS 2018 EU – Proceedings of 5th Annual DFRWS Europe, vol. 24, pp. S29–S37 (2018). https://doi.org/10.1016/j.diin.2018.01.005
7. Beverly, R., et al.: Forensic carving of network packets and associated data structures. Digit. Investig. **8**(Suppl.), S78–S89 (2011). https://doi.org/10.1016/j.diin.2011.05.010
8. Bhat, W.A., Wani, M.A.: Forensic analysis of B-tree file system (Btrfs). Digit. Investig. **27**, 57–70 (2018). https://doi.org/10.1016/j.diin.2018.09.001
9. Chen, Q., et al.: File fragment classification using grayscale image conversion and deep learning in digital forensics. In: Proceedings of 2018 IEEE Symposium on Security and Privacy Workshops, SPW 2018, pp. 140–147 (2018). https://doi.org/10.1109/SPW.2018.00029
10. Darnowski, F., Chojnaki, A.: Selected methods of file carving and analysis of digital storage media in computer forensics. Teleinform. Rev. **1**(2), 25–40 (2015)

11. Durmus, E., et al.: Image carving with missing headers and missing fragments. In: 2017 IEEE International Workshop on Information Forensics and Security, WIFS 2017, January 2018, pp. 1–6 (2017). https://doi.org/10.1109/WIFS.2017.8267665
12. Ezequiel, R., Haro, J.: Forensic tool to study and carve virtual machine hard disk file (2019)
13. Garfinkel, S.L., McCarrin, M.: Hash-based carving: searching media for complete files and file fragments with sector hashing and hashdb. In: Proceedings of Digital Forensic Research Conference, DFRWS 2015, USA, vol. 14, pp. S95–S105 (2015). https://doi.org/10.1016/j.diin.2015.05.001
14. Hand, S., et al.: Bin-carver: automatic recovery of binary executable files. In: Proceedings of Digital Forensic Research Conference, DFRWS 2012, USA, pp. S108–S117 (2012). https://doi.org/10.1016/j.diin.2012.05.014
15. Heo, H.S., et al.: Automated recovery of damaged audio files using deep neural networks. Digit. Investig. **30**, 117–126 (2019). https://doi.org/10.1016/j.diin.2019.07.007
16. Hiester, L.: File fragment classification using neural networks with lossless representations networks with lossless representations. Undergraduate Honors Theses, pp. 1–32 (2018)
17. Kadir, N.F.B.A.: Statistical byte frequency analysis for identifying JPEG. Universiti Teknologi Malaysia (2015)
18. Karresand, M., et al.: Creating a map of user data in NTFS to improve file carving. IFIP Adv. Inf. Commun. Technol. **569**, 133–158 (2019). https://doi.org/10.1007/978-3-030-28752-8_8
19. Laurenson, T.: Performance analysis of file carving tools. In: Janczewski, L.J., Wolfe, H.B., Shenoi, S. (eds.) SEC 2013. IAICT, vol. 405, pp. 419–433. Springer, Heidelberg (2013). https://doi.org/10.1007/978-3-642-39218-4_31
20. Liebler, L., et al.: On efficiency of artifact lookup strategies in digital forensics. Digit. Investig. (2019). https://doi.org/10.1016/j.diin.2019.01.020
21. Masoumi, M., Keshavarz, A., Fotohi, R.: File fragment recognition based on content and statistical features. Multimedia Tools Appl. **80**(12), 18859–18874 (2021). https://doi.org/10.1007/s11042-021-10681-x
22. van der Meer, V., et al.: A Contemporary Investigation of NTFS File Fragmentation. Radboud University, Nijmegen (2021)
23. Minnaard, W.: The Linux FAT32 allocator and file creation order reconstruction. Digit. Investig. **11**(3), 224–233 (2014). https://doi.org/10.1016/j.diin.2014.06.008
24. Mittal, G., et al.: FiFTy: large-scale file fragment type identification using neural networks **16**(Table I), 28–41 (2019). arXiv
25. Prade, P., et al.: Forensic analysis of the resilient file system (ReFS) version 3.4. Forensic Sci. Int. Digit. Investig. **32**, 300915 (2020). https://doi.org/10.1016/j.fsidi.2020.300915
26. Ravi, A., et al.: A method for carving fragmented document and image files. In: 2016 International Conference on Advances in Human Machine Interaction, HMI 2016, pp. 43–47 (2016). https://doi.org/10.1109/HMI.2016.7449170
27. Romano, L.M.P.C.: File carving in practice. Universidade do Minho (2015)
28. Sari, S.A., Mohamad, K.M.: A review of graph theoretic and weightage techniques in file carving. J. Phys. Conf. Ser. **1529**, 5 (2020). https://doi.org/10.1088/1742-6596/1529/5/052011
29. Sester, J., et al.: A comparative study of support vector machine and neural networks for file type identification using N-gram analysis. Forensic Sci. Int. Digit. Investig. **36**, 301121 (2021). https://doi.org/10.1016/j.fsidi.2021.301121
30. Shi, K., et al.: A novel file carving algorithm for National Marine Electronics Association (NMEA) logs in GPS forensics. Digit. Investig. **23**, 11–21 (2017). https://doi.org/10.1016/j.diin.2017.08.004
31. Uzun, E., Sencar, H.T.: Carving orphaned JPEG file fragments. IEEE Trans. Inf. Forensics Secur. **10**(8), 1549–1563 (2015). https://doi.org/10.1109/TIFS.2015.2416685

32. Vulinovic, K., et al.: Neural networks for file fragment classification. In: Proceedings of 2019 42nd International Convention on Information and Communication Technology, Electronics and Microelectronics, MIPRO 2019, pp. 1194–1198 (2019). https://doi.org/10.23919/MIPRO.2019.8756878

33. Yoo, B., et al.: A study on multimedia file carving method. Multimed. Tools Appl. **61**(1), 243–261 (2012). https://doi.org/10.1007/s11042-010-0704-y

34. Zha, X., Sahni, S.: Fast in-place file carving for digital forensics. In: Lai, X., Gu, D., Jin, B., Wang, Y., Li, H. (eds.) e-Forensics 2010. LNICSSITE, vol. 56, pp. 141–158. Springer, Heidelberg (2011). https://doi.org/10.1007/978-3-642-23602-0_13

35. Lee, H., Lee, H.-W.: Block based smart carving system for forgery analysis and fragmented file identification. J. Internet Comput. Serv. **2020**(3), 93–102 (2020)

Cascade Generalization Based Functional Tree for Website Phishing Detection

Abdullateef O. Balogun[1,2(✉)], Kayode S. Adewole[1], Amos O. Bajeh[1], and Rasheed G. Jimoh[1]

[1] Department of Computer Science, University of Ilorin, PMB 1515, Ilorin, Nigeria
{balogun.ao1,adewole.ks,bajehamos,jimoh_rasheed}@unilorin.edu.ng
[2] Department of Computer and Information Sciences, Universiti Teknologi PETRONAS, 32610 Bandar Seri Iskandar, Perak, Malaysia

Abstract. The advent of the web and internet space has seen its adoption for rendering various services -from financial to medical services. This has brought an increase in the rate of cybersecurity issues over the years and a prominent one is the phishing attack where malicious websites mimic the appearance and functionalities of another legitimate website to collect users' credentials required for access to services. Several measures have been proposed to mitigate this attack; blacklisting and variants of machine learning approaches have been employed, yielding good performance results. However, there is a need to increase the rate of identification of phishing attacks and reduce the rate of false positives. This study proposes the use of a functional tree (FT) machine learning approach to mitigate phishing attacks. FT, a hybridization of multivariate decision trees and discriminant function using constructive induction, uses logistic regression for splitting tree nodes and leaf prediction, unlike the conventional decision tree that simply split nodes based on the data. Furthermore, a variant of the FT is proposed based on cascade generalization (CG-FT). Three datasets with varied instance distributions, both balanced and imbalanced, are used in the empirical investigation of the performance of the proposed CG-FT. The results showed that FT has improved performances over some selected baseline classifiers. Relative to FT, the CG-FT techniques showed improvement in the detection of a phishing attack with Area Under the Curve (AUC) and True Positive rate (TP-rate) ranging from 98–99.6% and 92–97% respectively in the datasets. Also, the false-positive rate is reduced with values ranging from 1.7 to 6.1%. The proposed CG-FT showed improvement over all the other reviewed approaches based on studied performance metrics. The use of FT and its hybridization with cascade generalization (CG-FT) showed an improvement in performance in the mitigation of phishing attacks.

Keywords: Cascade generalization · Cybersecurity · Functional tree · Machine learning · Phishing attack

1 Introduction

The fast expansion and implementation of new technologies, smart gadgets, 5G connectivity, and so on has led to the proliferation of internet-based services. Some of the

© Springer Nature Singapore Pte Ltd. 2021
N. Abdullah et al. (Eds.): ACeS 2021, CCIS 1487, pp. 288–306, 2021.
https://doi.org/10.1007/978-981-16-8059-5_17

services are essential for day-to-day activities [1–3]. Several studies have reported that social networking and educational apps are some of the most popular and extensively used web-based services, with a large user base. The increasing number of people who utilise these web-based services demonstrates their popularity over the years. The purpose is to maximize the availability and accessibility of web-based services that are utilised regularly. Nonetheless, because there are no general cyberspace regulatory policies or mechanisms, the open access and use of web-based services or technologies on the internet creates opportunities for cyber-attacks [4, 5].

Cyber-attacks pose security weaknesses and threats for web-based services and their users, and also substantial information and financial losses. Phishing attacks on websites are a frequent form of these cyber-attacks. Cybercriminals have been setting up bogus websites to collect personal information from unsuspecting users for malicious purposes [2, 6, 7]. The website phishing assault is a serious cybersecurity issue that has overburdened the internet and has impacted web-based services and their users [8, 9].

Website phishing, according to [2], is a common deception in which an illegal website impersonates a legitimate website with the explicit aim of collecting data from unwary users. Consequently, phishing threats pose a serious risk to web-based services [10–12]. In 2018, the Anti-Phishing Working Group (APWG) identified 51,401 phishing websites on the internet. Also, in 2016, RSA reported that international organisations lost over $9 billion due to phishing scams [13, 14]. These incidents have demonstrated that phishing assaults from illegitimate websites are fast gaining popularity, resulting in huge monetary costs and difficulties, even while current remedies may be ineffectual in fixing the problem [10, 12, 15].

For detecting phishing websites, numerous cybersecurity experts and researchers have suggested and developed a range of anti-phishing solutions [16–18]. The prevention of website phishing threats using the blacklist method is one of these remedies. The Internet web browsers' blacklisting procedure checks the submitted universal resource locator (URLs) with previously logged phishing website URLs to assess its authenticity. A key disadvantage of the blacklist anti-phishing method is its failure to discover new phishing URLs owing to its reliance on accumulating blacklisted phishing URLs. [4, 19]. Moreover, cyber-attackers are adopting sophisticated methods that can quickly circumvent blacklisting procedures. Due to the fluidity of cyber-attacks, machine learning (ML)-based anti-phishing solutions can be used to assess the legitimacy of websites to accommodate the dynamism of phishing attempts on attributes emanating from websites. The goal is to offer robustness in distinguishing genuine websites from malicious scams [13, 16, 20]. Nonetheless, the successful application of the ML-based anti-phishing techniques is dependent on the performance of the adopted ML technique for identifying malicious websites.

Different ML approaches have been developed to detect phishing websites, with average accuracy rates and considerable false-positive rates [6, 21, 22]. This could be ascribed to the existence of data quality issues, like imbalanced datasets that have a detrimental influence on the performance of ML approaches [23, 24]. The dynamic of phishing websites demand increasingly powerful ML algorithms with a high phishing detection rate and low false-positive rates.

As a result, this research presents a cascade generalisation based Functional Tree (CG-FT) for detecting phishing websites. By using positive induction, FT merges a decision tree with a linear function, resulting in a decision tree with multivariate decision nodes and leaf nodes that employ discriminant functions to generate predictions.

This research has made the following scientific contributions:

1) The FT algorithm is used to detect legitimate and phishing websites.
2) The proposed CG-FT algorithm is used to classify legitimate and phishing websites; and
3) An experimental analysis of the detection performance of the proposed CG-FT with existing phishing methods.

Furthermore, this research aims to address the following research questions:

1) How efficient is the FT algorithm in detecting legitimate and phishing websites?
2) How efficient is the proposed CG-FT algorithm in detecting legitimate and phishing websites?
3) How efficient is the proposed CG-FT compared to existing phishing methods?

The rest of this article is organised as follows. Section 2 examines the related works. Section 3 illustrates the approach for the analysis, an explanation of the experimental technique, and the algorithms utilised. Section 4 discusses the research experiment and the analysis of the experimental data. Finally, Sect. 5 concludes and suggests further studies.

2 Related Works

This section investigates and analyses current phishing detection methods developed utilising different anti-phishing methods.

Alqahtani [6] used a novel association law induction approach to identify phishing websites. To assess the validity of a page, the suggested approach employs an association law method. The proposed method recorded a high accuracy value (95.2%) and f-measure value (0.9511) that are superior to DT and other experimented associative-based learning techniques. [8] developed a Multi-label Classifier-based Associative Classification (MCAC) technique that selects attributes from URLs. In another study, [9] enhanced MCAC by considering content-based properties (CBAC) of the URLs. The proposed CBAC recorded a high detection accuracy of 94.29% when tested. [11] generated and compared the performance of a fast Associative Classification technique (FACA) with selected AC-based techniques for phishing website detection. Their experimental findings indicate that FACA outperforms other AC approaches such as MCAR and CBA. The efficacy of these associative-based methods demonstrates their suitability for phishing detection. Nonetheless, their comparable performance in terms of detection accuracy is a drawback.

To detect phishing websites, [1] used a self-structuring neural network. Their model is built on an adaptive learning rate that changes before introducing new neurons and, as a result, the neural network framework. From their experimental results, the proposed method had an accuracy value of 94.07% on the training dataset, 92.48% on the testing dataset and 91.12% on validation datasets. A Deep Belief Network (DBN) was proposed by [5] to detect phishing websites. The proposed DBN generates robust hierarchical features using Restricted Boltzmann Machines (RBM). On testing, it was observed that the proposed DBN performed comparably to a decision tree (DT) and Random Forest (RF) classifiers. [4] developed a website phishing framework based on a genetic algorithm (GA) and a deep neural network (DNN). In the proposed framework, the GA was deployed to select relevant features while DNN was used for the classification process. The proposed framework was outperformed selected experimented baseline classifiers such as DT in their experiments. Similarly, [2] improved DNN using the bat meta-heuristics algorithm. The proposed method recorded a high accuracy value (96.9%) and performed comparably with some experimented methods. These findings indicate that DNN techniques are comparable to conventional ML classifiers at detecting phishing websites. [12] comparatively analysed the performance of selected conventional classifiers and some meta-learners in phishing detection. Likewise, [10] investigated the use of meta-classifiers to boost phishing website identification. Their respective results demonstrated that ensemble approaches outperformed single classifiers. Also, findings from [13] supported the use of meta-learners in phishing detection. [14] deployed a cumulative distribution function gradient (CDF-g) method to select relevant features for phishing detection. The detection accuracy of the RF assessment of proposed method was 94.6%. [18] suggested a function selection (FS) and ensemble learning system (ELM) based phishing method. The Random Forest Regressor (RFG) was used as the FS process, and majority voting was used to determine the ELM. According to the experimental findings, the proposed method has an accuracy value of 95.4%, a precision value of 0.935, and an f-measure value of 0.947 that outperformed some existing ML approaches such as NB, SVM, MLP.

According to the foregoing studies, there is a need for more reliable and efficient alternatives since most current approaches work adversely. As a result, this research proposes a CG-FT method for detecting phishing websites.

3 Methodology

In this section, the research methodology utilised will be presented. The proposed method examined phishing datasets, performance assessment measures and the experimental procedure is addressed in detail.

3.1 Functional Tree (FT) Algorithm

Functional Tree (FT), which is also known as a generaliza-tion of multivariate trees, is the merging of multivariate DTs and discriminant functions using a constructive in-duction approach [25]. FT includes attributes at the leaf and decision nodes. In certain situations, FT integrates at-tributes at both nodes and leaves while creating classifica-tion trees, just so decision nodes are produced using the classification tree's expansion and functional leaves are built when the tree is pruned [7, 25]. FT may be used to estimate the value of class variables in a given dataset for classification problems. Particularly, the dataset spans the tree from the root node to a leaf, expanding the dataset's range of attributes at each decision node utilizing node-built functions. The decision test of the node is then used to decide the path that the dataset will traverse. Eventual-ly, the dataset is labelled as a leaf using either the leaf-based function or the leaf-related constant [17, 25]. The main difference between DT algorithms and FT is that the former (DT) divides input data into tree nodes by examin-ing the value of some input features to a constant, where-as FT utilises logistic regression functions for internal node splitting and leaf prediction [26]. Figure 1 and Fig. 2 presents the pseudocode used by FT for developing and pruning a tree respectively.

Algorithm 1.
Function GrowTree (Dataset, Constructor)
1.   if Stop_Criterion (DataSet)
        - Return a Leaf Node with a constant value.
2.   Construct a model α using Constructor
3.   For each example $\vec{x} \in Dataset$
        - Compute $\hat{y} = \alpha(\vec{x})$
        - Extend $\vec{x}$ with new attributes $\hat{y}$
4.   Select the attributes of original as well as newly constructed attributes that maximizes some merit-functions
5.   For each partition i of the DataSet using selected attributes
        - $Tree_i = GrowTree\ (Dataset_i, Constructor)$
6.   Return a *Tree* as a decision node based on the selected attribute, containing the α model and descendants $Tree_i$
End Function

Fig. 1. Building a functional tree

3.2   Cascade Generalization Based Functional Tree (CG-FT) Method

Cascade generalization is an efficient process that operates on the base and meta-levels. In this step, to assess the ultimate ensemble outcome, a meta-level classifier trains a model directly from the projections of base-level classifiers [27]. Cascade generalization extends the dimensionality of the input space by using the predictions of the base-level classifiers. This is accomplished by appending the output of each of the base-level classifiers to each training example as a new function. As a result, all base and meta-level classifiers use the initial input features, with the meta-level classifiers having access to additional features (predictions from the base-level classifier) [27]. Figure 3 presents the pseudocode for the CG-FT method.

```
Algorithm 2.
Function Prune (Tree)
1.   Estimate Leaf_Error as the error at this node.
2.   If Tree is a leaf, Return Leaf_Error.
3.   Estimate Constructor_Error as the estimated error at α
4.   For each dependant i
           -   Let pᵢ the probability that an example goes through branch i
           -   Backed-up-Error += pᵢ × Prune(Treeᵢ)
5.   If argmin (Leaf_Error, Constructor_Error, Backed-up-Error)
           -   Is Leaf_Error
                       •   Tree = Leaf
                       •   Tree_Error = Leaf_Error
           -   Is Model_Error
                       •   Tree = Constructor Leaf
                       •   Tree_Error = Constructor_Error
           -   Is Backed-up-Error
                       •   Tree_Error = Backed-up-Error
6.   Return Tree_Error

End Function
```

Fig. 2. Pruning a functional tree

Algorithm 3. Cascade Generalization based Functional Tree (CG-FT) Algorithm

Input:

Training set $S = \{x_i, y_i\}, i = 1 \dots m, y_i \in Y, Y = \{c_1, c_2, \dots, c_k\}, c_k$ is the class label;
T=100   // Maximum Iteration
L: Initial labeled variables
A: Initial unlabeled variables
Z: Acceptance Threshold
X_i : Variable with Most Confident Predictions (MCP)
Base Learner= FT // As defined in Section 3.1

1.   **Initialization:**
     Train FT as base learner
2.   **For t = 1 to T** // loop for maximum iteration
     Use FT to select variables with MCP per iteration
     Remove X_i from A and add to Y
     Re-train FT as base learner on new L

Output: Predicted class labels on test datasets

Fig. 3. Pseudocode for the CG-FT method [28]

3.3 Website Phishing Datasets

During the experimentation process of this study, three phishing datasets were used. These databases are widely available and often used in current research [1, 12–14, 16]. Dataset 1 consists of 11,055 samples (4,898 phishing and 6,157 legitimate samples). with 30 definitive attributes that characterize the dataset [1]. Dataset 2 has 10,000 samples (5,000 phishing and 5,000 legitimate samples) and it consists of 48 attributes [12, 14].

Lastly, Dataset 3 comprises 1,353 samples (702 phishing, 548 real, and 103 suspicious) with 10 attributes. Dataset 3 differs from Datasets 1 and 2 in that it has three class codes. Refer to [1, 12–14, 16] for more detail on the phishing datasets.

3.4 Experimental Procedure

In this section, the experimental procedure (See Fig. 4) utilised in this study is presented.

The experimental procedure is intended to experimentally evaluate and validate the efficacy of the proposed method for detecting phishing websites. Three phishing datasets from the UCI repositories are utilised for training and testing the suggested method, and the K-fold (where k = 10) cross-validation (CV) approach is employed for phishing model creation and assessment. The 10-fold CV selection is based on its capacity to create phishing models while minimising the impact of the data sparsity or any form of data quality problems [24, 29–33]. Moreover, the K-fold CV technique allows each instance to be utilised repeatedly in both training and testing phases [34–39]. The suggested approach and the selected baseline classifiers (FT, NB, SMO, SVM, and Decision Table (Dec Table)) are then deployed on experimented datasets, using the 10-fold CV technique. The detection performances of generated phishing models are then evaluated

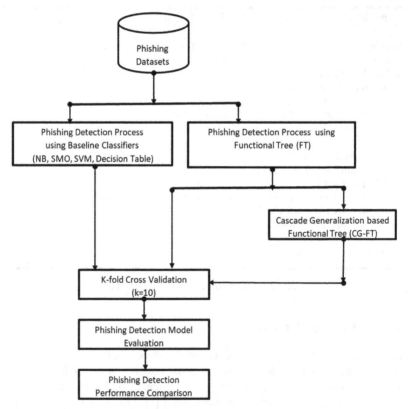

Fig. 4. Experimental procedure

and compared to other phishing detection approaches. In the same context, all tests were carried out using the WEKA machine learning tool [40].

3.5 Performance Assessment Measures

Accuracy, F-measure, Area under the Curve (AUC), false-positive rate (FPR), true positive rate (TPR), and Mathew's correlation coefficient (MCC) performance assessment measures are used to evaluate the detection capabilities of the built phishing models. The choice for these measures stems from the widespread and regular use of these assessment criteria for phishing website identification as reported in current studies [12, 13, 18–20, 41, 42].

i. Accuracy is the average degree to which all instances' actual labels are accurately predicted. It is calculated as shown in Eq. (1):

$$\text{Accuracy} = \frac{\text{TP} + \text{TN}}{\text{TP} + \text{FP} + \text{TN} + \text{FN}} \tag{1}$$

ii. The F-measure is the weighted arithmetic mean of the Recall (R) and Precision (P) values. It emphasises a classifier's capacity to maximise both the accuracy and recall simultaneously. The calculation of F-measure is represented by Eq. 2.

$$\text{F-measure} = \frac{2 \times \text{TP}}{2 \times \text{TP} + \text{FP} + \text{FN}} \tag{2}$$

iii. The AUC depicts the FP and TP rates on the X-axis and Y-axis respectively. AUC is not susceptible to plurality bias and does not neglect minority samples throughout its evaluation.

iv. The False Positive Rate (FPR) is the percentage of genuine samples that were misclassified as phishing attacks. Equation 3 shows the calculation for FPR.

$$\text{FPR} = \frac{\text{FP}}{\text{FP} + \text{TN}} \times 100 \tag{3}$$

v. The True Positive Rate (TPR) is the percentage of genuine phishing website occurrences that are accurately categorised as such. Equation 4 depicts the calculation for TPR.

$$\text{TPR} = \frac{\text{TP}}{\text{TP} + \text{FN}} \times 100 \tag{4}$$

vi. Mathews Correlation Coefficient (MCC) is a numerical proportion that gives a high score if the prediction yields good results in all four classes of the confusion matrix, in ratio to the level of the genuine and illegitimate samples in the phishing dataset. MCC can be computed as shown in Eq. 5.

$$\text{MCC} = \frac{\text{TP} \times \text{TN} - \text{FP} \times \text{FN}}{\sqrt{(\text{TP} + \text{FP}) \times (\text{TP} + \text{FN}) \times (\text{TN} + \text{FP}) \times (\text{TN} + \text{FN})}} \tag{5}$$

4   Results and Discussion

In this section, experimental results and findings concerning the experimental procedure (See Fig. 4) on studied datasets (See Sect. 3.3) are presented and discussed.

4.1   FT and Selected Baseline Classifiers

In terms of accuracy and other performance assessment criteria, FT outperformed the baseline classifiers, as depicted in Table 1. Except in the case of AUC where the Decision Table baseline classifier slightly outperformed the FT based on the evaluation conducted using Dataset 1. FT achieved accuracy (95.50%), F-Measure (0.955), TP-Rate (0.955), FP-Rate (0.048) and MCC (0.909). The result obtained with FP-Rate shows that FT with 0.048 greatly reduced false classification of the phishing websites as against the baseline classifiers, which recorded higher values of FP-Rate (i.e. NB 0.098, SVM 0.059, SMO 0.078, and Dec Table 0.073). These findings suggest that the FT classifier performs well when used for phishing detection. This noteworthy result demonstrates the proposed methods' superiority over the existing baseline classification algorithms.

Table 1. Performance assessment of FT and selected baseline classifiers on Dataset 1

	FT	NB	SVM	SMO	Dec Table
Accuracy (%)	95.50	90.70	94.60	92.70	93.44
F-Measure	0.955	0.907	0.946	0.927	0.934
AUC	0.973	0.962	0.944	0.925	0.981
TP-Rate	0.955	0.907	0.946	0.927	0.934
FP-Rate	0.048	0.098	0.059	0.078	0.073
MCC	0.909	0.811	0.891	0.852	0.867

Similarly, on Dataset 2, the FT classifier outperformed the baseline classifiers as shown in Table 2. Except for the Decision Table classifier which achieved slight improvement in AUC (0.982). According to the result shown in Table 2, FT achieved an accuracy of 96.79%, F-Measure of 0.968, TP-Rate of 0.968, FP-Rate of 0.032 and MCC of 0.936 respectively. FT also shows a significant reduction in terms of false classification of phishing websites as compared with baseline classifiers. This pattern of results was also replicated when FT was evaluated using phishing Dataset 3 as shown in Table 3. This result implies that irrespective of the size of the dataset, the FT algorithm produced comparable results based on the three datasets for phishing detection.

4.2   Cascaded Generalization Functional Tree (CG-FT)

In this section, we compared the results of the proposed Cascaded Generalization Function Tree (CG-FT) with the FT classifier that shows a significant performance when compared with the baseline classifier. The goal is to ascertain the extent to which the

Table 2. Performance assessment of FT and selected baseline classifiers on Dataset 2

	FT	NB	SVM	SMO	Dec Table
Accuracy (%)	96.79	85.15	91.49	93.87	95.79
F-Measure	0.968	0.850	0.915	0.939	0.958
AUC	0.977	0.949	0.915	0.939	0.982
TP-Rate	0.968	0.852	0.915	0.939	0.958
FP-Rate	0.032	0.149	0.085	0.061	0.042
MCC	0.936	0.715	0.830	0.878	0.916

Table 3. Performance assessment of FT and selected baseline classifiers on Dataset 3

	FT	NB	SVM	SMO	Dec Table
Accuracy (%)	88.91	84.10	85.66	86.00	84.47
F-Measure	0.890	0.825	0.825	0.846	0.839
AUC	0.950	0.948	0.867	0.900	0.954
TP-Rate	0.889	0.841	0.857	0.860	0.845
FP-Rate	0.074	0.120	0.123	0.109	0.110
MCC	0.810	0.722	0.734	0.757	0.737

proposed CG-FT will outperform the FT classifier. Table 4 shows the results obtained with FT and the proposed CG-FT. Findings from these results show that the proposed CG-FT produced promising results and significantly outperformed the FT classifier on Dataset 1. CG-FT produced an accuracy of 96.99% as against 95.50% produced by FT. This pattern of improvement was replicated across the other evaluation metrics as shown in Table 4.

Table 4. Performance assessment of CG-FT and FT on Dataset 1

	FT	CG-FT
Accuracy (%)	95.50	96.99
F-Measure	0.955	0.97
AUC	0.973	0.996
TP	0.955	0.97
FP	0.048	0.032
MCC	0.909	0.939

Similarly, CG-FT outperformed the FT algorithm based on Dataset 2 evaluation when considering the different evaluation metrics used in this study. CG-FT achieved an accuracy of 98.27%, F-Measure of 0.983, AUC of 0.998, TP-Rate of 0.983, FP-Rate of 0.017 and MCC of 0.965 respectively as shown in Table 5. This is better when compare with FT results which show an accuracy of 96.79%, F-Measure of 0.968, AUC of 0.977, TP-Rate of 0.968, FP-Rate of 0.032 and MCC of 0.936 respectively. The results obtained in Table 5 is also similar to the results in Table 6 where the proposed CG-FT outperformed the FT classifier.

Table 5. Performance assessment of CG-FT and FT on Dataset 2

	FT	CG-FT
Accuracy (%)	96.79	98.27
F-Measure	0.968	0.983
AUC	0.977	0.998
TP	0.968	0.983
FP	0.032	0.017
MCC	0.936	0.965

Table 6. Performance assessment of CG-FT and FT on Dataset 3

	FT	CG-FT
Accuracy (%)	88.91	91.80
F-Measure	0.890	0.918
AUC	0.950	0.975
TP	0.889	0.918
FP	0.074	0.061
MCC	0.810	0.854

Figures 5, 6 and 7 show the trend in results obtained when comparing the proposed CG-FT with the FT algorithm. According to these figures, the superiority of CG-FT can be observed and this confirmed the acceptability of the proposed CG-FT algorithm over FT and baseline classifiers for phishing website detection.

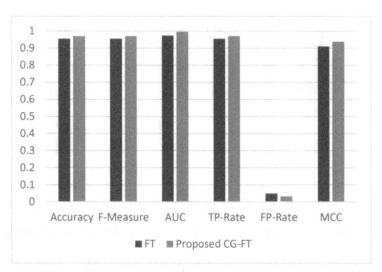

Fig. 5. Graphical representation of Performance assessment of CG-FT and FT on Dataset 1

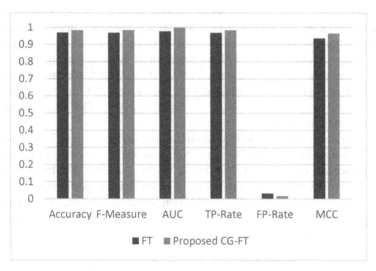

Fig. 6. Graphical representation of Performance assessment of CG-FT and FT on Dataset 2

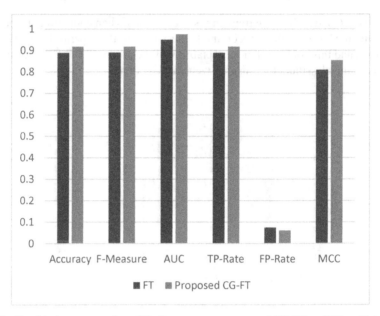

Fig. 7. Graphical representation of Performance assessment of CG-FT and FT on Dataset 3

4.3 Cascade Generalization Based Functional Tree (CG-FT) with Existing Methods

This section compares the performance of the proposed CG-FT with existing state-of-the-art methods for phishing website detection. We compare our proposed approach with different existing methods as shown in Table 7. According to the results in this Table 7, CG-FT outperformed current phishing detection methods, achieving an accuracy of 96.99%. The results obtained in the work of Al-Ahmadi and Lasloum [43], Alsariera, Elijah and Balogun [13], Ali and Malebary [22] and Vrbančič, Fister Jr and Podgorelec [2] are comparable to the proposed CG-FT result, however, CG-FT still outperformed these models in terms of accuracy on Dataset 1.

Table 8 shows the results obtained when the proposed approach (CG-FT) was compared with existing methods on Dataset 2. Similarly, CG-FT produced an accuracy of 98.27%, F-Measure of 0.983, AUC of 0.998, TP-Rate of 0.983, FP-Rate of 0.017 and MCC of 0.965 respectively, which shows the results with better performance when compared with existing approaches. The implication is that the proposed CG-FT achieved promising performance and can be used as a good candidate model for phishing website detection with a minimal false alarm rate.

Table 7. Performance assessment of CG-FT and current phishing methods on Dataset 1

Detection methods	Accuracy (%)	F-Measure	AUC	TP-Rate	FP-Rate	MCC
Aydin and Baykal [15]	95.39	0.938	0.936	-	0.046	-
Dedakia and Mistry [9]	94.29	-	-	-	-	-
Mohammad, Thabtah and McCluskey [1]	92.18	-	-	-	-	-
Ubing, Jasmi, Abdullah, Jhanjhi and Supramaniam [18]	95.40	0.947	-	-	0.041	-
Ali and Ahmed [4]	91.13	-	-	-	-	-
Verma and Das [5]	94.43	-	-	-	-	-
Hadi, Aburub and Alhawari [11]	92.40	-	-	-	-	-
Chiew, Tan, Wong, Yong and Tiong [14]	93.22	-	-	-	-	-
Rahman, Rafiq, Toma, Hossain and Biplob [12] (KNN)	94.00	-	-	-	0.049	-
Rahman, Rafiq, Toma, Hossain and Biplob [12] (SVM)	95.00	-	-	-	0.039	-
Chandra and Jana [10]	92.72	-	-	-	-	-
Folorunso, Ayo, Abdullah and Ogunyinka [20] (Stacking)	95.97	-	-	-	-	-
Folorunso, Ayo, Abdullah and Ogunyinka [20] (Hybrid NBTree)	94.10	-	-	-	-	-
Al-Ahmadi and Lasloum [43]	96.65	0.965	-	-	-	-
Alsariera, Elijah and Balogun [13]	96.26	-	-	-	0.040	-
Ali and Malebary [22]	96.43	-	-	-	-	-
Ferreira, Martiniano, Napolitano, Romero, Gatto, Farias and Sassi [44]	87.61	-	-	-	-	-
Vrbančič, Fister Jr and Podgorelec [2]	96.50	-	-	-	-	-
*CG-FT	**96.99**	**0.970**	**0.996**	**0.970**	**0.032**	**0.939**

*Indicates method proposed in this study.

Table 8. Performance assessment of CG-FT and current phishing methods on Dataset 2

Detection methods	Accuracy (%)	F-Measure	AUC	TP-Rate	FP-Rate	MCC
Chiew, Tan, Wong, Yong and Tiong [14]	94.60	-	-	-	-	-
Rahman, Rafiq, Toma, Hossain and Biplob [12] (KNN)	87.00	-	-	-	0.078	-
Rahman, Rafiq, Toma, Hossain and Biplob [12] (SVM)	91.00	-	-	-	0.067	-
*CG-FT	**98.27**	**0.983**	**0.998**	**0.983**	**0.017**	**0.965**

*Indicates method proposed in this study.

Based on Dataset 3 as shown in Table 9, the proposed CG-FT in this study also outperformed existing models used to detect phishing websites on Dataset 3. CG-FT achieved an accuracy of 91.80%, F-Measure of 0.918, AUC of 0.975, TP-Rate of 0.918, FP_Rate of 0.061 and MCC of 0.854 respectively. Therefore, the proposed model has shown superiority over the existing state-of-the-art approaches based on the evaluation results on Dataset 1, 2 and 3 respectively.

Table 9. Performance assessment of CG-FT and current phishing methods on Dataset 3

Detection methods	Accuracy (%)	F-Measure	AUC	TP-Rate	FP-Rate	MCC
Rahman, Rafiq, Toma, Hossain and Biplob [12] (KNN)	88.00	-	-	-	0.099	-
Rahman, Rafiq, Toma, Hossain and Biplob [12] (SVM)	87.00	-	-	-	0.087	-
*CG-FT	**91.80**	**0.918**	**0.975**	**0.918**	**0.061**	**0.854**

*Indicates method proposed in this study.

5   Conclusions and Future Works

One of the serious cyberattacks that have a global negative impact on internet users is phishing attacks. A website phishing operation has a catastrophic impact on internet users and web-based services in general. A website phishing attack allows an adversary to obtain sensitive information of victims which can be further utilized to perform fraudulent transactions or steal users identities. Numerous cybersecurity professionals and academics have proposed and created numerous anti-phishing techniques for detecting phishing sites. However, identifying phishing websites has been evasive due to the sophisticated methods being deployed by attackers. To address false alarm that is very common with existing state-of-the-art methods for phishing website detection, this study proposed a cascaded generalization functional tree algorithm called CG-FT. CG-FT leveraged the performance of the Functional Tree (FT) algorithm to produce superior classifiers that outperformed baseline models such as NB, SVM, SMO, and Decision Table as well as existing state-of-the-art methods for phishing website detection.

Answers to the research questions (RQs) stated in this study are supplied, and the following conclusion is reached based on the findings of this study.

RQ1: How efficient is the FT algorithm in detecting legitimate and phishing websites?

Implementations of the FT algorithm demonstrated substantial improvements in accuracy and false alarm reduction when compared to baseline approaches such as NB, SVM, SMO, and Decision Table. This performance is reproduced across the three datasets evaluated in this study.

RQ2: How efficient is the proposed CG-FT algorithm in detecting legitimate and phishing websites?

The proposed CG-FT leveraged the promising performance of the FT algorithm and through a novel improvement, CG-FT has shown a significant increase in accuracy as well as a reduction in error rate when compared with the FT algorithm for phishing website detection. This improvement was replicated considering the three datasets evaluated in this study.

RQ3: How efficient is the proposed CG-FT compared to existing phishing methods?

The performance of the proposed CG-FT is superior based on the performance assessment measures utilised in this study when compared with current phishing methods.

In the future, the authors want to test the proposed CG-FT on more phishing website datasets to determine its generalisation potential to diminish the risk of phishing websites. A deep learning model will also be considered for future research to produce a scalable phishing website detection algorithm.

References

1. Mohammad, R.M., Thabtah, F., McCluskey, L.: Predicting phishing websites based on self-structuring neural network. Neural Comput. Appl. **25**(2), 443–458 (2013). https://doi.org/10.1007/s00521-013-1490-z
2. Vrbančič, G., Fister, I., Jr., Podgorelec, V.: Swarm intelligence approaches for parameter setting of deep learning neural network: case study on phishing websites classification. In: Proceedings of the 8th International Conference on Web Intelligence, Mining and Semantics, pp. 1–8 (2018)
3. Adeyemo, V.E., Azween, A., JhanJhi, N., Mahadevan, S., Balogun, A.O.: Ensemble and deep-learning methods for two-class and multi-attack anomaly intrusion detection: an empirical study. Int. J. Adv. Comput. Sci. Appl. **10**, 520–528 (2019)

4. Ali, W., Ahmed, A.A.: Hybrid intelligent phishing website prediction using deep neural networks with genetic algorithm-based feature selection and weighting. IET Inf. Secur. **13**, 659–669 (2019)
5. Verma, R., Das, A.: What's in a URL: fast feature extraction and malicious url detection. In: Proceedings of the 3rd ACM on International Workshop on Security and Privacy Analytics, pp. 55–63 (2017)
6. Alqahtani, M.: Phishing websites classification using association classification (PWCAC). In: International Conference on Computer and Information Sciences (ICCIS), pp. 1–6. IEEE (2019)
7. Balogun, A.O., et al.: Improving the phishing website detection using empirical analysis of Function Tree and its variants. Heliyon **7**, e07437 (2021)
8. Abdelhamid, N., Ayesh, A., Thabtah, F.: Phishing detection based associative classification data mining. Expert Syst. Appl. **41**, 5948–5959 (2014)
9. Dedakia, M., Mistry, K.: Phishing detection using content based associative classification data mining. J. Eng. Comput. Appl. Sci. **4**, 209–214 (2015)
10. Chandra, Y., Jana, A.: Improvement in phishing websites detection using meta classifiers. In: 6th International Conference on Computing for Sustainable Global Development (INDIACom), pp. 637–641. IEEE (2019)
11. Hadi, W., Aburub, F., Alhawari, S.: A new fast associative classification algorithm for detecting phishing websites. Appl. Soft Comput. **48**, 729–734 (2016)
12. Rahman, S.S.M.M., Rafiq, F.B., Toma, T.R., Hossain, S.S., Biplob, K.B.B.: Performance assessment of multiple machine learning classifiers for detecting the phishing URLs. In: Raju, K.S., Senkerik, R., Lanka, S.P., Rajagopal, V. (eds.) Data Engineering and Communication Technology. AISC, vol. 1079, pp. 285–296. Springer, Singapore (2020). https://doi.org/10.1007/978-981-15-1097-7_25
13. Alsariera, Y.A., Elijah, A.V., Balogun, A.O.: Phishing website detection: forest by penalizing attributes algorithm and its enhanced variations. Arab. J. Sci. Eng. **45**(12), 10459–10470 (2020). https://doi.org/10.1007/s13369-020-04802-1
14. Chiew, K.L., Tan, C.L., Wong, K., Yong, K.S., Tiong, W.K.: A new hybrid ensemble feature selection framework for machine learning-based phishing detection system. Inf. Sci. **484**, 153–166 (2019)
15. Aydin, M., Baykal, N.: Feature extraction and classification phishing websites based on URL. In: IEEE Conference on Communications and Network Security (CNS), pp. 769–770. IEEE (2015)
16. Adeyemo, V.E., Balogun, A.O., Mojeed, H.A., Akande, N.O., Adewole, K.S.: Ensemble-based logistic model trees for website phishing detection. In: Anbar, M., Abdullah, N., Manickam, S. (eds.) ACeS 2020. CCIS, vol. 1347, pp. 627–641. Springer, Singapore (2021). https://doi.org/10.1007/978-981-33-6835-4_41
17. Pham, B.T., Nguyen, V.-T., Ngo, V.-L., Trinh, P.T., Ngo, H.T.T., Tien Bui, D.: A novel hybrid model of rotation forest based functional trees for landslide susceptibility mapping: a case study at Kon Tum Province, Vietnam. In: Tien Bui, D., Ngoc Do, A., Bui, H.-B., Hoang, N.-D. (eds.) GTER 2017, pp. 186–201. Springer, Cham (2018). https://doi.org/10.1007/978-3-319-68240-2_12
18. Ubing, A.A., Jasmi, S.K.B., Abdullah, A., Jhanjhi, N., Supramaniam, M.: Phishing website detection: an improved accuracy through feature selection and ensemble learning. Int. J. Adv. Comput. Sci. Appl. **10**, 252–257 (2019)
19. Abdulrahaman, M.D., Alhassan, J.K., Adebayo, O.S., Ojeniyi, J.A., Olalere, M.: Phishing attack detection based on random forest with wrapper feature selection method. Int. J. Inf. Process. Commun. (IJIPC) **7**, 209–224 (2019)
20. Folorunso, S.O., Ayo, F.E., Abdullah, K.-K.A., Ogunyinka, P.I.: Hybrid vs ensemble classification models for phishing websites. Iraqi J. Sci. 3387–3396 (2020)

21. Alsariera, Y.A., Adeyemo, V.E., Balogun, A.O., Alazzawi, A.K.: AI meta-learners and extra-trees algorithm for the detection of phishing websites. IEEE Access **8**, 142532–142542 (2020)
22. Ali, W., Malebary, S.: Particle swarm optimization-based feature weighting for improving intelligent phishing website detection. IEEE Access **8**, 116766–116780 (2020)
23. Balogun, A.O., Basri, S., Abdulkadir, S.J., Adeyemo, V.E., Imam, A.A., Bajeh, A.O.: Software defect prediction: analysis of class imbalance and performance stability. J. Eng. Sci. Technol **14**, 3294–3308 (2019)
24. Yu, Q., Jiang, S., Zhang, Y.: The performance stability of defect prediction models with class imbalance: an empirical study. IEICE Trans. Inf. Syst. **100**, 265–272 (2017)
25. Gama, J.: Functional trees. Mach. Learn. **55**, 219–250 (2004)
26. Witten, I.H., Frank, E.: Data mining: practical machine learning tools and techniques with Java implementations. ACM SIGMOD Rec. **31**, 76–77 (2002)
27. Gama, J., Brazdil, P.: Cascade generalization. Mach. Learn. **41**, 315–343 (2000)
28. Barakat, N.: Cascade generalization: one versus many. JCP **12**, 238–249 (2017)
29. Balogun, A.O., Bajeh, A.O., Orie, V.A., Yusuf-Asaju, W.A.: Software defect prediction using ensemble learning: an ANP based evaluation method. FUOYE J. Eng. Technol. **3**, 50–55 (2018)
30. Balogun, A.O., et al.: Empirical analysis of rank aggregation-based multi-filter feature selection methods in software defect prediction. Electronics **10**, 179 (2021)
31. Balogun, A.O., et al.: SMOTE-based homogeneous ensemble methods for software defect prediction. In: Gervasi, O., et al. (eds.) ICCSA 2020. LNCS, vol. 12254, pp. 615–631. Springer, Cham (2020). https://doi.org/10.1007/978-3-030-58817-5_45
32. Jimoh, R., Balogun, A., Bajeh, A., Ajayi, S.: A PROMETHEE based evaluation of software defect predictors. J. Comput. Sci. Appl. **25**, 106–119 (2018)
33. Xu, Z., Liu, J., Yang, Z., An, G., Jia, X.: The impact of feature selection on defect prediction performance: an empirical comparison. In: IEEE 27th International Symposium on Software Reliability Engineering (ISSRE), pp. 309–320. IEEE (2016)
34. Yadav, S., Shukla, S.: Analysis of k-fold cross-validation over hold-out validation on colossal datasets for quality classification. In: IEEE 6th International Conference on Advanced Computing (IACC), pp. 78–83. IEEE (2016)
35. Arlot, S., Lerasle, M.: Choice of V for V-fold cross-validation in least-squares density estimation. J. Mach. Learn. Res. **17**, 7256–7305 (2016)
36. Balogun, A.O., et al.: Search-based wrapper feature selection methods in software defect prediction: an empirical analysis. In: Silhavy, R. (ed.) CSOC 2020. AISC, vol. 1224, pp. 492–503. Springer, Cham (2020). https://doi.org/10.1007/978-3-030-51965-0_43
37. Balogun, A.O., et al.: Rank aggregation based multi-filter feature selection method for software defect prediction. In: Anbar, M., Abdullah, N., Manickam, S. (eds.) ACeS 2020. CCIS, vol. 1347, pp. 371–383. Springer, Singapore (2021). https://doi.org/10.1007/978-981-33-6835-4_25
38. Balogun, A.O., Basri, S., Abdulkadir, S.J., Hashim, A.S.: Performance analysis of feature selection methods in software defect prediction: a search method approach. Appl. Sci. **9**, 2764 (2019)
39. Balogun, A.O., et al.: Impact of feature selection methods on the predictive performance of software defect prediction models: an extensive empirical study. Symmetry **12**, 1147 (2020)
40. Hall, M., Frank, E., Holmes, G., Pfahringer, B., Reutemann, P., Witten, I.H.: The WEKA data mining software: an update. ACM SIGKDD Explor. Newsl **11**, 10–18 (2009)
41. Adewole, K.S., Akintola, A.G., Salihu, S.A., Faruk, N., Jimoh, R.G.: Hybrid rule-based model for phishing URLs detection. In: Miraz, M.H., Excell, P.S., Ware, A., Soomro, S., Ali, M. (eds.) iCETiC 2019. LNICSSITE, vol. 285, pp. 119–135. Springer, Cham (2019). https://doi.org/10.1007/978-3-030-23943-5_9

42. AlEroud, A., Karabatis, G.: Bypassing detection of URL-based phishing attacks using generative adversarial deep neural networks. In: Proceedings of the 6th International Workshop on Security and Privacy Analytics, pp. 53–60 (2020)

43. Al-Ahmadi, S., Lasloum, T.: PDMLP: phishing detection using multilayer perceptron. Int. J. Netw. Secur. Appl. **12**, 59–72 (2020)

44. Ferreira, R.P., et al.: Artificial neural network for websites classification with phishing characteristics. Soc. Netw. **7**, 97 (2018)

Comparison of Automated Machine Learning Tools for SMS Spam Message Filtering

Waddah Saeed[✉]

Center for Artificial Intelligence Research (CAIR), University of Agder,
Jon Lilletuns vei 9, 4879 Grimstad, Norway
waddah.waheeb@uia.no

Abstract. Short Message Service (SMS) is a very popular service used for communication by mobile users. However, this popular service can be abused by executing illegal activities and influencing security risks. Nowadays, many automatic machine learning (AutoML) tools exist which can help domain experts and lay users to build high-quality ML models with little or no machine learning knowledge. In this work, a classification performance comparison was conducted between three automatic ML tools for SMS spam message filtering. These tools are mljar-supervised AutoML, H2O AutoML, and Tree-based Pipeline Optimization Tool (TPOT) AutoML. Experimental results showed that ensemble models achieved the best classification performance. The Stacked Ensemble model, which was built using H2O AutoML, achieved the best performance in terms of Log Loss (0.8370), true positive (1088/1116), and true negative (281/287) metrics. There is a 19.05% improvement in Log Loss with respect to TPOT AutoML and 5.56% improvement with respect to mljar-supervised AutoML. The satisfactory filtering performance achieved with AutoML tools provides a potential application for AutoML tools to automatically determine the best ML model that can perform best for SMS spam message filtering.

Keywords: Short Message Service (SMS) · Spam filtering · Short text classification · Automatic machine learning · AutoML

1 Introduction

Short Message Service (SMS) is a very popular service that enables its users to send short text messages from one mobile device to another. However, mobile users can receive SMS spam messages.

According to [1,14], the huge number of mobile devices/users and the possibility of sending bulk SMS messages easily and with low cost are factors that contribute to the growth of SMS spam problem and attract malicious organizations for executing illegal activities and influencing security risks.

Content-based filtering has been extensively studied to combat SMS spam messages. This type of filtering uses techniques to analyze selected features extracted from SMS messages with the aim to filter spam messages.

© Springer Nature Singapore Pte Ltd. 2021
N. Abdullah et al. (Eds.): ACeS 2021, CCIS 1487, pp. 307–316, 2021.
https://doi.org/10.1007/978-981-16-8059-5_18

Various machine learning models have been utilized for SMS spam message filtering such as support vector machine (SVM) [2,3], multilayer perceptron [15], and deep learning [5,12].

Nowadays, many automatic ML tools (AutoML) exist. With these AutoML tools, domain experts are enabled to build ML applications without extensive knowledge of statistics and machine learning [17]. Furthermore, lay users with little or no ML knowledge can use user-friendly automated systems to build high-quality custom models [7]. In the literature of SMS spam message filtering, one work used an AutoML tool to make a classification performance comparison between various ML models built using that AutoML tool [13].

Clearly, to the best of our knowledge, there is no study comparing SMS spam message filtering performance of the best models built using AutoML tools. Therefore, this work carried out a comparison between three AutoML tools for SMS spam message filtering. These tools are mljar-supervised AutoML [11], H2O AutoML [9], and Tree-based Pipeline Optimization Tool (TPOT) AutoML [8]. The importance of this work is to investigate how good the classification performance using the three selected tools, how fast is the training process, and how much difference in the performance between these three tools.

The remainder of this paper is organized as follows. Related work is given in Sect. 2. Experimental settings are described in Sect. 3. Results and discussions are given in Sect. 4. Finally, conclusions and possible future works are highlighted in the last section.

2 Related Works

Content-based SMS spam filtering uses techniques to analyse selected features extracted from SMS messages with the aim to filter spam messages.

In [2,3], various classifiers were used to classify SMS messages. These classifiers were naive Bayes, C4.5, k-nearest neighbors, and SVM. Two tokenizers were used by the authors. In the first tokenizer, alphanumeric characters followed a printable character. Dots, commas, and colons were excluded from the middle of the pattern. The second tokenizer was represented by any sequence of characters separated by dots, commas, colons, blanks, tabs, returns, and dashes. It was found that better performance was achieved using the first tokenizer with accuracy equals 97.64%.

In [6], stylistic and text features were utilized with two SVM classifiers to filter SMS spam messages. An SMS message was classified as a spam message if both SVM classifiers classified the message as a spam message. It was found that the proposed methodology with two SVM classifiers was better than using one SVM classifier.

Multilayer perceptron with features selected by the Gini index (GI) method was used in [15]. According to the obtained results, the best AUC performance was around 0.9648, which was achieved with 100-features.

In [14], a classification performance comparison was conducted between ten feature subset sizes which were selected by three feature selection methods. SVM was used as a classifier and trained with the feature subset sizes selected by feature selection methods. Based on the obtained results, the features selected by information gain (IG) enhanced the classification performance of the SVM classifier with the ten feature subset sizes. The best result was achieved with only 50% of the extracted features. Based on that, it was concluded that the feature selection step should be used because using a big number of features as inputs could lead to degrading the classification performance.

In [16] the authors proposed a method based on the discrete hidden Markov model for two reasons. The first one is to use the word order information and the second reason to solve the low term frequency issue found in SMS messages. This proposed method scored 0.959 in terms of accuracy.

Deep learning models were used for SMS spam message filtering, for example, the works in [5,12]. In [5], the authors proposed a hybrid deep learning model based on the combination of Convolutional Neural Network (CNN) and Long Short-Term Memory (LSTM). The classifier was developed to deal with SMS messages that are written in Arabic or English. It was found that the proposed CNN-LSTM model outperformed several machine learning classifiers with an accuracy of 98.37%. The authors in [12] used CNN and LSTM models for classification. It was found that both models achieved higher classification accuracy compared to other ML models, with 3 CNN + Dropout being the most accurate model achieving an accuracy of 99.44%.

Nowadays, many automatic ML tools exist such as mljar-supervised AutoML [11], H2O AutoML [9], and Tree-based Pipeline Optimization Tool (TPOT) AutoML [8]. Domain experts can benefit from such AutoML tools because AutoML tools can enable them to build ML applications without extensive knowledge of statistics and machine learning [17]. Furthermore, lay users with little or no ML knowledge can use user-friendly automated systems to build high-quality custom models [7]. According to [7], there are four main steps in the AutoML pipeline: data preparation, feature engineering, model generation, and model evaluation. In data preparation step, the given data is prepared to be used to train and test ML models. In the second step, a dynamic combination of feature extraction, feature construction, and feature selection processes are used to come up with useful features that can be used by ML models. Search space and optimization methods are two main components in model generation step. The last step in the AutoML pipeline is evaluating the built ML models.

In the literature of SMS spam message filtering, one work used H2O AutoML to make a classification performance comparison between various ML models [13]. Based on the obtained results, it was found that the number of digits and existing of URL in SMS messages are the most significant features that contribute highly to detect SMS spam messages. It was also found that random forest is the best model for the used dataset with 0.977% in terms of accuracy.

Clearly, to the best of our knowledge, there is no study comparing SMS spam message filtering performance of the best models built using AutoML tools. Therefore, this work investigated the abilities of three AutoML tools for SMS spam message filtering.

3   Methodology

The methodology consists of two main steps: data collection and the setting used with the three automatic machine learning tools.

3.1   Data Used

In this work, the data used in the simulations is the post-processed data used in [14][1]. In [14], the data was collected from three works [3, 4, 10] then pre-processed by removing duplicate messages and non-English messages. The number of messages after the removal is 5,610 messages: 4,375 legitimate messages and 1,235 spam messages. Following that, as explained in [14], text pre-processing methods were used to reduce the number of extracted features including lowercase conversion, feature abstraction replacement, tokenization, and stemming.

There are 6,463 features in the data set. Therefore, in this work, features selected using the information gain (IG) method were used. IG was selected because its selected features helped SVM to achieve better results as reported in [14].

In this work, 25% of the data set was used as a test set. The data set was split in a stratified fashion. Three feature subset sizes were selected with sizes equal to 50, 100, and 200.

3.2   Settings Used with the Automatic Machine Learning Tools

The settings used with the automatic machine learning tools used in this work are described below.

mljar-supervised AutoML. It is an automated ML tool that works with tabular data [11]. Various ML models can be selected to be used for classification or regression tasks. In this work, nine models were used namely Baseline, Decision Tree, Random Forest, Xgboost, LightGBM, CatBoost, Extra Trees, Neural Network, and Nearest Neighbors.

The mljar-supervised AutoML has several steps that can be used in the process of searching for the best performing ML model in the ML pipeline. Not all ML models can be used in these steps. In this work, the steps with the ML model used are given below:

1. Using Baseline and Decision Tree models to get quick insights from the data.
2. The selected models except for Baseline and Decision Tree were trained with default hyperparameters.
3. Random Search step was used over a defined set of hyperparameters with the seven models in Step 2.
4. Golden Features (i.e., new-constructed features) were used with Xgboost, LightGBM, and CatBoost models.

---

[1] https://github.com/Waddah-Saeed/EnglishSMSCollection/blob/master/IG.zip.

5. New models based on Random Forest, Xgboost, LightGBM, CatBoost, Extra Trees, and Neural Network were trained on selected features.
6. The top two performing models were tuned further in what is called a hill-climbing step.
7. The last step is the ensemble step where all models from the previous steps were ensembled.

In this work, the command used to initialize AutoML object in mljar-supervised AutoML (version 0.10.6) is shown in Fig. 1:

```
automl = AutoML(
    algorithms = ["Baseline","Decision Tree", "Random Forest", "Xgboost", "LightGBM",
                  "CatBoost", "Extra Trees", "Neural Network", "Nearest Neighbors"],
    ml_task = "binary_classification",
    validation_strategy = {
        "validation_type": "kfold",
        "k_folds": 5,
        "shuffle": True,
        "stratify": True,
        "random_seed": seed
    },
    total_time_limit = hours * 60 * 60, explain_level = 2,
    golden_features = True, features_selection = True,
    start_random_models = 5,
    hill_climbing_steps = 2, top_models_to_improve = 2,
    eval_metric = 'logloss', random_state = seed,
    stack_models= True
)
```

Fig. 1. Initialize AutoML object in mljar-supervised AutoML.

H2O's AutoML. With H2O AutoML [9], various ML models based on Random Forest, Generalized Linear Model (GLM), Gradient Boosting Machine (GBM), Deep Learning (a fully-connected multi-layer neural network) can be built. In this work, the execution steps started with using the default settings with XGBoost, GLM, Random Forest, and Deep Learning models. Then, built an Extremely Randomized Trees (XRT) model. Following that, a grid search was used with XGBoost, GBM, and Deep Learning models. After that, learning rate annealing with GBM and learning rate search with XGBoost were used. Finally, two Stacked Ensembles were built. The code used to initialize AutoML object in H2O AutoML (version 3.32.1.3) is shown in Fig. 2.

TPOT. TPOT AutoML [8] is a tool that optimizes ML pipelines using genetic programming. Various ML models and their variations are evaluated by TPOT namely Naive Bayes, Decision Tree, Extra Trees, Random Forest, Gradient Boosting, Logistic Regression, Xgboost, Neural Network, and Nearest Neighbors. The code used to initialize AutoML object in TPOT (version 0.11.7) is shown in Fig. 3.

```
aml = H2OAutoML(max_runtime_secs = hours * 60 * 60,
                stopping_metric = "logloss", verbosity = "info", seed = seed,
                sort_metric = "logloss")
```

Fig. 2. Initialize AutoML object in H2O AutoML.

```
tpot = TPOTClassifier(scoring = 'neg_log_loss', cv = 5, verbosity = 2,
            max_time_mins = hours * 60, random_state = seed)
```

Fig. 3. Initialize AutoML object in TPOT.

General Settings. For a fair comparison between the tools, the following settings were used with the three tools:

– Cross-validation settings: Five folds were created with a stratified fashion. However, how the samples in these folds were selected from the training data are controlled by the tools.
– Performance metric: Log Loss was used as a performance metric.
– Training time: Two, three, and four hours were given to train the models using 50, 100, and 200 features, respectively.

4   Results and Discussion

This section reports and discusses the obtained results using the given methodology in the previous section. It starts with the classification performance comparison using three different feature subset sizes. Following that, the best classification performance for each feature size and for each tool are presented and discussed.

4.1   Classification Performance Comparison

The best model on the training set from each tool was used for prediction. The performance of the best model in each tool is shown in Table 1. It can be seen from Table 1 that the best model is the Gradient Boosting model built using the TPOT AutoML tool. The worst performance was using a Deep Learning model built using the H2O AutoML tool. The bad Log Loss value obtained by the Deep Learning model is because of the incorrect prediction as shown in the false positive component in Table 1.

Turning now to the results in Table 2 and Table 3, it seems that increasing the number of features helped the H2O AutoML to achieve better results. The Stacked Ensemble model is the best ML model using 100 and 200 features as shown in both tables. It is important to note that the Stacked Ensemble model that was built using the H2O AutoML with 200 features achieved the best performance in terms of Log Loss, true positive, and true negative metrics. It is a good combination because users want to avoid blocking their legitimate messages and ensure stopping spam messages.

Table 1, 2 and 3 reveal that the ensemble methods achieved the best performance in all cases with the mljar-supervised AutoML and in two cases with the H2O AutoML tools. However, the best performance achieved using the TPOT AutoML is with the Logistic Regression model.

Table 1. The classification performance comparison using 50 features.

Tool	Best model	Log loss	TP	FP	FN	TN	AUC
mljar-supervised	Stacked ensemble	1.2555	1085	42	9	267	0.9279
H2O	Deep learning	7.6809	**1091**	309	**3**	0	0.4986
TPOT	Gradient boosting	**1.1817**	1087	**41**	7	**268**	**0.9305**

Table 2. The classification performance comparison using 100 features.

Tool	Best model	Log loss	TP	FP	FN	TN	AUC
mljar-supervised	Stacked ensemble	**0.9109**	1087	**30**	7	279	**0.9483**
H2O	Stacked ensemble	1.0093	1084	31	10	278	0.9453
TPOT	Logistic regression	1.1817	1085	41	9	268	0.9295

Table 3. The classification performance comparison using 200 features.

Tool	Best model	Log loss	TP	FP	FN	TN	AUC
mljar-supervised	Stacked ensemble	0.8863	**1088**	30	**6**	279	0.9487
H2O	Stacked ensemble	**0.8370**	**1088**	**28**	**6**	**281**	**0.952**
TPOT	Logistic regression	1.034	1086	34	8	275	0.9413

With regards to the training time, as shown in Table 4, both the TPOT AutoML and mljar-supervised AutoML used the entire given time, while the H2O AutoML finished the training before the time-limit.

4.2 Best Classification Performance Comparison

As shown in Table 5, Stacked Ensemble models achieved the best performance with 100 and 200 features. As mentioned above and shown in Table 6, the Stacked Ensemble model that was built using the H2O AutoML with 200 features achieved the best classification performance. There is a 19.05% improvement in Log Loss with respect to the TPOT AutoML and 5.56% improvement

Table 4. Training time comparison. Time reported in H:MM format.

Tool	Feature size		
	50	100	200
mljar-supervised	2:01	3:01	4:04
H2O	1:20	2:03	2:41
TPOT	2:01	3:00	4:00

with respect to the mljar-supervised AutoML. The detail of the obtained training results for the best model is shown in Table 7. It can also be seen in Table 6 that the best performance was achieved with 200 features with all tools.

Table 5. The best classification performance comparison for each feature subset size.

Features subset size	Tool	Best model	Log loss
50	TPOT	Gradient boosting	1.1817
100	mljar-supervised	Stacked ensemble	0.9109
200	H2O	Stacked ensemble	**0.8370**

Table 6. Best classification performance comparison for each tool.

Feature subset size	Tool	Best model	Log loss	Improvement (%)
200	TPOT	Logistic regression	1.034	19.05
200	mljar-supervised	Stacked ensemble	0.8863	5.56
200	H2O	Stacked ensemble	**0.8370**	--

Table 7. Training results for the best model.

Metric	Value
Log loss	0.0766522
TP	3257
FP	24
FN	67
TN	859
AUC	0.994897
Training time (in millisecond)	2738
Prediction time per row (in millisecond)	0.288793

5   Conclusions and Future Works

In this work, the classification performance for SMS messages using three automatic ML tools was conducted. These tools are mljar-supervised AutoML, H2O AutoML, and TPOT AutoML. Three feature subset sizes were used with these tools. The main results of this work are summarized as follows:

- The Stacked Ensemble model that was built using the H2O AutoML with 200 features achieved the best performance in terms of Log Loss, true positive, and true negative metrics. There is a 19.05% improvement in Log Loss with respect to the TPOT AutoML tool and 5.56% improvement with respect to the mljar-supervised AutoML tool.
- Ensemble models (i.e., Stacked Ensemble and Gradient Boosting) achieved the best performance for each feature size.
- The best performance achieved with all tools was with 200 features.

The satisfactory filtering performance achieved with AutoML tools provides a potential application for AutoML tools to automatically determine the best ML model that can perform best for SMS spam message filtering. For future work, this work can be further extended by including more automatic ML tools, adding more features, and increasing training time-limit.

Acknowledgement. The source code for this work is available in https://github.com/Waddah-Saeed/SMS-Spam-Filtering-AutoML.

References

1. Abayomi-Alli, O., Misra, S., Abayomi-Alli, A., Odusami, M.: A review of soft techniques for SMS spam classification: methods, approaches and applications. Eng. Appl. Artif. Intell. **86**, 197–212 (2019). https://doi.org/10.1016/j.engappai.2019.08.024
2. Almeida, T., Hidalgo, J.M.G., Silva, T.P.: Towards SMS spam filtering: results under a new dataset. Int. J. Inf. Secur. Sci. **2**(1), 1–18 (2013)
3. Almeida, T.A., Hidalgo, J.M.G., Yamakami, A.: Contributions to the study of SMS spam filtering: new collection and results. In: Proceedings of the 11th ACM Symposium on Document Engineering, pp. 259–262 (2011)
4. Delany, S.J., Buckley, M., Greene, D.: SMS spam filtering: methods and data. Expert Syst. Appl. **39**(10), 9899–9908 (2012)
5. Ghourabi, A., Mahmood, M.A., Alzubi, Q.M.: A hybrid CNN-LSTM model for SMS spam detection in Arabic and English messages. Future Internet **12**(9) (2020). https://doi.org/10.3390/fi12090156
6. Goswami, G., Singh, R., Vatsa, M.: Automated spam detection in short text messages. In: Singh, R., Vatsa, M., Majumdar, A., Kumar, A. (eds.) Machine Intelligence and Signal Processing. AISC, vol. 390, pp. 85–98. Springer, New Delhi (2016). https://doi.org/10.1007/978-81-322-2625-3_8
7. He, X., Zhao, K., Chu, X.: AutoML: a survey of the state-of-the-art. Knowledge-Based Systems **212**, 106622 (2021)

8. Le, T.T., Fu, W., Moore, J.H.: Scaling tree-based automated machine learning to biomedical big data with a feature set selector. Bioinformatics **36**(1), 250–256 (2020)

9. LeDell, E., Poirier, S.: H2O AutoML: scalable automatic machine learning. In: 7th ICML Workshop on Automated Machine Learning (AutoML), July 2020

10. Nuruzzaman, M.T., Lee, C., Choi, D.: Independent and personal SMS spam filtering. In: 2011 IEEE 11th International Conference on Computer and Information Technology, pp. 429–435. IEEE (2011)

11. Płońska, A., Płoński, P.: Mljar: state-of-the-art automated machine learning framework for tabular data. Version 0.10.3 (2021). https://github.com/mljar/mljar-supervised

12. Roy, P.K., Singh, J.P., Banerjee, S.: Deep learning to filter SMS spam. Future Gener. Comput. Syst. **102**, 524–533 (2020). https://doi.org/10.1016/j.future.2019.09.001

13. Suleiman, D., Al-Naymat, G.: SMS spam detection using h2o framework. Proc. Comput. Sci. **113**, 154–161 (2017). https://doi.org/10.1016/j.procs.2017.08.335. The 8th International Conference on Emerging Ubiquitous Systems and Pervasive Networks (EUSPN 2017)/The 7th International Conference on Current and Future Trends of Information and Communication Technologies in Healthcare (ICTH-2017)/Affiliated Workshops

14. Waheeb, W., Ghazali, R.: Content-based SMS classification: statistical analysis for the relationship between number of features and classification performance. Comput. Sist. **21**(4), 771–785 (2017)

15. Waheeb, W., Ghazali, R., Deris, M.M.: Content-based SMS spam filtering based on the scaled conjugate gradient backpropagation algorithm. In: 2015 12th International Conference on Fuzzy Systems and Knowledge Discovery (FSKD), pp. 675–680. IEEE (2015)

16. Xia, T., Chen, X.: A discrete hidden Markov model for SMS spam detection. Appl. Sci. **10**(14) (2020). https://doi.org/10.3390/app10145011

17. Zöller, M.A., Huber, M.F.: Benchmark and survey of automated machine learning frameworks. J. Artif. Intell. Res. **70**, 409–472 (2021)

Deep Learning Approach for Detecting Botnet Attacks in IoT Environment of Multiple and Heterogeneous Sensors

Abdulkareem A. Hezam[1] ⓘ, Salama A. Mostafa[1](✉) ⓘ, Azizul Azhar Ramli[1] ⓘ,
Hairulnizam Mahdin[1] ⓘ, and Bashar Ahmed Khalaf[2] ⓘ

[1] Faculty of Computer Science and Information Technology, Universiti Tun Hussein Onn
Malaysia, 86400 Parit Raja, Johor, Malaysia
AI180287@siswa.uthm.edu.my, {salama,azizulr,hairuln}@uthm.edu.my
[2] Department of Medical Instruments Engineering Techniques, Bilad Alrafidain University
College, Ba'aqubah 32001, Diyala, Iraq
bashar@bauc14.edu.iq

Abstract. The impacts of Distributed-Denial-of-Service (DDoS) are doubtlessly major and continue to grow along with the growth of Internet-of-Things (IoT) devices. So many solutions have been contributed to detecting and mitigating this attack, specifically in IoT devices, yet the threat still exists and is bigger than ever. Denial of service attacks are often carried out by flooding a targeted computer or resource with phony requests in an attempt to overwhelm systems and prevent a few or all genuine requests from being completed; this is known as botnet attacks. There have been so many attempts to solve such puzzle-like middle-box and Artificial Intelligence (AI) solutions through machine learning (ML). The new botnets are so complex where for example, the Mirai botnet can mutate on a daily basis. This paper proposes a deep learning (DL) approach that consists of three DL algorithms, namely, recurrent neural network (RNN), convolutional neural network (CNN), and Long short-term memory (LSTM)-RNN to counter DDoS attacks targeting IoT networks. These algorithms are tested by implementing a real-world N-BaIoT dataset that has been collected by infecting nine IoT devices with two of the most dangerous DDoS botnets (Mirai and Bashlite). Subsequently, the three algorithms are compared in terms of accuracy, precision, recall, and f-measure. The results show that the RNN has achieved the highest accuracy of 89.75% among the three algorithms, followed by the LSTM-RNN and the CNN.

Keywords: Distributed Denial of Service (DDoS) · Internet of Things · Deep learning · Classification · Convolutional neural network (CNN) · Recurrent neural network (RNN) · Long short-term memory-recurrent neural network (LSTM-RNN)

1 Introduction

A massive scaled Distributed-Denial-of-Service (DDoS) botnet attack in 2016 has compromised over 100,000 IoT devices targeting Dyn DNS infrastructure [1]. Another one

© Springer Nature Singapore Pte Ltd. 2021
N. Abdullah et al. (Eds.): ACeS 2021, CCIS 1487, pp. 317–328, 2021.
https://doi.org/10.1007/978-981-16-8059-5_19

was used against Carphone Warehouse in 2015. It is utilized as a distraction method to the security system, which gave the hackers access to 2.4 million customers' personal information. This host-based attack turns the hacked device into a zombie and takes advantage of being a trusted source to hack a targeted network system. DDoS represents the attempt of hackers to render computers or networks' assets by interfering with the services of a host connected to the Internet. It is a targeted operation that focuses on assaulting websites by receiving more traffic than the website, and the server can handle. The server CPU operates in maximum workload, which slows down the performance of the running applications, including antiviruses and Internet protection applications. The huge capacity of the attack leaves the firewall paralyzed, which makes it easy for the hacker to get into the device aimed to hack. It might result in freezing the website and the server, and hence every device of this network is under attack [2].

The severity of such an attack can impact on a huge scale. The massive growth of IoT devices and the ignorance of some manufacturers on the security of these devices could result in a tremendous issue regarding trusting new technology whose primary job is to make our lives easier. The problem is that DDoS impacts are doubtlessly major, and they will continue to grow along with the growth of IoT applications. Many solutions have been contributed to detecting and mitigating this attack, specifically in IoT devices, yet the threat still exists and is bigger than ever. One of which is using a machine learning (ML) pipeline that captures the traffic and identifies whether it is benign or there is an attack [3].

Accordingly, the recommended method for detecting DDoS in IoT traffic is to build a ML pipeline that performs the data collection, feature extraction, and binary classification activities specified in the paperer for IoT traffic DDoS detection. While the features are designed to take advantage of IoT-specific network behaviors, they also take into consideration networks flow characteristics such as packet length, inter-packet intervals, and protocol type [3]. Yet, this method is more likely to be outdated where it focused on the early steps of the infection. New IoT devices (e.g., smartwatches) connect to some public free Wi-Fi. The malware is installed in the device at the moment of pairing. Mirai worm is a mutant, so it cannot be detected by the ML pipeline method as this method is in the first layer of defense. A new way has been proposed which focuses on the later steps of infection [4]. The solution is to add last layer security using a deep autoencoder. This method takes snapshots at the step of lurching the attack. It instantly detects the compromised device and makes an alert recommending disconnecting the infected device until being sanitized.

This research aims to study several aspects of the attack mechanisms and explain the way that IoT servers could be hacked using DDoS botnets. It reviews the currently offered solutions and perceives where these solutions have fallen out. Subsequently, it studies the effectiveness of the deep learning (DL) approach that consists of three DL algorithms, namely, RNN, CNN, and LSTM-RNN in handling DDoS attacks targeting IoT networks. These algorithms are tested by implementing a real-world N-BaIoT dataset that has been collected by infecting nine IoT devices with two of the most dangerous DDoS botnets (Mirai and Bashlite). These three classifiers were experimented with and compared to one another to see which classifier would perform the best. The comparison between those classifiers was made using a confusion matrix of accuracy, precision, recall, and F-1 score.

2 Related Work

This section reviews the most recently released methods of detecting DDoS botnets. So much effort and many researchers have devoted great work to mitigate such threats, especially in an IoT environment. The threat still exists now more than ever with the help of insecure IoT devices. Lots of methods are created on a daily basis to mitigate such threats, like adding more bandwidth so servers or websites do not get overwhelmed or building redundancy into infrastructure. Yet, the development of DDoS is way more powerful than such prevention methods. However, ML has been the best solution to detect and mitigate DDoS attacks. There have been so many published papers on solving the problem of DDoS attacks in IoT environments using ML. State-of-art solutions have been increasing rapidly, as the studies have shown in [5–9], and [4, 10–13], but DDoS methods of attacking are changing and coping with any new defense systems. They may be described as not primitive anymore where the new botnets have become so complex and sophisticated to be detected.

The work of [14] results in a solution based on a built ML pipeline that collects data, extracts features and conducts binary classification for IoT traffic DDoS detection. It makes use of IoT network behavior and network flow characteristics such as packet length, interpacket intervals, and protocol. The ML algorithms used are K-nearest neighbors (KNN), Support vector machine with a linear kernel (LSVM), decision tree (DT), random forest (RF), and artificial neural network (ANN). The results were excellent, with an accuracy of more than 0.999 in identifying assaults. However, focusing only on the first stages of dissemination and contact with the command-and-control server allows the botnet to continue expanding. Such malware like Mirai is so sophisticated and can mutate daily, making it hard to spot [15]. As proposed, the main reason for the insecurity of IoT devices is that they do not possess enough memory [16].

The work of [17] proposes a system using a sequential architecture framework to detecting DDoS attacks. The system showed remarkable results and performance, achieving 99% accuracy for botnet detection using three ML algorithms of ANN, J48 DT, and NB classifiers [17]. The system is divided into two phases. The first is Model Builder, where it conducts 1) data collection, 2) data organization, 3) model training, and 4) feature selection. The second phase is the Attack detector, where it detects the attack sequentially. As the data gets to the pre-processing phase, it runs into two steps. The first is to encode the packets sent, and the second is to extract the packet's features. Then it shall detect the attack based on the information given by the feature extraction step. Table 1 shows a summary of the related work solution model, evaluation methods, datasets, and testing results.

Table 1. Comparison between DDoS defense methods

Ref.	Model	Evaluation	Accuracy	Datasets
[14]	KNN	Accuracy, time and efficient	0.999	Their own
	LVSM	Accuracy and recall	0.991	
	DT	Accuracy and efficient	0.999	
	DF	Accuracy and efficient	0.999	
	ANN	Accuracy	0.999	
[17]	NB	Accuracy	0.858	N-BaIoT
	ANN	Accuracy	0.991	
	DT	Accuracy	0.990	
[18]	CNN	Accuracy	0.943	Their own
	LSTM-RNN	Accuracy and time	0.948	N-BaIoT

3   Research Methodology

In this research, the data mining research methodology is mainly used for achieving the research objectives. Data mining research methodology is the abbreviation of the Cross-industry standard process for data mining which refers to the process model that gives a system to the carrying-out data mining project. Data mining research methodology process model means to do large mining projects, more reliable, less expensive, more repeatable, quicker, and more achievable. The research methodology, consisting of four main steps: collection, preparation, feeding the data to the classifier, and evaluating the results. Each step consists of some other sub-steps, for instance, the stage of preparing the dataset. At this stage, the data should be first cleaned (dealing with missing values). Then a feature scaling stage will take place before splitting the data into testing and training. At the very last step of preparing the data, we reshaped the data to the shape expected by the network simulation program. Then to define and encode the labels, three DL algorithms: RNN, CNN, LSTM-RNN, are used in this work. In that manner, a third main step is to take place to feed them to the model and start the training stage. Eventually, the final stage of evaluating the result and calculating the confusion matrix is used as the comparison phase.

3.1   Dataset

The research of [4] provided an N-BaIoT dataset by infecting nine IoT devices (i.e., doorbell, thermostat, baby monitor, security camera, and webcam) with the most recent DDoS malware like Mirai and Bashlite. The N-BaIoT dataset offers better tests and studies of DDoS attacks as it includes real IoT traffic data. Table 2 shows a description of the N-BaIoT dataset. During his study, the deep autoencoder is trained on benign cases with normal behavior, and in this manner, normal senses are reconstructed. But it failed to rebuild anomalous observations (unknown behavior). At the time when the reconstructive bug is gathered, the observed data is categorized as abnormalities. A threshold value is utilized to separate benign from harmful behavior. The framework is evaluated on one dataset, in which the anomalous traffic could be properly distinguished.

The researchers made trace traffic of the dataset available on the Irvine online repository of the University of California and are available on "DATASET". A portion of the N-BaIoT dataset, Ecobee-Thermostat, Philips-B120N10-Baby Monitor, are utilized for this research. SimpleHome-XCS7-1002-WHT-Security camera, provision-PT-838-Security-Camera. The contents of the N-BaIoT dataset of features, their description, and datatype are described in Table 2 [4].

Table 2. Dataset description [4].

No	Feature	Description		Type
1	H	Host of this packet's recent traffic (IP)		Float
2	MI	Recent traffic from the host of this packet (IP + MAC)		Float
3	HH	Recent traffic between the packet's source host (IP) and destination host		Float
4	HH-jit	Statistics describing the jitter in the transmission between the packet's source host (IP) and destination host		Float
5	HpHp	Recent communication between the packet's source host and port (IP) and the packet's destination host and port		Float
6	Time-frame Lambda decay factor in the damp window	How much of the stream's recent history is captured in these data	L5	Float
			L3	
			L1	
			L0.1	
			L0.01	
7	Extracted statistics from the packet stream:	Weight	The stream's weight	Float
		Mean	-	
		Std	-	
		Radius	A measure of how different the two streams' variations are from one another	
		Magnitude	The origin of the two streams' meanings may be found at their intersection	
		Cov	An estimation of the covariance between two streams	
		pcc	An estimated correlation among two streams	
8	Classes	Benign	Normal traffic	
		Bashlite	UDP, SYN, SCAN, ACK, UDPPLAIN	
		Mirai	COMBO, JUNK, SCAN, TCP, UDP	

This research aims to utilize DL classifiers to classify requests made through this dataset and test the performance and effectiveness of the classifiers in categorizing requests into normal or several kinds of attacks.

3.2 Deep Learning Algorithms

In this work, we investigate the suitability of the DL algorithms in detecting DDoS attacks in IoT environments. This work uses three deep learning algorithm techniques, RNN, CNN, and LSTM-RNN, to classify DDoS attacks. This section describes the architecture of the classifiers used in this research. The selected DL algorithms are summarized in the following:

Recurrent Neural Network (RNN): This is a type of neural network in which the output of previous steps is fed into the current step. All the inputs and outputs in the traditional neural network are free of each other, but in situations such as when it is necessary to predict the subsequent expression of a phrase, final words are requested, and thus previous words must be remembered. RNN then emerged and resolved this problem with the help of a hidden layer. The main and important aspect of RNN is the hidden state that retains some sequence data. Suppose a deeper network is built with one layer, three hidden levels, and one layer of output. Each hidden layer will therefore have weight and partial bias, like another neural network, assuming that the weight and partial biases are (w1, b1), (w2, b2) for the second hidden layer, and (w3, b3) for the third hidden layer for hidden layer 1. This means that each layer is separate from the other layers. For example, the prior outputs are not remembered [19].

Convolutional Neural Network (CNN): It is a deep learning algorithm. Although it is mainly used for image classification, it can be used for time series datasets using (ConvNet 1D) which will give input and output of 2 dimensional where the first dimension is the timesteps, and the other one is the value of acceleration. The architecture of a ConvNet is comparable to the link network of neurons in the human brain and was inspired by the Visual Cortex. Individual neurons react to stimuli in a limited part of the visual field called the receptive field alone. A collection of identical fields covering the whole visual area [20]. For instance, the argument input shape (115, 3) indicates 115-time steps with three data points in each time step. These three data points represent acceleration along the x, y, and z axes. Kernel size is set to 5, signifying the width of the kernel, and kernel height is set to the number of data points in each time step [21]. To summarize all that has been said so far, convolution is a mathematical process that converts a tensor, matrix, or vector into a more compact one. For example, if you have n dimensions, you may sum up your input matrix in that dimension and then sum up all n dimensions in the other dimensions [22]. Conv1D and Conv2D summarize (convolve) a set of data in one or two dimensions, respectively.

$$bi = \sum_{j=m-1}^{0} ai + j * wj \tag{1}$$

where $i = [1, n - m + 1]$.

Long-Short Term Memory Recurrent Neural Network (LSTM-RNN): The standard design of this DL algorithm, among others, consists of three layers: an input layer, a recurrent LSTM layer, and an output layer. A layer called the input layer is linked with a layer called the LSTM layer. The recurrent connections in the LSTM layer are made simply from the cell output units to the cell input units and between the input gates, output gates, and forget gate. The output units of the cells are also linked to the network's output layer as an extra connection. Without taking into account the biases, the total number of parameters N in a typical LSTM network with one cell in per memory block may be calculated as follows:

$$N = n_c \times n_c \times 4 + n_i \times n_c \times 4 + n_c \times n_o + n_c \times 3 \qquad (2)$$

The number of input units is represented by n_c, while the number of output units is represented by n_o. The Short Term Memory architecture was inspired by error analysis in current RNNs, which showed that vast distances from existing structures had changed rapidly because of a recorded background error [19]. An LSTM layer has a number of blocks, known as memory blocks, that are repeatedly linked. We may consider these squares as a differentiable version for sophisticated PC memory chips. Each includes at least one repeatedly linked memory cell and three multiplicative units, which provide continuous analog writes, reads, and resets for the cells' input, output, and forget gates. The net can only work with the cells via the gates.

3.3 Implementation Setting

Each classifier used has been pretty much put to the same test using the same parameters except for the obvious ones that follow each classifier. However, some of the shared parameters are shown in Table 3.

Table 3. Shared parameters.

Batch size	Input	Learning-rate	Learning-rate	Optimizer
1024	115,1	0.001	0.001	Adam
Epochs	Verbose	Activation	Linear function	Output
100	1	SoftMax	ReLU	11

3.4 Evaluation Metrics

A confusion matrix was used to assess the performance of the classifiers. The confusion matrix is defined as a table to describe the classifier's performance. The pre-processing categorization is based on all the estimates of 115 characteristics. A relative description of the evaluation steps is provided below:

Accuracy: The percentage of the total number of forecasts was accurate. Where TN = true negative as the formula describes.

$$accuracy = \frac{TP + TN}{TP + TN + FP + FN} \tag{3}$$

Recall: Sometimes referred to as sensitivity. It is a fraction of the total number of relevant occurrences found. It thus relies on an understanding and significance of measurement.

$$recall = \frac{TP}{TP + FN} \tag{4}$$

Precision: Where P is a formula, the percentage of the positive instances anticipated is calculated. Where TP = true positive, FP = false positive. Where TP = true positive. And some similar characteristics are shared with recall since it is too dependent on a comprehension and relevance measure.

$$precision, p = \frac{TP}{TP + FP} \tag{5}$$

F-1 Score: It shows the relation between precision and recall.

$$F1 = 2 \times \frac{Precision \times recall}{Precision + recall} = \frac{TP}{TP + \frac{1}{2}(FP + FN)} \tag{6}$$

4 Results and Discussion

This research initially implements three DL classifiers: RNN, CNN, and LSTM-RNN and studies their performance in classifying DDoS attacks using the N-BaIoT dataset. However, the dataset was not used fully as we just use four IoT devices from the nine devices that are proposed in [4]. The selected devices of this study result in four datasets which are Ecobee-Thermostat (D1), Philips-B120N10-Baby-Monitor (D2), Provision-PT-838-Security Camera (D3), and SimpleHome-XCS7-1002-WHT-Security-Camera (D4). Table 4 shows the outcomes of the three DL classifiers using the 10-folds training and testing data split approach.

The results are typical in the 10-folds split type test because every classifier scores an overall accuracy of 89%. However, by looking at Table 4, we see that each dataset has achieved different results for each classifier. Yet, the Philips-B120N10-Baby-Monitor (D2) dataset has achieved the highest results for a very obvious reason: the dataset's size is bigger than the rest. By observing Table 4, the RNN has achieved the highest overall

Table 4. The results of the RNN, CNN, and LSTM-RNN with 10-folds split type.

Device	Accuracy	Error	Precision	F1-score	Recall
RNN					
D1	0.8832	0.1806	0.9283	0.8788	0.9077
D2	0.9221	0.1209	0.9559	0.8803	0.9078
D3	0.8905	0.1674	0.9569	0.8809	0.9085
D4	0.8942	0.1628	0.9561	0.8802	0.9081
Overall	0.8975	0.15792	0.9493	0.8800	0.9080
CNN					
D1	0.8822	0.1918	0.9383	0.8705	0.8995
D2	0.9214	0.1342	0.9283	0.8682	0.8948
D3	0.8897	0.1631	0.9362	0.8777	0.9047
D4	0.8930	0.1818	0.9470	0.8717	0.9001
Overall	0.8965	0.1677	0.9374	0.8720	0.8997
LSTM-RNN					
D1	0.8790	0.3511	0.8608	0.7566	0.7906
D2	0.9173	0.1471	0.8843	0.7362	0.8040
D3	0.8931	0.1681	0.9242	0.8446	0.8783
D4	0.8897	0.1785	0.8905	0.7903	0.8422
Overall	0.8947	0.2112	0.8899	0.7819	0.8287

accuracy of 89.75%, precision of 94.93%, recall of 90.80%, and f1-score of 88.00%, and lowest error rate of 15.79% as compared with the other two classifiers. Consequently, we see that CNN has archived the second-best results in all the evaluation metrics scores and surpasses the LSTM-RNN.

Subsequently, Table 5 shows the outcomes of the three DL classifiers using the 65 training and 35 testing data split approach. The overall accuracy results and error rates are similar to the results that are obtained based on the 10-folds cross-validation. However, CNN surpasses the other algorithms in all the other evaluation metrics scores in which it achieves the highest precision of 93.48%, recall of 89.91%, and f1-score of 87.08%.

Finally, Fig. 1 compares the results of the RNN, CNN, and LSTM-RNN using the approach of 10-folds and 65–35% training and testing data split.

Table 5. The results of the RNN, CNN, and LSTM-RNN with 65–35% split type.

Device	Accuracy	Error	Precision	F1-score	Recall
RNN					
D1	0.8847	0.1753	0.7017	0.5071	0.5889
D2	0.9214	0.1203	0.7575	0.5415	0.6364
D3	0.8913	0.1688	0.8469	0.7198	0.759
D4	0.8949	0.1654	0.6715	0.5771	0.6552
Overall	0.8980	0.1574	0.7444	0.5863	0.6598
CNN					
D1	0.8853	0.1955	0.9420	0.8694	0.8965
D2	0.9207	0.1371	0.9182	0.8701	0.8981
D3	0.8913	0.1602	0.9468	0.8785	0.9058
D4	0.8938	0.1848	0.9325	0.8652	0.8963
Overall	0.8977	0.1694	0.9348	0.8708	0.8991
LSTM-RNN					
D1	0.8802	0.2341	0.8526	0.7931	0.8381
D2	0.9179	0.1357	0.8782	0.7860	0.8381
D3	0.8949	0.1793	0.9044	0.8206	0.854
D4	0.8882	0.2530	0.8767	0.7736	0.8114
Overall	0.8953	0.2005	0.8779	0.7933	0.8354

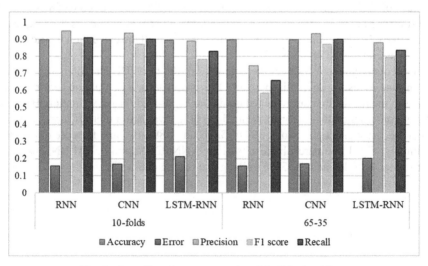

Fig. 1. Overall performance results of the DL classifiers.

5 Conclusion

DDoS assaults are a serious danger to everyone who uses the Internet, and they are difficult to identify because of the spoofing methods used by the attackers to disguise their identities. Based on the history of DDoS botnets, we may conclude that Mirai and Bashlite will not be the last and most powerful. These botnets have been developed and circumvented based on traditional mitigation techniques such as increasing bandwidth or performing traffic extraction. Cloud computing is in danger of DDoS assaults that are originating from the Internet of Things (IoT) or other network platforms attached to the cloud services. IoT devices are fundamentally insecure, yet, some IoT systems have high resistance to DDoS attacks due to the deployment of advanced detection models. In this work, three types of deep learning (DL) algorithms are deployed in constructing DDoS detection models. The RNN, CNN, and LSTM-RNN have proven very worthy in performing the DDoS detection and give an overall accuracy of 89.75%, 89.65%, and 89.47%, respectively, indicating that it is a solid way to dealing with DDoS. As it is observed from the results, RNN has achieved the highest overall performance, followed by the CNN, and the LSTM-RNN has achieved the lowest overall performance. More work has to be done to discover more innovative methods to halt DDoS attacks or mitigate their risk. The future work considers finding appropriate combinations of DL algorithms that can reduce the error rate and false alarm of detecting DDoS attacks.

Acknowledgment. This paper is supported by the Center of Intelligent and Autonomous Systems (CIAS), Faculty of Computer Science and Information Technology, Universiti Tun Hussein Onn Malaysia (UTHM).

References

1. Abhishta, A., van Rijswijk-Deij, R., Nieuwenhuis, L.J.: Measuring the impact of a successful DDoS attack on the customer behaviour of managed DNS service providers. ACM SIGCOMM Comput. Commun. Rev. **48**(5), 70–76 (2019)
2. Mirkovic, J., Reiher, P.: A taxonomy of DDoS attack and DDoS defense mechanisms. ACM SIGCOMM Comput. Commun. Rev. **34**(2), 39–53 (2004)
3. Doshi, R., Apthorpe, N., Feamster, N.: Machine learning DDoS detection for consumer internet of things devices. In: 2018 IEEE Security and Privacy Workshops (SPW), pp. 29–35. IEEE (2018)
4. Meidan, Y., et al.: N-BaIoT—network-based detection of IoT botnet attacks using deep autoencoders. IEEE Pervasive Comput. **17**(3), 12–22 (2018)
5. Khalaf, B.A., et al.: An adaptive protection of flooding attacks model for complex network environments. Secur. Commun. Netw. **2021**, 1–17 (2021)
6. Maseer, Z.K., Yusof, R., Bahaman, N., Mostafa, S.A., Foozy, C.F.M.: Benchmarking of machine learning for anomaly based intrusion detection systems in the CICIDS2017 dataset. IEEE Access **9**, 22351–22370 (2021)
7. Azizan, A.H., et al.: A machine learning approach for improving the performance of network intrusion detection systems. Ann. Emerging Technol. Comput. (AETiC) **5**(5), (2021)
8. Zulhilmi, A., Mostafa, S.A., Khalaf, B.A., Mustapha, A., Tenah, S.S.: A comparison of three machine learning algorithms in the classification of network intrusion. In: Anbar, M., Abdullah, N., Manickam, S. (eds.) ACeS 2020. CCIS, vol. 1347, pp. 313–324. Springer, Singapore (2021). https://doi.org/10.1007/978-981-33-6835-4_21

9. Khalaf, B.A., Mostafa, S.A., Mustapha, A., Mohammed, M.A., Abduallah, W.M.: Comprehensive review of artificial intelligence and statistical approaches in distributed denial of service attack and defense methods. IEEE Access **7**, 51691–51713 (2019)
10. Al-Othman, Z., Alkasassbeh, M., Baddar, S.A.-H.: A state-of-the-art review on IoT botnet attack detection. arXiv preprint arXiv:2010.13852 (2020)
11. Ahmed, M.E., Kim, H.: DDoS attack mitigation in internet of things using software defined networking. In: Proceedings of 3rd IEEE International Conference on Big Data Computing Service and Applications, BigDataService, pp. 271–276 (2017)
12. Metz, R.: Finding insecurity in the internet of things. Technol. Rev **119**(2), 76–77 (2016)
13. Suo, H., Wan, J., Zou, C., Liu, J.: Security in the internet of things: a review. In: Proceedings of 2012 International Conference on Computer Science and Electronics Engineering, ICCSEE 2012, vol. 3, pp. 648–651 (2012)
14. Doshi, R., Apthorpe, N., Feamster, N.: Machine learning DDoS detection for consumer internet of things devices. In: Proceedings 2018 IEEE Symposium on Security and Privacy Workshops, SPW, pp. 29–35 (2018)
15. Kolias, C., Kambourakis, G., Stavrou, A., Voas, J.: DDoS in the IoT: Mirai and other botnets. Computer **50**(7), 80–84 (2017)
16. Jia, Y., Zhong, F., Alrawais, A., Gong, B., Cheng, X.: Flowguard: an intelligent edge defense mechanism against IoT DDoS attacks. IEEE Internet Things J. **7**(10), 9552–9562 (2020)
17. Soe, Y.N., Feng, Y., Santosa, P.I., Hartanto, R., Sakurai, K.: Machine learning-based IoT-botnet attack detection with sequential architecture. Sensors **20**(16), 4372 (2020)
18. Parra, G.D.L.T., Rad, P., Choo, K.K.R., Beebe, N.: Detecting Internet of Things attacks using distributed deep learning. J. Netw. Comput. Appl. **163**, 102662 (2020)
19. Ab Aziz, M.F., Mostafa, S.A., Foozy, C.F.M., Mohammed, M.A., Elhoseny, M., Abualkishik, A.: Integrating elman recurrent neural network with particle swarm optimization algorithms for an improved hybrid training of multidisciplinary datasets. Expert Syst. Appl. **183**, 115441 (2021)
20. Kashinath, S.A., et al.: Review of data fusion methods for real-time and multi-sensor traffic flow analysis. IEEE Access **9**, 51258–51276 (2021)
21. Wu, J.: Introduction to convolutional neural networks. Natl. Key Lab Novel Softw. Technol. **5**(23), 495 (2017)
22. Maseer, Z.K., Yusof, R., Mostafa, S.A., Bahaman, N., Musa, O., Al-rimy, B.A.S.: DeepIoT.IDS: hybrid deep learning for enhancing IoT network intrusion detection. CMC-Comput. Mater. Continua **69**(3), 3945–3966 (2021)

Detect & Reject for Transferability of Black-Box Adversarial Attacks Against Network Intrusion Detection Systems

Islam Debicha[1,2]($\boxtimes$) , Thibault Debatty[1] , Jean-Michel Dricot[2] , Wim Mees[1] ,
and Tayeb Kenaza[3]

[1] Royal Military Academy, Rue Hobbema 8, 1000 Brussels, Belgium
{thibault.debatty,wim.mees}@rma.ac.be
[2] Université libre de Bruxelles, Avenue Franklin Roosevelt 50,
1050 Brussels, Belgium
{Islam.Debicha,jean-michel.dricot}@ulb.be
[3] École Militaire Polytechnique, Bordj El-Bahri 17, 16111 Algiers, Algeria
tayeb.kenaza@emp.mdn.dz

Abstract. In the last decade, the use of Machine Learning techniques in anomaly-based intrusion detection systems has seen much success. However, recent studies have shown that Machine learning in general and deep learning specifically are vulnerable to adversarial attacks where the attacker attempts to fool models by supplying deceptive input. Research in computer vision, where this vulnerability was first discovered, has shown that adversarial images designed to fool a specific model can deceive other machine learning models. In this paper, we investigate the transferability of adversarial network traffic against multiple machine learning-based intrusion detection systems. Furthermore, we analyze the robustness of the ensemble intrusion detection system, which is notorious for its better accuracy compared to a single model, against the transferability of adversarial attacks. Finally, we examine Detect & Reject as a defensive mechanism to limit the effect of the transferability property of adversarial network traffic against machine learning-based intrusion detection systems.

Keywords: Intrusion detection · Machine learning · Adversarial attacks · Transferability · Black-box settings

1 Introduction

The computer and networking industry is becoming increasingly important due to their growing use in various fields, which in turn leads to an escalation in the occurrence of cyberattacks. As a result, security is becoming a key concern of any network architecture and an active research topic. Intrusion Detection Systems (IDS) are one of the solutions presented to enhance network security by analyzing the traffic to identify any suspicious activity.

In order to detect intrusions, there are mainly two approaches: the first one is based on comparing traffic with a list of all known attack patterns, also called signature-based

© Springer Nature Singapore Pte Ltd. 2021
N. Abdullah et al. (Eds.): ACeS 2021, CCIS 1487, pp. 329–339, 2021.
https://doi.org/10.1007/978-981-16-8059-5_20

intrusion detection. Intuitively, this method gives excellent accuracy when dealing with known attacks, however, this type of detector is incapable of detecting zero-day attacks, which is essentially what motivates the use of the second type of intrusion detection techniques, called anomaly-based intrusion detection. The latter approach relies on modeling the normal behavior of network traffic and later examining new traffic against this baseline.

Anomaly-based intrusion detection has been extensively studied, with most research using Machine Learning (ML) techniques to create a trustworthy model of activity due to their high accuracy, including deep learning which is considered a state-of-the-art technique in this field. However, recent studies have shown that machine learning in general, and deep learning in particular, are vulnerable to adversarial attacks where the attacker seeks to fool the models by inserting slight but specially crafted distortions into the original input [2].

Research in the field of computer vision, where this vulnerability was first discovered, has shown that adversarial images designed to fool a specific model can, to some extent, fool other machine learning models [14]. This is known as the transferability property of adversarial attacks. By exploiting this property, an attacker can build a surrogate intrusion detection system, create adversarial traffic for that detector, and then attack another intrusion detection system without even knowing the internal architecture of that detector, leading to a black-box attack.

To avoid this kind of vulnerability, we are conducting this research and the following are our contributions in this paper:

- To the best of our knowledge, this is the first study to examine the transferability of adversarial network traffic between multiple anomaly-based intrusion detection systems with different machine learning techniques in black-box settings.
- In addition, we construct an ensemble intrusion detection system to examine its robustness against the transferability property of adversarial attacks compared to single detectors.
- Finally, we investigate the effectiveness of the Detect & Reject method as a defensive mechanism to mitigate the effect of the transferability property of adversarial network traffic against machine learning-based intrusion detection systems.

2   Background

2.1   Related Work

Studies have shown that incorporating machine learning techniques can help improving the performance of intrusion detection systems. Aslahi-Shahri et al. [4] have proposed and explained the implementation of an intrusion detection system based on a hybrid support vector machine (SVM) and genetic algorithm (GA) method. In [6], the authors have proposed a novel evidential IDS based on Dempster-Shafer theory to take into account source reliability. Vinayakumar et al. [20] have proposed a highly scalable intrusion detection framework using deep neural networks (DNNs) after a comprehensive evaluation of their performance against classical machine learning classifiers. Alamiedy et al. [3] proposed an improved anomaly-based IDS model based on a multi-objective gray wolf optimization (GWO) algorithm, in which GWO is used as a feature selection technique. Ghanem et al. [7] have proposed a cyber-intrusion detecting system classification with MLP trained by a hybrid metaheuristic algorithm and feature selection based on multi-objective wrapper method. In [8], the authors proposed a new binary classification model for intrusion detection, based on hybridization of Artificial Bee Colony algorithm (ABC) and Dragonfly algorithm (DA) for training an artificial neural network (ANN) in order to increase the classification accuracy rate for malicious and non-malicious traffic in networks. Nevertheless, we noticed that little or no attention was paid to the effect of adversarial attacks when proposing these solutions.

Szegedy et al. [18] was the first work to report the vulnerability of DNN to adversarial samples where they introduced imperceptible adversarial perturbations to handwritten digits images and succeeded to fool the DNN model with high confidence. This discovery has prompted a number of studies in the computer vision community, where several attacks and defenses have been proposed [9,10,12]. There are some works [11,14,22] dealing with the transferability of adversarial attacks. However, these studies were specifically designed for the field of image classification, where this particular vulnerability was first detected.

In recent studies, the effect of adversarial attacks on intrusion detection systems has been investigated. Wang [21] Inspected the performance of state-of-the-art attack algorithms against deep learning-based intrusion detection on the NSL-KDD dataset. Pawlicki et al. [15] evaluated the possibility of deteriorating the performance of a well-optimized intrusion detection algorithm at test time by generating adversarial attacks and then offers a way to detect those attacks.

Through our literature review, we did not find any studies on the transferability of adversarial network traffic between multiple anomaly-based intrusion detection systems with different machine learning techniques in black-box settings. Hence, we propose to conduct this study in order to fill this gap. Notice that in our recent work [5], we investigated the effectiveness of adversarial training as a defense for intrusion detection systems against these attacks.

2.2 Adversarial Attacks

Despite their considerable success in achieving high accuracy, machine learning algorithms in general and deep learning, in particular, have proven vulnerable to adversarial attacks, where crafting an instance with small intentional perturbations can lead a machine learning model to make an erroneous prediction [18].

The idea of generating adversarial examples is quite intuitive. It can be seen as the inverse process of gradient descent where, for a given input x and its label y, one tries to find model parameters θ that maximize the accuracy of the model by minimizing the loss function J. On the other hand, the adversarial examples are generated in order to minimize the accuracy of the model. Given the parameters θ, the loss function J is differentiated with respect to the input data x so as to find an instance x', as close to x as possible, that maximizes the loss function J.

One of the earliest and most popular adversarial attacks is called the Fast Gradient Sign Method (FGSM) [9]. This attack uses a factor ϵ to limit the amount of distortion in the original instance such that $\|x' - x\| < \epsilon$. One can think of ϵ as the attack strength or the size of the introduced perturbation. An adversarial instance x' is devised like following:

$$x' = x + \epsilon \nabla J_x(x, y, \theta) \tag{1}$$

Projected Gradient Descent (PGD) [12] is another adversarial attack and is basically an iterative extension of FGSM applying the attack repeatedly. However, PGD initializes the instance, at each iteration, to a random point in the ϵ-ball around the original input.

Adversarial attacks can be classified into two types based on the attacker's knowledge of the attacked system: White-box setting where the attacker has full knowledge of the internal architecture of the attacked system. Black-box setting where the attacker has no knowledge of the internal architecture of the attacked system. In this paper, we create adversarial network traffic records against a DNN-based IDS in a white-box setting, and then the rest of the experiments are conducted in a black-box setting where we use these adversarial instances to attack the other ML-based IDSs without having access to their internal architecture or training data.

3   Proposed Approach

Previous work has shown that the accuracy of a DNN-based IDS can be significantly reduced when exposed to adversarial attacks [5,15,21]. In this section, we construct a DNN-based IDS and five other ML-based IDSs to examine whether the same adversarial instances designed for a DNN-based IDS can be transferred to other ML-based IDSs, which are trained on a different data set, without knowing anything about their internal architectures. We also build an ensemble intrusion detection by clustering the five ML-based IDSs to study whether having multiple classifiers voting prediction can be a defense against the transferability property of adversarial attacks. Finally, we implement the Detect & Reject method as a defense mechanism for the intrusion detection system and evaluate its robustness to transferable adversarial examples.

3.1   NSL-KDD Dataset

Many research papers in the intrusion detection community have used the NSL-KDD dataset to demonstrate the performance of their proposed approaches and this is very useful as it creates a common basis for comparison between these approaches. Published in 2009 by [19], this dataset is an improvement of the well-known KDD-CUP'99 which has a fundamental problem of record redundancy which leads to the bias of classifiers towards frequent records. This problem has been solved in the NSL-KDD dataset by proposing a balanced version of KDD-CUP'99 by removing the redundancy, thus providing a more accurate comparative analysis of the performance of different proposed intrusion detection frameworks.

The dataset contains 41 network traffic characteristics, covering three aspects: basic characteristics, content characteristics, and traffic characteristics. Many attacks are covered in this dataset; they can be further classified into four families of attacks: denial-of-service (DoS) attacks, probe attacks (Probe), root-to-local (R2L) attacks, and user-to-root (U2R) attacks. We use KDDTrain+ in our experiments by dividing it into 80% and

20% for training and test data respectively. The training data is divided into two almost equal parts A and B to train the DNN-based IDS separately from other ML-based IDSs so as to examine the transferability property. The data used in the experimental part are summarized in Table 1 and their partitioning is illustrated in Fig. 1.

Table 1. Summary of the network traffic dataset.

	Normal	DoS	Probe	R2L	U2R
Training data A	26938	18371	4663	398	21
Training data B	26937	18371	4662	398	21
Test data	13468	9185	2331	199	10

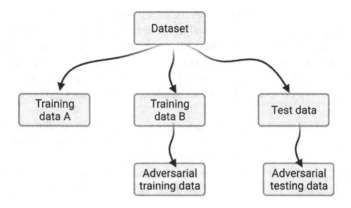

Fig. 1. The partitioning of the dataset for training and testing of IDS

3.2   Preprocessing

The network traffic included in this dataset is heterogeneous and contains both numerical and categorical values. Many machine learning algorithms do not support categorical values, hence the need for the numericalization step that transforms these categorical inputs into numerical values. In the case of the NSL-KDD dataset, the categorical features are "flag", "protocol type" and "service". Another important aspect is feature scaling, which consists of converting all features to the same scale to ensure that all features contribute equally to the result and also to help the gradient-based ML algorithms converge faster to the minima. We restrict our study to a binary classification where we consider any type of attack as "intrusion" and the rest as "normal" traffic.

3.3   Building Anomaly-Based Intrusion Detection Systems

TensorFlow [1] is used to build the DNN-based IDS, it consists of two hidden layers with 512 units each. As an activation function, we use Rectified Linear Unit (ReLU) to increase the non-linearity. To prevent overfitting, a dropout layer with a 20% dropout rate is placed after each hidden layer. ADAM and categorical cross-entropy are used as an optimization algorithm and loss function respectively. In the end, the logits are converted to probabilities using a softmax layer. The final prediction is assigned to the highest probability class.

We acknowledge the use of Scikit-learn [16] to build five ML-based IDSs. The default settings were maintained. These five ML algorithms were selected due to their popularity in the ML community: Support Vector Machines (SVM), Decision Tree (DT), Logistic Regression (LR), Random Forest (RF), and Linear Discriminant Analysis (LDA). We also construct an ensemble IDS by grouping these five ML algorithms where the final prediction is made using the majority voting rule.

3.4   Transferability of Adversarial Attack in Black-Box Settings

In order to test the transferability property of adversarial attacks, we build a DNN-based IDS where we generate adversarial network traffic records in a white-box setting and then test them against five different ML-based IDSs. Note that the five ML-based IDSs are trained on a different dataset (Training data B) and the adversary records were generated without assuming any knowledge of the internal architecture of these five ML-based IDSs, which means that we are working under a black-box setting assumption.

Two adversarial attacks were implemented to generate adversarial network traffic records: FGSM and PDG. For this, we use Adversarial Robustness Toolbox (ART) [13]. The experiments are repeated by increasing the attack strength ϵ to investigate the amount of perturbation required for the adversarial attack to be transferred from the DNN-based IDS to the other five ML-based IDSs in black-box settings.

3.5   Defenses Against the Transferability of Adversarial Attacks

Since the ensemble technique is known to increase accuracy over a single classifier [17], we want to examine whether it can also increase its robustness against the transferability of adversarial attacks in a black-box setting. To do so, we construct an ensemble IDS based on the previous five ML-based IDSs and use the majority voting rule to obtain the final decision.

The second defense we consider is the Detect & Reject method [10], which involves training our IDSs to detect not only "abnormal" and "normal" traffic, but also a third class called "adversarial". Thus, whenever the IDS decides that a network traffic record is adversarial, it is rejected. We implement this method on the five ML-based IDSs and examine their robustness to the adversarial attack transferability property.

4   Experimental Results

In this section, we present the results of experimenting our appraoch. Subsection (A) illustrates the effect of the transferability property of adversarial attacks on the five ML-based IDSs. In subsection (B), we examine the robustness of the ensemble IDS against these attacks in black-box settings. Subsection (C) illustrates the robustness improvement of all IDSs after adding the detection and rejection mechanism to the five ML-based IDSs.

4.1 Transferability of Adversarial Attacks in Black-Box Settings

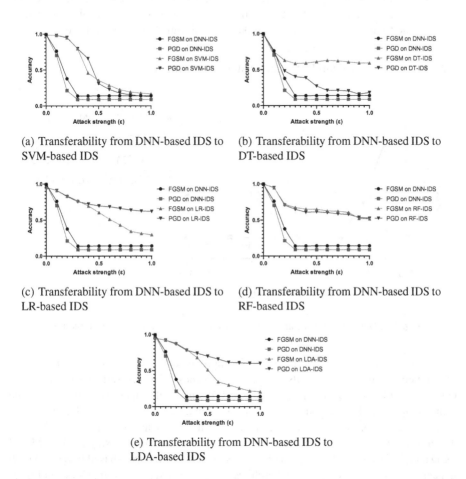

(a) Transferability from DNN-based IDS to SVM-based IDS

(b) Transferability from DNN-based IDS to DT-based IDS

(c) Transferability from DNN-based IDS to LR-based IDS

(d) Transferability from DNN-based IDS to RF-based IDS

(e) Transferability from DNN-based IDS to LDA-based IDS

Fig. 2. Transferability of adversarial attacks against ML-based intrusion detection systems in black-box settings

In this study, we use two adversarial attacks: FGSM and PGD to generate adversarial network traffic records from "Test data". These adversarial records are specifically designed to fool DNN-based IDSs since both attacks have access to the internal architecture of DNNs. As mentioned earlier, we train the DNN-based IDS using "Training data A", while the other 5 ML-based IDSs are trained using "Training data B". Adversarial traffic records are used at test time to attempt to mislead the IDSs. As shown in Fig. 2, increasing the attack strength (ϵ) further degrades the accuracy of the DNN-based

IDS. When testing these adversarial network traffic records on the five ML-based IDSs, we find that their accuracy decreases, even though the attacks do not have access to their internal architectures. We also note that although the accuracy of the ML-based IDSs did not deteriorate as much as the DNN-based IDSs, some models were more vulnerable than others. This may be due to their differentiability property, i.e., they are composed of differentiable elements, since the decision tree and the random forest, whose accuracies were least affected, are non-differentiable models that are not amenable to gradient descent due to their Boolean nature, unlike SVM or logistic regression for example.

4.2 Ensemble Intrusion Detection System Robustness

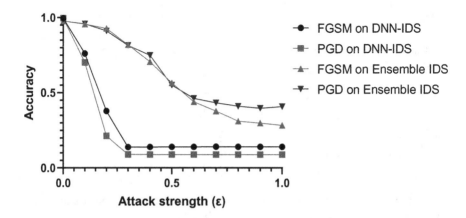

Fig. 3. Adversarial attack transferability from DNN-based IDS to Ensemble IDS

Since the ensemble technique is known to improve accuracy over a single model, we investigate whether it could also improve robustness. To this end, we construct an ensemble IDS based on the five ML-based IDSs using the majority voting rule. The same setup as in the previous experiment is maintained, which means that the 5 ML models used to build the ensemble model are trained using the "Training data B". The adversarial traffic records are generated from the "Test data" using the FGSM and PGD attacks. These adversarial records are designed to fool DNN-based IDS since both attacks can only access the internal architecture of the DNN model. As shown in Fig. 3, the ensemble IDS is not able to resist the transferability property of adversarial attacks, even though no information about the ensemble IDS was used to generate these adversarial records. This shows the ease of an evasion attack against an intrusion detection system without even knowing its internal architecture, simply by building a surrogate IDS (DNN-based IDS in our case) and generating adversarial network traffic for this surrogate model.

In practice, if we consider malicious network traffic, such as HTTP traffic that seeks to connect to dangerous URLs, like command-and-control [C&C] servers, an attacker could use adversarial attack techniques to disguise this malicious network traffic as normal traffic for the intrusion detection system while retaining its malicious aspects. This can be done by adding small amounts of specially designed data to that network traffic as a padding for example. Therefore, the attacker could evade the intrusion detection system.

4.3 Detect & Reject for Adversarial Network Traffic

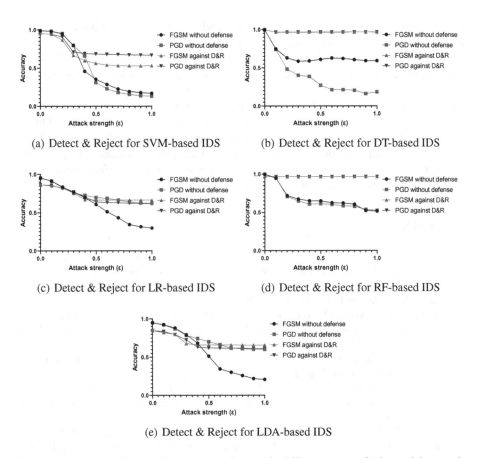

(a) Detect & Reject for SVM-based IDS

(b) Detect & Reject for DT-based IDS

(c) Detect & Reject for LR-based IDS

(d) Detect & Reject for RF-based IDS

(e) Detect & Reject for LDA-based IDS

Fig. 4. Detect & Reject as a defense against the transferability property of adversarial network traffic

In order to limit the effect of adversarial attacks in a black-box context, we implement the Detect & Reject method in each of the five ML-based IDSs. This method consists of re-training the model to detect not only "abnormal" and "normal" traffic but also "adversarial" traffic. PGD is used against "Training data B" to generate "Adversarial data". After that, the ML model uses a combination of "Training data B" and "Adversarial data" during the training phase to learn to distinguish the three classes. During the prediction phase, any network traffic record recognised as "adversarial" will be rejected. As shown in Fig. 4, all five ML-based IDSs have improved their robustness against adversarial attacks. Decision Tree and Random Forrest, which is an ensemble version of Decision Tree, have the highest detection rates of adversarial network traffic compared to the other IDSs.

5   Conclusion and Future Work

From an intrusion detection system perspective, adversarial attacks are a serious threat, as a small intentional perturbation of network traffic can mislead the system. To generate these adversarial records, the attacker must have access to the internal architecture of the machine learning model. However, by exploiting the transferability property of adversarial attacks, he can mislead other intrusion detection systems without having any knowledge about them. Ensemble IDSs, although known to improve model accuracy, are vulnerable to these attacks and thus cannot improve model robustness. On the other hand, Detect & Reject has shown through our experiments to be a suitable built-in defense for intrusion detection systems against adversarial attacks. An interesting future work would be to design more effective defenses to limit the effect of adversarial attacks against intrusion detection systems.

References

1. Abadi, M., et al.: TensorFlow: large-scale machine learning on heterogeneous systems (2015). https://www.tensorflow.org/. Software available from tensorflow.org
2. Akhtar, N., Mian, A.: Threat of adversarial attacks on deep learning in computer vision: a survey. IEEE Access **6**, 14410–14430 (2018)
3. Alamiedy, T.A., Anbar, M., Alqattan, Z.N.M., Alzubi, Q.M.: Anomaly-based intrusion detection system using multi-objective grey wolf optimisation algorithm. J. Ambient Intell. Hum. Comput. **11**(9), 3735–3756 (2020)
4. Aslahi-Shahri, B., et al.: A hybrid method consisting of GA and SVM for intrusion detection system. Neural Comput. Appl. **27**(6), 1669–1676 (2016)
5. Debicha, I., Debatty, T., Dricot, J.M., Mees, W.: Adversarial training for deep learning-based intrusion detection systems. In: ICONS 2021: The Sixteenth International Conference on Systems (2021)
6. Debicha, I., Debatty, T., Mees, W., Dricot, J.M.: Efficient intrusion detection using evidence theory. In: INTERNET 2020: The Twelfth International Conference on Evolving Internet, pp. 28–32 (2020)
7. Ghanem, W.A.H.M., et al.: Metaheuristic based IDS using multi-objective wrapper feature selection and neural network classification. In: Anbar, M., Abdullah, N., Manickam, S. (eds.) ACeS 2020. CCIS, vol. 1347, pp. 384–401. Springer, Singapore (2021). https://doi.org/10.1007/978-981-33-6835-4_26
8. Ghanem, W.A.H., Jantan, A., Ghaleb, S.A.A., Nasser, A.B.: An efficient intrusion detection model based on hybridization of artificial bee colony and dragonfly algorithms for training multilayer perceptrons. IEEE Access **8**, 130,452–130,475 (2020)
9. Goodfellow, I.J., Shlens, J., Szegedy, C.: Explaining and harnessing adversarial examples. arXiv preprint arXiv:1412.6572 (2014)
10. Grosse, K., Manoharan, P., Papernot, N., Backes, M., McDaniel, P.: On the (statistical) detection of adversarial examples. arXiv preprint arXiv:1702.06280 (2017)

11. Lu, Y., et al.: Enhancing cross-task black-box transferability of adversarial examples with dispersion reduction. In: Proceedings of the IEEE/CVF Conference on Computer Vision and Pattern Recognition, pp. 940–949 (2020)
12. Madry, A., Makelov, A., Schmidt, L., Tsipras, D., Vladu, A.: Towards deep learning models resistant to adversarial attacks. arXiv preprint arXiv:1706.06083 (2017)
13. Nicolae, M.I., et al.: Adversarial robustness toolbox v1. 0.0. arXiv preprint arXiv:1807.01069 (2018)
14. Papernot, N., McDaniel, P., Goodfellow, I.: Transferability in machine learning: from phenomena to black-box attacks using adversarial samples. arXiv preprint arXiv:1605.07277 (2016)
15. Pawlicki, M., Choraś, M., Kozik, R.: Defending network intrusion detection systems against adversarial evasion attacks. Future Gener. Comput. Syst. **110**, 148–154 (2020)
16. Pedregosa, F., et al.: Scikit-learn: machine learning in Python. J. Mach. Learn. Res. **12**, 2825–2830 (2011)
17. Rokach, L.: Ensemble-based classifiers. Artif. Intell. Rev. **33**(1), 1–39 (2010)
18. Szegedy, C., et al.: Intriguing properties of neural networks. arXiv preprint arXiv:1312.6199 (2013)
19. Tavallaee, M., Bagheri, E., Lu, W., Ghorbani, A.A.: A detailed analysis of the KDD cup 99 data set. In: 2009 IEEE Symposium on Computational Intelligence for Security and Defense Applications, pp. 1–6. IEEE (2009)
20. Vinayakumar, R., Alazab, M., Soman, K., Poornachandran, P., Al-Nemrat, A., Venkatraman, S.: Deep learning approach for intelligent intrusion detection system. IEEE Access **7**, 41525–41550 (2019)
21. Wang, Z.: Deep learning-based intrusion detection with adversaries. IEEE Access **6**, 38367–38384 (2018)
22. Xie, C., et al.: Improving transferability of adversarial examples with input diversity. In: Proceedings of the IEEE/CVF Conference on Computer Vision and Pattern Recognition, pp. 2730–2739 (2019)

Ensemble Feature Selection Approach for Detecting Denial of Service Attacks in RPL Networks

Taief Alaa Alamiedy[1,2] , Mohammed F. R. Anbar[1(✉)] , Bahari Belaton[3], Arkan Hamoodi Kabla[1], and Baidaa Hamza Khudayer[1,4]

[1] National Advanced IPv6 Centre, Universiti Sains Malaysia (USM), 11800 Gelugor, Penang, Malaysia
{taiefalamiedy,Arkan}@student.usm.my, anbar@usm.my,
baidaa@buc.edu.om

[2] ECE Department, Faculty of Engineering, University of Kufa, P.O. Box 21, Najaf, Iraq

[3] School of Computer Sciences, Universiti Sains Malaysia (USM), 11800 Gelugor, Penang, Malaysia
bahari@usm.my

[4] Information Technology Department, AlBuraimi University College, Buraimi, Oman

Abstract. The Internet of Things (IoTs) is regarded as a future trend following the Internet revolution. Many of us now use physical and electronic devices in our daily lives to perform and deliver specific services. All physical and electronic devices are linked together in IoT networks. Some of these devices, known as constrained devices, are battery-powered and operate in low-energy mode. Therefore, to allow communication and forward packets between constrained devices. The routing protocol for a low-power and lossy network (RPL) is proposed. RPL, on the other hand, is not an energy-aware protocol, making it vulnerable to a wide range of security threats. Denial of Service (DDoS) flooding attacks were the most significant attacks that targeted RPL. Hence, a reliable method for detecting DDoS flooding-based RPL attacks is required. In this paper, an ensemble Feature Selection (FS) approach for detecting DDoS attacks in RPL networks is presented. The proposed approach employs three bio-inspired algorithms to select the optimal subset of features that contribute to high detection accuracy. Furthermore, Support Vector Machine (SVM) is used as a classification algorithm to evaluate the subset of features produced by bio-inspired algorithms. Finally, the proposed approach is expected to significantly detect and identify DDoS flooding attack patterns in RPL networks.

Keywords: Intrusion detection · Machine learning · Internet of things security · LLN · RPL · Routing attacks · 6LoWPAN · Hello-flooding attacks

1 Introduction

Many researchers are drawn to this new era because of the rapid expansion of computer networks and Internet-based devices. Every appliance will be connected to other appliances as part of this revolution, and this group of connected devices will then form a

© Springer Nature Singapore Pte Ltd. 2021
N. Abdullah et al. (Eds.): ACeS 2021, CCIS 1487, pp. 340–360, 2021.
https://doi.org/10.1007/978-981-16-8059-5_21

network of connected devices. IoTs [1, 2] are a type of network that can be defined. IoT is a network of numerous sensors and actuators that provide various services such as sensing the environment, collecting information, analysing the gathered data, performing procedure actions, and so on. These devices can communicate and share information using a variety of protocols and communication techniques [3].

According to Cisco's recently renamed (annual Internet report) for the period (2018–2023) [4], Cisco predicts that network devices will grow significantly around the world, reaching 29.3 billion in 2023. This expansion will be accomplished through machine-to-machine technology and other forms of communication [4]. The statistics for IoT global growth obtained by the Cisco report are depicted in Fig. 1.

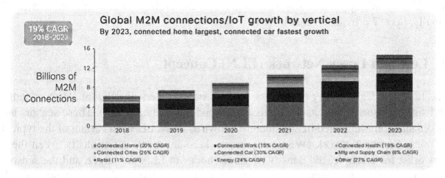

Fig. 1. IoT global growth by Cisco annual report [4].

The coronavirus disease (Covid-19) emerges in some countries at the end of 2019, specifically in December [5]. At the beginning of 2020, the virus quickly spread in most countries, and many countries implemented stringent measures and roles to prevent Covid-19 spread. These actions have ramifications for both the public and private sectors. Moving to digital techniques, which was the starting point for many challenges that the countries and people will face, is one of the proposed solutions to these issues and problems associated with these procedures.

Many studies [6–9] have been conducted to investigate the future impact of this crisis on the use of technology in various daily life activities. One of the current hot issues is the impact of Covid-19 on IoTs and their applications [10].

Furthermore, IoT plays an important role in limiting the spread of this crisis, and it has the potential to be used to prevent future disasters. Accent System, a Spanish company, developed an IoT-based contact tracing wristband to track people and determine if they were in close contact with the Covid-19 patient [11]. However, the security aspect of these techniques is critical in order to protect people's private information and prevent manipulation of the information until it reaches its destination.

This research aims to provide a new subset of features associated with the pattern of DDoS flooding attacks. Therefore, the following contributions are made to achieve this goal:

- Create a solid benchmark dataset with a variety of network scenarios (normal and attack traffic),
- Use three types of bio-inspired algorithms to select the optimal subset of features that contribute to high detection accuracy,
- Providing an intersection stage to extract the identical features previously obtained by bio-inspired algorithms results in an increase in detection accuracy,
- A classification algorithm based on SVM to classify the selected features.

The rest of the paper is organised as follows: Sect. 2 introduces the concept of Low Power and Lossy Networks, Sect. 3 reveals attacks in RPL networks, Sect. 4 reviews related studies to this research, Sect. 5 provides details about the methodology stages for the proposed approach, and Sect. 6 presents the evaluation and validation criteria. Finally, Sect. 7 provides a conclusion.

2   Low and Lossy Network (LLN) Concept

The IoT includes a variety of devices, such as smart meters, intelligent alarm systems, and small sensors (gas sensors, temperature, and humidity sensors). These sensors are linked and communicated in architecture known as LLN. LLN is a variant of the typical Wireless Sensor Network (WSN). However, there are many variations between these networks; for example, the density of sensor nodes in LLN are larger, and the sensors are considered as low power devices (low power operation, limited bandwidth, small memory size, and short radio range) [12, 13].

In addition, due to limited processing capability, there is a high likelihood of packet loss in LLN, and delay and transformed size are small compared to WSN. Despite such drawbacks, these networks communicate based on Internet Protocol (IP), which is still the best option for controlling and managing network sensors (nodes) [14].

Besides, as previously stated, the LLN is operated in low power mode. Therefore, it is critical to conserve the energy of such devices while forwarding and exchanging information between nodes. Many protocols have been proposed to facilitate communication between the resource-constrained devices in LLN. The routing protocol for a low-power and lossy network (RPL) was proposed. More information about the RPL protocol is provided in the following section.

2.1   Routing Protocol for Low Power and Lossy Network (RPL)

RPL was selected as a standard protocol for LLN by the Low Power and Lossy Networks Working Group (ROLL) in 2012 [15]. RPL has been standardised to function as an LLN network layer protocol. RPL is used in academic and industrial fields to conduct research and improve LLN performance. The ability of RPL to work with different constrained devices is the primary reason for its use in this type of network architecture. Moreover, RPL provides efficient routing between the constrained nodes. Additionally, this protocol promotes service quality [16, 17]. The RPL network is depicted in Fig. 2 as a basic concept.

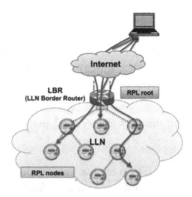

Fig. 2. The concept of RPL Network [18].

RPL is also a distance-vector and routing protocol designed for LLN. A protocol of this type calculates the distance and direction to any node in the network. Consequently, RPL forwards the packet between two nodes using the least expensive route with the shortest distance. The cost of reach to the destination is calculated using route metrics [19].

Terminologies of RPL Protocol. This section provides a brief overview of the network's RPL component.

Elements of the RPL Network. RPL manages the topology of the LLN network's nodes by constructing a Destination-Oriented Directed Acyclic Graph (DODAG). The DODAG is made up of nodes that are connected to one another and arranged in a tree-like structure [20]. Meanwhile, the sensor nodes are linked to the main node, which is known as the root or primary node. The root node collects and distributes information to all network nodes at the same time, connecting the RPL network to the external network. Therefore, such a node could be a border router or gateway, or it could be any other normal node in the network [21].

Furthermore, the root node is identified by an IPv6 address called DODAG ID, which is used to differentiate the DODAG from the other DODAGs in an RPL Instance. In addition, as mentioned in Sect. 2, the LLN network is used in a variety of IoT applications. As a consequence, in RPL, the DODAG is in charge of specific tasks or applications; for example, if two or more applications are running concurrently or independently; in this case, many DOGAGs would be used. This group of DODAGs is controlled by an RPL Instance, which may contain one or more DODAGs, and all DODAGs in this instance share the same ID, known as the Instance ID [22, 23].

Aside from that, each DODAG node is assigned a rank, the value of which is determined by a function known as the objective function. Some metrics are used to calculate the objective function. As the node gets further away from the node, the rank value decreases (the root node in the network has the lowest rank). The rank value, on the other hand, identifies the node's position in the network in relation to the root node [24, 25].

Traffic Types in RPL Network. The traffic direction in the RPL network is divided into three types: point to point (P2P), which occurs when two nodes exchange information, point to multi-point (P2MP), which occurs when traffic from the root node to other nodes, and multi-point to point (MP2P), which occurs when traffic generated from child nodes to the parent node [22, 23].

Control Messages in RPL Network. The RPL protocol uses five control messages to manage packet forwarding in the network. A brief explanation of these messages is provided below.

- DODAG Information Objects (DIO) are used to broadcast the required information to build the RPL Network. Such information includes the current RPL instance, the current rank of the node, the IPv6 address of the root [26], etc.
- Destination Advertisement Object (DAO) messages are used for advertising information required to construct the down routes and build the routing tables at the receiving nodes [24].
- DODAG Information Solicitation (DIS): this message is sent by nodes when they want to join the network and have not received a DIO message at that time. As a result, this new node sends a DIS message to their neighbour nodes inquiring whether or not there is any DODAG available to establish a connection with them [27].
- Destination Advertisement Object Acknowledgement (DAO-ACK): it is sent by the DAO recipient as a response to a DAO message [28, 29].
- Consistency Check (CC) message: the RPL protocol uses this type of message to verify the synchronicity of "security counter or timestamp between each pair of nodes" [30]. Figure 3 illustrates the RPL architecture.

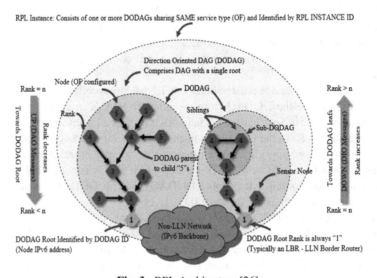

Fig. 3. RPL Architecture [26].

3 RPL Attacks

Various IoT applications necessitated the use of a security mechanism to ensure that information is delivered safely. Intrusion Detection System (IDS), authentication, and cryptography techniques can be used as the first defence line to meet such requirements. However, due to the limited resources of IoT sensors, these techniques are limited in their application. Therefore, adversaries can penetrate these devices and connect to the network as regular nodes. Afterwards, they can modify the operation of the comprised nodes to perform various types of attacks. As shown in Fig. 4, attacks in the RPL network can be classified into three types [31].

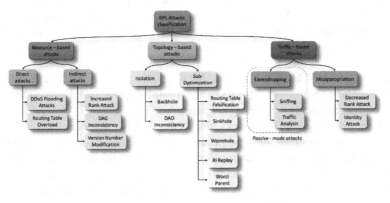

Fig. 4. Taxonomy of attacks against RPL network [31].

Resource-based attacks target the network's nodes' resources by forcing legitimate nodes to perform unnecessary actions in order to deplete their resources. These types of attacks aim to consume node energy, memory, or processing, reducing network lifetime by causing congestion in available links, eventually resulting in network failure [32, 33]. Topology-based attacks, on the other hand, aim to change the network's topology by isolating some nodes and changing the path of network traffic, resulting in collusion and destruction of the entire network [34, 35].

Eventually, the last band of attacks is known as traffic-based attacks. Such attacks targeted the network by employing techniques such as sniffing, capturing, and analysing network data, with the goal of infiltrating the network or stealing sensitive information [36]. As previously stated, the goal of this research is to detect DDoS flooding attacks classified as resource-based attacks. More information about this attack is provided in the subsection that follows.

3.1 Resource-Based RPL Attacks

There are two types of resource-based RPL attacks: direct and indirect attacks. In direct attacks, a malicious node(s) generates overload traffic directly to degrade network performance and drain their resources. In contrast, indirect attacks seek to cause the other nodes in the network to generate a large volume of traffic. For example, this attack could be carried out by creating loops in the RPL network to motivate the other nodes to generate traffic overhead. The section that follows discusses DDoS flooding attacks.

DDoS Flooding Attacks. DDoS Flooding attacks generate and launch a large volume of traffic in a network, causing nodes and links to become idle. Besides that, this attack can be carried out by an external or internal attacker. Internal DDoS flooding attacks are the focus of this research. Furthermore, in DDoS attacks, the attacks constantly send DIS messages to its neighbour nodes with its transmission area. As a matter of fact, DDoS attacks are also known as DIS flooding attacks. After receiving the DIS message, the victim node(s) would then reset their trickle timer, which is responsible for scheduling the send time of the packet in the network and with DIO messages to allow the malicious node to join the network, and this process continues, eventually exhausting the victim node(s) power resources and causing the network to fail.

Furthermore, during DDoS attacks, the victim node(s) are occupied with processing all of the requests, causing an additional overhead and preventing the nodes from performing their legitimate operations. Moreover, this attack could send unicast DIS messages to a single node or broadcast DIS messages to multiple nodes to its neighbour. In both cases, this attack causes network congestion and RPL node saturation [31]. Figure 5 depicts a basic DDoS Flooding attack scenario.

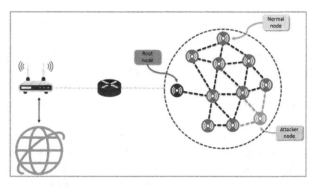

Fig. 5. DDoS flooding attack scenario.

4 Literature Review

This section discusses the studies that support the proposed approach. To detect and prevent attacks in RPL networks, the researchers used various mechanisms. As demonstrated in the following studies, such techniques include intrusion detection-based, trusted-based, and cryptography-based solutions.

In the study of Napiah et al. [37], the authors proposed a CHA-IDS, the proposed approach used a centralised IDS to detect Hello flood, Wormhole, and Sinkhole attacks, the authors used compression header data to extract the significant traffic features for both individual and combined attacks. In addition, for the feature selection stage, the best step-by-step strategy with a correlation-based approach was employed to select the important features. The authors then evaluated the selected features that used six machine learning algorithms. SVM, Decision Trees (J48), Random Forest (RF), Logistic Regression (LR), Multi-layer Perceptron (MLP), and Naive Bayes are just a few examples of these algorithms. However, the proposed model's main drawbacks include high memory resource consumption, energy consumption, and the inability to effectively identify the attacker.

The authors [38] devise a new IDS known as RIDES. For detecting DoS attacks in IP-based WSNs, the proposed approach includes hybrid IDS that includes anomaly and signature-based IDS. In addition, the attack pattern was detected by the anomaly IDS using Cumulative Sum Control charts (CUSUM) with a predefined threshold. The second type, on the other hand, was employed to reduce the overhead associated with long signature code. The coding scheme was used for this step. The long signature codes were converted into short attack signatures in this scheme. Additionally, the authors used a distributed IDS to reduce communication and memory consumption, as well as the computational overhead on network nodes.

Kasinathan et al. [39] developed an IDS for detecting DoS attacks in the 6LoWPAN network. In the proposed approach, the open-source IDS (Suricata) was used for attack detection and pattern matching. In addition, the proposed approach used a probe node to passively sniff the transmission of packets in the network and forward the gathered information to the main IDS (Suricata IDS) for additional inspection and analysis. Aside from, to avoid communication overhead issues, the authors used a wired link to connect the probe node directly to the Suricata IDS.

The authors of [40] proposed a trust-based IDS (T-IDS) scheme in their research. The proposed approach aims to secure the RPL protocol, and this scheme used network nodes as monitoring nodes to detect suspicious activity. Correspondingly, these nodes share information with the other nodes in order to detect any abnormal activities. Furthermore, each node was given a unique ID, and the network was linked to a backbone router, which works with the monitoring node to detect attacks. The main limitation of this study is that it cannot accurately identify malicious nodes.

Airehrour et al. [41] proposed an embedded trust-based mechanism. The proposed mechanism aims to reduce blackhole attacks in IoT. The authors add the node's trust value to the Objective Function (OF). Therefore, in addition to the other metrics, the trust value plays a role in determining the optimal route. The number of transmitted and dropped packets used to compute the trust value. So, the node's Expected Retransmission (ETX), trust value, and rank value all play a role in route selection. If multiple packets were dropped, the proposed method would identify the suspicious node. However, because only one metric was used to identify the attacks, the proposed mechanism could not detect them accurately.

The authors of [42] developed a Trust-Aware RPL routing protocol. The proposed method is designed to detect selective forwarding and blackhole attacks. The proposed mechanism identifies malicious nodes based on packet drop rates. When the attacker executes blackhole or selective forwarding attacks, such a mechanism considers the drop rate of packets by the malicious node to be higher than that of the normal node. Besides, any node in the network's behaviour can reveal its level of trust. The author used trust value to evaluate the trustworthiness of nodes, which aids in the selection of the optimum path.

The authors of proposed a new coordinative-balanced clustering algorithm in their work [43]. The proposed method is designed to detect Hello-flooding and Version Number attacks. In this paper, the authors proposed a coordinative-balanced clustering (CBC) algorithm to extend the network's lifetime during DDoS attacks. The CBC algorithm aims to group each set of nodes into clusters. Accordingly, this process reduces end-to-end delay, reduces energy consumption, and extends node lifetime. In addition, the authors introduced an improved ant colony algorithm for detecting DDoS attacks. To detect attacks, such an algorithm employs node features. Hence, a secure route was used for data transformation during the selection of the best parent for data forwarding. The parent was chosen by combining residual energy and a scoring factor. Despite this, the proposed approach achieves positive results in terms of reducing packet delivery ratio, energy consumption, end-to-end delay, and packet loss rate. Nonetheless, the proposed deals with a limited number of attacks on nodes and suffers from a lack of high attack detection. Table 1 summarises the related studies.

To summarise, as previously stated, the researchers employ various mechanisms and techniques for detecting and mitigating RPL-based attacks. However, some of the proposed solutions are incapable of accurately detecting attacks; additionally, some of the proposed mechanisms use the nodes as monitoring agents, consuming the node's resources. Besides, some solutions add extra messages to the network, which creates overhead and consumes the available network bandwidth. Thus, the identified problem would be addressed in this research proposal, as presented in the proposed methodology section.

Table 1. The summary of related studies

Ref. & Year	Proposed Mechanism	Type of Attack	Performance Metrics	Limitations
Napiah et al. (2018) [37]	CHA-IDS	Hello flood, Wormhole, Sinkhole	–	High memory and energy consumption, as well as insufficient to effectively identify the attacker
Amin et al. (2009) [38]	RIDS	DIS Flooding Attacks	TPR, FPR, ROC	Packet delay causes a loss detection rate
Kasinatinathan et al. (2013) [39]	DoS Detection based IDS	DIS Flooding Attacks	TP	The centralised IDS increases the communication overhead and reduces detection of internal attacks
Medjek et al. (2017) [40]	Trust-based IDS	Sybil-Mobile Attack	TPR	It is unable to accurately identify malicious nodes
Airehrour et al. (2016) [41]	Embedded trust-based mechanism	Blackhole	–	It is used one metric to identify the attack which leads to low detection accuracy of attacks It only uses one metric to identify attacks, resulting in low detection accuracy
Airehrour et al. (2017) [42]	Trust-Aware RPL routing protocol	Selective Forwarding and Backhole Attacks	Packet Drop Rate	It is used only the trust metric evaluate the trustworthiness of nodes which cannot detect the malicious node(s) accurately
Alabsi et al. (2019) [43]	Coordinative-based clustering with enriched- ant-colony algorithm	DIS Flooding and Version Number Attacks	Energy consumption, packet loss rate, packet delivery rate	Limited number of attacks attack nodes, lack of high attack detection

5   Methodology of the Proposed Approach

This research proposes an ensemble feature selection method for detecting DDOS flooding attacks in the RPL Network. The proposed approach is divided into four stages: (i) Data Collection, (ii) Feature Extraction and Preparation, (iii) Ensemble Feature Selection-based Bio-Inspired Algorithms, and (iv) DDoS Attack Detection have used Support Vector Machines. The main architecture of the proposed approach is depicted in Fig. 6.

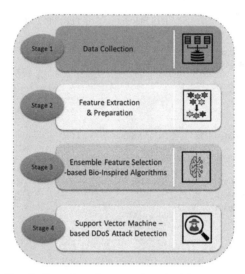

Fig. 6. Overview of proposed methodology stages.

More information about these stages is provided in the subsections that follow.

5.1   Stage 1: Data Collection

The primary goal of this stage is to construct the network environment and capture packets from traffic between network nodes. Following that, many processes would be performed on these packets in order to extract valuable information, as illustrated in the list of points below.

- Setup the network parameters and scenarios: the goal of this step is to initialise the network parameters. Such parameters include the design of various network architectures such as (star, mesh, and hybrid). Following that, the number of normal and malicious nodes is determined. Other parameters such as the number of transmitted packets and simulation time/speed are also specified. Additionally, as previously stated, this research focuses on detecting DDoS flooding attacks. As a result, two network scenarios are required. The first scenario gathers normal network traffic, which is later used as a baseline for evaluation, while the second scenario combines normal and DDoS flooding attack traffic.

- Network traffic generation: this step is carried out with the help of the network simulation environment Cooja [44]. When the simulation begins, all of the network's nodes begin exchanging messages in order to build the RPL network. Moreover, the simulation scenarios are run numerous times to ensure the reliability and validity of the proposed approach. Consequently, any errors that may occur during the experiments would be minimised.
- Capturing and labelling network traffic: Once the simulation begins, the network traffic is captured and labelled for further analysis. Wireshark [45] is a programme that sniffs and collects information from network traffic. Following that, the Wireshark programme saves all network scenario data into separate files. Finally, each file associated with the running scenario is labelled.

5.2 Stage 2: Feature Extraction and Preparation

Following the collection of network traffic, packets are extracted and analysed to identify the pattern of normal and suspicious activities. The points that follow provide more information about this stage.

- Extraction of dataset features: In this step, the Wireshark programme is used to extract features from network packets, and then the extraction tool is used to extract features based on observations and examples from previous studies. Following that, the features would be aggregated and saved as CSV. files. This procedure is carried out for all network scenarios.
- Data Cleaning: This is a critical step in any machine learning or deep learning project. The missing values are compensated in this step by calculating the average of the record values and removing irrelevant values.
- Data Encoding: The dataset includes a variety of features. These features include various types of information such as the alphabet, numbers, symbols, and so on. To analyse different types of information at the same time, ML techniques take a long time and require a lot of system resources. Furthermore, the performance of ML techniques may be impacted. To avoid these troubles, the data encoding process is used to map different data formats into a numerical format.
- Data normalization: This step reduces the range of values in the features. During the training and prediction phases, this process aids the classification algorithm. This process also aids in avoiding dataset biasing, which affects the performance of the classifier used to build the model. The records of the dataset features are scaled in this research. The boundary of each record, on the other hand, falls between (0) and (1). To scale each record of dataset features, use the Equation below.

$$y = \frac{x - x_{min}}{x_{max} - x_{min}}$$

Where y represents the normalised (new) value, x represents the existing value in the feature's record, and x_{max} and x_{min} represent the maximum and minimum values in each record, respectively.

5.3 Stage 3: Ensemble Feature Selection-Based Bio-inspired Algorithms

The proposed ensemble FS model identifies an optimal subset of features that contribute to high detection accuracy. Several researchers [46, 47] used bio-inspired algorithms to solve a variety of real-world optimisation problems. In this research, we used three bio-inspired algorithms that produced significant results in detecting network attacks [48, 49]. The algorithms chosen are used to obtain an optimal number of traffic features with high detection accuracy. Figure 7 depicts the architecture of ensemble FS-based bio-inspired algorithms.

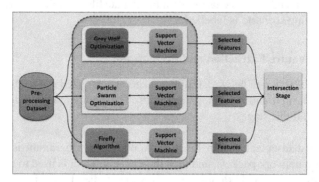

Fig. 7. The architecture of ensemble FS-based bio-inspired algorithms

The process of selecting the subset of a new feature is a difficult one. It is difficult to do it efficiently, especially when the data is complex in terms of a high dimension of features [50]. Therefore, bio-inspired metaheuristic algorithms are well suited to dealing with this issue. These algorithms produce useful results in a reasonable amount of time and effort. In this research, we used three different types of bio-inspired algorithms to detect network attacks and achieved significant results [51, 52]. More information about these algorithms can be found in the subsections below.

Particle Swarm Optimisation (PSO). The Particle Swarm Optimisation (PSO) was invented by Russell Eberhart and James Kennedy [53]. PSO is a computational method based on the locomotion of fish schools and bird flocks. PSO was created as a result of a large number of interpretations performed using computer simulations. This method employs a collection of particles to form a swarm. The swarm then passes through the field of research to find the best solution.

However, each particle in the research scope modifies its "travelling" to match its own travelling experiences as well as the travelling experiences of the other particles. The random generation of particles contributes to the launch of the PSO, which indicates the speed of the search. The particles would then be assessed in terms of fitness. Following that evaluation, two major tests are performed. The first test is called personal best (*pbest*), and it compares particle experiences to one's own. The second test, known as global best (*gbest*), compares the fitness of particles to other swarm experiences.

Following that, the best particle is retained as a result of these two critical tests. The termination criteria are then met. PSO algorithm was used to solve many different types of optimisation algorithms; additionally, PSO is used to detect several network attacks and produce impressive results.

Grey Wolf Optimisation (GWO) Algorithm. Mirjalili et al. [54] proposed the GWO algorithm. This algorithm was inspired by the hunting behaviours of grey wolves in terms of leadership skills. In addition, there are four types of wolves: Alpha, Beta, Delta, and Omega.

As flock leader, Alpha must make a decision. Even though they are not the strongest, they are the best at managing the pack. This is due to the importance of pack management over strength. Beta, on the other hand, is regarded as a lower-level wolf within the pack. Beta serves as Alpha's advisor and plays an important role in assuming Alpha's position in the event that Alpha dies or is incapacitated in some other way. Alpha's decisions are also supported by Beta and the rest of the pack. Furthermore, Beta provides Alpha with feedback on the pack's members to help Alpha make decisions.

Omega, on the other hand, is regarded as the pack's lowest-level wolf. Omega is a scapegoat in the pack, so its existence is critical to the pack's permanence. Omega indirectly preserves and satisfies the other members of the pack.

Last but not least, the rest of the pack is represented as Delta. Delta is made up of scouts, sentinels, elders, hunters, and caretakers. Thus, according to this hierarchy, the hunting process consists of three major steps:

1. Tracking, chasing, and approaching the prey,
2. Stopping the prey's movement through pursuing, encircling, and harassing it,
3. Attacking the prey.

Eventually, the GWO algorithm displays the illustrated hierarchy and hunting procedures. The GWO algorithm mimics these procedures in order to face and solve huge engineering problems. On the other hand, this algorithm has been used as a feature selection technique to detect different types of attacks, then generating a new acceptable subset of features that could contribute to improving detection accuracy [48].

Firefly Optimisation Algorithm. FFA algorithm was proposed by Xin She Yang [55]. It is a metaheuristic algorithm for feature selection. The main idea behind this algorithm was inspired by the communication behaviour of tropical fireflies. Also, it is based on the concept of idealised flashing pattern behaviour. This algorithm's mathematical model was built using the following rules:

1. All of the fireflies are unisex.
2. There is a proportional relationship between the brightness and attractiveness of fireflies.
3. The brightness of fireflies is limited and influenced by the environment of the objective functions.

In terms of the maximisation problem, the brightness may be proportional to the objective function value. However, there are two critical aspects of firefly's regular algorithm. First, consider the light intensity formulation. Second, the attractiveness shifts.

Consequently, the brightness of the firefly would be determined by the encoded objective feature landscape. Also, the light intensity difference must be described, and the attractiveness adjustment must be developed.

Intersection Stage. In this research, we used three bio-inspired algorithms (GWO, PSO, and FFA) to generate three significant feature sets (SF1, SF2, and SF3). Each algorithm selects a subset of features and uses an SVM classifier to evaluate them. Following that, each subset of the chosen features is introduced into the intersection stage. The intersection stage is used to reduce the selected features that resulted from those three algorithms, and only the synonymous features group a new subset known as SF4, SF5, and SF6. The number of proposed variants for intersections used in this stage is shown in Table 2.

Table 2. Type of intersections used in this stage.

Intersection No	Intersection Type	Output
1	SF1 ∩ SF2	SF4
2	SF1 ∩ SF3	SF5
3	SF2 ∩ SF3	SF6

Finally, SVM is again used to evaluate produced Intersection subsets to select the optimum subset of characteristics that contribute to the best detection accuracy as presented in Fig. 8.

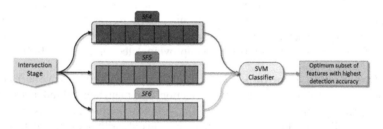

Fig. 8. A summary of intersection stage

5.4   Stage 4: Support Vector Machine-Based DDoS Attack Detection

SVM is used in this stage to evaluate the features chosen in Stage 2. SVM is a ML classification algorithm proposed by [53]. SVM performs well in classifying complex and noisy datasets. SVM also demonstrates its ability to process input data without prior knowledge, making it useful for dealing with a variety of datasets. Furthermore, many types of classification algorithms fall into local minimum traps, which the SVM could avoid.

Further to that, SVM supports two types of classifications: single and multi-class, and it can predict multiple behaviours at the same time. These advantages compel researchers to evaluate their approach using a SVM classifier. SVM operations are classified into two types: linear and nonlinear. The linear type is used to classify simple datasets, while the nonlinear type is used to deal with complex and complicated datasets. The kernel function is used in nonlinear equations. This function is classified into three types: polynomial, gaussian, and gaussian radial basis function (GRBF). The kernel function chosen is determined by the type of dataset that would be inserted into the classifier. The most popular is GRBF, which has a small number of control parameters and produces excellent results. Finally, SVM has been used by various researchers to classify network traffic into normal and abnormal classes, and the results seem to be impressive [56].

6 Evaluation and Validation of Proposed Approach

We used the confusion matrix, which describes the performance of the classification model, to evaluate the proposed approach's efficiency level in detecting DDoS flooding attacks in the RPL network. To obtain the performance level shown in Table 3, the confusion matrix employs four metrics which include True positive (TP), true negative (TN), false positive (FP), and false negative (FN). Meanwhile, other factors such as accuracy, sensitivity, precision, and F-measure could be derived from these metrics.

Table 3. Confusion Matrix

		Predicted	
		Normal	Attack
Actual	Normal	(TP)	(FN)
	Attack	(FP)	(TN)

TPR is used to determine the amount of normal data that is observed to be normal data. It is calculated as follows:

$$TPR = \frac{TP}{TP + FN}$$

TNR is used to calculate the amount of attack data that is recognised as attack data. It is calculated as follows:

$$TNR = \frac{TN}{TN + FP}$$

FPR is used to estimate the amount of attack data that is recognised as normal data. It is calculated as follows:

$$FPR = \frac{FP}{FP + TN}$$

FNR is used to estimate the amount of the normal data that is classified as attack data. It is calculated as follows:

$$FPR = \frac{FP}{FP + TN}$$

Accuracy is expressed as a percentage. The percentage then refers to the degree to which the records are correctly predicted. It is calculated as follows:

$$Accuracy = \frac{TPR + TNR}{TPR + TNR + FPR + FNR}$$

Precision is defined as the ratio of correct decisions. It can be calculated by dividing the TP by the sum of the FP and TP. It is calculated as follows:

$$Precision = \frac{TPR}{TPR + FPR}$$

Sensitivity is defined as the number of TP evaluations divided by the total number of positive evaluations. It is calculated as follows:

$$Sensitivity = \frac{TPR}{TPR + FPR}$$

The F-measure is a test for accuracy. It refers to the equilibrium that exists between precision and sensitivity. It is calculated as follows:

$$F - Measure = \frac{2 * (Precision * Sensitivty)}{Precision + Sensitivity}$$

7   Conclusion

In this paper, an ensemble feature selection approach for detecting DDoS flooding attacks in the RPL network is proposed. The proposed method employs various bio-inspired algorithms to select the optimal subset of features that contribute to high detection accuracy. In addition, SVM is used as a classification algorithm by ML algorithms to evaluate the selected features. Furthermore, an intersection stage is proposed to find intersected features from the generated subsets produced by bio-inspired algorithms in order to improve the selected subsets of dataset features. Moreover, new feature subsets are generated based on the set of intersection types, which are then passed to the SVM classifier to seek the optimal feature set with the highest detection accuracy. Finally, the proposed approach is expected to achieve high DDoS attack detection accuracy with an optimal subset of features associated with the pattern of DDoS attacks.

Acknowledgment. This research was pursued under the Research University (RU) Grant, Universiti Sains Malaysia (USM) No: 1001.PNAV.8011107.

References

1. Al-Hadhrami, Y., Hussain, F.K.: DDoS attacks in IoT networks: a comprehensive systematic literature review (2021)
2. Alamiedy, T.A., Anbar, M., Al-Ani, A.K., Al-Tamimi, B.N., Faleh, N.: Review on feature selection algorithms for anomaly-based intrusion detection system. In: Saeed, F., Gazem, N., Mohammed, F., Busalim, A. (eds.) Recent Trends in Data Science and Soft Computing. Advances in Intelligent Systems and Computing, pp. 605–619. Springer, Cham (2019). https://doi.org/10.1007/978-3-319-99007-1_57
3. Mahmoud, R., Yousuf, T., Aloul, F., Zualkernan, I.: Internet of things (IoT) security: Current status, challenges and prospective measures. In: 2015 10th International Conference for Internet Technology and Secured Transactions, ICITST 2015, pp. 336–341. IEEE (2016)
4. Cisco: Cisco Annual Internet Report (2018–2023). Comput. Fraud Secur. 2020, 4 (2020)
5. Fields, B.K.K., Demirjian, N.L., Gholamrezanezhad, A.: Coronavirus Disease 2019 (COVID-19) diagnostic technologies: a country-based retrospective analysis of screening and containment procedures during the first wave of the pandemic (2020). https://doi.org/10.1016/j.clinimag.2020.08.014
6. Whitelaw, S., Mamas, M.A., Topol, E., Van Spall, H.G.C.: Applications of digital technology in COVID-19 pandemic planning and response (2020)
7. Chick, R.C., et al.: Using technology to maintain the education of residents during the COVID-19 pandemic. J. Surg. Educ. **77**, 729–732 (2020). https://doi.org/10.1016/j.jsurg.2020.03.018
8. Kaharuddin, Ahmad, D., Mardiana, Rusni: Contributions of technology, culture, and attitude to English learning motivation during COVID-19 outbreaks. Syst. Rev. Pharm. **11**, 76–84 (2020). https://doi.org/10.31838/srp.2020.11.13
9. Alashhab, Z.R., Anbar, M., Singh, M.M., Leau, Y.B., Al-Sai, Z.A., Alhayja'a, S.A.: Impact of coronavirus pandemic crisis on technologies and cloud computing applications. J. Electron. Sci. Technol. **19**, 25–40 (2021). https://doi.org/10.1016/j.jnlest.2020.100059
10. Lueth, K.L.: The impact of Covid-19 on the Internet of Things Part 2. https://iot-analytics.com/the-impact-of-covid-19-on-the-internet-of-things-part-2/
11. Ligero, R.: Accent Systems developed a connected wristband to contain Covid-19. https://accent-systems.com/blog/accent-systems-developed-connected-wristband-technology-contain-covid19/?v=75dfaed2dded
12. Chen, Y., Chanet, J.P., Hou, K.M., Zhou, P.: A context-aware tool-set for routing-targeted mutual configuration and optimization of LLNs through bridging virtual and physical worlds. In: New and smart Information Communication Science and Technology to support Sustainable Development (NICST 2014) (2014). 5 p.
13. Ammar Rafea, S., Abdulrahman Kadhim, A.: Routing with energy threshold for WSN-IoT based on RPL protocol. Iraqi J. Comput. Commun. Control Syst. Eng. 71–81 (2019). https://doi.org/10.33103/uot.ijccce.19.1.9
14. Tennina, S., Gaddour, O., Koubâa, A., Royo, F., Alves, M., Abid, M.: Z-Monitor: A protocol analyzer for IEEE 802.15.4-based low-power wireless networks. Comput. Netw. **95**, 77–96 (2016). https://doi.org/10.1016/j.comnet.2015.12.002
15. Fallis, A.: RFC6550 RPL: IPv6 routing protocol for low-power and lossy networks. J. Chem. Inf. Model. **53**, 1689–1699 (2013)
16. Palattella, M.R., et al.: Standardized protocol stack for the internet of (important) things (2013)
17. Mahmoud, C., Aouag, S.: Security for internet of things: a state of the art on existing protocols and open research issues. In: ACM International Conference Proceedings Series (2019). https://doi.org/10.1145/3361570.3361622

18. Kim, H.S., Cho, H., Kim, H., Bahk, S.: DT-RPL: diverse bidirectional traffic delivery through RPL routing protocol in low power and lossy networks. Comput. Netw. **126**, 150–161 (2017). https://doi.org/10.1016/j.comnet.2017.07.001

19. Tian, H., Qian, Z., Wang, X., Liang, X.: QoI-Aware DODAG construction in RPL-based event detection wireless sensor networks. J. Sens. **2017** (2017). https://doi.org/10.1155/2017/1603713

20. Xiao, W., Liu, J., Jiang, N., Shi, H.: An optimization of the object function for routing protocol of low-power and Lossy networks. In: 2014 2nd International Conference on Systems and Informatics, ICSAI 2014, pp. 515–519 (2015). https://doi.org/10.1109/ICSAI.2014.7009341

21. Lamaazi, H., Benamar, N., Jara, A.J.: RPL-based networks in static and mobile environment: a performance assessment analysis. J. King Saud Univ. - Comput. Inf. Sci. **30**, 320–333 (2018). https://doi.org/10.1016/j.jksuci.2017.04.001

22. Ma, G., Li, X., Pei, Q., Li, Z.: A security routing protocol for internet of things based on RPL. In: Proceedings - 2017 International Conference on Networking and Network Applications, NaNA 2017, pp. 209–213. Institute of Electrical and Electronics Engineers Inc. (2017)

23. Le, A., Loo, J., Lasebae, A., Vinel, A., Chen, Y., Chai, M.: The impact of rank attack on network topology of routing protocol for low-power and lossy networks. IEEE Sens. J. **13**, 3685–3692 (2013). https://doi.org/10.1109/JSEN.2013.2266399

24. Raoof, A., Matrawy, A., Lung, C.H.: Routing attacks and mitigation methods for RPL-based internet of things. IEEE Commun. Surv. Tutor. **21**, 1582–1606 (2019). https://doi.org/10.1109/COMST.2018.2885894

25. Al-Fuqaha, A., Guizani, M., Mohammadi, M., Aledhari, M., Ayyash, M.: Internet of things: a survey on enabling technologies, protocols, and applications. IEEE Commun. Surv. Tutor. **17**, 2347–2376 (2015). https://doi.org/10.1109/COMST.2015.2444095

26. AlSawafi, Y., Touzene, A., Day, K., Alzeidi, N.: Hybrid RPL-based sensing and routing protocol for smart city. Int. J. Pervasive Comput. Commun. **16**, 279–306 (2020). https://doi.org/10.1108/IJPCC-11-2019-0088

27. Winter, T., Thubert, P.: RPL: IPv6 routing protocol for low power and lossy networks, draft-ietf-roll-rpl-04.txt. IETF, Internet Draft (work progress) (2009)

28. Fatima-Tuz-Zahra, Jhanjhi, N.Z., Brohi, S.N., Malik, N.A.: Proposing a rank and wormhole attack detection framework using machine learning. In: MACS 2019 - 13th International Conference on Mathematics, Actuarial Science, Computer Science and Statistics Proceedings (2019). https://doi.org/10.1109/MACS48846.2019.9024821

29. Fatima-Tuz-Zahra, Jhanjhi, N.Z., Brohi, S.N., Malik, N.A., Humayun, M.: Proposing a hybrid RPL protocol for rank and wormhole attack mitigation using machine learning. In: 2020 2nd International Conference on Computer and Information Sciences, ICCIS 2020, pp. 1–6. IEEE (2020)

30. Perazzo, P., Vallati, C., Arena, A., Anastasi, G., Dini, G.: An implementation and evaluation of the security features of RPL. In: Puliafito, A., Bruneo, D., Distefano, S., Longo, F. (eds.) ADHOC-NOW 2017. LNCS, vol. 10517, pp. 63–76. Springer, Cham (2017). https://doi.org/10.1007/978-3-319-67910-5_6

31. Mayzaud, A., Badonnel, R., Chrisment, I.: A taxonomy of attacks in RPL-based internet of things (2016)

32. Wallgren, L., Raza, S., Voigt, T.: Routing attacks and countermeasures in the RPL-based internet of things. Int. J. Distrib. Sens. Netw. **2013**, 11 (2013). https://doi.org/10.1155/2013/794326

33. Alzubaidi, M., Anbar, M., Hanshi, S.M.: Neighbor-passive monitoring technique for detecting sinkhole attacks in RPL networks. In: Proceedings of the 2017 International Conference on Computer Science and Artificial Intelligence - CSAI 2017. ACM Press, New York (2017)

34. Alzubaidi, M., Anbar, M., Chong, Y.W., Al-Sarawi, S.: Hybrid monitoring technique for detecting abnormal behaviour in RPL-based network. J. Commun. **13**, 198–208 (2018). https://doi.org/10.12720/jcm.13.5.198-208

35. Alzubaidi, M., Anbar, M., Al-Saleem, S., Al-Sarawi, S., Alieyan, K.: Review on mechanisms for detecting sinkhole attacks on RPLs. In: ICIT 2017 - 8th International Conference on Information Technology, Proceedings, pp. 369–374. Institute of Electrical and Electronics Engineers Inc. (2017)

36. Pongle, P., Chavan, G.: A survey: attacks on RPL and 6LoWPAN in IoT. In: 2015 International Conference on Pervasive Computing: Advance Communication Technology and Application for Society, ICPC 2015 (2015)

37. Napiah, M.N., Bin Idris, M.Y.I., Ramli, R., Ahmedy, I.: Compression header analyzer intrusion detection system (CHA - IDS) for 6LoWPAN communication protocol. IEEE Access **6**, 16623–16638 (2018). https://doi.org/10.1109/ACCESS.2018.2798626

38. Amin, S.O., Siddiqui, M.S., Hong, C.S., Lee, S.: RIDES: Robust intrusion detection system for IP-based Ubiquitous Sensor Networks. Sensors **9**, 3447–3468 (2009). https://doi.org/10.3390/s90503447

39. Kasinathan, P., Costamagna, G., Khaleel, H., Pastrone, C., Spirito, M.A.: Demo: an IDS framework for internet of things empowered by 6LoWPAN. In: Proceedings of the ACM Conference on Computer & Communications Security, pp. 1337–1339 (2013). https://doi.org/10.1145/2508859.2512494

40. Medjek, F., Tandjaoui, D., Romdhani, I., Djedjig, N.: A trust-based intrusion detection system for mobile RPL based networks. In: Proceedings - 2017 IEEE International Conference on Internet of Things, IEEE Green Computing and Communications, IEEE Cyber, Physical and Social Computing, IEEE Smart Data, iThings-GreenCom-CPSCom-SmartData 2017, pp. 735–742. Institute of Electrical and Electronics Engineers Inc. (2018)

41. Airehrour, D., Gutierrez, J., Ray, S.K.: Securing RPL routing protocol from blackhole attacks using a trust-based mechanism. In: 26th International Telecommunication Networks and Applications Conference, ITNAC 2016, pp. 115–120. Institute of Electrical and Electronics Engineers Inc. (2017)

42. Airehrour, D., Gutierrez, J., Ray, S.: A trust-aware RPL routing protocol to detect blackhole and selective forwarding attacks. Aust. J. Telecommun. Digit. Econ. **5** (2017). https://doi.org/10.18080/ajtde.v5n1.2

43. Alabsi, B.A., Anbar, M., Manickam, S., Elejla, O.E.: DDoS attack aware environment with secure clustering and routing based on RPL protocol operation. IET Circuits Devices Syst. **13**, 748–755 (2019). https://doi.org/10.1049/iet-cds.2018.5079

44. Autonomous Networks Research Group: Cooja Simulator – Contiki. http://anrg.usc.edu/contiki/index.php/Cooja_Simulator

45. Wireshark Foundation: Wireshark Â Go deep. https://www.wireshark.org/

46. Pazhaniraja, N., Paul, P., Roja, G., Shanmugapriya, K., Sonali, B.: A study on recent bio-inspired optimization algorithms. ieeexplore.ieee.org (2017)

47. Rai, D., Garg, A.K., Tyagi, K.: Bio-inspired optimization techniques-a critical comparative study **38**, 1–7 (2013). https://doi.org/10.1145/2492248.2492271, dl.acm.org

48. Alzubi, Q.M., Anbar, M., Alqattan, Z.N.M., Al-Betar, M.A., Abdullah, R.: Intrusion detection system based on a modified binary grey wolf optimisation. Neural Comput. Appl. **32**(10), 6125–6137 (2019). https://doi.org/10.1007/s00521-019-04103-1

49. Alamiedy, T.A., Anbar, M., Alqattan, Z.N.M., Alzubi, Q.M.: Anomaly-based intrusion detection system using multi-objective grey wolf optimisation algorithm. J. Ambient Intell. Human. Comput. **11**(9), 3735–3756 (2019). https://doi.org/10.1007/s12652-019-01569-8

50. Altaher, A.: Malware detection based on evolving clustering method for classification. Sci. Res. Essays **7**, 2031–2036 (2012). https://doi.org/10.5897/sre12.001

51. Razak, M.F.A., Anuar, N.B., Othman, F., Firdaus, A., Afifi, F., Salleh, R.: Bio-inspired for features optimization and malware detection. Arab. J. Sci. Eng. **43**(12), 6963–6979 (2017). https://doi.org/10.1007/s13369-017-2951-y

52. Soliman, O.S., Rassem, A.: A network intrusions detection system based on a quantum bio inspired algorithm. Int. J. Eng. Trends Technol. **10**, 370–379 (2014). https://doi.org/10.14445/22315381/ijett-v10p271

53. Clerc, M.: Particle Swarm Optimization (2010). https://doi.org/10.1002/9780470612163

54. Safaldin, M., Otair, M., Abualigah, L.: Improved binary gray wolf optimizer and SVM for intrusion detection system in wireless sensor networks. J. Ambient Intell. Human. Comput. **12**(2), 1559–1576 (2020). https://doi.org/10.1007/s12652-020-02228-z

55. Yang: Firefly algorithm - Google Scholar. https://scholar.google.com/scholar?cluster=3276324836150250709&hl=en&oi=scholarr

56. Mohammadi, M., et al.: A comprehensive survey and taxonomy of the SVM-based intrusion detection systems (2021)

Intrusion Detection Model for Imbalanced Dataset Using SMOTE and Random Forest Algorithm

Reem Alshamy[1]([✉]) [iD], Mossa Ghurab[1], Suad Othman[1], and Faisal Alshami[2]

[1] Faculty of Computer and IT (FCIT), Department of Computer Science, Sana'a University, Sana'a, Yemen

[2] Software Colleague Northeastern University, Shenyang 110819, Liaoning, China

Abstract. Dynamic environments such as networks prone to various types of attacks, therefore fast and robust solutions are needed to deal with rapidly changing attacks. Intrusion Detection Systems (IDSs) play a vital role in cybersecurity to detect any attack or threat in the network. This paper introduced the IDS model using the Synthetic Minority Oversampling Technique and Random Forest algorithm (IDS-SMOTE-RF) to detect different types of attacks. In this model, we have used SMOTE Technique to deal with a class imbalanced problem and RF classifier that has improved performance to detect types of attack. In the experiment, we used the NSL-KDD dataset to train and test the model and introduced a comparison between the IDS-SMOTE-RF model with Adaboost (AB), Logistic Regression (LR), and Support Vector Machine (SVM) classifiers based on accuracy, precision, recall, f1-score, and time metrics for both binary and multi-class classification. The results of the experiment showed that the IDS-SMOTE-RF model achieved high accuracy compared with previous relevant work and was efficient for Big Data.

Keywords: Intrusion Detection System (IDS) · Imbalanced dataset · NSL-KDD dataset · IDS-SMOTE-RF model

1 Introduction

Recently, the number of Internet users has grown, which has led to the created a large number of data and the emergence of various types of attacks, this large amount of data is called Big Data. However, big data includes not only the volume but also the variety and velocity, among other aspects, involved in concepts that are still being defined [1]. The big challenge facing network engineers and researchers today is to identify malicious activities in a host or over a network. The cyber-security research area looks at the ability to act proactively to mitigate or prevent attacks.

IDS is placed at a strategic point in the network where it monitors all traffic and analyzes traffic to detect potential attacks [2]. IDS can be defined as an intrusion detection process which is to find events violation of security policies in computer networks and usually located within the network to monitor all internal network traffic [3]. Mostly, IDS

© Springer Nature Singapore Pte Ltd. 2021
N. Abdullah et al. (Eds.): ACeS 2021, CCIS 1487, pp. 361–378, 2021.
https://doi.org/10.1007/978-981-16-8059-5_22

follows one of the two major detection methods: Signature-based IDS and Anomaly-based IDS. Additionally, many researchers have suggested hybrid detection methods. The Signature-based detection method is designed to detect known attacks that are preloaded in the IDS datasets. Anomaly-based detection is an effective way to detect unknown attacks. The Hybrid detection is combined two methods to overcome disadvantages in signature-based detection and obtain advantages for anomaly-based detection [4, 5]. To detect unknown attacks, researchers have paid great attention to introduce other techniques in detect network intrusion, and machine learning techniques are one of the most used.

In recent years, many studies used machine learning algorithms to intrusion detection such as Support Vector Machine (SVM), Decision Tree (DT), Neural Network (NN), Deep Neural Network (DNN), Naïve Bayes (NB), K Nearest Neighbor (KNN), and other algorithms. However, the machine learning traditional tools take a long time in learning and classifying data. Using Big Data tools and machine learning algorithms in IDS can solve many challenges such as develop accurate IDS and speed [6]. In this paper, we use Anaconda tool in network IDS to reduce computation time and achieves accurate classification for each attack. For this purpose, we propose a model for IDS named the IDS-SMOTE-RF to detect specific attack. Firstly, the data preprocessing method is used on the NSL-KDD dataset to drop features that have 0 values and to convert categorical data to numerical data, and then standardization in the dataset is done to improve classification efficiency. Secondly, SMOTE method is used to enhance the detection accuracy for each attack because the NSL-KDD dataset has a class imbalance problem. Thirdly, RF classifier is used for data classification. Additionally, we introduce a comparison RF classifier with AB, LR, and SVM classifiers on Anaconda platform based on accuracy, precision, recall, f1-score, and time metrics for both binary and multi-class classification problems.

The remainder of this paper is structured as follows: A review of relevant works is introduced in the "Related works" section. In the "Proposed approach" section, we provided the proposed the IDS-SMOTE-RF model for IDS. Furthermore, each step in the IDS-SMOTE-RF model is introduced. Results and discussion are mentioned in the "Results and discussion" section. Finally, conclusions and directions for future work are presented in the "Conclusion" section.

2 Related Works

There are many approaches proposed for IDS to improve attacks detection and it used Big Data tools for analyzing and storing data in IDS. In this section, we summarize some previous relevant works that used Big Data tools to solve the multi-class, binary, or both classification problems in IDS.

Othman et al. [7] proposed a new approach by combining different machine learning (DT and RF) algorithms and feature selection methods in a Big Data environment. They used a full UNSW-BN15 dataset with feature selection and without feature selection methods.

Bandyopadhyay et al. [8] used Information Gain (IG) and DT classifiers. The IG reduced the dimension of the features, and also produced a high detection rate in both multi-class and binary classification problems. They evaluated the performance of DT, RF, LR, and NB classification algorithms using the Anaconda environment. The overall performance comparison was evaluated on NSL-KDD dataset in terms of accuracy, precision, recall, f1 measure, and construction time for building models for both multi-class and binary classification.

Saravanan et al. [9] proposed model based on Big Data platform for network intrusion detection by using LR, DT, SVM, and SVMwithSGD to classify data into normal or attack. They used Chi-square as a feature selection for selecting the features from network security events data. Moreover, they used the NSL-KDD dataset to evaluate the performance of proposed model in terms of AUPR and AUROC metrics and tabulated the training and testing time of each algorithm.

Haggag et al. [10] proposed Deep Learning Spark IDS (DLS-IDS) model on the NSL-KDD dataset. They used SMOTE to dealing with imbalance class and LSTM to detect intrusions behaviors. The DLS-IDS model found that the use of LSTM with SMOTE improved attack detection accuracy. They focused on multi-class and binary classification problems.

Devan et al. [11] proposed model namely XGBoost–DNN for network IDS using NSL-KDD dataset. The XGBoost–DNN model contained three steps: normalization, feature selection, and classification. They used XGBoost technique for feature selection and DNN for classification network intrusion. Moreover, they applied a Softmax classifier to classify data into normal or attack.

Kanimozhi et al. [12] used Artificial Neural Networks (ANN) on the CSE-CIC-IDS2018 dataset. The proposed system provided an outstanding performance of Accuracy score and an average area under ROC and an average False Positive rate.

Gao et al. [13] proposed an adaptive ensemble learning model. The key idea of this model is to use ensemble learning to gather the advantages of different algorithms. They compared the obtained results with other research papers and other algorithms that were used the same dataset. The whole NSL-KDD dataset was used to training and testing the proposed model by using Python programming language with a Scikit-learn and tensorFlow library.

Othman et al. [6] proposed intrusion detection model using SVM and Chisqselectore to select and reduce features. In the proposed method has been used Apache Spark platform to process data on Big Data environment. The authors focused on binary classification.

Nanda et al. [14] compared SVM, KNN, and DT algorithms over Normal, Dos, R2L, and U2R attacks on the NSL-KDD dataset. The features selection method was applied by using a correlation-based method. The results of the comparison between the different types of attacks that can be detected in Anaconda environment are shown, and KNN algorithm achieved high accuracy in network IDS.

Peng et al. [15] proposed a clustering method to determine which one is normal behavior or not. The KDDCup1999 dataset was used to test the proposed model. They combined between Principal Component Analysis (PCA) with Mini Batch K-means. The PCA was applied to improve the clustering efficiency and reduce dimension and the Mini Batch Kmeans method was used for the clustering. PMBKM method can be used for IDS over a Big Data environment.

Manzoor et al. [16] suggested a real-time network IDS based on SVM and Apache Storm framework. The KDD99 dataset was used to train and evaluate the proposed approach. They used LibSVM and one-versus-one used for multi-class classification. The proposed method was feasible for stream processing of network traffic data for the detection of network intrusion with high accuracy.

From previous works, we noted that IDS suffer from the problem of Big Data, and researchers have solved this problem in two strategies to deal with this Big Data:

- Researchers used the full dataset and implemented the proposed approach using Big Data tools such as Apache Spark, Anaconda, and Apache Storm tools [4].
- Others used sampling technique to identify relevant input samples for training instead of using the full training dataset [17].

Table 1 displays comparative between related works based on some criteria such as the algorithms, tools, dataset, and the classification problem.

Table 1. A comparative of related works.

Work	Algorithms	Dataset	Tool	Classification problem
[7]	DT, RF and GBT	UNSW-NB15	Apache Spark	Binary
[8]	DT, RF, LR and NB	NSL-KDD	Anaconda	Both
[9]	LR, DT, SVM, and SVMwithSGD	NSL-KDD	Apache Spark	Binary
[10]	MLP, RNN and LSTM	NSL-KDD	Apache Spark	Both
[11]	DNN, LR, SVM and NB	NSL-KDD	Anaconda	Binary
[12]	Artificial Neural Networks	CSE-CIC-IDS2018	Anaconda	Binary
[13]	DT, RF, KNN, DNN and MultiTree	NSL-KDD	Anaconda	Multi-class
[14]	SVM, KNN and DT	NSL-KDD	Anaconda	Multi-class
[15]	Mini Batch Kmeans	KDD99	Anaconda	Binary
[16]	C- SVM	KDD99	Apache Storm	Multi-class

3 Proposed Approach

3.1 IDS-SMOTE-RF Proposed Model

In this section, we describe the IDS-SMOTE-RF model and techniques used in the proposed model. The steps of the IDS-SMOTE-RF model can be summarized as follows:

Step 1: Load the NSL-KDD dataset.
Step 2: Data preprocessing.
Step 3: Train IDS-SMOTE-RF model by using SMOTE method and RF classifier on the NSL-KDD training dataset.
Step 4: Test IDS-SMOTE-RF model by using RF classifier on the NSL-KDD testing dataset.
Step 5: Results analysis.

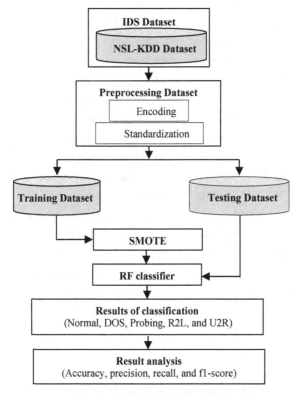

Fig. 1. IDS-SMOTE-RF model.

The steps of the IDS-SMOTE-RF model for intrusion detection are shown in Fig. 1.

Data Description. The NSL-KDD dataset was used to evaluate IDS-SMOTE-RF model. The number of instances that were used is equal to 125,973. The NSL-KDD dataset is an enhanced version of the KDD99 dataset and is recommended by Tavallaee in 2009 [18–20]. It is one of the most popular datasets that was used in training and evaluating IDS [21, 22]. This dataset contains 42 features. The NSL-KDD dataset has four categorical features, four binary features, and 34 Numeric features. Table 2 illustrates the NSL-KDD dataset features and types of features.

Table 2. NSL-KDD dataset features.

Features	Type	Features	Type
1. duration lenght	Numeric	22. count	Numeric
2. protocol_type	Categorical	23. is_guest_login	Binary
3. service	Categorical	24. serror_rate	Numeric
4. flag	Categorical	25. srv_count	Numeric
5. dst_bytes	Numeric	26. rerror_rate	Numeric
6. urgent	Numeric	27. srv_serror_rate	Numeric
7. logged_in	Binary	28. same_srv_rate	Numeric
8. wrong_fragment	Numeric	29. srv_rerror_rate	Numeric
9. src_bytes	Numeric	30. srv_diff_host_rate	Numeric
10 land	Binary	31. diff_srv_rate	Numeric
11. lroot_shell	Numeric	32. dst_host_srv_count	Numeric
12. hot	Numeric	33. dst_host_count	Numeric
13. lnum_compromised	Numeric	34. dst_host_same_srv_rate	Numeric
14. num_failed_logins	Numeric	35. dst_host_diffsrv_rate	Numeric
15. lsu_attempted	Numeric	36. dst_host_same_src_port_rate	Numeric
16. lnum_root	Numeric	37. dst_host_srv_diff_host_rate	Numeric
17. lnum_file_creations	Numeric	38. dst_host_serror_rate	Numeric
18. lnum_shells	Numeric	39. dst_host_srv_serror_rate	Numeric
19. lnum_access_files	Numeric	40. dst_host_rerror_rate	Numeric
20. num_outbound_cmds	Numeric	41. dst_host_srv_rerror_rate	Numeric
21. is_hot_login	Binary	42. class	Categorical

The class feature marks the attack type of the connection consists of 23 classes that include 22 attacks and one normal. The 23 classes are grouped into five classes: Normal, U2R, R2L, Probe, and DOS. Out of 22 different types of attack, there are eight types of attack in R2L, six types of attack in Denial of service (DOS), four types of attack in U2R, and four types of attack in Probe. Table 3 demonstrates different distributions of attacks into one of five main categories.

Table 3. NSL-KDD attack types.

Class	Attack type
Normal	Normal
DOS	teardrop, neptune,back, land, smurf, pod
Probe	portsweep, ipsweep, satan, nmap
R2L	guess_passwd, phf, warezmaster, spy, multihop, ftp_write, warezclient, imap
U2R	buffer_overflow, loadmodule, perl, rootkit

Figure 2 displays the distributions of instances in different types of attacks for both training and testing datasets.

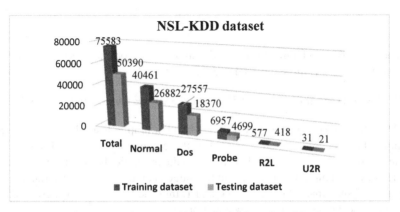

Fig. 2. The distributions of instances in the NSL-KDD dataset.

Data Preprocessing. It is a crucial step that helps to enhance the quality of data to help the extraction of meaningful insights from the data. It suitable for a building and training model. In order to obtain value from the dataset and make it suitable for a building and training the IDS-SMOTE-RF model, we need to first prepare or preprocess the dataset. In this step we used some techniques for data preprocessing that illustrated below:

Transformation. The transformation was performed in order to convert the data into suitable forms for machine learning algorithms. Firstly, the categorical features in dataset are converted to numeric features. Secondly, one-hot encoder method uses to encode categorical features as a one-hot numeric array and derives the categories based on the unique values in each feature. The example of the output of this method the protocol_type feature has three distinct values namely: tcp, udp, and icmp. The protocol_type feature value can be encoded as [1, 0, 0], [0, 1, 0], and [0, 0, 1] and the 41-dimensional of the original the NSL-KDD dataset is mapped into the 122-dimensional.

Standardization. In machine learning, the standardization of datasets is very significant for algorithms that use Euclidean distance. If they are not standardized, there is a potential that features that have values in a larger range may have been given greater importance. Since not every feature can be represented in the same measurement range, features of different sizes will have a negative impact on machine learning algorithms. This can be avoided by standardization by converting data to the same range. It is useful as it helps improve the prediction performance of the model [23]. Several of the features of the NSL-KDD dataset have many values. Values for some features have large ranges between the minimum and maximum values. Such as the duration feature, where the minimum is 0 and the maximum value is 58,329 making the feature values incomparable and unsuitable for processing. Moreover, in the IDS-SMOTE-RF model, we used StandardScaler. The StandardScaler is Standardize features by removing the mean and scaling to unit variance. The StandardScaler uses a following formula to standardize data.

$$z = \frac{x - u}{s} \tag{1}$$

Where z – the standardized value of the sign, x is the original vector, u is the mean of the vectors, and s is the standard deviation.

Model Classifier. In this section, we introduce SMOTE method and RF classifier.

SMOTE. The SMOTE founded by Chawla [24]. It is a simple cluster-based oversampling technique that has been widely accepted in the community [25, 26]. It chooses two samples of the minority class and then assigns it the properties between the two samples. For each of the feature, the difference in the value is obtained and then a random value r is generated such that it lies between 0 and 1, thus the features of the new sample are generated in accordance to the below equation:

$$x_{ni} = \min(x_{ji}, x_{ki}) + |x_{ji} - x_{ki}| \times r \tag{2}$$

Where x_{ni} is the ith feature of the nth new sample and x_j, x_k are the random two samples of the minority class and $r \in (1, 0)$ thus, a set of oversampled values is obtained. Using this technique the two classes are made almost equally proportioned. This simple algorithm ensures that the correlation among the features is conserved even when a large number of synthetically created samples are added to the dataset. The SMOTE suitable for data that have class imbalance. Therefore, the authors used SMOTE to solve class imbalance problem and achieve accurate classification. The SMOTE was applied once for binary classification and once for multi-class classification. The distribution of data in different classes before and after applying SMOTE method in binary classification is shown in Fig. 3. Figure 4 shows the distributions of instances in different attacks before and after SMOTE that applied on the training dataset.

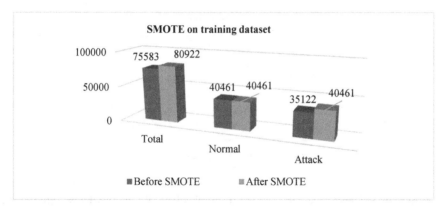

Fig. 3. Results of SMOTE method on training dataset in binary classification.

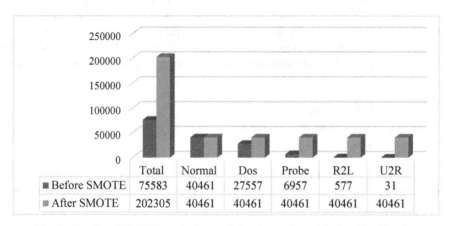

Fig. 4. Results of SMOTE method on training dataset in multi-class classification

Random Forest Classifier. The RF is an ensemble learning algorithm combines multiple machine learning models to produce one model [27]. The RF classifier is an ensemble learning algorithm for classification and prediction [28]. It was founded by Breiman [29]. The RF is combining tree classifiers to predict new unlabeled data. The predictor depends on a constant that denotes the number of trees in the forest; the features are selected randomly, and each number of the set (trees) here, they represent one forest, and each one of these forests represents a prediction class. In this algorithm, random feature selection will be selected for each tree. Random Forest architecture is displayed in Fig. 5 [30].

Many classification trees will be produced by using RF classifiers, and each separate tree is built by different parts of the general dataset. After each tree classifies an unlabeled class, the new object will be applied and each tree will vote for a decision. The forest chosen as the winning class is based on the highest number of recorded votes. The number of votes is calculated as follows:

Random Forest algorithms:

Decision Forest

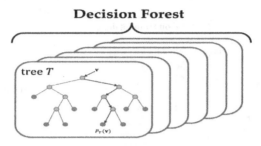

Fig. 5. Random Forest Architecture.

If there is a dataset, we need to split n samples from the whole dataset, giving the number of trees. Each dataset sample needs to be classified; for each instance, this is randomly split among all predictor classes to reach an approximately optimal split. The RF classifier is a meta estimator that fits several decision tree classifiers in different subsamples of the dataset and uses an average to improve the predictive accuracy and control overfitting. The subsample size is always the same as the sample size of the original input. The following parameters must be properly adjusted to reach the highest accuracy:

- The number of trees in the forest.
- The function to measure the split quality.
- The samples that are used when building trees.

In this paper, we used RF classifier because it can be deal with binary and multi-class classification problems and SMOTE method to improve accuracy for the minority class.

3.2 Evaluation Metrics

The confusion matrix as a basis for the performance evaluation is widely used in intrusion detection. The confusion matrix consists of four evaluation values which are TN, TP, FN, and FP.

The performance of our proposed model is evaluated in four terms of accuracy, precision, recall, f1-score, and time. The accuracy is calculated as [31]:

$$\text{Accuracy} = \frac{\text{TP} + \text{TN}}{\text{TP} + \text{TN} + \text{FN} + \text{FP}} \tag{3}$$

The precision is calculated as [32]:

$$\text{Precision} = \frac{\text{TP}}{\text{TP} + \text{FP}} \tag{4}$$

The Recall is calculated as [33]:

$$\text{Recall} = \frac{\text{TP}}{\text{TP} + \text{FN}} \tag{5}$$

The F1-score is calculated as [32]:

$$\text{F1-score} = 2 * \frac{\text{Precision} * \text{Recall}}{\text{Precision} + \text{Recall}} \tag{6}$$

4 Results and Discussion

In this section, the authors show the results of Big Data the IDS-SMOTE-RF model that is used for intrusion detection. The main programming language was Python using on Anaconda platform. The performance analysis of the IDS-SMOTE-RF model using the NSL-KDD dataset is performed in two ways as follows:

1. Binary classification: classify data into normal or attack class.
2. Multi-class classification: classify data into one of five classes (Normal, DOS, Probe, R2L, and U2R).

4.1 Evaluation Based on Binary Classification

In the experiment, the SMOTE method is used to solve class imbalanced problem. The results and distribution of data in different classes before and after applying SMOTE method is shown in Fig. 3. After that, RF classifier is used to classify data. Table 4 illustrates the accuracy of the IDS-SMOTE-RF model for each class and Fig. 6 illustrates Confusion matrix of the IDS-SMOTE-RF model in binary classification (Normal and Attack).

Table 4. Accuracy of the IDS-SMOTE-RF on each class in binary classification.

Model	Normal	Attack
IDS-SMOTE-RF model	**99.96**	**99.80**

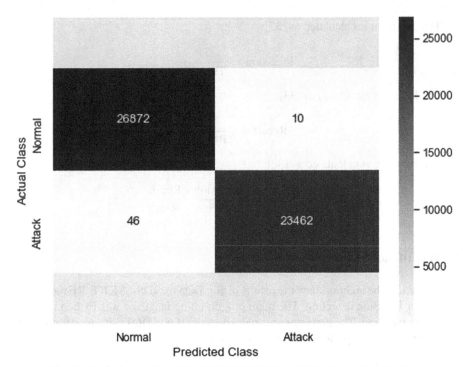

Fig. 6. Confusion matrix of the IDS-SMOTE-RF model in binary classification.

In addition, other classifiers have been applied to compare them with our proposed classifiers. The overall metrics of our proposed model are accuracy: 99.89, precision: 99.88, recall: 99.89, and f1-score: 99.88 for binary classification. Table 5 and Fig. 7 summarize the results of the IDS-SMOTE-RF model with other classifiers in binary classification.

Table 5. Comparison results in binary classification with other classifiers.

Classifier	Accuracy	Precision	Recall	F1-score
LR	97.27	97.28	97.27	97.27
AB	99.13	99.13	99.13	99.13
SVM	99.26	99.26	99.26	99.26
IDS-SMOTE-RF model	**99.89**	**99.88**	**99.89**	**99.88**

Finally, the proposed model was compared with some previous research works. Table 6 and Fig. 8 summarize the results of comparison with other works in binary classification.

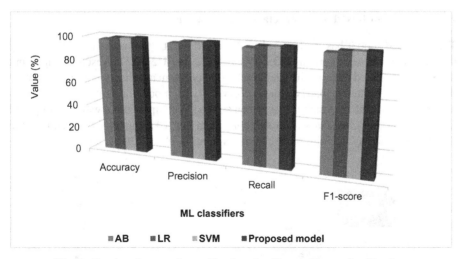

Fig. 7. Results of comparison with other classifiers in binary classification.

Table 6. Comparison results in binary classification with other works.

Method	Accuracy
DT [8]	90.9
SVMwithSGD [9]	91.1
XGBoost–DNN [11]	97.6
IDS-SMOTE-RF model	**99.89**

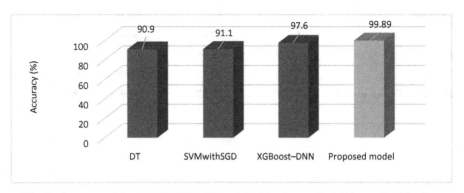

Fig. 8. Accuracy of the IDS-SMOTE-RF model with other works in binary classification.

4.2 Evaluation Based on Multi-class Classification

The proposed model has been tested to detect different types of attacks and classify data into five classes (Normal, DOS, Probe, R2L, and U2R). The results of applying the SMOTE method to solve the data distribution problem are shown in Fig. 4. Figure 9 illustrates the Confusion matrix of the IDS-SMOTE-RF model for multi-class classification. In addition, other classifiers have been applied to compare them with our proposed classifiers to multi-class classification. Table 7 and Fig. 10 summarize the results of the IDS-SMOTE-RF model with other classifiers in multi-class classification.

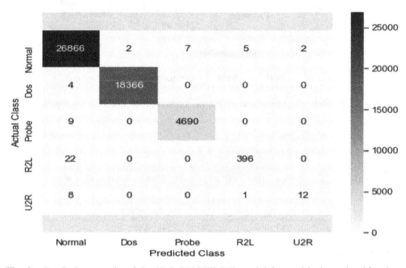

Fig. 9. Confusion matrix of the IDS-SMOTE-RF model for multi-class classification.

Table 7. Performance comparison of the IDS-SMOTE-RF model with other classifiers in multi-class classification.

Classifier	Accuracy	Precision	Recall	F1-score
AB	75.86	87.96	75.86	81.02
LR	97.23	98.55	97.23	97.72
SVM	97.82	98.95	97.82	98.25
IDS-SMOTE-RF model	**99.88**	**99.87**	**99.88**	**99.87**

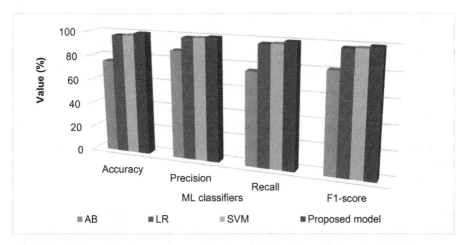

Fig. 10. Results of comparison with other classifiers in multi-class classification.

Finally, the proposed model was compared with some previous research works to multi-class classification. Table 8 summarizes the results of the IDS-SMOTE-RF model and other previous works.

Table 8. Accuracy of the IDS-SMOTE-RF model and other works in multi-class classification.

Method	Accuracy
DT [8]	85.4
MultiTree [13]	85.2
LSTM [10]	96.63
IDS-SMOTE-RF model	**99.88**

In the IDS, there is a high real-time requirement for the analysis of Big Data, which requires not only high evaluation metrics but also as short detection time as possible, it is crucial for measuring the efficiency of network security applications. Table 9 demonstrates the training and testing times for the proposed model with other classifiers for binary and multi-class classification. The results were shown the proposed model reduced the training and testing time so the proposed model can be dealing with Big Data effectively.

In "Propose approach" section we displayed the IDS-SMOTE-RF steps and Anaconda Big Data tool which are used in the implemented proposed model to make the model efficient for Big Data. The results of the experiment model are illustrated in Fig. 6 and Fig. 9 for each class in both binary and multi-class classification. We used RF classifier with SMOTE method to achieve high detection for each attack. The result of the experiment showed that our proposed model has high performance. According to the comparison in Table 6 and Table 8 between the IDS-SMOTE-RF model and other

Table 9. Training and testing times for the IDS-SMOTE-RF model with other classifiers.

Classifier	Binary classification		Multi-class classification	
	Training time (s)	Testing time (s)	Training time (s)	Testing time (s)
LR	3.940	**0.100**	22.138	1.072
AB	9.250	1.420	29.840	1.700
SVM	61.219	19.954	435.616	299.133
IDS-SMOTE-RF model	6.450	**0.710**	23.520	**0.980**

researcher's methods in both binary and multi-class classification based on accuracy the IDS-SMOTE-RF is the best classifier. Table 9 showed the results based on training and predicting time. According to the comparison in Table 9 between the IDS-SMOTE-RF model and other classifiers based on predicting time the IDS-SMOTE-RF model is the best classifier.

5   Conclusion

In this paper, the IDS-SMOTE-RF model for network intrusion detection that can deal with Big Data was introduced. The proposed model used the Anaconda tool which can process and analyze data with high performance using the NSL-KDD dataset. In the proposed model, we used SMOTE method to deal with the class imbalance problem on training data and RF algorithms to classify data into normal or specific attack (Dos, Probe, R2L, and U2R). The results of experiment showed that our model has high performance and speed for both binary and multi-class classification. In future work, we can improve the accuracy detection rate for each type of attack and reduced computation time. Additionally, we can apply this model on a recent dataset to cover modern types of attacks.

References

1. Basgall, M.J., Naiouf, M., Fernández, A.: FDR2-BD: a fast data reduction recommendation tool for tabular big data classification. Electronics **10** (2021)
2. Ju, A., Guo, Y., Ye, Z., Li, T., Ma, J.: HeteMSD: a big data analytics framework for targeted cyber-attacks detection using heterogeneous multisource data. Secur. Commun. Netw. **2019** (2019)
3. Kim, K., Aminanto, M.E., Tanuwidjaja, H.C.: Network Intrusion Detection Using Deep Learning: A Feature Learning Approach. Springer, Heidelberg (2018)
4. Alshamy, R., Ghurab, M.: A review of big data in network intrusion detection system: challenges, approaches, datasets, and tools. J. Comput. Sci. Eng. **8**, 62–75 (2020)
5. Othman, S.M., Alsohybe, N.T., Ba-Alwi, F.M., Zahary, A.T.: Survey on intrusion detection system types. Int. J. Cyber-Secur. Digit. Forensics **7**, 444–463 (2018)
6. Othman, D.M.S., Hicham, R., Zoulikha, M.M.: An efficient spark-based network anomaly detection. Int. J. Comput. Digit. Syst. **9**, 1–11 (2020)

7. Othman, S.M., Ba-Alwi, F.M., Alsohybe, N.T., Al-Hashida, A.Y.: Intrusion detection model using machine learning algorithm on Big Data environment. J. Big Data **5**(1), 1–12 (2018). https://doi.org/10.1186/s40537-018-0145-4

8. Bandyopadhyay, S., Chowdhury, R., Banerjee, P., Dey, S.D., Saha, B.: A Decision Tree Based Intrusion Detection System for Identification of Malicious Web Attacks. Preprints.org. (2020)

9. Haggag, M., Tantawy, M.M., El-Soudani, M.M.S.: Implementing a deep learning model for intrusion detection on apache spark platform. IEEE Access (2020)

10. Devan, P., Khare, N.: An efficient XGBoost–DNN-based classification model for network intrusion detection system. Neural Comput. Appl. **32**(16), 12499–12514 (2020). https://doi.org/10.1007/s00521-020-04708-x

11. Kanimozhi, V., Jacob, T.P.: Artificial intelligence based network intrusion detection with hyper-parameter optimization tuning on the realistic cyber dataset CSE-CIC-IDS2018 using cloud computing. In: 2019 International Conference on Communication and Signal Processing (ICCSP), pp. 0033–0036. IEEE (2019)

12. Saravanan, S.: Performance evaluation of classification algorithms in the design of apache spark based intrusion detection system. In: 2020 5th International Conference on Communication and Electronics Systems (ICCES), pp. 443–447. IEEE (2020)

13. Gao, X., Shan, C., Hu, C., Niu, Z., Liu, Z.: An adaptive ensemble machine learning model for intrusion detection. IEEE Access **7**, 82512–82521 (2019)

14. Nanda, N.B., Parikh, A.: Network intrusion detection system: classification, techniques and datasets to implement. Int. J. Future Revol. Comput. Sci. Commun. Eng. **3**, 106–109 (2018)

15. Peng, K., Leung, V.C.M., Huang, Q.: Clustering approach based on mini batch kmeans for intrusion detection system over big data. IEEE Access **6**, 11897–11906 (2018)

16. Manzoor, M.A., Morgan, Y.: Real-time support vector machine based network intrusion detection system using Apache Storm. In: 2016 IEEE 7th Annual Information Technology, Electronics and Mobile Communication Conference (IEMCON), pp. 1–5. IEEE (2016)

17. Suthaharan, S.: A single-domain, representation-learning model for big data classification of network intrusion. In: Perner, P. (ed.) MLDM 2013. LNCS (LNAI), vol. 7988, pp. 296–310. Springer, Heidelberg (2013). https://doi.org/10.1007/978-3-642-39712-7_23

18. Tavallaee, M., Bagheri, E., Lu, W., Ghorbani, A.A.: A detailed analysis of the KDD CUP 99 data set. In: 2009 IEEE Symposium on Computational Intelligence for Security and Defense Applications, pp. 1–6. IEEE (2009)

19. Ghurab, M., Gaphari, G., Alshami, F., Alshamy, R., Othman, S.: A detailed analysis of benchmark datasets for network intrusion detection system. Asian J. Res. Comput. Sci. **7**, 14–33 (2021)

20. NSL-KDD dataset. https://www.unb.ca/cic/datasets/nsl.html. Accessed 16 Dec 2020

21. Ferrag, M.A., Maglaras, L., Moschoyiannis, S., Janicke, H.: Deep learning for cyber security intrusion detection: approaches, datasets, and comparative study. J. Inf. Secur. Appl. **50** (2020)

22. Jaber, A.N., Anwar, S., Khidzir, N.Z.B., Anbar, M.: A detailed analysis on intrusion identification mechanism in cloud computing and datasets. In: Anbar, M., Abdullah, N., Manickam, S. (eds.) ACeS 2020. CCIS, vol. 1347, pp. 550–573. Springer, Singapore (2021). https://doi.org/10.1007/978-981-33-6835-4_37

23. Tunduny, T.K.: A HIV/AIDS viral load prediction system using artificial neural networks (2017)

24. Chawla, N.V., Bowyer, K.W., Hall, L.O., Kegelmeyer, W.P.: SMOTE: synthetic minority over-sampling technique. J. Artif. Intell. Res. **16**, 321–357 (2002). https://doi.org/10.1613/jair.953

25. Tanha, J., Abdi, Y., Samadi, N., Razzaghi, N., Asadpour, M.: Boosting methods for multi-class imbalanced data classification: an experimental review. J. Big Data **7**, 1–47 (2020)

26. Patil, A., Framewala, A., Kazi, F.: Explainability of SMOTE based oversampling for imbalanced dataset problems. In: 2020 3rd International Conference on Information and Computer Technologies (ICICT), pp. 41–45. IEEE (2020)
27. Brown, G.: Ensemble Learning. Encyclopedia of Machine Learning, vol. 312 (2010)
28. Araar, A., Bouslama, R.: A comparative study of classification models for detection in IP networks intrusions. J. Theor. Appl. Inf. Technol. **64** (2014)
29. Breiman, L., Friedman, J., Stone, C.J., Olshen, R.A.: Classification and Regression Trees. CRC Press (1984)
30. Obeidat, I., Hamadneh, N., Alkasassbeh, M., Almseidin, M., AlZubi, M.: Intensive preprocessing of KDD Cup 99 for network intrusion classification using machine learning techniques. International Association of Online Engineering (2019)
31. Ye, K.: Key feature recognition algorithm of network intrusion signal based on neural network and support vector machine. Symmetry **3** (2019)
32. Al-Qatf, M., Lasheng, Y., Al-Habib, M., Al-Sabahi, K.: Deep learning approach combining sparse autoencoder with SVM for network intrusion detection. IEEE Access **6**, 52843–52856 (2018)
33. Shone, N., Ngoc, T.N., Phai, V.D., Shi, Q.: A deep learning approach to network intrusion detection. IEEE Trans. Emerg. Top. Comput. Intell. **2**, 41–50 (2018)

Optimized Stacking Ensemble Model to Detect Phishing Websites

Badiea Abdulkarem Mohammed[1,2](✉) and Zeyad Ghaleb Al-Mekhlafi[1]

[1] College of Computer Science and Engineering, University of Ha'il, Ha'il 81481, Saudi Arabia
b.alshaibani@uoh.edu.sa
[2] College of Computer Sciences and Engineering, Hodeidah University, Hodeidah, Yemen

Abstract. Phishing attacks are security attacks that do not affect only individuals or organisations websites, but it may affect Internet of Things (IoT) devices and networks. IoT environment is an exposed environment for such attacks. Attackers may use thingbots software for dispersal hidden junk emails that not noticed by users. Machine and deep learning and other methods were used to design detection methods for these attacks. However, there still a need to enhance the detection accuracy. An optimized ensemble classification method for phishing website detection is proposed in this study. A Genetic Algorithm (GA) was used to optimize the ensemble classification method by tuning the parameters of several ensemble Machine Learning (ML) methods, including Random Forest, AdaBoost, and XGBoost. These were accomplished by ranking the optimized classifiers to pick out the best classifiers as a base for stacking ensemble method. A phishing website dataset that made up of 4898 phishing websites and 6157 legitimate websites was used for this study experiments. As a result, detection accuracy was enhanced and reached 97.16%.

Keywords: Phishing websites · Ensemble classifiers · Optimization methods · Genetic algorithm

1 Introduction

Cybercrimes became a concern of many organisations and researchers in the recent years. Phishing is a type of cybercrimes that considers as one of the most dangerous types. In phishing, the attackers stole the user's credentials and information by using false emails or websites that look like original ones. This type of attacks became a concern because it affects many internet users and organisations. In phishing, a legitimate website of a selected organisation is faked by the attacker and then distributed to victims via fake or junk emails or via posted URLs in social media and networks, or any medium of communication. This may lead victims to click on the links in that emails or posts and they will be redirected to the fake website [1, 2].

Internet of Things (IoT) environments are more exposed to phishing threats. In IoT, the devices are highly connected and IoT sensors which can be considered as an easy attacker medium. As mentioned in [3], the smart routers, TVs, and fridges were between

© Springer Nature Singapore Pte Ltd. 2021
N. Abdullah et al. (Eds.): ACeS 2021, CCIS 1487, pp. 379–388, 2021.
https://doi.org/10.1007/978-981-16-8059-5_23

the 25% of junk emails hosts. Furthermore, attackers may use thingbots software of an IoT device for dispersal junk emails without sending any viruses or Trojans. This can be done without the user perceptive, as the functionality of the IoT device may not be affected [4]. Therefore, the literature introduced several methods to increase the security of IoT environment. However, there is no effective phishing detection method, which can effectively detect phishing emails and websites [2, 5]. The literature introduced some phishing websites detection approaches and methods in the IoT environment. For example, a light-weight deep learning method was introduced in [6]. This method suggests the use of a detection sensor to detect phishing websites. The detection sensor can work in real-time and have a feature to save the energy consumption. With this proposed system, IoT devices do not need to install anti-phishing software. Moreover, the detection sensor only needs to be installed once in a location between the devices and the internet local router. This method considered somewhat efficient and can be installed in the router directly.

Several techniques were used phishing websites detection. Deep learning [7, 8], Convolution and Deep Neural Network (CNN and DNN), Long Short-Term Memory (LSTM) [7], Genetic Algorithm (GA) [8], Machine Learning (ML) [9–11], and other methods were utilized to enhance the accuracy of phishing website detection approaches. The results of these studies exhibited that the suggested approaches gained significant enhancement in terms of sensitivity, specificity, accuracy, and other measures in comparison with other state-of-the-art approaches. However, there still a need to enhance the detection accuracy.

An optimized ensemble classification model for phishing websites detection is proposed in the present study. To build the proposed model, The GA was used. This includes three main stages that are training, ranking and testing. First, training was used to train the classifiers (Random Forest, AdaBoost, and XGBoost). In this step, no optimization method was applied. In second step, GA is used to optimize these classifiers to select the optimal values of the model parameters that can be used to increase the whole accuracy of the classifiers. Next, optimized classifiers employed as the stacking ensemble method base classifiers based on their ranking. Finally, test dataset is generated by collecting a new websites and used to foresee the ultimate class label of the websites.

The organization of this study is as follows. An overview of the related literature is presented in Sect. 2. The methodology and materials were disused in Sect. 3. The finding of the experiments of the present study are presented in Sect. 4. In the same section, the finding are explained and compared with related literature. In Sect. 5, the conclusion of the present study is summarised in which the results and recommendations are presented.

2   Related Literature

Various research have formerly been performed in phishing detection field. Information from related literature have been intensely reviewed to help in motivating the methodology of the present study. This related literature can be organized as follow:

2.1   IoT- Based Phishing Detection Methods

Several millions of connected IoT devices suffer from serious security issues that menace the IoT web safety [12]. Therefore, it is highly necessary to protect these IoT devices against several kinds of attacks (e.g. phishing). The target of phishing attack usually are unconventional networks for instance the IoT [2]. In [13], the main cyber menaces for the IoT industry (IIoT) have been examined and have been identified as 5 kinds of attacks, the first kind was phishing. Phishers apply compromised attacks in critical infrastructures such as IoT, an advanced approaches combining zero-days malware with social engineering and they also use other functionality that developed on remote web sites to attack IIoT systems. The front-end level is used by attackers to access the IIoT.

Several methods were proposed in IoT environment to detect phishing websites. Parra et al. suggested in [14] a framework that based on cloud and deep learning comprises two tools: cloud-based temporal LSTM and Distributed CNN. The first tool was used for the detection of phishing as an IoT micro-security device, whereas the second tool was employed on the back-end to Botnet attacks detection and realize convolution neural network embeddings for the detection of distributed phishing attacks on IoT devices. Results from experiments demonstrated that the first tool could achieve 94.3% detection accuracy with CNN and 93.58% with F-score for phishing attacks.

Mao et al. talked in [15] about the main security concerns in intelligent IoT systems and discovered that phishing is from the most frequent types of attacks. As a proposed solution that based on ML, an automated page-layout-based approach was developed by them to detect phishing websites. Detecting phishing websites in this approach is based on gaining the page layout resemblance by using aggregation analysis. In their experiments, four ML methods were employed, and the results showed improved precision.

In [16], Virat et al. thoroughly discussed the security issues in IoT, arguing that its devices are not intelligent, making the problem solving difficult and requiring adequate methods of detection the main challenge of IoT security. Deogirikar, as well as Vidhate have also investigated several vulnerabilities, which have endangered the IoT technology [17]. They have reviewed different IoT attacks and how to reduce their production and damage level in IoT and they have accomplished extensive research to find effective solutions.

2.2   ML-Based Detection Methods

The detection methods for several cybersecurity issues widely utilized the AI and ML. Several methods that based on AI and ML with good detection ability were offered for detecting phishing websites. Al-sariera et al., for example, proposed new AI-based schemes that considered new methods of phishing mitigation [18]. Four meta-learner methods were introduced based on the extra-tree base classifiers that were applied on data sets of phishing website. The results from the previous experiments show that the proposed models achieved 97% accuracy and the false-positive rate were reduced to 0,028.

In the context of hyperlinks contained in HTML, Jain and Gupta in [19] proposed a new approach to detect Phishing Websites. This method brings several new hyperlink characteristics together and divides them into twelve types that are used in ML models training. The method was applied with several ML classifiers to a phishing website dataset. Experimental results showed that 98.4% accuracy was achieved with a logistic regression classifier in the proposed model. This procedure is a solution in the client-side that needs no support from third parties. Another phishing website detection model was introduced by Feng via a neural system [20]. This model used a Monte-carlo technique during the training stage and accuracy that was achieved reached 97.71%, with False Positive Rate reaching 1.7%, signifying that the suggested model is worthy in comparison to other ML methods of phishing websites detection.

In order to predict phishing websites, Aburub and Hadi in [21] used association rules. The phishing multi-class Association Rule system was employed with a dataset that contains 10,068 legitimate and phishing websites, which is comparable to other associative classification methods. Their findings showed that their method gained acceptance rate of detection. Likewise there have been other ML-based methods using selection techniques [22, 23], ensemble classifiers [24], hybrid deep learning and ML methods [25] and other methods.

3   Materials and Methods

The present section presents and explains the suggested genetic-based ensemble classifier technique for enhancing the phishing website detection. The methodology that followed in the present study is shown in Fig. 1. Three main stages constitute the methodology of the present study, training, ranking, and testing stages. These stages are more discussed in the following sub-sections. Training stage aims to train the classifiers (Random Forest, AdaBoost, and XGBoost) without optimization. The purpose after that is twofold: first, to get an overview of the ensemble classification performance before optimisation and second, to discover which of the phishing website characteristics are most valuable. The GA then used to optimize the above-mentioned classifiers. Here, the GA was used to increase the whole accuracy of the suggested model by selecting the optimal values of model parameters. Next, in the ranking stage, the stacking method was used to arrange the optimized classifiers and build ensemble classifier. In the testing phase, a testing data were gathered and used.

The methodology in [26] have been followed in order to excerpt the features of the websites. The Malware and Phishing Blacklist of the PhishTank database of verified phishing pages has been gathered from a range of benign and malicious websites [27]. A Python script is created with the Whois, urllib, ipaddress, requests and Beautiful Soup libraries so that remove the features that were used in the dataset of training (abnormality-based features, domain-based features, bar-based features and HTML and JavaScript features). Subsequently, these features were ultimately provide into the classifiers to forecast the website's ultimate label of the class.

The experiments in the present study was conducted on a public dataset available in the UCI ML Repository [28]. Scripts were written in Anaconda environment under windows 10 64-bit. Python 3.6 language were used. The employed dataset that were used in these experiments comprises of 6157 legitimate websites (56%) and 4898 phishing websites (44%). The number of minority class was increased by the oversampling

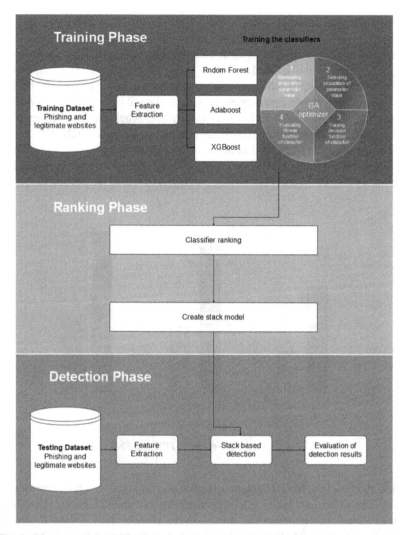

Fig. 1. The proposed optimized stacking ensemble model for phishing website detection

technique to imbalance the dataset. The features of dataset (30 features) can be classified into 4 groups: address bar-based (12 features), HTML and JavaScript-based (5 features), abnormality-based (6 features), and domain-based (7 features).

To assess the ensemble model, specific performance measures were utilized. These measures are classification accuracy, recall, precision, F-score, false negative rate (FNR) and false positive rate (FPR). Commonly, numerous researches used these measures to evaluate the phishing website detection systems performance [11].

In order to evaluate the suggested method accurately, 10-fold cross-validation were used with all the conducted experiments with optimized or non-optimized classifiers. The normality of each fold were also checked.

4   Findings and Discussions

This section describes the results for each technique before comparisons with the related works are presented and discussed.

As mentioned above, 10-fold cross validation was used to train a set of ensemble classifiers. The experiment was first conducted without the use of GA. The performance of the default configuration classifier is shown to have the highest precision compared with other classifiers. Random Forest classification achieved approximately 97% accuracy. The rest of the classifiers achieved an accuracy of 93% to 94.61%.

Figure 2 shows FPR and FNR. It was found that Random Forest achieved distinguished FPR (0.05) and FNR (0.02). AdaBoost achieved the second range.

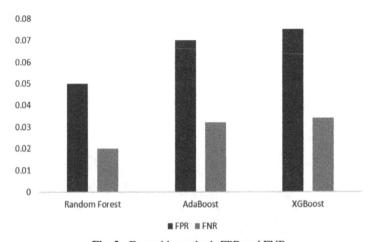

Fig. 2. Ensemble methods FPR and FNR

While all classifiers have demonstrated good performance, several parameters have to be adjusted to achieve better assessment results. For each classifier, it's relatively difficult to adjust such parameters. The GA in the present study is used to adjust the parameters of classifiers. In the area of algorithm parameter search, the GA has shown good results [29]. For configuring the GA the following parameters were used (see Table 1).

The confusion matrices of Random Forest and XGBoost are shown in Figs. 3 and 4, respectively.

In Fig. 4b, it is noticeable that the classifier GA-XGBoost has been optimized to the greatest benefit. 95.94% of cases have been detected correctly as a 'phishing website' class, representing the TP measure and 4.06% of instances incorrectly as 'legitimate' class, which is the FP measure. Furthermore, 98.04% of instances were detected as the "legitimate" class representing the TN measure, whereas the FN measure represented incorrectly 1.96% of detected instances as a "phishing website" class. It is possible to conclude that the GA-XGBoost classification system has achieved a high TP rate and a low FP. The results for other performance measures are listed in Table 2.

Table 1. GA parameter settings that used in the present study

Parameter	Value
Population size	24
Generations	10
Mutation rate	0.02
Early stop	12
Crossover rate	0.5

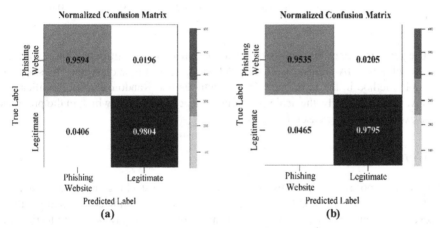

Fig. 3. Normalized Random Forest confusion matrix for the phishing website: (a) without optimized parameters; (b) with optimized parameters

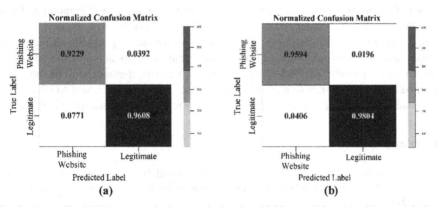

Fig. 4. Normalized XGBoost confusion matrix for the phishing website: (a) without optimized parameters; (b) with optimized parameters

Table 2. Performance evaluation of phishing website detection

Classifier	Class name	Precision	Recall	F-score
GA-Random Forest	Phishing website	0.964	0.941	0.951
	Legitimate	0.952	0.973	0.964
	Weighted Average	0.959	0.957	0.959
GA-XGBoost	Phishing website	0.975	0.958	0.965
	Legitimate	0.967	0.980	0.972
	Weighted Average	0.970	0.970	0.970
	Legitimate	0.955	0.963	0.958
	Weighted Average	0.953	0.953	0.953

The performance of these classifiers was classified after the training phase, with the best model being GA-XGBoost. This model was used as a base classifier of a stacking ensemble method in the next stage. In the meta-learner, Random Forest classification was investigated. Finally, the achieved accuracy reached 97.16%, which in the previous phase exceeds the other ensemble methods.

5 Conclusions

This paper proposes to detect phishing sites an optimized stacking ensemble model.

The optimization method has been used to identify the optimized parameter values of several ensemble learning methods by using a GA. Training, ranking and testing are the three stages the form the proposed model. In the training stage, several ensemble learning methods have been trained, including Random Forest, Adaboost, XGBoost, without using the GA method. GA then used to optimize these classifiers by selects the optimum model parameter values and enhances whole precision. In the ranking phase, certain classifier were used as basis classifier for a stacking ensemble method. These classifiers was the best ensemble methods (GA-Random Forest). Finally, new websites were compiled in the testing phase and used as a test data set to guess the ultimate label of the class (legitimate or phishing). The experiments findings demonstrate a superior performance compared with other machine-based detection methods with the proposed optimized stacking ensemble method. The accuracy achieved amounted to 97.16%. In future work, 6 classifiers were planned to be optimized rather than the three in this work.

References

1. Al-Sarem, M., Saeed, F., Al-Mekhlafi, Z.G., Mohammed, B.A., Al-Hadhrami, T., et al.: An optimized stacking ensemble model for phishing websites detection. Electronics **10**(11), 1–18 (2021)
2. Gupta, B.B., Arachchilage, N.A.G., Psannis, K.E.: Defending against phishing attacks: taxonomy of methods, current issues and future directions. Telecommun. Syst. **67**(2), 247–267 (2017). https://doi.org/10.1007/s11235-017-0334-z

3. Gubbi, J., Buyya, R., Marusic, S., Palaniswami, M.: Internet of Things (IoT): A vision, architectural elements, and future directions. Futur. Gener. Comput. Syst. **29**(7), 1645–1660 (2018)
4. Roman, R., Najera, P., Lopez, J.: Securing the Internet of Things. Computer **44**(9), 51–58 (2011)
5. Tang, D.: Event detection in sensor networks. School of Engineering and Applied Sciences, The George Washington University, USA (2009)
6. Wei, B., Hamad, R.A., Yang, L., He, X., Wang, H., et al.: A deep-learning-driven light-weight phishing detection sensor. Sensors **19**(19), 1–13 (2019)
7. Somesha, M., Pais, A.R., Rao, R.S., Rathour, V.S.: Efficient deep learning techniques for the detection of phishing websites. Sādhanā **45**(1), 1–18 (2020). https://doi.org/10.1007/s12046-020-01392-4
8. Ali, W., Ahmed, A.A.: Hybrid intelligent phishing website prediction using deep neural networks with genetic algorithm-based feature selection and weighting. IET Inf. Secur. **13**(6), 659–669 (2019)
9. Chiew, K.L., Tan, C.L., Wong, K., Yong, K.S., Tiong, W.K.: A new hybrid ensemble feature selection framework for machine learning-based phishing detection system. Inf. Sci. **484**, 153–166 (2019)
10. Rao, R.S., Pais, A.R.: Detection of phishing websites using an efficient feature-based machine learning framework. Neural Comput. Appl. **31**(8), 3851–3873 (2018). https://doi.org/10.1007/s00521-017-3305-0
11. Ali, W., Malebary, S.: Particle swarm optimization-based feature weighting for improving intelligent phishing website detection. IEEE Access **8**, 116766–116780 (2020)
12. Khursheeed, F., Sami-Ud-Din, M., Sumra, I.A., Safder, M.A.: Review of security mechanism in internet of things (IoT). In: IEEE 3rd International Conference on Advancements in Computational Sciences (ICACS), Lahore, Pakistan, pp. 1–9. IEEE (2020)
13. Tsiknas, K., Taketzis, D., Demertzis, K., Skianis, C.: Cyber threats to industrial IoT: a survey on attacks and countermeasures. IoT **2**(1), 163–218 (2021)
14. Parra, G.D., Rad, P., Choo, K.K., Beebe, N.: Detecting Internet of Things attacks using distributed deep learning. J. Netw. Comput. Appl. **163**(102662), 1–20 (2020)
15. Mao, J., et al.: Phishing page detection via learning classifiers from page layout feature. EURASIP J. Wirel. Commun. Netw. **1**, 1–14 (2019). https://doi.org/10.1186/s13638-019-1361-0
16. Virat, M.S., Bindu, S.M., Aishwarya, B., Dhanush, B.N., Kounte, M.R.: Security and privacy challenges in internet of things. In: IEEE 2nd International Conference on Trends in Electronics and Informatics (ICOEI), Tirunelveli, India, pp. 454–460. IEEE (2018)
17. Deogirikar, J., Vidhate, A.: Security attacks in IoT: a survey. In: IEEE International Conference on IoT in Social, Mobile, Analytics and Cloud (I-SMAC), Palladam, India, pp. 32–37. IEEE (2017)
18. Alsariera, Y.A., Adeyemo, V.E., Balogun, A.O., Alazzawi, A.K.: AI meta-learners and extra-trees algorithm for the detection of phishing websites. IEEE Access **8**, 142532–142542 (2020)
19. Jain, A.K., Gupta, B.B.: A machine learning based approach for phishing detection using hyperlinks information. J. Ambient. Intell. Humaniz. Comput. **10**(5), 2015–2028 (2018). https://doi.org/10.1007/s12652-018-0798-z
20. Feng, F., Zhou, Q., Shen, Z., Yang, X., Han, L., et al.: The application of a novel neural network in the detection of phishing websites. J. Ambient Intell. Hum. Comput. 1–15 (2018)
21. Aburub, F., Hadi, W.: A new association classification based method for detecting phishing websites. J. Theor. Appl. Inf. Technol. **99**(1), 147–158 (2021)
22. Gandotra, E., Gupta, D.: An efficient approach for phishing detection using machine learning. In: Giri, K.J., Parah, S.A., Bashir, R., Muhammad, K. (eds.) Multimedia Security. AIS, pp. 239–253. Springer, Singapore (2021). https://doi.org/10.1007/978-981-15-8711-5_12

23. Shabudin, S., Sani, N.S., Ariffin, K.A., Aliff, M.: Feature selection for phishing website classification. Int. J. Adv. Comput. Sci. Appl. **11**(4), 587–595 (2020)
24. Subasi, A., Molah, E., Almkallawi, F., Chaudhery, T.J.: Intelligent phishing website detection using random forest classifier. In: IEEE International Conference on Electrical and Computing Technologies and Applications (ICECTA), Ras Al Khaimah, United Arab Emirates, pp. 1–5. IEEE (2017)
25. Yu, X.: Phishing websites detection based on hybrid model of deep belief network and support vector machine. In: IOP Conference Series: Earth and Environmental Science, vol. 602, no. 1, pp. 1–9 (2020)
26. Patil, D.R., Patil, J.B.: Malicious web pages detection using feature selection techniques and machine learning. Int. J. High Perform. Comput. Netw. **14**(4), 473–488 (2019)
27. PhishTank. Developer information. http://phishtank.org/developer_info.php. Accessed 28 Feb 2021
28. Dua, D., Graff, C.: UCI machine learning repository. School of Information and Computer Science, University of California, Irvine, CA, USA. https://archive.ics.uci.edu/ml/datasets/Phishing+Websites. Accessed 10 Jan 2021
29. Jiang, Y., Tong, G., Yin, H., Xiong, N.: A pedestrian detection method based on genetic algorithm for optimize XGBoost training parameters. IEEE Access **7**, 118310–118321 (2019)

OSINT Explorer: A Tool Recommender Framework for OSINT Sources

Alwan Abdullah, Shams A. Laghari, Ashish Jaisan, and Shankar Karuppayah[✉]

National Advanced IPv6 Centre, Universiti Sains Malaysia, Glugor, Pulau Pinang, Malaysia
alwan@student.usm.my, {shamsularfeen,ashishjaisan}@nav6.usm.my,
kshankar@usm.my

Abstract. The Internet has had a profound impact on our daily lives since its inception. It has become a determining element in how we interact and do business, particularly in terms of our ability to access information, jobs, our ability to stay connected, our company's chances of survival, our ability to thrive in the workplace, and education, etc. There are several everyday problems for which the Internet provides resources, such as software and hardware solutions that we may rely on in times of crisis. The abundance of software and computational services offered by the Internet has introduced new challenges for what was previously unknown, i.e., within the plethora of resources available, users cannot work out which tool to use to solve the problem. The collection and review of freely accessible material, often from online sources that are freely accessible to the general public, is referred to as open-source intelligence (OSINT). With the plethora of OSINT tools available, it has become difficult for users to choose the best tool for the given problem. This article presents a framework for identifying OSINT tools that are most appropriate for solving given problems. The proposed framework is user-friendly and provides tools based on MIME types or advanced search features. The framework has been evaluated by subject experts and has shown to be an invaluable resource for end-user tool recommendations.

Keywords: Open-source intelligence · OSINT · Cybersecurity · Open-source information

1 Introduction

With the Internet's never-ending growth and the amount of data available on it, it has become a place where sensitive information is stacked for professional and personal collaboration. If the data were to be compromised, the damages would be catastrophic. Cybercriminal aims to obtain sensitive information from personal and professional cooperation and use it to their financial benefits. With every activity in cyberspace, there will be a trail of data. This data can be useful for performing forensic analysis to gain information on the culprit. The intelligence cycle is where the intelligence is obtained, produced, and made available to the user.

There are various intelligence collection disciplines [1] (ICD) including Human Intelligence (HUMINT), Signals Intelligence (SIGINT), Imagery Intelligence (IMINT),

© Springer Nature Singapore Pte Ltd. 2021
N. Abdullah et al. (Eds.): ACeS 2021, CCIS 1487, pp. 389–400, 2021.
https://doi.org/10.1007/978-981-16-8059-5_24

Measurement and Signatures Intelligence (MASINT), and Open-Source Intelligence (OSINT).

OSINT is the category on which we will be focusing our research in this study. With OSINT, a trail of available information can track and gather information about that cyber-criminal and help track and prevent future attacks. Open-Source Intelligence (OSINT) is a collection of public records from open-source data outlets such as mass media, news networks, forums, etc., along with sophisticated compilation and analysis techniques [2]. The information found helps the analysts to achieve their goals. For example, Law enforcement agencies gathering intelligence using online public resources to prevent crimes. OSINT is now commonly adopted by governments and by Intelligence agencies for carrying out their investigations and fighting against cybercrime [3]. However, it is not only used for state relations but referred instead to many different purposes. Researchers have claimed that up to 90 [4] percent of the Soviet Union's intelligence was obtained from open-source material. It has become easier to gather vast volumes of data with the advent of electronic records and arrange information to satisfy the needs of everyone, including researchers and adversaries.

Information collected from open sources may also provide beneficial clues about the operations and resources of an enterprise. Open access materials may also offer information on corporate dynamics, technological procedures, and analysis practices that are not otherwise accessible. It's also possible to derive sensitive data or trade secrets as open-source data is collected. This is particularly valid for research that has been published in professional and academic journals. Analyzing journal papers written by various scientific agency members will also derive a substantial interpretation of research and development activities.

Finally, information gathered from open sources is often time-sensitive and may only be accessible in the early phases of a disaster or emergency. However, there are downsides to using open-source intelligence; for example, in military or research publications, papers sometimes reflect a potential or ideal capacity rather than a real ability. Censorship can also restrict the disclosure of crucial knowledge required to arrive at a thorough interpretation of an enemy's actions, or the press may be used as part of an attempt to mislead deliberately. OSINT has several information sources some are listed below:

- government data and public reports, budgets, hearings, telephone directories, press conferences, websites, and speeches
- commercial data and images, financial and industrial evaluations, as well as databases
- Photos and videos, including metadata

However, there are many tools out there and a new researcher who does not know about OSINT Tool; thus, it will be challenging to navigate and decide which tool is helpful for him and which is not. This study aims to create a tool recommender system for OSINT sources. The proposed framework aims to help researchers pick which OSINT tools are relevant to the data they have to process. Furthermore, this study attempts to create a file validator to validate the file's file signature and check if the file has been altered with malicious code. The tool recommender framework is a web-based system for users to discover and learn which tool to choose given a specific input MIME type.

The paper is further organized into sections. Section 2 describes the history and related work in depth. Section 3 details the proposed framework's methodology. Section 4 details the framework's implementation. The assessment methodology is discussed in Sect. 5, and the findings and future work are discussed in Sect. 6.

2 Background and Related Work

This section discusses NATO categories for the information and intelligence, Intelligence Collection Disciplines (ICD), the latest Intelligence Disciplines (OSINT), and the OSINT Framework [5]. The OSINT framework was created to gather information from freely available tools and materials. The aim is to assist users in locating free OSINT tools.

2.1 Open-Source Intelligence

OSINT refers to all publicly accessible information, which encompasses both online and offline resources. OSINT relied on publicly accessible sources, while ICD sources, such as SIGINT, HUMINT, and so on, are often private. The authors of [6] suggested a paradigm for integrating Digital Forensic Intelligence (DFINT) with Open-Source Intelligence (OSINT). The authors have outlined it as follows:

1. Commence (Scope/Tasking), The concentration, goals, and scope of the study are outlined to allow for the planning and guidance of the overall evaluation
2. Prepare, gathering equipment and expertise, including network security, legal authority approval, and covert considerations
3. Identify and collect, identify devices with potential evidence, and undergo examination and documentation according to policies
4. Data Reduction by Selective Imaging (DRbSI), a digital forensic subset of data is collected from the identified device or media
5. Quick Analysis and Entity Extraction, analyzing, and extracting an entity using software (e.g., Internet Evidence Finder, RegRipper, and Bulk Extractor). After using the proposed framework (DFINT + OSINT), the authors extracted the data from the dataset they were using. Then they proceeded to the next stage by using Maltego CE to expand their knowledge about the asset that lies within their extracted data. It resulted in additional data matches, expanding their knowledge related to the test data entities, including associated URL locations with references to the email addresses and entities contained within the dataset.

The preceding outline demonstrated the process by which OSINT was integrated into DFINT. The author began by defining the issue and the desired outcome. The second phase was to take the necessary steps to establish the framework, such as obtaining permission from the appropriate legal body. The next stage was to find and acquire devices that could contain evidence. Data Reduction by Selective Imaging was the fourth phase (DRbSI). After completing all of these processes, the author collected data using the proposed framework and utilized Maltego CE to further improve understanding of the retrieved data.

OSINT is a valuable resource that researchers and cybersecurity specialists may use. Regrettably, a plethora of instruments prohibit people from completely benefiting from it. As a result, we strive to make it simpler for cybersecurity specialists to employ OSINT techniques and accomplish their objectives.

2.2 Nato Classification

NATO Has classified information and intelligence into four categories [7] based on the type of information. This classification will help to understand which type of information falls into which category.

1. Open-Source Data (OSD): OSD is the raw data that coming from a primary source, can be satellite images, a photo, or a personal letter.
2. Open-source information (OSINF): OSINF comprises data that can be assembled, usually by providing some sort of filtering and validation. OSINF is Generic knowledge, which is typically widespread Distributed. Newspaper, Books, Broadcasting, and regular general updates are part of this world of OSIF.
3. Open-Source Intelligence (OSINT): OSINT is material that has been purposely found, discriminated against, distilled, and disseminated to a small group, usually the commander and his immediate staff, to resolve a particular problem. In other words, OSINT extends the validated intelligence method to the vast range of open sources of information and generates intelligence.
4. Validated OSINT (OSINT-V): OSINT-V is the knowledge that can be applied to a very high degree of confidence. It can be generated by an all-source intelligence specialist, with access to confidential intelligence sources, whether working for a nation or a coalition staff. It may also come from an open-source protected source, in which case questions about its authenticity cannot be raised (images of aircraft landing at an airport and the information is broadcasted in the media).

2.3 OSINT Framework

OSINT Framework [8] is a web-based framework that recommends OSINT tools to help people find free OSINT tools based on sources. The user can find various OSINT sources and their tools. Some may require money to unlock additional features. The creator has categorized the tools into four categories:

(**T**)   Indicates a link to a tool that must be installed and run locally
(**D**)   Google Dork
(**R**)   Requires registration
(**M**)   Indicates a URL that contains the search term, and the URL itself must be edited manually

The author has created the website with an information security point of view. Since then, the response was outstanding, and the author stated that the framework would be extended, and new features will be added. However, in its present state, the OSINT Framework does not cover all OSINT sources and its associated tools.

3   Proposed Framework

In this section, we will be discussing the proposed framework.

OSINT framework required a rule-based recommender system to recommend tools to the user base on the input that the user provides. The proposed system has three-step. The first step is Preprocessing data resource that contains categories, tools, mapping process, and ratings. Categories contain the OSINT sources, tools will contain OSINT tools, mapping will be the connection between the categories and the tools, and the last one will be the rating that the user will provide for the OSINT tools. The second step will be the recommender mechanism which contains user input. The user will have three options for the input: upload a file(s), input a keyword(s), or dropdown menu. The upload function will have two mappings on the front end to determine the MIME type for the file. Fig. 1 represents the proposed framework.

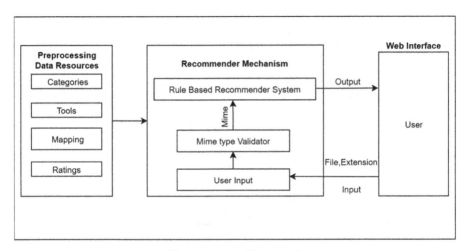

Fig. 1. Proposed framework

Next is MIME type validator. MIME type validator has two functions designed to detect and verify the file MIME type of the uploaded file the first one is:

1. File signature: This mapping was designed to determine the file MIME type based on the signature for the uploaded file(s). For instance, a user may have a *.docx file that has been renamed to png/image. The modified png/image extension has no effect on the highlighted file, and the original *.docx file may still be retrieved using the proposed framework. There is a possibility that the user may upload a file with a signature that is not included in the framework's library. The system will then switch to the second MIME detection algorithm.

2. MIME-type J.S.: This function is designed as a fallback mechanism for situations when the first function cannot correctly detect the file MIME type. This mechanism will send the file extension without checking the file signature. For example, if an image file ends with.png, the function will conclude the file MIME type as a png. If

both MIME detection algorithms provide inconsistent results, a popup window will prompt the user to choose the MIME type for which the user desired the response. Otherwise, the user will be redirected to the result page. Once the user provides input to the framework, an SQL statement will be sent to query the information stored in the database and fetch the results. The database population can be done either manually or automated (more on that in Sect. 4).

The final step will be the web interface where the user can view the results (tools) Fig. 2 represent the full flow of the system.

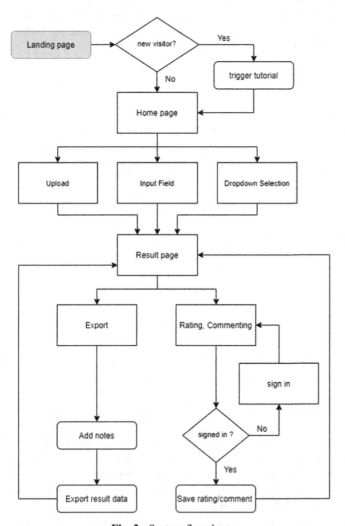

Fig. 2. System flowchart

4 The Implementation Steps

4.1 Scraping

This section outlines how we scraped the Github repository [9]. The proposed system enables users to enter the sources manually or through the use of a scraper. We extracted approximately 81 sources from the website [9] using a scraper tool. A scraper is a software program used to extract data from websites. The scraper is used to automate the process; otherwise, manually entering each item would be a tedious and time-consuming process. Scraping is an automated process, and it will be repeated on a periodic basis. After scraping is complete, the newly scraped tools will be added to the database alongside the current tools. In addition, Node.js is employed in the framework. Node.js an open-source, cross-platform framework that uses JavaScript language. Node.js is designed to build scalable network applications.

After installing Nodejs, we scraped the GitHub repository [9] using the Cheerio library [9]. Cheerio is a JavaScript library that enables users to extract data from websites and export it in any format desired. Cheerio is built on top of fb55/htmlparser2 [10], a parser for HTML pages that allows for user customization of the output data structure. The scraper is a script that was coded using NodeJS and Cheerio to scrape the HTML and store them into the database.

4.2 Store into the Database

After the first step is done, the next step is to import the data into the database. MySQL was used as the OSINT framework database. MySQL is an open-source relational database management system [11]. We utilize MySQL as the choice of the database because it was ranked top 10 free relational database management systems [11]. Using MySQL will enable the user to create, delete or modify the tables inside the database, and control the user access to the database. We will be exporting the scraped data into SQL format and import it into our MySQL database. represents the database structure.

4.3 Laravel

For the proposed framework, we used Laravel. Laravel is a web application framework using PHP language. We used HTML, CSS, and JavaScript for the front end of our proposed framework.

4.4 OSINT Framework Modules

The following list will be representing the modules that are included in the proposed OSINT Framework.

1. Tutorial module: The tutorial module appears the first time, and it is intended to assist users in becoming familiar with the OSINT framework.

- Automated activation: this will trigger once the user has visited the web platform for the first time. Once the user visits the web platform, the system will search for the tutorial cookie on the local system. The framework relies on cookies to keep track of user sessions. The absence of a cookie on the local machine indicates that the user has never visited the website before; as a result, a tutorial will be launched to assist the user in becoming familiar with the system.
- Manual activation: Alternatively, users may access the tutorial by clicking on the button located in the top right corner.

2. User-input module: Users may interact with the system in two ways: assisted search and manual selection.

   a. **Assisted search:** a first option available for the user, and it's divided into two sub options
   Upload a file(s): The user can upload a file using the upload file button. The user may also upload multiple files at once, and based on the binary signature [12], the framework will check for the signature in its signature library. If it finds it, it will send the extension to the backend to fetch the result. Suppose the binary signature is not available in the signature library as some files like JavaScript files don't have a fixed binary signature. In that case, it will send the file extension to the backend. Once the file extension is sent to the backend, it is mapped to the OSINT category mapping, and the user is redirected to the result page to view the results.
   Input field search: This is the second option that the users can use to search for tools. With this option, the user needs to input a keyword, for example, pcap. Additionally, the framework provides the user with the option of inputting multiple keywords at once, separated by commas.
   b. **Manual selection:** last option available to the user is to select an OSINT category from a dropdown list.

3. Result module: this module is responsible for getting the search query from the user-input module, fetching the result, and sending it to the frontend. The following options are available to the user:

   a. **Export results:** this feature allows users to export and store results in a variety of different formats. This feature is available to users so they may view results offline.
   b. Instead of searching for each MIME type separately, users may search for many MIME types at the same time. Naturally, the final page will include the results of each MIME-type specified. The framework provides options to the users to filter the results by one or more MIME types.

4. Feedback modules: The users' feedback into the system is the most important module in the framework to improve accuracy and effectiveness. The users may suggest improvements based on their experience and interaction with the system; for example, users may suggest a new tool to be added to the database or report a tool listed

in a wrong category or point to a not working tool. Comments posted by users are another type of user feedback to the system. This feature allows users to report a tool that is in the incorrect category or isn't functioning. Ratings are another type of feedback that may influence the results, i.e., the tool with the most 5-star ratings, for example, will be at the top of the result page.

5   Design of Evaluation

We developed a case study questionnaire and circulated it to evaluate the OSINT framework and its usefulness. We have employed the evaluation model similar to the study [13], in which the authors gathered expert opinions from three domain experts. The questionnaire was designed with two primary objectives: the first was to determine if the system was functional and operating correctly, and the second was to get feedback from evaluators assessing the user interface and ease of use. Four distinct scenarios were created in order to attain the desired results.

- Scenario 1 (File Validator)

    The first scenario was for the upload function. This scenario aimed to test the upload MIME type functionality. The upload function was built to help users find tools for the files by extracting the files' MIME type. The upload functionality has a map to determine the file MIME type from the extension. For example, a user has a png image file; however, the extension has been modified to docx. The user will follow the docx extension as shown by the operating system in the file listing, and the file has an MSWord icon. When the user opens the file, the default application associated with docx would be M.S. Word, which will open the file but fail to render it properly because it is not a docx file. This scenario is designed to test and identify the real application associated with the file. That is, in this case, it is image software. We have provided nine different files that have been altered with random extensions to conceal the identity of the real file. For example, file#1 is a png image file with a docx extension. The system evaluators have been provided nine files to test the functionality of the system in this scenario. The evaluators were supplied with the URL to the framework in order to access the framework and complete the tasks stated in scenario one. The questionnaire included the predicted outcome, and evaluators were required to validate it.

- Scenario 2 (Input field)

    The first scenario is only applicable when users have files and are unaware of the tools associated with those files. For situations when users know the MIME type or file extension, scenario one is not useful. When users are aware of the MIME or file extension, the framework includes capabilities that allow them to explore the tools without uploading files by entering the MIME or file extension in the search box. The questionnaire included the predicted outcome, and evaluators were required to validate it.

- Scenario 3 (Rating)

Scenario three aims to test the tools' rating functionality. In addition to the structured questions, the respondents are also provided a text box to freely write their experiences, shortcomings, and improvements to better the framework. These comments are later reviewed by the administrator and acted upon as deemed fit. The questionnaire included the predicted outcome, and evaluators were required to validate it.

- Scenario 4 (Filter System)

Scenario four is designed to get user feedback on the filtering functionality. After the user obtains the result, a comprehensive list of tools may appear. The questionnaire included the predicted outcome, and evaluators were required to validate it.

6   Results

In this section, we will be sharing the result of the evaluation. In the introduction, we ran a test for the tutorial we had. The tutorial functionality was design to trigger automatically the first time the user visits the website. After that, a cookie will be stored in the user browser preventing the tutorial from automatically triggering.

The Expert-I had some issues because we have given him a shortened URL it does not work. After he notified us, we fixed it by removing the shortened URL, and the next two experts had no issue with the tutorial function.

As stated in Sect. 5, three experts have tested and evaluated the framework [13], who have experience using OSINT tools for cybersecurity.

The experts agreed with the anticipated output provided to them in the evaluation form. The study's findings were established by the evaluators using the evaluation form questionnaires, and the same questionnaires were shared with all of the experts who tested out the framework. Base on the feedback we received, it was concluded that the system is working, and the research objectives have been achieved. Expert-I, Expert-II, and Expert-III were keen to try and use the framework to find tools.

The overall usability of the Framework was evaluated further with another questionnaire. this questionnaire was answered by the experts and the results are visualized in Fig. 3. The following are the questions provided to the experts.

1. The Framework is interactive and easy to use
2. The Framework has all the basic functionalities
3. I can see myself using and benefiting from Framework

As you can see in Fig. 3, the experts gave scores on scale of one to five. The average score the ease of use and interactivity of the framework is 4.6 out of 5. The availability of basic functionality got an average of 3.6 out of 5. The usability and benefits of the framework averaged 4.6 out of 5.

Another question we gave them did you have any suggestions to improve the system? And Expert-I has suggested adding more descriptions for the tools on the result page, and in doing so, it will be easier for the user to understand what each tool does. A similar suggestion we had was from Expert-II, where they suggested the same suggestion as Expert-I. Expert-I made another suggestion is to view the comments that users leave on the tools in doing so the other user can view the comment. Based on the comments received, we have improved the system user interface to make it easier for them to navigate the framework and understand it better.

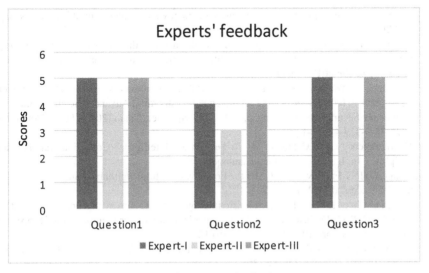

Fig. 3. Experts' feedback

7 Conclusion and Future Work

Open-source information is a multi-factoring approach for data collection, analysis, and decision-making in an intelligence environment open to the public. OSINT has been around for a long time, but the problem that users face is that finding tools is complicated, and since there are many tools, users can't find the correct tools that can help them with their data. Additionally, for users who are not familiar with OSINT tools, it might take them hours to find one tool that can help them.

With that, an OSINT framework was designed to help users with finding tools. Additional features can quickly help users find tools for their files by uploading the file to the recommender system to find tools to help them with their file(s). The framework also has other features, such as getting input on the MIME type or manual selection. With this framework, finding tools for a new user has been solved since we have collected a large number of tools and mapped them to specific categories, and we can recommend them according to their needs. However, some features can be added to improve the framework.

Future studies can add these features to further improve the framework. Future studies can improve the mapping by adding more file-MIME signatures to improve the upload file-MIME detection. Since it's a web-based framework, future studies can go one step further and design software solutions for windows or mobile devices to recommend tools based on the device's operating system. Thus, instead of visiting the website, they can use the app to fetch the OSINT tools.

References

1. Intelligence Cycle. https://www.intelligencecareers.gov/icintelligence.html,last. Accessed 11 April 2021
2. Glassman, M., Kang, M.J.: Intelligence in the internet age: the emergence and evolution of open source intelligence (OSINT). Comput. Hum. Behav. **28**, 673–682 (2012). https://doi.org/10.1016/j.chb.2011.11.014
3. Tabatabaei, F., Wells, D.: OSINT in the context of cyber-security. In: Akhgar, B., Bayerl, P., Sampson, F. (eds.) Open Source Intelligence Investigation. Advanced Sciences and Technologies for Security Applications, pp. 213–231. Springer, Cham (2016). https://doi.org/10.1007/978-3-319-47671-1_14
4. The Interagency OPSEC Support Staff: Section 2 - Intelligence Collection Activities and Disciplines. In: Intelligence Threat Handbook (1996)
5. lockfale/OSINT-Framework: OSINT Framework. https://github.com/lockfale/osint-framework. Accessed 11 April 2021
6. Quick, D., Choo, K.K.R.: Digital forensic intelligence: data subsets and open source intelligence (DFINT+OSINT): a timely and cohesive mix. Futur. Gener. Comput. Syst. **78**, 558–567 (2018). https://doi.org/10.1016/j.future.2016.12.032
7. Kernan, W.F., (SACEUR), E.: NATO OSINT Handbook v1.2, vol. 136, p. 1306 (2002). https://doi.org/10.1001/archsurg.136.11.1306
8. Lockfale: OSINT Framework. https://osintframework.com/
9. jivoi/awesome-osint: Acurated list of amazingly awesome OSINT. https://github.com/jivoi/awesome-osint. Accessed 11 April 2021
10. Forgiving HTML and XML parser. https://github.com/fb55/htmlparser2/. Accessed 19 January 2021
11. Top 10 Free Relational Database Management Systems (RDBMS) in 2020 - Reviews, Features, Pricing, Comparison - PAT RESEARCH: B2B Reviews, Buying Guides & Best Practices. https://www.predictiveanalyticstoday.com/top-free-relational-database-management-system-rdbms/. Accessed 19 January 2021
12. Bielska, A., Noa Rebecca Kurz, Yves Baumgartner, V.B.: Open source intelligence tools and resources handbook, vol. 148, pp. 148–162 (2020)
13. Anbar, M.F.R.: Graphical Web Based Tool for Generating Query from Star Schema (2009)

Propose a Flow-Based Approach for Detecting Abnormal Behavior in Neighbor Discovery Protocol (NDP)

Abdullah Ahmed Bahashwan[(✉)] ⓘ, Mohammed Anbar[(✉)] ⓘ,
Selvakumar Manickamⓘ, Iznan Husainy Hasbullahⓘ,
and Mohammad A. Aladailehⓘ

National Advanced IPv6 Center (NAv6), Universiti Sains Malaysia (USM),
11800 Gelugor, Penang, Malaysia
bahashwan@student.usm.my, {anbar,selva,iznan,m_aladaileh2003}@usm.my

Abstract. Neighbour Discovery Protocol is vulnerable to various attacks, such as DoS flooding attack that uses excessive amount of Router Advertisement (RA) and Neighbour Solicitation (NS) messages to flood the network, causing congestion and breaking down the network. There are several existing approaches to detect RA and NS DoS flooding attacks. However, these approaches either rely on a packet-based traffic representation, which is inefficient for high-speed networks; or static threshold, which leads to high false-positive rate. Thus, this work proposes a flow-based approach with innovative design to detect RA and NS DoS flooding attacks. The proposed approach utilizes flow-based traffic representation to accommodate high-speed networks. Also, the proposed approach utilizes three algorithms to address the existing approaches' drawbacks: Entropy-Based Algorithm (EBA), Adaptive Threshold algorithm, and rule-based technique. The EBA is more sensitive and more appropriate for detecting abnormal network traffic. The Adaptive Threshold algorithm can be defined as dynamic values that are used as a baseline for NDP abnormal behavior. Finally, the rule-based technique can operate as a classifier of network traffic behavior and generate specific rules for detecting abnormal NDP-based attacks.

Keywords: Intrusion Detection System (IDS) · NDP abnormality · RA DoS flooding attack · NS DoS flooding attacks · Network traffic representation

1 Introduction

Internet Protocol version 4 (IPv4) addresses have been exhausted due to the rapid increases of internet users and emerging technologies, such as wireless applications, Internet-of-Things (IoT), and cloud computing [1–4]. All mentioned technologies expedited the exhaustion of IPv4 addresses in 2011. To overcome the IP address exhaustion problem, IPv6 was engineered and touted as a promising

© Springer Nature Singapore Pte Ltd. 2021
N. Abdullah et al. (Eds.): ACeS 2021, CCIS 1487, pp. 401–416, 2021.
https://doi.org/10.1007/978-981-16-8059-5_25

new internet protocol to replace IPv4 [5]. In addition, IPv6 is equipped with new features, such as stateless address auto-configuration, enormous IP addresses space, and mobility. All stated key features are enabled in any IPv6 networks or IPv6 nodes by default. Currently, many enterprises like Google and Facebook added IPv6 connectivity to their service offerings [6,7].

The IPv6 defines two main protocols, Internet Control Messages protocol version six (ICMPv6) and Neighbour Discovery Protocol (NDP). The ICMPv6 is the foundation of the IPv6 because it is accountable for several critical operations. For instance, ICMPv6 works as an intermediate director between the routers and nodes. Also, ICMPv6 plays a vital role in acknowledging the sender of any problems on the routing path. As an example, in case there is a router that wants to forward a packet to the distention node and this packet is too big. ICMPv6 is an essential and core protocol for IPv6 since the ICMPv6 protocol is encapsulated in IPv6 packets [8,9]. Figure 1 presents the ICMPv6 in IPv6 packet.

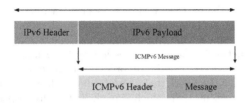

Fig. 1. Illustrates the ICMPv6 encapsulation in IPv6 Packet.

In addition, ICMPv6 also has two types of messages: ICMPv6 error messages and ICMPv6 informational messages. The ICMPv6 error messages begin at 1 and end at 127, while the ICMPv6 information messages begin at 128 and end at 255 [10]. Table 1 illustrates both message types.

Table 1. ICMPv6 information and error messages types

ICMPv6 messages	
Error messages	Informational messages
Destination Unreachable - Type 1	Echo Request - Type 128
Packet is Big - Type 2	Echo Reply - Type 129
Time Exceeded - Type 3	Router Solicitation - Type 133
Parameter Problem - Type 4	Router Advertisement - Type 134
Private Experimentation - Type 100	Neighbor Solicitation - Type 135
Private Experimentation - Type 101	Neighbor Advertisement - Type 136
Reserved for Expansion - Type 127	Redirect - Type 137
	Private Experimentation - Type 200
	Reserved for Expansion - Type 255

ICMPv6 follows a novel protocol called the NDP protocol. The NDP allows IPv6 nodes to discover other nodes on same link-local network [11]. The NDP functions on top of ICMPv6 because it utilizes five information messages, as mentioned in RFC 4861 [12], described below:

- Router Solicitation (RS) message, Type 133, is sent by hosts to the routers in the network via all-routers multicast address after successful IPv6 address configuration via Stateless Address Autoconfiguration (SLAAC).
- Router Advertisement (RA) message, Type 134, is sent by routers after start up or in response to RS message requests. Routers use this message to notify other nodes of their presence in the network. The RA message also conveys crucial information to other nodes like network prefix and Maximum Transmission Unit (MTU).
- Neighbor Solicitation (NS) message, Type 135, is used by hosts to inquire the link-layer address of newly joined nodes in a link-local network. This message assists Duplicate Address Detection (DAD) process to check the uniqueness of the host's IP address or to check the reachability of neighbors.
- Neighbor Advertisement (NA) message, Type 136, announces any changes to hosts IP addresses or media access control (MAC) addresses to other nodes in link-local network. This message is also used to respond to NS messages sent by others.
- Redirect Message (RM), Type 137, is used to forward network traffic from one router to other router [11,13].

The NDP is a fundamental protocol in IPv6 that allows IPv6-enabled hosts in the network to automatically configure their own IPv6 address and communicate with each other in the absence of network-wide verification entity. However, without authentication feature, the NDP is well-known as a vulnerable protocol that are susceptible to a variety of threats and attacks. For example, an internal attacker can spoof NDP messages to attempt a Denial of Service (DoS) attack [14].

The key contribution of this proposed approach is to come out with an effective flow-based traffic representation approach to detect abnormal NDP traffic in IPv6 networks due to NS and RA DoS flooding attacks. Additionally, the use of flow-based traffic representation accommodates high-speed networks. Other than an entropy-based algorithm, the proposed approach also adopts a dynamic threshold algorithm and a rule-based algorithm. Finally, the proposed approach attempts to address the limitation of our previous approach [15].

The overall structure of the proposed approach is as follows. Section 2 presents the background of the proposed flow-based approach. Section 3 covers the related works. Section 4 discusses the design of the proposed flow approach, followed by the discussion of the proposed flow approach in Sect. 5. Finally, Sect. 6 concludes the paper and presents several future works.

2   Background

This section presents the background of the proposed approach by introducing NDP-based DoS attacks (i.e., NS DoS attack and RA DoS attack) and the different types of network traffic representation (i.e., packet-based and flow-based).

2.1   NDP Based Attacks

The lack of authentication exposes the NDP to a variety of threats and attacks. As a result, attackers can easily use and exploit the NDP's five messages to execute several attacks. There are two main types of attacks on NDP: Man-in-the-Middle (MiTM) and Denial of Service (DoS) attacks. The replay attack, spoofed NA messages, and spoofed RA messages are all part of MiTM attack type. ICMPv6 flooding attacks (i.e., RA and NS DoS flooding attack), Smurf attack, and Duplicate Address Detection (DAD) attack are all part of DoS attack types [16]. Figure 2 illustrates the taxonomy of NDP-based attacks.

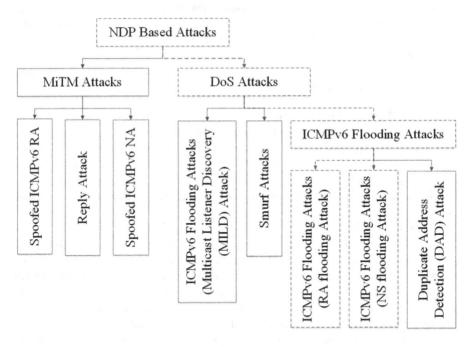

Fig. 2. Taxonomy of NDP based attacks [16].

The proposed approach only covers RA DoS flooding attack and NS DoS flooding attack since they are considered the major threat against IPv6 networks. In those attacks, the perpetrator floods the network with a large volume of abnormal traffic causing congestion that breaks down the network [16]. The following subsection discusses the RA and NS attacks in more detail.

RA-DoS Flooding Attack

The RA message is an ICMPv6 information message. RA message plays many vital roles in IPv6 networks. For example, a router utilized RA message to update other routers about their presence on the networks and offers network prefix information to newly joined IPv6 hosts to generate their IPv6 address using SLAAC [14].

Figure 3(A) illustrates the RA and RS message exchanges between nodes in IPv6 local network. The default gateway node sends RA messages to the multicast group (FF02::1) targeting all IPv6 nodes in the network. This allows all nodes on IPv6 local network to configure their routing table and default getaway address accordingly. The perpetrator exploits this condition to impersonate the default gateway by sending spoofed RA messages containing false prefix values into the network [14].

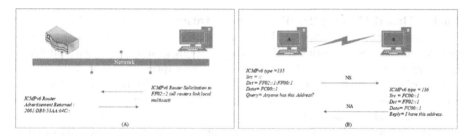

Fig. 3. (A) Presents the stateless address auto-configuration, (B) Illustrates the NS and NA exchange messages between nodes

NS-DoS Flooding Attack

The NS message is a type of ICMPv6 information message used to validate IPv6 addresses and verify the local neighbor's link layer address. In a normal scenario, any node in a link-local network can send NS messages at any time to request the destination node's link layer address. Similarly, a node attempting to resolve an IPv6 address also transmits NS message to the destination node. As soon as the destination node receives the NS message, it instantly responds with an NA message and updates its neighbor cache table. Figure 3(B) illustrates how nodes in the IPv6 network exchange NS and NA messages.

The NS DoS flooding attack occurs when the target nodes are forced to create redundant fake entries that map the MAC address and IPv6 address in their neighbor cache tables. As a result, the fake entries will exhaust the kernel memory because the neighbor cache table is a finite resource; therefore resulting in targeted nodes to be unreachable. Consequently, the NS messages are transmitted to the multicast group (FF02::1), all nodes on the same network that have been getting the spoofed NS messages immediately refresh their neighbor caches table correspondingly. In summary, the attack is only successful because the victim node believes that the attacker node is trustworthy and dependable [15,16].

2.2   Representation of Network Traffic

Recently, advancement in network technologies lead to faster network speed and higher bandwidth along with the number of users, which increase the network throughput that has to be considered by any intrusion detection systems. There are two categories of IDS: host-based intrusion detection system (HIDS) and network-based intrusion detection system (NIDS). The NIDS is more capable of handling high-rate network compared to HIDS. NIDS has two types based on the network traffic representation used: packet-based NIDS and flow-based NIDS [15,17]. The subsequent subsections discuss both forms in detail.

Packet-Based (NIDS) Traffic Representation

Packet-based NIDS is a popular IDS approach that performs deep packet inspection on all captured network traffic, including ingress and egress, without filtration and skipping any packet. So, these systems capturing the packets as it is representing. TCP Dump and Wireshark are two examples of software tool commonly used for capturing network traffic, and they are typically placed at the edge point of the network [18].

The packet-based NIDS has some advantages over flow-based NIDS due to these systems having access to complete network packet information, including the entire "packet header and payload", of all ingress and egress traffic allowing deep packet inspection. However, there are also some disadvantages since the advent of high speed networks that require NIDS to process a huge volume of network traffic packets which adds more complexity, which are extremely ineffective [15].

Flow-Based (NIDS) Traffic Representation

A flow is a sophisticated approach to represent network traffic. It is defined in RFC3917 as a pair of endpoints' IP addresses passing through monitoring or detecting systems within a specific time intervals [19]. IPv4 flow has five network traffic attributes: protocol type (i.e., UDP or TCP), source and destination addresses, and source and destination port numbers. The IPv4 flow construction cannot be used to represent ICMPv6 network traffic since there are no source and destination ports. For that reason, [15] used the source IP address, destination IP address, and ICMPv6 message type (i.e., RA = 134 and NS = 135) attributes to represent the ICMPv6 traffic flow.

Flow-based traffic representation has some advantages over packet-based traffic representation, such as (i) create smaller size datasets resulting in faster analysis of network traffic, (ii) eliminates extra network details, and (iii) more suited for high speed networks. Many researchers have demonstrated the superiority of flow-based NIDS over packet-based NIDS, such as [15,18,19]. Table 2 compares the strengths and weaknesses of flow-based and packet-based NIDS.

Table 2. Comparison of flow-based and packet-based traffic representation.

Flow-based NIDS	Packet-based NIDS
Strengths	
- In this approach inspect only the packet header	- Deep packet Inspecting (header and payload)
- Maintaining the privacy	- The data is immediately presented at NIDS, which means no delay
- Suitable for high-speed networks	
- Lightweight flow-based NIDS	
Weaknesses	
- Not all data will be filtered	- Inspect all the network traffic without filtration
- Extra preprocessing to construct the network flows	- In case of encrypted payload, signature matching will be impossible
- In flow-based, there are delays in data catching and accessibility to the NIDS	- Exposing the confidential information
	- Heavyweight packet-based NIDS
	- Not efficient for high-speed networks

3   Related Works

IDS protects computer networks by monitoring the traffic and identifying malicious attempt at breaking into the networks. There are various types of IDSs implemented to detect NDP attacks. This section discusses three types of IDSs, including Monitoring tools, Rule-based IDSs, Signature-based IDSs, Statistical-based IDSs (i.e., Entropy-based IDS), and Machine Learning-based IDSs. Figure 4 illustrates the taxonomy of existing IDSs.

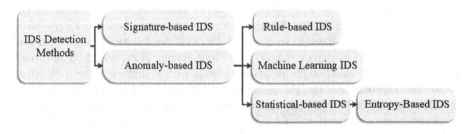

Fig. 4. Taxonomy of IDS detection methods.

There are many ICMPv6 monitoring tools designed to monitor network traffic for abnormal ICMPv6 message behavior and inform the system administrator. The most common monitoring tools are [20–22]. However, monitoring tools lack scalability and are not a proper IDS since they are not designed to take any action against suspicious activities identified. Signature-based IDSs, such as [23–25], depend on particular patterns to identify and detect attacks. SIDS typically stores hundreds or thousands of signature patterns and every pattern represents an exact type of attack. These systems can only detect attacks according to predefined signatures stored in their databases. However, SIDSs are not efficient in detecting ICMPv6 DDoS and DoS attacks because of their function limitations and predefined signatures stored in their databases. Also, SIDS cannot detect zero-day attacks [18].

Rule-Based IDSs, such as [6,26,27], rely on a predefined knowledge of network traffic behavior to identify and detect attacks, and then trigger an alert if abnormal behavior was detected. According to [26,27], those approaches work well to detect DoS attacks and Man-in-the-middle attack. However, they are resource consuming, particularly in the case of DDoS and DoS attacks. [6] proposed a rule-based technique for detecting ICMPv6 anomalous behaviors. However, their approach utilizes rule-based technique with predetermined threshold values, resulting in high false-positive rates.

Machine learning-based IDSs are a broad topic in IDSs. These systems utilize machine learning to automatically build an advanced detection model [28]. Because of machine learning's efficiency in learning attack behaviors, it has been widely deployed in various IDSs to identify a variety of attacks, including NDP attacks. [5] proposed a technique to detect the presence of RA flooding attacks in IPv6 networks. However, the technique only detect RA attacks. Meanwhile, [11] proposed a framework to detect ICMPv6 echo request DDoS attacks using a back-propagation neural network algorithm. However, the approach is designed to detect ICMPv6 echo request DDoS attacks. [29] proposed an approach to detect RA flooding attacks by using several classification techniques, and their proposed approach achieved an acceptable detection accuracy for detecting RA flooding attacks. [30] proposed an approach to detect RA flooding attacks using the SVM algorithm. [18] proposed a flow-based approach to detect ICMPv6 DDoS attacks, and their approach achieved an acceptable detection accuracy.

Another type of IDS detection method is based on statistical methods (i.e., Entropy-based IDS). It is one of the most effective detection mechanisms nowadays. The entropy is the most efficient network traffic feature that indicate the presence of abnormal traffic. Many researchers have proposed entropy-based IDSs to detect NDP attacks, such as [14,15]. [14] used entropy algorithm and adaptive threshold to detect RA DoS flooding attack. However, their approach relies on a packet-based traffic representation, which is inefficient for high speed networks. The proposal by [15] uses a combination of entropy, static threshold, and flow-based traffic representation to detect RA and NS attacks. However, this approach uses a static threshold which leads to high false-positive (FP) rates. Table 3 summarizes the limitations and weaknesses of related works.

Table 3. limitations of existing mechanisms

Mechanisms	Limitations
Signature-based IDS	
[23–25]	- Limited to IPv6 signatures attacks
	- Unable to understand IPv6 features
	- Powerless to spot the zero-day attack
	- Unable to detect DDoS attacks
Rule-based IDS	
[26,27]	- Using the probe packets that will consume the network bandwidth
[6]	- Rule-based technique with predetermined threshold values
Machine learning-based IDS	
[5]	- Detect RA flooding attacks
[11]	- Detect ICMPv6 ECHO Request Attack only
[29]	- Detect RA flooding attacks with acceptable detection accuracy
[30]	- Detect RA DoS flooding attack only
[18]	- Achieved acceptable detection accuracy
Statistical (entropy)-based IDS	
[14]	- This approach relies on a packet-based method, which is inefficient for high-rate networks
[15]	- This approach uses a static threshold which leads to increases in the False Positive (FP) rates

4   Design of Proposed Flow-Based Approach

This section underlines the proposed flow-based approach, which comprises three phases to detect NDP abnormality from RA and NS attacks. Figure 5 illustrates the proposed flow approach architecture.

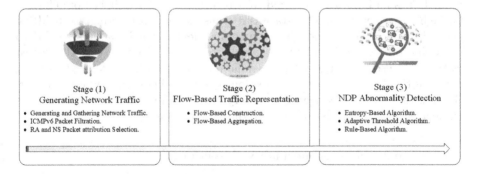

Stage (1)
Generating Network Traffic
- Generating and Gathering Network Traffic.
- ICMPv6 Packet Filtration.
- RA and NS Packet attribution Selection.

Stage (2)
Flow-Based Traffic Representation
- Flow-Based Construction.
- Flow-Based Aggregation.

Stage (3)
NDP Abnormality Detection
- Entropy-Based Algorithm.
- Adaptive Threshold Algorithm.
- Rule-Based Algorithm.

Fig. 5. Architecture of proposed approach

4.1   Stage 1- Gathering and Capturing Network Traffic

The first stage of the proposed flow-based approach involves gathering and collecting network traffic. It comprises three steps, as follows.

Capturing Network Traffic

This step involves capturing the required network traffic via the monitoring host using the Wireshark packet capture tool. The captured network traffic includes both normal and anomalous traffic, which are then stored as datasets. Then the datasets serve as the input to the next step.

ICMPv6 Packet Filtration

This step removes irrelevant network traffic from the dataset to reduce the dataset's size. The filtration process starts by filtering out non-ICMPv6 traffic, followed by additional pre-processing to only retain the RA and NS messages in the datasets, which are then passed to the next step.

RA/NS Packets Attribution Selection

This stage selects the crucial network traffic features to be used in the subsequent stage. The features selected include source and destination IP addresses, ICMPv6 message types (i.e., RA or NS), and the time interval for detecting RA and NS DoS flooding attacks. To detect RA DoS flooding attacks, the features selected are source and destination IP addresses, ICMPv6 message types (i.e., RA), network prefix, and the time interval for detecting the attack. All features selected in this step will be used to create traffic flow representation in Stage 2.

4.2   Stage 2 - Flow-Based Traffic Representation

In general, there are two ways to represent network traffic: packet-based and flow-based. This research uses the flow-based traffic representation for several reasons. First, to protect confidential information by removing certain network details. Second, it is an innovative method to detect attacks. Third, it is more efficient for high speed networks. This stage is responsible for constructing the ICMPv6 network traffic features including source and destination IP address, ICMPv6 message types (i.e., RA and NS), network prefix, and time interval. All selected features are used to construct flow traffic representation format before passing it to the third stage for attack detection based on abnormal traffic behaviour. Besides, the flow will be aggregated every one second since there are a massive number of packets for just one second during the attack time [15].

4.3   Stage 3 - NDP Abnormality Detection

This stage adopts three advanced algorithms to detect RA and NS DoS attacks effectively. The algorithms are described in the following subsections.

Entropy-Based Algorithm

The entropy-based algorithm is considered one of the most effective techniques and most suitable for detecting abnormal network traffic. It is commonly used especially in network security field due to its efficiency in measuring the probability of incoming traffic flow into the network. Therefore, this research employs entropy-based algorithm to determine the distribution uncertainty of the network traffic features (i.e., source and destination IPv6 address, ICMPv6 message types "RA and NS" and network prefix) [15]. The main reason for deploying such an algorithm is to measure the randomness of the network traffic features. Equation 1 presents the entropy equation used.

$$H(X) = -\sum_{1-i}^{n} P_i \, log_2 \, P_i.$$ (1)

As can be seen from Eq. 1, let us assumes that X personates the dataset and the $X = x1, x2, x3. . . . . . . xn$, whereas the Pi is the probability of xn in X. [16].

Dynamic/Adaptive Threshold Algorithm

The dynamic or adaptive threshold algorithm is a sophisticated algorithm that is used in many field. It uses dynamic values that can be deployed as a threshold to detect abnormal NDP traffic resulted from NS and RA DoS flooding attacks. The base threshold values are chosen dynamically according to network traffic behavior. Any variation that exceeds the baseline values are considered abnormal traffic activity. This research uses the adaptive threshold since it is an efficient algorithm to monitor the network traffic changes over a given time interval. The value of the threshold is set adaptively based on an estimate of the mean number of packets, which is computed from recent traffic measurement. Also, the threshold values are generated adaptively according to an estimate of the mean value from the previous network traffic flow. The threshold is calculated using Eq. 2:

$$X_n \geqslant (\alpha + 1).\mu_n - 1$$ (2)

Where X_n is the number of packets in the nth time interval and $\mu_n - 1$ is the mean rate calculated from measurements prior to n. Here $\alpha > 0$ is the parameter that indicates the percentage above the mean value that is considered to be an indication of anomalous behavior. However, after direct execution of Eq. 2, there would possibly resulted in many false-positives. For this reason, a minor modification is required to enhance its function to generate an alarm after a certain number of consecutive violations of the threshold [31–33] as shown in Eq. 3.

$$\sum_{i=n-k+1}^{n} [X_n \geqslant (\alpha+1).\mu_n - 1] \geqslant K$$ (3)

Whereas k is the certain number of repeated threshold violations. In this proposed approach, k is 3, indicating the maximum number of threshold violations before the alert is triggered [14]. This proposed approach going to use an exponentially weighted moving average (EWMA) to compute the mean μ_n entropy value. The control chart (EWMA) is used to identify a change of average process and it can be defined as:

$$\mu_n = \lambda \cdot \mu + (1 - \lambda) \cdot X_n \qquad (4)$$

Where λ parameter defines the rate at which prior data entered into the calculation of the EWMA statistic. And the value of $\lambda = 1.0$ indicates the recent measurement impacts the EWMS. Henceforth, when there is a large value of λ that is closer to 1.0, it gives more weight to recent data and less weight to older one. The recommended λ parameter is usually between 0.5 and 0.2 in the interval. Therefore, this research will use 0.1 as λ parameter [14,33].

Rule-Based Algorithm

Rule-based algorithm is commonly used in IDSs and to solve complicated problems. An IDS can use rule-based algorithm to generate specific rules for detecting abnormal NDP traffic behavior resulted from RA and NS DoS attacks. The main contribution of this approach is to compare the entropy algorithm function output with the dynamic threshold values, using a rule-based Algorithm 1, where k is the maximum number of threshold violation before alarm is triggered (k = 3). If the entropy of RA and NS network traffic features exceeds the adaptive threshold value continuously for k times, it is considered an abnormal behavior or an attack.

Algorithm 1: Detecting RA and NS DoS Flooding Attacks.

Count = 0
*IF Entropy of RA/NS Network Traffic Features (i.e., Source IP address, Network Prefix) > Adaptive Threshold **then***
count = count +1
*If (count ≥ k) **then***
Alert = turn
End if
End if

Algorithm 1 increases the detection accuracy of the proposed flow-based approach.

5 Discussion

The proposed flow-based detection approach aims to detect abnormal NDP traffic behavior resulted from NS and RA DoS flooding attacks. This section compares the proposed flow-based detection approach with the existing approaches.

Table 4 illustrates the comparison of the proposed approach against the existing ones. The comparison is based on several aspects: (i) dataset type (i.e., generated dataset), (ii) network traffic representation, (iii) technique used (i.e., Entropy and Static Threshold or Entropy and Adaptive Threshold), and (iv) attack type (NS and RA DoS attack).

Table 4. Qualitative Comparison approaches

Approach	Year	Generated dataset	Network traffic representation		Technique			NDP attack	
			Flow-based	Packet-based	Entropy and adaptive threshold	Entropy and static threshold	RA DoS flooding attack	RA and NS DoS flooding attack	
[14]	2019	✓		✓	✓		✓		
[15]	2021	✓	✓			✓		✓	
This approach	2021	✓	✓		✓			✓	

As seen in Table 3, [14] is an approach that only detect RA DoS attacks. It utilized an entropy-based algorithm and dynamic threshold. However, it relied on packet-based traffic representation, which is unsuited for high-speed networks. [15] proposed a flow-based approach to detect RA and NS attacks. But, it has a low precision rate because of many false-positive results due to relying on a static threshold value. Overall, the proposed approach attempts to address all existing limitations by proposing a dependable flow-based approach that achieves a high detection accuracy and low false-positive rates compared to existing approaches in detecting abnormal NDP traffic behaviour from RA and NS DoS attacks.

6 Conclusion and Future Work

The IPv6 networks are vulnerable to many type of attacks due to lack of authentication on one of its core protocols, the NDP. Attackers can easily exploit the RA and NS messages to perform DoS flooding attacks by injecting a massive volume of RA or NS messages into the network. Unfortunately, there are no reliable detection approaches to protect the network from such attacks currently. Thus, this research proposed an efficient and reliable flow-based approach to protect IPv6 networks. The proposed approach consists of three essential stages. The first stage involves capturing and preprocessing network traffic. Second stage entails converting the captured network traffic into flow-based representation. Finally, the third stage is where the abnormality in NDP traffic flow is identified and detected by adapting entropy-based algorithms, adaptive threshold algorithms, and rule-based technique. The proposed approach is expected to accomplish high detection accuracy and low false-positive rate in detecting NS and RA DoS flooding attacks. In future work, an implementation of the proposed flow-based approach will be conducted by address the limitation of existing detection approaches to detect the RA and NS DoS flooding attacks reliability and effectively.

Acknowledgment. This work is supported by Ministry of Higher Education Malaysia under Fundamental Research Grant Scheme with Project Code: FRGS/1/2019/ICT03/USM/02/3.

References

1. Al-Ani, A., Anbar, M., Al-Ani, A.K., Hasbullah, I.H.: DHCPv6Auth: a mechanism to improve DHCPv6 authentication and privacy. Sādhanā **45**(1), 1–11 (2020). https://doi.org/10.1007/s12046-019-1244-4
2. Bahashwan, A.A.O., Manickam, S.: A brief review of messaging protocol standards for internet of things (IoT). J. Cyber Secur. Mob. **8**, 1–14 (2019). https://doi.org/10.13052/2245-1439.811
3. Bahashwan, A.A., Anbar, M., Abdullah, N.: New architecture design of cloud computing using software defined networking and network function virtualization technology. In: Saeed, F., Mohammed, F., Gazem, N. (eds.) IRICT 2019. AISC, vol. 1073, pp. 705–713. Springer, Cham (2020). https://doi.org/10.1007/978-3-030-33582-3_66
4. Bahashwan, A.A., Anbar, M., Abdullah, N., Al-Hadhrami, T., Hanshi, S.M.: Review on common IoT communication technologies for both long-range network (LPWAN) and short-range network. In: Saeed, F., Al-Hadhrami, T., Mohammed, F., Mohammed, E. (eds.) Advances on Smart and Soft Computing. AISC, vol. 1188, pp. 341–353. Springer, Singapore (2021). https://doi.org/10.1007/978-981-15-6048-4_30
5. Anbar, M., Abdullah, R., Al-Tamimi, B.N., Hussain, A.: A machine learning approach to detect router advertisement flooding attacks in next-generation IPv6 networks. Cogn. Comput. **10**(2), 201–214 (2018)
6. Saad, R.M., Anbar, M., Manickam, S.: Rule-based detection technique for ICMPv6 anomalous behaviour. Neural Comput. Appl. **30**(12), 3815–3824 (2018)
7. Bahashwan, A.A., Anbar, M., Hanshi, S.M.: Overview of IPv6 based DDoS and DoS attacks detection mechanisms. In: Anbar, M., Abdullah, N., Manickam, S. (eds.) ACeS 2019. CCIS, vol. 1132, pp. 153–167. Springer, Singapore (2020). https://doi.org/10.1007/978-981-15-2693-0_11
8. Anbar, M., Abdullah, R., Saad, R., Hasbullah, I.H.: Review of preventive security mechanisms for neighbour discovery protocol. Adv. Sci. Lett. **23**(11), 11306–11310 (2017)
9. Elejla, O.E., Belaton, B., Anbar, M., Alabsi, B., Al-Ani, A.K.: Comparison of classification algorithms on ICMPv6-based DDoS attacks detection. In: Computational Science and Technology. LNEE, vol. 481, pp. 347–357. Springer, Singapore (2019). https://doi.org/10.1007/978-981-13-2622-6_34
10. Tayyab, M., Belaton, B., Anbar, M.: ICMPv6-based DoS and DDoS attacks detection using machine learning techniques, open challenges, and blockchain applicability: a review. IEEE Access **8**, 170529–170547 (2020)
11. Al-Ani, A.K., Anbar, M., Al-Ani, A., Ibrahim, D.R.: Match-prevention technique against denial-of-service attack on address resolution and duplicate address detection processes in IPv6 link-local network. IEEE Access **8**, 27122–27138 (2020)
12. Al-Ani, A.K., Anbar, M., Manickam, S., Al-Ani, A., Leau, Y.-B.: Preventing denial of service attacks on address resolution in IPv6 link-local network: AR-match security technique. In: Computational Science and Technology. LNEE, vol. 481, pp. 305–314. Springer, Singapore (2019). https://doi.org/10.1007/978-981-13-2622-6_30

13. Elejla, O.E., Anbar, M., Belaton, B.: ICMPv6-based DoS and DDoS attacks and defense mechanisms. IETE Tech. Rev. **34**(4), 390–407 (2017)
14. Shah, S.B.I., Anbar, M., Al-Ani, A., Al-Ani, A.K.: Hybridizing entropy based mechanism with adaptive threshold algorithm to detect RA flooding attack in IPv6 networks. In: Computational Science and Technology. LNEE, vol. 481, pp. 315–323. Springer, Singapore (2019). https://doi.org/10.1007/978-981-13-2622-6_31
15. Bahashwan, A.A., Anbar, M., Hasbullah, I.H., Alashhab, Z.R., Bin-Salem, A.: Flow-based approach to detect abnormal behavior in neighbor discovery protocol (NDP). IEEE Access **9**, 45512–45526 (2021). https://doi.org/10.1109/ACCESS.2021.3066630
16. Anbar, M., Abdullah, R., Saad, R.M.A., Alomari, E., Alsaleem, S.: Review of security vulnerabilities in the IPv6 neighbor discovery protocol. In: Information Science and Applications (ICISA) 2016. LNEE, vol. 376, pp. 603–612. Springer, Singapore (2016). https://doi.org/10.1007/978-981-10-0557-2_59
17. Elejla, O.E., Anbar, M., Belaton, B., Hamouda, S.: Labeled flow-based dataset of ICMPv6-based DDoS attacks. Neural Comput. Appl. **31**(8), 3629–3646 (2018). https://doi.org/10.1007/s00521-017-3319-7
18. Elejla, O.E., Anbar, M., Belaton, B., Alijla, B.O.: Flow-based IDS for ICMPv6-based DDoS attacks detection. Arab. J. Sci. Eng. **43**(12), 7757–7775 (2018). https://doi.org/10.1007/s13369-018-3149-7
19. Quittek, J., Zseby, T., Claise, B., Zander, S.: Requirements for IP flow information export (IPFIX), RFC 3917,10.17487/RFC3917, October 2004. https://www.rfc-editor.org/rfc/pdfrfc/rfc3917.txt.pdf
20. Beck, F., Cholez, T., Festor, O., Chrisment, I.: Monitoring the neighbor discovery protocol. In: 2007 International Multi-Conference on Computing in the Global Information Technology (ICCGI 2007), p. 57. IEEE (2007)
21. Lecigne, C.: NDPWatch, Ethernet/IPv6 address pairings monitor. http://ndpwatch.sourceforge.net/. Accessed 11 May 2021
22. Morse, J.: Router Advert MONitoring Daemon. http://ramond.sourceforge.net/. Accessed 11 May 2021
23. Paxson, V.: Bro: a system for detecting network intruders in real-time. Comput. Netw. **31**, 2435–2463 (1999)
24. Roesch, M.: Snort: lightweight intrusion detection for networks. In: Lisa, vol. 99, no. 1, pp. 229–238 (1999)
25. Suricata: Suricata-open source IDS/IPS/NSM engine. https://suricata-ids.org. Accessed 02 Apr 2021
26. Barbhuiya, F.A., Biswas, S., Nandi, S.: Detection of neighbor solicitation and advertisement spoofing in IPv6 neighbor discovery protocol. In: Proceedings of the 4th International Conference on Security of Information and Networks, pp. 111–118. ACM (2011)
27. Bansal, G., Kumar, N., Nandi, S., Biswas, S.: Detection of NDP based attacks using MLD. In: Proceedings of the Fifth International Conference on Security of Information and Networks, pp. 163–167. ACM (2012)
28. Alalousi, A., Razif, R., AbuAlhaj, M., Anbar, M., Nizam, S.: A preliminary performance evaluation of K-means, KNN and EM unsupervised machine learning methods for network flow classification. Int. J. Electr. Comput. Eng. **6**(2), 778 (2016)
29. Elejla, O.E., Belaton, B., Anbar, M., Smadi, I.M.: A new set of features for detecting router advertisement flooding attacks. In: 2017 Palestinian International Conference on Information and Communication Technology (PICICT), pp. 1–5. IEEE (2017). https://doi.org/10.1109/PICICT.2017.19

30. Zulkiflee, M., Azmi, M., Ahmad, S., Sahib, S., Ghani, M.: A framework of features selection for ipv6 network attacks detection. WSEAS Trans. Commun. **14**(46), 399–408 (2015)

31. Aladaileh, M., Anbar, M., et al.: Entropy-based approach to detect DDoS attacks on software defined networking controller. Comput. Mater. Continua **69**(1), 373–391 (2021)

32. Bošnjak, S., Cisar, S.M.: EWMA based threshold algorithm for intrusion detection. Comput. Inf. **29**, 1089–1101 (2010)

33. Al-Adaileh, M.A., Anbar, M., Chong, Y.-W., Al-Ani, A.: Proposed statistical-based approach for detecting distribute denial of service against the controller of software defined network (SADDCS). In: MATEC Web of Conferences, vol. 218, p. 02012. EDP Sciences (2018)

Securing Software Defined Networking Using Intrusion Detection System - A Review

Noor Al-Mi'ani$^{(\boxtimes)}$ ⓘ, Mohammed Anbar ⓘ, Yousef Sanjalawe ⓘ,
and Shankar Karuppayah ⓘ

National Advanced IPv6 Centre of Excellence (NAv6), Universiti Sains Malaysia,
11800 USM Penang, Malaysia
`{anbar,kshankar}@usm.my`

Abstract. For the time being, the advances of the Internet technologies in respect of a wide-spread development and the fixed nature of traditional networks have the restricted capacity to satisfy organizational business requirements. Software-Defined Networking (SDN) as a new network architecture presented to overcome these challenges and issues of the existing network topologies and provide peculiar features. However, these programmable and centralized architectures of SDN suffer from new security threats, which require innovative security approaches and techniques such as Intrusion Detection Systems (IDSs). Currently, most of the IDS of SDN are implemented with a machine learning method; however, a deep learning method is also being utilized to satisfy better detection performance. Still, no recent comprehensive review of IDS has been conducted; therefore, this article provides an inclusive and detailed overview and analysis of the SDN with its security issues and attacks and IDS-based on deep learning as a solution for the security issue, to highlight their strengths and weaknesses, and then derive future research directions from these shortcomings.

Keywords: Attacks · Controller · Intrusion detection system · Security · Software defined networking

1 Introduction

Typically, computer networks involved extensive network devices; including switches, routers, and middle boxes (traffic-processing tools apart from forwarding). As multiple servers and hosts were interrelated through network devices and middle boxes, the features were vendor-oriented with proprietary alternatives. In this vein, network operators were accountable for modifying every device (for network and security event management) (Alanazi et al. 2019). Manual device modifications with low-level device-based syntax proved tedious, intricate, time-consuming, and erroneous as operators needed to be consistently present for device configurations. The drawbacks induced network interruptions (ONF 2008; Colville and Spafford 2010) following the absence of conventional IP networks in computerized readjustments (Benson et al. 2009). Although the present network dynamics required automatic incorporation into the current condition,

© Springer Nature Singapore Pte Ltd. 2021
N. Abdullah et al. (Eds.): ACeS 2021, CCIS 1487, pp. 417–446, 2021.
https://doi.org/10.1007/978-981-16-8059-5_26

the conventional IP network hampered dynamic network configuration following the present condition. Additionally, control and data planes were incorporated into internal network devices (within the conventional networks), thus minimizing dynamism and versatility. Low programmability and centralized control in conventional networks also caused complexities involving novel service deployment without disrupting continuous services (Chen et al. 2009). The situation could deteriorate following big network sizes (Kim et al. 2012). As network size expansion and heterogeneity could instigate further intricacies, the issues required a novel technique to facilitate network device and application deployments.

The recent advent of Software Defined Networking (SDN) development addressed the aforementioned barriers by decoupling network control from the device data plane (ONF 2013). Network intelligence in SDN was sequentially centralized within a software-oriented entity (controller) and network devices (switches and routers) as a simplified forwarding device. Essentially, forwarding devices involved flow rules for incoming packet processes following the match fields under flow tables (source and destination IPs and protocol). The devices could then be controller-programmed with a standard interface, including OpenFlow (McKeown et al. 2008a), NETCONF (Enns et al. 2011), and ForCES (Halpern et al. 2010). Network operators could also denote high-level network policy incorporation (involving the controller) into switches with the applications operating on the controller. Given that an SDN controller could gather the flow statistics from network switches, authentic global network conditions could be outlined with flow statistics assessment (application deployments involving the controller) (Tootoonchian et al. 2010; Van Adrichem et al. 2014; Mann et al. 2012; Zhong et al. 2017) towards significant network architecture simplification and efficient network management.

The SDN denoted a novel-networking trend that distinguished the control plane from the data counterpart. Specifically, SDN involved three planes: data, control, and management. The term SDN (initially coined at Stanford University) has garnered much scholarly and industrial attention regarding SDN-oriented research (McKeown et al. 2008b). Figure 1 presents SDN architecture where distinct control and data planes facilitated network application deployments following present network prerequisites. Under SDN, Open Networking Foundation (ONF) implied an industrial organization established by multiple service providers and network vendors to enable software-oriented standards (ONF), scholars were also actively engaged in SDN development and deployment (Yap et al. 2009; Openflow network research center). Notably, SDN was recommended to resolve all network intricacies by decoupling control and data planes and generating moderate data plane devices. The SDN was typically formed following four aspects:

- Control and data plane isolation: the planes must be rationally isolated and linked through an interface. Specifically, the control element was omitted from forwarding devices and assigned to an external entity;
- Network programmability: an open Application Programmable Interface (API) denoted a fundamental SDN architecture component where software and scripts could conveniently access and readjust network components;

- Network abstraction: network digitization for any high-hierarchy components. Despite services and applications for the entire network condition, physical qualities and resources proved irrelevant for modifications and computations;
- Logically centralized control: all forwarding devices of a domain were connected to a controlling entity under specific policies.

However, securing the SDN from the attacks is still a challenging and resource-intensive process that diminishes the Quality-of-Service (QoS) of the provided services and in managing the whole network. This is even more so, given the actuality that there are various types of attacks on SDN. Therefore, any effort to secure SDN against attacks needs to be considered in a comprehensive understanding along with SDN features.

The contributions of this review article are: (i) comprehensive review of SDN features and possible security concerns and attacks; (ii) a synthetic analysis of recent IDS based on deep leaning on SDN; and (iii) suggestions of future works in the field of IDS on SDN to enrich the research community.

The remainder of this paper is organized as follows. Section 2 provides a research background on SDN and its architecture, possible threats, and Vulnerabilities. Section 3 conducts a synthetic analysis and discussion of IDS-based deep learning on SDN. And finally, Sect. 4 concludes the article and provides future research directions, respectively.

2 Background

2.1 The SDN Architecture

The SDN denoted a developing network architecture for effective network infrastructure to (a) eliminate vertical integration using the bifurcating control plane (network control logic) from the data counterpart (underpinning routers and switches forwarding network traffic using network control logic) and (b) construct simplified packet-forwarding devices through isolation (network control logic incorporated into rationally centralized controllers and network switches) for versatility, implementation rate, programmability, and basic network management. Nevertheless, SDN architecture could improve network security using centralized controllers, worldwide network tangibility, and customized traffic-forwarding rules (Ahmad et al. 2015). The primary study focusses in SDN encompassed centralized control where policies could be reflected for different network status and implemented in the data plane with southbound API (SBI). The SDN also provided worldwide palpability and programmability towards computerized networking device modifications following the present network condition. Essentially, the SDN architecture involved three layers (Ahay et al. 2019) (see Fig. 1):

The SDN Plane Layer

1. Application Layer: Involved all business and security application management, such as metering, routing, QoS, load balancer, Intrusion Detection Systems (IDS), Intrusion Prevention Systems (IPS), firewall incorporation, and mobility management

(vital software services monitored by the aforementioned layer). The layer also corresponded to a lower counterpart through northbound application interfaces (Voellmy et al. 2012).

2. Control Layer: Mediated application and data layers and encompassed the Network Operating System (NOS) controller to monitor general network workability. In this vein, a rationally centralised controller denoted complete network management and decision-making on routing, flow-forwarding, and packet-dropping with programming (Dhamecha and Trivedi 2013; Gude et al. 2008). Specifically, the controller implied a rationally centralised and physically distributed context interconnected with the west and east-bound interfaces through SBIs, including OpenFlow (Todorov et al. 2020) and NetConf (Kreutz et al. 2014); Notably, the rational centralisation of the control logic provided three specific advantages. For example, the centralisation indicated simplification with fewer errors in network policy configurations with advanced languages and software components compared to low-level device-specific modifications. Additionally, a control programme could automatically respond to spurious network condition alterations to sustain advanced policies. Information on worldwide network conditions simplified the complex development of networking roles, services, and applications (Kreutz et al. 2014).

3. Data Layer: The essential role encompassed packet-forwarding (following the policies or regulations delegated and established by the controller) and involved physical network devices involving switches, routers, access points, and digital switches (OpenvSwitch, Indigo, Pica8, Nettle, and Open Flow) (Voellmy and Hudak 2011; Stallings 2013; Hu et al. 2014).

The SDN Interfaces
The APIs significantly influenced SDN with plane communications. Essentially, APIs reflect SDN architectural elements to push modifications or knowledge to forwarding components or applications (Latif 2020). Figure 1 presents various APIs with specific SDN aspects:

1. Southbound API: The southbound API (SBI) was an SDN catalyst that offered a communication protocol (between control and data planes). In this regard, API was employed to push modification updates and incorporate flow entries into the data plane with abstract network device roles for the control plane. Primary southbound interface complexities included heterogeneity, vendor-oriented network components, and language specifications (McKeown et al. 2008b).

2. Northbound API: Northbound APIs (NBIs) significantly affected application developers by offering a typical controller-management plane interface and underpinning device knowledge for application development towards a controllable and versatile SDN (Kreutz et al. 2014).

3. East and Westbound API: Eastbound APIs were utilized for knowledge import-export among distributed controllers while the westbound counterpart facilitated legacy network device (router) interactions with controllers (Bahashwan and Manickam 2019).

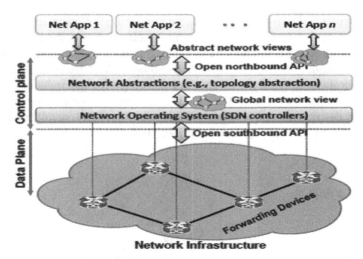

Fig. 1. SDN Architecture (Kreutz et al. 2014)

Based on the SDN notion (Shenker et al. 2011), the network could be classified into three essential abstractions: forwarding, distribution, and specification. As a ubiquitous component in many computer architecture and systems, abstractions were vital study instruments in computer science and information technology (Alkhatib et al. 2014). Typically, the forwarding abstraction should enable any forwarding behavior favored by the network application (control programme) while omitting underpinning hardware details. OpenFlow implied the actualization of one such abstraction (at par with a "device driver" in an operating system) (Singh and Behal 2020; Costa et al. 2021).

Abstract distribution should protect SDN applications from distributed condition vagaries by converting the aforementioned issue into a logically centralized counterpart. The actualization required a general distribution layer (NOS). Specifically, the layer was accountable for integrating control commands with forwarding devices and gathering forwarding layer condition data (network devices and connections) for a worldwide network application perspective (Singh and Behal 2020). The last abstraction involved specifications facilitating network application for favorable network behaviors without accountability for behavioral implementation using digitized alternatives and network programming languages. The techniques outlined abstract readjustments under specific applications following a simplified and abstract network model from a global and physical network modification perspective by the SDN controller (Singh and Behal 2020).

The SDN Controllers
A controller denoted an essential SDN control plane feature to primarily manage underpinning network component traffic with specific instructions or flows (Casellas et al. 2020). As fundamental controller roles proved similar (topology information, statistics, notifications, and device management) despite potential variances in controller elements, controllers employed extensive southbound interfaces, including OpenFlow and Open Daylight. The controllers were also provided with northbound interfaces to

operate different applications with inadequate standardization compared to the southbound counterparts. Among the various controller classifications, the key determinant was architecture where controllers were either centralized or distributed (Ahmad and Mir 2021). A single entity was accountable for all network device management in centralized controllers, whereas several entities collaborated for underpinning component management in distributed controllers. On another note, east or westbound interfaces were the key determinants of distributed environments. The SDN controller was implied as the SDN "Network Brain" (Stancu et al. 2015) (see Fig. 2).

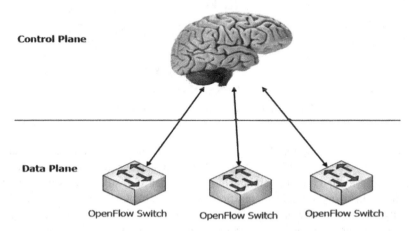

Fig. 2. SDN Controllers (Stancu et al. 2015)

Controllers Types

The most relevant controller classification elements either followed a centralized or distributed SDN controller (Kreutz et al. 2014). A centralized controller implied an entity in forwarding device management while the distributed counterpart denoted multiple control components across the system.

Controller Vulnerabilities

As a fundamental SDN element, inappropriate controller management within the control plane might potentially lead to a single point of attack and failure. Given that controllers highlighted the data flow occurrence in data planes, attacked or manipulated controllers potentially led to a poor network (Pradhan and Mathew 2020). Centralised controllers possibly resulted in attacks for controller access for flow regulation shifts in devices (Benton et al. 2013) and network experiences following novel threats or fraudulent entries (Shalini and Vetriselvi 2018).

Specific controller weaknesses are listed as follows (Pradhan and Mathew 2020):

1. Weak authentication: Low authentication reflected circumstances with fairly weak verification processes compared to shielded property values.

2. Incomplete encryption: Encryption employed intricate mathematical formulae to secure information from external parties and the conversion of documents, messages, and files into unintelligible texts. Although encrypted information generally required a decryption key, hackers could override verification protocols and access high-profile information in some contexts, thus resulting in unauthorized entries.
3. Information disclosure: Disclosure occurred when an application did not sufficiently secure sensitive and confidential knowledge from external parties, thus resulting in network traffic control.

2.2 The SDN Threats and Vulnerabilities

Although SDN technology could be acknowledged (security-wise) for easing or completely alleviating specific commonly-exploited risks and vulnerabilities in traditional networks, novel vulnerabilities and threat vectors (underlying the new architecture) were indicated. For example, control and data plane isolations and the rational centralization of network astuteness outlined a single failure point that could be manipulated to completely undermine SDN (Ahmad et al. 2015). Notably, SDN encountered multiple complexities from various factors. The first part of this section presents specific intricacies and a generalized overview of the most palpable attack surfaces and threat vectors determined in SDN architecture planes and interfaces. The middle section encompasses a thorough elaboration of the aforementioned intricacies, impacts, and implications following attack-surface and threat-vector manipulations in SDN architecture. The final part presents a list of typical attacks and deviant behaviors targeting SDN architecture layers.

The SDN Challenges

1. Centralised Controller: The SDN offered a rationally centralised control plane for networks. Specifically, the network controller retained a worldwide network perspective and programmes that forwarded devices following the policies outlined in the application layer. Although controllers were initially formed as single devices, distributed controllers have recently been implemented to adapt to scalability and reliability prerequisites in real-life contexts. In the study context, every forwarding device set was delegated to particular controllers under the master or slave deployment model (Chakraborti et al. 2021, Aladaileh et al. 2021).
2. Open Programmable Interfaces: The three primary programmable SDN interfaces involved (a) control plane application, (b) east and westbound control plane, and (c) control to data plane. Notably, the open interfaces enabled SDN programmability compared to conventional counterparts. For example, the NBI facilitated SDN applications to incorporate policies into the network control plane (REST APIs). Additionally, (b) denoted an interface permitting interactions among various interrelated controllers that might or might not be operating under the same domain. Meanwhile, (c) highlighted SBI as the most advanced and emphasized SDN interface to date (Chan et al. 2020).

3. Forwarding Device Management Protocol: The aforementioned protocol and Open-Flow catalyzed the modification and management of programmable forwarding devices. For example, the OFConfig protocol could be employed to construct an OpenFlow-facilitated device and various logical forwarding counterparts (to be initiated atop the aforementioned device). Another protocol example was OVSDB (Chakraborti et al. 2021).

4. Third-party Network Services: The SDN controller aided external network service integrations and performance as an operating system for convenient customization, formation and innovation, and low proprietary service costs. For example, external services could interact with a controller through internal APIs or open NBIs. The applications could also be incorporated as part of the controller module (NOX and POX) or instigated at run-time (OpenDayLight) based on the utilized controller (Shin et al. 2014).

5. Virtualized Logical Networks: Network Function Virtualisation (NFV) was established through the close integration of service providers with software-oriented networks without existential reliance on SDN. Summarily, NFV digitalized network services (initially hardware-oriented) and emphasized network service optimization by decoupling network roles (DNS and caching) (Mijumbi et al. 2015).

Attack Surfaces and Threat Vectors in SDN

Each network, protocol, device, or layer engaging with SDN could result in intentional or innocent misuse. Occasionally, { } was leveraged to highlight system errors or reveal subtle deviant behaviors. As such, each SDN component or layer within the architecture implied a possible threat vector or attack surface (Chica et al. 2020). Given that SDN architecture isolated network policy connotations and storage from applications and practices, the attacks (emphasizing five primary SDN components) were duly classified in line with the effects on network regulation, application, and practice architecture (Shaghaghi et al. 2020).

1. Implementation Attacks: Attacks focusing on the SBI and the data plane elements of a software-oriented network were classified under 'Implementation Attack' (urRasool et al. 2020). Notably, three distinct attacks (device, protocol, and side-channel) could be instigated to undermine data planes.

2. Policy Attack: 'Policy attacks' denoted the threats emphasizing SDN capacities to outline and contain appropriate network regulations. An attacker intending to focus on network policy levels strived to undermine SDN control and implementation strategies. Consequently, an attacker could manipulate network knowledge (shared with applications) and undermine decision-making processes.

3. Enforcement Attacks 'Enforcement attacks' strived to hamper effective software-based network instructions (when, where, and how network policies should be regulated). Therefore, attacks emphasizing control plane, SBI, and NBI might be connected to counterparts focusing on policy regulations.

The SDN Security Complexities

Security complexities in SDN (computer network security management) proved to be challenging as network administrators needed to offer overall security to protect the network from internal and external parties. For example, unauthorized access could be limited within the network through firewall applications in the application layer. Regardless, firewalls merely provided network protection by implementing preconceived security policies. Despite efficient security management strategies to combat the aforementioned intricacies, centralized controllers (Abubakar and Pranggono 2017) reflected a security threat in SDN architecture. Regarding the control plane, controllers provided an abstract perspective of applications for current resource utilization in the data plane. For example, attackers could readjust network controller regulations and prevent authentic users from accessing resources if the controller was undermined. The substantial security intricacies instigated by controller attackers involved service denial, data alteration and leakage, and illegal network access. In illegal access and data reconfiguration, attackers were disguised as controllers to exploit and alter network operations for complete network control.

Regarding the data plane, every OpenFlow switch encompassed distinct forwarding tables consisting of packet-management regulations. Intruders could be skeptical of the applied action in each packet through packet-processing time assessment. For example, the duration to process a packet from one port to another would be shorter than processing a packet from port to controller. In this vein, attackers possibly garnered more network knowledge upon determining the packet nature. Inauthentic controller requests could also increase under the manipulations and deter legal users from accessing network resources (data leakage). As external applications (in the application plane) could be incorporated into the application layer, deviant applications could be instigated for controller access. Ineffective (buggy) applications also led to severe security conundrums in SDN architecture. One of the efficient strategies for security issue management in SDN was the integration of IDS with SDN architecture.

2.3 Intrusion Detection System

The IDS significantly influenced network infrastructure security. Essentially, IDS (Hamed et al. 2018; Al-E'mari et al. 2020; Aladaileh et al. 2020) monitored network setting and identified suspicious network processes. The general aspects outlining IDS effectiveness were precision, dependability, and identification rate. Meanwhile, successful IDS provision included data-mining, machine-learning, and deep-learning methods. In this regard, multiple IDS were developed for networks with the following complexities:

1. False attack identification.
2. Failed recognition of unidentified attacks.
3. Inability to process large data.

Much research is currently being performed on IDS development with minimal false alarm rates and higher precision (Masduki et al. 2015). Ideally, an IDS must reflect precision, performance, error tolerance, timelessness, and measurability (Garg and Maheshawri 2016). Most IDSs typically demonstrated structures involving (a) a data-collection module with potential proof of attack, (b) an analysis module on attack identification following data processing, and (c) an attack-reporting strategy. The input data in every system component within the data-collection module could be obtained and assessed to determine typical interactional behaviors, thus identifying preliminary deviant behaviors. Given that the assessment module could be integrated with different strategies, DL techniques could assume novel attacks (often contradictory to past attacks) as DL strategies could astutely forecast potential unidentified attacks using currently authorized samples (Al-Garadi 2020). Figure 3 presents general IDS elements following DL algorithms.

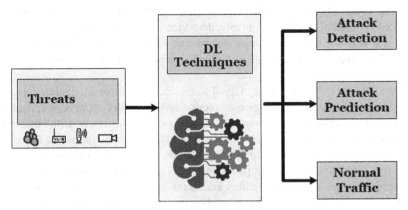

Fig. 3. Role of Deep Learning (DL) Based IDS (Asharf et al. 2020).

The IDS Design Choices

Following Fig. 4, the primary variances in IDS design alternatives relied on the following aspects: (a) data sources (host, network, or hybrid-oriented data input), (b) detection Methods (signature, anomaly, specification and hybrid), (c) Time of detection (online or offline), (d) architecture (categorized as centralized and distributed architecture),and (e) environment (wired, wireless, or Adhoc networks) (Vasilomanolakis 2015).

The IDS Data Source

Following the monitoring and assessment strategy, IDS data sources were classified into two types (see Fig. 4):

1. Host Based IDS (HIDS): The first implemented ID (Dacier and Wespi 1999) was operated (as an agent on individual hosts) to monitor the computer and relevant logs based on the conventional picture. The primary HIDS drawback implied that only HIDS-oriented computer systems were monitored.
2. Network Based IDS (NIDS): NIDS Essentially, NIDS was utilized to analyze traffic arrival and departure between system nodes. As such, NIDS investigated network traffic to determine illegal access, deviant behavior, and subsequent network attack.

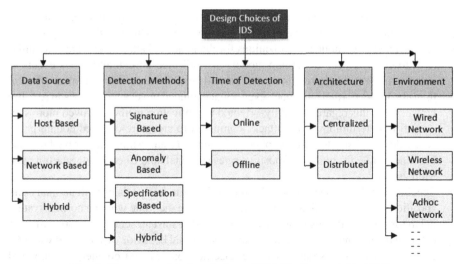

Fig. 4. Taxonomy of design choices of IDS (Vasilomanolakis 2015).

Notably, the IDS system employed signature and anomaly-oriented identification strategies (Al-Maksousy et al. 2018). Detection Methods of IDSs.

The IDS Detection Methods

The IDS identification strategies could be categorized into four systematic types (Wanda 2020) (see Fig. 4) as elaborated below:

1. Signature-Based Detection Techniques: Signature-oriented identification methods encompassed multiple attack signatures and compared network traffic or system outcomes to the repository. For example, identification alerts were sounded upon match detection. Despite adequate precision against determined attacks for which signatures were presented in the repository, the strategy failed to identify zero-day (novel) attacks. Notwithstanding the inefficiencies against current attack alterations (Keshk et al. 2019, 2020; Vacca 2012), specific studies (Liu et al. 2011) recommended methods to resolve signature-based deficiencies with Artificial Immune System (AIS). The method developed detectors that depended on attack signatures or trends with immune cell models (to identify if a packet was normal or deviant) through self or non-self-component categorization. Additionally, the system could adopt novel trends following consistent system monitoring. Although resource limitations in signature-related IDS were resolved using a separate Linux machine with an adapted Suricata-based signature IDS version (Kasinathan et al. 2013a), no clues (to update the attack signatures) were discovered. Hence, Kasinathan et al. (2013a) expanded the research published in Kasinathan et al. (2013b) by recommending signature-matching reconfiguration methods.
2. Anomaly-Based Detection Techniques: The aforementioned techniques fundamentally depended on an ordinary behavior profile for the assessed environment (Keshk

et al. 2020, 2018). The baseline was subsequently employed for ongoing system outcome comparisons. Any deviations beyond the permitted threshold were reported by raising an alert without categorizations for the identified attack form. Despite initiatives to utilize machine-learning models that reflected normal and attack events as behavioral identification counterparts, normal profile construction was more efficient than absorbing normal and attack events that excluded novel attack events in real-life networks. In this regard, anomaly-oriented identification methods proved more successful in determining novel attacks compared to signature-oriented counterparts. Regardless, one shortcoming implied intricacies in establishing the normal behavior baseline profile for high false-positive rates (Mitchell and Chen 2014; Scarfone and Mell 2007).

3. Specification-Based Detection Techniques: The fundamentals of both anomaly and specification-oriented identification methods were the same where a normal system behavior was specifically profiled and compared against present system outcomes for external deviation identification. Regardless, normal behavior was imbibed with ML in anomaly-oriented strategies while specification-oriented counterparts required manual specifications using a repository of regulations with connected deviation ranges by human specialists (Amaral et al. 2014). Consequently, false-positive rates were lowered compared to the anomaly counterpart (Mitchell and Chen 2014). Following the advantageous absence of learning phases upon sets of rule specifications (Amaral et al. 2014), the methods lacked diverse context adaptability and erroneous specifications (Butun et al. 2013).

4. Hybrid-Based Detection Techniques: The aforementioned methods utilized a mix of previous strategies to counter drawbacks and optimize current and novel attack benefits. For example, (Raza et al. 2013) recommended SVELTE, an IDS for IP-linked IoT systems employing RPL as a routing protocol in 6LoWPAN networks. The IDS was developed with a fusion of anomaly and signature-oriented identification methods for storage and processing prerequisite equilibrium for both strategies. In this vein, signature-oriented identification storage rates and the anomaly counterpart-computing price required balancing.

3   Related Works

This section provides an analysis of prior works related to IDS-based on deep learning methods in detail.

3.1   Deep Learning-Based Security Models

a. **Traffic Classification-based IDS**

Tang et al. (2020) recommended a deep learning (DL) strategy for network intrusion detection system (DeepIDS) in the SDN architecture. Specifically, the models were trained and assessed using the NSL-KDD dataset (with 80.7% and 90% precision) for a fully-connected Deep Neural Network (DNN) and Gated Recurrent Neural Network (GRU-RNN), respectively. Research experiments affirmed that the DL method potentially catalyzed flow-oriented anomaly identification in the SDN context. In this vein, the suggested model analyzed system performance through throughput, latency, and resource utilization. Although DeepIDS failed to impact the OpenFlow performance controller (a viable strategy), the method encountered certain complexities. For example, the technique failed to emphasize one particular attack type (DDoSIt) and offered relatively low ACC as opposed to other counterparts (with a complete 41-feature NSL-KDD dataset for model optimization and high identification and low false alarm rates). As such, DeepIDS required implementation in other OpenFlow controllers and an authentic testbed for future assessments.

On another note, Zhang et al. (2018) suggested a unique hybrid DNN-oriented implementation categorization strategy. Specifically, the processed data was utilized to train the hybrid DNN encompassing a stacked autoencoder (SAE) and softmax regression layer. Deep flow elements were automatically attainable from the SAE rather than manual feature identification and extraction, whereas the softmax regression layer was employed as a classifier to actualize the implementation categorization. Lastly, the simulation outcomes revealed that the recommended categorization technique was more successful with higher categorization precision than the support vector machine (SVM)-oriented counterpart. Although the strategy authenticated and assessed the suggested DL-oriented implementation categorization technique (following the Moore dataset), specific intricacies remained unsolved. For example, small-labelled data samples were needed without automated DL algorithm utilization towards implementation categorization. The training duration for the DNN was also fairly prolonged.

Ujjan et al. (2020) introduced a co-identification DL model with Snort IDS to identify unfavorable Internet of Thing (IoT) nodes in DDoS traffic using sFlow and polling-oriented traffic sampling at the data plane. The method assessed network overhead between the SDN controller and data-plane with every sampling application, thus enhancing IDS and DNN model capacity identification. First, sFlow and adaptive polling-oriented sampling were individually deployed to minimize processing and the network overhead of switches at the data plane. Second, Snort IDS and the SAE-DL model were collaboratively deployed to optimize identification precision at the control plane. Trade-offs among attack identification precision and resource overheads were then quantitatively examined upon implementing performance metrics on the gathered traffic streams. The recommended system assessment indicated higher identification precision (with 95% of True Positive and under 4% of False Positive rates) in the sFlow-oriented application as opposed to adaptive polling. Two model objectives were regarded: (1) to incorporate astute and periodic polling-oriented sampling only at SDN-facilitated edge switches (using real-time traffic streams to reduce the essential overhead) and (2) train an automated DL model through rule and signature-oriented real-time network datagrams for optimal DDoS identification precision.

On another note, Toupas et al. (2019a) recommended an SL model to practice a flow-oriented anomaly identification IDS for multi-class categorization. Specifically, a DNN model could determine unusual or deviant behavior in network traffic and categorize the traffic forms among 13 distinct cases. As such, the number of model input features was substantially minimized during data analysis and dataset pre-processing without undermining the performance. Following the updated CICIDS2017 dataset employed for training and assessment objectives, the experimental result with MLP for IDS revealed that the recommended model could attain an overall model precision of 99.95%. Specifically, accuracy reached 94.31%, recall or identification rates reached 95.62%, and the F1 Score reached 94.1% with a False Positive Rate of 0.05%. Although the (macro) average AUC value of all classes reached 0.99 on the particular dataset, the model encountered specific barriers. For example, the recommended model failed to assess different methods (AEs) for model execution sustainability. In this regard, the present dataset needed much enhancement and expansion with multiple network-oriented attack forms and model re-training (for identification) without minimizing the execution of all 13 classes. Notably, various architecture forms were disregarded as relevant alternatives, such as RNN (LSTM and GRU) implementation or CNN architecture.

Ravi (2020) presented a unique framework (an SDN-oriented prevention method involving phishing attacks) through deep machine learning with the CANTINA strategy (DMLCA) in cyberspace. In this vein, high identification precision was attained through the DMLCA approach using different parameters. Given that the machine learning strategy countered phishing attack issues SVM, the aforementioned approach efficiently resolved categorization complexities. For example, the CANTINA method facilitated solid hyperlinks by assessing term frequency (TF) and inverse document frequency (IDF). As the information retrieval algorithm enabled different document comparison, categorization, and retrieval, the simulation outcomes currently reflected improved performance compared to multiple techniques (an efficient means of forecasting phishing attacks in cyberspace).

Assis et al. (2021) recommended an SDN defense system following a single IP flow record evaluation through the GRU-based DL technique to identify DDoS and intrusion attacks. The suggested system strived to assess and determine individual-flow attacks (for improved precision on identification) and response rates (for alleviation processes). Specifically, the suggested system encompassed two primary elements: detection and mitigation modules. The detection module served to identify attack occurrences, whereas the mitigation counterpart strived to minimize network impacts and users. For example, the suggested model was assessed against some distinct machine learning strategies over two public datasets (CICDDoS 2019 and CICIDS 2018) that indicated high identification rates and assessed flow (per second), thus demonstrating GRU as a viable method for the recommended system. Notwithstanding, the suggested GRU technique implied specific barriers. For example, the technique could only identify anomalies without means to reduce computational expenditure and elevate alleviation results. The introduced strategy also proved incompatible with other learning methods.

Elsayed et al. (2020) recommended DDoSNet (an IDS. Specifically, a novel DL method was suggested following RNN-AE to categorize input traffic into normal or deviant forms. In this vein, the suggested DL model could minimize data dimensionality by mechanically deriving input data features. The model was specifically assessed with the novel CICDDoS2019 dataset. Although DDoSNet provided the highest assessment metrics involving recall, accuracy, and F-score as opposed to current renowned classical ML methods, the aforementioned strategy encountered specific intricacies. For example, the recommended model was yet to analyze other dataset performances. In addition, the strategy employed a binary categorization framework to classify input traffic into normal and deviant forms. In this vein, distinct categorizations of every individual attack form and the expansion of a multi-class categorization framework proved necessary.

Nguyen and Kim (2020) suggested a unique algorithm involving a network intrusion detection system (NIDS) with an enhanced feature subset [explicitly chosen using a thorough genetic algorithm (GA)-oriented search] and fuzzy C-means clustering (FCM). The NSL-KDD dataset was duly employed for the algorithm through the bagging (BG) classifier and CNN model (as an efficient extractor) with GA and five-fold cross-validation (CV) for CNN model structure selection. The deep-feature subset derived from the chosen CNN model was integrated with the BG classifier for performance authentication with the five-fold CV. The advanced feature set attained by the three-layered feature development (through GA, FCM, CNN extractors and hybrid CNN and BG learning techniques) substantially enhanced the final identification performance. Highly credible authentication performance outcomes (attained with the five-fold CV protocol for the recommended algorithm) denoted a well-established application in a practical computer network setting (NIDS). Regardless, the research limitation included much time consumption following the incorporation of an extensive GA-oriented search technique for relatable feature subset and efficient CNN structure selection. The reiterative five-fold CV protocol also needed long periods of practical simulation. Consequently, the input data could prove incongruent with potential demonstrations of a biased algorithm (towards the predominated category) when implemented in practical computer network settings.

Zhang et al. (2020) recommended a unique categorical in congruency in technology processing for large-scale datasets known as SGM [an integration of Synthetic Minority Over-Sampling Technique (SMOTE) and under-sampling for clustering following the Gaussian Mixture Model (GMM)]. Specifically, a flow-oriented intrusion identification model (SGM-CNN) was developed to integrate incongruent class processing with CNNs and examine the influence of various convolution kernels and learning speed on model performance. The suggested model benefits were validated with UNSW-NB15 and CICIDS2017 datasets. Resultantly, SGM-CNN obtained an identification rate of 99.74% and 96.54%, respectively, for binary and multi-class categorization on the UNSW-NB15 dataset while an identification rate of 99.85% was demonstrated for a 15-class categorization on the CICIDS2017 dataset. Following five incongruent processing techniques and two categorization algorithms, SGM-CNN offered an efficient alternative towards incongruent intrusion identification and outperformed advanced intrusion identification counterparts. Nonetheless, the recommended model required other feature selection strategy examinations for high identification performance.

Garg et al. (2019) introduced a hybrid DL-oriented anomaly identification scheme for suspicious flow identification in social multimedia settings following two modules: 1) an anomaly identification module that enhanced the limited Boltzmann machine and gradient descent-oriented SVM towards suspicious activity identification and 2) an end-to-end data transmission module to fulfil the stringent QoS prerequisites of SDN. Lastly, the recommended scheme was experimentally analyzed on both real-time and TIET, KDD'99, and CMU datasets for workability involving anomaly identification and data transmission (vital for social multimedia). For example, a big-scale assessment over a Carnegie Mellon University (CMU)-oriented insider threat dataset was executed to determine performance involving deviant event identification (identity theft, profile duplication, and confidential data gathering). Upon analysis using real-time and benchmark datasets, the suggested model resulted in substantial results against the present advanced counterparts. Although the recommended scheme attained a remarkably high identification rate (>99%) over TIET, KDD'99, and CMU datasets, the recommended framework required expansion to various application domains (Smart Grids, Intelligent Transportation Systems, Unmanned Aerial Vehicles, and Smart Homes).

Zhang et al. (2019) suggested a novel intrusion identification network under DL [parallel cross CNN (PCCN)] to perform all three-feature integrations for high identification outcomes encompassing highly incongruent suspicious flow samples. In this vein, PCCN could imbibe flow features with lesser samples, thus implying an enhanced authentic flow feature extraction algorithm. The experimental outcomes on the CICIDS2017 dataset indicated that the authentic flow feature extraction algorithm substantially decreased feature dimensions, accelerated model convergence, and attained positive identification outcomes. Additionally, the recommended model identified unusual flows with minimal samples and demonstrated high generalizability for diverse elements. Lastly, higher metrics were adopted to reflect model efficiency. Nevertheless, the PCCN model demonstrated specific restrictions, such as necessary DL algorithm utilization for flow novelty identification and high identification performance. The model also required an algorithm that could identify attack classifications that were intangible within the dataset (highly crucial for network safety under present large-scale data settings).

Qin et al. (2019) introduced a deviant network traffic categorization strategy following CNN and Recurrent Neural Network (RNN) [incorporated into the Graphic Process Unit (GPU) and facilitated TensorFlow]. Initially, the method involved model development under CNN and RNN that could mechanically garner authentic elements and categorize the deviant network flow in the SDN context. Three common attacks were then simulated with mininet and pox through python. Lastly, the experiment was conducted to validate model efficiency. The proposal was also assessed with three datasets (CTU-13, CSIC, and sim_data). Although the model could attain high precision, recall, and F1-score, the outcomes remained flawed with further room for improvement. For example, the first exploration avenue for enhancement required model utilization in SDN settings. Present assessments were performed through real-life backbone network traffic to indicate extended model benefits.

Zhang et al. (2019) recommended an intrusion identification model following CNN. Specifically, SMOTE and the Edited Nearest Neighbors (ENN) algorithm were incorporated for network traffic equilibrium. The method was concluded as a CNN-oriented IDS for mechanical feature derivation and recommended utilizing over-sampling-under-sampling integrative strategies for incongruent data issue resolution for NID. Lastly, the ENN strategy was incorporated into the pipeline following the SMOTE application (for a cleaner space) using the NSL-KDD dataset for model assessment. In this vein, the recommended SMOTE-ENN-oriented CNN IDS model obtained 83.31% of precision. Moreover, the U2R detection rate (from 26% to 77%) was substantially enhanced. Regardless, the recommended CNN model indicated restrictions that were only deemed appropriate for intrusion identification on incongruent network traffic.

Boukria and Guerroumi (2019) recommended anomaly-oriented IDS with a DL method to conserve the SDN control layer-infrastructure layer interaction channel (against false data injection attacks) and identify possible SND southbound side attack attempts. The flows circulating within the SDN network were assessed using logarithm functions and minimum or maximum scalar methods to normalize flow aspects while Relu and Softmax functions were manipulated for flow categorization. The suggested system was measured using the CICIDS2017 dataset on an experimental platform through Mininet context-ONOS controller integrations. Although the recommended technique offered improved attack identification performance with 99.6% precision, the strategy remained flawed with much room for enhancement (improving recommended alternatives for multiple attack identification) and other solutions for SDN network security (integrations of multi-controllers with other technologies).

Su et al. (2020) suggested that a unique traffic anomaly identification model (BAT-MC) address low precision and feature-engineering issues involving intrusion identification using two BLSTM learning phases and emphasis on time-series elements (for intrusion identification through the NSL-KDD dataset). Specifically, the BLSTM layer linked forward and backward LSTM for feature extraction on the traffic bytes of every packet towards packet vector generation. The packet vectors were subsequently organized for network flow vector construction. Meanwhile, the attention layer was employed for feature-learning involving the network flow vector with packet vectors. The aforementioned feature-learning process was mechanically fulfilled through DNN without feature-engineering technologies. For example, the BAT-MC strategy was assessed by KDDTestC and KDDTest-21 datasets. Meanwhile, the NSL-KDD dataset outcomes implied that the BAT-MC model obtained 84.25% precision in time-series data determination. The standard classifier comparisons demonstrated the potential of BAT-MC model outcomes as opposed to other present DL-oriented strategies. Although the BAT-MC model was predictably a formidable instrument for intrusion identification issues, the recommended model reflected restrictions requiring model-testing on real datasets.

Toupas et al. (2019a) recommended a DL model (a neural network encompassing multiple stacked fully connected layers) to incorporate a flow-oriented anomaly IDS for multi-class categorization. A DNN model was employed for unusual or deviant behavior identification (a possible cyber-attack) in network traffic and traffic type categorization among 13 distinct cases with the upgraded CICIDS2017 dataset for training and assessment. Resultantly, the recommended model could attain promising outcomes on multi-class categorization regarding precision, recall (identification rates), and False Positive rates (false alarm rates) on the particular dataset to substantially minimize model input elements without undermining model performance. Nevertheless, the outcomes denoted much room for enhancement (assessing further input element reduction) through multiple strategy assessments, including AEs or Principal Component Analysis (PCA) and Independent Component Analysis (ICA). The present dataset could also be enhanced and expanded with multiple network-oriented attack forms and model re-training for successful identification without lowering the original 13-class performance. Lastly, various architecture form performance proved necessary to address pertinent issues.

Azizjon et al. (2020) suggested a DL technique for effective and versatile IDS formation through a one-dimensional CNN (1DCNN). Notably, two-dimensional CNN techniques reflected substantial performance in image-object detection encompassing computer vision fields. For example, traffic data was gathered and labelled using normal and anomalous traffic records from various network sources. A good data element representation was subsequently attained through DL methods that eventually facilitated a monitored categorization for substantial outcomes. The model assessment was performed on the UNSW NB15 IDS dataset for strategy efficiency. Regarding performance-oriented comparison studies, machine learning-related Random Forest (RF), SVM models, and 1D-CNN were manipulated with multiple network parameters and architecture. Consequently, the 1D-CNN model outperformed the state-of-arts methods in terms of precision, recall, and F-score when trained on holistic data instead of incongruent counterparts. Notably, RF attained the highest precision upon operation. Although performance robustness involving big-scale data and computational advantages rapidly facilitated model feature-learning, the method encountered specific intricacies, such as the necessity for other DL algorithm implementations (GRU, MLP, and ANN).

Malik et al. (2020a) recommended a control plane-oriented orchestration for different advanced threats and attacks. The suggested strategy encompassed a hybrid Cuda-facilitated and DL-catalyzed architecture that employed the indicative power of LSTM and CNN for successful and timely multi-vector threat and attack identification. Currently, an advanced CICIDS2017 dataset and standard performance evaluation metrics were utilized to meticulously assess the recommended strategy by thoroughly comparing the recommended method against hybrid DL-architecture development and present benchmark algorithms. The framework reflected the high precision of mild and dynamic cyber threats and attack identification. Although the model reflected 98.6% identification precision, two restrictions were perceived: (1) the necessity to incorporate multiple DL models for successful and timely identification of dynamic cyber threats and (2) the need to organise the control plane for multiple potential roles (timely prevention and the alleviation of underpinning big-scale distributed systems and IoT).

Lee et al. (2020) presented a DL-facilitated intrusion detection and prevention system (DL-IDPS) to deter secure shell (SSH), brute-force, and distributed denial-of-service (DDoS) attacks in SDN. Four DL models (MLP, CNN, LSTM, and SAE) were chosen and compared under the recommended IDS for network attack detection using packet length sequences and packet headers as pertinent elements. Following the MLP model utilization in DL-IDPS for both SSH brute-force and DDoS attack identification, the suggested DLIDPS could attain almost 99% precision in deterring SSH and brute-force attacks and negate almost 100% of DDoS-attacking packets against the victim host. Several model paths could be regarded (real-time DL-IDPS implementation in dual mode) as flow-oriented IDPS failed to offer thorough packet knowledge to the SDN controller. For example, Programming Protocol Independent Packet Processors (P4) could be incorporated for network packet processing at the switch level for a novel study method (for improved precision and execution involving DL-facilitated IDSs in SDN). The suggested real-time DL-IDPS also required incorporation for intricate scenarios encompassing multiple SDN switches.

Following Kaur et al. (2020) recommendation of an image-oriented deep neural model, this study intended to offer a precise real-time intrusion identification framework with image-based DNN (deep image learning) to derive optimal dataset elements (to be fed to the multi-layer convolutional network for intrusion type forecasts). This research employed two public and comprehensive datasets (CICIDS2017 and CSECIC-IDS2018) to gauge different attack forms, such as brute force (FTP and SSH), DoS (GoldenEye, Hulk, and SLowloris) and web attacks, intrusion, SQL injection, DDoS attack, and bot. Specifically, a CNN model was utilized for various attack categorization and attributes. Regarding accurate forecasts, the model could precisely categorize and characterize 99% and 97.5% of the attacks in CICIDS2017 and CSE-CIC-IDS2018, respectively. Regardless, the method encountered specific barriers, such as the necessity for attack assessments with distinct DL models (RNN and LSTM) for outcome comparisons against deep-image learning counterparts towards a robust DL model (for attack categorization and characterization.

As Pakanzad and Monkaresi (2020) introduced a hybrid method with CNN and LSTM networks for enhanced IDS execution, this research aimed to offer a strategy to precisely categorize deviant traffic based on attack forms. Data pre-processing was initially executed where records with null or infinity values were omitted from the dataset. As the three data elements denoted symbolic values, value digitization was required for appropriate network training (protocol type, flag, and service) through a one-hot encoder. The minimum-maximum role was subsequently employed for dataset normalization into [0, 1] ranges. Additionally, the data was reconfigured into one dimension for a multiple-layer (Conv1D, MaxPooling1D, Dropout, LSTM, and Dense) 1D-CNN implementation. Categorization performance following the dense layer revealed that the RELU activation role reflected improved performance than other activation counterparts. In the research context, the outcomes were authenticated using NSL-KDD and CICIDS2017 datasets. In this vein, the model could attain multiple categorization precision for NSL-KDD and CICIDS2017 datasets at 98.1 and 96.7, respectively. Specifically, convolutional LSTM network outcomes (with much potential) proved comparable with the research results.

Given that Sinha and Manollas (2020) recommended a DL model integrating specific CNN advantages with Bi-directional LSTM (Bi-LSTM) data involving spatial and temporal feature-learning, this study aimed to suggest a hierarchical model through 1DCNN and Bi-LSTM layer integrations. Specifically, CNN was employed to gauge the integration of spatial or high-level dataset elements, Bi-LSTM layers (primarily an RNN subcategory), and long temporal data feature durations for attack predictions (performed for binary classification to forecast the extent to which attacks occurred and precise attack categories). Concerning multi-category attack forecasting, the evaluation was performed on five classes [DoS, Probe (Probing Attacks), R2L (Root to Local Attacks), and U2R] in NSL-KDD. Meanwhile, 10 classes were employed in multi-category attack forecasts under UNSW-NB15, (Normal, DoS, Exploits, Generic, Reconnaissance, Worms, Shellcode, Analysis, Backdoor, and Fuzzers). Consequent training and assessment of NSL-KDD and UNSW-NB15 datasets provided high identification and fairly lower False Positive rates. The recommended model outperformed multiple advanced NID systems that leveraged machine learning or DL models. Nonetheless, this method encountered specific barriers, such as model optimization necessities to examine potential U2R and Worms attack categories using the honeypot system assessment.

Mhamdi *et al.* (2020) suggested a hybrid autonomous DL method with SAE and One-class SVM (SAE-1SVM) for Distributed Denial of Service (DDoS) attack identification. As SAE imbibed legitimate traffic trends and compressed input data into a lower dimension, the lower-dimensional and higher-level data proved more appropriate for OC-SVM processing. The ICIDS2017 dataset emphasis on DoS, Heartblead, Slowloris, Slowhttptest, Hulk, GoldenEye, and DDoS attacks was particularly selected. Resultantly, the recommended algorithm could attain (on average) 99.35% precision with a small set of flow elements. Although SAE-1SVM indicated a substantial reduction of processing time while sustaining high identification rates, the method encountered specific intricacies. For example, the strategy was not executed in an authentic SDN testbed for a more thorough assessment and did not identify other network attack types.

Ahn et al. (2020) recommended a technique to outline DL-oriented traffic categorization functionality as an Explainable artificial intelligence (XAI) approach under a genetic algorithm. A dominant feature identification strategy was recommended to elaborate on the recommended DL-oriented traffic classier operation mechanism by quantifying the essentiality of every element. Additionally, the genetic algorithm was leveraged for feature-selection mask generation for vital elements in the whole feature set. A DL-oriented traffic classier was employed with an approximate precision of 97.24% to highlight the recommended technique. The fundamentals of every element (derived from the aforementioned technique) were also introduced by stating the dominance rate. Notwithstanding, the method remained flawed with much room for enhancement, including a vital feature selection algorithm for ner-grained application-oriented traffic classifiers. The genetic algorithm convergence speed also required improvement to facilitate real-time essential feature selection.

Bai et al. (2020) recommended a DL method to identify SDN-based anomaly using OpenFlow by assessing multiple metrics (derived from the OpenFlow switch metadata) with four trained DL models towards multivariate time-series categorization (83.8% precision on average). Regardless, strategy execution that distinguished various anomaly forms and catalyzed metric and model optimization for incorporation into efficient SDN contexts (enterprise and cloud data centers and campus intranet) needed to facilitate SDN safety improvement.

Dinh *et al.* (2021) recommended an improved scheme to effectively and dependably identify and alleviate EDoS attacks. The recommended scheme encompassed online and offline stages through GRU implementation to determine intricate temporal data reliance connections and minimize gradient complexities in time series. First, the normal trends were rejected while the suggested scheme imbibed precise multivariate time-series representations. Next, the representations were employed to reconfigure input data. Lastly, potential modifications were utilized for anomaly identification and interpretation. The recommended scheme also presented a self-correcting threshold for minimal error rates while current alternatives typically utilized a hard threshold for anomaly analysis, thus elevating the error rates. An experiment was performed with various simulated EDoS attacks on a renowned cloud-computing platform (OpenStack) and an ONOS-based SDN controller. The offline model module was trained with tuned hyperparameters through the SMD dataset in the research context for cloud users to avoid different EDoS attacks (slow HTTP/SYN flooding, database API requests, Yo-Yo, and Slowloris). Although cloud service provider services reflected improvement, the recommended scheme required enhancement for a thorough comparison against other EDoS defence systems with more assessment prerequisites for specific EDoS attacks.

b. **Routing Optimization based IDS.**

Zhang et al. (2019) recommended a deep reinforcement learning (DRL)-oriented controller synchronization framework that utilized DNNs to generalize policy prediction synchronization or Multi-Armed Cooperative Synchronization (MACS). The MACS facilitated controllers in comprehending synchronization policies following previous experiences for optimal performance (through controller synchronization). The assessment outcomes asserted outstanding DNN capacities in abstracting latent trends within the distributed SDN context and reflecting high superiority to MACS-oriented synchronization policies (56% and 30% performance enhancement over ONOS and greedy SDN controller synchronization heuristics). Notwithstanding, the recommended MACS required more enhancement, including more effective policies that gradually optimized performance improvement through controller synchronization.

Shu et al. (2020) suggested a collective IDS following SDN distribution by positioning a distributed SDN controller on every base station. Essentially, GAN was explored through successful collective IDS strategy designs to resolve the biased flow issue following the incorporation of distributed SDN into CIDS. Consequently, multiple SDN controllers could mutually train an efficient intrusion identification model for the whole Vehicular Ad hoc Network (VANET) instead of a local sub-network (for rigorously-proved accuracy in both IID and non-IID circumstances). Optimization-oriented performance assessment was also conducted with theoretical and experimental analyses on KDD99 and NSL-KDD dataset adoptions in specific analyses. The detailed experimental outcomes affirmed that CIDS proved successful in intrusion identification for VANETs. Additionally, the suggested CDSA encompassed restrictions in various m-values that affected performance. As lower m-values indicated higher efficiency and interaction costs among SDNs (a trade-off at present), adequate m-values proved necessary for efficiency-interaction expenditure congruencies.

Xiao et al. (2019) suggested a NID model under CNNIDS for specific network traffic data. Method redundancy with irrelevant network traffic data features was initially omitted with distinct dimensionality minimization techniques. The dimensionality minimization data features were mechanically retrieved with CNN, whereas other intrusion detection-oriented knowledge was derived from monitored learning. As the KDD-CUP99 dataset assessed the recommended CNN model performance, the recommended CNNIDS model significantly enhanced the categorization identification performance of intrusion network traffic to decrease the categorization duration and complement real-time IDS prerequisites. In the study context, the recommended CNNIDS model successfully identified NID with dimensionality minimization (AC, DR, and FAR at 94.0%, 93.0%, and 0.5%, respectively). As the study limitation reflected poor identification rates and feature-learning complexities within a few attack classifications (U2R; R2L), novel sample data were deemed crucial in perpetuating adversarial network strategies for multiple attack category feature detection.

Subba (2015) recommended a Neural Network-oriented NIDS framework for real-time anomaly identification in current network traffic. Essentially, the suggested framework utilized a convex Logistic Regression cost role, stochastic gradient descent, and simulated annealing for an optimized real-time anomaly identification framework. Resultantly, the updated UNSW-NB15 dataset indicated that the suggested Neural Network-oriented NIDS framework outperformed other NIDS counterparts with Decision Tree, SVM, and Voting Ensemble Methods by optimizing different NIDS framework-based hyper parameters (activation roles, regularization terms, gradient descent repetitions, and hidden layer nodes). Although the recommended NIDS framework attained high identification rates against multiple current network attacks with fairly low false alarm rates, the framework remained flawed with much room for improvement, including the necessity of NIDS framework development and assessment following RNN, Long Short Term Memory (LSTM), and CNN.

Following Khan et al. (2019) recommendation of a NID model, this study suggested a strategy integrating CNN and Softmax algorithms to mechanically derive efficient intrusion sample elements for precise categorization. Resultantly, the KDD99 datasets implied that the recommended model potentially enhanced human intrusion identification precision and human IDS execution. As high precision occurred with the rise of epoch numbers, the suggested model reflected higher performance as opposed to SVM and Deep Belief Network (DBN) counterparts. Notwithstanding, the aforementioned method encountered specific intricacies, such as the necessity of multiple DL algorithms (GRU, MLP, and ANN) applications.

C. **Resource Management-based IDS**

Wang et al. (2018) suggested an SDN-HGW framework to improve smart home network distribution and facilitate the SDN controller. For example, the recommended SDN-HGW expanded the access network control (a smart home network) for enhanced end-to-end network management. Notably, the recommended SDN-HGW could obtain distributed implementation awareness through data traffic categorization within a smart home network. For example, SDN-HGW framework essentialities denoted DataNet (a DL-oriented encrypted data packet classier). The recommended DataNets were constructed using three strategies (MLP, SAE, and CNN). An open dataset with over 20, 000 packets from 15 applications was employed to design and assess the recommended DataNets. Resultantly, DataNets proved applicable to the SDN-HGW framework with precise packet categorization in SDN HGW and high computational effectiveness for real-time processing in a smart home network. In this vein, the recommended SDN-HGW required enhanced DataNet performance and implementation (towards improved network resource management and novel corporate strategies) without undermining service providers or users' privacy and security (Table 1).

Table 1. Summarize the most recent studies that used deep learning algorithms to detect attacks in SDN

Reference	Algorithm	Dataset	Controller	Findings	Shortcomings
Tang (2020)	(DN) and GRU-RN)	NSL-KDD	POX controller	High accuracy	- Low ACC - Low detection rate and high false alarm rate
Zhang et al. (2018)	(SAEs) and (SR)	Moore data set		High classification accuracy	The time consumption is large
Ujjan et al. (2020)	(SAE) s	sFlow and adaptive polling based sampling individually	RYU-SDN-Controller	High detection accuracy	High crucial overhead
Toupas et al. (2019a)	(DNNs)	CICIDS 2017	–	High accuracy	It needs a more comprehensive dataset
Assis et al. (2021)	(GRU)	CICDDoS 2019 and the CICIDS 2018	SDN Controller	Promising detection rates	- Detect the occurrence of anomalies but can't identify, - High computational cost
Elsayed et al. (2020)	RNN	CICDDoS2019	mininet and flood controller	High evaluation metrics	Low classify each attack type
Nguyen and Kim (2020)	(GA), (FCM) and (CNN)	NSL-KDD	–	High quality feature set and high detection performance	High time consumption
Zhang et al. (2020)	(SMOTE) and (GMM)	NSW-NB15 and CICIDS2017 datasets	–	An effective solution to imbalanced intrusion detection	Low detection performance
Garg et al. (2019)	(BM) and SVM	TIET, KDD'99 and CMU datastes	SDN Controller	High detection rate over the considered datasets	Lacks diversity of application domains
Zhang et al. (2019b)	(CNN)	CICIDS2017	–	-Reduces the feature dimension -Good detection results	Low detection performance
Qin et al. (2019)	(CNN) and (RNN)	(CTU-13, CSIC and sim_data) datasets	–	High accuracy, recall and F1 score	The model is not implemented within SDN environment
Zhang et al. (2019a)	(DNNs)	CAIDA AS-27524" dataset and real dataset	ONOS and greedy SDN controller	Rendering significant superiority to MACS which are 56% and 30% performance improvements	low performance
Boukria and Guerroumi (2019)	Relu and Softmax functions	CICIDS2017	ONOS controller	Gives a good performance in terms of attack detection	Detects a limited number of attacks
Su et al. (2020)	(BLSTM)	KDDTestC and KDDTest-21 dataset	–	Good accuracy	It needs to test their modeon a real dataset
Toupas et al. (2019a)	(DNN)	CICIDS2017	–	Promising results on multi-class	It needs to improve dataset with more types of network based attacks
Azizjon et al. (2020)	(CNN)	UNSW NB15 IDS dataset	–	High Accuracy, Recall, F-score RF	It needs to apply other deep learning algorithms

(continued)

Table 1. (*continued*)

Reference	Algorithm	Dataset	Controller	Findings	Shortcomings
Malik et al. (2020b)	(LSTM) and (CNN)	CICIDS2017	–	High detection accuracy	It can't detect evolving cyber threats
Lee et al. (2020)	MLP, CNN, LSTM and SAE	The packet-based dataset was captured	SDN controller	High detection accuracy	It needs to improve both accuracy and performance
Kaur et al. (2020)	(CNN)	CICIDS2017 and CSECIC-IDS2018	–	classify and characterize 99% and 97.5% attacks	It needs to analyze these attacks with different deep learning models
Pakanzad and Monkaresim (2020)	(CNN) and (LSTM)	NSL-KDD and CICIDS2017 datasets	–	High detection accuracy	It needs to improve performance
Sinha and Manollas (2020)	(CNN)	NSL-KDD and UNSW-NB15 datasets	–	Good performance	It needs more optimization
Mhamdi et al. (2020)	(SE) and (SAE-1SVM)	ICIDS2017	–	High detection accuracy	The model doesn't implemented in SDN environment
Ahn et al. (2020)	(GA)	A dataset was created used statistical features	–	High detection accuracy	Low convergence speed of the genetic algorithm
Bai et al. (2020)	(DNN)	Network traffic(real dataset)	ONOS Controller	Good accuracy of 83.8%	It needs to optimize the metrics and model
Dinh et al. (2021)	(RNN)	Network traffic(real dataset)	ONOS SDN controller	Decrease EDoS attacks	Low performance detection for particular EDoS attacks
Khan et al. (2019)	(CNN) and (SRA)	KDD99 datasets	–	Good accuracy and improve the performance	it needs to apply other deep learning algorithms such as GRU, MLP and ANN
Shu et al. (2020)	GAN and EGBAD	KDD99 NSL-KDD	OpenFlow-SDN-Controller	Is efficient and effectiveness in intrusion detection for VANETs	Low performance
Xiao et al. (2019)	(AE) and (CNN)	KDD-CUP99 dataset	–	-Good classification detection performance - reduces the classification time	Low detection rate
Subba (2019)	(BPNN)	UNSW-NB15 dataset	–	High detection rate and low false alarm rate	It needs to develop and evaluate NIDS frameworks based on Neural Network algorithm
Hu et al. (2020)	(CNN)	Moore dataset	OpenFlow-SDN-Controller	Outperforms three benchmarks on recall ratio, precision ratio, F value and stability	- High computation complexity - Decreases the applicationawareness speed to some extent
Ravi (2020)	(DNN) with CANTINA approach and (SVM)	–	–	An effective way to predict the phishing attack	Low detection performance
Wang et al. (2018)	(MLP), (SAE) and (CNN)	Open dataset	SDN Controller	Accurate packet Classification - High computational efficiency	Low performance of DataNets

4   Conclusion and Future Directions

This article introduces an overview of IDS on SDN by illustrating the strengths and weaknesses of each IDS. Moreover, this article provides a new classification taxonomy of the existing IDS-based deep learning on SDN. Also, it highlights the shortcomings of several IDSs which could be addressed by using better and more efficient, and/or optimized methods that might enhance detection performance. Finally, researchers in such fields might also take the advantages and strengths of existing IDS by hybridizing or enhancing them to provide a comparable IDS against attacks on SDN. However, from the limitations of the existing studies, we can draw some future directions, including minimizing the operation overheads during attack detection, sophisticated Quality-of-Service management for data traffic implementations, integration with blockchain to ensure data security and integrity.

References

ONF: Open networking foundation (2014). https://www.opennetworking.org/. Accessed 14 April 2021. n.d. vi, 16

Clayman, S., Maini, E., Galis, A., Manzalini, A., Mazzocca, N.: The dynamic placement of virtual network functions. In: 2014 IEEE Network Operations and Management Symposium (NOMS), pp. 1–9. IEEE (2014, May)

Mann, V., Vishnoi, A., Kannan, K., Kalyanaraman, S.: CrossRoads: seamless VM mobility across data centers through software defined networking. In: 2012 IEEE Network Operations and Management Symposium, pp. 88–96. IEEE (2012, April)

Zhong, H., Fang, Y., Cui, J.: Reprint of LBBSRT: an efficient SDN load balancing scheme based on server response time. Future Gener. Comput. Syst. **80**, 409–416 (2018)

Ahmad, I., Namal, S., Ylianttila, M., Gurtov, A.: Security in software defined networks: a survey. IEEE Commun. Surv. Tutor. **17**(4), 2317–2346 (2015)

Sahay, R., Meng, W., Jensen, C.D.: The application of software defined networking on securing computer networks: a survey. J. Netw. Comput. Appl. **131** 89–108 (2019)

Voellmy, A., Kim, H., Feamster, N.: Procera: a language for high-level reactive network control. In: Proceedings of the first Workshop on Hot Topics in Software Defined Networks, pp. 43–48. (2012, August)

Dhamecha, K., Trivedi, B.: SDN issues–a survey. Int. J. Comput. Appl. **73**(18), 30–35 (2013)

Gude, N., et al.: NOX: towards an operating system for networks. ACM SIGCOMM Comput. Commun. Rev. **38**(3) 105–110 (2008a)

Todorov, D., Valchanov, H., Aleksieva, V.: Load balancing model based on machine learning and segment routing in SDN. In: 2020 International Conference Automatics and Informatics (ICAI), pp. 1–4. IEEE (2020, October)

Kreutz, D., Ramos, F.M., Verissimo, P.E., Rothenberg, C.E., Azodolmolky, S., Uhlig, S.: Software-defined networking: a comprehensive survey. Proc. IEEE **103**(1), 14–76 (2014)

Colville, R.J., Spafford, G.: Top Seven Considerations for Configuration Management for Virtual and Cloud Infrastructures (2010). http://img2.insight.com/graphics/no/info2/insight_art6.pdf. Accessed 15 May 2020

Voellmy, A., Hudak, P.: Nettle: taking the sting out of programming network routers. In: Rocha R., Launchbury J. (eds.) Practical Aspects of Declarative Languages. PADL 2011. LNCS, vol. 6539, pp. 235–249. Springer, Berlin, Heidelberg (2011). https://doi.org/10.1007/978-3-642-18378-2_19

Stallings, W.: Software-defined networks and openflow. Internet Protoc. J. **16**(1), 2–14 (2013)

Hu, F., Hao, Q., Bao, K.: A survey on software-defined network and openflow: from concept to implementation. IEEE Commun. Surv. Tutor. **16**(4), 2181–2206 (2014)

Latif, Z., Sharif, K., Li, F., Karim, M.M., Biswas, S., Wang, Y.: A comprehensive survey of interface protocols for software defined networks. J. Netw. Comput. Appl. **156**, 102563 (2020)

Bahashwan, A.A.O., Manickam, S.: A brief review of messaging protocol standards for internet of things (IoT). J. Cyber Secur. Mobil. 1–14 (2019)

Shenker, S., Casado, M., Koponen, T., McKeown, N.: The future of networking, and the past of protocols. Open Netw. Summit **20**, 1–30 (2011)

Alkhatib, H., et al.: IEEE CS. IEEE Computer (2014)

Singh, J., Behal, S.: Detection and mitigation of DDoS attacks in SDN: a comprehensive review, research challenges and future directions. Comput. Sci. Rev. **37**, 100279 (2020)

Costa, L.C., et al.: OpenFlow data planes performance evaluation. Perform. Eval. 102194 (2021)

Casellas, R., Martínez, R., Vilalta, R., Muñoz, R.: Abstraction and control of multi-domain disaggregated optical networks with OpenROADM device models. J. Lightwave Technol. **38**(9), 2606–2615 (2020)

Benson, T., Akella, A., Maltz, D.A.:. Unraveling the complexity of network management. In: Proceedings of the 6th USENIX Symposium on Networked Systems Design and Implementation, ser. NSDI 2009, Berkeley, CA, USA, 2009, pp. 335–348 (2009)

Ahmad, S., Mir, A.H.: Scalability, consistency, reliability and security in SDN controllers: a survey of diverse SDN controllers. J. Netw. Syst. Manag. **29**(1), 1–59 (2020). https://doi.org/10.1007/s10922-020-09575-4

Stancu, A.L., Halunga, S., Vulpe, A., Suciu, G., Fratu, O., Popovici, E.C.: A comparison between several software defined networking controllers. In: 2015 12th International Conference on Telecommunication in Modern Satellite, Cable and Broadcasting Services (TELSIKS), pp. 223–226. IEEE (2015, October)

Pradhan, A., Mathew, R.: Solutions to vulnerabilities and threats in software defined networking (SDN). Procedia Comput. Sci. **171**, 2581–2589 (2020)

Benton, K., Camp, L.J., Small, C.: OpenFlow vulnerability assessment. In: Proceedings of the second ACM SIGCOMM Workshop on Hot Topics in Software Defined Networking, pp. 151–152 (2013, August)

Shalini, S., Vetriselvi, V.: Intrusion detection system for software-defined networks using fuzzy system. In: Mandal, J., Saha, G., Kandar, D., Maji, A. (eds.) Proceedings of the International Conference on Computing and Communication Systems. Lecture Notes in Networks and Systems, vol. 24, pp. 603–620. Springer, Singapore (2018). https://doi.org/10.1007/978-981-10-6890-4_59

Chakraborti, S., Ray, A.M., Chatterjee, S.R., Chakraborty, M.: Software-defined network vulnerabilities. In: Chakraborty, M., Singh, M., Balas, V.E., Mukhopadhyay, I. (eds.) The "Essence" of Network Security: An End-to-End Panorama. LNNS, vol. 163, pp. 215–239. Springer, Singapore (2021). https://doi.org/10.1007/978-981-15-9317-8_9

Chan, R., Tan, F., Teo, U., Kow, B.: Vulnerability assessments of building management systems. In: Staggs, J., Shenoi, S. (eds.) Critical Infrastructure Protection XIV. ICCIP 2020. IFIP Advances in Information and Communication Technology, vol. 596, pp. 209–220. Springer, Cham (2020). https://doi.org/10.1007/978-3-030-62840-6_10

Shin, S., et al.: Rosemary: a robust, secure, and high-performance network operating system. In: Proceedings of the 2014 ACM SIGSAC Conference on Computer and Communications Security, pp. 78–89 (2014, November)

Mijumbi, R., Serrat, J., Gorricho, J.L., Bouten, N., De Turck, F., Boutaba, R.: Network function virtualization: state-of-the-art and research challenges. IEEE Commun. Surv. Tutor. **18**(1), 236–262 (2015)

Chica, J.C.C., Imbachi, J.C., Vega, J.F.B.: Security in SDN: a comprehensive survey. J. Netw. Comput. Appl. **159**, 102595 (2020)

Chen, X., Mao, Z.M., Van der Merwe, J.: ShadowNet: a platform for rapid and safe network evolution. In: Proceedings of the 2009 Conference on USENIX Annual Technical Conference, p. 3 (2009, June)

Shaghaghi, A., Kaafar, M.A., Buyya, R., Jha, S.: Software-defined network (SDN) data plane security: issues, solutions, and future directions. In: Gupta, B., Perez, G., Agrawal, D., Gupta, D. (eds.) Handbook of Computer Networks and Cyber Security, pp. 341–387. Springer, Cham (2020). https://doi.org/10.1007/978-3-030-22277-2_14

ur Rasool, R., Wang, H., Ashraf, U., Ahmed, K., Anwar, Z., Rafique, W.: A survey of link flooding attacks in software defined network ecosystems. J. Netw. Comput. Appl. 102803 (2020)

Abubakar, A., Pranggono, B.: Machine learning based intrusion detection system for software defined networks. In: 2017 seventh International Conference on Emerging Security Technologies (EST), pp. 138–143. IEEE (2017, September)

Hamed, T., Ernst, J.B., Kremer, S.C.: A survey and taxonomy of classifiers of intrusion detection systems. In: Daimi, K. (ed.) Computer and Network Security Essentials, pp. 21–39. Springer, Cham (2018). https://doi.org/10.1007/978-3-319-58424-9_2

Masduki, B.W., Ramli, K., Saputra, F.A., Sugiarto, D.: Study on implementation of machine learning methods combination for improving attacks detection accuracy on Intrusion Detection System (IDS). In: 2015 International Conference on Quality in Research (QiR), pp. 56–64. IEEE (2015, August)

Garg, A., Maheshwari, P.: A hybrid intrusion detection system: a review. In: 2016 10th International Conference on Intelligent Systems and Control (ISCO), pp. 1–5. IEEE (2016, January)

Al-Garadi, M.A., Mohamed, A., Al-Ali, A.K., Du, X., Ali, I., Guizani, M.: A survey of machine and deep learning methods for internet of things (IoT) security. IEEE Commun. Surv. Tutor. **22**(3), 1646–1685 (2020)

Asharf, J., Moustafa, N., Khurshid, H., Debie, E., Haider, W., Wahab, A.: A review of intrusion detection systems using machine and deep learning in internet of things: challenges, solutions and future directions. Electronics **9**(7), 1177 (2020)

Vasilomanolakis, E., Karuppayah, S., Mühlhäuser, M., Fischer, M.: Taxonomy and survey of collaborative intrusion detection. ACM Comput. Surv. (CSUR) **47**(4), 1–33 (2015)

Al-Maksousy, H.H., Weigle, M.C., Wang, C.: NIDS: neural network based intrusion detection system. In: 2018 IEEE International Symposium on Technologies for Homeland Security (HST), pp. 1–6. IEEE (2018, October)

Kim, H., Schlansker, M., Santos, J.R., Tourrilhes, J., Turner, Y., Feamster, N.: Coronet: fault tolerance for software defined networks. In: 2012 20th IEEE international conference on network protocols (ICNP), pp. 1–2. IEEE (2012, October)

Wanda, P.: A survey of intrusion detection system. Int. J. Inform. Comput. **1**(1), 1–10 (2020)

Keshk, M., Sitnikova, E., Moustafa, N., Hu, J., Khalil, I.: An integrated framework for privacy-preserving based anomaly detection for cyber-physical systems. In: IEEE Transactions on Sustainable Computing (2019)

Vacca, J.R.: Computer and Information Security Handbook Newnes, London (2012)

Keshk, M., Turnbull, B., Moustafa, N., Vatsalan, D., Choo, K.K.R.: A privacy-preserving-framework-based blockchain and deep learning for protecting smart power networks. IEEE Trans. Ind. Inf. **16**(8), 5110–5118 (2020)

Liu, C., Yang, J., Chen, R., Zhang, Y., Zeng, J.: Research on immunity-based intrusion detection technology for the Internet of Things. In: 2011 Seventh International Conference on Natural Computation, vol. 1, pp. 212–216. IEEE (2011, July)

Kasinathan, P., Pastrone, C., Spirito, M.A., Vinkovits, M.: Denial-of-Service detection in 6LoW-PAN based Internet of Things. In: 2013 IEEE 9th International Conference on Wireless and

Mobile Computing, Networking and Communications (WiMob), pp. 600–607. IEEE (2013a, October)

Kasinathan, P., Costamagna, G., Khaleel, H., Pastrone, C., Spirito, M.A.: An IDS framework for internet of things empowered by 6LoWPAN. In: Proceedings of the 2013 ACM SIGSAC Conference on Computer & Communications Security, pp. 1337–1340 (2013b, November)

Keshk, M., Moustafa, N., Sitnikova, E., Turnbull, B.: Privacy-preserving big data analytics for cyber-physical systems. Wirel. Netw. 1–9 (2018). https://doi.org/10.1007/s11276-018-01912-5

Mitchell, R., Chen, I.R.: A survey of intrusion detection techniques for cyber-physical systems. ACM Comput. Surv. (CSUR) **46**(4), 1–29 (2014)

Scarfone, K., Mell, P.: Guide to Intrusion Detection and Prevention Systems (IDPS). Recommendations of the National Institute of Standards and Technology (2007). http://csrc.nist.gov/publications/nistpubs/800-94/SP800-94.pdf

McKeown, N., et al.: OpenFlow: enabling innovation in campus networks. ACM SIGCOMM Comput. Commun. Rev. **38**(2), 69–74 (2008b)

Amaral, J.P., Oliveira, L.M., Rodrigues, J.J., Han, G., Shu, L.: Policy and network-based intrusion detection system for IPv6-enabled wireless sensor networks. In: 2014 IEEE International Conference on Communications (ICC), pp. 1796–1801. IEEE (2014, June)

Butun, I., Morgera, S.D., Sankar, R.: A survey of intrusion detection systems in wireless sensor networks. IEEE Commun. Surv. Tutor. **16**(1), 266–282 (2013)

Raza, S., Wallgren, L., Voigt, T.: SVELTE: real-time intrusion detection in the Internet of Things. Ad Hoc Netw. **11**(8), 2661–2674 (2013)

Tang, T.A., Mhamdi, L., McLernon, D., Zaidi, S.A.R., Ghogho, M., El Moussa, F.: DeepIDS: deep learning approach for intrusion detection in software defined networking. Electronics **9**(9), 1533 (2020)

Zhang, C., Wang, X., Li, F., He, Q., Huang, M.: Deep learning–based network application classification for SDN. Trans. Emerg. Telecommun. Technol. **29**(5), e3302 (2018)

Ujjan, R.M.A., Pervez, Z., Dahal, K., Bashir, A.K., Mumtaz, R., Gonzá-lez, J.: Towards sFlow and adaptive polling sampling for deep learning based DDoS detection in SDN. Future Gener. Comput. Syst. **111**, 763–779 (2020)

Hu, N., Luan, F., Tian, X., Wu, C.: A novel SDN-based application-awareness mechanism by using deep learning. IEEE Access **8**, 160921–160930 (2020)

Toupas, P., Chamou, D., Giannoutakis, K.M., Drosou, A., Tzovaras, D.: An intrusion detection system for multi-class classification based on deep neural networks. In: 2019 18th IEEE International Conference on Machine Learning and Applications (ICMLA), pp. 1253–1258. IEEE (2019a, December)

Ravi, R.: A performance analysis of Software Defined Network based prevention on phishing attack in cyberspace using a deep machine learning with CANTINA approach (DMLCA). Comput. Commun. **153**, 375–381 (2020)

Assis, M.V., Carvalho, L.F., Lloret, J., Proença Jr., M.L.: A GRU deep learning system against attacks in software defined networks. J. Netw. Comput. Appl. **177**, 102942 (2021)

Enns, R., Bjorklund, M., Schoenwaelder, J., Bierman, A.: Rfc 6241, network configuration protocol (netconf). Internet Engineering Task Force (IETF) (June 2011)

Elsayed, M.S., Le-Khac, N.A., Dev, S., Jurcut, A.D.: Ddosnet: a deep-learning model for detecting network attacks. In: 2020 IEEE 21st International Symposium on A World of Wireless, Mobile and Multimedia Networks (WoWMoM), pp. 391–396. IEEE (2020, August)

Nguyen, M.T., Kim, K.: Genetic convolutional neural network for intrusion detection systems. Future Gener. Comput. Syst. **113**, 418–427 (2020)

Zhang, H., Huang, L., Wu, C.Q., Li, Z.: An effective convolutional neural network based on SMOTE and Gaussian mixture model for intrusion detection in imbalanced dataset (2020)

Garg, S., Kaur, K., Kumar, N., Rodrigues, J.J.: Hybrid deep-learning-based anomaly detection scheme for suspicious flow detection in SDN: a social multimedia perspective. IEEE (2019)

Zhang, Y., Chen, X., Guo, D., Song, M., Teng, Y., Wang, X.: PCCN: parallel cross convolutional neural network for abnormal network traffic flows detection in multi-class imbalanced network traffic flows. IEEE Ac-Cess **7**, 119904–119916 (2019a)

Qin, Y., Wei, J., Yang, W.: Deep learning based anomaly detection scheme in software-defined networking. In: 2019 20th Asia-Pacific Network Operations and Management Symposium (APNOMS), pp. 1–4. IEEE (2019, September)

Zhang, X., Ran, J., Mi, J.: An intrusion detection system based on convolutional neural network for imbalanced network traffic. In: 2019 IEEE 7th International Conference on Computer Science and Network Technology (ICCSNT), pp. 456–460. IEEE (2019b, October)

Boukria, S., Guerroumi, M.: Intrusion detection system for SDN network using deep learning approach. In: 2019 International Conference on Theoretical and Applicative Aspects of Computer Science (ICTAACS), vol. 1, pp. 1–6. IEEE (2019, December)

Su, T., Sun, H., Zhu, J., Wang, S., Li, Y.: BAT: deep learning methods on network intrusion detection using NSL-KDD dataset. IEEE Access **8**, 29575–29585 (2020)

Doria, A., et al.: Forwarding and control element separation (ForCES) protocol specification. RFC **5810**, 1–124 (2010)

Azizjon, M., Jumabek, A., Kim, W.: 1D CNN based net-work intrusion detection with normalization on imbalanced data. In: 2020 International Conference on Artificial Intelligence in Information and Communication (ICAIIC), pp. 218–224. IEEE (2020, February)

Malik, J., Akhunzada, A., Bibi, I., Imran, M., Musaddiq, A., Kim, S.W.: Hybrid deep learning: an efficient reconnaissance and surveillance (2020a)

Lee, T.H., Chang, L.H., Syu, C.W.: Deep learning enabled intrusion detection and prevention system over SDN networks. In: 2020 IEEE International Conference on Communications Workshops (ICC Workshops), pp. 1–6. IEEE (2020, June)

Al-E'mari, S., Anbar, M., Sanjalawe, Y., Manickam, S.: A labeled transactions-based dataset on the ethereum network. In: Anbar, M., Abdullah, N., Manickam, S. (eds.) Advances in Cyber Security. ACeS 2020. Communications in Computer and Information Science, vol. 1347, pp. 61–79. Springer, Singapore (2020). https://doi.org/10.1007/978-981-33-6835-4_5

Kaur, G., Lashkari, A.H., Rahali, A.: Intrusion traffic de-tection and characterization using deep image learning. In: 2020 IEEE International Conference on Dependable, Autonomic and Secure Computing, International Conference on Pervasive Intelligence and Computing, International Conference on Cloud and Big Data Computing, International Conference on Cyber Science and Technology Congress (DASC/PiCom/CBDCom/CyberSciTech), pp. 55–62. IEEE (2020, August)

Pakanzad, S.N., Monkaresi, H.: Providing a hybrid approach for detecting malicious traffic on the computer networks using convolutional neural networks. In: 2020 28th Iranian Conference on Electrical Engineering (ICEE), pp. 1–6. IEEE (2020, August)

Sinha, J., Manollas, M.: Efficient deep CNN-BiLSTM model for network intrusion detection. In: Proceedings of the 2020 3rd International Conference on Artificial Intelligence and Pattern Recognition, pp. 223–231 (2020, June)

Mhamdi, L., McLernon, D., El-moussa, F., Zaidi, S.A. R., Ghogho, M., Tang, T.: A deep learning approach combining auto-encoder with one-class SVM for DDoS attack detection in SDNs. In: 2020 IEEE Eighth International Conference on Communications and Networking (ComNet) (2021)

Ahn, S., Kim, J., young Park, S., Cho, S.: Explaining deep learning-based traffic classification using a genetic algorithm. IEEE Access (2020)

Bai, X., Bai, J., Yang, X., Liu, H., Wang, B., Liu, Y.: A deep learning approach to detect anomaly in software-defined network. In: 2020 12th International Conference on Advanced Infocomm Technology (ICAIT), pp. 100–106. IEEE (2020, November)

Dinh, P.T., Park, M.: R-EDoS: robust economic denial of sustainability detection in an SDN-based cloud through stochastic recurrent neural network. IEEE Access **9**, 35057–35074 (2021)

Tootoonchian, A., Gorbunov, S., Ganjali, Y., Casado, M., Sherwood, R.: On controller performance in software-defined networks. In: 2nd {USENIX} Workshop on Hot Topics in Management of Internet, Cloud, and Enterprise Networks and Services (Hot-ICE 12) (2012)

Khan, R.U., Zhang, X., Alazab, M., Kumar, R.: An improved convolutional neural network model for intrusion detection in networks. In: 2019 Cybersecurity and Cyberforensics Conference (CCC), pp. 74–77. IEEE (2019, May)

Zhang, Z., Ma, L., Poularakis, K., Leung, K.K., Tucker, J., Swami, A.: Macs: deep reinforcement learning based sdn controller synchronization policy design. In: 2019 IEEE 27th International Conference on Network Protocols (ICNP), pp. 1–11. IEEE (2019, October)

Shu, J., Zhou, L., Zhang, W., Du, X., Guizani, M.: Collaborative intrusion detection for VANETs: a deep learning-based distributed SDN approach. IEEE Transactions on Intelligent Transportation Systems (2020)

Xiao, Y., Xing, C., Zhang, T., Zhao, Z.: An intrusion detection model based on feature reduction and convolutional neural networks. IEEE Access 7, 42210–42219 (2019)

Subba, B.: A Neural Network based NIDS framework for intrusion detection in contemporary network traffic. In: 2019 IEEE International Conference on Advanced Networks and Telecommunications Systems (ANTS), pp. 1–6. IEEE (2019, December)

Wang, P., Ye, F., Chen, X., Qian, Y.: Datanet: deep learning based encrypted network traffic classification in SDN home gateway. IEEE Access 6, 55380–55391 (2018)

Malik, J., Akhunzada, A., Bibi, I., Imran, M., Musaddiq, A., Kim, S.W.: Hybrid Deep Learning: An Efficient Reconnaissance and Surveillance Detection Mechanism in SDN (2020b)

Aladaileh, M.A., Anbar, M., Hasbullah, I.H., Chong, Y.W., Sanjalawe, Y.K.: Detection techniques of distributed denial of service attacks on software-defined networking controller–a review. IEEE Access 8, 143985–143995 (2020)

Alanazi, S. T., Anbar, M., Karuppayah, S., Al-Ani, A.K., Sanjalawe, Y.K.: Detection techniques for DDoS attacks in cloud environment. In: Piuri, V., Balas, V., Borah, S., Syed Ahmad, S. (eds.) Intelligent and Interactive Computing. Lecture Notes in Networks and Systems, vol. 67, pp. 337–354. Springer, Singapore (2019). https://doi.org/10.1007/978-981-13-6031-2_34

Mohammad, A., Mohammed, A., Hasbullah, H., Yousef, S.: Information theory-based approaches to detect DDoS attacks on software-defined networking controller a review. Int. J. Educ. Inf. Technol. 5, 83–94 (2021)

Using Genetic Algorithms to Optimized Stacking Ensemble Model for Phishing Websites Detection

Zeyad Ghaleb Al-Mekhlafi[1]([✉]) [iD] and Badiea Abdulkarem Mohammed[1,2] [iD]

[1] College of Computer Science and Engineering, University of Ha'il, Ha'il 81481, Saudi Arabia
[2] College of Computer Sciences and Engineering, Hodeidah University, 967 Hodeidah, Yemen

Abstract. Phishing attacks are security attacks that affect individuals and organ-isations websites. I addition, it may also devices and networks such as Internet of Things (IoT) devices and networks. IoT networks are exposed environment for phishing attacks. Thingbots software in IoT devices can be utilized by attack-ers for spreading hidden and unnoticed spam emails. Several approaches such as machine learning, deep learning and others were used to create and design detec-tion methods for phishing attacks. However, these methods detection accuracy still not enough and need to be enhanced. Anew proposed method for phishing website detection that based on optimized ensemble classification method is suggested in the present study. in this proposed method, A Genetic Algorithm (GA) was used to optimize the ensemble classification method by tuning the parameters of sev-eral ensemble machine learning methods, including Bagging, GradientBoost, and LightGBM. These were accomplished by ranking the optimized classifiers to pick out the best three models as base classifiers of a stacking ensemble method. A dataset of websites that made up of 44% phishing websites (4898) and 5\% legit-imate websites (6157) was used for the present study experiments. As a come out, with the proposed detection method, detection accuracy was enhanced and reached 97.16%.

Keywords: Phishing websites · Ensemble classifiers · Optimization methods · Genetic Algorithm

1 Introduction

Many organizations and researchers have been concerned about cybercrimes in the last few years. Phishing is one of the most dangerous types of cybercrimes. In phishing, attackers steal the credentials and information from the user by using false emails or websites. Such attacks became an issue because many internet users and organisations are affected. In phishing, the attacker fakes a legitimate Website of a selected organization, which then is sent to victims through fake or junk mail or via URLs posted in social media and networks or any media. This may lead victims to click on the links in that emails or posts and they will be redirected to the fake website [1].

The internet of things (IoT) is more vulnerable to phishing attacks because of the higher risk. The interconnected nature of IoT devices and IoT sensors makes them

© Springer Nature Singapore Pte Ltd. 2021
N. Abdullah et al. (Eds.): ACeS 2021, CCIS 1487, pp. 447–456, 2021.
https://doi.org/10.1007/978-981-16-8059-5_27

attractive to hack. Smart routers, TVs, and fridges constituted about 25% of junk email hosts as mentioned in [2]. In addition, IoT device thingbots software could be used by attackers to spread unwanted junk emails while at the same time sending no viruses or Trojans. It is not necessary for the user to be aware of it [3]. Thus, the literature introduced a number of security enhancements for IoT systems. The fact that there is no effective phishing detection method can completely stop people from falling victim to phishing attacks [1, 4]. We also discussed new approaches to detect phishing websites in the IoT environment, such as incorporating detection methods from literature. Let's take a look at one such method that was released [5]. Using this method, you could possibly detect phishing websites using a sensor. Detecting can happen in real time, and features are provided to reduce the energy use. IoT devices don't need to install anti-phishing software because of this proposed system. It must be in-installed only once between the devices and the internet router; there is no need to re-install the sensor after a relocation. This process can be installed in the router and appears to be moderately efficient.

A variety of approaches were used to try to find phishing websites. The data set for this analysis included over 3.3 million phishing websites, including some advanced techniques like Deep Learning [6, 7], Convolution, and Deep Neural Network (CNN and DNN), Long Short-Term Memory (LSTM) [6], Genetic Algorithm (GA) [7], Machine Learning (ML) [8–10], and other techniques. It can be concluded that suggested approaches such as improved sensitivity, specificity, accuracy, and other measures showed significant increases in comparison to other state-of-the-art approaches. But for now, there's still room for improvement in the detection accuracy.

A theoretical classification model that has been optimized for phishing website detection is described in the study presented here. The GA was used to build the proposed model. These are three primary stages, starting with training, then ranking, and finishing with testing. The first step was training the classifiers by doing practice problems (Bagging, GradientBoost, and LightGBM). No optimization technique was used in this step. The model optimization is performed in the second step, where GA is used to find the best parameters for the model to enhance the overall accuracy of the classifiers. Next, optimized classifiers (aka stacking ensembles) served as the base classifiers for the stacking ensemble method. In the end, a new set of websites is acquired and a classification is made based on their labels.

The study is organized as follows. A general overview of the literature surrounding the subject is presented in Sect. 2. In Sect. 3, the methodology and materials had been obsolete for some time. Section 4 contains a presentation of the findings of the experiments in this study. Those findings are discussed and compared to previous literature in the same section. In Sect. 5, the findings and recommendations of the study are summarized.

2   Related Literature

Various previous studies have been conducted in the field of phishing detection. Data pertaining to literature similar to the one being referenced was critically examined to assist in motivating the methodology of the present study. Arranged in the following order:

2.1 IoT- Based Phishing Detection Methods

A substantial number of IoT devices are vulnerable to severe security threats that put the integrity of the IoT web at risk [11]. There is therefore a great need to safeguard these IoT devices from various threats (e.g. phishing). Typically, phishing targets include unconventional networks such as the Internet of Things [1]. Creative idea in [12], the 5 major types of attacks identified in the IIoT, (Internet of Things) industry, have been examined and are referred to as phishing, the first of these attacks. Phishers apply compromised attacks in critical infrastructures, such as the Internet of Things (IoT), a way of doing things that uses zero-day malware combined with social engineering, and on top of that, they make use of features that exist on the web. Attackers use the front-end level to access IIoT.

Various methods were developed to combat phishing websites in the IoT environment. Parra et al. in [13] proposed a framework that utilizes cloud-based temporal LSTM and Distributed CNN as two distinct components. The first tool was utilized for IoT micro-security, detecting phishing attacks via security device implementations as a form of IoT device protection, whereas the second tool was utilized on the back-end to combat Botnet attacks and implement convolution neural network embedding for distributed phishing attacks on IoT devices. To demonstrate the performance of the tool, a scientific experiment yielded findings that stated that the tool could successfully detect phishing emails at a rate of 94.3% accuracy, while only garnering 93.58% accuracy for CNN detection.

According to Mao et al. [14], the biggest security concerns associated with intelligent IoT systems are phishing, and they discovered that this is one of the most frequently encountered types of attacks. Based on machine learning, a web-page layout-based approach to phishing detection was developed by them, which they implemented as a proposed solution. Gaining a page layout resemblance by using aggregation analysis is a key technique in detecting phishing websites in this approach. Precision was improved by using four different machine learning methods in their experiments.

The security issues in IoT have been thoroughly discussed in [15] by Virat et al. They assert that IoT devices are not intelligent, requiring methods of detection that are appropriate for the task. The vulnerabilities discovered by Deogirikar and Vidhate have put the IoT technology at risk as well [16]. They've conducted research on IoT attacks and have found ways to minimize their IoT production and damage levels.

2.2 Machine Learning-Based Detection Methods

A wide range of detection methods used AI and ML to locate cybersecurity issues. Many different methods for detecting phishing websites based on AI and ML were made available, each with strong detection abilities. For example, in a paper by Al-Sariera, Jr., and co-authors, new AI-based methods that incorporated new methods of phishing mitigation strategies were proposed [17]. Four extra-tree base classifiers were applied to phishing website data sets, resulting in four new meta-learner methods. The previous tests show that the models produced a 97% accuracy, with a 0.028% false positive rate.

A new method to identify phishing websites was proposed by Jain and Gupta in [18] in the context of hyperlinks in HTML. By organizing hyperlinks in this way, several new characteristics have been brought together and organized into twelve types that are used in machine learning model training. Several ML classifiers were used to train a phishing website classifier. Experimental results revealed that the proposed model could achieve 98.4% accuracy with a logistic regression classifier. This is a client-side solution that requires no third-party support. A neural system developed by Feng incorporates another phishing detection model [19]. In this particular case, the training was conducted using a Monte-Carlo technique, which yielded an accuracy of 97.71%, with a False Positive Rate of 1.7%, implying that the suggested model is preferable to other ML methods when it comes to detecting phishing websites.

Aburub and Hadi in [20] created association rules to help predict phishing websites.

This ten thousand legitimate and phishing websites dataset is comparable to other associative classification methods, which employs the phishing multi-class Association Rule system. They found that their detection method was accepted by a majority of the subjects. Additionally, there have been ML-based techniques that have employed various selection techniques [21, 22], ensemble classifiers [23], and hybrid deep learning and ML techniques [24].

3   Materials and Methods

The suggested genetic-based ensemble classifier technique is presented and explained in the present section. In the current study, you can see the methodology demonstrated in Fig. 1. The methodology employed in this study consists of three primary stages, training, ranking, and testing. As can be seen in the following sections, these stages are frequently mentioned. During training, we wish to give Bagging, GradientBoost, and LightGBM the ability to learn without needing optimization. To be able to use the data more efficiently, we first must make sure we have a general understanding of the ensemble classifications' overall performance, and then look into identifying which of the phishing website characteristics are most valuable. After implementing the GA, the GA was used to fine-tune the classifiers mentioned above. Using the GA, we improved the model's overall accuracy by picking the best parameters for our model. Following, in the ranking stage, the stacking method was employed to place the classifiers based on their accuracy, and to construct an ensemble classifier. At the outset, a sampling of the testing data was collected and employed.

[25] is based on following the methodology used in [26] in order to find out the features of the websites. From a range of sites containing both benign and malicious links, the list of verified phishing pages in the PhishTank database has been built. To remove the features that were present in the dataset of training, a Python script is made using Whois, urllib, ipaddress, requests, and Beautiful Soup (abnormality-based features, domain-based features, bar-based features and HTML and JavaScript features). Additionally, these attributes were made available to the classifiers, which were then used to predict the website's final class label.

In this study, the experiments were conducted on the UCI ML Repository dataset, which is publicly available [27]. Scripts were written in Anaconda under Windows 10 64-bit on a virtual machine using Anaconda. Python 3.6 was used, the language being Python 3.6. The dataset employed in these experiments includes both legitimate and

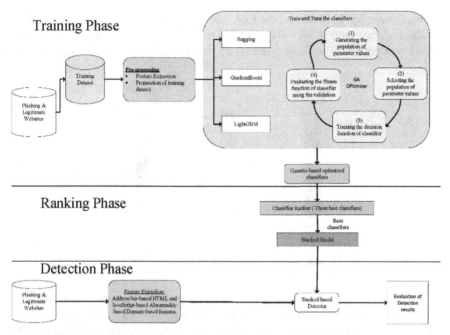

Fig. 1. A phishing website stack optimization model has been proposed.

phishing websites, which constitute 56% legitimate websites 44% phishing websites. The oversampling technique was used to make the dataset more imbalanced. For dataset (30 features), 12 features fall into the "address bar-based" category, 5 features into the "HTML and JavaScript-based" group, 6 features are classified as "abnormality-based," and the remaining two are split between "domain-based" and "web based" (7 features).

To evaluate the ensemble model, metrics specifically designed for the purpose were employed. This is the accuracy of the classification, the number of items recalled, the precision of the measurement, the F-score, and the false negative and false positive rates (FPR). Typically, many research projects used these evaluation metrics to examine the effectiveness of phishing website detection systems. 10-fold cross-validation were used in order to conduct accurate evaluations of the suggested method. Finally, each fold was evaluated to ensure the normality of the data.

4   Results and Discussion

The results of each experiment are explained in this section before a comparison with related work is presented. 10-fold cross validation was used to train an ensemble classifier set. To begin with, we didn't include optimization with GA in the experiment. The classifiers' performances were displayed, and it was found that the Bagging classifier yielded the best accuracy. Approximately 96.73% of the way to the target was correct. Classifiers with a remaining accuracy between 93% and 94.61% were the ones who received higher overall scores.

This figure (Fig. 2) illustrates the FPR (i.e. the false positive rate) and the FNR (i.e. the false negative rate) (FNR). Bagging had the best FPR and FNR with 0.07, which means it was notable. The Bagging had the lowest overall value, when measuring FNR (0.03).

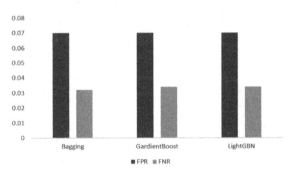

Fig. 2. Ensemble methods FPR and FNR

Overall, all classifiers demonstrated favorable results, but parameters must be fine-tuned to get better evaluation scores. It can be time-consuming to alter parameters for each classifier. The genetic algorithm is used to tune classifier parameters in the current study. There have been positive results in the area of algorithm parameter search, as demonstrated by the GA [28]. To configure the GA, the following parameters were used: (see Table 1).

Table 1. GA parameter settings that used in the present study

Parameter	Value
Population size	24
Generations	10
Mutation rate	0.02
Early stop	12
Crossover rate	0.5

The confusion matrices of GradientBoost and LightGBM are shown in Figs. 3 and 4, respectively.

With the help of the GA-GradientBoost classifier, we can observe in Fig. 3b that the GA-GradientBoost classifier got the most benefit from the optimization. The test determined that 95.94% of all identified instances as "phishing website", while the remaining 4.06% was identified as "legitimate". Moreover, they found that 98.04% of instances were deemed "legitimate" class, while only 1.96% of instances were deemed "phishing websites." We can conclude that GA-GradientBoost classifiers performed well, yielding TP rates that were above average and matching or even surpassing the FP rates. Table 2 shows the other measures of performance.

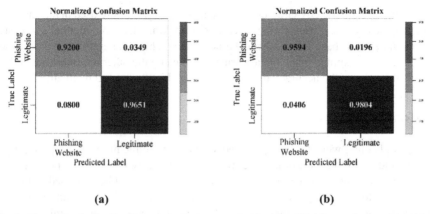

(a)   **(b)**

Fig. 3. Normalized GradientBoost confusion matrix for the phishing website: (a) without optimized parameters; (b) with optimized parameters

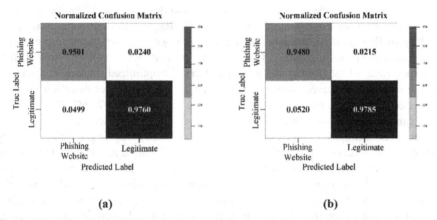

(a)   **(b)**

Fig. 4. Normalized LightGBM confusion matrix for the phishing website: (a) without optimized parameters; (b) with optimized parameters

Table 2. Performance evaluation of phishing website detection

Classifier	Class name	Precision	Recall	F-score
GA-GradientBoost	Phishing website	0.970	0.957	0.964
	Legitimate	0.968	0.975	0.971
	Weighted average	0.969	0.968	0.968
GA- Light GBM	Phishing website	0.951	0.942	0.947
	Legitimate	0.955	0.963	0.958
	Weighted average	0.953	0.953	0.953

The two classifiers, GA-GradientBoost and GA-Bagging, were used in the ensemble training. These models were further used in the stacking ensemble method's next step as base classifiers (base learners) for the next layer. The GradientBoost classification algorithm was examined in the meta-learner. After using the other ensemble methods in the previous phase, the accuracy reached 97.16%, which surpassed them all.

5 Conclusions

To detect phishing websites, an optimized stacking ensemble model is proposed in the present study. The optimization process was carried out by finding the optimized values for the parameters of several ensemble-learning methods. GA was used to find the optimized values. There were three stages in the proposed model: training, ranking and testing phases. The training stage was carried out by training several ensemble-learning classifiers (Bagging, GradientBoost, and LightGBM) that not yet optimized in this stage. Next to that, GA used to optimize these classifiers to select the optimal values of the model parameters and increase the whole accuracy. Ranking stage were assigned to select the best ensemble classifier (GradientBoost). These classifies was used as base classifier for a stacking ensemble method. Bagging and GB were used by the stacking method as meta-learners. Finally, testing stage was carried out to predict the final class label of testing dataset (phishing or legitimate websites). The finding from the experiments of the present study exhibited that the optimized stacking ensemble in the present study achieved greater performance compared to other detection methods that based on machine learning. The achieved accuracy reached 97.16%. To prove that the obtained improvements were statistically significant, a statistical analysis was performed. In addition, the findings showed that the proposed methods got higher accuracy comparing with recent studies that used the same phishing dataset. As a recommendation for future studies, more light detection method will be more accurate with IoT environments. Furthermore, using deep learning methods to investigate and improve the detection rate of phishing websites and using more phishing datasets is also advisable. For future work, an optimization is planned to be performed for six classifiers instead of the three in this study.

References

1. Gupta, B.B., Arachchilage, N.A.G., Psannis, K.E.: Defending against phishing attacks: taxonomy of methods, current issues and future directions. Telecommun. Syst. **67**(2), 247–267 (2017). https://doi.org/10.1007/s11235-017-0334-z
2. Gubbi, J., Buyya, R., Marusic, S., Palaniswami, M.: Internet of Things (IoT): a vision, architectural elements, and future directions. Futur. Gener. Comput. Syst. **29**(7), 1645–1660 (2018)
3. Roman, R., Najera, P., Lopez, J.: Securing the Internet of Things. Computer **44**(9), 51–58 (2011)
4. Tang, D.: Event detection in sensor networks. The George Washington University, School of Engineering and Applied Sciences, USA (2009)
5. Wei, B., Hamad, R.A., Yang, L., He, X., Wang, H., et al.: A deep-learning-driven light-weight phishing detection sensor. Sensors **19**(19), 1–13 (2019)

6. Somesha, M., Pais, A.R., Rao, R.S., Rathour, V.S.: Efficient deep learning techniques for the detection of phishing websites. Sādhanā **45**(1), 1–18 (2020). https://doi.org/10.1007/s12046-020-01392-4

7. Ali, W., Ahmed, A.A.: Hybrid intelligent phishing website prediction using deep neural networks with genetic algorithm-based feature selection and weighting. IET Inf. Secur. **13**(6), 659–669 (2019)

8. Chiew, K.L., Tan, C.L., Wong, K., Yong, K.S., Tiong, W.K.: A new hybrid ensemble feature selection framework for machine learning-based phishing detection system. Inf. Sci. **484**, 153–166 (2019)

9. Rao, R.S., Pais, A.R.: Detection of phishing websites using an efficient feature-based machine learning framework. Neural Comput. Appl. **31**(8), 3851–3873 (2018). https://doi.org/10.1007/s00521-017-3305-0

10. Ali, W., Malebary, S.: Particle swarm optimization-based feature weighting for improving intelligent phishing website detection. IEEE Access **8**, 116766–116780 (2020)

11. Khursheeed, F., Sami-Ud-Din, M., Sumra, I.A., Safder, M.A.: Review of security mechanism in Internet of Things (IoT). In: IEEE 3rd International Conference on Advancements in Computational Sciences (ICACS), Lahore, Pakistan, pp. 1–9 (2020)

12. Tsiknas, K., Taketzis, D., Demertzis, K., Skianis, C.: Cyber threats to industrial IoT: a survey on attacks and countermeasures. IoT **2**(1), 163–218 (2021)

13. Parra, G.D., Rad, P., Choo, K.K., Beebe, N.: Detecting Internet of Things attacks using distributed deep learning. J. Netw. Comput. Appl. **163**(102662), 1–20 (2020)

14. Mao, J., et al.: Phishing page detection via learning classifiers from page layout feature. EURASIP J. Wirel. Commun. Netw. **2019**(1), 1–14 (2019). https://doi.org/10.1186/s13638-019-1361-0

15. Virat, M.S., Bindu, S.M., Aishwarya, B., Dhanush, B.N., Kounte, M.R.: Security and privacy challenges in Internet of Things. In: IEEE 2nd International Conference on Trends in Electronics and Informatics (ICOEI), Tirunelveli, India, pp. 454–460 (2018)

16. Deogirikar, J., Vidhate, A.: Security attacks in IoT: a survey. In: IEEE International Conference on IoT in Social, Mobile, Analytics and Cloud (I-SMAC), Palladam, India, pp. 32–37 (2017)

17. Alsariera, Y.A., Adeyemo, V.E., Balogun, A.O., Alazzawi, A.K.: AI meta-learners and extra-trees algorithm for the detection of phishing websites. IEEE Access **8**, 142532–142542 (2020)

18. Jain, A.K., Gupta, B.B.: A machine learning based approach for phishing detection using hyperlinks information. J. Ambient. Intell. Humaniz. Comput. **10**(5), 2015–2028 (2018). https://doi.org/10.1007/s12652-018-0798-z

19. Feng, F., Zhou, Q., Shen, Z., Yang, X., Han, L., et al.: The application of a novel neural network in the detection of phishing websites. J. Ambient Intell. Humaniz. Comput. 1–15 (2018).https://doi.org/10.1007/s12652-018-0786-3

20. Aburub, F., Hadi, W.: A new association classification based method for detecting phishing websites. J. Theor. Appl. Inf. Technol. **99**(1), 147–158 (2021)

21. Gandotra, E., Gupta, D.: An efficient approach for phishing detection using machine learning. In: Giri, K.J., Parah, S.A., Bashir, R., Muhammad, K. (eds.) Multimedia Security. AIS, pp. 239–253. Springer, Singapore (2021). https://doi.org/10.1007/978-981-15-8711-5_12

22. Shabudin, S., Sani, N.S., Ariffin, K.A., Aliff, M.: Feature selection for phishing website classification. Int. J. Adv. Comput. Sci. Appl. **11**(4), 587–595 (2020)

23. Subasi, A., Molah, E., Almkallawi, F., Chaudhery, T.J.: Intelligent phishing website detection using random forest classifier. In: IEEE International Conference on Electrical and Computing Technologies and Applications (ICECTA), Ras Al Khaimah, UAE, pp. 1–5 (2017)

24. Yu, X.: Phishing websites detection based on hybrid model of deep belief network and support vector machine. IOP Conf. Ser. Earth Environ. Sci. **602**(1), 1–9 (2020)

25. Patil, D.R., Patil, J.B.: Malicious web pages' detection using feature selection techniques and machine learning. Int. J. High Perform. Comput. Netw. **14**(4), 473–488 (2019)

26. PhishTank, Developer information. http://phishtank.org/developer_info.php. Accessed 28 Feb 2021
27. Dua, D., Graff, C.: UCI machine learning repository. School of Information and Computer Science, University of California, Irvine, CA, USA. https://archive.ics.uci.edu/ml/datasets/Phishing+Websites. Accessed 10 Jan 2021
28. Jiang, Y., Tong, G., Yin, H., Xiong, N.: A pedestrian detection method based on genetic algorithm for optimize XGBoost training parameters. IEEE Access 7, 118310–118321 (2019)

Ambient Cloud and Edge Computing, SDN, Wireless and Cellular Communication

A Model to Detect Location Anomalies in a Cellular Network Using Travel Time and Distance Correlation

Rafia Afzal and Raja Kumar Murugesan[✉]

School of Computer Science and Engineering, Taylor's University,
Subang Jaya, Malaysia
afzalrafia@sd.taylors.edu.my, rajakumar.murugesan@taylors.edu.my

Abstract. Signaling System No. 7 (SS7) network standard was designed and built only for the networks of credible partners. By design, the signalling communication network neither protects the communication channel nor validates the network peers. The SS7 signalling network protocol has shortcomings such as the inability to verify the identity of the subscriber and their location, as well as the lack of an illegitimate message filtering system. Thus, an attackers could use these vulnerabilities to impose threats including intercepting mobile communications, performing account frauds, tracking subscribers and denial of service attacks. This study aims to develop a defensive model for anomaly detection by estimating the origin and destination with travel time correlation of incoming update location requests. The proposed method's performance is assessed using synthetic datasets, and the findings exhibit that the suggested model has higher anomaly detection accuracy with a low false alarm rate compared to existing methods.

Keywords: SS7 · Signaling network security · Telecommunication · Cellular network

1 Introduction

The mobile telecom networks use the Signalling System No. 7 (SS7), which act as a backbone of these networks for communication purposes. Moreover, it helps in managing bills of mobile service providers and other things simultaneously. The primary objective of SS7 is to establish a set of protocols to communicate, cooperate and provide services to their users for the telecommunication network elements. The global SS7 signalling security network has been regulated and fabricated, based on only trusted partners' network. For a very long era, it remained in the hands of these trusted parties as landline operators were only using it. The enhancement made in the network for new standards of communication and services, an Internet Protocol (IP) network-based signalling transport protocol (SIGTRAN) was developed for transferring message. The signalling communication network itself and by design does not either encrypt the communication

© Springer Nature Singapore Pte Ltd. 2021
N. Abdullah et al. (Eds.): ACeS 2021, CCIS 1487, pp. 459–468, 2021.
https://doi.org/10.1007/978-981-16-8059-5_28

channel or authenticate and verify peers of the entire network and now not even left isolated [6]. This disclosure of network is caused due to the design and the architecture requirement of roaming network of peers, which make this system vulnerable to attacks [8]. These vulnerabilities faced by users can be divided into four categories which are obtaining subscriber location information, spying or snooping, monetary mugging or account fraud and interruption and denial of subscriber service [11].

Hence, liberalization and shifting to IP make SS7 exposed towards grave outbreaks such as tracking subscribers' movements, conversational interference or eavesdropping, deception/spamming and subscriber's services interruption or denial at all and account frauds [3]. Several commercial signalling firewalls are currently being offered by companies working worldwide in the security domain, and also there has been significant work on Global System for Mobile Association (GSMA) level. However, they still lack the feature of a network being secure. As these commercial firewalls are only focusing on Home Public Land Mobile Network (PLMN) level protection to mitigate the risks. They are still not adequate and are hardly used as there are different ways of how the coverage could be evaded. This issue arises mainly because of lack of protection while subscribers are roaming and from a possibility of spoofing messages in SS7 Signalling Connection Control Part (SCCP) and Diameter protocols. Taking into consideration the fact that present defensive procedures such as the use of firewalls, filtering, and blacklisting, regrettably, these are not able to deliver satisfactory assurance of safety for SS7 [11].

This research aims to provide a defense model for anomaly detection in abrupt change in location of incoming messages requests. To address this issue, Cell-ID positioning technique is used. The dataset used for this research is simulated using an open-source attack simulator. Our main contributions are as follows:

- We present an overview of the Global System for Mobile communications (GSM) cellular network hierarchy with the Cell-ID components localization concept.
- We present a simple yet effective anomaly detection model for detecting abrupt location updates.

This paper is organized into the following sections. Section 2 provides a brief background of GSM network components. Section 3 highlights the literature review in terms of attack vectors with personifications. Section 4 presents the adopted methodology to detect anomalies. The results is in Sect. 5. While, Sect. 6 concludes the paper with some future directions.

2   Background

In this section, the GSM cellular network will first be briefly described before digging into details of cell ID components. The mobile networks are based on a number of geographically confined regions or cells covering a wider area. Each cell consists of a base station that sends data at a particular node. These areas are usually hexagonal cells that completely cover an area and are somewhat close to actual propagation patterns [1].

2.1 GSM Cellular Network Entities

There are 15 major conceptual entities comprising a GSM cellular network, which includes the Base Station System (BSS), the Mobile Station (MS), the Visitor Location Register (VLR) and the Mobile Switching Center (MSC) etc. This work does not cover the comprehensive explanation of these above mentioned units. Here is just a simplified example of GSM hierarchy, as shown in Fig. 1 that divides the entire GSM network into 5 localized service areas [7]. Each located area is specifically introduced as follows:

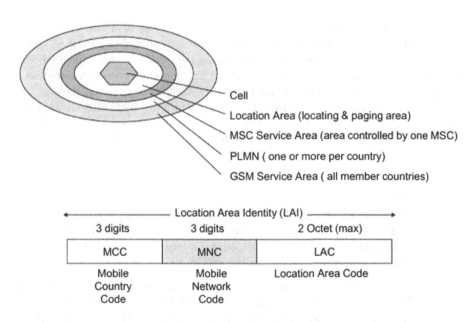

Fig. 1. GSM cellular network service areas

Cell: A cell is the geographic area served by a single base station responsible for continuous signals and data exchange in a mobile network with an MS. A global identification cell-ID (CI) is assigned to each cell that differentiates it from other cells [2].

Location Area: A geographical area of particular place is a larger region linked by one or more cells. Each cells is allocated a unique number known as a location area code (LAC). The LAC is used to verify the position of MS in this area by the communication system [2].

MSC/VLR Service Area: In GSM, there are many MSC/VLR service zones, all controlled by the same company and could be managed by a single MSC as well [2].

PLMN Service Area: In GSM, numerous MSC/VLR service areas are required at the same time by a mobile operator. These service areas are referred to as PLMN service areas. Generally, a country or a small region of a country or a group of countries may constitute a coverage area of a particular PLMN [2].

GSM Service Area: The GSM service area covers all PLMN services around the world. With the increase in number of BTSs worldwide, the GSM service area is continually expanding [2].

Cell-ID with Components: Cell-ID is a unique code a mobile device may detect and submit to a network (also referred to as a cell global identifier, CGI). It is a unique identification for mobile phone cells that enable linked phones to be found geographically. Whereabouts of any mobile phone connected to a particular cell tower can be identified using the Cell-ID of that cell tower.

A Cell-ID is uniquely identified by either combining LAC and CI alone or by using "Mobile Country Code (MCC)" and "Mobile Network Code (MNC)" tuple as well along with them, as seen in following Eq. 1 [2,10].

$$CellID = CGI = MCC + MNC + LAC + CI \tag{1}$$

In which:

1. In a GSM network, the MCC denotes the country to which a PLMN belongs.
2. In a GSM network, the MNC identifies the PLMN a user belongs to.
3. The location area of cell tower is known by a location area code (LAC).
4. The cell identification (CI) segregate a cell in a GSM network.

"MCC/MNC" tuple are defined by the International Telecommunication Union (ITU) and are both fixed. Tuples are available to the public in general, and we can retrieve practically any tuple from anywhere in the world in Cell. As an example, as previously stated, a CelCom Malaysia user's MCC and MNC are 502 and 198, respectively. We can acquired a full Cell-ID (i.e., 502198214545225) by extracting MCC (502), MNC (198), LAC (e.g., 2145) and a CI (e.g., 45225) the combination of LAC and CI alone uniquely identifies a cell in a cellular network.

3 Attack Vectors and Personifications

3.1 3G IMSI Catcher Using SendAuthenticationInfo

Unfortunately, the sendAuthenticationInfo message is used as genuine and legitimate message request while a subscriber is roaming, it cannot be blocked at the border [7,9].

3.2   Call Interception Using SendIdentification

The sendIdentification message request is only required during handovers within the internal network. It should be screened at the border since it has no legitimate use from external network [7,9].

3.3   Outgoing Traffic Interception Using InsertSubscriberData

The external networks should not send the insertSubscriberData message to the roaming operator's own network subscribers, However, it can be sent to external network subscribers travelling within the operator's network. It gets more difficult to filter such message requests at the border [7,9].

3.4   SMS Interception Using UpdateLocation

Unfortunately, when a subscriber roams outside of the operator's network the updateLocation message has a legitimate use case and cannot be screened at network boundaries [7,9].

3.5   Location Tracking Attack

Fortunately, there is no justification for receiving the anyTimeInterrogation message from an external networks, and should be blocked at the network's perimeter. if anyTimeInterrogation message is somehow filtered out at the network border, the attacker has provideSubscriberInfo message option as well that he can use to attack subscriber. however, he must have victim's IMSI (International Mobile Subscriber Identity) and MSC's address which he can get using sendRoutingInfoForSM message request, which delivers the MSC's Global Title (GT) address [7,9].

3.6   Frauds Using ProcessUnstructuredSS USSD

Unfortunately, in many circumstances, the operator enables this message to be received from other networks in case its roaming users want these services while visiting another country, making it difficult to filter such messages at the border [7,9].

3.7   Denial of Service Attack by Altering Subscriber Data

An attacker can deny a service to certain subscribers in a number of ways. The attacker can deactivate essential services or enable call barring for the target by using insertSubscriberData or deleteSubscriberData. Similarly, an attacker can use a cancelLocation message to deceive the network into disconnecting the subscriber from the network, preventing calls and SMSs from being sent. The attacker can alter allowed subscriptions of any subscriber by simply using MAP following messages requests "insertSubscriberData", "deleteSubscriber-Data" and "cancelLocation". For example, the attacker can rule out the phone and SMS call or even delete his record from VLR [7,9].

4   Methodology

In this section we will describe our methodology for anomaly detection. Figure 2 illustrate the flowchart.

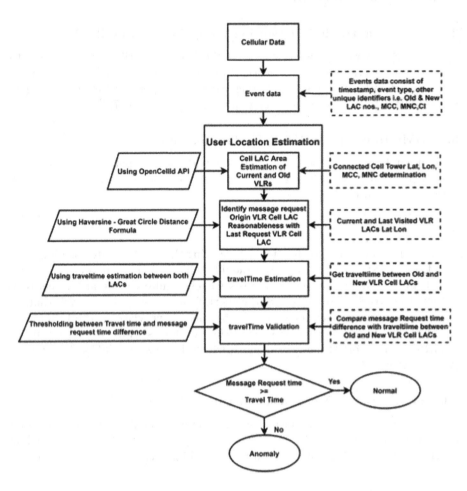

Fig. 2. Anomaly detection flow chart

4.1   Cellular Data and Feature Selection w.r.t. Event Data

An open-source SS7 attack simulator defined by Jensen et al. [4] was used. The simulator creates both normal and abnormal traffic to discover irregularities. The complex mode of the SS7 network simulator consists of three network operators, namely A, B and C. A victim is the first network provider (A), the second network operator (B) is a roaming network, while the third networking provider

(C) has an attacker. These operators interact with each other using thirteen standard messages, which do not involve an attack procedure that reflects the usual network traffic. Along with the regular messages, location tracking and call/SMS intercept attacks are carried out using UpdateLocation (UL) and ProvideSubscriberInfo (PSI) messages requests which target operator A's subscriber. The attacks are simulated by an attacker who is a subscriber from network operator C.

A set of features as illustrated below are selected to create a subscriber profile in network operator A. This profile is used to detect an abrupt change in the location of the subscriber and malformed parameters anomalies.

- Previous location updated
- Time since previous location update
- Distance traveled
- Message network origin address
- Message network destination address
- Time of the MAP message
- Location Area Code
- SCCP details
- Location of request generated
- Type of MAP message i.e. UL
- VIP Subscriber IMSI.

4.2   Detect Anomalous Updated Location Request by User Location Estimation

If an operator can maintain subscriber states, anomalies might be identified in the geographical movement of a single subscriber. For example, according to our simulation, the subscriber from operator A would travel at a consistent rate on daily basis. An anomaly occurs when an attacker uses the updateLocation (UL) message with a different location that is significantly far away from the subscriber's current location. This signals a journey between two far away locations in a very short period. To detect this anomalous behavior, the user location estimation is used. We achieve this by correlating the time and distance traveled by the subscriber from his last known VLR location to his current VLR location (updated by the attacker). Figure 2 illustrated flowchart to detect anomalous updated location requests. Time distance correlation are performed with the help of the attributes derived from the cellular event data. Following are the flowchart steps:

Cell LAC Area Estimation: The OpenCellId API [5] is used in this step. The APIs return the location coordinates for old and new VLR cell ids, which are then saved as the subscriber's old and new VLR address coordinates.

Find Distance Reasonableness Between Old and New VLR Addresses:
In this step, Great Circle Distance Haversine formula [12] is used to find distance between last known VLR cell id address to new request location update cell id address. These obtained distances are then correlated to find any irregularities in movement.

TravelTime Estimation: In this step Google Maps distance matrix API [5,12] is utilized to find travel time between last known VLR address to this new VLR address from where we have received update location request.

TravelTime Validation: The last step is to check if the time stamp difference is shorter than the minimum travel time between two updated locations, an anomaly was found indicating that the subscriber location has been abruptly changed.

5   Results

The proposed detection scheme's results are shown below. Based on the results in Table 1, we can conclude that the user location estimation check is a very useful method for detecting abnormal subscriber location update. The proposed anomaly detection model performs better than the existing methods in terms of detection rate, true positive rate, and false alarm rate. The proposed anomaly detection model has a higher accuracy and detection rate, and a true positive rate of 99.92% respectively and low false alarm rate of 18.18% compared to the existing methods such as Pattern Recognition ANN and Gen Regression ANN algorithm that are the closest in terms of performance as shown in Table 2.

Table 1. Proposed anomaly detection model results

	MAP UpdateLocation	
	True positive	True negative
Predicted positive	9	2
Predicted negative	0	2342
Accuracy	0.9992	
False positive rate	18.18	
Sensitivity	1.0000	
Precision	0.8181	

Table 2. Results comparison with existing techniques

Evaluation matrix algorithms	Detection rate %	False alarm rate %	True positive rate %
K-Means clustering [4]	100	49	75.25
SHESD algorithm [4]	100	43	57
Rule-based filtering [9]	98.8	33.2	66.8
Pattern recognition ANN [9]	99.58	24	76
Proposed model	**99.92**	**18.18**	**99.90**

6 Conclusion

With the expansion of the SS7 network, it has been progressively exposed to intruder along with new service providers, resulting in additional interfaces and potential threats to users' privacy. We have seen how SS7 vulnerabilities can easily be exploited if an attacker acquires access to the SS7 core network owing to a lack of built-in security measures. The implementation of new signalling messages for telephone mobility and sophisticated telecommunication services has resulted in further abuses and exploits such as subscriber targeting, call interception, SMS spamming, and denial of service attacks. In certain circumstances, location tracking down to the cell level and precise location tracking are also achievable. In an effort to find a new approach for detecting SS7 attacks, this research aims to provide a defense model for anomaly detection in abrupt change in new location of incoming messages requests to its last known location. To address this issue, Cell-ID positioning technique is used. The results shows that this technique gives higher accuracy in terms of location anomaly detection rate and low false alarm rate with respect to existing methods.

References

1. GSM Association: The mobile economy. Technical report, 35 (2018). https://doi.org/10.5121/ijcsit.2015.7409
2. ETSI: 3GPP Technical Specification 29.272 (2019). https://www.etsi.org/deliver/etsi_ts/129200_129299/129272/15.04.00_60/ts_129272v150400p.pdf
3. International Telecommunication Union(ITU)-T: ITU Workshop on SS7 Security. Technical report, International Telecommunication Union(ITU)-T (2016). http://www.itu.int/en/ITU-T/Workshops-and-Seminars/201606/Pages/default.aspx
4. Jensen, K., Nguyen, H.T., Do, T.V., Årnes, A.: A big data analytics approach to combat telecommunication vulnerabilities. Clust. Comput. **20**(3), 2363–2374 (2017). https://doi.org/10.1007/s10586-017-0811-x
5. Mahdizadeh, M.S., Bahrak, B.: A regression framework for predicting user's next location using call detail records. Comput. Netw. **183**, 107618 (2020)
6. Puzankov, S.: Stealthy SS7 attacks. J. ICT Stand. 39–52 (2017)
7. Rao, S.P., Holtmanns, S., Aura, T.: Threat modeling framework for mobile communication systems. arXiv preprint arXiv:2005.05110 (2020)

8. Shi, M.: ITU workshop on "SS7 Security" Geneva, Switzerland 29 June 2016. Technical report, June 2016
9. Ullah, K., Rashid, I., Afzal, H., Iqbal, M.M.W., Bangash, Y.A., Abbas, H.: SS7 vulnerabilities-a survey and implementation of machine learning vs rule based filtering for detection of SS7 network attacks. IEEE Commun. Surv. Tutor. **22**(2), 1337–1371 (2020)
10. Wang, Z., He, S.Y., Leung, Y.: Applying mobile phone data to travel behaviour research: a literature review. Travel Behav. Soc. **11**, 141–155 (2018)
11. Welch, B.: Exploiting the weaknesses of SS7. Netw. Secur. **2017**(1), 17–19 (2017)
12. Winarno, E., Hadikurniawati, W., Rosso, R.N.: Location based service for presence system using haversine method. In: 2017 International Conference on Innovative and Creative Information Technology (ICITech), pp. 1–4. IEEE (2017)

Analysing Security Concerns About the Massive Increase of Sharing Data over the Cloud During the Pandemic of Covid-19

Fatina Shukur[(✉)]

Department of Computer Science, University of Kufa, Kufa, Iraq
`fatinat.shukur@uokufa.edu.iq`

Abstract. With the unprecedented worldwide crisis of Covid-19, people with no choice have to change their lives, behaviours and the nature of their works. They have to adopt technology to continue their work, education, and communication. While more data are being uploaded, shared, processed, managed, and saved over the internet, there would be huge data generated frequently. Therefore, there is a big demand to use extra cloud capacity to access these data from everywhere at any time without restrictions. Also, to ensure use them safely and securely. Technology plays a vital role to overcome some of the challenges caused by Covid-19. For example, adopting cloud computing during pandemic has become double to handle the highest accelerating of process data through the cloud. However, the sudden and heavy use of cloud computing alerts the attack of cyber security. Therefore, this adds a threat to the security for different organisations around the world. Attackers are targeting vulnerable people who work, study, do personal business over the internet. In this research, we mainly analyse two types of data sources that have heavily uploaded to the cloud during Covid-19 time. These include data from educational institutes and business organisations. We propose a protocol with a sequence of steps-based a level of security required. We present three levels of security: high, medium, and low. Once a user or organisation identifies the desired security, the best match level of the security required will be easily selected accordingly. Our protocol is easy, affordable, and can be modified and adjusted. It can be used by a large popularity of people with different background and knowledge.

Keywords: Covid-19 challenges · e-learning · e-commerce · Cloud data · Authorisation

1 Introduction

Over a year ago, the World Health Organization (WHO) has announced the Corona virus is a global pandemic virus [15]. It is commonly called *Covid-19*. The quick spread of this virus is causing a sharp increase of people got infected and even dead. This is mainly due to gathering people or contact directly with each

© Springer Nature Singapore Pte Ltd. 2021
N. Abdullah et al. (Eds.): ACeS 2021, CCIS 1487, pp. 469–480, 2021.
https://doi.org/10.1007/978-981-16-8059-5_29

other. Therefore, the whole world has disrupted, and people have been asked to practice a social distance when they meet or stay at home, in order to minimise the spread of the virus and reduce the fatality rate. Accordingly, and to keep the main life activities going, governments at different countries have announced strict rules and proposed potential alternative solutions for their citizens. These broadly include the following aspects of

1. *Education*: learn from a distance electronically, (e-learning).
2. *Business*: work from home remotely, (e-commerce).
3. *Travelling*: enforce travel restrictions for both locally and globally.
4. *Healthcare*: support the healthcare sector to find a solution against Covid-19. To understand the nature of the virus and its characteristics, huge data from different populations are required to do lots of experiments. These data should be protected from any intrusion to avoid a life threatening.

We will be focusing on the first two aspects (education and business) as will be shown in Fig. 3, while the others are beyond the boundary of this research.

According to the above given aspects, this means attending classes is not allowed at schools, colleges, universities, and any other educational institutes. Thus, the entire education system has become electronically. Also, companies have shut down their buildings and their employees cannot work at their offices. They have to follow the policy of working from home if they can. Moreover, shops have closed, and customers have to make orders online.

To put the measures of the above aspects in place, we are, in fact, transforming our education and moving our business over the internet. As a result, our daily life meetings and communicating are based on using one of the video meeting applications such as Google Meets, Microsoft Teams, Zoom, and others [13]. Therefore, more data are being uploaded, shared, processed, managed, and saved online. Consequently, there will be huge data generated. As thus, there is a big demand to use cloud computing services such that to access and use these data safely and securely. Moreover, with the second and third waves of Covid-19, many more organisations have adopted cloud solutions, particularly with the cloud storage and the software services to cut the hardware usage as well as manage real time and big data workloads[1].

Generally speaking, in recent decades the use of cloud computing has grown rapidly, particularly with the diversity of cloud providers. Moreover, to tackle the crisis caused by Covid-19 [11] as explained above. Last year, 2020, showed a global exponential acceleration of cloud usage from all different types and sizes of companies even the start-up ones [5]. Also, to highlight the effect of this crisis over the cloud usage plans by organisations, a survey made by [7] showed that 90% of them have over cloud usage than their original plans. Therefore, some organisations are even struggling to predict their cloud costs correctly whilst Covid-19 is still existing and expanding over the world. Figure 1 [7] shows their average cloud costs were over budget estimate by 24%, and they expect further accelerate by 39% within a year. The main reason for this is the accelerating demand for extra cloud capacity in order to store and access the data as well as run applications.

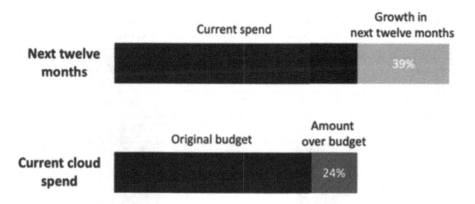

Fig. 1. Average cloud costs budget estimate during Covid-19 [7].

Globally, the expectation growth rate for the cloud computing market between 2021 and the next half decade, 2026 is from \$388.52 billion to \$784.80 billion [12] as shown in Fig. 2. While prediction of information security will be \$170.4 billion by 2022 [14].

This year, 2021, among the top leading vendors of cloud computing are Amazon Web Services (AWS), Microsoft Azure, Google Cloud Platform, IBM, Alibaba cloud, and many more [16].

The sudden and heavy use of cloud computing alerts the attack of cyber security, data- and network breaches as well as other challenges. In addition to more data are generating beside a set of challenges at the same time. Meanwhile, maintaining flexibility is also one of the top priorities for study or work remotely in the digital world. Therefore, we proposed a protocol for an online scheme based solution to deal with some of Covid-19 challenges.

The contributions of this paper are the following:

1. Introduce some of Covid-19 challenges based cloud data security
2. Analyse deeply the need to handle data over the cloud while highly increase the demand to adopt the cloud computing.
3. Present the above challenges that Covid-19 caused which include e-learning and remote working.
4. Propose a protocol of a multi authentication scheme to deal with the above challenges. We are, in fact, introducing a set of security levels to protect peoples' clouds accounts from unauthorised access by hackers and intruders. These levels are classified into three: high-, medium-, and low-levels. These levels can be selected based on people's desire and need. Hence, our proposed solution is feasible to be adopted by a large number of organisations or users with no complex mechanism and relatively low cost.
5. Moreover, our protocol is not only simple and affordable, but also, it can be adjusted easily by adding more steps or taking off steps at any step of the aforementioned security levels. Further, extra steps can be specified to certain users, applications, or scenarios when needed.

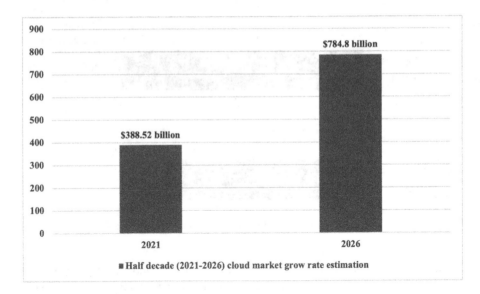

Fig. 2. Growth rate estimation of cloud market between this year and the next five years [12].

The structure of this paper is organised as follows. In Sect. 2, some of the challenges of sharing data over the cloud are analysed. We mainly focus on two aspects: education as well as business that deal with accessing data via the cloud (i.e., e-learning and e-commerce). Section 3 presents our proposed protocol with simple, appropriate, and sufficient solutions. Section 4 shows a discussion about attacks of cloud based different services during the pandemic of Covid-19. Finally, we draw our conclusions and set our future works at Sect. 5.

2   Challenges of Sharing Data over the Cloud

Through the unprecedented worldwide crisis of Covid-19, people with no choice have to change their lives and behaviours. Governments, companies, and institutions have to adopt technology to enable people to continue their work, education, and communication safely whilst staying at home or confirming the social distance. While many have swiftly transitioned to online facilities, neither all have given an adequate attention for security and privacy issues, nor have enough and good skills to protect themselves from being a prey of attackers. Many of them are listing within the education, business, and healthcare sectors as the most target data to get attacked. To meet the objective of this research, we will be presenting the first two sectors as follows:

2.1   Education (e-learning)

During the pandemic of Covid-19, millions of worldwide educational institutes are using mainstream live model at all different levels of learning and education

[6]. Lecturers at higher education and teachers at schools are delivering lessons and interacting with their students through a video/audio software. A software usually has features of online chat messages and sharing a digital screen. It could also have an option to record the video as well as save all the chatting messages. All these data (videos/audios, messages) could be automatically stored on the used software storage itself. In addition, they can be synchronised automatically via cloud-based software for an easy access by authorised staff/students. Such data can be vulnerable to cyber security attackers and breached because of the following:

1. At schools and universities, the popularity of users are young students who do not understand the risk behind cyber security attacks. Also, they might not even realise the existing of such threats. They do care about having fun when using technology based- an online service more than concern about its security threats. Such as playing games, share/exchange personal data/photos among their friends on social media.
2. We have a large number of educational institutes exist without a sufficient number of professional people in cyber security threats. In fact, it is impossible to have a balance between those high skilled people of internet concerns with the massive increase and quick transform to an online platform during this time of pandemic in particular.
3. As educational institutes have different experiences with remote learning. Generally speaking, we could have two cases: some institutes have to start from a scratch while others might have some repositories of digital contents. Therefore, the first case could face a sever cyberattack than the second case because it has to plan, design, implement, test, and run a digital system of remote learning program. In this case, the dedicated time, effort and priority will be given to create the system to support distance learning rather than keep it secure or maintain its security [3].

2.2 Business (e-commerce)

In order to mitigate the spread of Covid-19, working from home strategy has become the most acceptable and popular approach by people over the world. In addition to secure their jobs, and to keep the economy growing up.

Majority of people have to use their own devices for working at home. Such devices do not have the security details which are given by the government and public/private organisations offices that they use to have at work. Consequently, the system's security of these devices has become weak. Moreover, such weakness might also be caused by ignoring the notifications presented to people to keep updating their devices with the latest versions of the installed operating system as well as the supporting and running applications. Furthermore, working from home environment is, in fact, a new experience for many employees. It is, therefore, considered a more stressful environment as well as inconvenient to them. As a result, this leads to serious cyber-attacks in which hackers exploit such security loopholes.

Although a business community has already adopted the cloud into the market, Covid-19 pandemic has hugely boosted cloud computing services but without any restrictions [10]. These services become essential tools to collaborate team members of an enterprise remotely. On top of these services is to share data over the cloud, i.e., download, upload, exchange, store and process data.

With a big project, for example, some data are very large to be processed on a personal machine. Meanwhile, the data can no longer be accessed for processing via a local server. The unique alternative option is to shift such data to the cloud and access them from there. Not only for a storge purpose, but also to be accessed from everywhere by everyone with a prior and proper authorisation so that people can work together at the same time as if they are working at one place.

Due to the resources of weakness of security precaution (as explained above) with a massive increase of sharing data over the cloud during the Covid-19 crisis, data breaches are, in fact, not worse than the crisis itself. They are at the top list of the global risks by attackers as described in the following example:

Ransomware attack: Once the data are breached, they not only can get malicious encrypted, but also exfiltrated. Hackers usually demand for money from the owner of the data that can be a user, company or an organisation. If the bargaining did not get agreed, hackers threaten victims to reveal the data to public, share them with particular people who will misuse them, keep them or any other types of blackmail data methods. Moreover, it will be worst if the data got encrypted, they will most likely be lost [2].

3   Proposed Protocol: Cloud Security Levels Based Multi-authentication Policy

During Covid-19 and when many educational and non-educational organisations have moved to work/study from home, cloud computing has been adopted significantly. In addition to tolerate with the uncertainty of this time. Using the cloud is the best platform to access, process and save data/applications securely as we propose our solution and present it in Fig. 3.

The capacity and level of security can be easily adjusted to meet the organisations' requirements at any time when needed. Without an appropriate plan to address the cloud characteristics, organisations can be failed to substantial attacks. Therefore, we propose our protocol with a sequence of steps-based level of security required. i.e., our protocol is designed with a multi authentication policy. We broadly have three levels of security: high-, medium-, and low- level security as shown in Fig. 4. Data in the cloud will be unlocked upon a success of a multi authentication as described in the following steps:

- **Step1:** generate one-time random code and send it through a message on a given mobile number, or via an application

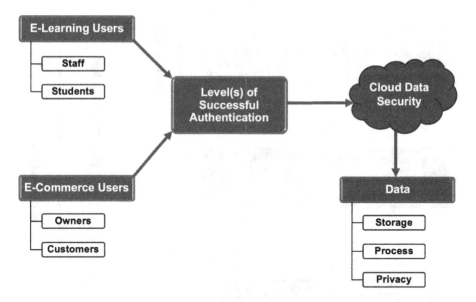

Fig. 3. Aspects of a successful authentication for cloud data security.

- **Step2:** use modality/multi-modalities of biometric data, such as face, voice, fingerprint, signature, etc.
- **Step3:** promote users to enter a passcode of six to eight digits/ characters at most prior to access their accounts.

Which level would be used, is determined by the desire of an organisation itself. To have a system that is more convenient, step one with a *low-level* security should be enough, and this would reduce the false rejections. Whereas to maintain a *high-level* security, it is, therefore, necessary to reduce the false acceptances. Then, a user has to pass the above three steps in sequence until get to unlock the cloud data. If a system considers a balance between false acceptances and false rejections, then, the *medium-level* security can be selected and used. In this case, steps two and three will be applied.

Fail to do any of the above three steps, (based on the level that will be chosen) after two succession attempts, will prevent the users from access their accounts. A user has to contact the authorisation centre to get registered as a new user. Also, one time access code within a certain time will be sent to the user prior to start the registration process.

4   Discussion: Cloud Services-Based Attacks During the Pandemic of Covid-19

Last year has had a major transformation of how companies operate and employees work and collaborate. As almost all industries used the collaboration tools

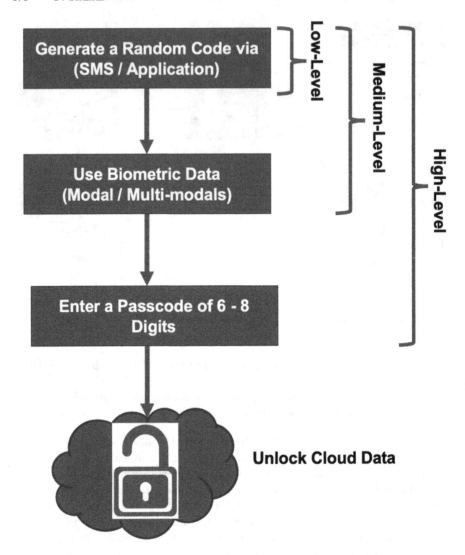

Fig. 4. Security levels based multi authentication policy.

remotely and all different levels of students have been taught though online virtual classes. Therefore, education and manufacturing sectors were among the highest usage of cloud services. They heavily depend on the cloud based different solutions and services such as using its collaboration, storage, and applications.

Figure 5 [9] showed the collaboration cloud from four applications services over the first four months of 2020. These applications are Zoom, Microsoft Teams, Slack, and Cisco. The following figure clearly present a dramatic increase of the cloud services by these applications after the first two months of 2020.

This means, after the widely spread of the corona virus, and when people have been asked to shift to digital world and work remotely.

Thus, cloud computing has become an essential tool for a successful digital migration. Such migration brings the cybercriminals attention to exploit any weakness at the new digital environment [4].

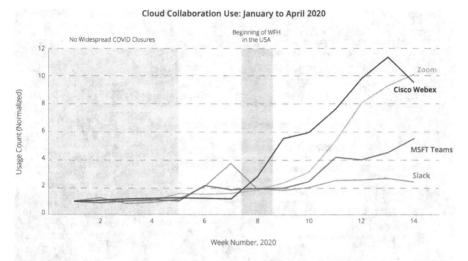

Fig. 5. Collaboration cloud of four applications services from January to April 2020 [9].

Recently, McAfee published a report to analyse cyber threats over the cloud throughout 2020 [8]. It gathered information from its over 30 million customers around the world for 10 countries as shown in Fig. 6. The customers are from different sectors including education, technology, estate agency, healthcare, bank, and others. It discovered more than 3 million cloud user accounts which have been externally attacked during the last year. The highest attacks rate was at the second quarter of last year, i.e., with the beginning of "stay at home and do stuff from there policy" among most countries. Although USA and New Caledonia have increased the attack rates during the second half of 2020, the rest eight countries have remained stable.

Figure 6 also shown that Thailand has the highest cloud attacks with 650,000 in the second quarter of 2020, and more than 500000 at both third and fourth quarters of last year. On the other hand, USA showed the least attacks among the given list of countries [8].

Generally speaking, as the pandemic still exists, attackers continue targeting vulnerable people who work, study, do personal business over the internet. Therefore, the best ways to deal with cyber attacks based cloud services, we recommend the following advice:

1. Educate users to avoid being a prey for most common cyber and cloud data attacks prior to their engagement with the digital world.

2. Build or improve security skills for users based on their age, education level, and need (i.e., to what extend they want to use the internet services).
3. Use our proposed protocol to protect users' accounts. It is simple, easy, and affordable.

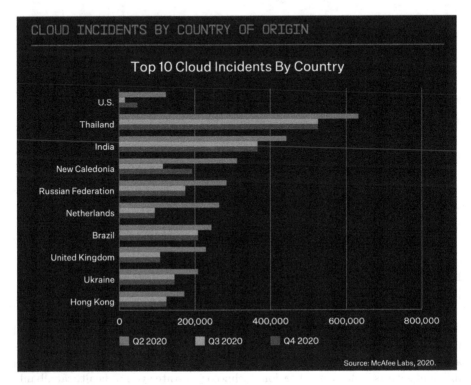

Fig. 6. McAfee analyses the cloud based attacks for 10 countries throughout 2020 [8]

5   Conclusion and Future Work

Governments, companies, and institutions have to adopt technology to enable people to continue their work, education, and communication safely whilst staying at home or confirming the social distance. While many have swiftly transitioned to online facilities, neither all have given an adequate attention for security and privacy issues, nor have enough and good skills to protect themselves from being a prey of attackers. Many of them are listing within the education and business sectors as the most target data to get attacked.

We proposed a multi authentication protocol to deal with some Covid-19 challenges. In fact, we introduced a set of security levels to protect peoples' clouds accounts from unauthorised access by hackers and intruders. We believe, maintaining flexibility is one of the top priorities for study or work remotely in a digital world. Moreover, it is a new environment for many people. Therefore, we set a three classifications of security levels. These included high-, medium-, and low-security levels. A security level can be selected easily based on people's desire and need. Hence, our proposed solution is feasible to be adopted by a large number of organisations/users with no complex mechanism, i.e., it is simple and affordable.

Many businesses, companies, and organisations, that have migrated their systems to the cloud during Covid-19 pandemic, would most likely remain using the cloud services even after the pandemic is over [1]. We could also conclude that Covid-19 itself has added a threat to the could computing security environment for different organisations over the world. Our future work is to implement our proposed protocol with different scenarios to measure its validity, and to what extent can be applied and by whom.

References

1. BBC: The role of cloud for companies in a post-pandemic world, a better tomorrow. http://www.bbc.com/storyworks/future/a-better-tomorrow/the-role-of-cloud-for-companies-in-a-post-covid-19-world. Accessed 03 June 2021
2. European-Data-Protection-Board: Guidelines 01/2021 on examples regarding data breach notification, 14 January 2021
3. Fernandez, A., Peralta, D., Herrera, F., Benítez, J.: An overview of e-learning in cloud computing. In: Uden, L., Corchado, R.E., De Paz Santana, J., De la Prieta, F. (eds.) Workshop on Learning Technology for Education in Cloud (LTEC 2012). Advances in Intelligent Systems and Computing, vol. 173, pp. 35–46. Springer, Heidelberg (2012). https://doi.org/10.1007/978-3-642-30859-8_4
4. He, W., Zhang, Z.J., Li, W.: Information technology solutions, challenges, and suggestions for tackling the COVID-19 pandemic. Int. J. Inf. Manag. **57**, 102287 (2021)
5. ITU-News: How cloud computing has supported the COVID-19 response, 01 June 2021. https://news.itu.int/how-cloud-computing-has-supported-the-covid-19-respons
6. Joia, L.A., Lorenzo, M.: Zoom in, zoom out: the impact of the COVID-19 pandemic in the classroom. Sustainability **13**(5), 2531 (2021)
7. Luxner, T.: Cloud computing trends: 2021 state of the cloud report, 15 March 2021. https://www.flexera.com/blog/cloud/cloud-computing-trends-2021-state-of-the-cloud-report
8. McAfee: McAfee labs threats report, April 2021
9. McAfee: Cloud adoption and risk report: work from home edition, May 2020
10. Oxford-Analytica: Pandemic will boost global use of cloud computing. Emerald Expert Briefings (OXAN-DB)
11. Penteo: Why is the demand for cloud services growing rapidly? https://www.linkeit.com/blog/accelerated-growth-in-the-demand-for-cloud-services. Accessed 03 June 2021
12. Research, Markets: Research and markets the world's largest market research store, June 2021. https://www.researchandmarkets.com/reports/5094093/cloud-computing-market-research-report-by-type#rela4-5136796

13. Soni, V.D.: Global impact of e-learning during COVID 19. Available at SSRN 3630073 (2020)
14. Varonis: Cybersecurity statistics and trends for 2021, 02 January 2021. https://www.varonis.com/blog/cybersecurity-statistics/
15. World Health Organization, et al.: Statement on the second meeting of the international health regulations emergency committee regarding the outbreak of novel coronavirus (2019-ncov) (2020)
16. Zdnet: Top cloud providers in 2021: AWS, Microsoft Azure, and Google Cloud, hybrid, SaaS players, 11 January 2021. https://www.zdnet.com/article/the-top-cloud-providers-of-2021-aws-microsoft-azure-google-cloud-hybrid-saas/

Intrusion Detection Systems in Fog Computing – A Review

Fadi Abu Zwayed[1]([⊠]) [iD], Mohammed Anbar[1] [iD], Yousef Sanjalawe[1,2] [iD], and Selvakumar Manickam[1] [iD]

[1] National Advanced IPv6 Centre of Excellence (NAv6), Universiti Sains Malaysia (USM), 11800 George Town, Penang, Malaysia
{anbar,selva}@usm.my
[2] Computer Science Department, Northern Border University, KSA, Arar, Saudi Arabia

Abstract. With the growing volume of network throughput, packet transmission and security threats and attacks in Fog computing, the study of Intrusion Detection Systems (IDSs) in this environment has grabbed a lot of attention in the computer science field in general, and security field in particular. Since Fog, computing can be depicted as an emerging cloud-like platform holding similar data, information, computation, storage resources and application services, but is principally distinct in that it is decentralized platform. Besides, as aforementioned, Fog Computing is capable of processing huge volume of data locally, operate on premise, that is totally portable, and can be installed on several heterogeneous hardware devices; thus these characteristics make it highly vulnerable for time and location-sensitive applications; and therefore vulnerable to security attacks targeting sensitive data, virtualization technique, segregation, network resources and others. Existing IDSs pose challenges and shortcomings such as consumption of huge computational resources, capricious intrusion categories, and so forth. However, there is a number of prior studies to highlight the existing IDS issues in Fog Computing, but still there is a need to provide more comprehensive review of the most recent studies conducted in the same area to provide a more elaborated clear image for a comprehensive review. Through the inclusive review and advanced organization of this article, a new taxonomy is provided to categorize recent IDSs in Fog Computing.

Keywords: Attacks · Fog Computing · IDS · Intrusion Detection System · Review · Shortcomings · Threats

1 Introduction

Fog computing denoted a novel pattern offering computational resources in a geographically distributed manner [1]. Specifically, fog computing provided service-based entry to computational resources with similar service models, such as cloud computing. Other technologies, including virtualization and containers) were employed to facilitate effective management and high resource usage. Unlike cloud computing (following several high-capacity data centers), fog computing utilized a big set of extensively distributed and heterogeneous resources with average capacity (fog nodes) [2, 3]. The primary fog

© Springer Nature Singapore Pte Ltd. 2021
N. Abdullah et al. (Eds.): ACeS 2021, CCIS 1487, pp. 481–504, 2021.
https://doi.org/10.1007/978-981-16-8059-5_30

computing benefit over the cloud counterpart indicated the proximity to end devices, such as sensors and actuators, smartphones, smart cameras, and Internet of Things (IoT) devices.

As other network topologies, Fog computing, as the complement of Cloud Computing (CC), can offer low-delay services between several mobile users and the CC. Nevertheless, devices of for computing might encounter security issues resulting the fog nodes being close to the end fog-users and having limited computing ability. Some of these issues might destroy the whole network and fog nodes as well; therefore, Intrusion Detection System (IDS) is one of the most effective solution that can handle this concern or mitigate its impact. IDS is a proactive security detection mechanism [4, 5], and can be utilized in the Fog Environment. However, IDSs in classical networks have been well investigated and studied in details, unfortunately directly utilizing them in the Fog Computing environment may be improper. Since fog nodes introduce massive volume of data at all times, and, therefore, implementing an IDS system in the Fog Computing environment is of radical importance. However, existing IDSs pose challenges and shortcomings such as consumption of huge computational resources, capricious intrusion categories, and so forth. However, there is a number of prior studies to highlight the existing IDS issues in Fog Computing, but still there is a need to provide more comprehensive review of the most recent studies conducted in the same area to provide a more elaborated clear image for a comprehensive review. Through the inclusive review and advanced organization of this article, a new taxonomy is provided to categorize recent IDSs in Fog Computing.

The paper is structured as follows: In the following section, background of Fog Computing, fog architecture, fog layers, fog characteristics, fog security issues and attacks are provided. Then, in Sect. 3 related works are categorized and discussed by highlighting shortcomings and to highlight their significance. Finally, in Sect. 4, we conclude by providing a discussion of the identified shortcomings, motivating future research.

2 Background

This section provides a background of Fog computing, its architecture, features and issues.

2.1 Fog Computing

As the aforementioned end devices generally encompassed highly restricted capabilities, end-device applications frequently required devices that are more advanced. One alternative involved cloud utilization as back-end applications. Regardless, the method resulted in high latency following the long network path between end devices and cloud data centers. As the network connection bandwidth of cloud data centers might pose another drawback, fog computing (fog nodes) utilization resulted in substantially lower latency and no cloud-level intricacies [6]. Fog computing was first coined in 2012 when CISCO denoted the term as "a highly-virtualized platform that provides computing, storage, and networking services between end devices and traditional cloud computing data centers, typically but not exclusively located at the edge of the network" [1]. Consequently, recent works of literature have highlighted the essentiality of fog computing [7–11].

[6] recommended a sound fog-computing connotation as follows: "Fog computing is a scenario where a huge number of heterogeneous (wireless and sometimes autonomous), ubiquitous, and decentralized devices communicate and potentially cooperate among them and with the network to perform storage and processing tasks without the intervention of third-parties. These tasks can be for supporting basic network functions or new services and applications that run in a sandboxed environment. Users leasing part of the devices to host the services received incentives for doing so." [9] developed a similar fog computing definition the following year by stating that "fog computing is a geographically-distributed computing architecture with a resource pool consisting of one or more ubiquitously-connected heterogeneous devices (edge devices) at the edge of the network and not exclusively seamlessly-backed by cloud services to collaboratively provide elastic computation storage and communication (and many other new services and tasks) in isolated environments to a large scale of clients in proximity."

2.2 Fog Architecture

This subsection presents an overview of fog architecture. Recent attempts to define the fog computing architecture model has garnered much scholarly attention as most relevant studies denoted a three-layer architecture involving cloud, fog, and IoT [8, 9, 12–14]. Additionally, the OpenFog combination implied a wider N-layer reference architecture [15] as a modification of the three-layer counterpart.

Three-Layer Architecture
The three-layer fog computing architecture fundamentals (illustrated in Fig. 1) originated from the primary fog computing notion as cloud computing expansion within the cloud-IoT spectrum [16]. The architecture demonstrated an intermediate layer (fog) to close the cloud infrastructure-IoT device gap. All the three layers underpinning the architecture are elaborated as follows [13]:

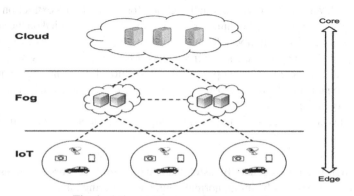

Fig. 1. 3-tier architecture of Fog computing.

The IoT Layer
The aforementioned layer involved IoT devices (sensors, smart vehicles, drones, smartphones, and tablets) and was widely geographically distributed for upper-layer data-sensing and delivery for containment or processing. Notwithstanding, computational devices with significant capacities (smartphones) potentially executed local processing before upper-layer engagement.

Fog Layer
The layer denoted the fog computing architecture baseline encompassing multiple fog nodes. Following the OpenFog consortium, a fog node implied "the physical and logical network element that implements fog computing services" [17]. For example, fog nodes could calculate, transfer, and temporarily contain data (to be identified anywhere between the cloud-end device spectrum). Consequently, fog nodes were explicitly associated with end devices for service provision. The nodes were also linked to the cloud infrastructure for service provision and attainment. For example, fog nodes potentially benefitted from cloud storage and computational capacities while offering users contextual knowledge.

Cloud Layer
The layer primarily encompassed centralized cloud infrastructure involving specific servers with high computational and storage capacities using various services. Unlike conventional cloud computing architecture, the fog counterpart involved computations or services that could be effectively transferred from cloud to fog layers for minimal cloud resource load and optimal effectiveness.

OpenFog N-Tier Architecture
The N-tier architecture suggested by the OpenFog Consortium (OpenFog, 2017) is presented in Fig. 2 and primarily established an internal fog layer structure under the three-layer architecture to facilitate industry players in Fog computing deployment within particular contexts. Albeit contextual fog software and system deployments, the key fog architecture determinants remained palpable in fog deployment. The three primary components involved endpoints or things, fog nodes, and cloud.

Given the fog layer construction with several fog node tiers (N-tiers), the nodes that moved away from end devices obtained higher computational capacities and astuteness. Every upper-level fog layer was gradually refined for relevant data extraction and high astuteness at every level. The tier number in a certain deployment relied on the contextual needs, such as end device numbers, the work load and form addressed by every tier, node capacities at every tier, and latency prerequisites. Moreover, fog nodes on every layer might be interconnected to develop a mesh for additional elements (resilience, error acknowledgement, and load equilibrium). As such, fog nodes could interact horizontally and vertically in the architecture.

Fog nodes could be classified following endpoint and cloud proximity in the N-tier vision:

- Lowest tier: Fog nodes generally instructed and monitored sensors and actuators with primary emphasis on obtaining, normalizing, and gathering data;

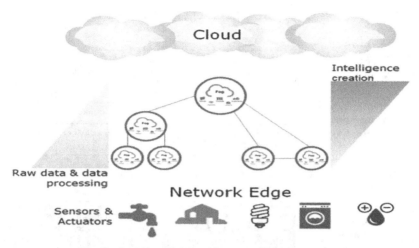

Fig. 2. OpenFog N-tier architecture of Fog Computing.

- Intermediate tiers: Fog nodes essentially emphasized data filtering, compression, and conversion from the lower layer. Typically, the nodes encompassed more analytical capacities;
- Highest tier: Fog nodes closest to the cloud generally undertook data aggregation and knowledge construction.

2.3 Fog Computing Layers

Fog computing denoted a method that conveyed certain data center operations to the network edge with restricted computing, retainment, and networking services between end devices and classic cloud computing data centers. Essentially, fog computing offered low and assumable latency for time-sensitive IoT implementations [18]. Fog computing architecture encompassed six layers: physical and virtualization, monitoring, pre-processing, temporary storage, security, and transport [19–22] (see Fig. 3).

The physical and virtualization layer encompassed various node forms (physical and digital nodes and digital sensor networks). The nodes were handled and sustained following certain types and service requirements. As such, various sensor forms were geographically distributed to detect the context and transfer the gathered data to upper layers through gateways for extended processing and filtering [15]. Regarding the monitoring layer, resource usage, sensor obtainability, fog nodes, and network components were assessed. All node performance measures (analyzing node-task performance, duration, and subsequent requirements) were assessed in the aforementioned layer. All application and service performance and conditions (deployed on infrastructure) and fog node energy consumption were duly evaluated [19]. Given that fog computing employed multiple devices with various power consumption levels, energy management strategies could be timely and successful [19, 21].

The pre-processing layer executed data management duties. The gathered data were subsequently evaluated with data-filtering and trimming for genuine knowledge extraction. As the aforementioned data was contained within the temporary storage layer,

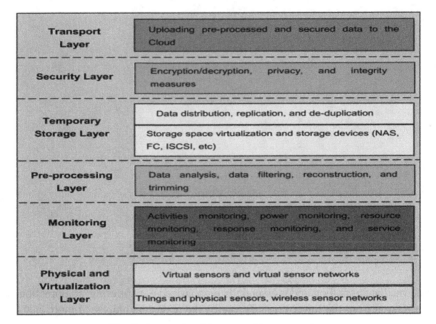

Fig. 3. Layered architecture of fog computing.

local storage was no longer needed in cloud transmission data and could be omitted from temporary media storage [21, 22]. Data encryption or decryption was highlighted in the security layer with integrity-based strategies for data protection against tampering. Regarding the transport layer, pre-processed data were uploaded to the cloud for the extraction and establishment of more insightful services [21, 22]. Notably, only a part of the gathered data was uploaded to the cloud for optimal power usage. In this vein, the gateway device linking IoT to cloud initiated data-processing before cloud delivery. In smart gateways, the data gathered from sensor networks and IoT devices were conveyed using the aforementioned gateways to the cloud. The cloud was consequently contained and employed to establish user services [23]. Following the restricted fog resources, a communication protocol was deemed necessary for efficiency, transportability, and customizability. In this vein, communication protocol selection relied on the fog application setting [24].

2.4   Fog Computing Characteristics

Fog computing offered various features in IoT devices (computation, processing, interaction, and containment) regarding closer user network edge devices. The offered service capacities indicated closeness to IoT devices and were the most essential and beneficial fog computing attribute as opposed to other conventional computing models [7]. Other attributes are listed as follows:

Low Latency and Real-Time Interactions

Fog nodes in close network edges obtained IoT device-generated data (sensors and devices), subsequently processing and retaining data with network edge devices in local network areas. Consequently, data movement across the Internet was substantially minimized with sustainable, high-speed, high-quality, and localized endpoint services [13] for low latency and real-time communication, specifically involving latency or time-sensitive applications [1].

Bandwidth Conservation

Cloud computing was primarily employed towards effective calculation and big storage capacity (resembling fog computing) that expanded to network edge services to process and contain the data produced and evaluated between end nodes and conventional cloud. The IoT device-generated data were subsequently collected and computed (data preprocessing, redundancy omission, data cleaning, and valuable knowledge extraction) and locally executed at the fog layer. A small portion of the insightful data was then uploaded to the cloud following data processing.

Mobility Support

The fog computing pattern denoted different interrelated IoT devices, including smartphones, vehicles, and smartwatches (versatility through frequent spatial mobility at the terminal layer) amid several static end devices (traffic cameras). In this regard, explicit fog computing-mobile device interactions proved crucial. Given that mobile device also indicated explicit intercommunication [25], mobile device access followed physical proximity based on specific communication technologies (ZigBee, Bluetooth, Near Field Communication (NFC), and Millimeter Wave Communication). The addressed complexities could prevent network connectivity disruptions due to mobility [6]. For enhanced system and service quality, fog computing architecture facilitated location-oriented mobility needs and administrators to monitor users, mobile device entries, and information access methods [26].

Heterogeneity

Fog nodes were derived from various elements and arranged in extensive contacts through physical or virtual nodes [27]. The nodes typically involved high-performance servers, edge routers, access points, gateways, and base stations. The fog computing platform was established by a multi-tiered hierarchical architecture (from edge to core). In different IoT applications (smart homes, vehicles, and cities), fog node resources and service interfaces proved extremely versatile and heterogeneous at various architecture hierarchy levels to respond to requirements on extensively distributed and low-latency applications [28].

Geographical Distribution and Decentralized Data Analysis

Although cloud computing denoted extensive geographical node distributions, fog nodes tended to be clustered. As a cloud computing extension, fog computing was also related to cloud and IoT devices (end users). In this vein, all fog layer nodes were distributed in extensively spread clusters. Certain nodes (servers, switches, access points, gateways, and routers) could be statically distributed. As a knowledge-processing and storage option in a centralized data center (away from end-users and IoT devices), the decentralized fog computing architecture confirmed the data analysis proximity to customers. The processing attribute could catalyze rapid big data analysis, enhanced location-oriented services, and high real-time decision-making capacities [27].

Interoperability
Due to the heterogeneous nature, fog nodes and IoT devices (end users) were derived from various providers that were generally incorporated into different settings. In this vein, fog computing should interoperate and collaborate with various providers to manage broad error-free service ranges for particular service facilitations [27].

Low Energy Consumption
Fog computing architecture enabled the geographical distribution of fog nodes as an essential cooling system for minimal heat following concentration [29]. Specifically, IoT devices were associated with dense fog nodes that potentially led to low paradigm-oriented power consumption, computational energy conservation, and minimal cost. Notably, low energy consumption in fog computing potentially facilitated greener computation.

Privacy Protection and Data Security
Fog computing offered services nearer to end-users (sensors, IoT devices, and mobile phones) to secure end-users with efficient outcomes following layer proximity. The computing also enabled data protection through encryption and separation. For example, fog nodes offered access to control policies, various encryption algorithms for security measures, integrity assessment for confidentiality, and isolation strategies to protect data privacy and avoid system upgrade risks [30].

2.5 Fog Computing Security Issues

As security and privacy should undeniably be regarded within every layer in fog computing system development, this study posed the following question: "What is novel regarding fog computing security and privacy?" Following fog computing attributes, further research proved necessary to manage the intricacies.

Trust and Authentication
Although data centers were generally owned by cloud service providers in cloud computing deployment, fog service providers could imply distinct parties following various deployment options: (a) Internet service providers or wireless carriers with a home gateway or cellular base station control might construe fog with current infrastructure, (b) cloud service providers who intended to extend cloud services to network edge could establish fog infrastructure, and (c) end-users with a local private cloud to minimize ownership cost could convert the cloud into the fog and lease additional resources. The versatility inevitably complicated fog trust circumstances.

Trust Model: Reputation-oriented trust model [31] was effective in ecommerce, peer-to-peer (P2P), user reviews, and online social networks. [32] recommended a holistic reputation system for resource selection in P2P networks with a distributed polling algorithm to evaluate resource dependability before downloading. Specific intricacies required alternatives to develop a reputation-oriented fog computing system, such as (a) consistent, novel, and specific identity attainment, (b) intentional and innocent misdemeanor management, and (c) reputation-oriented penalties and redemption. Trust models also followed unique hardware, such as Secure Element (SE), Trusted Execution Environment (TEE), or Trusted Platform Module (TPM) for trust utilization in fog computing applications.

Rogue Fog Node: A rogue fog node denoted a fog device or situations that were assumable legal and persuaded end-users for connections. Although a fog administrator might be authorized to handle fog-oriented contexts in an internal attack, the administrator might initiate a rogue fog situation compared to a legal counterpart. Relevant research [8] indicated man-in-the-middle attack viability in fog computing, wherein the gateway could either be undermined or substituted with a fake counterpart. Intruders could exploit incoming and outgoing end-user or cloud needs, stealthily gather or tamper user data, and conveniently launch further attacks upon connection. Artificial fog nodes were substantial threats to user data safety and confidentiality. The complexity proved challenging to resolve in fog computing following specific purposes: (a) intricate trust circumstances required various trust management schemes and (b) the versatile creation and omission of digital machine situations proved challenging to sustain a rogue node blacklist. A measurement-oriented technique facilitated clients to avoid linking rogue access point (AP) [33, 34]. The method leveraged the round-trip period between end-users and the DNS server to identify rogue AP from clients' perspectives.

Authentication: Authentication denoted an essential fog computing security component as services were provided to big-scale end-users using front fog nodes. Primary fog computing security intricacies were regarded as authentication at different fog node levels [8]. As conventional PKI-oriented authentication proved ineffective with low measurability [35], an affordable, safe, and user-friendly alternative was recommended for the authentication issue in local impromptu wireless networks that depended on physical pre-authentication contact in a location-restricted medium. Likewise, NFC could be employed to simplify the verification procedure regarding cloudlets [36]. The biometric verification in mobile and cloud computing (fingerprint, face, and touch or keystroke-oriented verification) would be advantageous for biometric application following fog computing verification.

Network Security
Based on the wireless concept in fog networking, wireless network security indicated major fog networking conundrums (jamming and sniffer attacks). The attacks could be regarded in wireless network study domains (excluded in the present study scope). Although manual network administrator configurations and network management traffic separation from constant data traffic required network trust [37], fog nodes were deployed at the network (Internet) edge and burdened network management, such as big-scale

cloud server sustenance cost (distributed across the network edge without convenient maintenance access).

Secure Data Storage

User data was outsourced in fog computing while user control over data was conveyed to fog nodes, hence presenting the same safety threats in cloud computing. Data authenticity proved challenging to establish as the outsourced data could be lost or inaccurately readjusted. Second, the uploaded data could be manipulated by illegal parties for unethical interests. Consequently, verifiable data storage services were recommended in the cloud computing context for cloud computing data protection. For example, homomorphic and searchable encryption denoted integrative strategies for cloud storage system integrity, privacy, and authenticity to permit clients' data storage-monitoring in unreliable servers.

Secure and Private Data Computation

Another crucial fog computing complexity involved attaining safety and confidentiality-sustaining computation (outsourced to fog nodes).

Verifiable Computing: Authenticated computing facilitated computing devices to offload computation roles to unreliable servers while sustaining authenticated outcomes. Other servers monitored the roles and reciprocated outcomes with evidence that the function was accurately executed. The term was duly formalized in [38]. Specifically, fog users should authenticate computation accuracy in fog computing to cultivate computation confidence (offloaded to the fog node).

Data Search: Confidential end-user data required encryption before outsourcing to the fog node, thus deterring efficient data usage services and data privacy protection. One of the most essential services implied keyword searches within encrypted data files. Some searchable encryption schemes were established for users to safely search through encrypted data using non-decrypted keywords. [39] recommended initial encrypted data search schemes for encryption secrecy, query separation, controlled searching, and hidden query support along with other scheme developments [40, 41].

Privacy

Private information (data, venue, or usage) leakage has garnered substantial attention when end users employed specific services (cloud computing, wireless network, and IoT). Privacy protection intricacies in fog computing (Security and Privacy Issues of Fog Computing) as fog nodes indicated end-users with more sensitive data than the remote clouds underlying the fundamental network. Consequently, privacy-protection methods were suggested in multiple settings, such as cloud [42], smart grid [43], wireless network [44], and digital social network [45].

Data Privacy: Privacy-protection algorithms in the fog network were operable between fog and cloud while the algorithms typically encompassed resource restrictions in end devices. Generally, fog nodes at network edges gathered sensor and end-device-generated confidential data. For example, homomorphic encryption could be employed for privacy-protection aggregation in non-decrypted local gateways [46]. Differential privacy could also be employed for the non-disclosure privacy of a random data entry in the dataset involving statistical queries.

Usage Privacy: Another privacy complexity denoted the utilization trend where a fog client employed fog services. In smart grids, smart meter reading would reveal many household data (the absence of household members at specific periods and the specific time the television was switched on) that undoubtedly compromised user privacy. Although privacy-protection strategies recommended smart metering [43, 47], the mechanisms proved irrelevant in explicit fog computing following the lack of reliable external parties (smart meter in a smart grid) or the absence of counterpart devices (battery). Given that fog nodes conveniently gathered end-user utilization statistics, a potential (albeit gullible) alternative was to encourage fog clients towards artificial task development and merging genuine counterparts among the dummies (to be offloaded into multiple fog nodes). Nevertheless, the alternative eventually increased fog clients' expenditure and resource and energy wastage. As such, smart application classification proved necessary to ensure the offloaded resource utilization preserved private data.

Location Privacy: Location privacy in fog computing primarily denoted fog clients' area confidentiality. As fog clients generally offloaded specific tasks to the closest fog node, the node with the offloaded work implied fog clients' proximity. If a fog client employed multiple fog services in various locations, the pathway might be revealed to fog nodes through hypothetical collisions. In this regard, individual and non-human area privacy was at risk with such associations.

Access Control

Access control was a valid instrument for system safety and user privacy protection. Conventional access control was typically responded to under the same trust domain. Following the cloud computing outsource nature, cloud computing access control was cryptographically incorporated for outsourced information. Notably, symmetrical key-based alternatives were non-measurable in crucial management.

2.6 Fog Computing Attacks

Following Fig. 4, malicious attacks reflected a substantial threat to fog computing. Following [48, 49], fog computing attacks were categorized as follows:

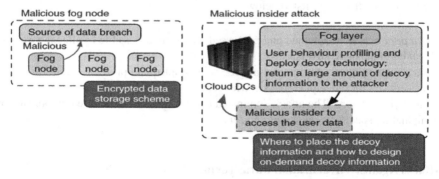

Fig. 4. Malicious attacker steals the end user's private key and illegitimately accesses

Attacks Against Network Infrastructure
Attacks under the aforementioned category emphasized fog network communication infrastructure elements. The attacks are listed as follows:

Denial-of-service (DoS): The DoS attacks were easily instigated as many IoT devices were not mutually verified. The undermined devices might demand unlimited fog node-processing or storage resources for legal devices to avoid fog service access;
Man-in-the-middle: An adversary dominated a network section and subsequently instigated attacks (eavesdropping and traffic insertion);
Rogue gateway: Adversaries potentially deployed personal gateways following the explicit fog network nature. As such, the rogue gateway was disguised as a legal counterpart and initiated specific attacks (man-in-the-middle).

Attacks Against Edge Data Center
The center hosts (managing multiple services) could be aimed through the following attacks:

Data leakage: An edge data center primarily contained and processed knowledge from the entities located within the area. Several weaknesses involving suspicious API, misconfiguration, or deviant insiders could be manipulated for data leakage;
Privilege escalation: The attack could be instigated by external adversaries that manipulated specific edge data center weaknesses or internal counterparts with unethical intentions;
Service manipulation: External adversaries dominated specific edge data center elements through privilege escalation or deviant actions by legal administrators. Hence, edge data center service exploitation was deemed possible;
Rogue data center: External and internal adversaries fully dominated the edge data center under the attack.

Attacks Against the Core Infrastructure
The following attacks are listed below:

Illegal data access: Contained and processed data were accessible by illegal parties or ethical but inquisitive adversaries;
Service manipulation: An internal adversary with adequate privileges could instigate rogue services for indecipherable knowledge;
Rogue infrastructure: The attack dominated certain core infrastructure components by manipulating specific weaknesses and services.

Attacks Against Virtualization Infrastructure
Similar to any physical host, digital machines could be dominated by deviant adversaries attempting to manipulate the offered resources. The attacks are listed as follows:

The DoS: A deviant digital machine could attempt to outrun the hosts' current computational and storage resources;

Resource misuse: A deviant digital machine could perform various unethical programmes that emphasized remote entities (seeking weak IoT or hosting botnet servers);

Data leakage: Most virtualization infrastructure at the edge data center incorporated APIs that offered physical and rational environmental information. For example, a deviant digital machine could attain knowledge of performance contexts if the APIs reflected insecurity;

Privilege escalation: Deviant digital machines potentially manipulated hosts' weaknesses to execute privilege elevation and exploit other counterparts;

VM manipulation: A host dominated by external or internal adversaries could initiate various attacks against hosted virtual machines (data leakage or computational work manipulations).

Attacks Launched by User Devices
The devices dominated by users could attempt to interrupt fog services. The following attacks are listed under the aforementioned category:

Data injection: An undermined device could generate artificial data upon request (sensors or vehicles reporting inaccurate values);

Service manipulation: A device potentially engaged in service provision (crowdsourcing services). Undermined devices under adversarial domination could exploit service results;

- Web-oriented attacks: Specific attacks (SQL injection, cross-site scripting and forgery requests, session or account-hijacking, and insecure explicit object references) could aim at weak digital applications hosted by the edge data centre and initiate different attacks (data leakage and deviant application implementations);
- Malware-oriented attacks: Adversaries could influence hosts or digital machines with various malware forms (rational bombs, Trojans, worms, spyware, and ransomware).

3 Related Works

This section provides a comprehensive discussion about prior works related to IDS in Fog Computing in details.

3.1 Deep Learning Based IDS

Sadaf and Sultana [50] recommended an intrusion detection approach (Auto-IF) following a deep learning method with Autoencoder (AE) and Isolation Forest (IF) in fog context. As fog devices encompassed attack differentiation from real-time normal packets, the aforementioned technique only emphasized the binary categorization of incoming packets. The recommended approach was authenticated on the benchmark

NSL-KDD dataset. Notably, the recommended intrusion detection method attained a high precision rate (95.4%) as opposed to advanced counterparts.

Moreover, Sudqi Khater et al. [51], introduced a lightweight intrusion identification model following a hidden-layer Multilayer Perceptron (MLP) model in fog computing. In ensuring lightness, the recommended feature extraction method employed an adjusted vector space representation through n-gram transformation. Additionally, a sparse matrix was implemented to compress the matrix formatting. Furthermore, the linear correlation coefficient (LCC) was utilized to substitute zero values. Joint knowledge feature selection was also utilized for minimal feature numbers. The recommended approach was assessed with the ADFA-LD dataset through a Raspberry Pi (resembling the fog device) for 94% precision, 95% recall, and 92% F1-measure in ADFA-LD and 74% precision, 74% recall, and 74% F1-measure in ADFA-WD. Notwithstanding, identification precision and computational effectiveness required much enhancement with additional elements or effective algorithms. One possible direction involved employing a more efficient learning algorithm than backpropagation. Performance assessment on various fog nodes could also be useful in MLP model-testing.

In [52], it was suggested an anomaly identification framework for IoT traffic in a fog setting with the VCDL technique to resolve the non-measurable nature of anomaly identification systems within IoT traffic. In a measurable anomaly identification framework, traffic records were distributed to several fog nodes to simultaneously learn IoT traffic elements. Furthermore, learning was executed with a VCDL network (trained using FCN) through feature extraction with VCN. The learned VCDL model was subsequently utilized by the master fog node to categories known and unknown IoT traffic anomalies. As the recommended anomaly identification framework was assessed with the Bot-IoT dataset under UNSW, the recommended framework in a fog setting affirmed the distributed anomaly identification with lower detection period than the centralized architecture. The recommended technique reflected substantial performance enhancement compared to advanced anomaly identification systems and traditional DL models. Precision-wise, the aforementioned framework also demonstrated substantial performance of the chosen features compared to other counterparts. Notwithstanding, the recommended model posed precision-oriented limitations concerning class incongruences.

Moreover, SaiSindhuTheja and Shyam [53], suggested an effective DoS attack identification system that employed the Oppositional Crow Search Algorithm (OCSA) that integrated Crow Search Algorithm (CSA) and Opposition Based Learning (OBL) approaches to respond to similar issue types. Essentially, the recommended system encompassed two stages: feature selection with OCSA and categorisation through the Recurrent Neural Network (RNN) classifier. Vital elements were then chosen with the OCSA algorithm and conveyed to RNN classifiers. Notably, incoming data was categorised using the RNN classifier in subsequent testing processes to ensure standard data isolation (saved in cloud) and undermined data omission through the KDD cup 99 dataset. Resultantly, the recommended method outperformed other traditional counterparts by 98.18%, 95.13%, 93.56%, and 94.12% regarding precision, recall, F-measure, and accuracy, respectively. The suggested work also outperformed current counterparts by an average of 3% for all applied metrics. The approach emphasis concerned minimal feature selection that potentially influenced precision.

Furthermore, Abdel-Basset et al. [54] recommended a forensics-oriented DL model (Deep-IFS) to determine IIoT traffic intrusions. Regarding the model, local representations were gauged with a local gated recurrent unit (LocalGRU) to present an MHA layer for global representation (sustainable reliance). A residual link between layers was structured for knowledge loss prevention. Another obstacle involving present IIoT forensics frameworks concerned restricted big IIoT traffic data management measurability and performance through IIoT devices. The complexity was resolved by executing and training the recommended Deep-IFS in a fog computing context. Specifically, the infiltration detection proved measurable through computation and IIoT traffic data distribution across worker fog nodes for model training. For example, the master fog node shared training parameters and aggregated worker nodes output. The aggregated categorization output was then delivered to the cloud platform for attack mitigation. Scientific outcomes on the Bot-IIoT dataset revealed that distributed Deep-IFS could efficiently manage Big IIoT traffic data as opposed to current centralized DL-oriented forensics methods.

In this regard, the outcomes authenticated the Deep-IFS robustness across different assessment measures. The experimental assessment revealed that Deep-IFS obtained higher precision with G2 training than employing the complete feature set. Essentially, Deep-IFS allowed simplified data interaction between fog nodes and lowered overheads for a useful decision support framework in facilitating people and IIoT service providers towards trustworthy and secure data interaction. Regardless, the recommended model posed specific shortcomings. First, learning from unlabeled traffic was disrupted as Deep-IFS was trained with supervision. Consequently, this study strived to extend Deep-IFS by learning from unlabeled traffic through semi-supervised learning (generative networks). Notwithstanding, the recommended framework disregarded data privacy strategies (a vital component of sensitive industrial implementations).

Additionally Zhou et al. [55], presented an integrated CNN-RNN framework through astute recommendation methods for online medical pre-diagnosis facilitation. A CNN-oriented classifier was developed for textural feature extraction at the sentence level while an RNN-oriented model was developed to gauge the possible trends and correlations at a dialogue level. An astute suggestion approach was subsequently structured to offer patients with mechanical clinic navigation and pre-diagnosis recommendations in a data-driven manner. Experiments following the authentic data revealed model efficiency and online medical pre-diagnosis facilitation strategies. Regardless, high-dimensional and health-oriented data management and the development of assessment experiments for more intricate circumstances in online medical data settings required much improvement.

3.2 Machine Learning Based IDS

A study by Souza et al. [56] suggested a hybrid binary categorization technique (DNN-kNN) with high precision and recall rates derived from Deep Neural Networks (DNN) and the k-Nearest Neighbor (kNN) algorithm. Regarding the two-stage identification technique within the architecture, the first-level categorization approach should have high accuracy and recall rates (the most substantial number of potential intrusive events was categorized as intrusive). Based on the public NSL-KDD and CICIDS2017 databases, the recommended approach proved successful with classic machine learning and advanced methods. The proposed method in the study context attained 99.77% and 99.85% precision for the CICIDS2017 and NSL-KDD datasets, respectively. In this vein, the recommended hybrid approach could attain higher accuracy regarding classic machine learning methods and recent intrusion identification advancements for IoT systems. Although the technique was efficient with a low overhead involving memory and processing costs, the method required event grouping capacities in particular attack forms for second-level identification operation. Nevertheless, much improvement was required as the employed method within the architecture attribute selection module disregarded the work.

Furthermore, studies conducted by Illy et al. [57], recommended multiple learner integrations to construct ensemble learners that improved identification precision. Specifically, the first level executed an anomaly identification that substantially minimized categorization latency, whereas the second level performed attack categorization for accurate prevention measures through Decision Tree (DT) and a parametric and nonparametric algorithm. Resultantly, the recommended IDS proved more efficient than sophisticated counterparts on the NSL-KDD dataset. Summarily, 85.81% and 84.25% precision were attained for binary and attack categorizations, respectively. A deployment architecture was also recommended where anomaly identification was executed in fog nodes for quicker detection and responses. Although attack categorization in the cloud benefitted from multiple resources to operate a more intricate ensemble (for improved categorization) that navigated intrusion prevention tasks, the recommended method needed further improvement. For example, examining more diverse base learners and different integration techniques could significantly enhance the envisioned outcomes.

Further, research by Kumar et al. [58] recommended a distributed ensemble design-oriented IDS with fog computing for IoT network protection. Particularly, the model demonstrated the fog computing working architecture to deflect attacks in the IoT context. The suggested identification system followed three essential stages. The first stage (data pre-processing) encompassed feature mapping that transformed categorical attributes to numerical elements, imputed missing data with mean and "unknown" values, feature normalization with the Standard Scaler (measured elements to a particular scale), and feature selection with mutual knowledge and optimised feature set selection. The second stage (an anomaly identification method) implemented a random forest (RT)-oriented ensemble technique with K-NN, XGBoost, and Gaussian naive Bayes algorithms for improved overall identification rates. The third stage (incoming IoT network traffic) was employed for assessment.

The IoT system was permitted to utilise normal traffic while the administrator was alerted for deviant activities. Essentially, the cloud server stored log information for such unusual traffic towards efficient intrusion response mechanism activation. The recommended model performance was subsequently assessed with UNSW-NB15 and real IoT-based datasets, such as the Distributed Smart Space Orchestration System (DS2OS). Resultantly, the recommended distributed IDS with UNSW-NB15 attained improved identification rates: up to 71.18% for backdoor, 68.98% for analysis, 92.25% for reconnaissance, and 85.42% for DoS attacks. Likewise, the DS2OS dataset identification rate was up to 99.99% for the majority of attack vectors. Nevertheless, several complexities were encountered. For example, the method failed to implement various deep learning approaches and construct a prototype that authenticated the formal security parameters of the overall model. As such, subsequent integrations potentially improved the overall IoT security in different IoT implementations.

Moreover, Pani et al. [59] recommended the Flower Pollination Algorithm (FPA) for intrusion detection feature selection. Notably, FPA proved beneficial in long-distance pollination that evaluated several elements and flower consistency for more pertinent feature detection. The recommended FPA performance was subsequently assessed with different IoT IDS categorization. Additionally, FPA demonstrated improved convergence processes and chose pertinent feature identification. Essentially, FPA was incorporated into the intrusion identification strategy for high IoT network effectiveness. A virtual IoT setting was established following DS2OS for synthetic data creation. Given the FPA advantage in long-distance pollination and flower consistency for efficient feature analysis, IoT network features were chosen and incorporated into the classifier for attack identification. Classifiers, including Logistic Regression (LR), Support Vector Machine (SVM), DT, RF, and Artificial Neural Network (ANN) were used for network intrusion identification. Resultantly, the recommended FPA technique with ANN reflected 99.5% precision in identification while the current ANN reflected 99.4% precision in identification. Notwithstanding, this study employed limited datasets and samples.

3.3 Optimization Based IDS

In [60], it was recommended a novel hierarchical and distributed intrusion detection system (HD-IDS). Specifically, the system followed a distributed fog architecture with three hierarchical network levels (home and residential area and fog operation center networks) for smart-metering infrastructure against false data injection attacks within the smart grid. As the system involved three protection and detection levels (with IDS application at every network level), the complexity was addressed with stochastic modelling under the Markov chain process. The recommended HD-IDS alternative proved advantageous with expansive simulations in various performance metrics as opposed to centralized architecture. The recommended system could only utilize and apply three hierarchical network levels following distinct real-world traces although the application corresponded to real-world electricity consumption traces in iToronto, Canada.

Furthermore, Lawal et al. [61] suggested an IoT-oriented hybrid anomaly mitigation framework with fog computing towards rapid and precise anomaly identification. Specifically, signature and anomaly-oriented identification techniques were utilized for two distinct modules. The signature-oriented module employed an attack source database (blacklisted IP addresses) for quicker identification during attacks from the blacklisted IP address, whereas the anomaly-oriented counterpart utilized a radical gradient-enhancing algorithm for precise network trace flow categorization (normal or otherwise). The recommended modules were assessed with a BoT-IoT dataset. Resultantly, the signature-oriented module attained attack identification (minimally six times quicker) compared to the anomaly-oriented counterpart in every assessment. For example, the anomaly-oriented module employed the XGBoost classifier towards attack identification with 99% precision with minimally 97% for average recall, precision, and F1 score regarding binary and multiclass categorization. Although the classifier indicated 0.05 following false-positive rates, the recommended work required further examination of other botnet attack elements for additional framework signatures.

Moreover, Huang et al. [62] examined a generalized service replicas placement problem that applied to different industrial contexts. The problem was formulated into a multi-objective model using two scheduling objectives: deployment cost and service latency. Concerning problem-solving, an ant colony optimization-oriented alternative known as multi replicas Pareto ant colony optimization (MRPACO) was suggested to attain the non-dominated Pareto front and satisfactory performance of both objectives: 1) deployment cost and 2) service latency. The improvement encompassed a new heuristic formulation and effective technique for a viable alternative in the restricted problem. Resultantly, the recommended technique outperformed the baseline regarding precision and solution diversity. As the study limitation indicated a sole emphasis on latency for the final inference outcome, model application to simulations without authentic data led to inaccurate outcomes.

Additionally Zedadra et al. [63], offered an initial comprehension of technical swarm intelligence algorithm features to present a novel astute level to IoT-oriented systems by examining the possibility of acknowledging SI-oriented IoT systems. Current swarm intelligence-oriented algorithms and IoT-oriented systems with SI-based algorithms were introduced with key implementations. Lastly, swarm intelligence and IoT-oriented system convergence patterns were outlined to present how essential IoT-oriented system prerequisites could be managed with SI-oriented algorithms and insightful guidelines into appropriate SI-oriented algorithm application in IoT-based systems.

Further, research by Almaiah et al. [64] presented a scheme where Frequency Particle Swarm Optimization (FPSO) was employed in examining digital forensics Particle Swarm Optimization (PSO) to identify and categories the APT attack (Shamoon attack) in a fog setting. The method utilized four stages. Meanwhile, an optimal feature set was derived from feature extraction. As optimal weight features were forecasted with FPSO, the weighted elements were clustered with K-means clustering and categorized under the KNN classifier to retain proof without undermining the examined structure of online gathering, detection, and authentication for historical event reconstructions.

The method performance was assessed through a confusion matrix with subsequent outcomes. For example, the recommended IDF-FPSO performance was analyzed with the confusion matrix and comparisons against different existing classifiers (SVM, KNN, Naïve Bayes, and DTs) in performance assessment with a confusion matrix and accuracy, specificity, sensitivity, recall, precision, F-measure, and G-mean values. Although KNN-FPSO classifiers nearly attained the precision of 0.99998, the recommended scheme limitation proved only efficient for Shamoon attacks instead of other counterparts.

Furthermore, Rahman and Wen [65] recommended a MITM attack identification framework that existed between fog nodes and cloud and vice versa through swarm intelligence optimization methods or the Dragonfly Algorithm (DA) to be incorporated into the ifogsim simulator platform. The recommended framework encompassed three phases. The first phase involved problem development, planning, and dataset description. The second phase encompassed structure and application (DA identification on the ifogsim simulator platform), model flowchart, and pseudocode. Meanwhile, the third phase entailed performance assessment and application (experimental setup and performance metric and evaluation). Predictably, DA could identify any deviant attacker who aimed to infiltrate the pertinent knowledge oscillating from fog node to cloud or vice versa and incorporate false knowledge in fog computing setting. Although DA was extended for MITM attack identification at the edge of fog devices in fog computing settings, the method posed specific limitations. For example, the recommended approach only concerned ifogsim without application to an authentic system or dataset for precise outcomes. Additionally, data flow from fog to cloud and vice versa failed to manipulate the data flow between fog device edges in fog computing contexts.

A study by Kesavamoorthy and Soundar [66] recommended a technique to identify and counter DDoS attacks with autonomous multi-agent systems. The agents interemployed PSO for efficient interaction and precise decision-making. Specifically, DDoS attacks were identified with multiple agents that inter-communicated and updated the coordinator agent. The scenario was assessed by the coordinator agent with entropy and co-variance strategies for DDoS attack detection. For example, the controlling agent would operate in real-time and monitor cloud resources and networking at the aforementioned stage [67]. Any unusual occurrences potentially induced action within identification and recovery agents. Although the suggested system could deter different DDoS attack forms with 98% precision, the recommended technique required much improvement (more optimization with stochastic-based filtering in the attack identification stage) for real network application.

Further, research by Al Hwaitat et al. [68] presented an improved PSO version (Improved PSO algorithm) to improve the identification of jamming attack sources over randomized mobile networks. Improved PSO normalized entity positions and squared ensuing fraction values for quicker position updates and optimal swarm location. Essentially, improved PSO algorithm was assessed with two experiments. Regarding the first experiment, improved PSO (compared to PSO, GWO, and MFO) was the optimum algorithm in attaining the jamming attack location. Concerning the second experiment, improved PSO was measured against PSO in a mobile network setting (to ascertain that improved PSO was more optimal than PSO) to attain mobile network locations with minimal coverage areas. The improved PSO algorithm also enhanced jamming attack identification effectiveness and source node detection for jamming attacks. Notwithstanding, this study posed limitations in addressing jamming attack complexities on wireless networks.

4 Conclusion and Future Work

In Fog Computing environment, more than one collaborative users' edge devices perform storage and communication tasks, and manage configurations needed. This article provides a broad discussion and analysis of Fog Computing architecture, and possible related potential security challenges and attacks. Then, it discusses the intrusion detection systems used to mitigate the impact of these issues in Fog environment, by analyzing the recent prior works in the field and highlight their challenges and shortcomings comprehensively. As aforementioned, Fog Computing is an extremely virtualized platform since it allows storage and computing services through the nearest edge devices. Basically, it handles the challenge of low latency. However, being distributed and open architecture, Fog Computing is of course vulnerable security threats and attacks.

This article provides a deep analysis the Fog Computing environment from a general to detailed aspect. The related intrusion detection systems used in Fog environment are also summarized in detail and the discussions about open security are provided, and future work is highlighted. As Fog Computing is distributed and remotely operated, the new security challenges that are not mentioned and analyzed in the centralized Cloud, need to be considered. In sum, considering the limitations of the existing works and research trends, it is vital to develop a suite of elaborate security mechanisms. A lot of security challenges seem to remain open.

References

1. Bonomi, F., Milito, R., Zhu, J., Addepalli, S.: Fog computing and its role in the internet of things. In: Proceedings of 1st ACM Mobile Cloud Computing Workshop, MCC 2012, pp. 13–15 (2012). https://doi.org/10.1145/2342509.2342513
2. Sanjalawe, Y., Anbar, M., Al-E'mari, S., Abdullah, R., Hasbullah, I., Aladaileh, M.: Cloud data center selection using a modified differential evolution. Comput. Mater. Continua **69**, 3179–3204 (2021). https://doi.org/10.32604/cmc.2021.018546
3. Iorga, M., Feldman, L., Barton, R., Martin, M.J., Goren, N., Mahmoudi, C.: Fog computing conceptual model. NIST Spec. Publ. **500–325**, 1–13 (2018). https://doi.org/10.6028/NIST. SP.500-325
4. Aladaileh, M.A., Anbar, M., Hasbullah, I.H., Chong, Y.W., Sanjalawe, Y.K.: Detection techniques of distributed denial of service attacks on software-defined networking controller-a review. IEEE Access. **8**, 143985–143995 (2020). https://doi.org/10.1109/ACCESS.2020.301 3998
5. Al-E'mari, S., Anbar, M., Sanjalawe, Y., Manickam, S.: A labeled transactions-based dataset on the ethereum network. In: Anbar, M., Abdullah, N., Manickam, S. (eds.) ACeS 2020. CCIS, vol. 1347, pp. 61–79. Springer, Singapore (2021). https://doi.org/10.1007/978-981-33-6835-4_5
6. Vaquero, L.M., Rodero-Merino, L.: Finding your way in the fog: towards a comprehensive definition of fog computing. Comput. Commun. Rev. **44**, 27–32 (2014). https://doi.org/10.1145/2677046.2677052
7. Chiang, M., Zhang, T.: Fog and IoT: an overview of research opportunities. IEEE Internet Things J. **3**, 854–864 (2016). https://doi.org/10.1109/JIOT.2016.2584538
8. Stojmenovic, I., Wen, S.: The fog computing paradigm: scenarios and security issues. In: 2014 Federated Conference on Computer Science and Information Systems, FedCSIS 2014, pp. 1–8 (2014). https://doi.org/10.15439/2014F503
9. Yi, S., Hao, Z., Qin, Z., Li, Q.: Fog computing: platform and applications. In: Proceedings of 3rd Workshop on Hot Topics in Web Systems and Technologies, HotWeb 2015, pp. 73–78 (2016). https://doi.org/10.1109/HotWeb.2015.22
10. Chen, X., Wang, L.: Exploring fog computing-based adaptive vehicular data scheduling policies through a compositional formal method - PEPA. IEEE Commun. Lett. **21**, 745–748 (2017). https://doi.org/10.1109/LCOMM.2016.2647595
11. Kitanov, S., Janevski, T.: Fog networking for 5G and IoT. In: 5G Mobile: From Research and Innovations to Deployment Aspects, pp. 45–69 (2017)
12. Lin, J., Yu, W., Zhang, N., Yang, X., Zhang, H., Zhao, W.: A survey on internet of things: architecture, enabling technologies, security and privacy, and applications. IEEE Internet Things J. **4**, 1125–1142 (2017). https://doi.org/10.1109/JIOT.2017.2683200
13. Hu, P., Dhelim, S., Ning, H., Qiu, T.: Survey on fog computing: architecture, key technologies, applications and open issues. J. Netw. Comput. Appl. **98**, 27–42 (2017). https://doi.org/10.1016/j.jnca.2017.09.002

14. Ni, J., Zhang, K., Lin, X., Shen, X.S.: Securing fog computing for internet of things applications: challenges and solutions. IEEE Commun. Surv. Tutor. **20**, 601–628 (2018). https://doi.org/10.1109/COMST.2017.2762345

15. Liu, L., Guo, X., Chang, Z., Ristaniemi, T.: Joint optimization of energy and delay for computation offloading in cloudlet-assisted mobile cloud computing. Wirel. Netw. **25**(4), 2027–2040 (2018). https://doi.org/10.1007/s11276-018-1794-0

16. Amairah, A., Al-Tamimi, B.N., Anbar, M., Aloufi, K.: Cloud computing and internet of things integration systems: a review. Adv. Intell. Syst. Comput. **843**, 406–414 (2019). https://doi.org/10.1007/978-3-319-99007-1_39

17. Wang, H., et al.: Architectural design alternatives based on cloud/edge/fog computing for connected vehicles. IEEE Commun. Surv. Tutor. **22**, 2349–2377 (2020). https://doi.org/10.1109/COMST.2020.3020854

18. Shi, Y., Ding, G., Wang, H., Eduardo Roman, H., Lu, S.: The fog computing service for healthcare. In: 2015 2nd International Symposium on Future Information and Communication Technologies for Ubiquitous HealthCare, Ubi-HealthTech 2015, pp. 70–74 (2015). https://doi.org/10.1109/Ubi-HealthTech.2015.7203325

19. Mukherjee, M., Shu, L., Wang, D.: Survey of fog computing: fundamental, network applications, and research challenges. IEEE Commun. Surv. Tutor. **20**, 1826–1857 (2018). https://doi.org/10.1109/COMST.2018.2814571

20. Aazam, M., Huh, E.N.: Fog computing and smart gateway based communication for cloud of things. In: Proceedings of 2014 International Conference on Future Internet of Things and Cloud, FiCloud 2014, pp. 464–470 (2014). https://doi.org/10.1109/FiCloud.2014.83

21. Aazam, M., Huh, E.N.: Fog computing micro datacenter based dynamic resource estimation and pricing model for IoT. In: Proceedings of International Conference on Advanced Information Networking and Applications, AINA, April 2015, pp. 687–694 (2015). https://doi.org/10.1109/AINA.2015.254

22. Muntjir, M., Rahul, M., Alhumyani, H.A.: An analysis of internet of things (IoT): novel architectures, modern applications, security aspects and future scope with latest case studies. Int. J. Eng. Res. Technol. **6**, 422–447 (2017)

23. Aazam, M., Hung, P.P., Huh, E.N.: Smart gateway based communication for cloud of things. In: 2014 IEEE 9th International Conference on Intelligent Sensors, Sensor Networks and Information Processing, Conference Proceedings, IEEE ISSNIP 2014 (2014). https://doi.org/10.1109/ISSNIP.2014.6827673

24. Marques, B., MacHado, I., Sena, A., Castro, M.C.: A communication protocol for fog computing based on network coding applied to wireless sensors. In: Proceedings of 29th International Symposium on Computer Architecture and High Performance Computing Work, SBAC-PADW 2017, pp. 109–114 (2017). https://doi.org/10.1109/SBAC-PADW.2017.27

25. Rodríguez Natal, A., et al.: LISP-MN: mobile networking through LISP. Wirel. Pers. Commun. **70**, 253–266 (2013). https://doi.org/10.1007/s11277-012-0692-5

26. Hassan, M.A., Xiao, M., Wei, Q., Chen, S.: Help your mobile applications with fog computing. In: 2015 12th Annual IEEE International Conference on Sensing, Communication and Networking, SECON Workshop 2015, pp. 49–54 (2015). https://doi.org/10.1109/SECONW.2015.7328146

27. Kai, K., Cong, W., Tao, L.: Fog computing for vehicular ad-hoc networks: paradigms, scenarios, and issues. J. China Univ. Posts Telecommun. **23**, 56–96 (2016). https://doi.org/10.1016/S1005-8885(16)60021-3

28. Hong, K., Lillethun, D., Ramachandran, U., Ottenwälder, B., Koldehofe, B.: Mobile fog: a programming model for large-scale applications on the internet of things. In: Proceedings of 2nd, 2013 ACM SIGCOMM Workshop on Mobile Cloud Computing, MCC 2013, pp. 15–20 (2013). https://doi.org/10.1145/2491266.2491270

29. Zhang, Y., Niyato, D., Wang, P., Kim, D.I.: Optimal energy management policy of mobile energy gateway. IEEE Trans. Veh. Technol. **65**, 3685–3699 (2016). https://doi.org/10.1109/TVT.2015.2445833

30. Jalali, F., Hinton, K., Ayre, R., Alpcan, T., Tucker, R.S.: Fog computing may help to save energy in cloud computing. IEEE J. Sel. Areas Commun. **34**, 1728–1739 (2016). https://doi.org/10.1109/JSAC.2016.2545559

31. Jøsang, A., Ismail, R., Boyd, C.: A survey of trust and reputation systems for online service provision. Decis. Support Syst. **43**, 618–644 (2007). https://doi.org/10.1016/j.dss.2005.05.019

32. Damiani, E., De Capitani Di Vimercati, S., Paraboschi, S., Samarati, P., Violante, F.: A reputation-based approach for choosing reliable resources in peer-to-peer networks. In: Proceedings of ACM Conference on Computer and Communications Security, pp. 207–216 (2002). https://doi.org/10.1145/586110.586138

33. Han, H., Sheng, B., Tan, C.C., Li, Q., Lu, S.: A measurement based rogue AP detection scheme. In: Proceedings of IEEE INFOCOM, pp. 1593–1601 (2009). https://doi.org/10.1109/INFOCOM.2009.5062077

34. Han, H., Sheng, B., Tan, C.C., Li, Q., Lu, S.: A timing-based scheme for rogue AP detection. IEEE Trans. Parallel Distrib. Syst. **22**, 1912–1925 (2011). https://doi.org/10.1109/TPDS.2011.125

35. Balfanz, D., Smetters, D.K., Stewart, P., Wong, H.C.: Talking to strangers: authentication in ad-hoc wireless networks. In: Proceedings of 9th Annual Network and Distributed System Security Symposium, pp. 7–19 (2002)

36. Bouzefrane, S., Mostefa, A.F.B., Houacine, F., Cagnon, H.: Cloudlets authentication in nfc-based mobile computing. Proceedings of 2nd IEEE International Conference on Mobile Cloud Computing, Services, and Engineering, MobileCloud 2014, pp. 267–272 (2014). https://doi.org/10.1109/MobileCloud.2014.46

37. Tsugawa, M., Matsunaga, A., Fortes, J.A.B.: Cloud computing security: what changes with software-defined networking? In: Jajodia, S., Kant, K., Samarati, P., Singhal, A., Swarup, V., Wang, C. (eds.) Secure Cloud Computing, pp. 77–93. Springer, New York (2014). https://doi.org/10.1007/978-1-4614-9278-8_4

38. Gennaro, R., Gentry, C., Parno, B.: Non-interactive verifiable computing: outsourcing computation to untrusted workers. In: Rabin, T. (ed.) CRYPTO 2010. LNCS, vol. 6223, pp. 465–482. Springer, Heidelberg (2010). https://doi.org/10.1007/978-3-642-14623-7_25

39. Song, D.X., Wagner, D., Perrig, A.: Practical techniques for searches on encrypted data. In: Proceedings of IEEE Computer Society Symposium on Research in Security and Privacy, pp. 44–55 (2000). https://doi.org/10.1109/secpri.2000.848445

40. Wang, C., Cao, N., Ren, K., Lou, W.: Enabling secure and efficient ranked keyword search over outsourced cloud data. IEEE Trans. Parallel Distrib. Syst. **23**, 1467–1479 (2012). https://doi.org/10.1109/TPDS.2011.282

41. Cash, D., et al.: Dynamic searchable encryption in very-large databases: data structures and implementation. In: Citeseer (2014)

42. Cao, N., Wang, C., Li, M., Ren, K., Lou, W.: Privacy-preserving multi-keyword ranked search over encrypted cloud data. IEEE Trans. Parallel Distrib. Syst. **25**, 222–233 (2014). https://doi.org/10.1109/TPDS.2013.45

43. Rial, A., Danezis, G.: Privacy-preserving smart metering. In: Proceedings of the ACM Conference on Computer and Communications Security, Chicago, IL, USA, pp. 49–60 (2011)

44. Qin, Z., Yi, S., Li, Q., Zamkov, D.: Preserving secondary users' privacy in cognitive radio networks. In: Proceedings of IEEE INFOCOM, Toronto, ON, Canada, pp. 772–780. Institute of Electrical and Electronics Engineers Inc. (2014)

45. Novak, E., Li, Q.: Near-Pri: private, proximity based location sharing. In: Proceedings - IEEE INFOCOM, Toronto, ON, Canada, pp. 37–45. Institute of Electrical and Electronics Engineers Inc. (2014)

46. Lu, R., Liang, X., Li, X., Lin, X., Shen, X.: EPPA: an efficient and privacy-preserving aggregation scheme for secure smart grid communications. IEEE Trans. Parallel Distrib. Syst. **23**, 1621–1632 (2012). https://doi.org/10.1109/TPDS.2012.86

47. McLaughlin, S., McDaniel, P., Aiello, W.: Protecting consumer privacy from electric load monitoring. In: Proceedings of the ACM Conference on Computer and Communications Security, Chicago, IL, USA, pp. 87–98 (2011)

48. Roman, R., Lopez, J., Mambo, M.: Mobile edge computing, Fog et al.: a survey and analysis of security threats and challenges. Futur. Gener. Comput. Syst. **78**, 680–698 (2018). https://doi.org/10.1016/j.future.2016.11.009

49. Khan, S., Parkinson, S., Qin, Y.: Fog computing security: a review of current applications and security solutions (2017). https://journalofcloudcomputing.springeropen.com/articles/10.1186/s13677-017-0090-3

50. Sadaf, K., Sultana, J.: Intrusion detection based on autoencoder and isolation forest in fog computing. IEEE Access **8**, 167059–167068 (2020). https://doi.org/10.1109/ACCESS.2020.3022855

51. Khater, B.S., Wahab, A.W.B.A., Idris, M.Y.I.B., Hussain, M.A., Ibrahim, A.A.: A lightweight perceptron-based intrusion detection system for fog computing. Appl. Sci. **9**, 178 (2019). https://doi.org/10.3390/app9010178

52. Bhuvaneswari Amma, N.G., Selvakumar, S.: Anomaly detection framework for internet of things traffic using vector convolutional deep learning approach in fog environment. Futur. Gener. Comput. Syst. **113**, 255–265 (2020). https://doi.org/10.1016/j.future.2020.07.020

53. SaiSindhuTheja, R., Shyam, G.K.: An efficient metaheuristic algorithm based feature selection and recurrent neural network for DoS attack detection in cloud computing environment. Appl. Soft Comput. **100**, 106997 (2021). https://doi.org/10.1016/j.asoc.2020.106997

54. Abdel-Basset, M., Chang, V., Hawash, H., Chakrabortty, R.K., Ryan, M.: Deep-IFS: intrusion detection approach for industrial internet of things traffic in fog environment. IEEE Trans. Ind. Inform. **17**, 7704–7715 (2021). https://doi.org/10.1109/TII.2020.3025755

55. Zhou, X., Li, Y., Liang, W.: CNN-RNN based intelligent recommendation for online medical pre-diagnosis support. IEEE/ACM Trans. Comput. Biol. Bioinform. **18**, 912–921 (2021). https://doi.org/10.1109/TCBB.2020.2994780

56. de Souza, C.A., Westphall, C.B., Machado, R.B., Sobral, J.B.M., Vieira, G.S.: Hybrid approach to intrusion detection in fog-based IoT environments. Comput. Netw. **180**, 107417 (2020). https://doi.org/10.1016/j.comnet.2020.107417

57. Illy, P., Kaddoum, G., Moreira, C.M., Kaur, K., Garg, S.: Securing fog-to-things environment using intrusion detection system based on ensemble learning. In: IEEE Wireless Communications and Networking Conference, WCNC, Marrakesh, Morocco. Institute of Electrical and Electronics Engineers Inc. (2019)

58. Kumar, P., Gupta, G.P., Tripathi, R.: An ensemble learning and fog-cloud architecture-driven cyber-attack detection framework for IoMT networks. Comput. Commun. **166**, 110–124 (2021). https://doi.org/10.1016/j.comcom.2020.12.003

59. Pani, A.K.: An efficient algorithmic technique for feature selection in IoT based intrusion detection system. Indian J. Sci. Technol. **14**, 76–85 (2021). https://doi.org/10.17485/ijst/v14i1.2057

60. Chekired, D.A., Khoukhi, L., Mouftah, H.T.: Fog-based distributed intrusion detection system against false metering attacks in smart grid. In: IEEE International Conference on Communications, Shanghai, China. Institute of Electrical and Electronics Engineers Inc. (2019)

61. Lawal, M.A., Shaikh, R.A., Hassan, S.R.: An anomaly mitigation framework for IoT using fog computing. Electronics **9**, 1–24 (2020). https://doi.org/10.3390/electronics9101565

62. Huang, T., Lin, W., Xiong, C., Pan, R., Huang, J.: An ant colony optimization-based multi-objective service replicas placement strategy for fog computing. IEEE Trans. Cybern. 1–14 (2020). https://doi.org/10.1109/tcyb.2020.2989309

63. Zedadra, O., Guerrieri, A., Jouandeau, N., Spezzano, G., Seridi, H., Fortino, G.: Swarm intelligence-based algorithms within IoT-based systems: a review. J. Parallel Distrib. Comput. **122**, 173–187 (2018). https://doi.org/10.1016/j.jpdc.2018.08.007

64. Hwaitat, A.K.A.L., Manaseer, S., Al-Sayyed, R.M.H., Almaiah, M.A., Almomani, O.: An investigator digital forensics frequencies particle swarm optimization for detection and classification of APT attack in fog computing environment (IDF-FPSO). J. Theor. Appl. Inf. Technol. **98**, 937–952 (2020)

65. Rahman, G., Wen, C.C.: Mutual authentication security scheme in fog computing. Int. J. Adv. Comput. Sci. Appl. **10**, 443–451 (2019). https://doi.org/10.14569/IJACSA.2019.0101161

66. Kesavamoorthy, R., Ruba Soundar, K.: Swarm intelligence based autonomous DDoS attack detection and defense using multi agent system. Clust. Comput. **22**(4), 9469–9476 (2018). https://doi.org/10.1007/s10586-018-2365-y

67. Alanazi, S.T., Anbar, M., Karuppayah, S., Al-Ani, A.K., Sanjalawe, Y.K.: Detection techniques for DDoS attacks in cloud environment: review paper. In: Piuri, V., Balas, V.E., Borah, S., Syed Ahmad, S.S. (eds.) Intelligent and Interactive Computing. LNNS, vol. 67, pp. 337–354. Springer, Singapore (2019). https://doi.org/10.1007/978-981-13-6031-2_34

68. Al Hwaitat, A.K., et al.: Improved security particle swarm optimization (PSO) algorithm to detect radio jamming attacks in mobile networks. Int. J. Adv. Comput. Sci. Appl. **11**, 614–625 (2020). https://doi.org/10.14569/IJACSA.2020.0110480

Review of Data Integrity Attacks and Mitigation Methods in Edge Computing

Poornima Mahadevappa🅙 and Raja Kumar Murugesan(✉)🅙

Taylor's University, Subang Jaya, Malaysia
poornimamahadevappa@sd.taylors.edu.my,
rajakumar.murugesan@taylors.edu.my

Abstract. In recent years, edge computing has emerged as a promising technology due to its unique feature of real-time computing and parallel processing. They provide computing and storage capability closer to the data source and bypass the distant links to the cloud. The edge data analytics process the ubiquitous data on the edge layer to offer real-time interactions for the application. However, this process can be prone to security threats like gaining malicious access or manipulate sensitive data. This can lead to the intruder's control, alter, or add erroneous data affecting the integrity and data analysis efficiency. Due to the lack of transparency of stakeholders processing edge data, it is challenging to identify the vulnerabilities. Many reviews are available on data security issues on the edge layer; however, they do not address integrity issues exclusively. Therefore, this paper concentrates only on data integrity threats that directly influence edge data analysis. Further shortcomings in existing work are identified with few research directions.

Keywords: Data Integrity · Data Security · Edge computing · Edge Data Analytics

1 Introduction

Edge computing is the advancement of cloud computing by bringing computation and networking ability closer to edge devices. This extended computing paradigm has addressed the challenges of increased digitalization due to billions of ubiquitous devices. Edge computing facilitates the resources to ubiquitous devices according to user requirements in real-time and reduces the burden of voluminous data on the cloud. This is achieved by the highly virtualized edge layer between the cloud and ubiquitous devices providing network, storage and compute services [1]. Currently, various applications in healthcare, VANET (Vehicular Adhoc Network), smart grid, smart transport, smart cities, augmented reality are adopting edge computing and the inability of cloud to meet stringent latency requirements is achieved [2–5]. It is forecasted that by 2025 edge computing market revenue will be up to 28 billion U.S dollars[1]. As evidence, localized computing power on edge can grow exponentially soon.

---

[1] https://www.statista.com/statistics/948744/worldwide-edge-computing-market-size/.

© Springer Nature Singapore Pte Ltd. 2021
N. Abdullah et al. (Eds.): ACeS 2021, CCIS 1487, pp. 505–514, 2021.
https://doi.org/10.1007/978-981-16-8059-5_31

Edge computing is defined as distributed computing paradigm that has network, compute, and storage capacity at the edge of the network through small data centres closer to the users. The current landscape integrates Internet of Things (IoT) devices with the cloud through the edge computing layer by filtering, preprocessing, and aggregating data generated by IoT devices [6]. The edge computing layer includes edge nodes, actuators, sensors geographically distributed on the edge layer. They provide mobility, location-awareness, interoperability, heterogeneity, and real-time responses to applications deployed over the edge computing layer. This potentially brings several advantages like lower latency, less bandwidth utilization, and increased energy efficiency. Overall, this makes edge computing appropriate for computation-intensive and latency-sensitive applications. There are also few drawbacks that are acknowledged in the existing literature like low individual computing power, unreliable devices and limited load balancing capacity [7, 8]. Hence, the pros and cons must be considered while developing edge-based applications. In Addition, the access technology in edge computing is mainly through wireless gateways with 1-hop distance Wi-Fi or cellular connections. In various scenarios, autonomous communication such as Machine-to-Machine (M2M), Device-to-Device (D2D), Car-to-Infrastructure (C2I), Car-to-Car (C2C) is used among users and devices continuously [9]. The communication scenarios and the distributed features of edge computing make it vulnerable to many security threats and issues.

Edge computing is subjected to several security challenges. It can be prone to many malicious activities like malicious access or manipulation of sensitive data. Like, the wireless networking technology can be broken by malicious users without physical contact to determine the resource location and access the data. Finally, limited resources make it challenging to adopt enhanced data protection models [10]. The above challenges motivate a need for developing an efficient data security system in the edge computing layer. Although most threats are inherited from the cloud, breaking network access, unknown stakeholders or determining resource locations are specific threats that arise in edge computing. This demands a particular study on data security issues in edge computing. It can be noted that [11–13] are complete reviews on data security, privacy, and trust issue, and there are no reviews, particularly on data integrity issues. In edge computing, computation details are not transparent like a cloud; malicious users can unknowingly tamper, hide, or remove data. More importantly, users are unaware of the stakeholders processing it. This affects data integrity and disturbs the edge data analysis. Thereby this review focuses mainly on data integrity issues and identifies the shortcomings in existing work.

In the remainder of this paper, an overview of edge data analytics and security issues arising from data analysis are discussed. Later a review on data integrity issues is analyzed, and research gaps are identified. Finally, research directions towards developing a secure data framework are proposed.

1.1 Edge Data Analytics

Edge data analytics (EDA) includes a data stream (DS) from the ubiquitous devices sent to edge nodes (EN) that are typically close to their sources. The communication channel at the proximity ensures that data is processed without delay. Each edge node maintains appropriate data processing models to update the data analysis and infer real-time interactions to the applications. The data models transmit processed data to the nearby edge server. This approach includes the parallel processing of data streams to foster the scalability of the system. The processed data are aggregated at the edge servers (ES) and broadcasted to all the edge nodes for accurate inference. The generic data analysis process is illustrated in Fig. 1 [14]. The security threats during this process can affect data quality and accuracy. While data is processed on the edge nodes, data owners lose complete control over their data. This can also lead to malicious intruders gaining control over the network. Finally, few infringements here can cause data theft or tamper with storage devices [11]. Therefore, while benefiting from the edge computing paradigm from various IoT applications, ensuring security to data present at the edge layer becomes the most valuable research in secure edge data analytics.

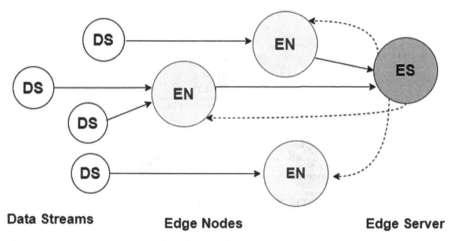

Fig. 1. Edge data analytics

Observation #1: During data traversal from IoT devices to edge servers, end-users lose complete ownership of their data. In case of a security breach, their data can be mishandled by intruders. Lack of service agreements like in cloud computing can create uncertainty among end-users in this regard.

2 Data Security Issues

Securing data from external threats is an evolving research area since the early days of computers and their usage. The primary concern while securing data is to ensure reliability, consistency, and accessibility to the authorized personnel. To achieve this, the CIA triad is widely used in information technology. The origin of the CIA triad is deeply rooted in the military security system that focuses on protecting internal information from external threats. In academia and information security research, this approach is an important asset for protecting information [15]. The three categories of the CIA triad that are the foundation for the data protection system are: confidentiality, integrity, and accessibility and is represented as shown in Fig. 2. They are identified as follows:

1. **Confidentiality** – It is the level of privacy that is required at each level of data processing. The attacker can observe the data pattern through traffic analysis and infer the data. Monitoring unauthorized supervision of end-users data is a security measure to achieve confidentiality.
2. **Integrity** – It is a kind of data sabotage where attackers alter or modify intentionally. Compromising data integrity can be achieved mainly during data outsourcing, where data owners lose complete control. Data validity against undesired changes assures integrity.
3. **Availability** – It is a way of preventing authorized users from referring to or modify data. The attacker can hack the data resources and gain complete control over them. Data must be reachable to required processing nodes to ensure availability.

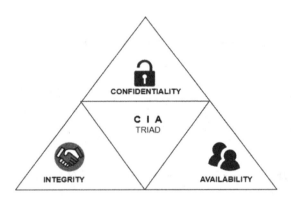

Fig. 2. Data Security Triad – CIA

Many critical security threats are growing concerns in information technology. But attacks that affect data integrity can have a severe effect that can mislead the data analysis process and deceive real-time interaction provided by the edge nodes. Therefore, addressing data integrity attack is challenging and crucial to establish trust between the end-users and the application running on edge computing. A complete understanding of the system with intelligence is required to make this attack effective [16].

2.1 Data Integrity Issues

The goal of the data integrity attack is to mislead the operator with erroneous data. To achieve these, attackers can create malicious data through spam or false data injection. Hence, in this section, existing security mechanisms that address these threats are analyzed to identify their pros and cons and tabulated in Table 1. Spam can be defined as sending an irrelevant, inappropriate and unsolicited message to several users to exploit sensitive information [16]. Fog augment, and Machine Learning (ML) based spam detection tool detects spam in both incoming and outgoing Short Message Service (SMS). It is an efficient tool to identify spam SMS that is illegitimately installed on mobile devices due to malware. Various ML classifiers and data preprocessing termed as a filter in this tool assist significantly in identifying spam on mobile devices and cloud servers. The fog computing layer is used only to perform classification and identification and has no specific role in data processing [17]. Deep learning-based multistage and elastic spam detection on mobile social networks like Twitter, Facebook, and Sina Weibo, significantly improve real-time quality of service. Initial detection is performed on mobile terminals, and later the result with the message is passed to the cloud server. The server extensively computes to identify and confirm the spam through the detection queue. The computational time and resources in the detection queue may incur superfluous resources [18].

Wi-Fi enabled a mesh of cloudlets to secure data during transmission, storage and processing on mobile devices and remote clouds. This framework includes hierarchical intrusion detection and prevents spam/virus attacks between cloud, edge, and mobile devices. Collaborative intrusion detection and MapReduce spam filtering process does predictive security analyses at the backend, emphasizing real-time response towards intrusions through the trusted remote cloud [19].

Data injection is an attack akin to spam where legitimate data is modified, altered, or injected with false data to affect the data processing efficiency. Paillier homomorphic encryption scheme is used to secure data from false injection and modification attacks on the edge computing layer. This includes three phases in terms of key generation, encryption, and decryption. Without having a third-party trust assigning authority, data privacy is obtained in the edge computing layer. This approach is more efficient than traditional methods, but when the number of IoT devices increases, the edge nodes' computation overhead increases gradually [20]. S-CLASSIFIER is a false data injection detector on edge nodes. It includes four components – data controller to transmit sensory data, indicator to indicate connectivity between nodes and sensors, aggregator to receive collective data from the data collector and finally, a detector responsible for classifying the data and deciding whether it is good or bad. In case of detecting bad data, the detector issues an alarm to the other node, blocking them from further data transmission. The Support Vector Machine (SVM) method makes this method simple and efficiently divides train data on edge nodes [21]. Comparatively, a third-party auditor is used to audit data integrity through a homomorphic authenticator. Bilinear pairing keys are used along with the homomorphic authenticator for auditing multimedia data. This includes seven phases of key generation, data uploading, backup, recovery, and auditing. This is later outsourced for a third-party auditor to validate storage proof using a public key. Although this approach is efficient in recovering data, resource consumption and time computation may be more for this redundant process [22].

There are many other methods that are suitable for smaller attack areas [23], specific models for healthcare applications [24, 25] or a model with only conceptual design [26]. These recent advances show that addressing data integrity attacks is a hot topic in edge computing. Since these attacks can obstruct the normal operation of the network without being detected, the intention of these attacks can be to gain control over the system, establish undetectable errors, or malicious intent of exploiting the system. Therefore, addressing these attacks is crucial to ensure data privacy and confidentiality. Additionally, most existing methods include complex computations, expensive pre-computation steps, multiple execution of single steps, or outsourcing computation to third-party authorities.

These approaches for resource and computation limited edge computing can be challenging and affect the data processing efficiency. It can also be observed that identifying any form of intrusion when the data enter the edge layer can greatly reduce the intensity of the attack. Overall, there is a need for secure data framework that can detect the intrusion at an early stage and diminish the attack without adding complex computational load on the edge nodes.

Table 1. Review on existing security mechanism to address integrity issues in Edge Computing

Ref	Method	Evaluation	Pros/Cons
[17]	Fog Augmented and ML-based SMS spam detection system generated by malware on mobile devices	5 ML classifiers and filters are used to identify spam on mobile devices and cloud servers. Based on the user preference, appropriate spam filters are recommended	The data preprocessing performed is termed as a filter, which assists greatly in identifying spam
[18]	Deep learning-based multistage and elastic spam detection in mobile social network	A server's detection queue with a timer identifies and elastically abandon the spam data received from mobile terminals. Edge computing handles computational resources for multistage detection	Real-time message detection significantly improves the service, but multistage detection consumes enormous resources
[19]	Wi-Fi enabled mesh of cloudlets to secure cloud by pervasive mobile users	Hierarchically trusted secure framework emphasizing to remove malicious attacks and filter spam from mobile devices	Collectively performs intrusion detection and spam reduction. Effectively offload task between cloud and cloudlets
[20]	Paillier homomorphic encryption scheme against data injection attack	Protects sensitive information through 3 stage cryptographic operations and uses blinding factors to enhance data privacy	Reliable and efficient security framework to ensure data integrity in edge computing. However, it increases the computational load on edge devices
[21]	S-CLASSIFIER an edge node detector to identify false data injection in smart grid	ML-based classifier identifies the attack during data transmission, and sub-controller on the edge nodes takes the decision immediately to mitigate the attack by issuing an alarm	Edge nodes detect the attack at a faster rate and prevent it

(continued)

Table 1. (*continued*)

Ref	Method	Evaluation	Pros/Cons
[22]	Homomorphic authenticator to audit data integrity on multimedia data	Stores historical data in a one-way lined information table. Third-party auditor audits the stored data to ensure data integrity, recovery and recure from replay attack	Significantly support data recovery and backup in the cloud and determines it can be applied in a real-time scenario for multimedia security
[23]	Constraint-based false data injection model	Linear and nonlinear based two models are used to identify a complicated and straightforward attack	Better for smaller attack area
[24]	Data integrity preservation in healthcare applications	A transaction dependency graph is used to monitor the transaction and identify intrusions initially. Later, using a damage assessment algorithm on serializable history, data integrity is verified	Intrusion detection significantly monitors unauthorized access in the edge layer

Observation #2 – Complex security frameworks provides security to the edge framework but overload the edge nodes. Thereby it makes it challenging for the edge nodes to retain their characteristics, especially the real-time responsiveness. This can significantly affect the future adoption of edge computing in any application.

Observation #3 – Cryptographic techniques, outsourcing validation externally, and maintaining multiple logs increase the edge nodes' time and resource utilization through frequent interactions. These interactions unknowingly can create an opportunity for the intruders to let them understand the system's working.

3 Future Research Directions

Future research directions that could leverage the existing solutions to achieve data integrity in the edge layer are listed below:

- **Designing reputation management model of edge nodes** – The decentralized edge computing framework collect, process, and analyze data frequently on the edge layer. As noted in observation #1, edge data analytics lack users' confidence in their data. The potential loopholes are mainly due to malicious users gaining access to the network. Therefore, creating fairness among the participating nodes and users can patch these loopholes [27]. A scalable reputation-based security mechanism can be more suitable considering historical interaction and frequent peers' updates.

- **Adopting Federated Learning algorithms** – Edge computing is the most feasible technology due to its local computation to reduce data intensity on the cloud. As mentioned in observation #2, overloading edge nodes can affect the feasibility gradually. Federated Learning, a distributed machine learning approach, facilitates training large amounts of data on ubiquitous devices. This approach significantly improves the data analysis process; thereby, adopting this can complement edge computing and address the fundamental problem of privacy, ownership, and locality data.
- **Adopting Fine-Grained data consistency enhancing model** – Following observation #3, the multiple interactions due to complex cryptography or third-party security measures leads intruders to gain access to the network. Adopting a straightforward fine-grained data consistency model can reduce the interactions between the nodes and achieve secure collaboration. This approach is proved to be efficient in cloud computing [28]. Therefore, adopting a similar approach can provide data tracking and enhance interoperability between heterogenous edge nodes.

4 Conclusions

With the proliferation of IoT devices, edge computing is becoming an emerging technology to manage ample data through local edge data analytics and offering resources. Alongside the security concern due to proximity, data handling is also progressing. Therefore, there is a paramount need to address the data security issue to sustain edge computing. This paper addresses security issues that affect data integrity, influencing data efficiency on the edge layer. Existing security methods available to address this are reviewed to identify the gaps in current research. Lastly, future research directions towards data security, privacy and secure data analytics are directed.

References

1. Osanaiye, O., Chen, S., Yan, Z., Lu, R., Choo, K.K.R., Dlodlo, M.: From cloud to fog computing: a review and a conceptual live VM migration framework. IEEE Access. **5**, 8284–8300 (2017). https://doi.org/10.1109/ACCESS.2017.2692960
2. Mutlag, A.A., Abd Ghani, M.K., Arunkumar, N., Mohammed, M.A., Mohd, O.: Enabling technologies for fog computing in healthcare IoT systems. Futur. Gener. Comput. Syst. **90**, 62–78 (2019). https://doi.org/10.1016/j.future.2018.07.049
3. Pereira, J., Ricardo, L., Luís, M., Senna, C., Sargento, S.: Assessing the reliability of fog computing for smart mobility applications in VANETs. Futur. Gener. Comput. Syst. **94**, 317–332 (2019). https://doi.org/10.1016/j.future.2018.11.043
4. Ning, Z., Huang, J., Wang, X.: Vehicular fog computing: enabling real-time traffic management for smart cities. IEEE Wirel. Commun. **26**, 87–93 (2019). https://doi.org/10.1109/MWC.2019.1700441
5. Verba, N., Chao, K.-M., Lewandowski, J., Shah, N., James, A., Tian, F.: Modeling industry 4.0 based fog computing environments for application analysis and deployment. Future Gener. Comput. Syst. **91**, 48–60 (2019). https://doi.org/10.1016/j.future.2018.08.043
6. Yousefpour, A., et al.: All one needs to know about fog computing and related edge computing paradigms: a complete survey. J. Syst. Archit. **98**, 289–330 (2019). https://doi.org/10.1016/j.sysarc.2019.02.009

7. Mahadevappa, P., Murugesan, R.K.: Study of container-based virtualisation and threats in fog computing. In: Anbar, M., Abdullah, N., Manickam, S. (eds.) ACeS 2020. CCIS, vol. 1347, pp. 535–549. Springer, Singapore (2021). https://doi.org/10.1007/978-981-33-6835-4_36

8. Mukherjee, M., Shu, L., Wang, D.: Survey of fog computing: fundamental, network applications, and research challenges. IEEE Commun. Surv. Tutor. **20**, 1826–1857 (2018). https://doi.org/10.1109/COMST.2018.2814571

9. Gedeon, J., Brandherm, F., Egert, R., Grube, T., Muhlhauser, M.: What the fog? edge computing revisited: promises Applications and Future Challenges. IEEE Access **7**, 152847–152878 (2019). https://doi.org/10.1109/ACCESS.2019.2948399

10. Mann, Z.A.: Data protection in fog computing through monitoring and adaptation. Infosys.tuwien.ac.atPaperpile (2018)

11. Liu, D., Yan, Z., Ding, W., Atiquzzaman, M.: A Survey on secure data analytics in edge computing. IEEE Internet Things J. **6**, 4946–4967 (2019). https://doi.org/10.1109/JIOT.2019.2897619

12. Zhang, J., Chen, B., Zhao, Y., Cheng, X., Hu, F.: Data security and privacy-preserving in edge computing paradigm: survey and open issues. IEEE Access. **6**, 18209–18237 (2018). https://doi.org/10.1109/ACCESS.2018.2820162

13. Noura, H., Salman, O., Chehab, A., Couturier, R.: Preserving data security in distributed fog computing. Ad Hoc Netw. **94**, 101937 (2019). https://doi.org/10.1016/j.adhoc.2019.101937

14. Aral, A., Erol-Kantarci, M., Brandić, I.: Staleness control for edge data analytics. Proc. ACM Meas. Anal. Comput. Syst. **4**, 1–24 (2020). https://doi.org/10.1145/3392156

15. Coss, D., Samonas, S.: The CIA strikes back: redefining confidentiality, integrity and availability in security. J. Inf. Syst. Secur. **10**, 21–45 (2014)

16. Jang-Jaccard, J., Nepal, S.: A survey of emerging threats in cybersecurity. J. Comput. Syst. Sci. **80**, 973–993 (2014). https://doi.org/10.1016/j.jcss.2014.02.005

17. Bosaeed, S., Katib, I., Mehmood, R.: A fog-augmented machine learning based sms spam detection and classification system. In: 2020 5th International Conference on Fog and Mobile Edge Computing FMEC 2020, pp. 325–330 (2020). https://doi.org/10.1109/FMEC49853.2020.9144833

18. Feng, B., Fu, Q., Dong, M., Guo, D., Li, Q.: Multistage and elastic spam detection in mobile social networks through deep learning. IEEE Netw. **32**, 15–21 (2018). https://doi.org/10.1109/MNET.2018.1700406

19. Shi, Y., Abhilash, S., Hwang, K.: Cloudlet mesh for securing mobile clouds from intrusions and network attacks. Proc. - 2015 3rd IEEE International Conference on Mobile Cloud Computing, Services, and Engineering MobileCloud 2015, pp. 109–118 (2015). https://doi.org/10.1109/MobileCloud.2015.15

20. Zhang, Y., et al.: Privacy-preserving data aggregation against false data injection attacks in fog computing. Sensors. **18**, 2659 (2018). https://doi.org/10.3390/s18082659

21. Xun, P., Zhu, P., Zhang, Z., Cui, P., Xiong, Y.: Detectors on edge nodes against false data injection on transmission lines of smart grid. Electron. **7**, 1–12 (2018). https://doi.org/10.3390/electronics7060089

22. Liu, D., Shen, J., Vijayakumar, P., Wang, A., Zhou, T.: Efficient data integrity auditing with corrupted data recovery for edge computing in enterprise multimedia security. Multimedia Tools Appl. **79**(15–16), 10851–10870 (2020). https://doi.org/10.1007/s11042-019-08558-1

23. Tran, N.N., Pota, H.R., Tran, Q.N., Hu, J.: Designing constraint-based false data injection attacks against the unbalanced distribution smart grids. IEEE Internet Things J. 1–14 (2021). https://doi.org/10.1109/JIOT.2021.3056649

24. Alazeb, A., et al.: Data Integrity Preservation Schemes in Smart Healthcare, 1–27 (2021)

25. Alazeb, A., Panda, B.: Ensuring data integrity in fog computing based health-care systems. In: Wang, G., Feng, J., Bhuiyan, M.Z.A., Lu, R. (eds.) SpaCCS 2019. LNCS, vol. 11611, pp. 63–77. Springer, Cham (2019). https://doi.org/10.1007/978-3-030-24907-6_6

26. KashifMunir, A., Mohammed, L.: Secure Third Party Auditor(TPA) for ensuring data integrity in fog computing. Int. J. Netw. Secur. Its Appl. **10**, 13–24 (2018). https://doi.org/10.5121/ijnsa. 2018.10602
27. Nwebonyi, F.N., Martins, R., Correia, M.E.: Reputation-based security system for edge computing. ACM Int. Conf. Proc. Ser. (2018). https://doi.org/10.1145/3230833.3232819
28. Ye, X., Khoussainov, B.: Fine-grained access control for cloud computing. Int. J. Grid Util. Comput. **4**, 160–168 (2013). https://doi.org/10.1504/IJGUC.2013.056252

Security Issues and Challenges in SDN

Ali Haider Shamsan[✉] ⓘ and Arman Rasool Faridi ⓘ

Department of Computer Science, Aligarh Muslim University, Aligarh, U.P., India
ahtshamsan@myamu.ac.in, ar.faridi.cs@amu.ac.in

Abstract. Software Defined Network SDN is a programmable network with the new architecture of separating control functions from the switching devices. The new paradigm of SDN still not secured enough due to the differences in compared to the legacy network. SDN security is considered as key concern and challenge while it's unproven in regard to the single point of controlling and management – centralized controller - which it may become a target for attackers. This paper surveys the overview of SDN, and its characteristics, as well as, APIs interface in order to understand the background of SDN. The security issues and threats are surveyed with proposed solutions to those issues.

Keywords: SDN · DOS · OpenFlow · SDN security · Security issues

1 Introduction

Computer network consists of vast number of devices such as switches, routers, and different types of devices. As well as, many protocols are implemented to control the network and forwarding the packets. Designing the network and configuring the devices are considered as the core of building and operating the network. Thus, changing the configuration and updating the rules are done manually for all devices with highly restricted to complete all tasks smoothly [1]. So, programmable network concept has been born to facilitate and simplify network management and development. That concept is called Software Defined Network (SDN) [2].

Software Defined Network (SDN) is considered as revolutionary network. It is the best practice of virtualization in network era. The idea of SDN is to centralize the controlling of the network in a form of centralized controller and software programing, and to free the network nodes and devices from any controlling responsibility [3, 4]. SDN has some features over the legacy network: i) decoupling data and control plane which leads to create independent applications for specific purposes, ii) SDN provides complete information of the network which leads to enhance the network performance and utilization. That information is provided by centralized controller which has global view of the network [4]. iii) SDN is programmable network which can be configured by centralized controller via appropriate APIs and protocols, for that SDN is more flexible for troubleshooting. iv) SDN is a virtualized network which can be work physically and virtually [5]. SDN is considered as a centralized management based, so it provides various technologies and approaches [6].

© Springer Nature Singapore Pte Ltd. 2021
N. Abdullah et al. (Eds.): ACeS 2021, CCIS 1487, pp. 515–535, 2021.
https://doi.org/10.1007/978-981-16-8059-5_32

The features of SDN is made up of the need for reliable, flexible way to secure and manage the network. SDN changes the architecture of traditional network completely by decoupling and separating hardware of forwarding and then control logic. In that, routers and switches only forward the data traffic, while the control functions are done by logical controller which provides the abstraction of the whole network [7, 8].

In spite of all features of SDN, SDN security is considered as key concern and challenge while it's unproven in regard to the single point of controlling and management – centralized controller - which it may become a target for attackers. Some threats and vulnerabilities are caused by the programmability concepts.

Security refers to prevent attacks and detect intrusion [9]. By keeping focus on SDN features and architecture, it is more exposed to attacks than legacy network. SDN does not introduce security as part of its design, so, the security should be implemented as service to the network [7]. The current SDN standards do not describe the issues of security which are considered as the most critical issues for the network. security aspects of SDN differ in a point of view of researchers; some think that SDN can manage the security problems which can be introduced by implementing SDN [10], and it can be an advantage of implementing security regarding centralized controller [6]. On the hand, others think that SDN network will be more complex and cause difficulties to secure the network properly [10], and it may complicate the security problems [6] as all data traffic is detected by a central controller, which strengthen the security of SDN. In this regard, the new policies will be propagated overall the network, which will improve the network performance [11, 12]. In the same time, it is considered as a weakness that the controller will be easily targeted for attackers.

SDN could be affected by attacks of a legacy network, but the security of traditional network may not work properly on SDN because the separation of data and control planes forces switches to forward packets blindly according to the policies and rules which are governed by SDN controller. Moreover, the network can go down by untrusted hosts which can interrupt the controller by initiating flooding packets to the controller. In that, the whole network may go down [13].

This paper is structured as follows: Sect. 2 define the SDN and gives an overview of the programmable network. In Sect. 3, security fundamentals and SDN security will be covered with its pros and cons. Section 4 discusses the SDN security threats in different planes of SDN. Section 4.2 suggests some solutions to SDN security issues. Finally, this paper will conclude with some future recommendations in Sect. 5.

2   SDN Overview

Software Defined Network (SDN) is considered as new computer network methodology [1] which deploys and operates the network by programmable platform [5] of managing function of network controlling efficiently. It is a paradigm of network which improves new functions for controlling the network [1] which are allowed to be executed logically by the centralized controller [5] instead of the traditional way of managing network that every device has its own controlling interface which is provided by its vendor [1].

SDN provides an easy way of network administration than the traditional ways. It decouples physically data plane and control plane, while all network devices such as routers, switches, access point, etc. are considered as forwarding devices and they only forward packets [5] according to the policies of the controllers which is centralized logically to manage the whole network without any interventions by network administrator [14].

2.1 SDN Planes

Software defined network (SDN) has three planes which are Data plane, control plane, and application/ management plane, as shown in Fig. 1.

Data Plane

It contains all network hardware devices which are physically connected [1], and they are considered as forwarding devices that forward the packets over the network based on the Flow table which consists of rules of forwarding packets [3, 4], and those rules are configured, updated, programmed by the centralized controller [14]. Data plane communicates with the control plane and controller by southbound APIs [15]. Some management functionalities are implemented in this layer to help the controller in collecting information of the network, and to enable forwarding packets [8]. It is also known as physical infrastructure layer [1, 15] data forwarding layer [4], data layer [7, 8].

Control Plane

It is considered as the mind of the SDN network while it contains the controller which is responsible of controlling the whole network [4], and it provides the view of the network for application plane. So, programming data flow paths, and configuring the nodes are basically done by the controller in a control plane and pushed to network devices in data plane [12, 16]. It also translates and transfers the request of the users which comes from application layer [14] to be understandable to network devices [1]. SDN controller is a software platform which is deployed with specific software [4]. Control plane communicates with other planes through different APIs, it communicates with data plane via Southbound APIs [4], and with application plane through Northbound APIs [1].

Control plane supports multi-controllers to enhance the availability and scalability of the network. In that, every controller is responsible for specific process and specific portion of the network devices. For that, the controllers communicate between each other using eastbound and westbound APIs [4].

Application Plane

It contains the applications which come as respond to the requirements by users from various fields, either business, academic, or personal [4]. Those applications, services, policies are developed in this layer [1] by different vendors [6] fulfill the requirements and to work with the functions of SDN controller [4] Which enable changing and updating the network configuration from one point [1].

518   A. H. Shamsan and A. R. Faridi

It communicates with control plane via Northbound APIs. In that, the abstraction of the network and its physical resource are provided by the controller through Northbound APIs [4].

This layer provides various kinds of services and applications such as management, security, load balancing, WAN optimization, and net virtualization applications [4, 7, 8, 14].

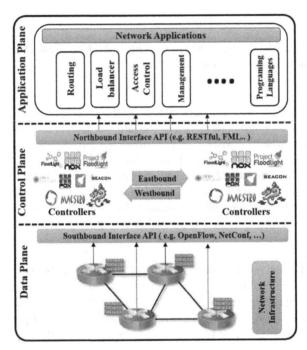

Fig. 1. SDN architecture planes and interfaces

2.2 SDN Interfaces

SDN has four Application Programming Interfaces (APIs) which are used to communicate between planes and controllers. Those interfaces are shown in Fig. 1.

Southbound API

It is an interface between data plane and control plane, it is used to communicate between the controller and network devices in the infrastructure layer [17, 18]. In the case of deploying the configuration on devices, updating routing flow table, or updating the rules, southbound APIs are used [19], as well as if network devices such as switch cannot decide about a packet, this packet automatically is sent to the controller through southbound APIs [1]. It is also used to exchange the policies and state of the network with a controller [20].

OpenFlow is the best example of southbound APIs, which is considered as a protocol to define the rules on forwarding devices [1, 20–22].

It Exchanges network state information and control policies with the CP and provides functions such as programmatic control of all device-capability advertisements, forwarding operations, event notifications and statistics reports.

Northbound API

It is the interface API, which is used to facilitate the communication between control plane and application plane [1, 21]. It can be used to manage the SDN controller by using some application to set the service and requirements [1]. The controller provides network view abstraction to applications through Northbound APIs [19]. Current controllers offer a quite broad variety of applications and northbound APIs [17, 18].

It enables applications to program the network, manages SDN system, and requests services from the network and controller [1], as well as to show the network behaviors and automation [22].

Eastbound/Westbound APIs

They are software APIs which provide the communication between multiple distributed controllers over several domains to coordinate decisions [19] and exchange the information. It enables managing distributed SDN architectures [21], which are considered as the extension of SDN structure [15, 23].

Every controller has its own East/westbound APIs to identify common compatibility and provide interoperability between controllers [18].

Particular data distributed mechanisms are required for this kind of APIs, as well as some communication protocols between controllers to support various functionalities services to effective reachability of controllers. Furthermore, the heterogenetic of controllers which need to communicate with others not only peer controller. In that, East/westbound APIs have to support different interfaces of different controllers with their requirements, services, infrastructure, and technologies to improve the interoperability [22], so that may improve the scalability of network with a vast number of controllers to exchange massive amount of information and data. In that, it is noticed that no standards available for east/westbound interfaces [22].

2.3   OpenFlow

It is considered as southbound API which is used to communicate between data plane and control plane in an SDN Network. It supports to manage the network devices such as switches, routers, access points, etc. without a need for vendor's programs of their devices [24].

Through OpenFlow, the controller can access to forwarding devices, and instruct those devices how to deal with packets and how to forward them, as well as to deploy the configurations and rules on network devices in data plane. OpenFlow is considered as controlling forwarding behavior of a wide network, and for that, many different tools and APIs are provided by different vendors to do the same function [25].

OpenFlow contains three components [21, 26]: OpenFlow controller, OpenFlow channel, OpenFlow switch.

OpenFlow Controller

It is responsible for managing the network devices in order to update instructions and distributed policies. It can edit flow table entries, either adding or removing. So, Open-Flow controller is able to handle packets easily. OpenFlow supports multiple controllers which enhance the reliability of the network [26]. As soon as the OpenFlow startup, all switches and controllers should be connected regarding their configuration [21].

OpenFlow Channel

It is an interface between OpenFlow controllers and OpenFlow switches, which is used to send a packet from the switch, and to manage switch configuration. It supports three messages types [21]: symmetric, asynchronous, and controller-to-switch. Symmetric is initiated and sent by controller or switch without solicitation. Asynchronous message is generated by the switch with information of changes in the status of switches and events of the network and send to the controller. The third type of message is a controller-to-switch message which is to inspect and manage switch status.

OpenFlow Switch

It consists of a flow table to forward the packet to the right destination, which has a list of entries with different fields such as header, counter, and action. Each field has different using [21]. Header comes with some information such as IP address, source, destination, etc. while counter counts the packet numbers and bytes, etc. Moreover, the process of matching the packet and forwarding entries is given by the action field [26].

3 Characteristics of Software-Defined Networks

As discussed in the previous sections, we can summarize SDN features and characteristics. Those characteristics may cause weakness, threats, and vulnerabilities to security, which may be used for targeting attacks toward the network [16]. The traits of SDN as follows:

Centralized Controller [7] *:* The controller in SDN is logically centralized which is considered as the essential feature of SDN [16]. In a traditional network, the controller is attached on every device which leads to complicate managing the network when each network component acts autonomously [26]. The instructions and rules of forwarding packets are provided by the controller to the forwarding devices of the network to allow them to decide about packets [26]. Moreover, controller abstracts the network view to application plane [27].

To guarantee redundancy, reliability, and scalability, the controller may be distributed to act as a cluster of controllers, while every controller behaves as a master of a group of slave switches in the mode of Master/slave architecture [16].

Open Programmable Interfaces [7]: The interfaces of SDN which are using for commutating between planes or between different controllers, either Southbound APIs, Northbound APIs or East-Westbound APIs are all open and programmable [16, 27]. Those APIs provide adequate control for all planes [26]. The Openness of SDN helps in developing and improving SDN technologies by allowing various researchers from different background to experiment and deploy new inventions and technologies. Hence, that will increase the speed of advancement of SDN [26], and introduce the novel solutions easily [16].

Simplify the Forwarding Devices: The forwarding devices of SDN are simplified while they are controlled by the centralized controller which is upgraded independently [16]. All network devices become forwarding device in SDN concerning the rules that set up and configured by the controller [27].

Switch Management Protocol [7]: The switch management protocol is the programmable interface mentioned above. Those protocols such as OpenFlow, NETCONF, RESTful, etc. are used to facilitate the management functions. Programmable devices and switches need to standardize the configuration to support multiple logical switches [16].

Third-Party Network Services: SDN architecture integrates with various services from different vendors which are provided by third-party. Those services run on the controller at a run-time level while the controller is working without needs for restarting the controller [16], and they are compatible with the environment platform. The third-party services using Northbound APIs to communicate with controllers due to they are installed in the application plane.

Virtualized Logical Networks: The infrastructure components of SDN can be virtualized to support initiating multiple virtual switches on the same physical devices [16]. Multi-tenancy of the network components helps in improving the performance, QoS, and Security. Virtualizing supports the agility of SDN services and network paradigm. The network services decouple from the physical network, so hosts unaware if the utilized resources are virtual or not, and differ than expected and designed [27].

Planes Separation [7]: The primary feature of SDN is the separation of planes. It decouples control plane from forwarding plane. All functions of forwarding reside in the data plane. The packet may be forwarded, discarded, consumed, and replicated in data plane. Hence, the planes are separated logically, and the control functions moved off of the forwarding devices to the centralized controller [26].

4 SDN Security

SDN security is considered as a cornerstone, while SDN is a controller centralized based which is easier to be attacked compared to the traditional network [4] with various methods of attacks. For instance, Denial of service attack, in which the attacker targets the center of the network [10] and send huge packets and requests which can lead to down the network due to the controller is down [27], while on the other hand, current network components are distributed not centralized [4].

According to SDN characteristics, SDN effectively monitors the traffic because of the way that a centralized controller can see the whole traffic. So, if there is any abnormal packet, it can be noticed easily [4]. As well as, it supports application security to be run on the application layer depending on the view of the network to improve the flexibility of management and security strategies for different equipment and applications [28]. Also, SDN can deal with attacks and vulnerabilities faster and more convenient [28]. As the nature of SDN of programmable-based, it is easy to program an application or software to deal and adjust with security threats immediately [4, 28]. For that, time will be saved, and the network will be maintained secured without waiting for an update from third-party providers or manufacturers-integrated patches [4]. SDN deals with complicated security and volatile threats effectively [28].

SDN architecture is designed for effectively monitoring security and analysis. In this perspective, SDN can achieve the forensics purpose of the network. It supports quick identifying security threat and analyzes it in order to update the current security policies by reprogramming the software to optimize the security level. SDN is more flexible to alter the policies which help to reduce the conflicting policies and misconfigurations, so that new policies can be defined and deployed on all resource components. SDN supports inserting security services for specific traffic which can be done by applied security applications such as firewall and Intrusion Detection Systems (IDSs). Therefore, SDN security will depend on the defined security policies [7].

As a nature of SDN and its characteristics, it has some defects which are caused reducing security [10], such as centralized controller which is easy to be targeted by attacks where most functions reside on the controller such as configuration, calculation of routing, and collecting network information. If the attackers seize the controller, that may affect the whole network which is governed by that controller, and most of network services will go down. Moreover, open programmable interfaces may cause some security threats [10], it may cause controller to be fully exposed to attackers who have information how to exploit the open interfaces that are provided by the controller for the application layer. The openness of SDN could be used for embedding malicious software or viruses, so, interfaces have to be secured carefully and evaluated regularly. Furthermore, by considering the architecture of SDN, many attack points are found. SDN entities are distributed over various locations, and they communicate with each other, which provide multiple possible points to be attacked, such as distributed SDN switches with long flow tables, the link between switches easily to be attacked especially wireless media which are used for transmiting data between different switches, almost this data is unencrypted which contains sensitive data. Also, SDN controllers are considered a critical target for attacks, and the link between different distributed controllers as well as switches. Hence, the transmitted data on the links are easy to be intercepted by attackers.

Moreover, SDN applications are considered as one of the critical points of attacks which are used to discover the controller and targeted it [4].

4.1 SDN Security Threats

Like any network technologies, SDN network paradigm has security requirements. It is similar to a traditional network paradigm, and it is carrying confidential data [29]. While SDN architecturally differs from legacy network. Likewise, the security issues and threats may occur in different manners which arise the security challenges [30], and some of the security issues related to the SDN characteristics which are discussed earlier [16]. Therefore, security level should be maintained as a traditional network [29], but security tools of traditional network may not be work properly in SDN [18]. In this section, the security issues of SDN will be discussed, as well as summarized in Table 1.

Unauthorized Access
As the nature of SDN controllers which is logically centralized and physically distributed as multiple controllers [16]. In the case of a single controller, the necessary level of security can be maintained. However, with multiple controllers, access and authorization are more complex [12, 16]. The data plane is accessed by multiple controllers, while applications in the application plane from multiple sources can access the controllers with read-write permission of network status. The attackers can access to the network resources and operation in the case of impersonating application or controller [16], which increase the possibility of unauthorized access which may lead to configure the network nodes [12], hacking, or stealing data [14].

DoS/DDoS Attacks
Denial of Service (DoS) or Distributed Denial of Service (DDoS) are utilizing the network resource by fake request packets, which leads to denying the legitimate packets to be processed [31]. In SDN network, there are various types of DoS/DDoS attacks which target the availability of SDN resources [32] either controller, network switches, or their links, due to SDN introduced the architecture- related security weakness of combining the separation of plans and centralizing the controller [16].

The controller could be overwhelmed in the case of flooding it with flow-decision requests which lead to obstructing the ability of the controller to process any legitimate request [16, 29]. The entire network functionality may be downed by targeting the controller as a central point of the network. The functions of network may be available temporary when the controller went down, but this case will not be for long time. When the request timeout is completed, it may be sent again to the controller which is not unable to process the request; therefore, the whole network may go down.

Another way of DoS is the switch flow-table entry flooding which occurs in the data plane. Due to the flooding of the flow entries which are targeting devices of data plane, those devices will be unable to process new legitimate entries, and the flow table fills with false entries. As one of the issues of data plane devices that they are not able to differentiate between request packets either legitimate or illegitimate. Consequently, the flow buffer of the switches will be filled with such a request which leads to denying the network services [32].

Hijacked/Rogue Controller
SDN controller is considered as a brain of network which controls the whole network. If an attacker can hack or get access to the controller, he/she will be able to manage any process of the network such as changing the destination of the packet or stopping it not to reach the actual destination. It can operate a node in the network to act as "Man-in-the-Middle", which allows the attacker to inspect, alter, or drop the packet [29]. Moreover, rogue controller could be registered in control plane which can affect the availability, configuration, rules, and policies of the network, as well as, the attacker can violate the integrity and confidentiality of data.

Malicious Applications
The malicious application is considered as a serious issue in SDN due to the open framework of SDN which is integrated with third-party vendors of applications [14]. Such applications may have the same impact of compromised controller [16] as the applications work as deep inspection of a packet which may cause risk and can control the whole network capitalizing the information collected by inspection technique. Furthermore, malicious applications can threaten either integrity or confidentiality of stored information which is located in a centralized data center [29].

Control-Data Plane Link Attacks
The link between control and data plane could be targeted by attacking and introduce more security issues. As its nature of optional TLS/SSL of OpenFlow [16], it is considered as susceptible to many attacks such as black-hole attacks and Man-in-the-Middle [32], as well as DoS attacks [18]. A black-hole attack is the type of attack which drops the packets whose received from node instead of forwarding them to the controller which leads to unavailability of network services and down the network communications [1, 7, 15], and it could be done when the malicious node is established between data and control planes [32]. On the other hand, Man-in-the-Middle is considered malicious node which is manipulating the packet before forwarding them to the controller and vice-versa, and include spoofing SDN and controller ports [4]. It attacks the integrity of the packets between controller and network devices [29].

Eavesdropping Attacks
Eavesdropping attack is gathering meaningful information in order to do intrusive attacks. It could be done by gaining access to the network to inspect and capture packets. It can be carried out at the data plane, as well as could be carried out on the communication between control and data planes, and control and application planes. In order to inspect packets in the data plane, attacker may use the OpenFlow integrated mode of ease-of-use for listening [29].

4.2 Solutions

SDN security solution should be targeted to eliminate the threats and Issues which have a serious impact on all layers of SDN. There are many proposed solutions against each threat and issue. Most of those solutions depend on software solutions [16] such monitoring systems with specific security policies in order to monitor the network traffic to detect the malicious [14]. On the other hand, there some security architectures are proposed to be a reference to develop security tools and functions. However, still some threats and issues not getting much attention such as Data leakage and modifications [16].

Further details of the security solutions are provided as follows, and summarized in Table 1:

Unauthorized Access

In the Unauthorized access attack, there is two possible access which may be unauthorized; unauthorized applications, and unauthorized controllers. There are some proposed solutions to solve the issues of unauthorized access. In order to secure distributed controllers, the controller must be secured by TLS, and securing the transmission flow by a signature algorithm which will be done by a centralized trusted manager for the purpose of checking the signature and passing the messages [33].

For protecting controllers and eliminating the unauthorized access attacks of SDN control plane, an SDN structure is proposed to secure the network is capitalizing Byzantine mechanism. The secure structure supports multiple controllers in order to improve scalability and reliability, and to tolerance the fault [34].

However, In order to minimize the serious failure of SDN controller which is considered as a point of failure, switches and controllers setup hierarchically. In the case of hierarchal system, the work is divided between switch fabric and root controller which assumed to be trusted. The impacts of malicious applications might be limited with hierarchal architecture [35].

For the permission of applications, the PermOF is proposed by [36] with a mechanism of isolation to apply for the permissions at the APIs. It helps reduce attacks from control plane and protect the network by applying limited privileges of applications.

Moreover, in order to secure the interface between control and application plane (control-application API), the mechanism of check permission is implemented which is called OperationCheckpoint [37]. The (SEK) Security Enforcement Kernel is introduced by Security Enhanced SE-Floodlight which authenticate the Northbound APIs digitally through pre-signing the OpenFlow application to get permission to query or modify the network. the singing in is verified by SEK digitally at runtime [38].

To prevent unauthorized hosts from accessing the network, the proposed mechanism of access control and authentication concerning credentials of hosts. This mechanism is called AuthFlow which is implemented with RADIUS server, Authenticator, and OpenFlow controller [39].

Denial of Service DoS

Due to the separation of control and data plane in SDN, some weakness related to DoS introduced on the switch flow or on the controller. Number of Proposed solutions to solve this issue either targeting the data plane, control plane or both.

A solution AVANT-GUARD targets the communication between control and data plane based on TCP is proposed by [40] in order to solve the bottleneck of flow requests which are sent to the controller through mechanism of migration connection [16], and it is activating flow rules with specific predefined conditions which are enabled by Actuating Triggers [29]. The Connection Migration also removes the TCP SYN flood attack by ensuring that session handshake established successfully, and not allowing any request to the controller till the current request is completed, as well as remove the field sessions of TCP. Moreover, it prevents the DoS of sending requests of completed TCP handshake. However, Actuating Trigger mechanism reduce the number of requests transmitted to the controller by activating flow rules which are defined in advanced.

Paulo Fonseca et al. [41] present a solution to prevent DoS attacks of control plane – CPRecovery. It is considered as a way to offer network resilience. This replication components allow changing to the backup or secondary controller in the case of failing the primary controller due to an external attack on the primary controller, which leads to overwhelm the network.

Virtual Source Address Validation Edge (VAVE) mechanism is an IP Spoofing DoS solution which is data plane oriented. To protect against IP Spoofing, it uses the abilities of updating the rules dynamically, and the SDN capabilities of analyzing the traffic. Incoming packet is sent to the controller to be validating the source in the case of not matching with predefined OpenFlow rules. So, the traffic from that source will be stopped if any IP Spoofing is detected [42].

In some cases, if there are some missing entries in the flow table or the list of rules not full, some legitimate packets may be dropped. To solve this issue, VAVE and AVANT-GUARD or CPRecovery should be implemented in parallel [29].

Ident++ protocol avoids bottleneck caused by central controller, and it is used to protect SDN against DoS. It is used to solve DoS capitalizing the characteristics of SDN in order to overcome the SDN attacks. So the SDN-DoS can be prevented and reduced in the use of SDN features such as distributed control and dynamic flow table [43].

FlowRanger is proposed in [44]. It is an algorithm of prioritizing the requests for DoS Attack of control plane. FlowRanger implements the scheduling system of priority with the key metric of each node of the network as a first level, and the controller uses the FlowRanger to evaluate the node values which are received with request and prioritize those separate queues.

The major challenge of the provided solutions of DDoS/DoS is that they work after the attack happened and trying to deal with the attacking results. So that the network may go down temporarily before it recovers by the applied anti-attacking mechanism. In [45] a proposed scheme tries to stop the attacking in the first 500 packets. Although, this amount of packets in this particular time may lead the controller to go down. However, there is a tradeoff between the level of security solutions and the performance of the network [29].

Hijacked/Rogue Controller
The proposed solutions of unauthorized access can be effective with this attack. If the SDN network protected from unauthorized access that will prevent any Hijacked/Rogue Controller Mitigations which consider the getting access to the network is the first step to harm the network by any kind of this attack such as manage the network, change the destination, or operate nod as a man-in-the-middle.

One more solution can protect all SDN layers (data, control, and application) and the link between them. It installs flow rules in switches to guarantee authenticity, integrity, and validity. PERM-GUARD [46] manages the permissions of flow-rules productions for both controllers and applications. If any flow-rules are pushed out to the network by either controllers or applications, those controllers or applications are required to follow some means of identity signatures which one of them with controller or application in order to authenticate themselves to the authority system, or the request will be considered as illegitimate if signature not matched.

However, it may not stop the attackers from trying to connect to the network or hijack the controllers, but it will not allow them to make malicious changes to the structure of the network.

Malicious/Compromised Applications

Another serious security issue is malicious applications which have been developed with malicious in order to grant access and permission for attackers to control the network. In the same way, vulnerabilities caused by the buggy codes in the applications may be exploited by attackers to access to the network. To solve this issue, an identity authentication and a trusted connection should be established before the control packets are exchanged. The authentication mechanism should be applied to guarantee that all devices are eligible to receive the control messages and updates. Therefore, the contents will not be seen by the malicious applications unless they have all credentials.

FortNOX is a mechanism to monitor the flow-rules of applications to be inserted in devices in the network [38]. A proposed mechanism FortNOX determines the security authorization of OpenFlow applications by applying role-based authentication. If the new flow rules are not matched with the current flow rules which already exist on the receiving devices, those rules will be discarded and dropped without adding to the devices. But if the new rules with high priority, the current rules will be replaced even if there was conflict. The priority of the rules depends on the producer of the rules which they are: OF Operator, OF Security, and OF Application. However, FortNOX can enforce to overriding the new rules even if they are conflicted with existed ones. This is to ensure that new rules add by malicious applications to the network will be detected and prevented [29]. This mechanism has a limitation of solving priority enforcement and application identification, as well as the determination of suitable authorization level [16]. Moreover, some security applications will not operate properly if a hardcode is implemented such as application with dynamically modifying the flow [32], which may be the future improvement of this mechanism [47].

A robust secure and high-performance network operating system NOS which ran on top of control layer in multiple instance ways is ROSEMARY solution of malicious applications which is proposed by [47] as micro-NOS architecture. The running applications in SDN environment are executed individually to isolate every application effectively in order to protect control plane from any threats or vulnerabilities of the application. It aims to improve the resilience of controller to malicious applications and buggy codes by close monitoring of resources and transmitted packets of deployed applications on the network. As well as the application monitoring platform is provided by ROSEMARY to monitor malicious application activities. The network application is separated from trusted computing using NOS. ROSEMARY is considered as an advanced solution of security problem of malicious application. However, it is noticed that low level of computational overhead [29].

legoSDN [48] is a proposed solution to isolate failed applications which are considered as vulnerable and key of application attack-based. It provides a mechanism to isolate malicious applications from the network in order to protect the network from any damaged caused by those applications, and to avoid the controller crash which is caused by crash of applications.

LegoSDN is considered as similar to ROSEMARY in the way of isolating between SDN application and control planes. The application in ROSMARY is implemented individually, while in LegoSDN all applications are gathered in one plane.

Another solution is proposed in [37] which is considered as the application control system of SDN known as OperationCheckpoint. It deals with both policies and rules of the network which are pushed out to data-path, and the underlying information of the network which is read by the SDN applications.

It applies a wide group of user-defined permissions including all OF tasks. Any application needs to be deployed, it must be matched with a specific set of defined permissions. so any action of applications out of those permissions will be prevented unless authorized operator or administrator enforce it. That leads to banned malicious applications from executing malicious commands on the data layer devices or capturing sensitive packets. Network operators create set of permissions by declaring necessary functionality in order to ensure they know the behaviors of each application.

In comparison to proposed solutions of malicious applications, OperationCheckpoint seems the wide way for protecting SDN from malicious applications due to its permission system [29].

There is an advantage of SDN of allowing common APIs between controllers and applications, which eliminate the possibility of vulnerabilities due to poor coding of middleware.

Control Plane and Data Plane Link Attack
OpenFlow is a famous protocol of SDN which work as southbound API has some specifications of using TLS in communications and data transmission between control and data plane, but using TLS is optional which means most of controllers do not support it or not enforce it. Therefore, to ensure the security of the link, TLS should be enforced by control to provide encrypted transmissions and entities authentications on both ends.

Furthermore, in order to stop and eliminate the threats and attacks in this link, such as black hole and Man-in-the-Middle attacks, a methodology of Bro IDS is proposed to secure this link [49]. Ryu-based controller integrated with Bro IDS which uses techniques of packet inception in order to determine source, destination, and payload configuration of the received packets using signature-based IDS. This signature is predefined and configured in the controller to check all packets either known or unknown packets against the signature. However, the downside of this mechanism is a slow response because of the extra load caused by integrating controller with IDS.

This link could be protected using traditional security ways due to the main threats of this link are traditional network threats such as black-hole and man-in-the-middle [29]. Also, communication can be secured by cryptography [18], and in order to guarantee

Table 1. SDN security issues and solutions summary.

Issue	Targeted layer	Affected Interface	Impact on Security	Solutions	References	Note
Unauthorized Access	Data, control, application	Southbound (ctrl-Data)	Confidentiality, integrity	• Secured by TLS, and signature algorithm[33]. • SDN secure structure supports multiple controllers by Byzantine mechanism [34]. • Switches and controllers setup hierarchically [35] • PermOF is isolation mechanism to apply for the permissions at the APIs. • Mechanism of check permission is implemented which is called OperationCheckpoint [37]. • SE-Floodlight authenticates the Northbound APIs [38]. • AuthFlow is a mechanism of access control and authentication concerning credentials of hosts.[39]	[12,14 16,33-39]	Configure the network nodes, hacking, or stealing data.
DOS	Data, control	Southbound (ctrl-Data)	Availability	• AVANT-GUARD [40] solve the bottleneck of flow requests. • CPRecovery [41] is a way to offer network resilience. • (VAVE) a mechanism is an IP Spoofing DoS solution. • Ident++ protocol avoids bottlenecks caused by a central controller. • FlowRanger [44]. It is an algorithm for prioritizing the requests. • Applied anti-attacking mechanism. In [45] a proposed scheme tries to stop the attacking.	[16,29, 31,40-42, 44,45]	• Utilizing the network resources. • The controller could be overwhelmed in the case of flooding it with flow-decision requests. • Flow-table entry flooding.

(continued)

Table 1. (*continued*)

Attack	Plane	Interface	Security property	Solutions	References	Description
Hijacked/ Rogue Controller	Data, control	South-bound and north-bound	Confidential-ity, integrity	PERM-GUARD [46] manages the permissions of flow-rules productions for both controllers and applications. [33,35,37,,38].	[29,33,35, 37,38,46]	• Manage any process of the network. • Change the destination of the packet. • Operate a node in the network to act as "Man-in-the-Middle. • The rogue controller could be registered in the control plane.
Malicious Applications	control, applica-tion	North-bound, west/east-bound	integrity, confidentiality	• FortNOX [38] is a mechanism to monitor the flow rules of applications • ROSEMARY [47] robust secure and high-performance network operating system NOS. • legoSDN [48] isolate failed applications • OperationCheckpoint [37] application control system of SDN.	[14,16,18,29, 37,38,47]	• Black-hole attacks, Man-in-the-Middle, and DoS attacks compromise the controller. • Deep inspection of a packet may cause risk and can control the whole network.
Control-Data Plane Link Attacks	Control, Data	South-bound	Availability, integrity	Bro IDS [49] which uses techniques of packet interception TLS/SSL	[1,4,7,15, 16,18,29,49]	• Susceptible to many attacks such as black-hole attacks(drops the packets instead of forwarding them to the controller); and Man-in-the-Middle[32](manipulating the packet before forwarding them); DoS attacks [18].
Eavesdrop-ping Attacks	Data	South-bound, north-bound	Confidential-ity, integrity	• A Random Route Mutation [50]. Its idea is to change the data flow randomly. • Combat-Sniff [51], which works as detection and pro-active defense mechanisms	[29,50,51]	• Inspect and capture packets. • The attacker may use the Open-Flow integrated mode of ease-of-use for listening

trust between controller and network devices, association mechanisms should be used with automated, dynamic, and assured devices [18].

Eavesdropping Attack

As the passive nature of Eavesdropping attack which is easy to be established in the network to sniff and listen to the packet traffic, it is difficult to detect and defend it due to the similarity between the legitimate node and eavesdropping nodes [29]. The centralized nature of SDN increases the difficulty of detecting and protecting with the possibility of new attack platforms.

A Random Route Mutation approach is presented in [50] as a passive approach in data plane and the link of control-data plane. Its idea is to change the data flow randomly with keeping some information such as destination IP in order to complicate the process of tracing the packet flow. According to the author that the result of simulations, which is done on NOX controller, this mechanism, is effective and sufficient to reduce the packet eavesdropping, and it's suggested for SDN.

Another solution is proposed in [51] as Combat-Sniff which works as detection and pro-active defense mechanisms. It scans for eavesdropping as an active-detection mechanism, and prevent malicious as pro-active defense. It takes samples of flow entries randomly in order to check the integrity and to stopping attackers not to store illegitimate flow entry in the cache of the switches. One of the purposes of this mechanism is to keep the confidentiality of information of packet traffic by not allowing switches to check the content of packets, only switches aware about forwarding routs. This solution is reasonable to identify the illegitimate flows by using random samples of flow-entry [29].

Due to the passive of eavesdropping attack, it seems difficult to be defended, but still traditional protecting systems such as IDS and IPS can be used to detect this attack, and the node uses for eavesdropping [29]. The proposed solutions [50, 51] may reduce the impacts of this attack. Encryption and authentication mechanism should be implemented to ensure the only legitimate data and flows travel through the network.

5 Conclusion

Software-defined network SDN is considered as a new concept of network which centralized controlling functionalities and separated them from the network devices in the way of using devices for forwarding packets according to the rules and policies set by the controller. The new Architecture of SDN that separated data plane from control plane is considered immature regarding security.

In this paper, we surveyed the possible security issues and challenges of SDN, the suggested and proposed solutions for every issue which already proposed previously. The way of designing this paper is to look overview of SDN and its planes.

Security of SDN is affected by some factors such as APIs interfaces that are supported by SDN such as southbound, northbound, westbound, eastbound interfaces. The open interfaces are considered as one of the points of attacks. That is the reason for surveyed them in this paper. Moreover, in this paper, other factors are included, such as SDN characteristics and OpenFlow protocol. Those characteristics may cause weakness, threats, and vulnerabilities to security, which may be used for targeting attacks toward the network.

The security issues and threats which are discussed in this paper are the most common and serious issues. For each of those issues, many proposed solutions are mentioned and surveyed. Those suggested solutions don't protect the whole SDN; only each one targets one problem. So, the combination of mechanism should be implemented paralleled.

There are many proposed solutions against each threat and issue. Most of those solutions depend on software solutions such as monitoring systems with specific security policies to monitor the network traffic to detect the malicious. On the other hand, there some security architectures are proposed to be a reference to develop security tools and functions.

SDN security still needs to get more attention to enhance the use of traditional protecting mechanisms, devices, and systems which are not working properly in SDN due to the new different architecture of SDN. Improving the criteria of SDN security will increase the portion of spread and usage of SDN. However, SDN still one of the best tools to secure different environments with centralizing all security policies and rules in the controller.

This paper concludes that pure SDN solutions should be developed to overcome the security issues, still some threats and issues not getting much attention, such as Data leakage and modifications. As well as, Hardware-based solutions should be adopted for SDN due to the high performance of those devices. Finally, there is a trade-off between network performance and applying more security mechanisms. So, it needs to be balanced.

This paper recommends that there should be a separate security plane which will be responsible for securing the whole network of SDN. This plane should be designed to be connected to all planes in the way of parallel to three planes.

References

1. Imran, A.: SDN controllers security issues, ayesha. Master thesis, University of Jyväskylä (2017)
2. Nunes, B.A.A., Mendonca, M., Nguyen, X.N., Obraczka, K., Turletti, T.: A survey of software-defined networking: past, present, and future of programmable networks. IEEE Commun. Surv. Tutor. **16**, 1617–1634 (2014). https://doi.org/10.1109/SURV.2014.012214.00180
3. Wan, J., et al.: Software-defined industrial internet of things in the context of industry 4.0. IEEE Sens. J. **16**, 7373–7380 (2016)
4. Shu, Z., Wan, J., Li, D., Lin, J., Vasilakos, A.V., Imran, M.: Security in software-defined networking: threats and countermeasures. Mob. Netw. Appl. **21**(5), 764–776 (2016). https://doi.org/10.1007/s11036-016-0676-x
5. Tripathy, B.K., Das, D.P., Jena, S.K., Bera, P.: Risk based security enforcement in software defined network. Comput. Secur. **78**, 321–335 (2018). https://doi.org/10.1016/j.cose.2018.07.010
6. Ageyev, D., Bondarenko, O., Alfroukh, W., Radivilova, T.: Provision security in SDN/NFV. In: 2018 14th International Conference on Advanced Trends in Radioelecrtronics, Telecommunications and Computer Engineering (TCSET), pp. 506–509. IEEE (2018)
7. Sezer, S., Scott-Hayward, S., Kaur, P.: Are we ready for SDN? Implementation challenges for software-defined networks. IEEE Commun. Mag. **51**, 36–43 (2013). https://doi.org/10.1109/MCOM.2013.6553676

8. Kaur, R., Singh, A., Singh, S., Sharma, S.: Security of software defined networks: taxonomic modeling, key components and open research area. IEEE IInternational Conference Electrical, Electronics, and Optimization Techniques, pp. 2832–2839 (2016)
9. Hussein, A., Elhajj, I.H., Chehab, A., Kayssi, A.: SDN security plane: an architecture for resilient security services. In: Proceedings - 2016 IEEE International Conference on Cloud Engineering Workshop, IC2EW 2016, pp. 54–59 (2016). https://doi.org/10.1109/IC2EW.201 6.15
10. Dacier, M.C., König, H., Cwalinsk, R., Kargl, F., Dietrich, S.: Security challenges and opportunities of software-defined networking. IEEE Secur. Priv. 15, 96–100 (2017). https://doi.org/ 10.1109/MSP.2017.46
11. Scott-Hayward, S.: Design and deployment of secure, robust, and resilient SDN controllers. In: Proceedings of 2015 1st IEEE Conference on Network Softwarization, pp. 1–5 (2015). https://doi.org/10.1109/NETSOFT.2015.7258233
12. Scott-Hayward, S., O'Callaghan, G., Sezer, S.: SDN security: a survey. In: SDN4FNS 2013 - 2013 Working on Software Defined Networks Future Networks and Services (2013). https:// doi.org/10.1109/SDN4FNS.2013.6702553
13. Dhawan, M., Poddar, R., Mahajan, K., Mann, V.: S PHINX: detecting security attacks in software-defined networks. In: NDSS 2015, pp. 8–11 (2015). http://dx.doi.org/10.14722/ ndss.2015.23064
14. Patil, V., Patil, C., Awale, R.N.: Security challenges in software defined network and their solutions. In: 2017 8th International Conference on Computing, Communication and Networking Technologies, pp. 1–5 (2017). https://doi.org/10.1109/ICCCNT.2017.8203978
15. Akhunzada, A., Ahmed, E., Gani, A., Khan, M.K., Imran, M., Guizani, S.: Securing software defined networks: taxonomy, requirements, and open issues. IEEE Commun. Mag. 53, 36–44 (2015). https://doi.org/10.1109/MCOM.2015.7081073
16. Scott-Hayward, S., Natarajan, S., Sezer, S.: A survey of security in software defined networks. IEEE Commun. Surv. Tutor. 18(1), 623–654 (2016). https://doi.org/10.1107/S05677394700 00293
17. Kreutz, D., Ramos, F.M.V., Veríssimo, P.E., Rothenberg, C.E., Azodolmolky, S., Uhlig, S.: Software-defined networking : a comprehensive survey. 103 (2015). https://doi.org/10.1109/ JPROC.2014.2371999
18. Kreutz, D., Ramos, F.M.V., Verissimo, P.: Towards secure and dependable software-defined networks, vol. 42, pp. 55–60. ACM (2013)
19. Bera, S., Misra, S., Vasilakos, A.V.: Software-defined networking for internet of things: a survey (2017)
20. Li, J., Li, D., Yu, Y., Huang, Y., Zhu, J., Geng, J.: Towards full virtualization of SDN infrastructure. Comput. Netw. 143, 1–14 (2018). https://doi.org/10.1016/j.comnet.2018. 06.014
21. Li, W., Meng, W., Kwok, L.F.: A survey on OpenFlow-based software defined networks: security challenges and countermeasures. J. Netw. Comput. Appl. 68, 126–139 (2016). https:// doi.org/10.1016/j.jnca.2016.04.011
22. Xie, J., et al.: A survey of machine learning techniques applied to software defined networking (SDN): research issues and challenges. IEEE Commun. Surv. Tutor. 1 (2018). https://doi.org/ 10.1109/COMST.2018.2866942
23. Akhunzada, A., Khan, M.K.: Toward secure software defined vehicular networks: taxonomy, requirements, and open issues. IEEE Commun. Mag. 55, 110–118 (2017). https://doi.org/10. 1109/MCOM.2017.1601158
24. Open Networking Foundation: Software-Defined Networking : The New Norm for Networks. ONF White Paper, vol. 2, pp. 2–6 (2012)
25. Farhady, H., Lee, H., Nakao, A.: Software-defined networking: a survey. Comput. Netw. 81, 79–95 (2015). https://doi.org/10.1016/J.COMNET.2015.02.014

26. Göransson, P., Black, C., Culve, T.: Software Defined Networks A Comprehensive Approach. Morgan Kaufmann (2017)
27. Garg, G., Garg, R.: Review on architecture & security issues of. Int. J. Innov. Res. Comput. Commun. Eng. **2**, 6519–6524 (2014)
28. Fan, X., Lu, Z., Ju, L., Mu, D.: The research on security SDN south interface based on OTR protocol. In: 2016 16th International Symposium on Communications and Information Technologies, ISC 2016, pp. 629–633 (2016). https://doi.org/10.1109/ISCIT.2016.7751709
29. Spooner, J.: A review of solutions for SDN-exclusive security issues. Int. J. Adv. Comput. Sci. Appl. **7**, 113–122 (2016)
30. Sharif, W.: A practical framework for finding software vulnerabilities in SDN controllers (2017)
31. Raghav, P., Dua, A.: Enhancing flow security in Ryu controller through set operations. 2017 3rd IEEE International Conference on Computer and Communications, ICCC 2017, vol. 2018-Janua, pp. 1265–1269 (2018). https://doi.org/10.1109/CompComm.2017.8322746
32. Spooner, J.: A review of solutions for SDN-exclusive security issues, vol. 7, pp. 113–122 (2016)
33. Othman, O.M., Okamura, K.: Securing distributed control of software defined networks. Int. J. Comput. Sci. Netw. **13**, 5–14 (2013)
34. Li, H., Li, P., Guo, S., Nayak, A.: Byzantine-resilient secure software-defined networks with multiple controllers in cloud. IEEE Trans. Cloud Comput. **2**, 436–447 (2014). https://doi.org/10.1109/TCC.2014.2355227
35. Yu, D.: Authentication for resilience: the case of SDN (transcript of discussion). In: Christianson, B., Malcolm, J., Stajano, F., Anderson, J., Bonneau, J. (eds.) Security Protocols 2013. LNCS (LNAI and LNB), vol. 8263, pp. 45–53. Springer, Heidelberg (2013). https://doi.org/10.1007/978-3-642-41717-7_7
36. Wen, X., Chen, Y., Hu, C., Shi, C., Wang, Y.: Towards a secure controller platform for openflow applications, p. 171 (2013). https://doi.org/10.1145/2491185.2491212
37. Scott-Hayward, S., Kane, C., Sezer, S.: OperationCheckpoint: SDN application control. In: Proceedings - International Conference on Network Protocols, ICNP, pp. 618–623 (2014). https://doi.org/10.1109/ICNP.2014.98
38. Porras, P., Cheung, S., Fong, M., Skinner, K., Yegneswaran, V.: Securing the software defined network control layer. In: Proceedings of 2015 Network and Distributed System Security Symposium, pp. 8–11 (2015). https://doi.org/10.14722/ndss.2015.23222
39. Pemasaran, D., Niaga, D.A.N.: AuthFlow: authentication and access control mechanism for software defined networking diogo (2014)
40. Shin, S., Yegneswaran, V., Porras, P., Gu, G.: AVANT-GUARD: scalable and vigilant switch flow management in software-defined networks. ACM. (2013). http://dx.doi.org/10.1145/2508859.2516684
41. Fonseca, P., Bennesby, R., Mota, E., Passito, A.: A replication component for resilient OpenFlow-based networking. In: Proceedings of 2012 IEEE Network Operations and Management Symposium, NOMS 2012, pp. 933–939 (2012). https://doi.org/10.1109/NOMS.2012.6212011
42. Yao, G., Bi, J., Xiao, P.: Source address validation solution with OpenFlow/NOX architecture. In: Proceedings - International Conference on Network Protocol, ICNP, pp. 7–12 (2011). https://doi.org/10.1109/ICNP.2011.6089085
43. Naous, J., Stutsman, R., Mazieres, D., McKeown, N., Zeldovich, N.: Delegating network security with more information, p. 19 (2009). https://doi.org/10.1145/1592681.1592685
44. Wei, L., Fung, C.: FlowRanger: a request prioritizing algorithm for controller DoS attacks in software defined networks. In: IEEE International Conference on Communication, vol. 2015-Septe, pp. 5254–5259 (2015). https://doi.org/10.1109/ICC.2015.7249158

45. Mousavi, S.M., St-Hilaire, M.: Early detection of DDoS attacks against SDN controllers. In: 2015 International Conference on Computer Networking and Communications, ICNC 2015, pp. 77–81 (2015). https://doi.org/10.1109/ICCNC.2015.7069319
46. Wang, M., Liu, J., Chen, J., Mao, J.: PERM-GUARD : authenticating the validity of flow rules in software defined networking (2015). https://doi.org/10.1109/CSCloud.2015.89
47. Shin, S., et al.: Rosemary: A robust , secure , and high-performance network operating system categories and subject descriptors. In: Proceedings of 2014 ACM SIGSAC Conference on Computer and communications security - CCS 2014, pp. 78–89 (2014)
48. Chandrasekaran, B., Tschaen, B., Benson, T.: Isolating and tolerating SDN application failures with LegoSDN, pp. 1–12 (2016). https://doi.org/10.1145/2890955.2890965
49. Zanna, P., O'Neill, B., Radcliffe, P., Hosseini, S., Ul Hoque, M.S.: Adaptive threat management through the integration of IDS into software defined networks. 2014 International Conference on Network of the Future NOF 2014 – Working on Smart Cloud Networks Systems, SCNS 2014. (2014). https://doi.org/10.1109/NOF.2014.7119792
50. Duan, Q., Al-Shaer, E., Jafarian, H.: Efficient random route mutation considering flow and network constraints. In: 2013 IEEE Communications and Network Security, CNS 2013, pp. 260–268 (2013). https://doi.org/10.1109/CNS.2013.6682715
51. Jiang, F.: Combat-sniff: a comprehensive countermeasure to resist data plane eavesdropping in software-defined networks. Am. J. Netw. Commun. 5, 27 (2016). https://doi.org/10.11648/j.ajnc.20160502.13

Governance, Social Media, Mobile and Web, Data Privacy, Data Policy and Fake News

CLH: Approach for Detecting Deep Fake Videos

Amrita Shivanand Hedge, M. N. Vinutha, Kona Supriya, S. Nagasundari[(✉)],
and Prasad B. Honnavalli

C-ISFCR, Department of CSE, PES University, Bangalore 560085, India

Abstract. Deep Fakes are the media that takes the person's image in an existing photograph, audio recording, or video and replaces them with another person's likeness by making use of synthetic intelligence and device mastering. In this era, everybody can get easy access to software packages and tools to create deep fake videos. Existing techniques are constructed with the usage of the lip synchronization, mouth features artifacts and are commonly designed for detection of single frames. The proposed model, CLH (CNN+LSTM hybrid model) considers various parameters such as eye blinking, blurriness, skin tone, skin color, changes in lighting, lip syncing, and position to detect the fake videos. The CLH model employs "Convolutional Neural Networks (CNN)" and "Long Short-Term Memory (LSTM)" for detecting a deep fake video. The original videos and deep fake (high quality + low quality) videos were used in training the model. Datasets such as Celeb-DF, face forensics ++, Deep fake TIMIT, and fake videos developed by Facebook were used to train and evaluate the model, so that an efficient model is constructed. The proposed CLH model achieved a high accuracy of more than 90% and a low false positive rate of less than 5%. The CLH model is also compared with other models on the market and analyzed to understand the significance of the work.

Keywords: Deepfake · Video and image forensics · Image classification · Deep learning

1 Introduction

Deep Fakes are media that use Artificial Intelligence and Machine Learning to replace a person's image in a current photograph, audio recording, or video with someone else's image. The hyper-realistic images produced by the videos are barely visible to the naked eye. Deep learning involves the training of generative neural network architectures including generative adversarial networks and autoencoders which becomes the foundation to create deep fakes. Because of the ease with which these deep fake videos can be shared on social media, they trigger serious social issues.

Fake videos would most likely spread outside of the celebrity community as a new technique to allow unskilled individuals with a small collection of photos to create deep fakes. Deep Fakes aren't just for videos; deepfake technology can also be used to create convincing but entirely fictional images from scratch. Audio may also be deep-faked to build voice skins or voice copies of individuals.

© Springer Nature Singapore Pte Ltd. 2021
N. Abdullah et al. (Eds.): ACeS 2021, CCIS 1487, pp. 539–551, 2021.
https://doi.org/10.1007/978-981-16-8059-5_33

The modern patterns and improved methods of creating fake videos on the internet have made it much easier to identify and prevent harmful socio-economic consequences. These are often used by competitors or opponents to bring down the image of socially conscious individuals in an overly negative way. In a broader sense, it may be used to spoof terrorism, blackmail, and even harassment.

Recent public scandals, such as the splicing of celebrity faces onto pornographic recordings, have prompted the creation of automated methods to detect deep fake videos. As a result, a Deep Learning model is developed to effectively detect these types of videos, capable of detecting even the tiniest objects generated by cutting- edge strategies.

The main aim of this paper is to develop a deep learning model that can detect deep fake images with high accuracy. CLH model aims to reduce the model's false positive rate while also improving its accuracy. The model's consistency is maintained such that it produces reliable results across a wide variety of datasets. As a result, the CLH model would be more effective and easier to identify deep fake images, which have become a major challenge in today's digital environment.

As the CLH model uses Deep Learning techniques to detect Deep Fake videos and multiple combinations of the same to interpret and enhance the outcomes and out- put of this work, related work is discussed in the Sect. 2. Data preprocessing is explained in Sect. 3. The proposed approach, algorithm, and mathematical equations in Sect. 4, and experimental results and performance analysis in Sect. 5. Finally, Sect. 6 wraps up the paper and outlines future plans.

2   Deepfake Detection

This section presents a review of previous research on deep fake video detection and analysis methods, with a focus on deep learning techniques.

In 2018 Darius Afchar [1], et al. proposed an approach to detect and recognize face tampering in motion pictures automatically and effectively, with a focus on two recent procedures used to create hyper realistic forged images, Face2Face and Deep-Fake. As a result, this paper uses a deep learning approach and enumerates two networks, in which one has fewer layers, to recognize mesoscopic characteristics. They tested those fast networks on a current dataset as well as a dataset they created from online videos. Their tests infer that their model can detect Deep Fakes with a rate of around 98%, and Face2Face videos with a rate of around 95% under extreme conditions.

In the year 2018, David Guera et al. [2] made use of ML-based unfastened software tools or devices which made the process clean known as "deep fake" videos to develop convincing face swaps in videos that depart from a few indications of manipulation. A convolutional neural network is used to extract body-level features, which are then used to train a recurrent neural network (RNN) to recognize whether or not a video has been challenged for improvement. This paper proposes a temporal sensitive model for detecting deep fake videos dynamically which can effectively predict whether a video has already been subjected to some kind of forgery with as little as two seconds of video data using a convolutional LSTM structure.

In 2019, Pavel, et al. Advanced VGG [3] and facenet-based recognition algorithms were found to be vulnerable to Deepfakes, and it was also impossible to distinguish those types of videos from legitimate videos, with an equivalent error rate of up to 95%. Many conventional face swap detection approaches were also evaluated and calculated, and it was discovered that the lip-sync technique fails to identify mismatches with the existence of inconsistencies between lip movement and speech. In fact, with an equivalent error rate of 8.97%, the SVM classifier-based approach with image quality measures can better recognize high quality Deep Fake videos.

In the year 2020, Mousa, et al. [4] crafted and carried out using a deep learning model approach to identify Deep Fake videos by setting them apart, analyzing and testing lip/mouth motion, and a deep-fake detection technique for mouth attributes (DFT-MF). In comparison to several other studies in this field, tests of the DFT-MF model on datasets containing both fake as well as real videos yielded positive and favorable classification results. CNN was used to detect fake videos, taking into account the characteristics obtained as a biological signal from the mouth. Their research is most likely superior to that of others. Their study probably was improved and better than other methodologies; the findings were compared to illustrate these success results.

In June 2020 Dang et al. [5] proposed a methodology for processing and developing attribute maps for classification tasks using a consideration approach. In digital media forensics, identifying distorted facial images and videos is a subject of great importance, since cutting-edge face synthesis and manipulation techniques are now available. As a result, identifying distorted face pictures and pinpointing manipulated areas is unavoidable and long overdue. Finally, the authors depict that using their attention technique has improved the precision of the detection of facial forgery and manipulations with respect to localization of facial regions.

In mid-2020 Steven Fernandes et al. [6] addressed deep-fake video detection with an Advanced Attribution Based Trust (ABC) metric. Recent improvements in generative adversarial networks (GAN) have resulted in the detection of false images, a difficult and time-consuming task. The basic ABC metric is used to classify deep-fake videos in this study. The ABC metric does not require any access to training data or training of optimization methods on different validation data. For actual images, the obtained ABC values are not less than 0.94. Since the deep-fake videos have low ABC ratings, they are detected easily. They obtained an overall average validation accuracy of more than 96% on all three datasets.

Most strategies rely solely on the facts contained in a single photograph, analyzing frames one by one, and failing to take advantage of temporal details in images. 'Action-Recognition' is a field of study that has delved further into the use of facts and information across multiple frames in a video. The goal of Oscar de Lima, et al. [7] work is to implement video classification strategies that take advantage of 3D feedback to the Deep Fake classification problem. Since the networks make decisions by adding temporal knowledge, these methods differ from previously designed methods. R3D, in particular, outperformed all the other networks, including I3D, that are capable of action recognition.

The article published in 2020 by Siwei Lyu et al. [8], narrates how few of the difficulties that exist in deep fake identification are examined and addressed. The author also addressed the measures that must be taken to obtain the most effective detection methods. For widespread realistic adoption, typical running efficiency, accuracy of detection, and, most importantly, FPR rate must all be improved. Forgery vendors and digital media forensic researchers are constantly working on competencies.

3   Research Problem

New patterns and sophisticated methods of creating fake videos on the internet have made them much more difficult to spot, resulting in harmful socio-economic consequences. Most of the time, these fake videos are used by competitors/enemies to kill the image of socially conscious people in an unfairly negative way. So, a Deep Learning model, capable of detecting even the tiniest objects produced by advanced techniques is developed to detect these types of videos in an effective manner. The main goal of this paper is to create a deep learning model that can effectively detect deep fake images. The proposed model focuses more to reduce the model's false positive rate while improving its accuracy.

4   Design of CLH Model: A Hybrid of CNN and LSTM

Data is gathered from a variety of sources, including real-time data sets. The video is then used as input. The frames from the video are extracted. The face is detected, and several features (Eye Blinking, Lip Syncing, Blurriness, Quality, Skin Tone and Color, Lighting Change) are extracted. Irrelevant frames are deleted before preprocessing to ensure smooth and clean processing, which reduces overall complexity.

The cleaned data is processed, and as part of the preprocessing, data reduction will be performed to delete all noisy data and unnecessary columns so that it does not contribute to or affect the model's training. The CLH model will then be trained using the combined CNN and LSTM hybrid approach and experimented with various optimizers such as Adam optimizer, SGD, adagrad and RMSProp (Fig. 1).

The basic thought behind a hybrid model is to prepare the CLH model to handle huge datasets. CLH model comprises two deep learning models Convolutional neural networks (CNN) and LSTM. CNN accepts pictures as an input and allocates the significance to different parts of the picture. LSTM is a manufactured repetitive neural network which measures whole successions of inputs dissimilar to different models. Video manipulation and analysis performed frame by frame produces low level artefacts that manifest as inconsistent temporal artefacts in deep fake images, which lack temporal coherence.

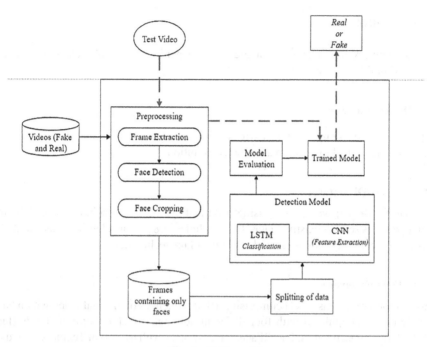

Fig. 1. CLH model

The Fig. 2 enumerates the different processes that must be performed as a part of the proposed work.

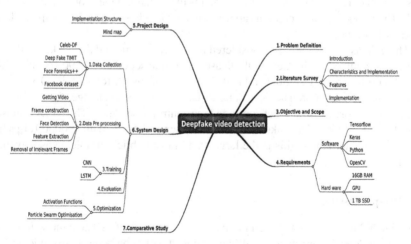

Fig. 2. Mindmap of deep fake video detection

5   Methodology

Various network architectures that are used to perform Deepfake classification are described in this section.

5.1   Data Collection

Data collection is a huge bottleneck for deep learning. Gathering and identifying right data works is critical to develop an effective solution.

5.1.1   Celeb-DF dataset

This dataset [9, 10] was created using a refined synthesis algorithm that reduces the visual artefacts seen in existing datasets. It includes 408 actual celebrity videos and 795 synthesized celebrity videos created using deepfake techniques.

5.1.2   Face Forensics

This is a forensics dataset [11] comprising 1000 sequences of original video which have already been manipulated with four different automated manipulation methods (face manipulation): Deep Fakes, Face2Face, Face Swap as well as Neural Textures. The data came from 977 YouTube images with a trackable mostly frontal face and no occlusions, enabling automated tampering methods to create realistic forgeries.

5.1.3   Facebook dataset

This is another recent dataset [12] that contains high-quality videos obtained from Facebook. The preview dataset contains approximately 5k videos, while the complete dataset contains 124k videos.

Three datasets are primarily considered in this work. True and deep fake synthesized videos are included in the Celeb DF dataset. This dataset contains 590 specific videos from YouTube as well as 5639 related deepfake videos. A total of 1000 videos are included in the Face Forensics ++ dataset. Deepfake, face exchange, face 2 face, and neural surfaces are the four most common face control procedures. The DFDC dataset is a Facebook-facilitated deep fake recognition challenge dataset. With 1000000 clips from 3246 paying entertainers, this is the largest and most publicly usable dataset available right now.

5.2   Pre-processing

Celeb-DF V2 is the dataset chosen in this work. It consists of 590 genuine videos, 5639 deep fake videos. To pre-measure all the videos, it would be better to exclude any data that could divert our attention away from what was significant. Since the only piece of the casing that is integrated in an inserted video is over top of the face, so the model consists of face cropping, much like the casing-based deep fake recognition strategies (Fig. 3).

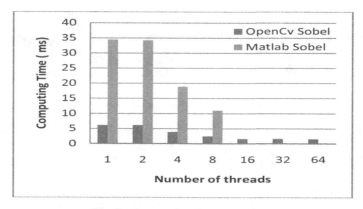

Fig. 3. Computation time comparison

OpenCv library is used for frame extraction as the processing time taken by openCv library is less when compared with Matlab sobel as demonstrated in the diagram above. This entailed cropping each frame to remove the face, then re-stacking the cropped frames into a video. It also implied that all of the images would have to be the same size, and the model didn't extend the source between these frames to fit this frame size, ensuring that the videos were free of distortion. Before deciding on RetinaFace, tried Haar Cascades, the BlazeFace. Because of their high rate of false positives, Haar Cascades are unsuitable for our model. BlazeFace didn't fit for us because it jittered a lot because it drew its bouncing boxes in a jumbled manner between frames. RetinaFace's forward pass is slower than BlazeFace's videos (Figs. 4 and 5).

Fig. 4. Dataset before preprocessing

5.3 DFT MODEL

As a reference point, one non-transient classification technique was used. Unmasking Deep Fake videos with basic features [13] is a technique that relies on detecting

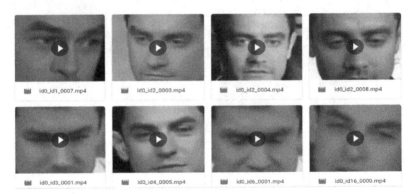

Fig. 5. Dataset after preprocessing

statistical artefacts in GAN-generated images. The image's discrete Fourier shift is registered, and the 2D amplitude spectrum is compressed into an element vector of 300-1 using azimuthal averaging technique. These element vectors will then be ordered using a simple/easy parallel classifier such as Logistic Regression. To successfully identify unlabeled datasets, this technique can also be combined with another technique such as k means clustering (Fig. 6).

Data Preprocessing

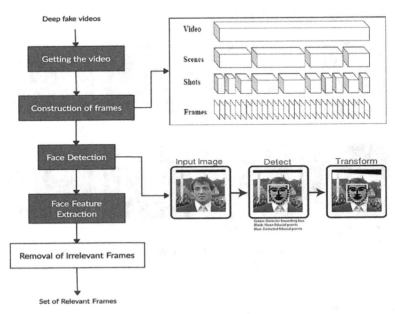

Fig. 6. Data preprocessing

6 Implementation of CLH Model

6.1 Model Training

The CLH model was prepared on 1000 plus of both genuine and fake videos from the Celeb-DF dataset. x recordings from Facebook and x recordings from FaceForensics++ dataset. fv used to include extraction and grouping investigation separately (Figs. 7 and 8).

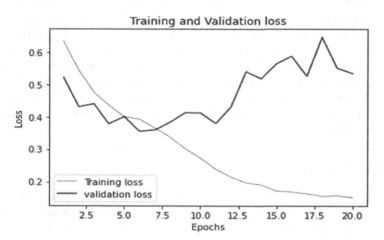

Fig. 7. Training & validation loss

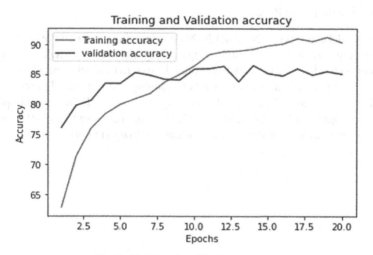

Fig. 8. Training & validation accuracy

For feature extraction, CNN was used. CLH gets the InceptionV3 [14] with a fully connected layer at the network's highest point that is not considered, allow the model to get a clear in-depth representation of every frame using the ImageNet pre-prepared model. CLH doesn't calibrate the network [3]. Following the last pooling layers, the 2048-dimensional entity vectors are used as the subsequent LSTM input. CLH can expect a succession of CNNs to include vectors of information outlined as data and a 2-node neural network with the probabilities of the grouping being relevant for a deep fake video or an untampered video using the LSTM for sequence processing. The aim of the model is to recursively deal with grouping in a significant way and is the main problem that CLH must solve. For this issue, CLH uses a 2048 wide LSTM unit with a drop out chance of 0.5, which can do exactly what is required. Here, CLH model considers an arrangement of 2048 dimensional ImageNet feature vectors during planning. The LSTM is followed by a 512 layer fully connected layer with a drop out chance of 0.5. Eventually, CLH processes the probabilities of the edge succession being either real or deep fake by making use of a softmax sheet. The LSTM module structure is considered to be a temporary component in the CLH pipeline. Since the model contains both CNN and LSTM with video processing, the calculation time is more. To accomplish the most elevated precision, various activation functions and optimizers are applied to deep learning models.

6.2 Model Testing

When the model is prepared well, to check if it's yielding the pertinent outcome, the testing dataset is fed into the CLH. Testing accuracy and false positive rate is determined to gauge the effectiveness of the model. In other words, testing accuracy and false positive rate is determined to quantify the productivity of the model.

6.3 Optimization and Result

Since the model consists of CNN and LSTM deep learning models, there is a lot of scope for optimizing the results. All Existing deep learning models did not focus on optimizing the output and delivering the consistent model. So CLH model focused on achieving consistency and maximum accuracy for both training and testing. CLH model trained with different activation functions like relu, sigmoid, Leaky Relu etc. and optimizers like SGD, Adagrad, Adam, RMSProp etc. CLH got the best result with >91% accuracy for leaky Relu as activation function and Adam optimizer (Fig. 9).

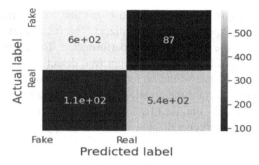

Fig. 9. Confusion matrix

6.4 Comparative Analysis

The Fig. 10 demonstrates the comparative analysis of the existing models with the CLH model. Accuracy parameter is compared with other models. First bar indicates the accuracy of the proposed CLH model with an accuracy of 85.59% as training accuracy obtained by executing the model with 30 epochs. CLH has achieved 91% of testing accuracy.

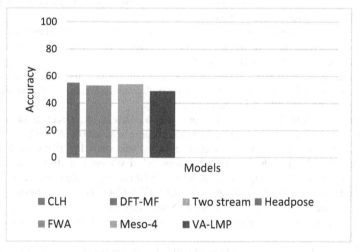

Fig. 10. Comparative analysis of accuracy

7 Conclusion

The presented CLH model has been successfully used to identify a wide range of deep fake images. Instead of using a single frame as an input, CLH model uses a series of cropped videos from the given video. This aids CLH model in capturing and incorporating temporal information as well as detecting objects within video frames. CLH has demonstrated superiority over previous baselines and state-of-the-art approaches in more than five separate experiments on optimizers. The Adam optimizer is used in the CLH model to increase the model's overall performance. To summarize, the proposed CLH model is a generalizable model with improved detection efficiency to overcome the limitations in previous state-of-the-art techniques. CLH hopes that this research will serve as a steppingstone toward the creation of more generalized deepfake detectors, and that future research will continue to question and refine current deep fake detection methods to make them more generalizable and standard approaches.

References

1. Afchar, D., Nozick, V., Yamagishi, J., Echizen, I.: MesoNet: a compact facial video forgery detection network. In: 2018 IEEE International Workshop on Information Forensics and Security (WIFS), pp. 1–7. IEEE, Hong Kong (2018)
2. Güera, D., Delp, E.J.: Deepfake video detection using recurrent neural networks. In: 2018 15th IEEE International Conference on Advanced Video and Signal Based Surveillance (AVSS), pp. 1–6. IEEE, Auckland (2018)
3. Korshunov, P., Marcel, S.: Vulnerability assessment and detection of deepfake videos. In: 2019 International Conference on Biometrics (ICB), pp. 1–6. IEEE, Crete (2019)
4. Jafar, M.T., Ababneh, M., Al-Zoube, M., Elhassan, A.: Forensics and analysis of deepfake videos. In: 2020 11th International Conference on Information and Communication Systems (ICICS), pp. 053–058. IEEE, Irbid (2020)
5. Dang, H., Liu, F., Stehouwer, J., Liu, X., Jain, A.K.: On the detection of digital face manipulation. In: Proceedings of the IEEE/CVF Conference on Computer Vision and Pattern recognition, pp. 5781–5790. IEEE, Seattle (2020)
6. Fernandes, S., et al.: Detecting deepfake videos using attribution-based confidence metric. In: Proceedings of the IEEE/CVF Conference on Computer Vision and Pattern Recognition Workshops, pp. 308–309. IEEE, Seattle (2020)
7. de Lima, O., Franklin, S., Basu, S., Karwoski, B., George, A.: Deepfake detection using spatiotemporal convolutional networks. arXiv preprint arXiv:2006.14749 (2020)
8. Lyu, S.: Deepfake detection: current challenges and next steps. In: 2020 IEEE International Conference on Multimedia & Expo Workshops (ICMEW), pp. 1–6. IEEE, London (2020)
9. Li, Y., Yang, X., Sun, P., Qi, H., Lyu, S.: Celeb-DF: a large-scale challenging dataset for deepfake forensics. In: Proceedings of the IEEE/CVF Conference on Computer Vision and Pattern Recognition, pp. 3207–3216. IEEE, Seattle (2020)
10. Celeb Deep fake Dataset. https://github.com/yuezunli/celeb-deepfakeforensics. Accessed 2 May 2021
11. Faceforensics Dataset. http://kaldir.vc.in.tum.de/faceforensics_download_v4.py. Accessed 2 May 2021
12. Deepfake detection Challenge Dataset. https://dfdc.ai/. Accessed 2 May 2021
13. Guarnera, L., Giudice, O., Battiato, S.: Deepfake detection by analyzing convolutional traces. In: Proceedings of the IEEE/CVF Conference on Computer Vision and Pattern Recognition Workshops, pp. 666–667. IEEE, Seattle (2020)
14. Mitra, A., Mohanty, S.P., Corcoran, P., Kougianos, E.: A novel machine learning based method for deepfake video detection in social media. In: 2020 IEEE International Symposium on Smart Electronic Systems (iSES) (Formerly iNiS), pp. 91–96. IEEE, Chennai (2020)

15. Ding, X., Raziei, Z., Larson, E.C., Olinick, E.V., Krueger, P., Hahsler, M.: Swapped face detection using deep learning and subjective assessment. EURASIP J. Inf. Secur. **2020**(1), 1–12 (2020). https://doi.org/10.1186/s13635-020-00109-8
16. Dolhansky, B., Howes, R., Pflaum, B., Baram, N., Ferrer, C.C.: The deepfake detection challenge (DFDC) preview dataset. arXiv preprint arXiv:1910.08854 (2019)

Consumer Information Sharing in Facebook: The Negative Role of Perceived Privacy Risk

Bui Thanh Khoa[(⊠)] and Nguyen Duong Thuc Vi

Industrial University of Ho Chi Minh City, Ho Chi Minh City, Vietnam
buithanhkhoa@iuh.edu.vn

Abstract. The growth of social commerce has opened a new business model and enhanced electronic word-of-mouth sharing. However, how the information is shared and exchanged and how to improve consumers' benefits based on their information sharing on social commerce is still an unexplored path. Therefore, this paper aims to identify the key factors affecting consumer information sharing on Facebook and propose solutions to improving customer engagement with the brand through information sharing on Facebook. Data were collected through a survey of 200 Facebook users in Vietnam. SPSS software was adopted to analyze the survey data. Finding reveals that extraversion, neuroticism, hedonic value, arousal, and brand love positively impact customer information sharing, and perceived privacy risk has a negative effect on the customer information sharing on the Facebook brand page. There are managerial implications regarding social media strategies for companies or brand managers to achieve better customer engagement on Facebook brand pages through information sharing.

Keywords: Perceived privacy risk · Information sharing · Extraversion · Neuroticism · Hedonic value · Arousal · Brand love · Social commerce

1 Introduction

The development of social networking technology has increased human connectivity through interaction, communication, and information sharing [1, 2]. Facebook is the most visited website in most countries around the globe; the number of Facebook users in the world is 2,879,570,777, accounting for 36.6% total world population on June 30, 2021; among that, Viet Nam has 75,940,000 Facebook users, accounting for 77.4 percent of the country's total population [3]. Also, according to a survey of 2000 Facebook users, nearly one-third of all Facebook users share information every day [4]. Although social media's primary purpose is to build a bridge between users, come along with education, information, entertainment - which is also the essential function of the mass media, it has applied in business's marketing strategy [5, 6]. Social media marketing opened up a new way for people to explore, read and share information and other news, images, and videos. It combines sociology and technology in marketing activities, turning one-to-many marketing into many-to-many marketing [7]. Facebook has become a valuable means for the business to target and reach potential customers online. Therefore, more

© Springer Nature Singapore Pte Ltd. 2021
N. Abdullah et al. (Eds.): ACeS 2021, CCIS 1487, pp. 552–567, 2021.
https://doi.org/10.1007/978-981-16-8059-5_34

than 200 million small businesses worldwide use Facebook's tools [8]. In addition, many companies use Facebook fan pages to reach their potential customers and use this site to build and manage customer relationships.

On the other hand, Facebook is to satisfy the user's information-seeking needs. Ultimately, word-of-mouth recommendation has always been one of the most trusted sources in marketing. According to Bloch, Sherrell and Ridgway [9], there are two general reasons consumers gather information: they want to gain knowledge and experience pleasure from it. Because Facebook can meet both consumers' needs, there is no doubt that Facebook is a more popular social networking site (SNS) for customers and businesses. According to Kaplan and Haenlein [10], the interactive and social media's structural characteristics stimulates continuous conversations between marketers and customers for all three phases of the purchase process: pre-purchase (i.e., problem or need recognition, gather information), purchase (i.e., alternative evaluation), and post-purchase (i.e., after-sales services). Although there have been some prior studies researched about information sharing factor on SNS on post-purchase stage [11], how information or news is disseminated and exchanged, and how to enhance consumer's brand experience through information sharing on SNS, especially on Facebook is an essential and unexplored path on post-purchase stage. Therefore, considering a lack of research on this matter, this study aimed to identify the factors affecting consumer information sharing in the post-purchase stage by proposing a theoretical model and justifying the hypotheses. The significance of the study is pointed out in theoretical and practical contributions. In theoretical contributions, this study has explored the impact of four dimensions, i.e., affections, personal traits, value perception, and perceived privacy risk, on the consumer information sharing in social networking site as Facebook; in which, perceived privacy risk is highlighted as a negative influence factor toward customer's sharing behavior in the digital age. Moreover, this research proposed some managerial implications for businesses to improve their performance through consumer information sharing on the Facebook page.

Besides the introduction, this paper began with a literature review and the hypotheses development. After that, the research approach, data analysis, and findings were then given. Finally, the study concluded the research result, its limitations, and further research.

2 Literature Review

2.1 Social Commerce and Information Sharing

Lu, Fan and Zhou [12] identified social commerce as the use of social media platforms to convey the various transactions and activities of e-commerce. Another definition of social commerce offered by Liang and Turban [13] is a subset of e-commerce that employs Web 2.0 tools to facilitate online interaction and contributions of online users to buy products and services.

When Facebook first launched Facebook Marketplace back in 2016, it finally set foot into social commerce. Furthermore, Facebook Shops allows businesses to make a personalized online store where customers can access Facebook and Instagram from May 2020. Businesses can make a catalog of their products and link to purchase either on the retailer's website or directly within Facebook Messenger, Instagram Direct, or Whatsapp, and Facebook had made a big move forward, to the birth of social commerce in a way that has so far been untapped.

Information sharing refers to the rapid flow of pertinent news from one person to another [14]. Because of the popularity of social media, today's online users have evolved into active information producers [15]. Customers can give their options to generate consumers' content for reviewing or evaluating a product or service on the business page. That action is one of the kinds of electronic word of mouth (eWOM) on social commerce. eWOM is any customer's positive or negative feedback in the online environment [16]. In the digital era, consumers joined various SNS groups or communities to exchange information and opinions about the products; as a result, marketers can indirectly influence users' attitudes toward brands [17, 18]. Kaplan and Haenlein [10] stated that social media's features appear in all three stages of the marketing process. Therefore, eWOM potentially influences consumer behavior. More precisely, consumers tend to engage in eWOM sharing most relevant to the post-purchase stage, when consumers have already obtained practical knowledge related to their shopping behavior as product/service's quality or customer service [11].

2.2 Hypotheses Development

Affections

Arousal refers to how an individual feels stimulated or active [19], often related to emotional responses. Fiore, Dennis and Kim [20] stated that emotional responses are subjective feelings states that occur within an individual due to instant stimuli. WOM intention is significantly influenced by emotion (i.e., arousal), according to researchers interested in the emotional and cognitive aspects of WOM [21]. Therefore, the research believes that arousal is positively engaged with consumer information sharing, thus:

H1a. Arousal has a positive impact on consumer information sharing on Facebook.

Carroll and Ahuvia [22] stated that brand love is the degree of passion, emotional attachment, which the customer gives to a brand if they are satisfied with the product/service quality. Therefore, brand love will build a consumer's long-term relationship with the brand. In addition, the self-image and self-esteem motives also create the customer's brand love [23]. Moreover, brand love comprises consumers' use of the brand to express their current and desired significant aspects [24]. Several studies have also indicated that users love to talk about their purchases and shopping experiences on social media. Thus, consumers are more likely to engage on the Facebook page if they like the brand. Therefore, the hypothesis H1b is proposed:

H1b. Brand love has a positive impact on consumer information sharing on Facebook.

Personal Traits

Many researchers have begun investigating the impact of personality on Internet usage, which contains five dimensions of personality traits [25]. Previous studies support that many users of the Internet, especially online activities in general related to personality traits [26], and neuroticism and extraversion are the two personality traits that are significantly related to online activities [27]. Thus in this study, those two personality traits investigate how they relate to information sharing behavior on Facebook.

Extraversion describes a sociable person who experiences positive emotions in his/her life [28]. The high extraversion people participate in more groups on Facebook and have several social capitals in SNS [25]. Extroverts are more likely to participate in Facebook social activities [29]. Especially when it comes to brand engagement, they are more likely linked to the interaction mode of broadcasting, which is likes and comments on Facebook [25]. Because extroverted individuals make all types of online contact, they often publicize their daily activities on Facebook [30]. Therefore, there is a possibility that extraversion personal traits are more likely to share information on Facebook. Thus, the following hypothesis is proposed:

H2a. Extraversion has a positive impact on consumer information sharing on Facebook.

Neuroticism is characterized by a person's proclivity to experience mental anguish and heightened threat sensitivity. Neuroticism is an anxious, nervous person who is exceedingly emotional and overreact to all types of stimuli [31]. Neuroticism is more likely to exert control over the information that is disseminated. Shen, Brdiczka and Liu [29] found out that high neurotic people are more likely to share personal information – they post more self preferences and generate more albums. People with more significant neurotic tendencies are more likely to post accurate personal information [25]. Therefore, neuroticism is positively influenced consumer information sharing on Facebook. Hence, the following hypothesis:

H2b. Neuroticism has a positive impact on consumer information sharing on Facebook.

Value Perception
In customer engagement on Facebook brand pages, many prior pieces of research have investigated seeking hedonic value such as fun and enjoyment. For instance, Nguyen and Khoa [32] have found that hedonic value is the primary motivator of online brand community participation. In order to satisfy customer's hedonic gratification, the brand page needs to generate fun, exciting, and entertaining content [33]. When users feel pleasant, they are more motivated to tell others about their experiences and thus encourage friends and relatives to use the service [34]. Therefore, the hypothesis proposed is as follows:

H3a. Hedonic value has a positive impact on consumer information sharing on Facebook.

According to Sweeney and Soutar [35], social value is the socially recognized or enhanced social self-concept generated by using a trendy and innovative product or service that not only allows the user to interact with people who are similar to them but also can signal that the user belongs to a specific social class. Because social values often involve interpersonal interactions, many Facebook users using them to maintain interpersonal relationships [36]. Facebook provides communication tools, i.e., text, media including videos and photos, for users to interact and communicate with one another to maintain and widen their social networks [37]. Therefore, people tend to share information on Facebook to maintain interpersonal relationships, thus strengthening their social position [38]. Moreover, individuals with a sociable personality often share information because they want others to share their joy and have a good time while using the platform. As such, the social value may enhance with consumer information sharing on Facebook. Thus, the hypothesis proposed is as follows:

H3b. Social value has a positive impact on consumer information sharing on Facebook.

Perceived Privacy Risk
Perceived privacy risk describes beliefs about individuals' potential uncertain negative consequences as they self-disclose their privacy information [39, 40]. In SNS, privacy is one of the most critical factors influencing users' social interactions. People tend to disclose their information in SNS to get the benefits; however, they do not know this information could be used illegally and without the transaction purpose. The users expose much personal information without using Facebook's privacy settings [41]. As a result, user's privacy risks are linked to their SNS usage behaviors. Furthermore, some Facebook users have high privacy concerns as they understand that they could not wholly control the sharing of information; thus, those concerns negatively influence the willingness of users to share personal information on the Internet [42]. Therefore, the more Facebook users' privacy risk, the less personal information they can share online. As a result of the increased privacy risks, user's attitudes toward online information sharing will degrade, thus:

H4. Perceived privacy risks negatively affect consumer information sharing on Facebook.

3   Research Methodology

The variables were evaluated using scales adapted from previous research studies, with minor wording changes to make them more appropriate for the target context. Participants were asked to evaluate how much they agreed with various statements through the 5-point Likert scale, with 1 indicating "strongly disagree" and 5 indicating "strongly agree" for all the variables except the arousal construct. The arousal scale (AA) includes six items: intense-stagnant, uneasy-boring, aroused-unaroused, motivated-relaxed, excited-calm, wide awake-sleepy [19], brand love scale (AB) was taken from Carroll and Ahuvia [22]. The extraversion (PE) and neuroticism (PN) items were adapted from Price, Kabadayi and Angela Hausman [25]. Social value (VS) and hedonic value (VH) were drawn from Jahn, Verma and Kunz [43]. There were five items to measure perceived privacy risk (PR) [44]. Finally, the information sharing factor (IS) was five items [45].

This study applied quantitative research. The data collection method was purposive, which chose the respondents through the screening questions as a level of Facebook adoption or shopping times in Facebook. The respondents in the survey belong the age of 18–45, who are familiar with Facebook and online shopping. Data was collected through an online survey through Google Form, distributed on Facebook and email in Viet Nam from March to May 2021. After discarding unusable observations, a final net sample of 200 observations was obtained.

Table 1. Demographics of the respondents

Measure	Items	Frequency	Percent
Gender	Male	99	49.5
	Female	87	43.5
	Other	14	7.0
Age	18–22	80	40.0
	23–27	65	32.5
	28–32	30	15.0
	32–45	25	12.5
Job occupation	Student	74	37.0
	Office worker	68	34.0
	Government official	33	16.5
	Businessperson	25	12.5
Monthly income	Less than 130$	65	32.5
	130–300$	47	23.5
	300–650$	72	36.0
	650$+	16	8.0

Table 1 summarizes the respondent's demographic profiles. SPSS software version 20.0 was used to analyze the multiple regression model and test the proposed hypotheses, as Fig. 1.

4 Results

The exploratory factor analysis (EFA) was conducted via Principal Axis Factor analysis with varimax rotation to examine the underlying structure of those 32 items measuring constructs affecting customer information sharing in Facebook. In addition, a reliability score and factor loading were presented in Table 2.

Cronbach's alpha coefficient (CA) of the social value construct was $0.539 < 0.7$; thus, it was dropped. Therefore H3b was not supported. Two items, PE6: "I see myself as someone with a strong personality" and AA6: "wide awake - sleepy", were eliminated because Corrected Item - Total Correlation was less than 0.3 [46]. The other item, PN2: "I see myself as someone unhappy", was also eliminated because the factor loading value was less than 0.5 [47].

Regression analysis was used to test hypotheses H1a, H1b, H2a, H2b, H3a, and H4. Table 3 showed that all models have a significant relationship with significant values

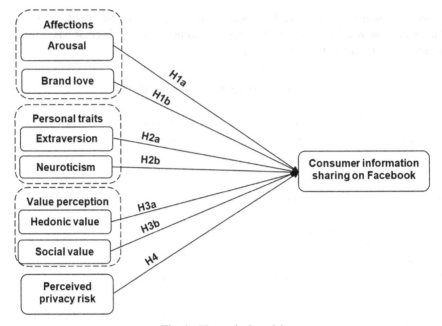

Fig. 1. Theoretical model

were less than 0.05. Variance Inflation Factor (VIF) coefficients were low, ranged from 1.172 to 1.495, and lower than 3. This result proved that the regression model did not violate the hypothesis of multicollinearity; the model had statistical significance.

In Table 4, Adjusted R Square was 0.996, and the significance of the ANOVA test was 0.00, which means six independent variables explained 99.6% of the change in information sharing in the research model. Additionally, Durbin Watson was 1.801, which belonged from 1.746 to 2.387 (n = 200, k = 6, and sig. = 0.01); hence, there was no autocorrelation in the multiple regression model.

This study added insights into the influence of research factors (affections, personal traits, value perception, and perceived privacy risk) on consumers' information sharing. According multiple regression result, arousal had the positive impact on the information sharing ($B_{AA} = 0.207$, sig.$_{AA} = 0.00$), hence, hypothesis H1a was supported in 99% of confidence level; brand love positively affected on the consumer's information sharing in SNS ($B_{AB} = 0.202$, sig.$_{AB} = 0.00$), therefore, hypothesis H1b was supported in 99% of confidence level; extraversion and neuroticism positive influenced on consumer's information sharing on Facebook ($B_{PE} = 0.202$, sig.$_{PE} = 0.00$; $B_{PN} = 0.175$, sig.$_{PN} = 0.00$), consequently, H2a and H2b were accepted in 99% of confidence level. H3a also was supported in 99% confidence level because the hedonic value positively affected the consumer's information sharing in Facebook ($B_{VH} = 0.20$, sig.$_{VH} = 0.00$). Lastly, perceived privacy risk was proved to negatively impact information sharing ($B_{PR} = -0.114$, sig.$_{PR} = 0.001$); hence, hypothesis H4 was accepted at a 95% confidence level.

Findings reveal that hedonic value had the most robust statistical relationship with information sharing behavior (Beta = 0.342), proving that hedonic value remains the

Table 2. Reliability and Factor loading of scale items

Construct		Items	Statistic		Factor loading	CA
			Mean	SD		
Affections	Arousal	AA1: intense-stagnant	3.37	0.84	0.689	0.714
		AA2: uneasy-boring	3.41	0.91	0.749	
		AA3: aroused - unaroused	3.4	0.78	0.779	
		AA4: motivated-relaxed	3.44	0.83	0.835	
		AA5: excited - calm	4.07	0.88	0.594	
	Brand love	AB1: The Facebook page of the brand is fantastic	3.32	0.85	0.603	0.806
		AB2: The brand brings me joy	3.34	0.83	0.601	
		AB3: It is a fantastic brand	3.34	0.91	0.786	
		AB4: The brand evokes a positive emotion	3.34	0.89	0.726	
		AB5: This is one of my favorite brands	3.35	0.92	0.789	
Personal traits	Extraversion	PE1:...myself as someone talkative	3.5	0.96	0.808	0.703
		PE2:...myself as someone who generates much enthusiasm	3.36	0.87	0.772	
		PE3:...myself as someone who is sometimes timid/inhibited	3.53	0.96	0.785	
		PE4:... myself as a quiet person	3.39	0.88	0.671	
		PE5:...myself as a reserved person	3.5	0.9	0.678	
	Neuroticism	PN1:...myself as someone who is calm and can manage stress properly	3.25	0.88	0.623	0.738
		PN3:...myself as a strained person	4.1	0.89	0.693	

(*continued*)

Table 2. (*continued*)

Construct	Items	Statistic		Factor loading	CA
		Mean	SD		
	PN4:...myself as a worrisome person	3.42	0.84	0.73	
	PN5:...myself to be emotionally stable and not easily offended	3.56	0.95	0.828	
Social value	VS1: This Facebook brand page help me meet people who share my interests	3.03	1.22	x	0.539
	VS2: I can make new friends on this Facebook brand page	3.02	1.16	x	
	VS3: On this Facebook brand page, I can learn more from others	2.9	1.21	x	
	VS4: On this Facebook brand page, I can interact with others	2.95	1.22	x	
Hedonic value	VH1: It is fun to read the Facebook brand page's content	3.32	0.91	0.832	0.872
	VH2: I feel excited when reading the Facebook brand page's content	3.3	0.82	0.835	
	VH3: The Facebook brand page's content is enjoyable	3.26	0.88	0.845	
	VH4: The Facebook brand page's content makes me feel entertaining	2.45	0.97	0.799	
Perceived privacy risk	PR1: Overall, I see no real risk to my privacy when using Facebook	3.49	0.85	0.641	0.865

(*continued*)

Table 2. (*continued*)

Construct	Items	Statistic		Factor loading	CA
		Mean	SD		
	PR2: I am scared that something terrible will happen to me as a result of my Facebook presence	3.44	0.85	0.777	
	PR3: I am comfortable with sharing personal information on Facebook	3.48	0.83	0.74	
	PR4: Overall, I believe that publishing my personal information on Facebook is dangerous	4.28	0.87	0.644	
	PR5: Overall, I have the high perceived privacy risks associated with using Facebook	4.1	0.94	0.614	
Information sharing	IS1: On Facebook, I participate in a lot of information/knowledge sharing activities	3.46	0.7	0.778	0.752
	IS2: I usually spend hours on Facebook updating new information	3.44	0.67	0.691	
	IS3: I post updates on my Facebook very often	3.34	0.66	0.674	
	IS4: On Facebook, I tend to share my experience or understanding with others	3.44	0.66	0.562	
	IS5: When I am on Facebook, I usually enjoy sharing my knowledge and information with others	3.28	0.76	0.53	

Table 3. Result of regression

Model	Unstandardized		Standardized	t	Sig.	Collinearity	
	B	Std. Error	Beta			Tolerance	VIF
PE	0.202	0.003	0.316	68.529	0.000	0.836	1.195
PN	0.175	0.003	0.274	53.174	0.000	0.669	1.495
AB	0.202	0.003	0.299	58.922	0.000	0.69	1.45
VH	0.200	0.003	0.342	74.895	0.000	0.853	1.172
AA	0.207	0.003	0.304	60.869	0.000	0.712	1.404
PR	−0.114	0.004	−0.215	3.4220	0.001	0.457	1.188

a. Dependent Variable: IS

Table 4. Model summary

Model	R	R^2	Adjusted R^2	Std. error of the estimate	Change Statistics					Durbin-Watson
					R^2 change	F change	df1	df2	Sig. F change	
1	.998ª	.997	.996	.02654	.997	9323.286	6	193	.000	1.801

most decisive factor affecting information sharing, attracting people to visit the brand page, and making them stay [38]. Next, customers with extraversion personality traits are more willing to participate in Facebook conversations than neurotic individuals. The previous study of Price, Kabadayi and Angela Hausman [25] added that "sharing" does not stop by like and comment on Facebook. The research result also proved that perceived privacy risk negatively impacted information sharing, and this factor's effect is lower than that of the benefits, consistent with Krasnova, Spiekermann, Koroleva and Hildebrand [46].

5   Conclusion

Consumers are using social media to interact with peers and companies on social media platforms; as a result, users share their information, knowledge, and experiences with other people [47]. Sometimes their information sharing includes feedback about products quality which they already used or brand-related information. When social commerce became a popular digital marketing trend and proliferated in many countries [48], companies started to care more about enhancing customer engagement through information sharing. If consumers share positive information about the brand or the products, it can lead to peer pressure on other users, create a positive attitude toward a brand, and affect its brand choice. Therefore, this research explored what factors affect consumer information sharing in the post-purchase stage and suggests solutions for improving customer engagement with the brand through information sharing on Facebook.

5.1 Theoretical Contributions

This study used SPSS to test the proposed hypotheses and corresponding hypotheses. Final result support six of seven hypotheses with significant relationships between analyzed constructs. Finding reveals that extraversion, neuroticism, hedonic value, arousal, brand love, and perceived privacy risk impact customer information-sharing behaviors. Our study results are consistent with many previous studies [21, 25, 38]. This study contributes to the scientific literature in various ways and provides practical brand management and social media marketing professionals with practical implications.

It contributes a new perspective to the existing literature on information sharing on social media. Although information sharing is a popular topic that many researchers already shed light on, studying information sharing in the post-purchase stage is an essential and unexplored path. Furthermore, many previous studies only focused on one aspect, such as personal traits or value perception. Therefore, this research extends existing research by combining all the factors that showed significant affection in previous studies.

Finally, this study can provide more insights into customer behavior on Facebook for brand managers by pointing out how personal traits can affect users by sharing information or what benefit drives users to engage on the brand page and attract users to visit and engage more on the fan page.

5.2 Managerial Implications

As mentioned above, consumers will engage more and share more information if they find it entertaining enough. Therefore, brand managers should focus on building entertainment and joyful content. It can be whether demonstrate brand's theme as fun, entertain or write/share funny posts. Besides, brand managers should learn more about gamification, a game-design element recently added to Facebook. Gamification can bring users joy and entertainment as it allows users to engage in playful activities.

Extraversion customers are more likely to participate on Facebook than neurotic individuals. Moreover, because individuals' Facebook profile pages and postings can also be used to predict their personality [49], brand managers can use it to determine which type of personal traits their primary users have in common. From that, they can develop strategies to suit their primary target audience.

Arousal and brand love connect with information sharing; specific arousal and brand love positively impact information sharing; brand managers can strategically use this data to plan their marketing campaigns strategically. For example, a brand wishing to grow relationships with potential consumers may want to post helpful information on its social media pages so that SNS users who visit the page are encouraged to interact with the brand. Moreover, people are drawn to fan pages if the content is attractive enough for them. So brand managers can develop content strategies that are not only informative but also fun, entertain. The brand can also use catchy headlines to stimulate users to read the article and interact more on the pages.

For customers who already bought the product from the brand, providing customers with a positive experience and a good impression is necessary for any brand. Brand love plays an important role here because if the customers love the brand, they will have a better brand experience. A brand loved by customers will improve the performance of its Facebook page. Chen, Papazafeiropoulou, Chen, Duan and Liu [50] stated that customers would keep supporting the brand and develop a strong bond. In order to develop brand love for users, brands must build up their trust first by these activities: First, selling quality products and improving the product continuously. There is no doubt that a product is what customers care about when it comes to brand; if their product is good, customers will trust the brand and eventually love it, they also can have re-purchase intention. Second, building up a good image on social media by doing volunteering activities (for example, donation, create a charity fund) and aim to sustainable values, as users starting to care more about nature (climate protection, for example) and equality in social (gender, education). If the brand proves to be a good company because of its products and what it did for communities, it will leave a good impression on customers and eventually develop their love for the brand.

Because perceived privacy risk negatively impacted information sharing (Beta = − 0.215), which means the lower level of privacy risk customers perceive, the more they are willing to share their information on the Facebook brand page. As a result, brands can get more interactions and better interaction with their customers and collect more helpful business plan insights. To reduce customers' perceived privacy risk, the brand needs to build trust to feel trustworthy enough and safe to share its information on the brand page. Besides, brands must protect the privacy of their customer's personal information and have a method to prevent their consumer's data from leaking to a third party. For example, brands can state that they do not and will never provide their customer's data to a third party without their permission. In this way, the brand can gain more trust from customers and reduce their perceived privacy risk.

5.3 Limitations and Further Research

Several limitations lead to directions for further research. First, the research topic is only applied for Facebook brand pages, not all the SNS platforms; thus, the findings cannot be applied to other types of consumption. Moreover, in the survey about arousal factors; as a result, the outcome may vary depending on the context. Thus, further research could focus on various situational contexts (for example, intention to visit a specific brand fan page) or product categories (i.g., electronics, automobiles, healthcare, entertainment) or expand to other SNS platforms such as Instagram and Twitter. Second, the research is examined using the purposive sampling method, which did not achieve high accuracy, and the statistics were not reliable enough. Therefore, further studies can be carried out with a broader scope and combining probability sampling methods to increase the accuracy of the results. Finally, this study used a self-report online survey method to determine personality traits. As a result of this process, the traits indicating participant's intent to act on social media could differ from their actual personality traits. However, one advantage of technological developments is that weblogs and digital data can easily monitor and track consumer behaviors [21]; thus, further research could use digital data to determine the precise personality characteristics of users.

References

1. Nie, N.H.: Sociability, interpersonal relations, and the internet: reconciling conflicting findings. Am. Behav. Sci. **45**, 420–435 (2001)
2. Khoa, B.T., Ha, N.M., Ngoc, B.H.: The accommodation services booking intention through the mobile applications of generation Y: an empirical evidence based on TAM2 model. In: Ngoc Thach, N., Ha, D.T., Trung, N.D., Kreinovich, V. (eds.) ECONVN 2021. SCI, vol. 983, pp. 559–574. Springer, Cham (2022). https://doi.org/10.1007/978-3-030-77094-5_43
3. Miniwatts Marketing Group: Internet 2021 Usage in Asia - Internet Users, Facebook Subscribers & Population Statistics for 35 countries and regions in Asia. https://www.internetworldstats.com/stats3.htm. Accessed 14 June 2021
4. Fractl: Average Facebook User Sharing Habits Study. https://www.frac.tl/work/marketing-research/facebook-user-sharing-habits-study. Accessed 10 June 2021
5. Khoa, B.T., Ly, N.M., Uyen, V.T.T., Oanh, N.T.T., Long, B.T.: The impact of social media marketing on the travel intention of Z travelers. In: 2021 IEEE International IOT, Electronics and Mechatronics Conference (IEMTRONICS), pp. 1–6. IEEE (2021). https://doi.org/10.1109/IEMTRONICS52119.2021.9422610
6. Khoa, B.T., Oanh, N.T.T., Uyen, V.T.T., Dung, D.C.H.: Customer loyalty in the Covid-19 pandemic: the application of machine learning in survey data. In: Somani, A.K., Mundra, A., Doss, R., Bhattacharya, S. (eds.) Smart Systems: Innovations in Computing. SIST, vol. 235, pp. 419–429. Springer, Singapore (2022). https://doi.org/10.1007/978-981-16-2877-1_38
7. Turban, E., Outland, J., King, D., Lee, J.K., Liang, T.-P., Turban, D.C.: Electronic Commerce 2018. Springer, Cham (2018). https://doi.org/10.1007/978-3-319-58715-8
8. Facebook: Facebook Reports Fourth Quarter and Full Year 2020 Results (2021). https://s21.q4cdn.com/399680738/files/doc_news/Facebook-Reports-Fourth-Quarter-and-Full-Year-2020-Results-2021.pdf
9. Bloch, P.H., Sherrell, D.L., Ridgway, N.M.: Consumer search: an extended framework. J. Cons. Res. **13**, 119–126 (1986)
10. Kaplan, A.M., Haenlein, M.: Users of the world, unite! The challenges and opportunities of Social Media. Bus. Horiz. **53**, 59–68 (2010)
11. Zhang, K.Z.K., Benyoucef, M.: Consumer behavior in social commerce: a literature review. Decis. Support Syst **86**, 95–108 (2016). https://doi.org/10.1016/j.dss.2016.04.001
12. Lu, B., Fan, W., Zhou, M.: Social presence, trust, and social commerce purchase intention: an empirical research. Comput. Hum. Behav. **56**, 225–237 (2016). https://doi.org/10.1016/j.chb.2015.11.057
13. Liang, T.-P., Turban, E.: Introduction to the special issue on social commerce: a research framework for social commerce. Int. J. Electron. Commer. **16**, 5–14 (2011)
14. Ko, H., Cho, C.-H., Roberts, M.S.: Internet uses and gratifications: a structural equation model of interactive advertising. J. Advert. **34**, 57–70 (2005). https://doi.org/10.1080/00913367.2005.10639191
15. Nov, O., Naaman, M., Ye, C.: Analysis of participation in an online photo-sharing community: a multidimensional perspective. J. Am. Soc. Inf. Sci. Technol. **61**, 555–566 (2009). https://doi.org/10.1002/asi.21278
16. Hennig-Thurau, T., Gwinner, K.P., Walsh, G., Gremler, D.D.: Electronic word-of-mouth via consumer-opinion platforms: what motivates consumers to articulate themselves on the internet? J. Interact. Mark. **18**, 38–52 (2004)
17. Hair, N., Clark, M., Shapiro, M.: Toward a classification system of relational activity in consumer electronic communities: the moderators' tale. J. Relatsh. Mark. **9**, 54–65 (2010). https://doi.org/10.1080/15332660903552238

18. Khoa, B.T.: The role of mobile skillfulness and user innovation toward electronic wallet acceptance in the digital transformation era. In: 2020 International Conference on Information Technology Systems and Innovation (ICITSI), pp. 30–37. IEEE (2020). https://doi.org/10.1109/ICITSI50517.2020.9264967

19. Mehrabian, A., Russell, J.A.: An Approach to Environmental Psychology. MIT Press, Cambridge (1974)

20. Fiore, A.M., Dennis, C., Kim, J.: An integrative framework capturing experiential and utilitarian shopping experience. Int. J. Retail. Distrib. Manag. **35**, 421–442 (2007). https://doi.org/10.1108/09590550710750313

21. Kim, A.J., Johnson, K.K.P.: Power of consumers using social media: examining the influences of brand-related user-generated content on Facebook. Comput. Hum. Behav. **58**, 98–108 (2016). https://doi.org/10.1016/j.chb.2015.12.047

22. Carroll, B.A., Ahuvia, A.C.: Some antecedents and outcomes of brand love. Mark. Lett. **17**, 79–89 (2006). https://doi.org/10.1007/s11002-006-4219-2

23. Albert, N., Merunka, D., Valette-Florence, P.: When consumers love their brands: exploring the concept and its dimensions. J. Bus. Res. **61**, 1062–1075 (2008). https://doi.org/10.1016/j.jbusres.2007.09.014

24. Batra, R., Ahuvia, A., Bagozzi, R.P.: Brand love. J. Mark. **76**, 1–16 (2012). https://doi.org/10.1509/jm.09.0339

25. Price, K., Kabadayi, S., Angela Hausman, D.: Consumer – brand engagement on Facebook: liking and commenting behaviors. J. Res. Interact. Mark. **8**, 203–223 (2014). https://doi.org/10.1108/jrim-12-2013-0081

26. Amichai-Hamburger, Y.: Internet and personality. Comput. Hum. Behav. **18**, 1–10 (2002). https://doi.org/10.1016/s0747-5632(01)00034-6

27. Amichai-Hamburger, Y., Vinitzky, G.: Social network use and personality. Comput. Hum. Behav. **26**, 1289–1295 (2010). https://doi.org/10.1016/j.chb.2010.03.018

28. Butt, S., Phillips, J.G.: Personality and self reported mobile phone use. Comput. Hum. Behav. **24**, 346–360 (2008). https://doi.org/10.1016/j.chb.2007.01.019

29. Shen, J., Brdiczka, O., Liu, J.: A study of Facebook behavior: what does it tell about your neuroticism and extraversion? Comput. Hum. Behav. **45**, 32–38 (2015). https://doi.org/10.1016/j.chb.2014.11.067

30. Correa, T., Hinsley, A.W., De Zuniga, H.G.: Who interacts on the web?: the intersection of users' personality and social media use. Comput. Hum. Behav. **26**, 247–253 (2010)

31. Kroencke, L., Geukes, K., Utesch, T., Kuper, N., Back, M.: Neuroticism and emotional risk during the COVID-19 pandemic. J. Res. Pers. **89**, 104038 (2020)

32. Nguyen, M.H., Khoa, B.T.: Customer electronic loyalty towards online business: the role of online trust, perceived mental benefits and hedonic value. J. Distrib. Sci. **17**, 81–93 (2019). https://doi.org/10.15722/jds.17.12.201912.81

33. Albayrak, T., Karasakal, S., Kocabulut, Ö., Dursun, A.: Customer loyalty towards travel agency websites: the role of trust and hedonic value. J. Qual. Assur. Hosp. Tourism **21**, 50–77 (2019). https://doi.org/10.1080/1528008x.2019.1619497

34. Carpenter, J.M., Sirakaya-Turk, E., Meng, F.: Efficacy of hedonic shopping value in predicting word of mouth. In: Tourism Travel and Research Association: Advancing Tourism Research Globally 2011 International Conference, University of Massachusetts Amherst (2016)

35. Sweeney, J.C., Soutar, G.N.: Consumer perceived value: the development of a multiple item scale. J. Retail. **77**, 203–220 (2001). https://doi.org/10.1016/s0022-4359(01)00041-0

36. Raacke, J., Bonds-Raacke, J.: MySpace and Facebook: applying the uses and gratifications theory to exploring friend-networking sites. Cyberpsychol. Behav. **11**, 169–174 (2008). https://doi.org/10.1089/cpb.2007.0056

37. Chang, Y.P., Zhu, D.H.: Understanding social networking sites adoption in China: a comparison of pre-adoption and post-adoption. Comput. Hum. Behav. **27**, 1840–1848 (2011)

38. Yu, J., Zo, H., Kee Choi, M., Ciganek, A.P.: User acceptance of location-based social networking services. Online Inf. Rev. **37**, 711–730 (2013). https://doi.org/10.1108/oir-12-2011-0202
39. Vimalkumar, M., Sharma, S.K., Singh, J.B., Dwivedi, Y.K.: 'Okay google, what about my privacy?': User's privacy perceptions and acceptance of voice based digital assistants. Comput. Hum. Behav. **120**, 106763 (2021)
40. Khoa, B.T.: The impact of the personal data disclosure's tradeoff on the trust and attitude loyalty in mobile banking services. J. Promot. Manag. **27**, 585–608 (2020). https://doi.org/10.1080/10496491.2020.1838028
41. Ayaburi, E.W., Treku, D.N.: Effect of penitence on social media trust and privacy concerns: The case of Facebook. Int. J. Inform. Manag. **50**, 171–181 (2020)
42. Dinev, T., Hart, P.: An extended privacy calculus model for e-commerce transactions. Inf. Syst. Res. **17**, 61–80 (2006). https://doi.org/10.1287/isre.1060.0080
43. Jahn, B., Verma, R., Kunz, W.: How to transform consumers into fans of your brand. J. Serv. Manag. **23**, 344–361 (2012). https://doi.org/10.1108/09564231211248444
44. Malhotra, N.K., Kim, S.S., Agarwal, J.: Internet users' information privacy concerns (IUIPC): the construct, the scale, and a causal model. Inf. Syst. Res. **15**, 336–355 (2004)
45. Hajli, N., Lin, X.: Exploring the security of information sharing on social networking sites: the role of perceived control of information. J. Bus. Ethics **133**(1), 111–123 (2014). https://doi.org/10.1007/s10551-014-2346-x
46. Krasnova, H., Spiekermann, S., Koroleva, K., Hildebrand, T.: Online social networks: why we disclose. J. Inf. Technol. **25**, 109–125 (2010). https://doi.org/10.1057/jit.2010.6
47. Khoa, B.T., Huynh, L.T., Nguyen, M.H.: The relationship between perceived value and peer engagement in sharing economy: a case study of ridesharing services. J. Syst. Manag. Sci. **10**, 149–172 (2020). https://doi.org/10.33168/JSMS.2020.0210
48. Khoa, B.T., Nguyen, H.M.: Electronic loyalty in social commerce: scale development and validation. Gadjah Mada Int. J. Bus. **22**, 275–299 (2020). https://doi.org/10.22146/gamaijb.50683
49. Ehrenberg, R.: Science & society: what a Facebook 'like' reveals: researchers predict personal traits using social media data. SciN **183**, 14 (2013)
50. Chen, H., Papazafeiropoulou, A., Chen, T.-K., Duan, Y., Liu, H.-W.: Exploring the commercial value of social networks. J. Enterp. Inf. Manag. **27**, 576–598 (2014). https://doi.org/10.1108/jeim-05-2013-0019

SQL Injection Prevention in Web Application: A Review

Joanna Hazaline Binti Johny, Wafa Athilah Fikriah Binti Nordin, Nurrina Mizana Binti Lahapi, and Yu-Beng Leau[✉]

Faculty of Computing and Informatics, Universiti Malaysia Sabah, Kota Kinabalu, Malaysia
{BI18110016,BI18110022,BI18110117}@student.ums.edu.my,
lybeng@ums.edu.my

Abstract. A web application is a software system that provides its users with an interface via a web browser on any operating system. Despite the increasing popularity of web applications, the security threat in web applications has become more diverse, resulting in more severe damage. In poorly designed web applications, malware attacks, particularly SQL injection attacks, are common. This vulnerability has been known for over two decades and remains a source of concern to this day. In this paper, we summarize fourteen different types of SQL injection attacks and their consequences for web applications. The primary goal of our research is to examine the various methods for preventing SQL injection. This paper presents an analysis of the best preventative mechanism against SQL injection attacks.

Keywords: SQL injection attack · Web application · Prevention mechanism

1 Introduction

Web technology advancements in recent years have resulted in an increase in the number of web applications running on the internet. A web application is a software system that provides an interface to its users via a web browser on any operating system and serves daily essential services such as online banking, web-based email, social networking, and many others. Because the service is available to almost everyone, one of the most significant benefits that web applications provide to people is that it can be accessed almost anywhere. A tremendous amount of data is stored in the web applications database in order to supply a large number of users around the world because a large amount of data and information, including confidential and private data in the web server's database, as well as data belonging to the website itself issued via web applications every day [1, 2].

Despite the growing popularity of web applications, the security threat in web applications has become more varied, resulting in more serious damage. This flaw allows unauthorized users to gain unrestricted access to confidential and private data stored on a specific web-based system. Malware attacks, particularly SQL injection attacks, are common in poorly designed web applications. According to the Open Web Application Security Project (OWASP), a global security organization dedicated to application

© Springer Nature Singapore Pte Ltd. 2021
N. Abdullah et al. (Eds.): ACeS 2021, CCIS 1487, pp. 568–585, 2021.
https://doi.org/10.1007/978-981-16-8059-5_35

software security research, SQL injections have been rated as the most dangerous vulnerability of web-based systems over the last two decades [3]. Structured Query Language Injections (SQLi) is a type of code injection used to attack database-driven web applications. It is an attack on a database via a website, typically on a text field. In this attack, malicious code was embedded in strings and then passed to the database backend for parsing and execution. In this attack, the malicious code generated database query results and harvested confidential information such as credentials account data and internal business data [4].

1.1 History and Exploitation of SQL Injection Vulnerabilities

The SQL injection vulnerability was discovered in 1998 and has been known for more than two decades, and it remains a source of concern for security experts today. When the vulnerability was first discovered in December 1998, Jeff Forristal, a well-known security professional, described a Microsoft SQL server as having the potential to gain access to sensitive data by using normal user input commands such as "name" and "telephone number" in Phrack magazine. Despite being described in 1998, SQL injection did not appear to gain traction in the information security industry until 2002. The four-year-old vulnerability drew attention immediately after the national event, as did the appearance of dangerous worms and virus outbursts on the internet at the time [5].

Since the sudden spotlight on SQL injection in 2002, there has been a lot of research and academic papers published and written to address SQL injection and other malware attacks. SQL injection attacks, like so many other aspects of computer technology, are infrequently consistent. According to the December 1998 issue of Phrack magazine, the SQL injection attacker purposefully attacked using the piggyback method on SQL statements in the user's input. The Piggyback method has long been recognized as an effective means of allowing unauthorized access to data stored in SQL databases. Several types of attacks, such as tautology-based, union-query, stored procedure, inference, and alternate encoding attacks, have been discovered that have the ability to penetrate the system and gain unauthorized data. Years later, tautology- and inference-based attacks appeared to be the most common SQL injection attacks in 2013 [5].

SQL injection attacks can also target desktop applications in addition to web applications. This SQL injection exploitation is possible as long as the databases are SQL-compatible. Attackers may insert the malicious query into a web form or by pasting the malicious query at the end of the URL in the browser's address bar. In a more unusual attack, an attacker may attempt to penetrate the malicious code via the HTTP header. For example, a module included in a web application can collect statistics about a user's activities such as IP address, type of browser, and language used, which information is then extracted from the HTTP link sent by the victim's browser and stored in a database for later inspection. SQL injection occurs when the stored procedure method is used in an attack as a string containing raw user input and the presence of dynamic SQL statements that are generated to access the database using input information [6].

The SQL injection attack procedure is depicted in Fig. 1 [7]. In a SQL injection attack, the attacker manipulates and changes the SQL statement by injecting a string-type input into the web application. This SQL vulnerability exploitation has the potential to cause

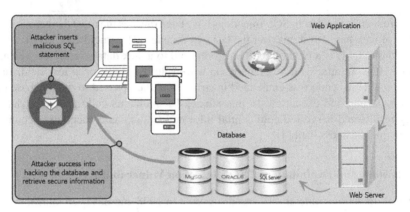

Fig. 1. The SQL injection attack procedure [7].

harm to the database in a variety of ways, including unauthorized database manipulation and confidential data retrieval. Because it can execute system-level commands, this attack has the potential to cause the system to deny the application's service. The SQL injection attack allows the attacker to bypass the authentication mechanism and gain complete access to the remote server's database. Nowadays, the majority of web applications store application data in SQL databases, and the majority of web applications use indeterminate SQL databases that run in the background. SQL syntax, like most programming languages, allows the database command to be varied based on the user's data. This enables remote users to enter data into the web application, which may be interpreted as a command, resulting in the user executing arbitrary commands on the database [6].

SQL injection attacks in web applications are classified into two types, according to the authors [6]. The first type of attack is a direct injection attack, which involves directly binding SQL statements. It is also known as first-order SQL injection because it attacks the SQL query's payload directly. The code is directly inserted into user input variables, which are then concatenated with the SQL statement before being executed. The second type of attack is an indirect attack, also known as a second-order injection attack, in which malicious code is placed on strings stored in a database table. The SQL statement is attached to the saved string, and the SQL malicious code is executed. The injection procedure works by terminating the string in the text before calling another command. Second-order SQL injection attacks are divided into two stages: storing the payload's attack in the file system or database and constructing the SQL syntax query statement using the payload's attack from the file system or database. User registration and user information functions, for example, in a web application, can lead to second-order SQL injection attacks. The attack payload is loaded into the database's user registration function in this function, while the user information modification function extracts the attack payload from the database, resulting in the formation of a SQL query that causes a second-order injection attack [8].

1.2 Statistics and Real Cases

According to the 2020 Vulnerability Statistics Report, SQL injection in web applications accounts for 12% of the most common critical risk vulnerabilities in 2019 for internal or non-public facing systems, while 42% of cases are reported for vulnerabilities in internet-facing or public-facing systems. SQL injection exploits account for 2.2% of the most common full-stack vulnerabilities in 2019, while vulnerabilities discovered through unauthenticated assessments of public internet-facing systems account for 20.3% of web application-related vulnerabilities, including SQL injection attacks [9]. Over the last 20 years, the majority of SQL injection attacks have targeted large corporations' websites, businesses, and social media platforms. Some of these attacks resulted in major data breaches (Fig. 2).

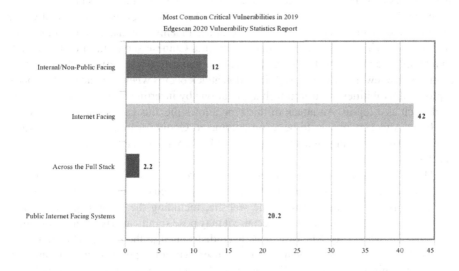

Fig. 2. Most common critical vulnerability for SQL injection in 2019

Every year since the SQL injection issue first surfaced, there has been more than one case reported. An SQL injection attack was discovered on the Guess.com website in March 2002, according to SecurityFocus, an online computer security news portal. Over 200,000 private records have been exposed as a result of the vulnerability, which allows anyone with the correct URL to obtain every customer's name, credit card number, and expiration date retrieved from the website's database [10]. The Web Application Security Consortium published a report on data breaches caused by SQL injection in January 2006. The vulnerability caused havoc on the official website of the Rhode Island government, which believes the attack was carried out by a Russian hacker. The vulnerability allegedly allowed attackers to steal private information such as credit card data belonging to individuals doing online business with state agencies. The website's hosting service provider claimed they only lost 4113 credit card numbers, but the attackers claimed they stole 53,000 credit card numbers from users [11].

Hackers defaced the Microsoft U.K. website in June 2007. A SQL injection attack on the Microsoft UK website was reported by The Register, a British technology news website. The attackers were successful in their attack because they replaced some information on the website with several graphics related to Saudi Arabia within Microsoft's UK domain site. The incident's attackers used SQL injection in a specific field on the table that will be read each time a new page is loaded by inserting HTML code into it, which will most likely succeed if the page used Microsoft's SQL Servers [12]. On September 19, the same year, an anti-American computer hacking group successfully gained access to at least two Army Web servers. The hackers, who go by the alias "m0sted", are from Turkey. On January 26, a breach occurred at the McAlester munitions plant, according to records. Users were redirected to a page with a protest against climate change. Soon after the breaches, officials from the defense department and other investigators launched an ongoing criminal investigation into the hacks [13].

According to a Taiwanese security firm, in May 2008, websites throughout China and Taiwan were hit by a mass SQL injection attack that implanted malware in thousands of Web sites. The attack is being launched from a Chinese server farm that has made no attempt to conceal its IP addresses. The vast majority of the servers affected are in China, with a few in Taiwan. A SQL injection attack occurs when an attacker attempts to exploit vulnerabilities in custom web applications by inserting SQL code into an entry field, such as a log-in. An attack of this type allows the attackers to gain access to the database. Attackers appear to be using automated Google searches to find vulnerable websites. The attack targeted sites such as SouFun.com, a real estate website, and Myc ar168.com [14].

The official Malaysian Kaspersky Antivirus website was hacked in July 2008 by Turkish hackers known as "m0sted". The attackers claimed that the attack was motivated by "patriotism". Several pages on the website, including the home page, have been defaced, which concerns end-users because it may pose significant risks since evaluation copies of the Kaspersky Antivirus have been distributed to the public. The authorities assumed that the attackers could have infected users who attempted to download antivirus files from legitimate websites. Kaspersky's file repository by uploading a malware-infected version of antivirus [15]. In August 2009, the US Department of Justice charged Albert Gonzalez, an American citizen, and two unnamed Russians with stealing data from 130 million credit and debit card payment systems, including Heartland Payment System and convenience store chain 7-Eleven. It is thought to be the largest case of identity theft in American history [16].

Yahoo, the former web portal, appears to have been the victim of a data breach. Over 450,000 plain text login credentials were stolen by a group of hackers claiming responsibility for the attack. They claimed to have used union-based SQL injection to gain access to the Yahoo subdomain. This attack was directed at a poorly designed web application that does not properly inspect the text entered into the user input field and search boxes. The service in question appears to be Yahoo Voice, also known as Associated Content [17]. TalkTalk, a British telecommunications company, was fined heavily in October 2015 for failing to protect its customers' confidential information. The attackers were able to take advantage of TalkTalk's system's lack of security due to the company's poor website security configuration. The attacker gained access to 156,959 users' private information, including bank account information [18]. SQL injection and other vulnerabilities were discovered in Fortnite, a popular online battle game, in January 2019. A SQL injection weakness, cross-site scripting (XSS) bug, web application firewall bypass issue, and most critically, an OAuth account takeover vulnerability have all been discovered in Fortnite. The breach allows the attackers to view the players' contacts and conversations throughout the game. This attack results in a significant breach of the user's privacy, which the attackers may exploit [19].

2 Types of SQL Injection Attack and Its Implications

A SQL injection attack occurs when an attacker injects SQL queries into form fields or other parameters of a web application in order to gain access to the system. The web application is vulnerable to this type of attack due to a lack of input validation, resulting in serious web security issues. The attacker can generate malicious input containing commands that can manipulate the database of the web application. SQL injection attacks, according to Pattewar et al. [21], can be carried out by first studying how the targeted database works. In the input field, random values are inserted to see how the server responds. Following that, an input value is generated using the acquired data, which the server interprets and executes as a SQL statement. SQL injection attacks can wreak havoc on a web application in a variety of ways. Using SQL injection, an attacker could bypass authentication, gain access to, and alter a database containing sensitive information. It's also possible that the system won't be able to load the application at all. SQL injection attacks [7, 20] can be carried out in a variety of ways, including:

1. Tautologies: This type of attack works by inserting code into a conditional SQL statement in such a way that it always evaluates to true, such as (1 = 1) or (- -). This method is commonly used to access databases without requiring authentication on websites. The tautology attack is demonstrated in the query below:

```
SELECT * FROM employees WHERE employee_ID= '1' OR '1=1' --' AND
employee_password= '1234';
```

2. Piggy-backed Query: The attacker in this type of attack appends additional query statements to the original query concatenated by ";." This method is particularly dangerous because it allows an attacker to inject almost any SQL statement. The following query exemplifies the piggy-backed query attack:

```
SELECT employee_password FROM employeeTable WHERE employee_ID=
'user1' AND employee_password = 0; DROP employeeTable;
```

3. Logically Incorrect: This attack takes advantage of an incorrectly executed query on the database. It will display database error messages, which typically contain

critical information that allows an attacker to determine the application's database details. The following query example demonstrates a logically incorrect attack:

> SELECT * FROM employeeTable WHERE employee_ID= '1111' AND employee_password = '1234' AND CONVERT (char, no);

4. Union Query: To carry out this attack, insert a UNION query into a target parameter to combine two or more queries. The union query attack is demonstrated in the query below:

> SELECT * FROM employeeTable WHERE employee_ID= '1111' UNION SELECT * FROM userTable WHERE user_ID= 'admin' AND password= '1234';

5. Stored Procedures: An attacker can manipulate the stored procedures in the database using this method. For both authorized and unauthorized users, the process will return true or false results. The stored procedure attack is demonstrated in the query below:

> SELECT username FROM userTable WHERE username= 'user1' AND password= ' '; SHUTDOWN;

6. Blind Injection: This attack occurs when programmers fail to hide any error messages, exposing the database application. By asking true/false questions in SQL statements, the attacker can infiltrate the database via error messages. The blind injection attack is demonstrated in the query below:

> SELECT password FROM userTable WHERE username= 'user' and 1=0 -- AND password = AND pin= 0
> SELECT info FROM userTable WHERE username= 'user' and = 1 -- AND password = AND password= 0

7. Timing Attacks: In this type of attack, the attacker can retrieve information by observing the time delays of database responses. The time delay is obtained through the if condition statement, and the keyword WAITFOR causes the database to delay its response by a specified amount of time. The timing attack is demonstrated in the query below:

```
declare @ varchar (8000) select @s = db_name () if (ascii (substring (@s, 1, 1)) &
(power (2, 0))) > 0 WAITFOR delay '0:0:5'
```

8. Alternate Encodings: The attacker modifies the injection query by encoding it in hexadecimal, ASCII, or Unicode. This allows the attacker to bypass the input filter, which looks for a specific "bad character" in input queries. The following query example demonstrates the alternate encodings attack:

```
SELECT accounts FROM userTable WHERE login= ' ' AND pin = 0; exec (char
(0x73687574646f6f776e))
```

9. Fast Flux SQL Injection Attack: The attacker intends to phish and steal information from the database. Phishing is a type of social engineering attack in which an attacker pretends to be a third party in order to obtain sensitive information from a user. Because typical phishing hosts can be easily identified by looking up the public Domain Name Server (DNS) or IP address, attackers use the Fast Flux technique. This is a DNS method for concealing phishing and malware distribution sites behind the constantly changing network of the affected host [7] (Fig. 3).

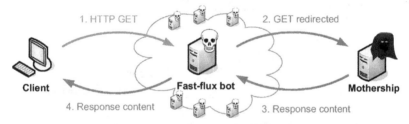

Fig. 3. Fast flux attack [7].

10. SQL Injection + DDoS (Distributed Denial of Service) Attacks: This attack causes a server to freeze and overuse its resources, preventing a user from accessing it. SQL commands such as encode, compress, and join could be used in SQL injection to track DDoS attacks. For the SQLI DDoS attack, the following sample code is shown:

```
select tab1 from (select decode (encode (convert (compress (post) using latin1),
concat(post, post, post, post)), sha1(concat (post, post, post, post))) as tab1 from
table_1);
```

11. SQL Injection + DNS (Domain Name Service) Hijacking: This type of attack is used by attackers to insert the SQL query into a DNS request, capture it, and upload it to the internet. The following sample code demonstrates this attack:

```
do_dns_lookup((select top 1 password from userTable) + '.inse6140.net');
```

12. SQL Injection + XSS (Cross-site Scripting): The attacker injects malicious code, which is the XSS script, into the web application's input fields. It will then run and attempt to connect to the application's database. The iframe command is used to extract data from a database, for example:

```
print "<html>" print "<h1>Most recent comment</h1>" <iframe src =
http://evil.com/xss.html> print "</html>"
```

13. SQL Injection using Cross-Domain Policies of Rich Internet Application (RIA): The cross-domain policy enables web client applications such as Java, Adobe Flash, and Adobe Reader to access data from multiple domains. The cross-domain policy is depicted in the figure below [7] (Fig. 4).

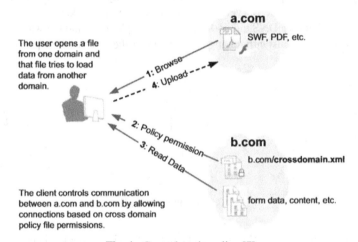

Fig. 4. Cross domain policy [7].

The code below shows that the web application is vulnerable to SQL injection using cross-domain policies attacks:

```
<allow-access-from domain="*.sub1.doaminA.com"/> <allow-access-from
domain="*.domainC.com"/> <allow-access-from domain="*"/>
```

14. SQL Injection + Insufficient Authentication: Because of an inexperienced user or administrator, the attacker can access sensitive data without first authenticating the user's identity. To insert SQL injection code, the attacker takes advantage of security parameters that have not been initialized.

As we can see, there are numerous SQL injection attack methods that can have serious consequences. For example, attackers can use SQL injection to log in as a regular user while bypassing the authentication of a trusted user such as a database administrator. They will impersonate the administrator in order to gain access to all database privileges. Then they can make changes to sensitive data in the database. For example, the attacker may purposefully transfer funds to their account or delete critical information. As a result, the confidentiality and integrity of the data would be jeopardized, resulting in a corrupted database. SQL injection can also be used by attackers to determine what type of database is being used in the backend, allowing them to execute database-specific attacks to exploit flaws in that database administration. To summarize, SQL injection attacks can result in data breaches, data alteration, complete database control, and control of the entire host system for the attacker.

3   Existing Mechanism of SQL Injection Attack Prevention

3.1   Prevention of SQL Injection Attack with Machine Learning Approach

The author [22] created a machine learning-based solution to detect and prevent SQL injection threats. To prevent SQL injection attacks during runtime monitoring, the Support Vector Machine (SVM) algorithm is used. When a new query is submitted by a user, the SVM is used to determine whether it contains any malicious expressions. When the application's home page is switched to the test page, the goal of this approach is to detect and prevent SQL injection attacks. The SVM algorithm was trained with all conceivable harmful phrases to create a model. The level of training data is used to train classifiers in predictive analytics web applications. The level of training data will be specified by a SQL token and a matrix or dictionary keyword property. Attack signatures will take the form of SQL injection attack tokens and positive symbols at the injection point, whereas a genuine web request will take the form of data that the application expects.

Another study developed a system that serves as a proxy to protect against SQL injection threats by combining SQL Injection Free Secure (SQL-IF) with the Naive Bayes model [23]. This mechanism's workflow begins with receiving input data in the form of HTTP requests and user-agents, which are then validated using the SQL-IF method. If no attacks are found, the data will be double-checked using the Naive Bayes technique before being sent to the web server for processing. This hybrid mechanism is then investigated to determine the effect of constant (K) on SQL-if, a number of datasets on the Naive Bayes method in terms of accuracy and web page efficiency. According to the research, the small constant (K) values in SQL-IF influenced the large dataset used in the Naive Bayes technique, resulting in an improved accuracy score of 90 for SQL injection attack prevention. In terms of efficiency, both SQL-IF and the Naive Bayes technique result in a faster average web page load time.

Based on extensive local and global research, the authors [24] proposed a SQL injection detection solution based on a natural language processing model and deep learning framework. Convolutional neural networks (CNN) and multilayer perceptron (MLP) were the two models investigated in this study. Prior to the model training procedure, the training data was sanitized using recursive decoding and lexical analysis. The dataset is tested after the model has been trained to ensure that it is accurate. The experiment results show that these two models are effective at detecting SQL injection attacks. Performance will vary slightly since various neural networks have different application contexts. These models will be used by the machine to automatically understand the language model aspects of SQL injection intrusions in order to avoid SQL injection attacks (Table 1).

Table 1. Comparison method of machine learning

Method	Strength	Weakness	Type of attack prevented
Applied machine learning predictive method [22]	The proposed method demonstrated fair results that can be evaluated empirically in big data environment	Unable to use multiclass classifiers to define groups of various types of SQL injection attack	Defend SQL injection attack during runtime monitoring
SQL-IF and Naïve Bayes method [23]	Yield high accuracy in preventing SQL injection attacks	Slows down web page load performance	Manual and tool-based SQL injection attacks
Deep learning technique [24]	The mechanism can detect and prevent first-order SQL injection attack accurately and efficiently	Does not focus on advanced SQL injection attack methods such as hybrid and second-order attack for future studies	First-order SQL injection attacks

3.2 Prevention of SQL Injection Attack with Cryptography Approach

A study looked at three different preventative approaches, including input validation using query tokenization and log maintenance during the login phase, parameterized queries, and RC4 and blowfish method encryption of sensitive information values at the back-end database [25]. The first method allows single-word inputs by comparing malicious symbols to a maliciously documented symbol set, which prevents nearly all SQL Injection attacks. For example, during the login process, the user may enter a single word rather than multiple words in order to detect suspicious behaviour if the user enters a multi-word username or password. The input is tokenized at the same time and a log file containing a list of different identified malicious symbols or tokens is kept. The entered input will be compared to a maliciously identified symbol set to validate the user login. This function would record the malicious user's IP address, as well as the date, time, and application page, for future use. The second mechanism is the well-known parameterized query, which requires the user to apply SQL query logic before entering the user input value, resulting in an unchanged query because the database already knows what the query would do. As a result, it will only accept valid usernames and passwords and will not allow direct user input value entry during the query development process because it does not use concatenation symbols, which are vulnerable to SQL injection attacks. The final option employs RC4 and blowfish encryption for the back-end database, which greatly improves the efficiency of encrypting the confidential field because both approaches have less time complexity than the AES algorithm. For example, when a new user registers, a unique secret key is generated and saved, and when the user logs in, the generated secret key is compared to the ones that have been saved. When a legitimate user logs in, their data is decrypted. Otherwise, it will be stored on the backend server, preventing the attacker from determining the absolute value. Because the RC4 algorithm is symmetric, it can encrypt and decrypt data using the same key. This feature provides more storage space for public keys. The RC4 and blowfish algorithms are also capable of encrypting sensitive data such as passwords and other personal information, ensuring data security and integrity. Because these three methods are used at the application level, they do not require any configuration and have a lower execution overhead.

A study by the authors [26] investigates how the MD5 and AES algorithms can potentially deter SQL injection attacks on web applications. The MD5 algorithm was created for digital signature applications that require a big file to be safely compressed before being encrypted with a private key using a public-key cryptosystem. whereas the AES algorithm is a symmetric encryption algorithm used to secure sensitive and unclassified resources because it works well in both software and hardware. The research describes a method that employs MD5, AES, and a combination of MD5 and AES algorithms, also known as the double encryption approach. The use of double encryption prevents attackers from needing the entire table name in order to access the database. Prior to testing these algorithms to prevent SQL injection attacks such as injected additional query, second-order SQL injection, bypass authentication, and authorised knowledge of databases, all data in the input field will be encrypted using the suggested algorithms, and the encryption time will be compared to determine which algorithms work faster. The study concluded that AES, MD5, and the double encryption approach effectively stopped all of the attempts.

The authors [27] used password encryption to prevent SQL injection attacks at the database storage level in their paper. The proposed method's goal was to encrypt the password text field using various mechanisms, preventing attackers from gaining access to the password and providing users with complete protection over their sensitive information. Following the user's login, the username and password are used to generate a hash, which is then compared to the initial hash. If all hashes are correct, the system will grant the user additional access to the web page. The database hashes are a combination of sha1 and salt. The password entered by the user during registration will be concatenated with the salt and a hash to form a salted hash before it is saved in the database table. If the intruder tries to decode the salted hash using the reverse hash lookups table, an error message such as "no value in sha1 database for this hash" will be displayed.

The paper by authors [28] proposes the use of the AES-128 algorithm in conjunction with Token-Base64. The AES-128 algorithm is used for encryption as well as defining the name and parameter, while token-base64 is used for decoding and encoding the token in the binary ciphertext produced by the AES-128 encryption process. The token is used to keep the user authentication of the client-side application up to date. These algorithms are combined and used in the client-server data transmission process. Six types of SQL injection attacks have been evaluated using HTTP GET or POST communication: tautology, union, illegal/logical invalid queries, piggyback queries, inference, and stored procedure. Black box testing was used in this study, and the SQL injection tools used were web cruiser and the pentest-tools URL-fuzzer web application to determine the URL addresses of web services that could be used as a SQL injection attack breach. According to the findings, the combination of AES-128 and token-Base64 algorithms prevented SQLIA in all 83 data connection attempts using HTTP GET or POST parameters (Table 2).

Table 2. Comparison method of cryptography approach

Method	Strength	Weakness	Type of attack prevented
RC4 and blowfish encryption [25]	Proposed mechanism has faster performance, requires no modification, and has less execution overhead	Unable to protect against second order SQL injection	Bypass authentication, unauthorized knowledge of database, and injected additional query
AES and MD5 algorithms [26]	Combination of AES and MD5 algorithms had better performance in terms of security in preventing SQL injection attack	Independent implementation of these algorithms is inefficient in improving web security	Bypass authentication, unauthorized knowledge of database, injected additional query, and second order SQL injection
Password encryption [27]	Mitigate a huge domain of SQL injection attack	Does not focus on advanced SQL injection attack methods such as hybrid and second-order attack for future studies	Unauthorized access at database storage level
AES-128 and token-base64 [28]	Improved the web service load time performance with a 31.26% increase in response time with 95% of the file size web services becomes greater	Does not improved the average grade in web services performance	Tautologies, Union, illegal/logical incorrect queries, piggyback queries, inference, and stored procedures

3.3 Prevention of SQL Injection Attack with Matching Algorithm

In a paper [29], a pattern matching method was used to detect and block SQL injection attacks on websites. The Aho-Corasick pattern matching scheme was used in this study to identify and protect a bank application from SQL injection threats. The proposed framework begins by tokenizing a user-generated query before passing it to a pattern matching algorithm for comparison and calculation of anomaly scores. If the anomaly score exceeds the threshold value, the administrator will be notified, otherwise the user will be able to access the website. This mechanism, which is used in Java, Apache Tomcat, and MySQL, detects and prevents SQL injection attacks such as tautologies, logically incorrect inquiries, union queries, piggy-backed queries, and alternative encoding.

A similar study developed a hybrid Aho-Corasick pattern matching algorithm technique to detect and avoid SQL injection attacks [30]. This mechanism was divided into two phases: static and dynamic. In the static phase, the SQL queries provided by the client are inspected using the Static Pattern Matching algorithm. If there is any type of data inconsistency, the dynamic phase will generate a new anomaly pattern and add it to the Static Pattern List. After that, the mechanism will use syntax awareness to convert tokenized queries into pattern matching syntax and discover anomalous scores for each query. If the anomaly score exceeds the threshold value, the attack pattern tokens will be removed and positive tainting will begin. After the attack pattern tokens have been removed, all tokens are merged, and the query is executed.

Another study used the Knuth-Morris-Pratt (KMP) string match algorithm to defend against SQL injection and cross-site scripting attacks [31]. If an attack is reported, the suggested method would compare the user's input string to a stored threat pattern derived from the development of SQL injection string pattern and parse tree design, which illustrates the structural pattern of several SQL injection and cross-site scripting attacks. A function named filter() is written to deter SQL injection and XSS attacks. This function includes additional features designed to detect any type of both attacks. For example, if at least one condition returns true, the filter will halt attackers, restart HTTP requests, and display a warning message. The method was tested with Apache Web Server and Internet Information Server (ISS). According to the test results, the suggested technique is capable of identifying and preventing attacks, recording attack records in the database, blocking attackers based on their MAC addresses, and displaying a blocked message. In summary, this research methodology is divided into five stages: creating a SQL injection string pattern, designing a parse tree, preventing SQL injection and cross-site attacks with the KMP algorithm, and developing a filter function.

A paper describes a method for detecting and preventing malicious code by using the Bitap string matching algorithm, which compares the user's input string to a stored pattern of injection text [32]. The algorithm begins by calculating a series of bitmasks, one for each pattern variable to compare user input with the proposed algorithm. To avoid any type of SQL injection attack, a function named filter() was created using the proposed algorithm based on the defined pattern. The function expects every input string to pass through it, and if at least one function returns valid, the user will be blocked. The proposed method was tested using a variety of metrics, including Boolean, union, comment, like-based, and cross-site scripting attacks. The techniques were found to effectively track and deter attacks, register attack entries in the database, block systems based on their MAC addresses, issue a blocked message, and deliver attack-related mail to tenants. This approach has been demonstrated to be more efficient than existing method as it is not limited to a certain type of attack as well as able to handle multiple forms of SQL injection and XSS attacks (Table 3).

Table 3. Comparison method of matching algorithm

Method	Strength	Weakness	Type of attack prevented
Pattern matching algorithm [29]	The proposed mechanism is able to detect several types of SQL injection attack to improve web security	Does not cover all types of SQL injection attacks on websites	Tautologies, logically incorrect inquiries, union queries, piggy-backed queries, and alternative encoding
Hybrid pattern matching algorithm [30]	Suggest useful corrupting changes from conventional spoiling and distinguish between genuine and fraudulent query using positive tainting	Unable to prevent encoded injection	Boolean-based, Union-based, Error-based, Batch query, like-based, and XSS attack
Knutt-Morris-Pratt algorithms [31]	Not confined to a single type of attack and capable of handling a variety of SQL queries	Used purposely vulnerable web application to test out the proposed method	Boolean-based, Union-based, Error-based, Batch query, like-based, encoded injection, and XSS attack
Bitap string algorithm [32]	Proposed method able to send notification of attack to tenants and provide better performance than existing techniques	Used a dummy website to test proposed technique	Boolean-based, Like-based, Comment-based, Union-based, XSS attack

4   Discussion

The study demonstrates three different mechanisms with various proposed methods against SQL injections, namely machine-learning-based method, cryptography method, and matching algorithm method. In the course of designing existing mechanisms, approaches and methods with significant advantages will be chosen. While each mechanism has advantages and disadvantages depending on the issues, this analysis supports the findings that preventative measures proposed using the cryptographic method can provide the best preventative mechanisms based on several methods proposed in various studies. The cryptography method is capable of preventing SQL injection attacks with minimal changes and lower execution overhead, improving web service loading time, mitigating large domains of attacks, and encrypting passwords for improved security performance. Meanwhile, the machine learning approach dealt with the SQL injection attack by predicting malicious expressions with trained models and data using machine learning algorithms. However, in order to produce high-quality models for preventing SQL injection attacks, this method heavily relies on data. The matching algorithm schemes addressed SQL injection attacks by comparing the query to the proposed algorithms and a stored injected query pattern; however, this methodology is frequently tested on purposefully created vulnerable websites only and is unable to cover all types of SQL injection attacks. In a nutshell, more research is required to develop more preventative measures against SQL injection attacks, particularly methods based on machine learning and matching algorithms.

5 Conclusion

This paper provides an overview of SQL injection attacks, including the reasons for their occurrence, the consequences, and the various types of attacks. In order to defend the web application against SQL injection attacks, a preventative technique is a vital component of security. To prevent SQL injection, we must recognize various security measures that can be used to mitigate the impact of such attacks. In general, the SQL injection attack prevention mechanism should validate and sanitize user inputs, encrypt private data, and keep the database up to date with the latest patches to prevent attackers from exploiting the weakness of an older version of the system. Based on previous research, this paper investigates and categorizes the existing security mechanisms used to prevent SQL injection attacks on web applications. Machine learning, cryptography, and matching algorithms are among the preventative methods investigated. Each existing mechanism's strengths and limitations are also thoroughly discussed. Machine learning is used to empirically analyze the preventative mechanism, emphasizing that its effectiveness is dependent on the amount of data used. The cryptographic method is one of the most widely used approaches for preventing SQL injection attacks. This method encrypts confidential data and stores the encrypted data in the database, whereas the matching algorithms method compares user input to matching algorithms and a stored injected query pattern. Based on the findings, it is possible to conclude that the cryptographic approach is the best mechanism for preventing SQL injection attacks. This method employs not only input validation but also parameterization queries to differentiate between malicious code and user input. Furthermore, this method employs the hashing method to encrypt data, such as passwords, to prevent attackers from accessing the data. For future research, the study should focus on analyzing the methods in a practical situation, such as implementing the existing mechanism to other domains of web application such as e-commerce, education system, or company business website.

References

1. Sharma, C., Jain, S.: SQL injection attacks on web applications. Int. J. Adv. Res. Comput. Sci. Softw. Eng. **7**, 24–26 (2017)
2. Mukhtar, B., Azer, M.: Evaluating the modsecurity web application firewall against SQL injection attacks. In: 2020 15th International Conference on Computer Engineering and Systems (ICCES), pp. 2–7 (2020)
3. Alenezi, M., Nadeem, M., Asif, R.: SQL injection attacks countermeasures assessments. Indon. J. Electr. Eng. Comput. Sci. **21**, 1121–1131 (2020)
4. Qian, L., Zhu, Z., Hu, J., Liu, S.: Research of SQL Injection Attack and Prevention Technology. In: 2015 International Conference on Estimation, Detection and Information Fusion (ICEDIF), pp. 303–306 (2015)
5. Horner, M., Hyslip, T.: SQL injection: the longest running sequel in programming history. J. Digit. Forensics Secur. Law **12**, 10 (2017)
6. Ma, L., Gao, Y., Zhao, D., Zhao, C.: Research on SQL injection attack and prevention technology based on web. In: 2019 International Conference on Computer Network, Electronic and Automation (ICCNEA), pp. 176–179 (2019)
7. Alwan, Z., Younis, M.: Detection and prevention of SQL injection attack: a survey. Int. J. Comput. Sci. Mob. Comput. **6**, 5–17 (2017)
8. Ping, C.: A second-order SQL injection detection method. In: Proceedings of 2017 IEEE 2nd Information Technology, Networking, Electronic and Automation Control Conference (ITNEC), vol. 2018-January, pp. 1792–1796 (2018)
9. Edgescan Fullstack Vulnerability Management: 2020 Vulnerability Statistics Report. Eoin Keary (2020)
10. Poulsen, K.: Guesswork Plagues Web Hole Reporting. https://www.securityfocus.com/news/346
11. Shezaf, O.: Russian hackers broke into a RI GOV website. https://web.archive.org/web/20110213051033/http://www.xiom.com/whid-2006-3
12. Ward, K.: Redmond channel partner online: hacker defaces Microsoft U.K. web page. https://web.archive.org/web/20071223181645/http://rcpmag.com/news/article.aspx?editorialsid=8762
13. McDougall, P.: Anti-U.S. hackers infiltrate army servers – informationweek. https://www.informationweek.com/architecture/anti-us-hackers-infiltrate-army-servers/d/d-id/1079964
14. Lemon, S.: Mass SQL injection attack hits Chinese websites. https://www.computerworld.com/article/2536020/mass-sql-injection-attack-hits-chinese-web-sites.html
15. Danchev, D.: Kaspersky's Malaysian site hacked by Turkish hacker | ZDNet. https://www.zdnet.com/article/kasperskys-malaysian-site-hacked-by-turkish-hacker/
16. BBC NEWS | Business | US man 'stole 130m card numbers'. http://news.bbc.co.uk/2/hi/americas/8206305.stm
17. Yap, J.: 450,000 user passwords leaked in Yahoo breach | ZDNet. https://www.zdnet.com/article/450000-user-passwords-leaked-in-yahoo-breach/
18. TalkTalk gets record £400,000 fine for failing to prevent October 2015 attack. https://web.archive.org/web/20161024090111/https://ico.org.uk/about-the-ico/news-and-events/news-and-blogs/2016/10/talktalk-gets-record-400-000-fine-for-failing-to-prevent-october-2015-attack/
19. Khandelwal, S.: Fortnite flaws allowed hackers to takeover gamers' accounts. https://thehackernews.com/2019/01/fortnite-account-hacked.html.
20. Hu, J., Zhao, W., Cui, Y.: A survey on SQL injection attacks, detection and prevention. In: CMLC 2020: 2020 12th International Conference on Machine Learning and Computing, pp. 483–488. Association for Computing Machinery, New York (2020)

21. Pattewar, T., Patil, H., Patil, H., Patil, N., Taneja, M., Wadile, T.: Detection of SQL injection using machine learning: a survey. Int. Res. J. Eng. Technol. (IRJET) **6**, 239–246 (2019)
22. Reddy, M., Latchoumi, T., Balamurugan, K.: Applied machine learning predictive analytics to SQL injection attack detection and prevention. Eur. J. Mol. Clin. Med. **7**, 3543–3553 (2020)
23. Hernawan, F., Hidayatulloh, I., Adam, I.: Hybrid method integrating SQL-IF and Naïve Bayes for SQL injection attack avoidance. J. Eng. Appl. Technol. **1**, 85–96 (2020)
24. Chen, D., Yan, Q., Wu, C., Zhao, J.: SQL injection attack detection and prevention rechniques using deep learning. J. Phys: Conf. Ser. **1757**, 012055 (2021)
25. Sonakshi, R.K., Gopal, G.: Prevention of SQL injection attacks using RC4 and blowfish encryption techniques. Int. J. Eng. Res. **V5**, 25–29 (2016)
26. Sood, M., Singh, S.: SQL injection prevention technique using encryption. Int. J. Adv. Comput. Eng. Netw. **5**, 5–8 (2017)
27. Sharma, K., Bhatt, S.: Efficient method to prevent SQL injection attacks using password encryption. IAETSD J. Adv. Res. Appl. Sci. **5**, 90–96 (2018)
28. Muttaqin, M.: Implementation of AES-128 and token-base64 to prevent SQL injection attacks via HTTP. Int. J. Adv. Trends Comput. Sci. Eng. **9**, 2876–2882 (2020)
29. Javali, P., Chougule, S.V.: SQL injection detection and prevention using pattern matching algorithm. Int. J. Adv. Res. Comput. Commun. Eng. **5**, 145–147 (2016)
30. Kashyape, M., Agrawal, A., Gahlod, S., Patil, S., Ranade, M., Wagh, P.: A hybrid approach for prevention of SQL injection attack using pattern matching Mitali. Int. Res. J. Adv. Eng. Sci. **2**, 194–197 (2017)
31. Abikoye, O.C., Abubakar, A., Dokoro, A.H., Akande, O.N., Kayode, A.A.: A novel technique to prevent SQL injection and cross-site scripting attacks using Knuth-Morris-Pratt string match algorithm. EURASIP J. Inf. Secur. **2020**(1), 1–14 (2020). https://doi.org/10.1186/s13 635-020-00113-y
32. Karthikeyan, N., Vivekanandan, R., et al.: A novel technique to detect and prevent SQL injection attacks using bitap string matching algorithm. High Technol. Lett. J. **27**, 252–264 (2021)

Threats on Machine Learning Technique by Data Poisoning Attack: A Survey

Ibrahim M. Ahmed[1](✉) and Manar Younis Kashmoola[2](✉)

[1] College of Science, University of Mosul, Mosul, Iraq
ibrahim_alhlima@uomosul.edu.iq
[2] College of Computer Science and Mathematics, University of Mosul, Mosul, Iraq
manar.kashmola@uomosul.edu.iq

Abstract. With the huge services provided by machine learning systems in our daily life, the attacks on these services are increasing every day. The attackers are trying to distort the functionality of these services and change their real duty by falsifying the function using the principle of intoxication. The poisoned system gives the unauthorized person the right to enter and exit the system as a legal person at anytime and anywhere. This could degrade the credibility of systems built using intelligent technologies. The paper extensively introduces the mechanisms of a data poisoning attack. Data poisoning attacks target systems based on machine learning technology, with explanations of the attack mechanisms targeting data sources and the intelligence model during either the training or testing phases. Defense methods presented by researchers in this field have also been described by defense strategies presented in the literature. The risks and effects caused by this attack are also described, and what are the future solutions that give opportunities for researchers working in this field to avoid and repel this attack perfectly.

Keywords: Data poisoning · Federated learning · Cybercriminals · Machine learning attack

1 Introduction

In an era of accelerated technical productivity, many challenges by the formidable security threats by cybercriminals are breaching privacy data [1]. The ability of the attackers differs from one to another depending on the target data type. Some of these data is an important treasure for many attack entities, especially sensitive data like government data, financial data, military data, and famous person data. With this increasing threat to data, there is a persistent need to increase security reinforcements by researchers and scientific institutions involved to provide security services [2]. The attackers set their strategies according to a specific mechanism, and this mechanism meets their desires to harm the victim. Such as data interruption, fabrication, modification, and interception. At a time when the artificial intelligence systems provide great services in technical development at all levels, attackers used their innovative experience and skills to lunch cybercriminals for the data on which are dependent on building intelligent systems. Thus,

© Springer Nature Singapore Pte Ltd. 2021
N. Abdullah et al. (Eds.): ACeS 2021, CCIS 1487, pp. 586–600, 2021.
https://doi.org/10.1007/978-981-16-8059-5_36

it leads to negative results called data poisoning [3]. These data poisoning attacks focus on systems that rely on machine learning. Machine learning uses the concept of training to solve a problem in a way that mimics human intelligence for problem-solving. The data poisoning attacks are used to divert the course of action from the intended target by data poisoning on which is the system trained [2, 4]. For diagnosing this attack, the researchers have conducted a lot of research in this area and have diagnosed the mechanisms of the attack [5].

The paper aims to clarify the vulnerability that cybercriminals exploit in intelligent systems in particular by poisoning data and models. The paper describes how to carry out a data poisoning attack, what are the detection mechanisms, and some defense methods that some researchers have adopted. Moreover, the paper describes the methods of electronic threats, through the focus on distorting data that are represented by its poisoning. The rest of the paper describes the data attack through the section on data poisoning techniques, some of the sections describe the attack on the model and the attack on the data sources. Finally, innovative ways to defend against these attacks, along with measures and benchmarks, are presented and assessed.

2 Method of Data Poisoning

Unauthorized access, destruction, disruption, or distortion of computers, fall under the term of cyberthreats. These threats target any intellectual property or any other form of sensitive data [6]. Disruption fabrication and modification events will lead to major disturbances in the work of the systems because of the problems they are caused [7]. The attacker's goals, varying between stealing, espionage, cutting. On the other hand, distortion or corrupting data will lead to erroneous results, which may lead to disastrous results [7]. The backdoor attack is one of the methods that exploit the deviation of any system from its real behavior. The goal of a backdoor attack is to attack a model of neural networks [8]. When an attacker activates a hidden backdoor, it will exploit the functioning of the system to carry out malicious activity. Which will be associated with data poisoning attacks through the concept of backdoor attacks based on poisoning, While the backdoor attack is active before and as shown in the Taxonomy of the two types in Fig. 1 [9].

Fig. 1. Taxonomy of Backdoor and poisoning attack [9]

Data poisoning is among the most relevant and emerging security threats that targeted data distortion. In these attacks, the attacker may target a small portion of the training data which are used either the learning algorithm or testing. These attacks can also facilitate subsequent system evasion. In many applications, data is collected from an unreliable environment, such as sensors, devices, or information from humans [5]. The performance of the learning algorithm will be degraded when the data poisoning targeted system training [10]. There are many methods of data poisoning, such as poisoning models or poisoning source data. These methods are faking and showing hostile acts as legitimate [11]. After that attacker enters and leaves systems as a legitimate member by using backdoors. Therefore, the researchers deliberately cover these approaches in several directions with a specific perspective on toxicology techniques.

2.1 Attacks on Model

This attack is the source of highlighting the data poisoning attack from the rest of the other attack strategies, by targeting machine learning systems, which is giving a bad impression to developers in this field because they do not believe in the idea of penetrating trained systems [12]. However, the poisoning attack is the most prominent and most effective attack on these systems [13]. There are many ways of attack on models such as federated learning, deep learning, regression learning, and traditional machine learning attack through the internet.

Attack on Federated Learning Model

Federated learning (F.L.) is an evolving paradigm for large-scale deep neural network distributed training; in which, the data of participants remains on their own devices and aggregated by the server [14]. Thus, parameters can be exchanged without affecting the data of the participants. These models were attacked by a poisoning attack since the training data is collected by the aggregator from different participants [15]. The attack on the federated learning model by the attacker targeting parameters that the system exchanges during the training process by poisonous parameters. These parameters work to divert the system's performance from its intended purpose. These studies exploit these models in the attack as a malicious participant [14]. Other researchers have clarified the risks to external training of federated learning systems by creating a malicious network trained file (anonymous neural network or BadNet). A new federal learning flaw that exploits the backdoor attack has been identified and evaluated [16].

Another form of attack on federated learning systems through poisoning attacks is by increasing the proportion of malicious participants [17]. Others have used false labeling schemes to incorporate an SSFL (Semi-Supervised Federation) system as a poisoning attack [18]. An open analysis of the federal learning system is also presented, focusing on the principles adopted through various attacks and exploring potential research methods exploited by attackers of these systems [19, 20].

Attack on Regression Learning Model

By injecting poisoned data into the training dataset, adversarial data poisoning is an effective attack against machine learning that compromises the integrity of the model. Although regression learning is used in many mission-critical systems, it is necessary to examine all elements of data poisoning attacks on regression learning. In Table 1, the actual scenarios in which data poisoning attacks pose a risk to the regression learning model have been presented.

Table 1. Comparison between an attack on model methodology.

Model types	Problem	Methodology	Environment
Federated learning	Investigations into model poisoning attacks on distributed learning systems [15]	Stochastic gradient descent algorithm	Fashion-MNIST dataset
	Define optimal attack strategies, Attack on Unified Learning (AT2FL), BadNets [16]	The measured attack strategies of AT2FL	MNIST [23]
	Directly influence the weights of the jointly learned model via model averaging of federated learning [17]	Stable aggregation evidently prohibits anyone from finding irregularities in the submissions of participants	Byzantine-tolerant distributed learning
	Negatively affected by these attacks and It has been demonstrated that with the increase in the proportion of malignant participants, in the semi-supervised learning community [18]	Cosine similarity and Wasserstein distance to pick customers with high-quality updates by device designs a minimax optimization-based customer filtering technique	MINIST, CIFAR10 [23, 24]
	Open analysis of this significant topic, from illustrating the intuitions [20]	Simple principles adopted by different attacks in (F.L.)	MINIST, CIFAR10 [27, 28]
Regression learning	Attacks of linear regression models to data poisoning attacks [21]	A LID (N-LID) based metric, for metric the local LID deviation of specific data depends on neighboring devices	House, Loan, Grid, machine Dataset [27–30]
	Their countermeasures to the linear regression model [22]	A new robust attack has been developed, so take a proactive approach that is significantly superior to the current robust regression methods	Health care [31], loan assessment, and real estate domains
Deep learning	Selective poisoning attack that reduces the accuracy of the selected class, by adding malicious data to the class [25]	The malignant training data used depends on the sample selected, while maintaining the accuracy of the remaining classes	MNIST, Fashion-MNIST [23]

(*continued*)

Table 1. (*continued*)

Model types	Problem	Methodology	Environment
	Weight poisoning attacks [26]	RIPPLES is the most powerful way to build back doors	(SST-2), Offens, Offens Eval, ron dataset [32–34]

It is clear from Table 1, that only 2–3% of the poison samples are included, the mean square error (MSE) rises so dramatically that it gives disastrous results in the regression learning model because it is used to represent systems that operate on the prediction principle. The researchers introduced a new defensive approach against model-targeting data poisoning attacks, which we fully analyzed [35, 36]. The researchers found a defense approach that successfully mitigates the assaults examined as a result of the trials conducted as shown in Table 1.

Attack on Deep Learning Model

Deep Neural Networks (DNNs) are providing many services that support modern technologies' convenience to the user. However, there is a significant risk to the DNN [25]. A poisoning attack reduces DNN's accuracy by inserting malicious data during the attack training process. The impact of the data poisoning attack on deep learning has become a major threat because it undermines the credibility of many systems that rely on it. The impact of a data poisoning attack on deep learning has become a major threat because it undermines the credibility of the many systems that depend on it [25].

The poisoning attack on the DNNs method was applied by adding malicious data to falsify the desired results. This method reduces the accuracy of the selected class. Malicious data was added to the Fashion-MNIST dataset [23] and the CIFAR10 dataset [24]. Others attacks on DNNs were using different attack methods, such as "Poisoning by weight", which is based on the "poisoning" of previously trained models that appear in a tailgate attack [22]. Others, however, have demonstrated that convolutional neural networks are maliciously trained, BadNets. This will provide output with the input chosen by the attacker [12].

A group of attacks targeted the mentioned above models are the federated learning model, deep learning model, and regression learning model. This is because a specific environment, a specific problem, and a specific methodology are used as described in Table 1.

2.2 Poisoning Attack on Data

In data distortion, many researchers have created attacks on machine learning systems. Some of them have created a detection and repellant mechanism for these attacks, while others have invented attack techniques to calibrate specific systems. Otherwise, some people attack data sources to verify the accuracy of this data and its collection mechanism [37].

Attack on the Source of Learning Data

Despite there are different sources of training data for intelligent systems, the methods of attackers who target these sources are different [38, 39]. Many attackers have devised methods for each type of data source to inflict the greatest damage in the process of teaching systems that the machine learning methods rely on as shown in Table 2.

Table 2. Attack on the source of learning data

Attacks	Methodology	Environment
Data poisoning attack taxonomy for truth inference in crowdsourcing [37]	Targeted attack and the untargeted attack with either heuristic attack-based attack optimization-based strategies	Real-world datasets [2]
Data poisoning assault against neighborhood-based approaches [38]	Attack on BPRMF and NCF by created fake users are inserted into original data	Amazon dataset [38]
Poisoning and backdoor hazard models and the relationships	Attack machine learning technique by the attack on training and testing	EMNIST dataset [3]
Attacks on data sterilization protections and near-neighbor anomaly detectors, training failures [39]	Entering just 3% of the poisoning data, these attacks increase the test error	Enron spam detection dataset [34], IMDB dataset [5]

It is clear from Table 2 that researchers provide perspective on how to conduct a data poisoning attack targeting data sources. This data poisoning attack was conducted using crowdsourcing [37]. This attack aims to exploit specific vulnerabilities by including the data of the fake users that were created in the original data [38]. Others have also developed three new data poisoning attacks that can circumvent a large variety of commonly used anomaly detectors based on their closest neighbors [39].

Attack Through Learning Stage

Another form of data poisoning is during the learning process. The attackers try to damage the Intelligent system by presenting false results during the training process. Such as the Lethean1 attack. Lethean1 Attack is a modern data poisoning technique that leads to catastrophic forgetting of the online form during the training [39]. Others have also produced a mathematical framework for Internet poisoning attacks based on optimal control. Within this mathematical framework, two algorithms were implemented that achieve near-perfect attack performance in both synthetic and real data experiments [40]. On the other hand, others have deliberately used additional mechanisms such as augmenting different data into the poisoning [41]. This type of attack also used a data poisoning attack on recommendation systems built with deep learning techniques that could be framed as an improvement problem by combining multiple inference techniques [31, 42].

With this form of attack, other researchers were interested in studying targeted poisoning attacks on standardized learning. An attacker can create homegrown models on machines of vulnerable workers [43]. As the attackers' mindsets varied, it was stated that part of the first poisoning attack targets the built-in Recommendations System (CBF). There are two types of attacks (access attack and target attack [44]. Trojan neural attack techniques targeting machine learning systems also one form of this attack [45]. A summary presented in Table 3 describes all attack poisoning learning models, methodology with details of each attacker's environment.

3 Defenses Against Poisoning Attack

Since the data poisoning attack is still one of the innovative modern attacks. The defense methods against this attack differ from the traditional methods used by many attackers. For every attack, there is a defensive method to be followed.

While regression learning systems were targeted during a data poisoning attack, researchers used linear regression models to increase resistance against data septic attacks [50]. For instance, regression models cannot withstand hostile attacks targeting large numbers of data sets. Thus, effective defense mechanisms have been proposed that are significantly superior to previous technology in terms of accuracy and computational costs over nonlinear regression models and implementation of N-LID in defense [17].

In the case of federated poisoning, others have created an efficient and secure IoT asynchronous federated learning system. The innovative principle is based on an asynchronous model that is being updated to improve communication efficiency [51]. Therefore, the IoT malicious cloud was unable to exploit a healthy hierarchical distribution of disruptive gradients [52].

A common defense mechanism called data sanitization defenses against targeted data poisoning and a defense perceptive attack algorithm have been also proposed [53, 54]. Presenting the challenge of increasing resistance to hostile training time attacks of carefully designed label flipping and the resulting turbulence will significantly reduce the efficiency of SVM ratings [55].

Others used meta neural analysis approaches as a modern paradigm for detecting trojans in neural networks (MNTD) [56, 57]. On the other hand, others have shown that recent data augmentation schemes can adapt the behavior of neural network training to reduce poisoning. By increasing samples of training data, these results indicate increased protection from poisoning [58]. Others review the state-of-the-art defense methods of data poisoning attacks.

Finally, others researchers have explained that there is a possibility of protection mechanisms by identifying Trojan neural horses. Thus, erasing the Trojan horse's features from the neural network model and bypassing it will provide some form of defense. It has also been shown that other forms of threats can be mitigated by using Trojan neurons to diagnose poisoning patterns [45]. Table 4 shows a comparison of defense methodology on data poisoning.

Table 3. Attack through the learning stage

Attacks type	Attacks method	Targeted	Environment
Lethean 1, data poisoning Attack [43]	Triggers disastrous forgetting of an online model	Training and testing phase	CIFAR 10 [24]
Online data poisoning attacks [44]	Evaluate attack algorithms NLP and DDPG against several baselines on synthetic and real datasets	Testing phase	Use 5 datasets for online logistic regression: [5], Breast Cancer [6], Cardiotocography [7], Sonar, and MNIST 1 [41]
Industrial Scale Data Poisoning via Gradient Matching [45]	Setup enforces clean-label attacks, meaning that the semantic label of a poisoned image is still unchanged	Training phase	CIFAR 10 [24]
Data Poisoning Attacks to Deep Learning-Based [46]	Baseline Attacks. We compare our poisoning attack to several existing poisoning attacks (Random Attack, Bandwagon Attack) and Poisoning Attack to MF-based Recommender		Three real-world datasets
Local Model Poisoning Attacks to Byzantine-Robust Federated Learning [47]	Local Model Poisoning Attacks (Attacking Krum, Attacking Trimmed Mean, Attacking Median)		MNIST [41]
Attack in neural collaborative filtering-based recommender systems [48]	To distort the recommender system, the objective function of availability attack should be able to measure the discrepancy of recommended results		On real data sets from Amazon [8], Twitter [9], and Movie Lens [10]

(*continued*)

Table 3. (*continued*)

Attacks type	Attacks method	Targeted	Environment
Threats Neuron Trojans [49]	Neural Trojan Attacks (Training Data Poisoning (Hiding Trojan Triggers)), Binary-Level Attacks		Image dataset

Table 4. Defense strategy against Data poisoning attack

Defense	Methodology	Environment
Defending regression learners against poisoning attacks [21]	Robust learners, N-LID based defenses-LID CVX	House, Loan, Grid and machine dataset [23–26]
Communication-efficient and attack-resistant federated edge learning for industrial internet of things [56]	Local differentially private asynchronous federated learning framework by using asynchronous local privacy mechanism (ALDP)	MNIST dataset [37]
Stronger targeted poisoning attacks against malware detection [58]	Data sanitization defenses, analysis of the optimal attack strategy proposed	Datasets Ransomware [11] and M-EMBER [54]
Defending distributed classifiers against data poisoning attacks [59]	LID called K-LID that uses kernel distance in the LID calculation, a weighted SVM against such attacks using K-LID, SDR-based surveillance system	MNIST, Acoustic, Ijcnn1, Seismic, Splice and OMNeT Dataset [12–16, 37]
Detecting AI trojans using meta neural analysis [60]	The modern paradigm for detecting Trojans in neural networks (MNTD) using meta neural analysis approaches	MNIST [37]. CIFAR10. SC. Irish MR
Novel defenses against data poisoning in adversarial machine learning [61]	One-class Support Vector Machines (OCSVMs) and regression models for new defenses	House, Loan, Grid and machine dataset [23–26]
STRONG data augmentation sanitizes poisoning and backdoor attacks without an accurate tradeoff [62]	Mixup and CutMix, SGD (DP-SGD) defense	CIFAR-10 [20]

4   Poisoning Threat Metrics and Criteria

Metrics and benchmarks are very important for evaluating the performance of any system for its safety from data poisoning attacks. Analysts follow several scenarios to make these measurements. The results of the criteria are symbolic as a basis for building a defense system against data poisoning attacks. By looking at the attack methods that researchers used in previous studies, it became clear that some of them conducted data poisoning attack scenarios and created a defense mechanism against their proposed scenarios [63]. Some of them used these attacks to find out the duration of the effect of poisoning the data on the results of systems [64, 65]. Other researchers have indicated the need for an equal comparison with the real risks from several attacks. Thus, there should be criteria that are used to diagnose methods of data poisoning [66]. A variety of criteria are needed to differentiate types of attacks, especially the difficulty in ranking them according to their effectiveness [67, 68]. While another researcher mentioned that data poisoning often represents a widespread threat to networks, the classification scenario has been emphasized as the cornerstone of data poisoning detection [69]. Identifying fraud that creates changes to the dataset without anyone realizing it (i.e. a model trained with a distinctive tag that distinguishes it from other models [70, 71].

5   Discussion and Assessment

The paper discusses how attackers can target a system based on machine learning or deep learning technology through a so-called data poisoning attack. Researchers who build their smart systems using machine learning techniques face significant challenges after such targeting by the reliability of the system results, training data may be poisoned or training parameters may be poisoned. Therefore, the followings have been found;

i.   Through the comprehensive study on the research presented in this field, the views of researchers vary. Some of them prepared the attack scenario and then created a method of discovery and response to it, and those who applied theories of discovery and repelling based on calibration of the data used.

ii. Attacks targeting the AI model are more complex than those targeting data sources. However, if the attacker succeeds in poisoning the AI model, the attacker will gain huge powers, controlling the system as a legitimate person without noticing any protection system. Attacks targeting data sources are easier than an attack targeting an AI model because it targets the available data, and this is different from an AI model. This will attack data sources in many ways, both at training time and in testing. This has been described in previous studies.

iii. As for the effects, the main effect of these attacks is the deviation of the workflow of the systems created by intelligent technologies from its true course.

6   Challenge and Recommendation

A comparison of studies presented by researchers is included in the literature. After conducting this comprehensive study describing the attackers' approach, whether towards attacking and poisoning data sources, or attacking and poisoning an AI model, several important things are raised.

i.   The data poisoning attack is of a dynamic and variable nature that varies from one environment to another, so it is difficult to detect it by anti-viruses in particular that work with the principle of matching models.
ii. Attacks targeting the AI model are more complex than those targeting data sources. However, if the attacker succeeds in poisoning the AI model, he will gain huge powers, controlling the system as a legitimate person without noticing any protection system for him.
iii. Attacks targeting data sources are easier than an attack targeting an AI model because it targets the available data, and this is different from an AI model. This will attack data sources in many ways, both at training time and in testing. This has been described in previous studies and illustrated in Fig. 2. However, these attacks are easier to detect than attacks targeting the AI model.
iv. Finally, a mechanism can be put in place to avoid a data poisoning attack, depending on the environment to be protected. We recommend several basic things to reduce the impact of a malicious data attack by focusing on selecting data sources from trusted and robust organizations to build smart systems based on behavior monitoring to detect anomalies in the system's work.

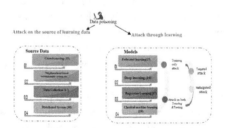

Fig. 2. Methodology of data poisoning

7   Conclusions

Now the world is motivated towards artificial intelligence to get great services by employing it in the structure of technology, such as smart cities, smart cars, monitoring and control, and others. This massive rush towards smart technologies has become a major concern after the emergence of a data poisoning attack targeting smart technologies. A data poisoning attack could stop the trend towards artificial intelligence. Therefore, this sensitive topic should receive great attention from researchers to determine the types of this attack and what are the ways to defend against this attack. In this paper, we define the risks and types of this attack that revolve around the target environment. A data poisoning attack targeting data sources is the most common and easiest for attackers to find, but the chances of it being detected are better than the second type targeting the smart model during the training and testing phases. Despite the danger of an attack targeting data sources, it is easier to detect compared to the other type because the parties responsible for standard data are obligated to periodically check their integrity, which makes it easier to discover traces of the attack on them. Whereas, an attack targeting a smart model is complex, difficult to detect, and has a significant impact. To detect these attacks and through our study, we concluded that methods for detecting anomalies in system behavior are the best methods for detecting a data poisoning attack.

Acknowledgment. The authors would like to thank the University of Mosul/ College of Computer Sciences and Mathematics for their provided facilities.

References

1. Amanuel, S.V.A., Ameen, S.Y.: Device-to-device communication for 5G security: a review. J. Inf. Technol. Inf. **1**(1), 26–31 (2021)
2. Khalid, L.F., Ameen, S.Y.: Secure IoT integration in daily lives: a review. J. Inf. Technol. Inf. **1**(1), 6–12 (2021)
3. Medak, T., Krishna, A.P.: Power controlled secured transmission using self organizing trusted node model. Int. J. Pure Appl. Math. **118**(24), 11–21 (2018)
4. Pitropakis, N., et al.: A taxonomy and survey of attacks against machine learning. Comput. Sci. Rev. **34**, 100199 (2019)
5. Goldblum, M., et al.: Data security for machine learning: data poisoning, backdoor attacks, and defenses. arXiv preprint arXiv:2012.10544 (2020)
6. Hamed, Z.A., Ahmed, I.M., Ameen, S.Y.: Protecting windows OS against local threats without using antivirus. Relation **29**(12s), 64–70 (2020)
7. Abd Al Nomani, M.M., Birmani, A.H.T.: Informational destruction crime; A comparative Study. PalArch's J. Archaeol. Egypt **17**(3), 2266–2281 (2020)
8. Yao, Y., et al.: Latent backdoor attacks on deep neural networks, pp. 2041–2055 (2019)
9. Li, Y., et al.: Backdoor learning: a survey. arXiv preprint arXiv:2007.08745 (2020)
10. Tang, D., Wang, X., et al.: Demon in the variant: statistical analysis of DNNs for robust backdoor contamination detection. In: 30th {USENIX} Security Symposium ({USENIX} Security 21) (2021)
11. Xia, Y., et al.: Weighted speech distortion losses for neural-network-based real-time speech enhancement. In: ICASSP 2020–2020 IEEE International Conference on Acoustics, Speech and Signal Processing (ICASSP). IEEE (2020)
12. Ning, J., et al.: Analytical modeling of part distortion in metal additive manufacturing. Int. J. Adv. Manuf. Technol. **107**(1–2), 49–57 (2020). https://doi.org/10.1007/s00170-020-05065-8
13. Ahmed, I.: Enhancement of network attack classification using particle swarm optimization and multi-layer perceptron. Int. J. Comput. Appl. **137**(12), 18–22 (2016)
14. Huang, J., et al.: An exploratory analysis on users' contributions in federated learning. arXiv preprint arXiv:2011.06830 (2020)
15. Tomsett, R., Chan, K.S., et al.: Model poisoning attacks against distributed machine learning systems (2019)
16. Gu, T., et al.: BadNets: evaluating backdooring attacks on deep neural networks. IEEE Access **7**, 47230–47244 (2019)
17. Bagdasaryan, E., et al.: How to backdoor federated learning. In: International Conference on Artificial Intelligence and Statistics. PMLR (2020)

18. Tolpegin, V., et al.: Data poisoning attacks against federated learning systems. In: Chen, L., Li, N., Liang, K., Schneider, S. (eds.) ESORICS 2020. LNCS, vol. 12308, pp. 480–501. Springer, Cham (2020). https://doi.org/10.1007/978-3-030-58951-6_24

19. Liu, Y., et al.: RC-SSFL towards robust and communication-efficient semi-supervised federated learning system. arXiv preprint arXiv:2012.04432 (2020)

20. Lyu, L., Yu, H., Yang, Q.: Threats to federated learning: a survey. arXiv preprint arXiv:2003.02133 (2020)

21. Weerasinghe, S., et al.: Defending regression learners against poisoning attacks. arXiv preprint arXiv:2008.09279 (2020)

22. Jagielski, M., et al.: Manipulating machine learning: poisoning attacks and countermeasures for regression learning. In: 2018 IEEE Symposium on Security and Privacy (SP). IEEE (2018)

23. Xiao, H., Rasul, K., Vollgraf, R.: Fashion-MNIST: a novel image dataset for benchmarking machine learning algorithms. arXiv preprint arXiv:1708.07747 (2017)

24. Recht, B., et al.: Do CIFAR-10 classifiers generalize to CIFAR-10? arXiv preprint arXiv:1806.00451 (2018)

25. Kwon, H., Yoon, H., Park, K.-W.: Selective poisoning attack on deep neural networks. Symmetry 11(7), 892 (2019)

26. Kurita, K., Michel, P., Neubig, G.: Weight poisoning attacks on pre-trained models. arXiv preprint arXiv:2004.06660 (2020)

27. Candanedo, L.M., Feldheim, V., Deramaix, D.: Reconstruction of the indoor temperature dataset of a house using data driven models for performance evaluation. Build. Environ. 138, 250–261 (2018)

28. Li, M., Mickel, A., Taylor, S.: Should this loan be approved or denied?: a large dataset with class assignment guidelines. J. Stat. Educ. 26(1), 55–66 (2018)

29. Makonin, S., Wang, Z.J., Tumpach, C.: RAE: the rainforest automation energy dataset for smart grid meter data analysis. Data 3(1), 8 (2018)

30. Purohit, H., et al.: MIMII dataset: sound dataset for malfunctioning industrial machine investigation and inspection. arXiv preprint arXiv:1909.09347 (2019)

31. Purushotham, S., et al.: Benchmarking deep learning models on large healthcare datasets. J. Biomed. Inform. 83, 112–134 (2018)

32. Wadawadagi, R., Pagi, V.: Fine-grained sentiment rating of online reviews with Deep-RNN. In: Chiplunkar, N., Fukao, T. (eds.) Advances in Artificial Intelligence and Data Engineering. Advances in Intelligent Systems and Computing, vol. 1133, pp. 687–700. Springer, Singapore (2021). https://doi.org/10.1007/978-981-15-3514-7_52

33. Fortuna, P., Soler-Company, J., Wanner, L.: How well do hate speech, toxicity, abusive and offensive language classification models generalize across datasets? Inf. Process. Manag. 58(3), 102524 (2021)

34. Apoorva, K.A., Sangeetha, S.: Deep neural network and model-based clustering technique for forensic electronic mail author attribution. SN Appl. Sci. 3(3), 1–12 (2021). https://doi.org/10.1007/s42452-020-04127-6

35. Huang, H., et al.: Data poisoning attacks to deep learning based recommender systems. arXiv preprint arXiv:2101.02644 (2021)

36. Shejwalkar, V., Houmansadr, A.: Manipulating the Byzantine: optimizing model poisoning attacks and defenses for federated learning (2021)

37. Tahmasebian, F., et al.: Crowdsourcing under data poisoning attacks: a comparative study. In: Singhal, A., Vaidya, J. (eds.) DBSec 2020. LNCS, vol. 12122, pp. 310–332. Springer, Cham (2020). https://doi.org/10.1007/978-3-030-49669-2_18

38. Chen, L., et al.: Data poisoning attacks on neighborhood-based recommender systems. Trans. Emerg. Telecommun. Technol. 32, e3872 (2020)

39. Koh, P.W., Steinhardt, J., Liang, P.: Stronger data poisoning attacks break data sanitization defenses. arXiv preprint arXiv:1811.00741 (2018)

40. Jianqiang, Z., Xiaolin, G., Xuejun, Z.: Deep convolution neural networks for Twitter sentiment analysis. IEEE Access **6**, 23253–23260 (2018)
41. Baldominos, A., Saez, Y., Isasi, P.: A survey of handwritten character recognition with MNIST and EMNIST. Appl. Sci. **9**(15), 3169 (2019)
42. Jain, A., Jain, V.: Effect of activation functions on deep learning algorithms performance for IMDB movie review analysis. In: Bansal, P., Tushir, M., Balas, V.E., Srivastava, R. (eds.) Proceedings of International Conference on Artificial Intelligence and Applications. AISC, vol. 1164, pp. 489–497. Springer, Singapore (2021). https://doi.org/10.1007/978-981-15-4992-2_46
43. Perry, E.: Lethean attack: an online data poisoning technique. arXiv preprint arXiv:2011.12355 (2020)
44. Zhang, X., Zhu, X., Lessard, L.: Online data poisoning attacks. In: Learning for Dynamics and Control. PMLR (2020)
45. Geiping, J., et al.: Witches' Brew industrial scale data poisoning via gradient matching. arXiv preprint arXiv:2009.02276 (2020)
46. Wang, Y., Chaudhuri, K.: Data poisoning attacks against online learning. arXiv preprint arXiv: 1808.08994 (2018)
47. Fang, M., et al.: Local model poisoning attacks to Byzantine-robust federated learning. In: 29th {USENIX} [17] Security Symposium ({USENIX} Security 20) (2020)
48. Zhang, Y., et al.: Towards poisoning the neural collaborative filtering-based recommender systems. In: Chen, L., Li, N., Liang, K., Schneider, S. (eds.) ESORICS 2020. LNCS, vol. 12308, pp. 461–479. Springer, Cham (2020). https://doi.org/10.1007/978-3-030-58951-6_23
49. Liu, Y., et al.: A survey on neural trojans. In: 2020 21st International Symposium on Quality Electronic Design (ISQED). IEEE (2020)
50. Aono, Y., et al.: Privacy-preserving logistic regression with distributed data sources via homomorphic encryption. IEICE Trans. Inf. Syst. **99**(8), 2079–2089 (2016)
51. Assegie, T.A.: An optimized K-nearest neighbor based breast cancer detection. J. Robot. Control (JRC) **2**(3), 115–118 (2021)
52. Amin, B., et al.: Intelligent neutrosophic diagnostic system for cardiotocography data. Comput. Intell. Neurosci. **2021**, 20–31 (2021)
53. Rezaei, M.R.: Amazon product recommender system. arXiv preprint arXiv:2102.04238 (2021)
54. Ramasamy, L.K., et al.: Performance analysis of sentiments in Twitter dataset using SVM models. Int. J. Electr. Comput. Eng. **11**(3), 2275–2284 (2088–8708) (2021)
55. Leung, J.K., Griva, I., Kennedy, W.G.: An affective aware pseudo association method to connect disjoint users across multiple datasets–an enhanced validation method for text-based emotion aware recommender. arXiv preprint arXiv:2102.05719 (2021)
56. Liu, Y., et al.: Towards communication-efficient and attack-resistant federated edge learning for industrial internet of things. arXiv preprint arXiv:2012.04436 (2020)
57. Siddiqui, M., Wang, M.C., Lee, J.: Data mining methods for malware detection using instruction sequences. In: Artificial Intelligence and Applications (2008)
58. Narisada, S., et al.: Stronger targeted poisoning attacks against malware detection. In: Krenn, S., Shulman, H., Vaudenay, S. (eds.) CANS 2020. LNCS, vol. 12579, pp. 65–84. Springer, Cham (2020). https://doi.org/10.1007/978-3-030-65411-5_4
59. Weerasinghe, S., et al.: Defending distributed classifiers against data poisoning attacks. arXiv preprint arXiv:2008.09284 (2020)
60. Xu, X., et al.: Detecting ai trojans using meta neural analysis. arXiv preprint arXiv:1910.03137 (2019)
61. Weerasinghe, P.S.L.: Novel defenses against data poisoning in adversarial machine learning (2019)

62. Borgnia, E., et al.: Strong data augmentation sanitizes poisoning and backdoor attacks without an accuracy tradeoff. arXiv preprint arXiv:2011.09527 (2020)

63. Gray, J., Sgandurra, D., Cavallaro, L.: Identifying authorship style in malicious binaries: techniques, challenges & datasets. arXiv preprint arXiv:2101.06124 (2021)

64. Sridhar, K., et al.: ICASSP 2021 acoustic echo cancellation challenge: datasets and testing framework. arXiv preprint arXiv:2009.04972 (2020)

65. Gu, L., et al.: Semi-supervised learning in medical images through graph-embedded random forest. Front. Neuroinf. **14**, 49 (2020)

66. Yang, L., et al.: Random noise attenuation based on residual convolutional neural network in seismic datasets. IEEE Access **8**, 30271–30286 (2020)

67. Asghari, H., et al.: CircMiner: accurate and rapid detection of circular RNA through the splice-aware pseudo-alignment scheme. Bioinformatics **36**(12), 3703–3711 (2020)

68. Panda, N., Majhi, S.K.: How effective is the salp swarm algorithm in data classification. In: Das, A.K., Nayak, J., Naik, B., Pati, S.K., Pelusi, D. (eds.) Computational Intelligence in Pattern Recognition. AISC, vol. 999, pp. 579–588. Springer, Singapore (2020). https://doi.org/10.1007/978-981-13-9042-5_49

69. Schwarzschild, A., et al.: Just how toxic is data poisoning? A unified benchmark for backdoor and data poisoning attacks. arXiv preprint arXiv:2006.12557 (2020)

70. Sablayrolles, A., et al.: Radioactive data: tracing through training. In: International Conference on Machine Learning. PMLR (2020)

71. Dang, T.K., Truong, P.T.T., et al.: Data poisoning attack on deep neural network and some defense methods, pp. 15–22 (2020)

Author Index

Printed in the United States
by Baker & Taylor Publisher Services